Communication
Yearbook

MICHAEL E. ROLOFF, Editor
GAYLEN D. PAULSON, Editorial Assistant

Communication
Yearbook

 Published Annually for the
International Communication Association

Sage Publications, Inc.
International Educational and Professional Publisher
Thousand Oaks ▪ London ▪ New Delhi

For information:

Sage Publications, Inc.
2455 Teller Road
Thousand Oaks, California 91320
E-mail: order@sagepub.com

Sage Publications Ltd.
6 Bonhill Street
London EC2A 4PU
United Kingdom

Sage Publications India Pvt. Ltd.
M-32 Market
Greater Kailash I
New Delhi 110 048 India

Printed in the United States of America

Library of Congress: 76-45943
ISBN 0-7619-2112-5
ISSN 0147-4642

00   01   02   03   04   05   06   7   6   5   4   3   2   1

Acquiring Editor: Margaret H. Seawell
Editorial Assistant: Sandra Krumholz
Production Editor: Astrid Virding
Editorial Assistant: Cindy Bear
Typesetter: Marion Warren
Indexer: Michael Ferreira
Cover Designer: Ravi Balasuriya

CONTENTS

THE INTERNATIONAL COMMUNICATION ASSOCIATION

The International Communication Association (ICA) was formed in 1950, bringing together academicians and other professionals whose interests focus on human communication. The Association maintains an active membership of more than 3,300 individuals, of whom some two-thirds are teaching and conducting research in colleges, universities, and schools around the world. Other members are in government, the media, communication technology, business, law, medicine, and other professions. The wide professional and geographic distribution of the membership provides the basic strength of the ICA. The Association is a meeting ground for sharing research and useful dialogue about communication interests.

Through its Divisions and Interest Groups, publications, annual conferences, and relations with other associations around the world, the ICA promotes the systematic study of communication theories, processes, and skills.

In addition to *Communication Yearbook,* the Association publishes the *Journal of Communication, Human Communication Research, Communication Theory, A Guide to Publishing in Scholarly Communication Journals, ICA Newsletter,* and the *ICA Membership Directory.*

For additional information about the ICA and its activities, contact Robert L. Cox, Executive Director, International Communication Association, P.O. Box 9589, Austin, TX 78766; phone (512) 454-8299; fax (512) 451-6270; e-mail icahdq@uts.cc.utexas.edu

Editors of the *Communication Yearbook* series:

Volumes 1 and 2, Brent D. Ruben
Volumes 3 and 4, Dan Nimmo
Volumes 5 and 6, Michael Burgoon
Volumes 7 and 8, Robert N. Bostrom
Volumes 9 and 10, Margaret L. McLaughlin
Volumes 11, 12, 13, and 14, James A. Anderson
Volumes 15, 16, and 17, Stanley A. Deetz
Volumes 18, 19, and 20, Brant R. Burleson
Volumes 21, 22, and 23, Michael E. Roloff

CONSULTING EDITORS

The following individuals helped make possible this volume of the *Communication Yearbook*. The editor gratefully acknowledges these scholars for the gifts of their time and wisdom.

EDITOR'S INTRODUCTION

WELCOME to Volume 23 of the *Communication Yearbook*. This collection continues the format of publishing state-of-the-art reviews of communication research. *Communication Yearbook* has established itself as an essential source for in-depth analyses of communication scholarship representing the broad array of research areas evident within the field. The chapters contained in this volume are of high quality and should be of interest to most communication researchers.

To help the reader understand this volume, I will describe the process by which the chapters were selected, the content of each chapter, and the individuals who played essential roles in putting together the volume.

CHAPTER CREATION

Approximately 18 months prior to the publication of this volume, a call for submissions was circulated. Drafts of chapters and proposals for chapters were solicited that would review important, specific areas of scholarship. An attempt was made to solicit reviews from across research specializations. To that end, copies of the call were sent to the leadership of all divisions and interest groups of the International Communication Association with a request that they identify potential contributors and circulate the call to the membership. I am grateful to those who assisted with these tasks. In addition, the call was sent to the editors of 20 newsletters published by organizations both within (e.g., National Communication Association) and outside the field of communication (e.g., Society for the Study of Personality and Social Psychology) most of which published it. Finally, given that dissertations are often a rich source for literature reviews, more than 100 letters were sent to professors at Ph.D.-granting institutions asking them to identify recently completed dissertations that contained quality literature reviews.

We received 31 new submissions and also considered 3 papers that were submitted to *Communication Yearbook 22* but were not completed by the deadline for publication. The proposed reviews reflected the diversity of our field and addressed issues in health communication, intercultural communication, interpersonal communication, legal communication, mass communication, organizational communication, political communication, public relations, and rhetoric. All 34 prospective chapters were subjected to blind review by at least two referees. Each referee was asked to make the following assessments: (a) Is the submission a literature review? (b) Is the literature worthy of review? (c) Is the review comprehensive and current? (d) Is there a coherent organizational pattern and procedure for conducting the review? (e) Are the conclusions clear and valid? (f) Is the review sufficiently critical? and (g) Does the review set forth future issues and directions for research? The authors of those proposals and papers that were judged to conform to each standard were encouraged to submit chapters, which were subjected to further evaluation. In most cases, the manuscripts went through several revisions.

The 10 chapters contained in this volume are those that survived this rigorous review process. They are truly a select group. Of the total, 7 were drawn from the 31 new submissions and 3 emerged from the projects originally proposed for *CY22*.

CHAPTER CONTENT

Although proposals were sought from all interest areas in communication, the selection of chapters was based entirely upon their judged quality. Had the proposals from a single interest area all been judged to be the best, *CY23* would have a singular focus. However, as testimony to the vibrancy of all of our research specializations, the chapters reflect the diverse interests that compose our field. Therefore, readers will find some chapters that fit into our formal divisional structures and some that blend two or more. Hence readers will likely find in-depth reviews focused on important topics in their own specializations and well-written syntheses that inform as to scholarship in other domains. I provide below a brief overview of the chapter contents.

Over the past decade, scholars have become interested in the relationship between communication and emotional processes. Accordingly, substantial research literatures exist that inform about this important relationship. Each of the first four chapters reviews one of those literatures. In Chapter 1, Planalp, Hafen, and Adkins review the rather voluminous body of research focused on messages of shame and guilt. They examine how shame and guilt are induced by messages as well as the effects of such messages on esteem, control, and connection. They do not confine their review to research conducted in a single context, but instead draw upon scholarship that informs about shame and guilt in intimate, family, organizational, and public discourse.

In a related topic, O'Keefe reviews the role of guilt in social influence situations in Chapter 2. His review indicates that messages can instill substantial guilt in their targets but that too much guilt can reduce persuasiveness. Anger and reactance can result from explicit attempts to instill guilt, and these reactions cut against the willingness to comply. O'Keefe notes that messages that forecast feelings of guilt rather than induce it may be more effective.

It seems intuitive that individuals try to avoid messages that would make them feel bad and instead expose themselves to those that would make them feel good. Research investigating selective exposure has generally supported this notion. However, under some conditions, individuals seek out media content that instills a negative mood. In Chapter 3, Zillmann identifies conditions under which individuals behave in a counterhedonic fashion and suggests alterations in current theorizing about selective exposure so as to incorporate these conditions.

In some cases, individuals may not be able to forecast when they might encounter negative messages. Hence they are exposed to ideas and images that are upsetting. Chapters 4 through 7 review the literatures examining particular aspects of problematic communication.

Individuals often seek assistance from others and typically do so with the hope and expectation that it will be forthcoming. However, the recipients of requests are not always willing or able to comply. In such cases, they must find a means of resisting compliance and, in some cases, in a socially appropriate manner. In Chapter 4, Ifert reviews the literature focused on compliance resistance. She examines taxonomies of compliance-resisting strategies as well as the factors that predict responses to particular request forms. She also examines the emotional reactions that accompany resistance.

Research focused on sexual harassment in the workplace has increased dramatically over the past decade. In Chapter 5, Jansma examines the literature with the goal of identifying organizational strategies for mitigating this common problem. To that end, she reviews literature that speaks to the frequency and forms of harassment, the factors that affect both the perception of harassment and tendency to act in a harassing manner, and, importantly, how individuals and organizations can combat harassment.

When encountering conflict, individuals enact behaviors designed to manage it. In Chapter 6, Kim and Leung examine cross-cultural influences on conflict management styles. In doing so, they note that a dominant focus on individualist perspectives has caused conflict scholars to overvalue confrontation and to devalue the more indirect and covert means of conflict management that are common in less individualist cultures. Moreover, Kim and Leung note that individuals who are bicultural (i.e., who blend individualist and interdependent perspectives) rather than culturally typed may be more flexible with regard to their styles, which increases their ability to manage conflicts.

Not all problematic communication arises from conflict between two people. In some cases, it arises from the negative impact of media images on the audience. In Chapter 7, Bishop reviews the literature that relates exposure to media images of thinness to body-image problems. His analysis reveals that the relationship is quite complex and that researchers are exploring it in a relatively simplistic fashion. He calls for research that more directly investigates the role of media images within the larger social environment, which contains other influences, such as family and friends.

Although dealing with problematic communication is an important facet of communication systems, members of such systems must also find a more general way of maintaining them. The final three chapters address this issue. In Chapter 8, Canary and Zelley examine research investigating how individuals maintain their personal relationships. They examine four lines of research, and their analysis points to the multifaceted role of communication in relational maintenance.

Decision-making groups face the challenge of managing their deliberations so as to reach conclusions within a context defined by member preferences and norms existing within the larger social system in which they are embedded. Structuration theory is a prominent framework used to analyze how groups accomplish their contextual goals, and four research approaches have emerged from it. In Chapter 9, Seyfarth reviews the findings associated with each approach and critiques their adequacy.

To remain a force in a social system, a member must find a way to communicate his or her perspectives to others. Indeed, to prevent alienation and to maintain social systems, one could argue that such communication should be promoted. The process of creating such messages is the core of public relations, and an extensive body of literature has focused on it. However, Miller notes in Chapter 10 that scholars have restricted their conception of public relations to a business history frame. She reviews literature drawn from a variety of sources and demonstrates that public relations did not emerge from a single source. Instead, public relations emerged from political and social activity as well as from business. Miller demonstrates that viewing public relations from a more expanded framework yields new insights into the process.

Although broadly cast, all of the chapters included here address issues that are important for communication researchers as well as for society as a whole. The reader will find that each chapter provides an excellent summary and critique of the literature. The authors have done a fine job.

ACKNOWLEDGMENTS

This is the last volume of my editorship, and I join the ranks of prior editors of the *Communication Yearbook*. I now turn over the reins to the able hands of William Gudykunst. I am confident that he will be an effective editor and that the *Communication Yearbook* will continue to be an important source of scholarship.

Throughout my term, I have received the support and cooperation of many people. Any success I have achieved must be shared with them. My able assistant editor, Gaylen Paulson, worked countless hours on all three *Yearbooks*. He computerized the review process, and his finely honed copyediting skills were invaluable. He kept me on track and was an effective problem solver. He deserves a great deal of credit for the completion of all three of these projects.

My colleagues from Northwestern and around the country also contributed to this endeavor. Dean David Zarefsky provided financial support from the School of Speech at Northwestern, as did the Department of Communication Studies. Two Northwestern staff members, Rita Lutz and Martha Kayler, helped me handle the internal paperwork necessary to keep the review process functioning. Professors Peter Miller, Linda Putnam, and James Ettema were extremely helpful in directing me to referees. Three doctoral students at Northwestern, Kari Soule, Joy Shih, and Lefki Anastasiou, assisted with copyediting tasks. I must also extend my appreciation to the many students who tolerated my delayed responses to their assignments and inquiries when my editorial duties beckoned.

Clearly, a volume such as this could not exist without submitters and reviewers. I am very appreciative of the interest expressed by those who sent in proposals, and I applaud the time and effort they expended on proposals that in some cases did not come to fruition. The referees provided thorough, insightful responses to the proposals, and most were completed in a timely fashion.

I want to acknowledge the assistance and support of the communication editor at Sage Publications, Margaret Seawell, and her assistant, Renée Piernot. They efficiently moved the volume through the production phase and were always effective and gracious problem solvers.

I am also very grateful to my predecessor, Brant Burleson. Brant was instrumental in establishing the literature review format for the *Communication Yearbook*. He created a strong foundation upon which I was able to build.

Finally, I must express my gratitude to my wife, Karen, and my daughters, Erika, Katrina, and Carlissa, for tolerating my periodic inattention to the travails of family life.

Michael E. Roloff

CHAPTER CONTENTS

1   Messages of Shame and Guilt

SALLY PLANALP
University of Montana

SUSAN HAFEN
University of Wisconsin–Eau Claire

A. DAWN ADKINS
Texas A&M University

U.S. society seems to be experiencing a dramatic wave of interest and public debate about shame and guilt. On one side, scholars decry the destruction of pride and self-esteem that shame and guilt can wreak on individuals, relationships, organizations, and nations; on the other side, scholars argue that a return to shame and guilt represents an attitude of awe or respect toward the values that are central to culture and to all human interaction. This review draws on the scholarly and popular literature on messages about shame and guilt to address this debate. Specifically, the authors review the grounds or bases for inducing shame and guilt in messages and then the consequences that messages of shame or guilt have for esteem, control, and connection at four levels of analysis: intimate dyads, families, organizations, and public messages. Finally, the authors pose a series of questions that can be used to frame the discussion of an ethics of shame and guilt messages.

> Though shame is a negative emotion in contrast
> with honor, this does not mean that it is bad to feel shame,
> to be shameless, is a profound vice, perhaps the worst of all vices.
> *Robert Solomon, "The Emotions of Justice," 1989*

> None of us is clean, and this is no excuse; our very dirtiness ties us to the earth, to
> life, and claims our commitment to make things better.
> *Frederick Turner, "Shame, Beauty, and the Tragic View of History," 1995*

AUTHORS' NOTE: An earlier version of this chapter was presented at the annual meeting of the Western States Communication Association, Denver, Colorado, February 1998. We thank several undergraduates who contributed to this project: Mary Fleming, Chris Garrison, Jana Knutson, Kathy Tannenbaum, and Melissa Wilson. A special thanks to Kim Beno, who searched the *Readers' Guide to Periodical Literature* for the popular magazine analysis.

Correspondence: Sally Planalp, Department of Communication Studies, University of Montana, Missoula, MT 59812; e-mail sallyp@selway.umt.edu

U.S. society seems to be experiencing a dramatic wave of interest and public debate about shame and guilt. On one side, scholars decry the destruction of pride and self-esteem that shame can wreak on individuals, relationships, organizations, and nations (Baum, 1987; Kaufman, 1992; Retzinger, 1991). On the other side, scholars argue that a return to shame is a return to traditional values and the need for privacy (Nathanson, 1992; Schneider, 1977). Kaufman and Raphael (1996), who call shame a "sickness of the soul," nevertheless believe that "our capacity for modesty and humility itself entirely depends on our willingness to surrender to shame, to hang our head" (p. 46). Wurmser (1987) states, "Shame is a fear of disgrace, but shame is also an attitude of awe or respect about the values central to culture and to all human interaction" (p. 66). Scheff (1995b) states that in the English language, shame is a *crisis* emotion that involves both extreme emotional pain and social disgrace; yet at the same time shame, "actual or anticipated, may be an almost continuous part of ordinary human contact" (p. 1053). We seem to have a similar ambivalence about guilt, although shame seems to have drawn more of the fire lately. No one wants to experience it, but no one wants others to be without it.

Shame and guilt messages are powerful emotional forces that are capable of bringing out the best and the worst in us all. They have played important roles in the major historical events of our times, for good and for ill, certainly having a significant impact on the Vietnam War and on the success of Amnesty International, to name just two examples. On a personal level, shame and guilt messages also help us to negotiate the intricacies of everyday interaction in our relationships with others (Lewis, 1992; Vangelisti, Daly, & Rudnick, 1991), and, on a broader social level, they are important elements in marital interaction, family communication, and organizational dynamics. They are also a part of U.S. popular culture, shaping our views of the roles these emotions play in our lives and especially how we should manage them.

Shame and guilt are of special interest to communication scholars because not only are they the "self-conscious" emotions (Tangney & Fischer, 1995), they are "socially conscious" emotions. Most often, people feel shame for having failed to live up to social expectations and guilt for having failed at social obligations (Lewis, 1993). Shame and guilt alert people that social bonds are being disrupted or transgressions have occurred so that they can take measures to repair them (Lewis, 1981). Miller and Leary (1992) argue that shame is the social counterpart to pain, and that it has served an important function in human evolution: "By sensitizing an individual to the opinions of the social group, such emotions ensured that one would be responsive to the criticism that forewarned abandonment" (p. 216). Shame can, indeed, be "one of the most painful emotions that it is possible for a human being to suffer" (Turner, 1995, p. 1060).

Most often, we manage our own and other people's shame and guilt through communication (sometimes relieving it, sometimes using it for our own purposes;

O'Keefe & Figgé, 1997). Shame messages are also powerful tools for childhood socialization (Izard, 1977, 1991; Lewis, 1971; Tomkins, 1963), and they continue to serve as powerful forces for social control among adults. Most people avoid transgressing social and moral codes (tempting as it may be) at least in part to avoid feeling shame and guilt afterward. Managing shame and guilt effectively through communication, however, is a special challenge because of the tendency for shamed or embarrassed people to want to withdraw from interaction (Izard, 1991) or even to hide from the shame itself by suppressing it (Retzinger, 1991). Unacknowledged shame is especially dangerous and has been linked to violence in conflicts ranging from marital quarrels to war (Scheff & Retzinger, 1991).

This profound ambivalence about messages of shame and guilt leads us to review the scholarly literature to understand it better and to find out how we might handle our messages of shame and guilt more wisely. Armon-Jones (1986) argues for a moral analysis of emotions so that we might use them more effectively for the benefit of individuals and social relations. We extend this argument beyond analyzing the moral value of emotions themselves to include the ways in which they are communicated to others, both between individuals and in general patterns of discourse in our society. It is unlikely that we will come away with clear answers, but we hope to inform the discussion and raise critical issues and concerns.

We consider below several types of connections between shame/guilt and communication: how these emotions are communicated both verbally and nonverbally, how they help to shape interaction patterns, how they are managed through communication, how they are a part of public discourse, and how shame and guilt messages may be judged critically and ethically. We review literature from the contexts of close relationships (friendship, marriage, parents and children), organizations, and public communication in the United States. In order to make the review manageable, we do not include the rather extensive literature on shame and guilt within individuals except insofar as it is necessary to define shame and guilt and link them to communication. We do not deal with shame and guilt's close cousin, embarrassment. We set aside issues involving shame and guilt in different cultures (especially concerning "face management" and shame versus guilt cultures) except as mentioned briefly. We do not review shame and especially guilt in therapeutic and legal settings and the extensive work in education, although we draw on this literature when it is relevant to other areas that we are reviewing. Even so, it is difficult to draw a clear boundary around this review because shame and guilt are often mentioned in passing or referred to by other names in many content domains. To compound the problem, communication has vague boundaries as well, so our task is one of reviewing the intersection of two fuzzy sets. To cope with this problem, we try to maintain a focus on messages, interaction, and public discourse about shame and guilt with an eye to their positive and negative functions and the moral concerns that they provoke.

SHAME AND GUILT PROCESSES

Shame and guilt command our profound ambivalence because they are the emotional points of negotiation between the self and society. We are guided by shame and guilt to be good (that is, to follow internalized standards of social conduct), and at the same time they make us feel bad. A shameless or guilt-free society would probably never work; yet, as individuals, we can fantasize about how nice it would be to live without shame or guilt. Still, as unpleasant as guilt and shame feelings can be, we are not forced to follow their dictates. We can challenge whether they are appropriate and whether their effects are worth the price, from the perspectives of individuals and of society.

Defining Shame and Guilt

Almost everyone, including scholars, struggles with understanding what *shame* and *guilt* mean, especially shame. When Lindsay-Hartz (1984) interviewed people about their experiences with shame and guilt, she found that they had difficulty defining the differences conceptually but were able to provide examples readily, although more eagerly for guilt than for shame. As one respondent said, "Well, I can think of an example [of shame], but I don't think I want to tell you about it" (p. 691). Tangney (1992) also observed that "when recalling shame experiences, respondents appeared generally less articulate and less efficient in their verbal productions" (p. 205). Izard (1991) notes that when people were asked, "Which emotion do you understand best?" (p. 345), shame came in last across the eight cultural groups that were studied.

Michael Lewis (1992) reviewed the scholarly literature distinguishing shame from guilt and concluded that Helen Block Lewis's distinction is most consistent with the empirical evidence (see especially Miller & Tangney, 1994; Tangney, 1992). Both shame and guilt result from failures and shortcomings, primarily moral ones, but shame is more global than guilt. With guilt, negative feelings are focused on the action, whereas with shame, the failure reflects on the entire self. One of the most concise distinctions between shame and guilt is that shame involves *being* whereas guilt involves *doing* (Barrett, 1995; Niedenthal, Tangney, & Gavanski, 1994). When people are ashamed, they feel that they are bad people; when people are guilty, they feel they have done something bad (or failed to do something good). A second important distinguishing characteristic is that guilt makes a person want to make amends, whereas shame makes a person want to escape or hide (Lewis, 1971; Retzinger, 1991, p. 41). Nathanson (1987b, p. 5) says that shame limits narcissism; guilt limits wrongful actions. The opposite of shame is high self-esteem or, in its extreme form, hubris; the opposite of guilt is pride (Lewis, 1993).

The terminology used in discussions of shame and guilt is not always consistent and is itself a matter of debate. For example, Izard (1977) reports that the characteristics *most commonly* reported for shame are "repents, atones, makes amends, changes, improves, does not repeat offense," with "retreats from others" being noted half as often (p. 398). Shame also seems to be more strongly associated with public dishonor, and guilt connotes private transgression (Gehm & Scherer, 1988; Solomon, 1990, pp. 294-295), although both are reported to be experienced more in the company of others than alone, with shame being about as common in solitude as guilt (Tangney, Miller, Flicker, & Barlow, 1996). Shame is usually thought to be more intense and aversive than guilt (Tangney, Miller, et al., 1996; Wicker, Payne, & Morgan, 1983), although Manstead and Tetlock (1989) found guilt to be less pleasant and higher in personal responsibility than shame. Guilt as an emotion (feeling guilty), of course, carries some connotations of responsibility and blame from its legal counterpart (being legally guilty). Our interpretation of these difficulties is that the terms *shame* and *guilt* (not to mention their family members, *embarrassment, humiliation,* and the like) are not used in entirely consistent ways by scholars or by the general public, so that we must simply choose the most useful working definitions for both and go from there. Yet, despite disagreements and subtleties here and there, many scholars can agree on the two primary differences between shame and guilt based on (a) global evaluation of the self versus specific evaluation of behavior and (b) the tendency either to hide or to repair.

Many of the measures of shame and guilt as states and shame- or guilt-proneness as dispositions share the same problems, according to Tangney (1996). Commonly used techniques are (a) projection tests (in which shame or guilt might be read into a hypothetical scenario, such as refusing a favor to a friend; Tangney, 1990), (b) self-report measures using Likert scales or adjective checklists (e.g., "Guilt and remorse have been a part of my life for as long as I can recall"), and (c) direct coding of behavior (e.g., criticism, abuse, ridicule). Many measures confound shame and guilt with each other and also may confound both shame and guilt with endorsement of moral standards (e.g., "One should not have sex relations before marriage," from the Mosher Forced-Choice Guilt Inventory). For scholars focusing on messages of shame and guilt, projective tests may be useful as a way of assessing people's tendencies to read shame or guilt into the messages. Coding systems, of course, are ideal for identifying shame and guilt in situ, but as Tangney (1996) points out, evidence of reliability and validity has been weak, in part because "people rarely articulate shame experiences spontaneously, without pointed inquiry from an interviewer" (p. 752). We might add that they may also be unwilling to admit shame and (to a lesser extent) guilt when it is present, or they may even be unaware of it themselves, making validity a nearly intractable problem. We will say more about coding systems later in this review when we address overt expressions of shame and guilt.

Components of Shame and Guilt Processes

To analyze shame and guilt, we use a framework of six components: (a) precipitating events, causes, objects, and grounds; (b) appraisals of precipitating events;
(c) effects on thought processes; (d) action tendencies and physiological reactions;
(e) expressions and actions; and (f) coping and management. Other theorists have
used similar schemes for many types of emotions (Edelmann, 1987; Frijda, 1986;
Shaver, Schwartz, Kirson, & O'Connor, 1987; Stein, Trabasso, & Liwag, 1993).
Izard (1991), for example, organizes the shame process into a similar set: (a) antecedent feelings, thoughts, and actions; and (b) consequent feelings, thoughts, and
actions. Fischer and Tangney (1995) use a similar scheme. Retzinger (1991) uses a
five-part shame process adapted from H. B. Lewis: stimulus, conscious content,
position of self in field, nature and discharge of hostility, and characteristic
defenses.

Precipitating Events/Causes/Objects/Grounds

Theorists struggle with what to call the events that produce, set off, or seem to
cause emotions. The terms *eliciting event* and *precipitating event* are used to refer
to events that trigger emotion, although they may be only the straws that break the
camels' backs. We can also talk about the "causes" of emotion, but that is a very
tricky case to make, especially given how many causes can contribute to an emotional state (Lazarus, 1991, pp. 171-213). Others refer to "objects" of emotion as
the perceived causes, although not necessarily actual causes. In the cases of shame
and guilt, theorists tend to agree that there is no set of standard and yet specific precipitating events, causes, or objects of shame or guilt. Many kinds of events and
messages can elicit shame or guilt, depending on how they are interpreted.
Tangney (1996) states that "there are very few, if any, 'classic' shame-inducing or
guilt-inducing situations" (p. 742), and Lewis (1993) concurs.
    Although it is difficult to find specific events, messages, or situations that elicit
shame and guilt, we can consider the general types of topics in messages that provoke shame or guilt, or what we will term the *grounds* for shame or guilt. These
will be central to our review and a key to our analysis of the ethics of shame and
guilt messages. Aristotle (1932) wrote about grounds for shame in ancient Greece,
although one gets the sense that he was prescribing rather than describing. His list
includes cowardice, injustice, licentiousness, greed, meanness, flattery, effemi-
nacy, a groveling mind, and boastfulness. Borg, Staufenbiel, and Scherer (1988)
argue that "in our culture, there seems to be a standard set of values such as intellectual achievement, moral rectitude, social skills, and dominance" (p. 83). These
sound similar although not identical to Aristotle's, and during the course of this
review we will add more.

Appraisal

Appraisal refers to the ways in which individuals interpret a message, event, or situation that set up an emotion (in this case, shame or guilt). In fact, emotions are defined in large measure (although not exclusively) in terms of the appraisals on which they are based (e.g., Roseman, Spindel, & Jose, 1990). Appraisals can be instantaneous or prolonged, conscious or unconscious, simple or very complex. Although cognitive appraisal processes play an important role in all emotions, Lewis (1993) argues that they play a more important role in shame and guilt because almost any event can produce either honor or shame, pride or guilt, depending on how it is appraised. In a certain sense, precipitating events fade seamlessly into appraisals because there are few if any "brute facts" or raw, uninterpreted events in the social world (Searle, 1969). In other words, shame- and guilt-producing messages are to be found, in large part, in the eye of the beholder (appraiser).

For both guilt and shame, "the decisive criterion . . . is the evaluation of the behavior *as highly incompatible with both internal and external norms*" (Gehm & Scherer, 1988, pp. 73). Both shame and guilt require two essential appraisals, one of failure and another of the self as the cause of the failure. That is why shame and guilt are commonly called the "self-conscious" or "self-evaluative" emotions (Lewis, 1993). With both shame and guilt, the individual focuses on a defective self in relation to another, often a judgmental other lurking in the psychic background. Retzinger (1995) writes of shame: "Self is the object of disappointment, defeat, rejection or fear of rejection, betrayal, judgmental comparison." The other appears "laughing, ridiculing, powerful, higher status, active, in control, unjust, hostile, unresponsive" (pp. 1105-1106). We get a similar picture with guilt (Baumeister, Reis, & Delespaul, 1995).

Both shame and guilt can also be felt *for* or *because of* others when the individual's identity is linked with a group, as is especially likely in cultures that foster "interdependent" rather than "independent" selves (Kitayama, Markus, & Matsumoto, 1995; Markus & Kitayama, 1991). Greenspan (1995) notes that guilt can be felt for actions that reflect indirectly on the self because of membership in a group or historical connections (such as the U.S. bombings of Hiroshima and Nagasaki). Liem (1997) found that for European Americans, shame centers on a self evaluated by others, but for first-generation (and to a lesser extent also second-generation) Asian Americans, shame centers on identification with the group, especially the family.

Because of the requirement that shame and guilt involve failures that reflect on the self, it is odd that neither seems to require the individual's having *control over the failure* (Borg et al., 1988). Guilt is not uncommon even in the complete absence of control over the wrongdoing, such as the much-discussed "survivor guilt" that individuals feel when they have survived some situation—the bombing of Hiroshima, HIV infection, corporate downsizing—that others have not (Baumeister,

Stillwell, & Heatherton, 1994, pp. 251-252). They feel guilty for benefiting from unfair or arbitrary selection processes over which they—and in many cases, any other human beings—had no control.

The essential distinction between shame and guilt, as addressed earlier, is that shame involves the whole person whereas guilt implicates specific behaviors. Niedenthal et al. (1994) have demonstrated this difference in a clever way by using counterfactual "What if . . . ?" questions. Experimental subjects were asked to imagine guilt scenarios such as letting a friend's bird die while pet-sitting and shame scenarios such as giving a wrong answer to an admired professor. Then they were asked, "What could have been different about you, your behavior, or any aspect of the situation so that the situation would have ended differently?" Those imagining the guilt scenarios wanted to change their behavior; those imagining the shame scenarios wanted to change themselves. Furthermore, if their counter-factual thinking was directed by statements that were presented to them, people who were induced to complete the statement "If only I were (not) . . ." felt more shame; those led to complete "If only I had (not) . . ." felt more guilt. These results have obvious implications for inducing guilt or shame in messages, such as when a parent says, "If you were only a responsible child," in contrast to "If you had only done the responsible thing," or when a child reads into a message, "If I had only been a good boy" compared with "If I had only done the good thing."

Because any event can generate either shame or guilt, depending on how widely the attribution spreads, individual differences in appraisal styles have been studied as an aspect of shame-prone and guilt-prone personalities. The Children's Inter-pretations of Interpersonal Distress and Conflict (CIIDC) test is especially realis-tic, is adaptable to different age groups, contrasts shame- and guilt-proneness, and does not confound them with belief in moral guidelines (as does, for example, the Mosher Forced-Choice Guilt Inventory; Tangney, 1996). The CIIDC is based on scenarios in which it is unclear whether the child transgressed or caused harm to others, and the test is to find out how much shame or guilt is inferred from (or read into) the situation. Tangney (1996) notes that this may be a measure that is espe-cially well suited to identifying a tendency toward misplaced or maladaptive guilt-proneness in children (that is, seeing guilt when others would not). We can speculate that the basic CIIDC procedure might be applicable to face-to-face com-munication, in which the shame- or guilt-producing intent of another's message is often unclear. A shame-prone personality should be especially likely to interpret ambiguous or neutral messages as shaming, and a guilt-prone personality should be likely to interpret such messages as guilt producing.

Effects on Thought Processes and Feelings

Some researchers have noted that shame can lead to the mind's going blank. Darwin (1872/1965) has called this "confusion of the mind"; he observed it in one person who gave an entire speech of gestures alone, without ever realizing that he literally said nothing. Izard (1991) argues that in less dramatic cases, the domination of self-awareness and self-imaging that is produced by shame results in a temporary inability to think logically. Miller and Tangney (1994) trace how mental confusion interferes with the use of self-reports to study shame: "Psychodynamic theorists might argue that one's most interesting and valuable experiences of shame are precisely those that one is least likely to recall" (p. 285), in part because of mental confusion but also because of repression. Guilt, on the other hand, tends to involve the individuals' "thinking of it over and over, wishing they had behaved differently or could somehow undo the bad deed that was done" (Tangney, Miller, et al., 1996, p. 1257).

Action Tendencies/Readiness and Physiological Reactions

The inclination to act (or in some cases not to act) is the quality that distinguishes emotion from thought, even if the inclination is not followed (Frijda, Kuipers, & ter Schure, 1989). One feels the urge to run, hide, hit somebody, jump up and down, scream—that is not just thinking, it is feeling. One's body also goes through physiological changes that prepare it to do something, to run or freeze in the case of fear, to fight against somebody or something in the case of anger, or to draw inward in the case of sadness. Although physiological changes were long thought to be the defining properties of emotion (James, 1884/1984; Schachter & Singer, 1962), and still are by some theorists (Ekman, Levenson, & Friesen, 1983), others consider action tendencies to be even more important (Frijda et al., 1989). In the case of moral emotions such as guilt and shame, Greenspan (1995) argues that we have access to "indirect knowledge of ethical properties as an inference from our felt tendency to act in certain ways" (p. 189). For example, feeling the urge to hide when we have said something stupid is a clue to the value we place on intelligence or verbal competence.

In the case of shame and guilt, action tendencies are the other crucial component that distinguish them (in addition to global or specific appraisals of self). Ashamed people have the urge to hide, to disappear, to crawl into a hole or, more generally, to withdraw from public scrutiny. As one of Lindsay-Hartz's (1984) respondents said: "Let me just cover myself up and nobody can see me. . . . Shame is just total—and you want to disappear" (p. 692). People feeling guilt, by contrast, have the urge to take action to fix the problem (Lewis, 1993; Tangney, Miller, et al., 1996). "I still—to this day . . . I wondered if I should try to go back to her now. . . . I'm wondering if I could undo this" (quoted in Lindsay-Hartz, 1984, p. 693). They may also feel both urges and suffer approach/avoidance conflicts (Ferguson, Stegge, & Damhuis, 1991).

Physiological changes due to shame and guilt are less clear, especially if blushing is ruled out by definition as only a part of their close cousin, embarrassment. Wicker et al. (1983, p. 36) note that individuals remember their faces as being more hot and flushed during shame experiences than during guilt experiences, but these authors do not differentiate shame from embarrassment. Izard (1991, p. 331) also says that shame is accompanied by blushing, but he seems to be referring to the general family of shame emotions, which includes embarrassment. Baumeister, Reis, and Delespaul (1995, p. 1267) found guilt to be positively correlated with unpleasant arousal states and negatively correlated with pleasant, relaxed feelings.

Verbal and Nonverbal Expressions

In many cases, shamed people do follow their urges to withdraw by quite literally leaving or escaping the situation. Other expressions of shame are more subtle, but they signal social withdrawal nonetheless: "Our heads droop, our eyes are cast down, and, blushing, we become briefly incapable of speech" (Nathanson, 1992, p. 134). We may curl up and make the body appear smaller (Izard, 1991, p. 330). We may use long pauses and stutter (Silverman, 1994). Alessandri and Lewis (1993, p. 339) coded the shame of 3-year-olds using the following indicators: body collapsed, corners of the mouth are downward/lower lip tucked between teeth, eyes lowered with gaze downward or askance, withdrawal from task situation, and negative self-evaluation (e.g., "I'm no good at this").

Morrison (1996) notes that he tunes in to key words that his clients in therapy use to describe themselves that reveal shame. They call themselves puny, invisible, "a nothing," pathetic, weak, ridiculous, stupid, dumb, idiots, freaks, or losers. Turner (1995) also notes that "euphemism is a dangerous sign. . . . if the pride were really felt there would be no need for the continual replacement of the distinguishing terms for certain ethnic groups by new euphemisms" (p. 1071). Notable by its absence is the failure to talk about shameful topics. As Morrison (1996) says, "Our secrets give us clues to our shame" (p. 120). Rimé, Finkenauer, Luminet, Zech, and Philippot (1996) report that the vast majority of intense emotional experiences (such as witnessing atrocities in Rwanda) are shared, but those that are not are the ones that elicit more intense feelings of shame and guilt. Balcom, Lee, and Tager (1995, p. 62) claim that a major indicator of shame is avoiding or having difficulty apologizing. More broadly, sensitivity to shame has been linked to shyness, social anxiety, communication apprehension, and other dispositional inclinations to avoid social contact (Crozier, 1990).

Retzinger (1995, pp. 1106-1112; see also Retzinger, 1991, pp. 69-75) provides an inventory of verbal, paralinguistic, and visual indicators or expressions of shame that can be used to code videotaped interactions. Verbal *code words* for shame fall into six general categories: (a) direct terms, such as *shame, embarrassment, humiliation,* and related terms; (b) references to abandonment, separation, and isolation; (c) references to ridicule; (d) references to inadequacy; (e) references to discomfort; and (f) references to a confused or indifferent state. Verbal *hiding behaviors* include (a) mitigation, (b) abstraction, (c) denial, (d) defensiveness, (e) verbal withdrawal, (f) distraction, (g) projection, and (h) fillers. Paralinguistic indicators are also hiding behaviors: (a) overly soft tone, (b) hesitation, (c) self-interruption, (d) pausing, (e) rapid speech, and (f) laughed words. Indicators of *disorganized thought* are (a) irregular rhythm of speech, (b) filled pauses, (c) stammering, and (d) fragmented speech. *Visual* cues to shame include (a) hiding behavior such as hand covering the face or gaze aversion, (b) blushing, or (c) control behaviors such as biting the tongue or false smiling. Retzinger (1995) argues that "the more categories (e.g., visual, verbal, paralanguage, etc.) involved, and the greater the number of cues from each category, the stronger the evidence for the particular emotion" (p. 1112).

Malatesta-Magai and Dorval (1992, pp. 173-174) also provide a coding scheme for shame and embarrassment together that includes four basic categories. The first is facial displays (blushing and an abashed or ashamed look). The second is hiding behaviors (covering the face, averting the face or body, especially the eyes, lowered head or eyes, and slumped or lowered posture). The third category is self-grooming/touching (touching face, head, hair, neck, clothes, jewelry). The fourth is verbal/vocal displays, which is the most elaborate category (direct statements, tone of shame, statements of submission, embarrassed or self-conscious laughter, low and less clear indicators such as lowered or trailing voice, disfluency, stuttering, false starts, particles, marked inhale or exhale, gasping, whining).

Verbal and nonverbal expressions of guilt are not as well documented as those for shame. Izard (1977) says that "two features may distinguish guilt from shame. In intense guilt, the person's face takes on a heavy look, while the hot, flushed face (blushing) is more characteristic of shame. Guilt typically affects a person's expression and demeanor for a considerably longer period of time than does shame" (p. 424). He describes a combination of approach and avoidance: "repents, atones, make amends, changes, improves, does not repeat offense (49%); is deliberately alone, retreats from others (22%); rationalize, forget it, escape from feelings (13%)" (p. 398).

Coping and Management

Managing, regulating, or coping with emotion is an integral part of the emotion process, but it is not really a separate component. Rather, it operates through the other components (Frijda, 1986). People try to manage their shame or guilt by working with the precipitating events, appraisals, physiological reactions/action tendencies, and expressions and messages. The most basic regulatory stance toward shame and guilt is to either acknowledge or deny the feelings. As we noted earlier, in the discussion of the effects of shame and guilt on thought processes, part of full-blown shame is a state of mental confusion that promotes denial (and vice versa—denial promotes mental confusion). Guilt, on the other hand, often involves obsessive thoughts about repair that promote acknowledgment (and vice versa—acknowledgment promotes guilt). This difference is consistent with various descriptions of the extensive psychotherapy that is needed to uncover shame before an individual can even begin to manage it (e.g., Morrison, 1996).

One of the most common and striking ways of managing shame and guilt is to denigrate others. Blaming the other seems to be more pronounced and probably more destructive for shame than for guilt. Proneness to shame has been found to be positively associated with the tendency to blame others, whereas proneness to "shame-free" guilt has been found to be negatively related to other-blame (Tangney, Wagner, Fletcher, & Gramzow, 1992). Conversely, other-oriented empathy has been found to be negatively related to shame-proneness but positively related to guilt-proneness (Tangney, 1991). As Retzinger (1991) notes, "Because of the virtual invisibility of shame, and its painfulness, it is easy to deny one's own feelings, to claim that the other is at fault" (p. 56). Baumeister et al. (1994) say that "one important strategy for dealing with guilt is to reduce fellow feeling with one's victims (e.g., by dehumanizing them)" (p. 259). Wurmser (1995) describes this more concretely: "You don't matter to me. What you've said doesn't count. That our relationship has been impaired doesn't mean anything to me. I feel very comfortable" (p. 197).

Such strategies may assuage the individual's own shame, but they only damage the relational bond further, even though many types of prosocial remedial strategies are also available, such as offering regrets, explanations, excuses, justifications, apologies, or simple verbal expressions of guilt or shame (Metts, 1997, p. 375). The research does not tell us how likely shamed or guilty people are to use these prosocial strategies, especially compared with people who are embarrassed (because the research generally does not discriminate among shame, guilt, and embarrassment). We might speculate, however, that shamed people would be least inclined to use remedial strategies because of the possibility of mental confusion and the tendency to withdraw rather than to try to make amends. Moreover, it is easy to imagine offering regrets, excuses, or apologies for actions for which one feels guilt (and certainly for actions that are embarrassing), but not for a self that is defective or inadequate.

Another way to manage painful emotions is to substitute one emotion for another (what Wurmser, 1995, calls "screen affects"). Anger is an especially good substitute for shame because it is less aversive and makes a person feel powerful and self-righteous rather than inadequate and immoral. Anger is the best-documented screen affect for shame, largely because shame-based anger has been linked to violence (Scheff & Retzinger, 1991; more on this later). Lewis (1971) notes that shame is hostility turned inward, but it involves disapproving others, so it can easily turn outward, resulting in rage. Tangney (1995a, p. 1140) has also found shame-proneness to be correlated with measures of anger, hostility, irritability, resentment, and suspicion. Other emotions can also screen shame as well; these include contempt, depression, love, envy, defiance, boredom, or even numbness (the absence of feeling) (Lewis, 1987, pp. 107-108; Wurmser, 1995, pp. 197-201).

Whereas other emotions can screen or reduce shame, shame may compound itself when an individual feels ashamed of being ashamed or ashamed that another person is ashamed, perhaps leading to pathological and protracted emotions (Scheff, 1995a). In addition, "guilt can turn into blame of others, which can turn into a renewed and intensified sense of guilt" (Johnson & Greenberg, 1994, p. 36). People may feel shame about guilt (the global "bad me" subsuming the specific "bad behavior"), but not vice versa (Lewis, 1993, p. 570).

When they are expressed openly, screen affects blend managing appraisals with managing expressions. As Izard (1991) describes it:

> One modification of the shame response is for the individual to simply take a quick look downward. Sometimes an individual may hold the head high, in effect, substituting the look of contempt for the look of shame. A person may look chronically humble so that a shame expression will not be so noticeable. Finally, a person may hold the head back, the chin out, but still have a downward cast of the eyes. (p. 332)

Wurmser (1995, pp. 197-198) describes the "strutting rooster" syndrome, "turning the tables" through ridicule, hiding through silence, and of course attacking others as ways of masking shame. For example, as one patient said: "I am so afraid to be laughed at that I could not open my mouth for weeks. But then I attack the other (mother, father, friend) 'You talk too loud, you eat too fast or with open mouth' " (quoted in Wurmser, 1995, p. 198).

A more direct way to deal with shame and guilt is, of course, to change one's actions or, better yet, to live up to the standards or avoid committing moral transgressions in the first place. Avoiding shameful or guilt-producing actions requires that one anticipate the shame or guilt that one would feel if one acted (or failed to act). Sometimes the outcomes are trivial (e.g., sending a holiday card in order to avoid guilt), and sometimes they are tragic (e.g., leaving the scene of an accident). Of course, it is impossible to estimate how strongly we are influenced by the shame or guilt that we anticipate because we probably make such judgments below the level of conscious awareness, but there is little doubt that shame and guilt are extremely aversive. Shame can make most people avoid violence and murder, but violence and murder are also the means some people use to avoid shame (Retzinger, 1991; Scheff & Retzinger, 1991).

Once a shame- or guilt-producing event has happened (or failed to happen, in the case of a sin of omission), an individual can try to cope with the problem by doing something to fix it. Guilt may lead people to make amends, or at least to apologize in order to repair the damage done to the relationship, but it also may lead them to avoid those they have transgressed against (although avoidance may be due to the influence of shame mixed with guilt) (Baumeister et al., 1994, pp. 257-258). Many of the coping or regulatory strategies that are a part of shame and guilt are attempts to manage their consequences, but consequences go well beyond the person to play an important role in close relationships, organizations, and public life, as we will explore in later sections of this review.

Consequences of Shame and Guilt

The effects of shame and guilt can be considered for the person who experiences them and for the larger society in terms of three fundamental concerns (similar to the three functions of guilt noted by Baumeister et al., 1994): (a) esteem (self-esteem for individuals and groups or national esteem for larger social entities), (b) control (of one individual over another, between the individual and society, and among groups in the society), and (c) connections (among individuals and larger social connections). Of course, all three consequences interact in a variety of ways that we discuss throughout this review, and the relationships among consequences for shame are different from those for guilt.

Esteem

The most notable consequence of shame or guilt is that it makes people feel bad about themselves or about the organization or group to which they belong. Shame clearly has a greater negative effect on self-esteem than does guilt. The effects of shame and guilt on esteem—be it self-esteem, group esteem, or national esteem—constitute one of the focal points of controversy in scholarly and public discussions, and we address these effects at length later in this review. As individuals and as a society, we do not make other people feel shame or guilt out of whim, but to enforce important ideals and moral rules.

Control

We use messages of shame and guilt to control others and to bring them in line with moral expectations. We "diss" people (shame them) or "lay guilt trips" on them for reasons, and part of the controversy involves whether we have good enough reasons for making people feel bad. We make our intimate partners feel guilty for neglecting us, we shame children for violating sex role expectations, we make others feel guilty for being overweight or smoking cigarettes, we shame organizations for their racism.

Connection

A final consequence of shame and guilt is the damage they cause to connections between people. Guilt makes people want to *repair* the connections; shame makes people want to *sever* those connections. Shame and guilt put people on notice that their behaviors or even their whole persons are unacceptable to society. Another important aspect of the controversy surrounding shame and guilt is the issue of whether social isolation is a threat (or, in the case of shame, an actual punishment) that is too strong for the crime. Moreover, once a person is isolated, there is no hope of further guilt or shame being effective.

In the sections that follow, we focus on how messages of shame and guilt function across several communicative contexts: in intimate dyads, in childhood socialization, in organizations, and in the public sphere. In particular, we focus on the grounds for shame and guilt and on their effects on esteem, control, and connection in order to lay the groundwork for an analysis of the ethics of shame and guilt messages.

MESSAGES OF SHAME AND
GUILT IN INTIMATE DYADS

Baumeister, Stillwell, and Heatherton (1995) make a persuasive case that guilt "should be understood as something that happens between people as much as it happens inside them" (p. 269). The same can be said for shame, but that is probably more obvious. Close relationships are an especially fruitful domain for studying social emotions because feelings are intensified when close relationships are threatened. When people feel inadequate in the eyes of those they care about, shame is more painful; when people hurt people who are important to them, guilt is sharper. Even "survivor guilt is felt most strongly and commonly vis-à-vis family members, relatives, and intimates" (Baumeister et al., 1994, p. 252). Moreover, in managing shame and guilt in dyadic relationships, people may be more acutely aware of the tensions inherent in fostering intimate connections, producing the behavioral changes they desire, and maintaining the self-esteem of everyone involved.

Precipitating Events and Grounds for
Shame and Guilt in Intimate Dyads

Guilt and shame are found often, but not exclusively, in individuals' interactions with other people (Tangney, Miller, et al., 1996). Children often feel guilty for fighting, inconsiderate behavior, lying, and other hurtful interactions with others (Williams & Bybee, 1994). But thoughts can trigger guilt too; in fact, Williams and Bybee (1994, p. 621) found that thoughts were the most common source of guilt for the 11th graders in their sample. Nevertheless, private guilt and shame are relatively rare, estimated in one study to make up only 10% of guilt experiences and 18% of shame experiences (Tangney, Miller, et al., 1996, p. 1259). Using the beeper method, Baumeister, Reis, and Delespaul (1995) found that Dutch students reported feeling guilty about 13% of their waking hours. Most guilt was mild and founded in interpersonal concerns, conflicts, and problems. In the same study, American students reported their experiences of guilt were less likely to be solitary (compared with being with other people and compared with other emotions) and more likely to involve close relationship partners.

The exact grounds (or moral transgressions) on which shame and guilt are based are not always obvious, but some are stated and others can be inferred. The U.S. undergraduates studied by Tangney (1992) reported lying (21% of guilt situations, 11% of shame situations), cheating (23%/5%), and stealing (19%/3%) as the only grounds with double-digit percentages; they also reported a wide variety of other grounds (infidelity; not helping others; breaking a diet; failure at work, school, or sports; socially inappropriate behavior or dress; sex; unspecified immoral action; hurting someone emotionally; crime; hurting someone physically; disobeying parents; damaging objects; and murder). With most categories it is impossible to know whether the transgression occurred in an intimate relationship or not (e.g., lying, cheating, stealing), but we can guess that the transgressions in other categories probably did (e.g., not helping others, hurting someone emotionally or physically, and disobeying parents). Baumeister, Reis, and Delespaul (1995) report that for their undergraduate sample, "the most common source of guilt . . . was neglecting someone . . . and two other common categories were romantic or sexual infidelities and being rude, mean, cold or nasty to someone" (p. 1264). Jones, Kugler, and Adams (1995) found five basic categories of relational transgressions for which their college student respondents felt guilty, in addition to another five that were nonrelational. The relational categories were (a) fantasy transgressions (e.g., wishing someone dead), (b) coercive transgressions (e.g., forcing a friend to smoke marijuana), (c) rebellion (e.g., doing things parents would disapprove of), (d) hostility (e.g., shouting angrily at a family member), and (e) deceit (lying to a friend). Specific events for college students included dating several men, leaving for the summer without saying good-bye to a close friend, saying something tactless, treating a friend badly, a summer romantic fling, and "a dumb argument on the phone" (Baumeister, Stillwell, & Heatherton, 1995); for 18- to 65-year-olds, specific events included breaking a promise to take a job, a respondent's overhearing two boys talking about her in a bar, never returning a borrowed item, a respondent's feeling responsible for her mother's death, a respondent's physically shaking his girlfriend and making her cry, a respondent's new boyfriend's telling her she was too thin, a respondent's giving her baby sister a fatal cold, and breaking off a relationship (Lindsay-Hartz, 1984).

Another approach to the question of grounds for shame and guilt is to ask on what grounds one person tries to make *others* feel ashamed or guilty in a close relationship. Studies by Baumeister, Stillwell, and Heatherton (1995) and Vangelisti et al. (1991) have addressed this issue with similar results. The violation of relationship obligations or norms is a very common ground for guilt, including neglecting the partner, failing to live up to an obligation, and betraying a romantic relationship. Baumeister et al. (1994) found that the "single largest category of guilt inductions was failure to pay sufficient attention to relationship partners. People would inform a relationship partner that they felt neglected by him or her, and the partner would then feel guilty and subsequently spend more time and energy on maintaining the relationship" (p. 249). Vangelisti and Sprague (1998) argue that guilt is based not so much on general moral standards, but on what might be termed a "relational conscience" (p. 145).

In general, the findings on grounds for shame and guilt in close relationships support the claim made earlier that it is difficult to find specific elicitors for shame and guilt, but general categories of moral transgression do summarize them, albeit vaguely. It seems that there are many ways to go wrong morally in close relationships, so that concise yet specific typologies may not be possible. Whether the general grounds for guilt and shame in interpersonal relationships derived primarily from student populations can be generalized to other age and occupational groups is as yet an open question. For example, Secouler (1992; see also Swift, 1991) found that for elderly women, loss of physical attractiveness and no longer being needed by others made them ashamed. It should also be noted that there is more systematic evidence for what makes people guilty (albeit in the form of self-reports) than there is concerning what makes people ashamed.

Consequences of Shame and Guilt Messages in Intimate Dyads

Wicker et al. (1983) provide a good starting point for understanding all three types of consequences of shame and guilt because they address the components explicitly, describe how the three are linked, and note differences between shame and guilt. In terms of *esteem,* they found that subjects "felt more active and felt greater control when guilty; they felt more submissive, inferior, inhibited, and lacking in status, power, and self-confidence when shamed" (p. 36). In terms of *connection:* "Subjects did seem to express greater alienation from others when ashamed. They reported a greater desire to punish others, compete with them, or hide from them with shame," and in turn, "other people were more likely to reject the raters, laugh at them, or abandon them" (that is, others were jeopardizing the connection as well) (p. 36). On the other hand, guilt's milder effect on self-esteem can goad an individual to repair the relationship with the other person. Both shame and guilt serve the function of social *control* by making people feel bad about transgression, but guilt can provoke a "desire for revenge, to rectify the power imbalance and/or return the pain received" (p. 37). Now we turn to each consequence separately as it applies to intimate dyads.

Control

Because shame and guilt are so aversive, they can be used very effectively to control others (O'Keefe & Figgé, 1997), although there may be a price paid in esteem and connection. Vangelisti et al. (1991) studied the many ways that people make one another feel guilty in conversations. Their examples probably sound disconcertingly familiar:

A: Are you going to watch the baby tomorrow while I'm at school?
B: No, I want to go fishing.
A: Fine. When he grows up and asks who daddy is, I'll say he never had time for you. (p. 10)

A: Sue, can I borrow your car?
B: No, I really don't like to loan out my car.
A: Well, I'm glad you appreciate all the times you've driven my car to work! (p. 11)

Vangelisti et al. found persuasion to be by far the most common reason for eliciting guilt in the conversations, followed by dominance as a distant second. There is also indirect evidence in Vangelisti et al.'s data that guilt is used by the less powerful or assertive member of the dyad as an alternative to direct confrontation. Socially unassertive and shy people found it relatively difficult to use guilt-inducing messages but reported using them more often than did their more assertive or less shy counterparts (Vangelisti et al., 1991). This finding is consistent with, although not directly supportive of, Baumeister et al.'s (1994) claim that "guilt may operate as an interpersonal influence technique that allows even a relatively powerless person to get his or her way" (p. 247). Baumeister et al. argue that guilt works best when the victim appears helpless, when the transgressor believes that the accusation is just, and when the transgressor cares about the victim. If not, the transgressor may feel resentful, manipulated, or unjustly accused, or simply may not care enough about the victim to be persuaded by guilt. Baumeister et al. "reiterate that inducing guilt appears to be a potentially costly technique for getting one's own way, and overdoing it can be extremely destructive" (p. 263).

On a personal level, guilt and shame serve the regulatory functions of directing attention away from the immediate rewards of actions to their long-term negative consequences, especially social ones (Baumeister, 1995). Appealing to anticipatory shame or guilt serves this function interpersonally, as when someone says, "Wouldn't you be really ashamed if you got caught cheating?" Appealing to and providing an outlet for people's existing guilt may also lead them to comply with a request, as O'Keefe and Figgé (1997) found in their meta-analysis of the "door-in-the-face" persuasive strategy. Making an initial request that is denied triggers guilt ("Can I use the car tonight, Mom?" "No!"), and making a second request that the other party can agree to reduces it ("Then can I at least invite Ricky over?" "Well, okay."). Expressing approval when another person makes sought-after changes (such as quitting smoking) can help alleviate guilt, and disapproval can start it up again if there is a relapse (Birkimer, Johnston, & Berry, 1993).

Shame has received less attention as a persuasive strategy, but certainly when a person is shamed for failure to live up to an ideal, this is an indirect form of persuasion or coercion. As Morrison (1996) says, "Ideals can either *serve* us or *enslave* us" (p. 70). He argues that attainable ideals promote growth and pride, but that harsh, demanding, or unattainable ideals lead to inevitable failures and possibly shame and despair.

In general, both shame and guilt support and enforce the moral status quo, but, as Izard (1991) notes, they are not beyond challenge: "Although efforts to avoid shame may subserve conformity, confronting and coping successfully with shame experiences can facilitate the development of autonomy, personal identity, and mutual love" (p. 343). Of course, shame and guilt serve control differently, with guilt focused on changing moral behaviors and shame focused on changing the person as a whole. In fact, self-reported moral behaviors (e.g., "I am honest in the way I deal with people" or "I have taken things I wanted without paying for them or returning them later") have been found to be positively associated with guilt-proneness but not associated with shame-proneness (Tangney, 1995a, p. 1139).

Esteem

It is obvious that messages of shame and guilt in close relationships affect the message receivers' self-esteem for the worse. Baumeister et al. (1994) note that "guilt also seems linked to a desire to enhance or recover self-esteem, suggesting that one aspect of guilt is a temporary loss of esteem" (p. 255). Tangney et al. (1992) write that "shame is an overwhelmingly painful experience that involves a clear threat to one's sense of self-worth and self-efficacy" (p. 673). Oversensitivity to shame and guilt in others' messages can also affect communication in maladaptive ways. Marriage therapists Johnson and Greenberg (1994) warn us that "shame causes problems because it is so painful to recognize, accept, and admit to, and there is such a temptation to shift the blame. When working affectively with couples where shame is a major dynamic, the therapist must always be on the lookout for self-esteem sinkholes—pockets of self-disgust and feelings of inadequacy and worthlessness" (p. 79). Tangney (1995a) contrasts shame and guilt in claiming that shame-proneness is associated with an array of psychological symptoms, but guilt-proneness is not. In her words, "Our guess is that guilt takes a turn for the worse when it becomes fused with shame" (p. 1141).

Baumeister et al. (1994, p. 247) claim that another principal function of guilt is to redistribute emotional distress within the dyad. The transgressor has presumably reaped some reward from the transgression at the expense of the victim. As Frijda (1994) states, "He walks in pleasure and I in suffering" (p. 263). Frijda is speaking of vengeance, but Baumeister and colleagues are saying that guilt works a kind of emotional vengeance by making the transgressor suffer as the victim has suffered. In addition, guilt inducers often feel better when their partners begin to feel and show guilt. One helpful consequence can be that guilt "brings partners into similar emotional states, which facilitates communication between them; and of course the improved communication may be beneficial for the relationship" (Baumeister, Stillwell, & Heatherton, 1995, p. 267). As one of Baumeister, Stillwell, and Heatherton's (1995) respondents described an episode when his mother made him feel guilty for making her worry: "We made up, of course, after lots of crying and explaining" (p. 267). One can easily imagine a comparable process of sharing shame by converting one's own shame to contempt as a way to bring the other down to one's own level and equalize the suffering, but with a quite different outcome. Rather than reaching out to one another, the individuals in a shamed pair are more likely to withdraw from one another, making communication and reconciliation even less likely than if the originally shamed partner had kept the shame to him- or herself.

At the interface between esteem and control is the syndrome of bypassed shame converted to anger, which makes people feel better (in both senses of the word—more pleasant and more morally correct), thus raising their esteem. Anger also gives one a sense of control over the situation, exerts control over the other person, and limits the other's control over oneself. Guilt does not seem to provoke the same enraged response (although there is a touch of hostility and resentment; Tangney et al., 1992, p. 674), suggesting that there may be more to the bypassed shame-anger link than simply an escape from negative feelings. One possibility is that shame is seen as too painful a punishment for what is perceived as a small offense. The shaming message is unfair in the mind of the person being shamed, so responding in anger is justified (see Tangney et al., 1992, p. 673). Another similar mechanism is that "shame also involves the imagery of a disapproving other, this hostility is easily redirected outward toward others who may be held in part responsible for the ugly feeling of shame" (Tangney, 1995a, p. 1135). Katz (1988) says that "righteousness is the essential stepping stone from humiliation to rage" (p. 23). Note that when anger is suffused with shame, it becomes so intense that the terminology switches from *anger* to *rage* or *fury* and shame is intensified into *humiliation,* which also places it further from self-blame and closer to other-blame. When humiliated, "I am acted on by one or more persons who morally assault me by challenging my competence or trying to ridicule me" (Katz, 1988, p. 27).

The bypassed shame-rage cycle has received considerable research attention because of its link to violence. It is mentioned in several major accounts of shame (e.g., Kaufman, 1992; first by H. B. Lewis, 1971, then by M. Lewis, 1992) and violence, especially domestic violence (Katz, 1988; Lansky, 1987; Retzinger, 1991; Scheff, 1994; Scheff & Retzinger, 1991). Lansky (1987) writes that "transactions in marriages characterized by domestic violence are typified by maneuvers that sharply increase shame in the system, that is, by *overt humiliation* as a typical transactional mode" (p. 340). One crucial ingredient to the shame-rage cycle is that the shame is often extremely fleeting, not even experienced consciously, and nearly always unacknowledged (Lewis, 1971). Its covert nature makes it very difficult to study, through either self-report or observation, and to manage, either by oneself or in therapy.

Retzinger (1991), however, has videotaped sequences showing individuals going from shame to anger to shame to anger, and so on, in a 5-second time span. She describes the cycle like this:

> When shame, the emotional signal of an impaired bond, is not acknowledged, escalation is likely. If intense shame is evoked but unacknowledged, rage is quick to follow. . . . The direction often taken is to perceive the self as a victim and the partner as the problem, rather than acknowledging feelings, joint involvement in the problem, and the need for love, care, and connection. (pp. 55-56)

Challenging messages that are likely to evoke shame-rage are interruptions, sarcasm, blame, criticism, interrogation, and threats (pp. 71-72), resulting in shame reactions such as denial, defensiveness, verbal withdrawal, and projection. "Disrespect is the medium for exchange of shame-rage between partners," says Retzinger (1991, p. 185). The verbal behaviors that Retzinger reports bear a striking resemblance to conflict styles that Gottman (1994, p. 414) identifies as precursors to divorce—criticism, contempt, defensiveness, and stonewalling.

It is easy to imagine dyads getting locked into reciprocal cycles of blaming/shaming messages, as described by Retzinger (1991). Tangney, Burggraf, and Wagner (1995, p. 360) offer a number of communicative strategies for escaping the cycle in therapy, but these strategies can also be extrapolated to other dyadic contexts. These include verbalizing the shame (which helps the individual to reflect on and reevaluate the shaming episode), using messages that elicit acceptance and understanding (thus rebuilding the interpersonal bridge), and even trying humor about some irony of the situation or about overreacting (which makes the shame seem less serious and threatening). Suggestions also come from the literature on marital therapy. Metts (1997, p. 378) proposes antidotes to Gottman's precursors to divorce, including not saying hurtful things, being willing to say you are sorry, acknowledging and praising one's partner, being positive, and being supportive. Balcom et al. (1995) advise using the common therapeutic techniques of making "I" statements instead of "we" statements (to avoid blaming) and letting one person talk without interruption, followed by the other person paraphrasing what he or she said. To address shame explicitly, they recommend the simple question, "What makes it so hard for you to apologize, to say, 'I'm sorry' or 'I'm wrong, I made a mistake'?" Confronting difficulties in apologizing "helps to develop, in small doses, tolerance for shame" and "begins the process of restitution and the development of empathy" (p. 62). The ultimate cure for shame and guilt, of course, is to work through the failure or transgression and reestablish the interpersonal bridge. In Morrison's (1996) poetic words, "Shame seems to disappear in the comforting cradle of belonging" (p. 78).

Connection

Shame and guilt would hold no dread if people did not care about the connections that they threaten. Kaufman (1992) calls shame "the alienating affect" (p. 6) and echoes the social nature of shame when he says that "the critical step occurs when one significant person somehow breaks the interpersonal bridge with the other" (p. 13). But as Izard (1991) notes: "In one respect we are anything but alienated. We are standing in flaming light before piercing eyes. However, we are quite alienated in the sense that we cannot easily reach out, touch, or communicate with the other person" (p. 334). Although guilt may not go so far as to threaten the bond itself, it does signal that the rules of relationship are threatened and "prompts and reminds people to pay attention to their loved ones, to refrain from hurting or injuring them, and so forth" (Baumeister, 1995, p. 123; see also Baumeister & Leary, 1995).

Vangelisti et al.'s (1991) examples show that control and connection are deeply intertwined in cases where people use guilt to persuade others to spend more time with them, give them more attention, or adhere to relational obligations and norms. If guilt leads to constructive action, it obviously motivates relationship-enhancing behavior (Baumeister et al., 1994). Shame, on the other hand, motivates relationship-damaging or relationship-destroying behaviors. We might say that guilt threatens the interpersonal bridge and leads people to try to repair it, whereas shame leads people either to withdraw the bridge or to cross it in order to attack.

Tangney (1995b) provides the largest body of evidence showing that being prone to guilt tends to have more prosocial effects on close relationships than does being prone to shame, because guilt tends to keep people constructively engaged, whereas shame often leads to avoidance (bearing in mind that this is true, at least in part, by definition). Proneness to shame tends to make a person focus on the self and to " 'short-circuit' feelings of other-oriented empathy" (Tangney, 1995b, p. 135), whereas proneness to guilt is positively associated with empathy (Tangney, 1991, 1995a). Tangney also notes the greater risk that shame will transform into anger and aggression, both verbal and physical. Johnson and Greenberg (1994) basically concur. They call the embarrassment-shame (guilt)-humiliation complex one of the "marriage-killer" emotions. They explain the dynamics:

> Shame separates people. We look down, cover our faces, look away, and go away when we feel shame. We also try to ward it off by arguing, getting mad, and blaming. But that only shames the other and leads to endless fights about who is to blame. Wiping dirt off yourself and onto your partner is a very costly way to get clean. (p. 78)

But they also say that "an important predictor of good outcomes is how willing the partners are, or can become, to engage each other, talk, deal openly, rather than withdraw" (p. 79).

Lindsay-Hartz's (1984) examples also affirm how shame promotes withdrawal whereas guilt promotes recompense. Shame "can lead lovers to flee love affairs, friends to cut off communications with friends, and patients to bolt from therapy" (p. 693). Guilt, by contrast, produces the urge to set things right. As one respondent said, "I'm wondering if after all this time, I could undo this—if it still is with me" (p. 693). Withdrawing is a common response to shame, whereas people who feel guilty are more likely to discuss the issue with their partners (Tangney, Wagner, Hill-Barlow, Marschall, & Gramzow, 1996, p. 805). Shame is also associated with the tendency to attack oneself or other people (Ferguson & Crowley, 1997; Tangney et al., 1992). As Tangney (1995a) says, "Not only are shame-prone individuals more prone to anger, in general, than their non-shame-prone peers. Once angered, they are also more likely to manage their anger in an unconstructive fashion" (p. 1140). Shame-proneness is related to "malevolent intentions; direct, indirect, and displaced aggression; self-directed hostility; and projected negative long-term consequences of everyday episodes of anger" (p. 1140). By contrast, guilt-proneness is associated with constructive ways of handling anger and positive long-term consequences (Tangney, 1995a, 1995b). Lopez et al. (1997) also found guilt-proneness to be positively associated with collaborative problem solving, whereas they found shame-proneness to be negatively related to collaboration and positively related to conflict avoidance.

Summary of Shame and Guilt Messages in Intimate Dyads

Retzinger (1991) claims that "shame is a normal and necessary part of human social organization. The way it is managed is the source of concern" (p. 199), and the same could be said of guilt. Our analysis of events that precipitate, or the grounds for shame and guilt, indicate that they are an array of moral transgressions that most of us would agree are shame- or guiltworthy. It is hard to argue in favor of neglecting one's close relationships, lying, defying one's parents, or hurting others emotionally. We should recognize, however, that these categories are based on self-reports and probably have a social desirability bias, in addition to any biases that might be associated with study samples made up primarily of college students. To be sure, some respondents have reported feeling guilty for sexual infidelity or murder, hardly socially desirable disclosures, but we also know that people will not tell anyone about many shameful events, so it is unlikely that researchers have tapped the full range of such events. Another problem that pertains more to shame than to guilt is that people are often unaware of their own shame or are unwilling to admit it even to themselves, so we are much less likely to know the precipitating events and grounds for shame than we are to know those for guilt.

Messages are used to induce shame and guilt often and probably very effectively as means of controlling ourselves and other people, though these messages are not without consequences for esteem and connections with others. In general, messages inducing guilt work toward connection by prompting remedial action, although not always. By contrast, nobody seems to have much good to say about shame and shaming messages because they work against connection by prompting avoidance, anger, and verbal and physical aggression. Especially dangerous in couples are the blaming/shaming sequences that some theorists argue are associated with domestic violence (and in any case can hardly be viewed as healthy). Both partners' becoming aware and tolerant of their own and their partners' shame and working together to rebuild the frayed bond seems to be the best way to manage shame in intimate dyads.

SOCIALIZATION OF SHAME AND GUILT IN CHILDREN

Grounds for Children's Shame and Guilt

Grounds for shame and guilt in children look similar to those for shame and guilt in adults, but they differ a bit due to developmental changes. Williams and Bybee (1994) found that fifth, eighth, and eleventh graders reported feeling guilty for interpersonal transgressions (such as fighting, arguments, disobedience, inconsiderate behavior, and lying) in addition to events that were not interpersonal (such as breaking objects, truancy, and stealing). This study, along with another (Graham, Doubleday, & Guarino, 1984; cited in Harris, 1989, p. 87), also found that feeling guilt about something that was not one's own fault declines with age, but still persists into adulthood (Baumeister et al., 1994).

Consequences of Shame- and Guilt-Inducing
Messages in Childhood Socialization

Control

Miller and Tangney (1994) sum up rather neatly the role of shame and guilt in childhood socialization: "By gradually teaching children to experience shame . . . a society inculcates respect for normative behavior that slowly reduces the need for external monitoring of individual conduct" (p. 273). In their work with second and fifth graders who responded to questions concerning stories about moral transgressions or social blunders, Ferguson et al. (1991) found that the second graders perceived both shame and guilt in terms of others' actions and opinions (e.g., ridicule), whereas the fifth graders showed evidence of having internalized the norms (e.g., feeling stupid and incapable). These results imply that messages used to manage (that is, induce or relieve) shame and guilt may have their greatest impacts in infancy and early childhood, but by late childhood children are guided more by their own internalized moral standards.

Ferguson and Stegge (1995, p. 182) discuss four general ways in which parents socialize shame and guilt in their children: (a) direct parental modeling of affective styles, (b) parental feedback to the child in emotion-eliciting situations, (c) parental communication to the child about how the parent perceives the child as actually being or behaving compared to expectations, and (d) parental attributional, emotional, and behavioral reactions to the child when an "ideal" or "ought" has been violated. The goal is "a constructive (albeit negative) emotion orientation in which the child critically accepts responsibility for untoward behavior but nonetheless maintains a sense of self-value and control" (p. 190).

Needless to say, there are many examples of parents who model shame and guilt messages badly. Malatesta-Magai and Dorval (1992) examined in detail a three-way family interaction in which the 12-year-old son used a shame-contempt sequence that he seemed to have learned and used as a defense against his mother's shaming messages and his father's contempt. Stierlin (1974) also provides several examples from his therapeutic practice of parents who work out their own shame and guilt issues through their children; Stierlin describes the children as "delegates in the service of their parents' superego" (p. 386). Ferguson and Stegge (1995) found that

> the parents of children who exhibited shame were hostile and provided little in the way of concrete feedback regarding what the children had done that was right or wrong. Importantly, too, the children responding with shame were the greatest disappointment to parents in domains involving attributes that are fairly difficult to change (e.g., temperamental characteristics, athletic prowess, and academic ability). (p. 190)

Harris (1989, p. 97) claims that when parents emphasize the harm that a child has done rather than being simply punitive or coercive, the child is more likely to anticipate feeling guilty after a transgression and to expect others to feel the same. Lewis (1992, p. 114) also adds that when parents assert power in forceful ways they may produce shame, making it hard for their children to focus on the message about morality (presumably via "mental confusion"), whereas reasoning with children helps them to examine their actions and try to repair the damage.

In addition to observations and reports of parent-child interactions, retrospective accounts of college students provide some evidence that parents' communicative styles influence their children's orientations to shame and guilt even into adulthood, but not in ways that are always simple. For example, Abell and Gecas (1997) found complex interactions among sex of child, sex of parent, and parenting style. For reasons that are not fully understood, "fathers' threats of withdrawal and loss of regard appear to weaken sons' connection to norms, whereas mothers' threats of withdrawal and loss of regard appear to strengthen sons' connection to norms" (p. 115). In a similar study, students who reported experiencing more shame were found to be likely to come from families perceived to be less cohesive and less expressive, with less intellectual/cultural orientation, less religious/moral orientation, less organization, and more conflict—in short, dysfunctional families (Pulakos, 1996). (Their dysfunction was validated by evidence that intact families had more cohesion, moral/religious emphasis, and organization and less conflict compared with families with divorced parents.) By contrast, students who reported experiencing more guilt came from families with more active/recreational orientations and better organization.

Esteem

Nathanson (1987a) argues for the benefits of shame in limiting narcissism and encouraging more realistic self-appraisal. Mild teasing and joking at displays of arrogance can serve this function. He argues that in healthy families, shaming is playful and mild and respects the bounds of self-esteem of each person (p. 261). In contrast, Lewis (1992, p. 110) believes that many instances of teasing and making someone the butt of jokes are in fact humiliating, especially when these are accompanied by nonverbal expressions of disgust, which he believes are used surprisingly often in the socialization of children.

Lewis (1992) is concerned about two potentially damaging ways in which shame and guilt messages affect children's self-esteem. First, he argues that inappropriately high achievement standards make it more likely that children will fail no matter what they do, thus leading to shame. The crucial factor, however, is whether the family humiliates and shames the child further or, alternatively, explains what he or she can do better (p. 99). In defense of shaming messages, Kaufman (1992, p. 22) argues that parents can be expected to set *reasonable* standards for the child to live up to in areas such as personal hygiene, use of language, respecting the property of others, respecting privacy, and keeping one's word. Children who do not live up to their parents' expectations (based on reasonable community norms) are rightfully shamed by parents who seek to teach them good citizenry.

Lewis (1992) is also concerned about two appraisal (or attributional) tendencies that can set up constructive or destructive shame or guilt. First, children who do not attribute blame to themselves for failure may experience too little shame or guilt; conversely, those who are too inclined to blame themselves may experience too much. Second, global attributions are more likely to foster shame, whereas specific attributions are more likely to foster guilt. Lewis argues that even positive global attributions, such as calling a child a "great kid," still foster global attributions, making it easier to move from "great kid" to "terrible kid" than from "great kid" to "terrible thing that you did." These two attributional tendencies may underlie the sex differences that have been found in some studies of children's socialization. Alessandri and Lewis (1993) found that "boys received more positive evaluations while girls received more negative ones" (p. 335) and that "signs of shame were positively correlated with number of negative parental evaluations" (p. 340). This was especially true for mothers who maltreated their children, with maltreated daughters showing "more shame when they failed and less pride when they succeeded than nonmaltreated girls" (a nonsignificant difference for boys; Alessandri & Lewis, 1996, p. 1857).

Connection

Lewis (1992) also comments on how love withdrawal produces shame through the same attributional processes—global attribution of failure. As Bowlby (1973) describes it, "An unwanted child is likely not only to feel unwanted by his parents but to believe that he is essentially unwantable" (p. 204; as quoted in Lewis, 1992, p. 115). Family members can be "put off" verbally as well as withdraw directly, leading to the same sense of love withdrawal. Scheff (1995a) believes that unacknowledged shame is a source of interminable conflict in families; it is a signal of alienation, but a signal that is ignored and denied: "Family members cycle through disrespectful words and gestures, shame, and anger, which leads to further disrespectful gestures, and on around the loop" (p. 411). Nathanson (1987a) concurs: "To the best of my knowledge, the verbal portion of a fight is only either shaming or 'guilting' " (p. 260).

Summary of Uses of Shame and Guilt
Messages in Childhood Socialization

As in the research on intimate dyads, the literature on shame and guilt in childhood socialization tends to grant the need and even the desirability of the use of shame and guilt as internalized and highly emotionally painful enforcers of social and moral values. The overriding concern for parents is how to use messages effectively to instill appropriate and constructive levels of shame and guilt. The key seems to be for parents to guide children's reasoning rather than simply coercing them, especially by threatening to withhold love or by showing contempt. In addition, messages that foster too little or too much self-blame or that carry globalizing judgments (whether good or bad) may foster unhealthy levels of shame or guilt. Acknowledging shame and avoiding disrespectful words and gestures may help families to avoid prolonged conflict and the instilling of dysfunctional levels of shame and guilt in children.

USE OF MESSAGES OF SHAME AND GUILT IN AND BY ORGANIZATIONS

Although research on emotions within organizations is increasing, shame and guilt have seldom been named explicitly, and it has been rarer still for them to have been the subject of research. Fineman's (1993a) anthology is a notable exception; in his own introductory chapter to the volume, Fineman (1993b) asserts that "the socially connected emotions of embarrassment, shame, and guilt are central to many aspects of organizational order . . . the motivational springs to self-control" (p. 17). Another exception is the psychoanalytic perspective of organizational communication—the "organizational unconscious" (Bion, 1959; De Board, 1978; Diamond, 1993; Kets de Vries, 1991; Schwartz, 1990). The absence of explicit mention of shame and guilt does not mean, however, that these emotions are absent from research studies—they simply go unnamed. As we identified the contexts in which shame and guilt have been named explicitly, we found many articles that discuss the same organizational communication phenomena without naming shame and guilt as emotional factors (for example, sexual harassment). In this section we point to identified grounds for organizational shame and guilt, reviewing primarily articles that explicitly name those emotions. We also include, to support those grounds, several studies in which shame and guilt appear to have a vital role but are not identified by name.

Grounds for Shame and Guilt in Organizations

The predominant grounds or antecedents for organizational shame and guilt that appear in the literature include the following categories: (a) psychodynamic neuroses based on family role transference (from the perspective of organizational psychoanalysis), (b) employee responsibilities, (c) racism, (d) sex roles and sexual harassment, (e) downsizing, and (f) gossip and graffiti. Within each of these overarching grounds (which include a wide range of related grounds), we have looked at how the organizations tried to manage their shame and guilt and how the consequences affected organizational or member esteem, control, and connection. Then, looking across the grounds, we have tried to understand the kinds of ethical dilemmas and decisions that these consequences imply.

Neuroses and Family Role Transference

Self-esteem, along with ego ideals and narcissism, is an important part of the unconscious life of organizations that Diamond (1993) explores, combining specific communication examples with organizational psychoanalysis. He describes how the staff members in a human services agency were shamed by the negative self-images that their boss projected on them. Baum (1987) describes a range of workplace behaviors that are unconsciously shame and guilt based, such as the subordinate who chooses not to challenge his boss's weak ideas on a proposal and feels shame rather than "confronting, feeling guilty, and being punished" (p. 82). In Baum's view, bureaucratic authority, "in the context of American beliefs about personal achievement, work, and success, appears to be most commonly interpreted by workers as a potentially shaming relationship" (p. 83). Although messages might negatively affect employee self-esteem, those effects serve the bureaucratic workplace, according to Baum, because shame and guilt are instruments of social control: "Workers who doubt their own efficacy and feel humiliated by organizational authority may not want to think about how power is exercised or what they might do to acquire it" (p. 84).

Psychoanalytic theory has given us the troubled organization (Kets de Vries & Miller, 1987), the neurotic organization (Kets de Vries & Miller, 1984), and the addictive organization (Schaef & Fassel, 1988), each with its concomitant communicative practices. The books written on these types of organizations address organizational neuroses resulting, in part, from the self-esteem issues of organization members (and, conversely, members' self-esteem problems created by organizational dynamics). This is hardly surprising to researchers with a postmodern bent, such as Barry and Hazen (1996), who believe that "the way we see our selves/bodies shapes the way we organize and create theories about organization" (p. 140). How, then, have "shamed bodies" written theory and instigated organizational practices? Morgan (1986) answers that question with a related, more specific question: "To what extent do our modes of organization institutionalize defense mechanisms relating to repressed sexuality?" He gives the example of the British "Factory Acts" of 1833, which led to the emphasis of "abstinence, restraint, and clean living" by the industrial masters (p. 209), and he speculates that the inspiration for Frederick Taylor's scientific management was an external manifestation of a "disturbed and neurotic personality" (p. 205). Taylor's well-documented nightmares and anal-compulsive obsessions may be interpreted as a classic Freudian example of unconscious struggles with repressed (shamed) sexuality.

Group members' unconscious fears and anxieties, manifested in feelings of inferiority, occupied Bion's (1959) groundbreaking research on groups in a military psychiatric hospital (see also the discussion of Bion's, Freud's, Klein's, and Lewin's work in De Board, 1978). Ashforth (1994) describes "petty tyranny in organizations" that fosters learned helplessness (p. 768). Although Ashforth does not mention shame directly, it can be associated with the behaviors listed: passivity, dependency, depression, helplessness, and self-depreciation. Kets de Vries

(1995), quoting Freud's description of people who are "criminals out of a sense of guilt" (p. 15), takes a clinical approach to understanding workaholism, work rivalries, and work anxieties as self-esteem problems related to guilt originating in members' families of origin.

Other organization studies that do not take deliberately psychoanalytic approaches nevertheless use the family metaphor to describe guilt-based organizational dysfunctions. Examples include a case study of "family" fights within a planning agency (Baum, 1991) and another of a university "divorcing" its president, who refused to acknowledge any personal guilt for university problems (Allen & Tompkins, 1996). In a third example, Pan American airline stewardesses who did not go along with a union slowdown because they wanted "to please in order to compensate for a flaw such as age, fatness, or homosexuality that they have been made to feel guilty about" (Hochschild, 1983, p. 130) were manipulated by upper management (parents) to vote against coworkers (siblings) through the use of internalized shame.

Leaders—as organizational surrogate parents by virtue of their accountabilities—are not only in a position to shame subordinates, they are also highly vulnerable to feelings of shame and guilt themselves. One example is the embarrassment experienced by some leaders when "mixing with the troops," due in part to what Gabriel (1997, pp. 329, 334) sees as the fantasies of leaders as "messiahs," which leaders cannot live up to. Gemmill and Oakley (1992) write about "the great leader myth" that leads to despair, disappointment, and disillusionment of members. Baum (1992) describes similar dynamics between mentors and protégés caught in the myths and fantasies surrounding idealized relationships. Applying psychoanalysis to the bonds between leaders and the led, Kets de Vries (1995) states that power "may lead to a regression to attachment-type behaviour which is itself based in early interaction patterns between mother and child" (p. 71).

Scholars who have written about guilt/shame-based organizational psychodynamics have focused on individual neuroses that create neurotic workplaces where depression, dependence, and self-depreciation are seen in both leaders and followers. When "family" is the metaphor used in association with shame or guilt, control, connection, and self-esteem all come into play as organizations (or their leaders) assume parental roles and organizational members are de facto "children." Although organizational neurosis as the antecedent of guilt in the workplace does not accrue any positive organizational outcomes, the ground of unfulfilled employee responsibilities has mixed outcomes; shame and guilt are both problematic and beneficial for the organization.

Employee Responsibilities

A wide range of organizational situations call for the use of shame and guilt to gain employee compliance. Workplace controls include internal pressure (guilt) and external pressure (shame) from coworkers to increase output (Lazear & Kandel, 1992). In their study of the Grameen (Cooperative) Bank in Bangladesh,

Papa, Auwal, and Singhal (1995) found that shame and guilt put pressure on people to repay their loans, particularly within the groups in which they worked. These authors critique the "concertive control system" that undergirds a dialectic of emancipation and subordination, reminiscent of the good shame/bad shame dialectic. At one end, the identification of the workers with the Grameen Bank provides empowering sustenance: They *are* the Grameen Bank; it is their "living body" (p. 211). Conversely, the Grameen Bank demands their total subordination, and disobedience can mean communal rejection. This evokes Wurmser's (1987) description of shame as "a fear of disgrace . . . but respect about the values central to culture and all human interaction" (p. 66). At the Grameen Bank those values—and the shame associated with violating them—are central to the members' survival and serve both to connect its members and to control them. In many mission-driven and highly demanding organizations, the tendency toward total absorption of the individual provides the grounds for guilt- or shame-based governance of employees' actions.

Inculcating a sense of guilt and shame can work better as an organizational control than can sanctions for deterrence. In a study of 410 Australian nursing homes, Makkai and Braithwaite (1994a) attempted to assess the effects of a range of sanctions on regulatory compliance, expecting a positive correlation with sanction severity. Instead, they found that the salient variable for compliance was not the severity of the sanctions but the emotionality of the directors/managers of the nursing homes (based on "guilt" scores on a self-administered questionnaire). For some managers, the threat of government sanctions inspired indignant "righteous resistance" rather than rational calculation of potential loss. Makkai and Braithwaite (1994a) call upon Scheff and Retzinger's (1991) theory that humiliation can be transformed into rage or defiance to explain "why deterrent threats are counterproductive with highly emotional actors" (p. 365). Compliance with standards was also predicated on the communication style of the inspectors, based on a scale of reintegrative versus stigmatizing shaming (Makkai & Braithwaite, 1994b). *Reintegrative* shaming, which focuses on the problem rather than blaming the wrongdoer, resulted in increased compliance, whereas *stigmatizing* shaming resulted in decreased compliance. In other words, shaming that was targeted to reduce the self-esteem of workers did not get the intended result of compliance from those workers.

In their study of legal and moral sanctions, Paternoster and Simpson (1996) gave four scenarios of corporate offenses (price-fixing, bribery, manipulation of sales statistics, and violation of EPA emission standards) to graduate students, who were asked to imagine themselves as managers of the offending corporations and then asked questions about their perceptions of the benefits and costs of each crime and their feelings of shame and moral evaluation of the act. Paternoster and Simpson conclude that legal sanctions and appeals to morality ("a sense of shame") are equally powerful sources of social control necessary for the organization. March (1994), in his primer on decision making, emphasizes the need for "such emotions as pride, shame, and embarrassment" to be internalized in the group, organizational, and societal identities of individuals (p. 65). Good decisions depend upon a "logic of appropriateness," and that logic must be imbued with moral content, which increases its emotionality. March's work on identity formation of organizational members presumes that good decision making depends upon individual and collective identities, which in turn rely on emotion-based sanctions and motives.

An example of the undesirable effects of guilt is the organizational cover-up by guilty gatekeepers (Rosen & Adams, 1974). Here guilt functions to control leakage of organizational secrets, which might serve the organization and the employee in the short term but serves neither in the long term. Employee performance evaluations can be sites of "shame, embarrassment, anger, and frustration," resulting in employees' hiding their errors to avoid negative performance appraisals (Becker, 1995, p. 29). Here is another example of organizational control gone awry due to the threat to employee self-esteem. In one case reported by Becker (1995), workers hid defective fabric in a wall. Employees' hiding problems to avoid being shamed by their mistakes (not to mention to avoid reduced paychecks in pay-for-performance work) has high business costs. Examples of organizational coercion that have been addressed in popular magazines include fear, guilt, and stigma used as informal controls (in *Forbes*; Sowell, 1993); the donations people make to organizations based on guilt; and the guilt customers feel when refusing to buy from a salesperson (in *Commonweal*; Byrne, 1992).

Shame and Guilt Appeals in Advertising

Guilt appeals are increasingly used as a persuasive tool to increase sales of products and services (Edell & Burke, 1987; Rossiter, Percy, & Donovan, 1991). Coulter and Pinto's (1995) study of guilt appeals made to working mothers concerning purchases of bread and dental floss found that moderate-guilt appeals elicited more guilt than did low- or high-guilt appeals. In the case of high-guilt appeals, an angry reaction to blatant manipulative messages created an inverse effect, resulting in weakened purchase intentions. Cockburn and Ormrod (1993) examined how microwaves were marketed in order to avoid embarrassing (shaming) men or women. The key was to let the engineered aspects of the product render microwaves sufficiently masculine so as not to embarrass men about their interest in a kitchen appliance while downplaying the engineering design so that women would not be embarrassed about their lack of technological competence.

These are all examples of the organization purposively inducing shame or guilt—directly or indirectly—as a means of controlling behavior. In the case of racism as the ground for organizational shame or guilt, the results have less to do with employee control than with employee esteem and connection.

Racism

Accusations of racism shame not only individuals, but organizations as well. Organizational prejudice and intolerance—based on what Goleman (1995, p. 231) calls "emotional illiteracy"—can result in multimillion-dollar lawsuits. Goleman provides as an example the Denny's restaurant chain, which suffered a $54 million settlement as a result of a class action suit on behalf of thousands of black customers who had suffered the indignities of antiblack prejudice (p. 155). As a result of the bad publicity (public shame), Denny's management scheduled diversity training for all the chain's employees. The precipitating event or antecedent in this case consisted of well-documented racist remarks and behaviors by Denny's employees; the problem was managed through diversity training, which constituted a type of apology.

Organizations that attempt to manage public shame by requiring organizational members to undergo diversity training, and thereby imply that members need to share the "guilt," often experience an angry backlash from employees who perceive the training as "guilt trips" (Lynch, 1997). Talking about such "white male backlash," one consultant empathized, "What white males feel is their dehumanization, the walking on eggshells, the rationalization, the apologies, the guilt" (quoted in Lynch, 1997, p. 69)—in short, they get a taste of what it is like to be members of a stigmatized group. The hostility toward what has become popularly known as "political correctness" has emerged, according to Schwartz (1993), from individuals' turning their inner feelings into a source of shame. He states that this shame, which is the metric of morality, "attaches to the identity. . . . [T]he white male is stigmatized, not for what he does, but for who he is: a white male" (p. 211).

Discussions of racism within organizations are particularly anxiety charged and can be psychologically debilitating, in part because no one wants to be accused of acting racist or to be a victim of racist acts (Bell & Nkomo, 1992; Pinderhughes, 1989). The former can produce guilt; the latter, shame. An expectant atmosphere, emotionally laden with potential feelings of guilt and shame (and anger at feeling shamed), makes diversity training programs challenging. Cox (1994, p. 11) suggests that managing diversity is based not only on legal obligations and economic performance goals, but also on expressed moral/ethical goals. Given that no trainee wants an immoral, unethical identity, participants use impression management skills to communicate their alignment with the goals of the training, thereby denying "the possibility of guilt for the non-appropriate attitudes or behaviors discussed throughout the workshop" (Workman, 1996, p. 17). Workman (1996) concludes that with the presence of moral judgment, employees have a greater need to save face (i.e., avoid shame) than to discuss and modify their own problematic attitudes and actions.

Karp and Sutton (1993) agree that diversity training programs are frequently guilt driven, which is

> problematic because on a moral level, nobody in the training program is personally responsible for the Holocaust or the enslavement of Africans. On a functional level, when people assume global responsibility for everything, they don't have to take personal responsibility for anything. . . . a focus on injustice and guilt tends to polarize the different groups into victims and oppressors. This polarization increases resent-

ment among groups, when the goal of diversity training ought to be to reduce it. (p. 33)

Speaking about multicultural education, Howard (1993) asserts that for "well-intentioned white Americans, guilt is a major hurdle" (p. 39). Guilt has a positive side—"it can be a spur to action, a motivation to contribute, a kick in the collective conscience"—but the "debilitating cycle of blame and guilt" needs to shift to "involvement, action, contribution, and responsibility" (p. 39). As a ground for shame and guilt, racism certainly qualifies, but shamed and guilt-ridden workplaces are not productive. The challenge is for organizations to manage diverse employee groups, within which racism will at least occasionally surface, in ways that do not re-create the "cycle of blame and guilt."

Additionally, any training that is "demystified"—that is, wherein participants openly explore their attitudes toward organizational practices, including the workshop itself—is too risky and is likely to create "feelings of awkwardness" (Hargie & Tourish, 1994, p. 1387; see also Elmes & Costello, 1992). In short, trainers (and potentially upper management) risk embarrassment if diversity training really questions management practices and policies, which would threaten top-down organizational control.

Sex Roles and Sexual Harassment

Closely related to organizational shame or guilt about historical racism are organizations' responses to sexism. Gherardi (1995) observes that the past several decades of gender-based prohibitions in the workplace, from discrimination to sexist language, have set in motion an organizational dynamic "from embarrassment, to shame, to a sense of guilt" (p. 149). The strategy of affirmative action is persuasive, in her estimation, not because of its threat of legal sanctions, but because of organizational susceptibility to feeling shamed. "Organizational sexualization" that can lead to harassment is derived from what Gherardi calls "heroic masculinity," a game of sexual identity and male ethos that creates "solidarity among the men, in both their manhood and the reciprocal admiration of their masculinity" (p. 54). The codes and language of this game are dependent upon male pride; conversely, the promulgation of male embarrassment/shame at violating the rules maintains the game.

The gendering of shame, guilt, and embarrassment is foregrounded in Pringle's (1988) study of secretaries in Australia; for example, Pringle notes that making tea and coffee for their bosses "provoked more passion than repetitive strain injury or sexual harassment" (p. 25). Embarrassed about this particular job duty, secretaries tried to define it in a way that maintained their self-esteem (saying that it is a reciprocal arrangement or that they do it voluntarily). Pringle notes that although sexual harassment is a legitimate topic of discussion for the secretaries, sexuality is not, "perhaps because of a certain embarrassment about what secretaries represent." Pringle suggests that rather than viewing secretaries as objects of sexual harassment, we need to see them as sexual subjects and "consider the power and pleasure they currently get in their interactions with people and raise the question of how they can get what they want on their own terms" (pp. 101-102). Such a stance evades gender shame through its focus on positive female self-identity.

The shame of sexual harassment is not easy to evade, given the reported occurrence of such harassment in the workplace: It has been estimated that 10% of women in the United States have quit at least one job due to sexual harassment, and when women who are sexually harassed at work stay in their jobs, the consequences are anxiety, tension, depression, and physical and mental illness (Abrams, 1992, as cited in Cox, 1994, p. 86; Gutek, Cohen, & Konrad, 1990). Clair (1993a, 1993b) gives accounts of organizational narratives to demonstrate how sexual harassment is "privatized" and "framed" to be perceived as a disparate interpersonal communication problem rather than as an institutional pattern of abusive power. Again, shame and guilt are not named specifically, but the implications are clear. For example, one male nurse who was a victim of sexual harassment described the assassination of his character and long-term damage to his relationships with women (Clair, 1994). Victims are told that their accusations will hurt their harassers' careers (Geist & Townsley, 1997, p. 22) and are given messages that normalize sexual harassment as an everyday event, "sweeping it under the rug," which protects the institution against lawsuits. Bingham (1994) believes that sexual harassment can be confronted through interpersonal communication, but acknowledges the difficulties involved with "incompatible goals" (e.g., not wanting to hurt the harasser's feelings; pp. 94-95).

Within academia, Oppedisano (1997) asserts that the responsibility for confronting sexual harassment belongs to faculty, and their failure to do so should make them feel guilty. After all, "wasn't that one of the reasons why tenure was established to enable faculty to speak out on issues without the fear of retaliation?" (p. 132). That faculty do not do so is a source of shame that they manage by staying "safely ensconced in our rhetoric and rubric, using these devices to distance ourselves from real involvement, from the pain that is right before our eyes if we chose to see" (p. 128). Oppedisano does not distinguish male from female faculty shame, but the "emotional labor" involved in managing feelings at work is shouldered more by women than by men (Gwartney-Gibbs & Lach, 1994; Hochschild, 1983). Crawford, Kippax, Onyx, Gault, and Benton (1992) agree that emotional well-being of others is the woman's burden. For example, women often apologize for others' discomfort, "even when they do not feel guilty" (p. 64). Writing on sexual harassment in education, Skaine and Skaine (1996) cite studies that show how male self-esteem and female self-esteem act oppositely in regard to men's and women's views of harassment. Men with low self-esteem tend to blame the harasser less than do men with high self-esteem. Women with low self-esteem are more critical of the harasser and more sympathetic to the victim than are women with high self-esteem, who are less critical of men who harass.

The dilemma here is that women take on organizational double duty—dealing with their own shame/guilt and then feeling responsible for managing the shame/guilt of everyone else. Like the ground of racism, sexual harassment is shameful, and the role that shame and guilt messages play needs to be studied. How and to whom organizations send those messages might make the cure more harmful than the illness. Male employees made to feel guilty about potentially harassing remarks may, as in the backlash against diversity training, react in ways that sever connections with female employees. As a power issue, sex roles are directly related to sexual harassment; women whose job duties lower their self-esteem are more vulnerable to harassment.

Downsizing

Downsizing is another arena for shame/guilt associated with self-esteem and connection: the shame associated with the loss of career identity and survivor guilt (Brockner, Davy, & Carter, 1985; Brockner et al., 1986). Commenting on the "downside of downsizing," Kets de Vries and Balazs (1997) describe the range of emotions experienced by survivors, including guilt, and the intense emotional reactions of the executive "executioners," which these authors categorize as "compulsive/ritualistic," "abrasive," "dissociative," "alexithymic/anhedonic," and "depressive." Although they do not name it, deep shame likely underscores those categories. This is the "self-blame" investigated by Miller and Hoppe (1994), who show that self-blame is more intense when layoffs are singular rather than spread across the workplace and that the intensity of psychological reactions (primarily anger) increases when terminations are perceived as unfair. The guilt of employees who have survived downsizing has been described in articles in such popular magazines as *Supervisory Management* (Brockner, 1986) and *People Management* (Doherty & Horsted, 1995).

In their "layoff" experiment with undergraduates—wherein some students participating in an extra-credit task were dismissed and others continued to work—Brockner et al. (1985) found that the "surviving coworkers" differed in their responses based on a self-esteem scale. Those with lower self-esteem felt the most remorse and developed more negative attitudes toward their coworkers, but the quantity of their work increased. Although this experiment contradicted the findings of earlier work by Brockner, in which only those with high or medium self-esteem increased their work, it did validate positive equity theory, which states that employees' behavior (work input) will reflect their sense of equity with work outcomes. Thus overpayment of wages results in employees' working harder—as does guilt over surviving downsizing. Brockner's work on downsizing is summarized in his book *Self-Esteem at Work: Research, Theory, and Practice* (1988) and has been updated in an article by Brockner and Wiesenfeld (1993). Unfortunately, Brockner's later work considers cognition rather than emotion, focusing on organizational justice rather than survivor guilt and remorse.

Not all experts agree that survivor guilt benefits the organization through positive equity theory. Executives who believe that surviving workers will be overwhelmingly grateful for their jobs have a rude awakening when they discover that, long after the downsizing, their greatest challenge is dealing with surviving employees who struggle with "pain, guilt, loneliness, depression, and job insecurity" (Caudron & Hayward, 1996, p. 39). Stoner and Hartman (1997) write about the need for "organization therapy" after downsizing, to overcome the many negative organizational impacts of downsizing: decreased employee satisfaction with their jobs, higher rates of absenteeism and turnover, and growing worker's compensation claims due to stress and anxiety. This therapy is based on communication as a remedy, breaking through the "survivor's facade" to the negative emotions— fear, betrayal, distrust, anger, sadness, depression, and guilt, to name a few—that employees may be suppressing. Caudron and Hayward (1996) also emphasize the urgency of honest, open, and frequent organizational communication after downsizing. Hartzell (1992) says that survivor guilt after downsizing can best be diminished by employees' asking themselves four major questions: (a) Was the layoff necessary? (b) Was the layoff conducted fairly? (c) Were those who were laid off treated humanely? (d) What is my status now?

Noer (1993) compares job loss to surviving a disaster, and Ehrlich (1991) likens it to grieving a loss, using Elisabeth Kübler-Ross's (1969) five stages of grief. One of the emotions described is guilt: "They were right to terminate me; I should have done a better job" (Ehrlich, 1991, p. 72). Ehrlich describes five case studies of job placement people who lost their jobs and watched the survivors also face guilt. The depression and guilt affected their job performance, feelings of control, and sense of personal well-being. Said one person who was laid off: "I knew how bad everyone felt, and I appreciated how some people came up to me right away and began to offer help. Others just couldn't deal with the whole thing and avoided me" (p. 73).

According to the research literature, downsizing causes survivor guilt, and—whether survivor guilt experienced from downsizing is suppressed, turned inward to depression, or expressed in anger and feelings of betrayal—the organization has a responsibility to help its members purge their guilt through communication. Missing here is any critical discussion of the organization's guilt as the downsizing executioner—or the guilt of its henchpersons. If survivors angrily blame the organization, rather than themselves, the organizational "therapy" might function less as catharsis than as internal public relations; this needs to be studied by organizational scholars as well as by human resource practitioners.

Gossip and Graffiti

Gossip and graffiti as illicit communication are also areas that might interest organizational scholars exploring workplace emotions. The common administrative admonition against "gossiping" has deep roots: In 14th- through 17th-century Britain, gossiping was proscribed by law, and gossipers were publicly shamed with stocks and ducking stools (Emler, 1994). One modern ramification is described by Hafen (1997) in her study of organizational gossip, in which interviewees admitted guiltily that they might listen to gossip, but said that they didn't pass it on. To be embodied as "a gossip" at work was to risk being a shamed person and, most likely, a female, because women were more likely than men to feel guilty about gossiping, although men as readily admitted to gossiping. Pringle (1988, p. 239) describes secretaries' embarrassment over gossiping, which gets redefined as female "bitching" but as male "joking" (see also Rosnow & Fine, 1976; Rysman, 1977; Spacks, 1986). Embarrassed/guilty or not, employees do gossip, and gossiping serves to connect people with grapevine knowledge and with a sense of belonging (Bach, 1983; Tannen, 1990; Ting-Toomey, 1979). Goodman and Ben-Ze'ev's (1994) edited book deals with the morality of gossip, vindicating gossip against its reputation as "moral contamination" (Bergmann, 1993). Although managers might seek to control the negative effects of gossip—its connecting effects among, say, union members is clearly to management's disadvantage—they also use it to "leak" information about individuals while simultaneously disavowing it (Hafen, 1997).

One way of avoiding the shame of gossip is to do it anonymously through graffiti. Nathanson (1992) describes the decaying of his own neighborhood, where graffiti took over the walls and billboards. One day a message appeared, written in perfect penmanship, "The name of the game is shame." Despite the defacing of other messages, this one remained, without being altered or defaced. Nathanson believes that it hit home: "When shame is identified as shame there can be change, however subtle and slow" (p. 458). Rodriguez and Nicotera's (1997) study of graffiti as organizational enculturation at one university shows how graffitists scold (i.e., attempt to shame) one another for writing on walls, even for incorrect grammar and spelling. It is apparent that graffiti are used as a way of managing/resisting anger and shame because of their focus on homosexuality, race, and gender. Graffiti function to "express individuals' sense of estrangement and powerlessness while simultaneously producing and reproducing individuals' connectedness with the linguistic community of which they are members" (Scheibel, 1994, p. 4).

Summary of Uses of Shame and Guilt
Messages in and by Organizations

This section on how shame and guilt are communicated (or repressed) within organizational contexts demonstrates the push-pull of shame and guilt to connect and control individuals and groups. Shame and guilt serve to reinforce organizational values and to provide a coercive control mechanism, encouraging people to repay loans, to make donations, and to contribute their share to group work. Public shame/guilt can prompt an organization to take actions against historical racism and sexism, such as requiring members to undergo diversity training. On the other hand, the backlash associated with feeling unfairly "shamed" can create resistance to such organizational actions. Issues of self-esteem, originating in the organization's collective "unconscious," can lead to neurotic, addictive, and troubled organizations that act out much as individuals or families do. Individuals within organizations can feel shamed because of harassment or can feel survivor guilt over downsizing, leadership guilt associated with not meeting the expectations of sub-ordinates, or guilt over poor performance.

Our review leads to further questions that call for more research. What are the ethics of shaming employees? How can the organization avoid making employees act in ways that penalize the organization in order to avoid their own guilt (e.g., hiding errors)? If part of maintaining self-control at work is the masking of feelings "to avoid embarrassment" (Putnam & Mumby, 1993, p. 50), how do we address these self-conscious emotions in ways that benefit rather than hurt the organization? The Grameen Bank provides an example of how internalized shame has worked for both the organization and its members. Gossip and graffiti exemplify ways in which organizational members resist shame, although to participate in either is a guilty act. Because we do bring our bodies to work, it is time that we examine the feelings that are embodied within us and the organizations that provide habitus for us. This kind of examination requires the "emotional intelligence" that Goleman (1995, p. 148) describes in his book of that title; he suggests that it is emotional intelligence that matters, and it is "managing with the heart" that will make the workplace more productive.

MESSAGES ABOUT SHAME AND
GUILT IN PUBLIC COMMUNICATION

To glimpse how the public has understood and reacted to various bases for shame and guilt over the past 50 years, we searched for articles dealing with shame and guilt in the *Readers' Guide to Periodical Literature,* which indexes mostly popular periodical publications, including newspapers, and some scholarly journals. We used a subject search of the bound *Readers' Guide* from 1940 to 1981 and a computerized keyword search for the years 1982 to 1997, including only articles for which shame and guilt were the subject or keywords. In every decade since the 1940s, guilt has spawned more articles than shame, although interest in shame increased dramatically beginning in the 1980s. These data support scholars who have claimed that the focus of American society has been on guilt rather than shame (Retzinger, 1991) and that the United States is a "guilt-based culture" in comparison to countries such as China and Japan, which are "shame-based cultures" (Benedict, 1946; Schneiderman, 1995). Not surprisingly, articles on guilt dropped in the 1960s and again in the 1990s as interest in shame increased. This surge of interest in shame is, as Scheff (1995b) has observed, "especially dramatic because it follows upon years of silence" (p. 1053). Whether or not the tide has turned in the 1990s is arguable, but certainly both scholarly and popular interest in shame has increased.

After reading titles, abstracts, and—when these were not sufficiently clear—the articles themselves, we grouped the topics for shame and guilt into the 10 categories shown in Table 1.1. The most significant changes in topics occurred in 20-year time spans. In the 1940s and 1950s, personal stories dominated articles about shame and guilt. In the 1960s and 1970s, self-help articles on shame and guilt appeared for the first time, along with increased interest in psychological traits, such as neurotic guilt versus healthy guilt. The 1960s and 1970s also showed religious concerns about shame and guilt, and parenting concerns appeared for the first time. In the 1980s and 1990s, parenting articles concerning guilt and shame jumped to the lead; psychology articles remained important at second place and religion was third.

Cultural Critiques of Shame and Guilt Messages in the United States

"The return of shame" has been a *Newsweek* cover story (Alter & Wingert, 1995) as well as the topic of lead articles in the *National Review* ("In Praise of Shame"; Lapin, 1995), *Atlantic Monthly* ("Shame"; Karen, 1992), and *Utne Reader* ("Innocence Lost"; Iggers, 1993). In academia as well, books about America's shame, lack of shame, or guilt culture have proliferated (Greenspan, 1995; Margalit, 1996; Morrison, 1996; Schneiderman, 1995; Sykes, 1992). Whether the writers argue for a return to shame or plead for the elimination of its damaging effects, both sides acknowledge the importance of the debate. Onlookers, less concerned with the moral consequences of a shaming versus shameless society, write about shame's impact on persuasion, using a Burkean analysis of the guilt-redemption cycle. In our review of this cultural critique of messages about shame and guilt in the United States, we first present the views of those who praise shame and guilt, then those of authors who range from rejecting shame and guilt to fearing their results. Finally, we discuss the work of those who view shame and guilt dispassionately as persuasive tools.

Shame and Guilt Are Good

Before we examine the "good shame" end of the dialectic as it is critiqued in American society, we need to clarify the distinction between shame and guilt cultures. Unlike the work in dyads and families, which distinguish between shame and guilt based on how globally each reflects on the self and how people tend to respond, cultural analyses of shame and guilt are based on the public (shame) versus private (guilt) distinction. Benedict (1946) claims that the United States embodies the ultimate guilt culture, based on individualism, whereas Japan is the ultimate shame culture, based on group collectivism/identity. A shame culture "provides a uniform code of conduct to promote civility, propriety, dignity, integrity, and honor," whereas a guilt culture "attempts to control behavior by passing laws and punishing transgression" (Schneiderman, 1995, p. 5). Schneiderman (1995) disagrees with Benedict's assessment that Americans are entirely guilt-prone; rather, taking a historical view, he believes that American society was shame based not only before the American Revolution, but afterward as well—attempting to extend "the practice of respect throughout the body politic rather than reserve it for an elite class of gentlemen" (p. 7).

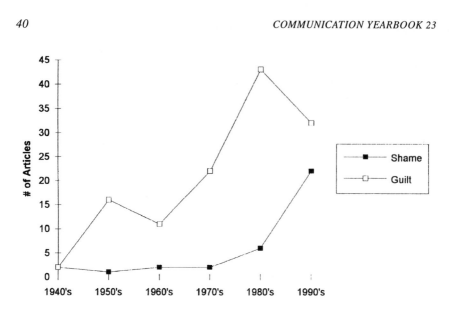

Figure 1.1. Articles on Guilt and Shame in the *Readers' Guide to Periodical Literature*

In our postmodern age, however, Schneiderman (1995) envisions a conflict of cultures, beginning with Watergate and the Vietnam War as "guilt narratives" built on "conflict and mystery" (pp. 80-82) wherein truth is more important than social order. Examples of guilt-based rather than shame-based public communication during this era are Defense Secretary McNamara's confession (in which he blamed others more than himself) and former President Richard Nixon's refusal ever to apologize publicly for the Watergate scandal. McNamara confessed his guilt in acquiescing to decisions that were unconscionable in the prosecution of the Vietnam War; however, Schneiderman notes that he felt no shame, merely the guilt of making a mistake, which he blamed on others, such as right-wing congressional hawks. In short, "McNamara did not feel the need to apologize. Instead, he confessed" (p. 72). In sharp contrast is the Confucian belief that the ruler alone is responsible for the suffering of the people (p. 21). On the other hand, Clinton's ceremonial recognition of Vietnam (p. 79) and, more recently, his public apology to African Americans for the Tuskegee medical experiments on African American men with syphilis demonstrate the dignity of publicly acknowledging shame regardless of individual guilt. In the perspective of shame cultures there is a greater connection among group members than is found in guilt cultures; hence to feel shamed in a shame culture is to experience a greater severance from the group and more emotional isolation than is the case in a guilt culture, where individualism is valued.

In the 1970s, Schneider (1977) drew upon religion to define the value of shame to society, quoting from the Talmud a verse that emphasizes the loveliness of shame because "whoever has a sense of shame will not sin so quickly" (p. 109). A

TABLE 1.1

Topics of Shame and Guilt Found in *Readers' Guide* Articles, 1940s-1990s
(in percentages)

Topic	1940s-1950s (n = 17)	1960s-1970s (n = 33)	1980s-1990s (n = 103)
Sex	0	0	4
Parenting	0	15	30
Politics	12	3	3
Ethics	6	6	8
Religion	12	24	13
Law	6	0	5
Stigmatized groups	6	9	10
Body	0	0	1
Psychology	6	34	20
Personal stories	40	9	0
Other	12	0	6

decade later, Schneider (1987), like others of that era, mourned the loss of shame: "We live in an era that treats shame itself with disrespect. We are valuing animals, and shame plays an important role in our system of values, despite the fact that what is valued changes from generation to generation" (pp. 194-195). Scheff (1995b) recounts the writings of Erasmus in the Middle Ages, who detailed manners of hygiene, etiquette, deference, and demeanor—the lack of which resulted in shame, but a kind of shame that was less disguised than in modern times. Nathanson (1992) declares shame to be "an auxiliary to the positive affects that power all society" (p. 454) and worries that the root of many of the problems of today's society—crime, civil disobedience, vulgarity, lack of simple courtesy—is a "disavowal of shame" (p. 472). He describes the societal development of shame in three steps: First, a human activity is declared "shameworthy" and disgusting; second, as the population slowly approves this new source of discomfort, it becomes a fit subject for humor (an example is the 1929 book *Is Sex Necessary?* by E. B. White, famed writer for the *New Yorker*); and third, once the society has accepted "the new balance of shame, exposure, and privacy," neither tension nor humor is associated with it (p. 449).

Lapin (1995) suggests increasing the "traditional use of ostracism and moral censure to reunite people of society and God" through the reteaching of shame and humiliation. Put differently, because the deadliest sin is pride, and pride must be cured by humility, a shaming society teaches its citizens humility (Margalit, 1996, p. 11). Charles Murray of the American Enterprise Institute agrees; his hot-button issue is the increase in the numbers of illegitimate children, which he claims would not be occurring if there were more stigma attached to unwed motherhood (cited in Rodenbaugh, 1995). Lasch (1992) states that the problem lies in the double meaning of shame as a "decent respect for privacy but also the fear of disgrace" (p. 29). The latter's association with the loss of self-esteem, based on the internalization of society's standards, has dominated the public's view of shame. Popular psychology tells us that it is better to be a culture of shamelessness than to have low self-esteem, a premise Lasch (1984) debates, stating that "selfhood expresses itself in the form of a guilty conscience, the painful awareness of the gulf between human aspirations and human limitations" (p. 258). The debate here is between the values of control and self-esteem. A fear of disgrace increases cultural control but diminishes individual self-esteem.

Villa-Vicencio (1997) uses the examples of Nazism and South African apartheid to describe the importance of guilt in bringing about either national reconciliation or serious political renewal. He describes Jaspers's (1947) four levels of guilt: (a) criminal guilt (breaking the law), (b) political guilt (using government policy), (c) moral guilt (feeling remorse and responsibility, unappeased by criminal or political propitiation), and (d) metaphysical guilt (involving human solidarity and responsibility for correcting the world's wrongs). Villa-Vicencio posits an essential relationship between confession of guilt and historical memory, saying that stories that "point to events that have hurt and healed, given life and death are not easy stories to tell" (p. 250). Thus it is necessary that government-appointed commissions hear the stories of victims; indeed, "the nation is obliged to hear them. It is in the encounter of telling, hearing, and understanding that the reconciliation process can begin" (p. 250). Swanson (1993) would like to put shaming stories in a "Hall of Shame" for those in society who retard or damage it—particularly educators. His two candidates are Lewis Terman, the originator of what Swanson sees as an elitist educational tracking system, and James Bryant Conant, who persuaded American educators to increase school size and drastically reduce the number of school districts.

An example of Jaspers's metaphysical guilt is shown in Greenberg's (1995) call for "citizens in service" to do something about children living in poverty. Greenberg advocates service learning projects for classrooms, quoting Marian Wright Edelman, the executive director of the Children's Defense Fund: "We are not all equally guilty, but we are all equally responsible" (p. 216). This sense of personal guilt/responsibility is what Solomon (1990) would equate with liberalism, which "is first of all a keen sense of personal guilt about one's own privileged place in the world" (p. 256). It is perhaps this liberal view of personal guilt over privilege that argues with the more traditional view that justice calls for shameful acts to reap a shaming penance.

Penance, as part of societal degradation ceremonies, is necessary to express the moral indignation of the society, according to Garfinkel (1956). Braithwaite (1989) proposes that nations with the lowest crime rates are those where shaming is used reintegratively to allow parties to pay community penance before they can experience forgiveness and return to the community. He presents historical lessons in good versus bad shaming: On the bad side, public executions in the late 17th through 18th centuries (scaffold hangings and beheadings) were in fact a war against the lower classes and resulted in attacks on the judges, executioners, and king—and felons were celebrated as heroes against tyranny. On the good side, community conferences in New Zealand and Australia apply the principle of reintegrative shaming through ceremony (Braithwaite & Mugford, 1994). Their success in dealing with juvenile offenders is based on the confrontation of offenders by those who most care for and respect those offenders. Here shaming produces less stigmatization and more reintegration because it is more victim centered, problem centered, and community centered.

Solomon (1990) also believes that caring about justice requires a sense of responsibility and includes not only the blaming emotions of shame, guilt, embarrassment, remorse, regret, and humiliation, but also the praising emotions of pride, self-love, and sense of honor. While valorizing shame, he nevertheless fears the harvest of vengeance and prefers compassion. He suggests that our sense of justice has become "hypocognated"—that is, as we talk less about it, we come to care about it less as well. Sykes (1992) takes a stand against the hypercognation of victimization, what he calls the "ideology of oppression" (p. 81). He worries that "while postmodern politics declares everyone guilty, postmodern politics lets almost everyone off the hook for just about everything" (p. 145) and blames society's abolition of sin and proliferation of psychological disorders. He calls for a "moratorium of blame" and an increase of self-control, based on the reestablishment of a "moral community" (pp. 252-253).

A belief in the value of shame to produce legitimate stigmatization can backfire, as Braithwaite (1993) makes clear. He argues that, in the case of gang members, stigmatization "can create criminal subcultures in which shame resides in complying with the law" (p. 15). He asserts "even in New York City, the best protection that citizens get is not from the police but from loving families who dispense disapproval effectively" (p. 15). Either through families or through group therapy in treatment centers, an adolescent sex offender "must experience feelings of guilt and enough self-disgust that he recognizes and stays away from high risk situations" (Lakey, 1994, p. 756).

Sanctions of shame (self-imposed, with feelings of remorse) and embarrassment (socially imposed, with violations of public norms) function much like legal sanctions (Grasmick & Bursik, 1990; Grasmick, Blackwell, Bursik, & Mitchell, 1993). Shaming penalties for criminals have been approved in Oregon and Florida, and one Houston judge makes criminals with "bad attitudes" clean stables—such penalties are made attractive by their cost-effectiveness in comparison with imprisonment (Gahr, 1997). Some studies show a deterrent effect from self-imposed shame. In one study examining tax cheating, theft, and drunk driving, interviewees were asked about the potential impacts of shame (defined as making oneself feel guilty or self-stigma), embarrassment (defined as losing the respect of significant others), and legal sanctions (punishment determined by a court); internalized shame was the greatest deterrent to all of the offenses except theft (Grasmick & Bursik, 1990). In another study involving littering, respondents showed an increased sense of shame and embarrassment after a statewide antilittering campaign (Grasmick, Bursik, & Kinsey, 1991). Shame also acts as a significant deterrent against drunk driving (Grasmick, Bursik, & Arneklev, 1993) and wife assault (Williams & Hawkins, 1989), but not against interpersonal violence: Interviewees who were asked to imagine that they had physically hurt someone on purpose perceived a threat of embarrassment, but not of shame (Grasmick, Blackwell, et al., 1993). The emotion of guilt also has no deterrent effects on psychopaths, who are even unable to identify guilt in stories about guilty protagonists (Blair et al., 1995). Men with low levels of "sex guilt" are more likely to act aggressively on their sexual fantasies (Porter, Critelli, & Tang, 1992).

Emotional verbal and nonverbal displays used by criminals during confessions and during the sentencing phases of trials send messages about their guilt. (The detailed media analysis of O. J. Simpson's facial expressions for signs of guilt is a case in point.) In two studies involving scenarios of a drunk driving accident, students viewed the driver more positively if he expressed remorse; however, apology strategies had only indirect effects on the recommended fine and sentence (Robinson, Smith-Lovin, & Tsoudis, 1994; Taylor & Kleinke, 1992). Another study that looked at accounts given to victims by offenders found that apologies were more likely to be offered after offenses that were due to negligence than after accidental or intentional offenses (Gonzales, Manning, & Haugen, 1992). Further, men's accounts were found to be less complex, less conciliatory, and more likely to be lies than were women's accounts.

Legally enforced shaming to control crime would distress Margalit (1996), who argues against public shaming (to be discussed further below, in the subsection on "bad shame"). One 1997 issue of *Social Research* included articles in response to Margalit's book by Lukes, Quinton, Ripstein, and Schick. Lukes (1997) worries that there is danger in taking humiliation and decency too seriously, because many forms of criticism risk giving offense; satirical humor, for example, has its place in the work of comedians such as Dean Swift and Lenny Bruce, despite the potential humiliation their monologues might create for specific (stigmatized) groups of people. Quinton (1997) refutes Margalit's contention that not recognizing an immigrant's language as an official language of the state is a sign of disrespect and thus humiliating. Ripstein (1997), while agreeing with Margalit that a decent society should not be a punitive society, does believe in appropriate institutional censure—for example, for the professor who humiliates a student in class, or the welfare official who asks intrusive questions about personal lives of applicants, or the prison official who allows prisoners to humiliate each other. He warns that "if society, through its institutions, decides to forgive one person for humiliating another, it is joining in the humiliation, rather than answering it" (p. 110).

Schick (1997) does not believe that exposure to shame, in itself, is necessarily bad; rather, what is wrong is "gloating" on the part of the humiliator, which Schick believes is intrinsic to real humiliation. For example, according to Schick, professionals who say they found it "humiliating" to be downsized from their jobs have not actually been humiliated unless others are gratified at their being fired. Other examples are the welfare recipient who might mistakenly imagine gloating by others, an elderly person who wrongly believes his or her lapses are mocked, or an unemployed person who can't find a job. These are sad situations in which something might indeed be wrong, but they are not, according to Schick, inherently humiliating situations. Humiliation must be accompanied by a gloating message (verbal or nonverbal) that implies that the gloater feels "above"—stronger or more fortunate than—the humiliated person.

If Margalit's (1996) concern is the negative effects on citizens' self-esteem from shaming, his opponents are concerned that those effects do not balance the need for individual freedom to satirize, the need for a common language for connection, or the importance of taking other factors into consideration, such as whether "gloating" has occurred and whether a ban on institutionalized shaming would constitute institutional "forgiveness." Overall, the perspective that public shame or guilt benefits society is based primarily on the usefulness of such shame or guilt for controlling conduct and increasing the societal connections among groups of people who are united in cultural values and norms. The counterpoint—that shaming persons or groups publicly is harmful to society—is focused on the stigmatizing degradation that occurs, which is an issue of self-esteem.

Shame and Guilt Are Bad

Morrison (1996) disagrees with Schneiderman (1995) that we have moved from a culture of shame to a culture of guilt and we need more shame. Morrison sees the reverse: Previous generations lived in a culture of guilt that prompted remorse and contrition; today we have a culture of shame, leading to alienation, divorce, disrespect, suicide and homicide, and shame-based depression. Margalit (1996) states the anarchist's view: that government is by definition humiliating, because to be governed is to bow to coercive institutions. That said, Margalit does not adopt this view, although he does use it to make the point that institutions (bureaucracies in particular), by virtue of their governing function, do need to be watched carefully for a propensity to shame citizens unjustifiably, merely for their failure to serve the institutions. Margalit describes the humiliation experienced by members of stigmatized groups, welfare recipients, and military and fraternity recruits during initiation rites. The litmus test, according to Margalit, is punishment, and whether a society cares about the dignity of its prisoners. Addressing punishment, Solomon (1990) asks why Western society has centralized vengeance and disregarded gratitude, such that our legal system is devoted to punishing the guilty and does nothing about rewarding those to whom we owe gratitude, who "help the system thrive" (p. 257). The law also serves to stigmatize groups (e.g., Colorado's 1992 referendum opposing gay rights), or, conversely, legislation of "hate laws" can affirm the rights of stigmatized groups (Kaufman & Raphael, 1996).

Social workers deal with the expressed shame of the groups most stigmatized in and by our society, such as disabled children and their siblings, AIDS patients and their families, prisoners, sexual abuse survivors and their victimizers, men who batter their wives, women in shelters, institutionalized schizophrenics, single parents, the institutionalized aged, the visually impaired, the elderly, bereaved children, and the homeless (Gitterman & Shulman, 1994). Understanding the disempowerment of societal messages that have instilled guilt, shame, and/or embarrassment in these groups is essential for social workers' communication skills. Other stigmatized groups that have been the targets of messages inducing shame or guilt include gay men and lesbians, for whom coming out of the closet is coming out of shame (Kaufman & Raphael, 1996; Penelope & Wolf, 1995); people who become disabled as adults and feel shamed about their loss of control (Kirshbaum, 1991; Parker, 1993); people who are "sent away" for detox or for treatment of mental breakdowns (Cronkite, 1994); and multiracial individuals who are forced to choose a racial identity, especially when their physical features are a composite (Comas-Diaz, 1996).

Guilt felt by individuals for acts they regret (or for the omission of actions they believe they should have taken) can be exacerbated by societal messages that are more punitive than healing. The guilt felt by rape victims can result in failure to report these crimes (Kellogg & Huston, 1995) and in men's doubting their masculinity (Lisak, 1994). Gay men and intravenous drug users with HIV/AIDS not only feel guilt about their behaviors, but have the double whammy of shame from society's disapproval of homosexuality and drug use and the shame of the disease itself (Rushing, 1995). Women who terminate pregnancies feel the guilt of letting down family members and of sinning against the fetus (Naziri & Tzavaras, 1993), whereas women who carry their pregnancies to term can feel the guilt of inadequate (real or perceived) prenatal care (Gregg, 1993).

If shame can cause someone to kill him- or herself (Shreve & Kunkel, 1991), then guilt for not being able to prevent that act haunts the victim's family and friends—fueled by the "shame" of suicide (Dalke, 1994; Miles & Demi, 1991). The recipients of organ donations must work through the guilt of being alive because they received those organs (i.e., benefiting from another's death; Chaturvedi & Pant, 1985). People who suffer from chronic fatigue express guilt about their inability to work or go to school, a feeling that is heightened by their contact with medical practitioners who do not believe that chronic fatigue is a "real" disease (Ware, 1992). These are all arenas where health communication entwines with public communication. Another is body shame resulting in anorexia and bulimia, which originates in the media's images of idealized bodies (Boskind-Lodahl, 1976; Brumberg, 1989; Chernin, 1981; Fredrickson & Roberts, 1997; Giddens, 1991). Public communication can also stigmatize those who associate with shamed targets, as Neuberg, Smith, Hoffman, and Russell (1994) learned; they found that individuals of higher status who associated with members of a stigmatized group were looked down upon more than were individuals of lower status. The trick, as Kaufman and Raphael (1996, pp. 58, 280) explain in the case of homosexuality, is to take the sources of shame—culture, internalized messages and scripts, and imprinted scenes—and invert them to sources of proud identity; to be a "cultural worker" by refusing the imposed silence and helping to disintegrate the power of shame to destroy lives.

An editorial in the *New Republic* has argued against the shaming of defendants at trials by the victims or families of the victims because this creates a carnival atmosphere and influences judges and juries based on emotion rather than reason ("Victim Justice," 1995). The American Civil Liberties Union argues that ostracizing and humiliating criminals, who have so little stake in society, is futile (Gahr, 1997). The other half of that equation is the victims' need to confront their offenders—in particular in the case of parents taking child molesters to court. There is cathartic value in using the legal process to shame perpetrators, so that parents can feel they have protected their children and victims can feel they have been taken seriously and faced their fears; however, courts may exacerbate family problems as "family members and associated professionals all take sides" (Jones, 1994, p. 253). Smith (1992) believes that the use of humiliation in the criminal justice system and in prisons will increase criminal behavior rather than reduce it. Programs that he cites that focus on restoration instead of retribution for criminal offenders include the Prison Fellowship in Pennsylvania and CHARLEE Family Care, designed for adolescent offenders. These programs increase care and support and reduce humiliation and degradation.

Ronald Potter-Efron and Patricia Potter-Efron, a psychotherapist team, agree. In their 1989 book, they describe the societal shame felt by members of nonmajority, marginalized groups who get the message that they are "defective and inferior" (p. 102). Such groups in U.S. society include women, old people, overweight people, alcoholics, the physically disabled, African Americans, Hispanics, Arabs, Native Americans, poor people, Jews, recent immigrants (especially Asians), rural people, adolescents, people of Eastern European ancestry, and homosexual/bisexual persons. Institutional shaming also occurs in churches, in schools, and in workplaces, where individuals are made to feel that they are sinful, dumb, and dead-ended. These authors suggest that the four aspects of American society that contribute to a person's shame are "(1) the unrelenting pressure to succeed, (2) too strong a focus on image and appearance, (3) prejudice and discrimination, and (4) institutional shaming" (p. 105).

Lamb (1992) suggests that society needs to avoid creating another generation of shame-based people, so that the inner child can heal. He is alarmed that shame (the feeling of being bad, wrong, or disgusting) has replaced guilt (the feeling of having done something wrong). A 1993 issue of the *Utne Reader* was devoted to American society's guilt-ridden relationship with food: eating meat, eating pesticides, eating fat, eating when others are starving, eating with food stamps, eating for status (Brazilian monkey brains but not Velveeta cheese), exploiting farmworkers, and destroying rural economies. Iggers (1993) says that "our eroticism and moral focus have migrated from our groins to our guts" (p. 58). The consequence of this guilt, according to Tisdale (1993), is that "our national obsession with weight loss has corrupted our relationship with food" (p. 64), not unlike the way strict cultural adherence to societal norms can corrupt relationships between people, cutting emotional ties.

Pressure to succeed and a focus on image affect nations as well as individuals. Prior to his invasion of Kuwait in 1990, Saddam Hussein announced, "No one can humiliate us" (quoted in Nathanson, 1992, p. 458). Kaufman (1992) describes the national shame of the Vietnam War and how its echo affected the reactions of U.S. citizens to the Gulf War; many rejected any connection between the two wars because "in so doing, they redeem a nation's honor from its past shame" (p. 237). In short, nations as well as individuals have to rebuild their self-esteem, having been publicly shamed. Further examples provided by Kaufman include Germany after Hitler's defeat and Great Britain after Argentina's invasion of the Falkland Islands, an event spread across newspaper headlines around the world, "Argentina HUMILIATES Great Britain" (p. 229). Kaufman claims that television magnifies national shame through its immediate and visual scenes of U.S. actions. Elsewhere, Nathanson (1992) argues that it is the media's increasing intrusion into our private lives via cameras, hidden microphones, computer databases, tabloid magazines, talk shows, and so on that has decreased our sense of privacy, thereby decreasing our sense of shame. Kaufman and Raphael (1996) believe that "shamelessness" and "fearlessness" are actually driven by acutely denied shame and fear—hence the media's magnification of shameful events (e.g., talk-show "shame-athons") might result in a counterreaction of shamelessness (p. 47).

Scheff is concerned with the shame-rage cycle and violence, not only for individuals and families but also for nations. He believes that humiliated fury was a primary motive behind France's entry into World War I (following that country's humiliating defeat in 1871) and the rise of Hitler (following Germany's humiliating defeat in World War I) (see Scheff, 1994; Scheff & Retzinger, 1991). Miller (1993) cites many examples from ancient Icelandic sagas of blood feuding, which was based on an ideology of avenging shame as a code of honor. He argues that today the honor ideology extends to the cultures of some urban black and Chicano males, Mafiosi, and "gangland, intergalactic, horror, or Clint Eastwood movies" (p. 9).

Scheff recommends handling shame issues between groups or nations much as one would handle such issues between people—by reestablishing the bond by minimizing secrecy and lying, recognizing interdependence by fostering cooperative interchange, acknowledging shame and guilt through sincere public apologies, and mediating disputes. Another example is the ritual of lustration (collective purification), as used by Braithwaite in Australia and New Zealand, by the Chinese at "speak bitterness" meetings, and by Pacific Islanders when they "disentangle" (Scheff, 1994, pp. 142-149; Watson-Gegeo & White, 1990).

Murphy (1990) addresses misdirected shame, rather than shame itself, as problematic. He gives as an example the speech that Robert Kennedy gave in Cleveland the day after Martin Luther King, Jr., was killed. Kennedy demanded that "each

American take individual responsibility for the disorder and work to remove this sickness from our soul" (quoted in Murphy, 1990, p. 402). Although this use of the jeremiad is a social control mechanism that can restore social harmony during crisis, it also "limits the scope of reform and the depth of social criticism" (p. 402), such that this time of "shame and sorrow" would be viewed as the growing menace of (individual) violent crime rather than as a function of a corrupt system. In other words, shaming messages have the potential to absolve the real villains, especially when they are societal institutions.

Shame and Guilt as Burkean Persuasion

Unlike the positions discussed above, in which shame and guilt (or the lack thereof) are seen as primary factors in society's ills, another perspective is that shame and guilt simply are. Although the scope of this chapter does not allow for a complete review of studies using Burke's guilt-redemption cycle, we would be remiss if we did not include examples of guilt used as a persuasive tool by politicians to sell a public agenda.

Burke (1951) broadens the traditional Aristotelian focus on persuasion to include identification. If shame is one of the most universal of all emotions and is intrinsic to humans' self-identities, then it makes sense that one of the most pervasive motivations for rhetoric is to appeal to our omnipresent guilt. Burke (1954/1965) writes that we purge and redeem ourselves in many social situations. Order is an outgrowth of "the spirit of hierarchy," which Burke (1966, pp. 15-16) relates to language, based on a hierarchy of being "up" or "down" in society and feeling guilty about either location (see also Mackey-Kallis & Hahn, 1994, for an explanation of Burke's linguistic-based cycle of guilt-redemption). In fact, Burke sees every violation of social hierarchy (laws, norms, values, expectations, categories) as a potential source of guilt or even shame. The purging of guilt can be accomplished only through three general means: the mortification of the self, the victimage of others, or transcendent reframing (e.g., with humor or a shift in perspective). Scapegoating is tempting; it arises "logologically" as humans attempt to manage their guilt, which arises from the myriad implicit covenants that are made, then inevitably broken, within any socioreligious order (Burke, 1961, pp. 172-241).

Scapegoating is more "medicinal" than self-mortification; it "cures" human guilt when "the individual properly realizes that he is not alone responsible for his condition" (Burke, 1967, pp. 202-203). Purging our guilt calls for a scapegoated victim to whom our sins can be transferred: "Order/Through Guilt/To Victimage/(hence: Cult of the Kill)" (Burke, 1961, p. 5). So pervasive is victimage that Burke (1954/1965) wonders whether "human societies could possibly cohere without symbolic victims which the individual members of the group share in common" (p. 285). At the level of nations, scapegoating replaces problem solving in what Burke (1961) calls tragic "cyclical compulsions of empire" that merely "process" rather than "resolve" guilt (p. 236). For example, Burke (1967) shows how well Hitler understood the political exigency of finding a "noneconomic explanation of economic phenomena" by blaming the Jews for Germany's problems (p. 201). In *Mein Kampf,* Hitler states that "the efficiency of the truly national leader consists primarily in preventing the division of the attention of a people, and always in concentrating it on a single enemy" (quoted in Burke, 1967, p. 193).

Burke (1950/1969) grapples with the notion of "pure persuasion," wherein the rhetor is not rewarded by any material outcomes other than the "satisfaction intrinsic to the saying" (p. 269). Writing about Burke's view of pure persuasion, Hagen (1995) calls it a "guiltless rhetoric" (p. 46)—that is, persuasion without any motive of gain. Much argumentation originates in what Burke (1954/1965) calls "hierarchical embarrassment," as people grapple with "what to question, how much to take on authority, how much to be merely polite about" (p. 278). When personal failures to measure up are experienced as transgressions, this becomes "hierarchical psychosis" (p. 279). A recent Burkean analysis of a public "hierarchical psychosis as guilt" is Moore's (1996) interpretation of Oregon Senator Bob Packwood's response to sexual misconduct charges. Packwood's strategic error, according to Moore, was shifting from a self-mortification rhetoric to one of victimage, with refutation and diversionary charges.

Similarly, Mackey-Kallis and Hahn (1994) use Burke to explain America's need to overcome the guilt of slavery through the North's defeat of the Confederacy, which embodied that guilt. Public messages of victimage are the primary means of redeeming the killings of war. President George Bush used that same rhetoric of war, Mackey-Kallis and Hahn argue, to shape the national drug problem, relying on an "us-them mentality" (p. 5). Bush used the war metaphor to make the drug problem an issue of national security, labeling drug lords, drug dealers, and partisan politicians as the encroaching enemy. The "war against drugs" metaphor also uses a guilt-based mortification of self-blame, with the "Just say no" slogan (Mackey-Kallis & Hahn, 1994, p. 17). Either way, guilt is the ploy for messages used to persuade the public to support national policies.

Not all rhetoric as persuasion relies on guilt, however. Foss and Griffin (1992) juxtapose Burkean rhetorical theory with feminist rhetorical theory, using Starhawk as an exemplar. Although Starhawk and Burke are in agreement about guilt's resulting from hierarchical structure, hierarchy, and thus guilt, is not inevitable for Starhawk. Rather than victimage or self-hatred, redemption can occur through "awakening to one's own immanent value" (Foss & Griffin, 1992, p. 341). An illustration of this is provided in Stewart's (1991) analysis of protest songs, which "address protestors as victimized, brave, powerful and valuable far more often than they address the opposition as victimizer, cowardly, weak, and worthless" (p. 252). These juxtaposed rhetorical positions ultimately reiterate the dialectic—not of shame, but of good/bad guilt.

Another, more pragmatic, approach to Burke's guilt-redemption cycle is shown in applications to organizations. Goodall, Wilson, and Waagen (1986) describe the performance appraisal interview as a "communication situation that determines a subordinate's survival or 'death' " (p. 83)—that is, the Burkean "symbolic kill." However, they point out, death can mean "transcendence" through promotion, and the guilt inherent in the "perfecting impulse of organizations" allows for goal setting and achievement (p. 84). Cheney (1983, p. 153) describes how organizational publications ("house organs") often urge employees to unite against a common enemy, usually some threat from the environment. This persuasion relies upon and encourages employee identification with the organization, using messages with an assumed "we" and the corresponding "they." Both Goodall et al. and Cheney note that guilt is used by organizations in ways that benefit the organizations and do not necessarily harm the members.

Summary of Public Communication
About Shame and Guilt

We found in our search that articles promoting public messages of shame and the need for an increase of guilt were clearly more numerous than those denouncing such messages. This trend corresponds with an increasing national concern with crime: the return of the death sentence, increases in the numbers of crimes counted as felonies, the sentencing of juveniles as adults, and so on. The need for shame and guilt corresponds with the need for control. Morrison (1996) believes that increased violence is in fact the outcome of too much shame in our society, such that "action, aggression, and retaliation" are the result of a failure to address social inequities (p. 198). The voices of dissent focus on the impact on self-esteem at the levels of health, group, and family communication. The question inherent in the differing premises of Margalit's (1996) and Morrison's (1996) books compared with Schneiderman's (1995) and Sykes's (1992) is whether increasing the public's sense of shame will increase national solidarity or result in more pockets of stigmatized isolation.

Margalit (1996) believes that a decent society is a pluralistic society where humiliation is not appropriate as "an institutional act of revenge" for violating social rules (p. 175). The stigmatizing of vulnerable groups as punishment destroys too many lives, and the loss of productive lives in turn hurts society. Solomon (1990, p. 287), on the other hand, argues that radical individualism has practically eliminated the importance of loyalty and honor (with its accompanying shame) as a necessity within a democratic society. However, he emphasizes the need for compassion, caring, and gratitude to play roles equal to that of shame in the cultivation of societal justice.

In other words, pluralistic values depend on a national orientation toward valuing individual differences. However, individualism robs groups or nations of allegiance to values of such import that to transgress those values is to feel shame; to adhere to those values is to feel a sense of pride, honor, and loyalty. The point Solomon is making is that without shame, there can be no honor. Schneiderman (1995) also argues for a return to a shame-based culture, where "the practice of respect confirms group membership" (p. 267). Self-respect, Lasch (1984) reminds us, must express itself in a "guilty conscience, the painful awareness of the gulf between human aspirations and human limitations" (p. 258). And, finally, Burke tells us that the public naming of guilt is necessary for societal redemption—be it by blaming others through victimization or blaming oneself through self-mortification.

ETHICS OF SHAME AND GUILT MESSAGES

Shame is the price humans pay for lives "fundamentally determined by an ethical code" and for a "series of profoundly felt rules" (Retzinger, 1991, p. 201). It also "maintains our commitment to a social determination of who we are" (Lindsay-Hartz, 1984, p. 700). Guilt "highlight[s] moral standards concerning what ought to be" and "supports the value of reconciling with others and being forgiven" (Lindsay-Hartz, 1984, pp. 701-702). Nevertheless, there remains considerable controversy surrounding the use of messages to manage shame and guilt. For example, is it "right" (good/moral/ethical) to make children feel guilty for not doing their homework? Was it a mistake to let the shame of illegitimacy dissipate into historical oblivion? Should we use public humiliation as punishment for crimes? The rhetoric surrounding these issues is confusing precisely because there are no clear guidelines. Perhaps the public dialogue about guilt and especially shame is becoming heated now because we do not understand guilt and shame well and because we are using them in different ways—a dangerous state for such powerful emotional forces.

We need to ask ourselves more frequently how we can manage shame and guilt through our messages in ways that are ethical. On the one hand, we do not want to extinguish, repress, or deny shame and guilt and, along with them, respect, awe, and humility toward our society's most precious values. For example, the silence that signifies a humbling shame is appropriate when drunk drivers are confronted by the mothers of the children they have killed or when an individual is acknowledging his or her own deficiencies at a craft or skill when being taught by an expert. Guilt is also an appropriate response to many actions, such as lying, theft, or hurting another person. Groups that encourage members to acknowledge their guilt include therapy groups, Alcoholics Anonymous, and religious groups. Messages that induce guilt can promote healthy behavioral changes, such as stopping smoking and starting exercising. Appeals to guilt are also used successfully to sell products and services, including the promotion of community service and donations. On the other hand, individuals can use messages to induce guilt or shame in order to satisfy their own egos or to manipulate the egos of others. For example, parents may shame their children indiscriminately or as a way to bolster their own egos, leaving the children feeling that they are totally worthless.

Our thinking about an ethics of shame and guilt messages leads us to close this essay with five questions. First, what *grounds* for shame and guilt should we encourage or discourage through messages? Here we need to reflect on important values in the culture. Are sex roles important enough to warrant shaming boys for playing with dolls? Can we tolerate citizens who feel no guilt for lying, cheating, or stealing? Lindsay-Hartz (1984, p. 702) argues that shame and guilt can be very dysfunctional if standards are inappropriate. For example, it may be healthier for Hispanics to work to change others' views of their ethnic group than to accept shame based on ethnicity. On the other hand, many grounds for shame and guilt are necessary for any society to function well. These include lying, cheating, stealing, failing to attend to close relationships, hurting others physically, price-fixing, and bribery. But alongside those are grounds that we judge to be less important, less necessary, and perhaps actively harmful grounds for shame, such as not owning certain consumer products, wearing socially inappropriate clothing, having a less-than-ideal body shape or size, being of a devalued race or ethnicity, being a survivor of a disaster or downsizing, being a victim of a crime, being poor, or being disabled. Many grounds, of course, lie in controversial areas—performing inadequately at work, failing to repay a loan, gender bending, gossiping, being on welfare, the sins of our forebears. It is not for us as authors to define the appropriate grounds for shame and guilt, but we do encourage more reflection and public debate on the actual in addition to the ideal grounds for shame that operate in society at all levels.

The second question we pose is whether shame and guilt are *acknowledged* both privately and publicly (where appropriate). Shame is more likely to be unacknowledged and hidden from oneself than is guilt, but both shame and guilt may never be acknowledged publicly despite several important reasons to do so. First, if shame and guilt are not acknowledged, it is not possible to reflect on their grounds or consequences. Children might never choose to disobey their parents or employees their bosses, stigmatized groups might never question the shame of their skin color or sexual orientation, organizations might ignore sexual harassment, and nations might never acknowledge their roles in massacres or genocide. Second, to acknowledge shame is to avoid the syndrome of shame-rage or humiliated fury that has been connected to domestic violence and war. Acknowledging shame seems to inhibit its immediate conversion into self-protective and other-blaming rage. Third, if shame and guilt go unacknowledged or are hidden, worse damage can be done than was caused by the original transgression. Hiding defective products or toxic chemicals or acts of family violence can perpetuate them. Disguising shame and guilt behind blaming, insulting, or demeaning others simply perpetuates shame and guilt—in oneself and others. Finally, admitting shame and guilt openly (especially through public apology) can be one step toward sharing the suffering between transgressor and victim. President Clinton's public apology to the victims of the Tuskegee syphilis experiments may not have taken away any physical suffering, but it may have contributed toward psychological and spiritual healing.

Our last three questions are tied to the consequences that shame and guilt messages have for esteem, control, and connection. In terms of *esteem*, we should ask if our standards are realistic and if the sanctions for violating them are appropriate.

On the one hand, holding children to unrealistic standards of achievement or punishing them for transgressions that are not clearly explained (especially in ways that are appropriate to their level of understanding) can be demoralizing rather than corrective. On the other hand, we might ask if all the praise that is lavished on children to improve their self-esteem actually undermines the humility they should feel at their own inadequacies and respect for the standards they should be meeting. The same dilemma applies to organizations. On the one hand, they may go too far in attempting to build self-esteem by managing their internal and external images at the expense of suppressing organizational inadequacies or failures. On the other hand, if organizations are not sometimes made to feel guilty or shamed for not meeting their goals, they might set the standards so low that there is no struggle. If we are afraid to threaten esteem, can we hope to build it by challenging it? The alcoholic who finally admits to secret drinking has faced shame and can now work toward feeling pride. The whistle-blowing employee who publicizes organizational mistakes ultimately helps the organization admit its guilt—for example, recalling defective products—and act with honor. At a societal level, national honor depends upon the nation's being willing to admit its mistakes and face the shame of violating its own creeds—be they humanitarian, democratic, or religious in foundation.

The fourth question is whether the person or entity being shamed or made to feel guilty has any *control* over the grounds. Considering that the function of shame is social control, it hardly seems appropriate to shame someone for something he or she cannot control, such as a disability (Lindsay-Hartz, de Rivera, & Mascolo, 1995, p. 297). Perhaps shame should be saved for transgressions such as smoking cigarettes or neglecting one's children. Shaming individuals or whole groups of people for fixed characteristics (such as race, gender, or status) keeps people in their place, perhaps rightfully so (as when parents shame children or religious leaders shame followers) and perhaps wrongfully so (as when dominant groups shame oppressed groups). We need to ask for whose benefit the control is being exerted. Ideally, shame and guilt should be used to foster collective values, not individuals' own personal goals. Do I shame my class for not doing the reading because I want them to try harder to learn or because I am irritated about having to lecture? Do employers give shaming performance appraisals to encourage employees to work better or simply to keep them in line? Do societies create laws to keep the homeless off the streets to help those without shelter or to pretend that such problems do not exist? In other words, how is shame shifted from organizations or societies to individuals who are less able to control the grounds for the shame?

Fifth, we should ask whether our messages of shame and guilt put at risk the *connections* among people and between people and the larger society. Without the shame that must coexist with honor, pride, and loyalty, groups do not cohere in solidarity. When managing messages of shame and guilt, one must always strive to preserve or to reestablish those connections. Without them, control and esteem are also at risk, because nobody can be controlled or feel a sense of secure esteem if he or she is alienated. But there is much hope that the damage to interpersonal and social bonds can be overcome by mutual caring and respect. We must remember Solomon's admonition to integrate compassion and caring along with just and responsible shaming. Braithwaite's model of "reintegrative shaming" is inspiring as a way of fusing contrition and connection.

This review can serve as a warning about the danger of two extremes: ignoring the value of shame and (re)acting against shame unwisely. At the time of this writing, the United States is considering taking military action against Iraq—action that is not condoned by most of the members of the United Nations. Nathanson (1992) has this to say about the possible import of such actions: "Faced with societal discontent [or problems at home], whole nations have been urged on courses of action designed by their leaders to reduce chronic shame. Is the public hungry for evidence of personal competence? A war might just be the thing" (p. 458). Although Nathanson gives as an example Saddam Hussein, his words can be applied to any nation: "As individuals, we can feel bigger when our nation annexes territory, humbles an enemy, develops a weapon that can destroy more people and lay waste more territory than ever before" (p. 458).

We want to end our discussion with an image of a healthy message of shame and guilt from the 1998 Olympics in Nagano, Japan. During the opening ceremonies, a legion of children ran into the center square, and running with them—holding the hand of one of the children—was a man who had lost both an arm and a leg as he was engaged in the work of removing land mines. The CBS announcer explained that his presence with the children symbolized for the Japanese people their atonement for acts of war in the past and their hopes for the children of the future in seeking peace.

REFERENCES

Abell, E., & Gecas, V. (1997). Guilt, shame, and family socialization. *Journal of Family Issues, 18*, 99-123.

Abrams, J. (1992, November 30). Study: Sexual harassment global. *Ann Arbor News*, p. A6.

Alessandri, S. M., & Lewis, M. (1993). Parental evaluation and its relation to shame and pride in young children. *Sex Roles, 29*, 335-343.

Alessandri, S. M., & Lewis, M. (1996). Differences in pride and shame in maltreated and nonmaltreated preschoolers. *Child Development, 67*, 1857-1869.

Allen, B. J., & Tompkins, P. K. (1996). Vocabularies of motives in a crisis of academic leadership. *Southern Communication Journal, 61*, 322-331.

Alter, J., & Wingert, P. (1995, February 6). The return of shame. *Newsweek, 125*, 21-25.

Aristotle. (1932). *The rhetoric of Aristotle* (L. Cooper, Trans.). Englewood Cliffs, NJ: Prentice Hall.

Armon-Jones, C. (1986). The social functions of emotion. In R. Harré (Ed.), *The social construction of emotions* (pp. 57-82). New York: Basil Blackwell.

Ashforth, B. (1994). Petty tyranny in organizations. *Human Relations, 7*, 755-866.

Bach, B. W. (1983, November). *Rumor and gossip in organizations: A review and analysis.* Paper presented at the annual meeting of the Speech Communication Association, Washington, DC.

Balcom, D., Lee, R. G., & Tager, J. (1995). The systemic treatment of shame in couples. *Journal of Marital and Family Therapy, 21,* 55-65.
Barrett, K. C. (1995). A functionalist approach to shame and guilt. In J. P. Tangney & K. W. Fischer (Eds.), *Self-conscious emotions: The psychology of shame, guilt, embarrassment, and pride* (pp. 25-63). New York: Guilford.
Barry, K., & Hazen, M. A. (1996). So you take your body to work? In S. M. Boje, R. P. Gephart, & T. J. Thatchenkery (Eds.), *Postmodern management and organization theory* (pp. 140-153). Thousand Oaks, CA: Sage.
Baum, H. S. (1987). *The invisible bureaucracy: The unconscious in organizational problem-solving.* New York: Oxford University Press.
Baum, H. S. (1991). Creating a family in the workplace. *Human Relations, 44,* 1137-1160.
Baum, H. S. (1992). Mentoring: Narcissistic fantasies and Oedipal realities. *Human Relations, 45,* 223-247.
Baumeister, R. F. (1995). Transcendence, guilt, and self-control. *Behavioral and Brain Sciences, 18,* 122-123.
Baumeister, R. F., & Leary, M. R. (1995). The need to belong: Desire for interpersonal attachments as a fundamental human motivation. *Psychological Bulletin, 117,* 497-529.
Baumeister, R. F., Reis, H. T., & Delespaul, P. A. E. G. (1995). Subjective and experiential correlates of guilt in daily life. *Personality and Social Psychology Bulletin, 21,* 1256-1268.
Baumeister, R. F., Stillwell, A. M., & Heatherton, T. F. (1994). Guilt: An interpersonal approach. *Psychological Bulletin, 115,* 243-267.
Baumeister, R. F., Stillwell, A. M., & Heatherton, T. F. (1995). Interpersonal aspects of guilt: Evidence from narrative studies. In J. P. Tangney & K. W. Fischer (Eds.), *Self-conscious emotions: The psychology of shame, guilt, embarrassment, and pride* (pp. 255-273). New York: Guilford.
Becker, B. A. (1995, September-October). How people experience evaluation of performance. *Compensation and Benefits Review, 27,* 28-31.
Bell, E. L., & Nkomeo, S. M. (1992). Re-visioning women managers' lives. In A. J. Mills & P. Tancred (Eds.), *Gendering organizational analysis* (pp. 235-247). Newbury Park, CA: Sage.
Benedict, R. (1946). *The chrysanthemum and the sword: Patterns of Japanese culture.* Boston: Houghton Mifflin.
Bergmann, J. R. (1993). *Discreet indiscretions: The social organization of gossip* (J. Bednarz, Trans.). New York: Aldine de Gruyter.
Bingham, S. G. (1994). Communication strategies for managing sexual harassment in organization: Understanding message options and their effects. *Journal of Applied Communication Research, 19,* 88-115.
Bion, W. R. (1959). *Experiences in groups.* New York: Basic Books.
Birkimer, J. C., Johnston, P. L., & Berry, M. M. (1993). Guilt and help from friends: Variables related to healthy behavior. *Journal of Social Psychology, 133,* 683-692.
Blair, R. J. R., Sellars, C., Strickland, I., Clark, F., Williams, A. O., Smith, M., & Jones, L. (1995). Emotion attributions in the psychopath. *Personality and Individual Differences, 19,* 431-437.
Borg, I., Staufenbiel, T., & Scherer, K. R. (1988). On the symbolic basis of shame. In K. R. Scherer (Ed.), *Facets of emotion: Recent research* (pp. 79-98). Hillsdale, NJ: Lawrence Erlbaum.
Boskind-Lodahl, M. (1976). Cinderella's stepsisters: A feminist perspective on anorexia nervosa and bulimia. *Signs, 2,* 342-356.
Bowlby, J. (1973). *Attachment and loss: Vol. 2. Separation.* New York: Basic Books.
Braithwaite, J. (1989). *Crime, shame and reintegration.* Cambridge: Cambridge University Press.
Braithwaite, J. (1993). Shame and modernity. *British Journal of Criminology, 33,* 1-18.
Braithwaite, J., & Mugford, S. (1994). Conditions of successful reintegration ceremonies: Dealing with juvenile offenders. *British Journal of Criminology, 34,* 139-171.
Brockner, J. (1986, February). The impact of layoffs on the survivors. *Supervisory Management, 31,* 2-7.
Brockner, J. (1988). *Self-esteem at work: Research, theory, and practice.* Lexington, MA: Lexington.

Brockner, J., Davy, J., & Carter, C. (1985). Layoffs, self-esteem, and survivor guilt: Motivational, affective and attitudinal consequences. *Organizational Behavior and Human Decision Processes, 36,* 229-244.

Brockner, J., Greenberg, J., Brockner, A., Bortz, J., Davy, J., & Carter, C. (1986). Layoffs, equity theory, and work performance: Further evidence of the impact of survivor guilt. *Academy of Management Journal, 29,* 373-384.

Brockner, J., & Wiesenfeld, B. (1993). Living on the edge (of social and organizational psychology): The effects of job layoffs on those who remain. In J. K. Murnighan (Ed.), *Social psychology in organizations: Advances in theory and research* (pp. 119-140). Englewood Cliffs, NJ: Prentice Hall.

Brumberg, J. J. (1989). *Fasting girls: The history of anorexia nervosa.* New York: New American Library.

Burke, K. (1951). Rhetoric—old and new. *Journal of General Education, 5,* 201-210.

Burke, K. (1961). *The rhetoric of religion: Studies in logoly.* Boston: Beacon.

Burke, K. (1965). *Permanence and change: An anatomy of purpose.* New York: Bobbs-Merrill. (Original work published 1954)

Burke, K. (1966). *Language as symbolic action: Essays on life, literature, and method.* Berkeley: University of California Press.

Burke, K. (1967). *The philosophy of literary form: Studies in symbolic action* (2nd ed.). Baton Rouge: Louisiana State University Press.

Burke, K. (1969). *A rhetoric of motives.* Berkeley: University of California Press. (Original work published 1950)

Byrne, K. (1992, May 22). The Perkins lady/man! The persuasiveness of guilt. *Commonweal, 119,* 5-6.

Caudron, S., & Hayward, D. R. (1996). HR to the rescue: Teach downsizing survivors how to thrive. *Personnel Journal, 75,* 38-45.

Chaturvedi, S. K., & Pant, V. L. (1985). Emotional reactions and long-term adjustments in renal transplant recipients. *Indian Journal of Psychological Medicine, 8,* 3-9.

Cheney, G. (1983). The rhetoric of identification and the study of organizational communication. *Quarterly Journal of Speech, 69,* 143-158.

Chernin, K. (1981). *The obsession: Reflections on the tyranny of slenderness.* New York: Harper & Row.

Clair, R. P. (1993a). The bureaucratization, commodification, and privatization of sexual harassment through institutional discourse. *Management Communication Quarterly, 7,* 123-157.

Clair, R. P. (1993b). The use of framing devices to sequester organizational narratives: Hegemony and harassment. *Communication Monographs, 60,* 113-135.

Clair, R. P. (1994). Resistance and oppression as a self-contained opposite: An organizational communication analysis of one man's story of sexual harassment. *Western Journal of Communication, 58,* 235-262.

Cockburn, C., & Ormrod, S. (1993). *Gender and technology in the making.* London: Sage.

Comas-Diaz, L. (1996). LatiNegra: Mental health issues of African Latinas. In M. P. Root (Ed.), *The multiracial experience: Racial borders as the new frontier* (pp. 167-190). Thousand Oaks, CA: Sage.

Coulter, R. H., & Pinto, M. B. (1995). Guilt appeals in advertising: What are their effects? *Journal of Applied Psychology, 80,* 697-705.

Cox, T., Jr. (1994). *Cultural diversity in organizations: Theory, research, and practice.* San Francisco: Berrett-Koehler.

Crawford, J., Kippax, S., Onyx, J., Gault, U., & Benton, P. (1992). *Emotion and gender: Constructing meaning from memory.* Newbury Park, CA: Sage.

Cronkite, K. (1994). *On the edge of darkness: Conversations about conquering depression.* New York: Doubleday.

Crozier, W. R. (Ed.). (1990). *Shyness and embarrassment.* Cambridge: Cambridge University Press.

Dalke, D. (1994). Therapy-assisted growth after parental suicide: From a personal and professional perspective. *Omega, 29,* 113-151.

Darwin, C. (1965). *The expression of the emotions in man and animals.* Chicago: University of Chicago Press. (Original work published 1872)

De Board, R. (1978). *The psychoanalysis of organizations: A psychoanalytic approach to behaviour in groups and organizations.* London: Tavistock.

Diamond, M. A. (1993). *The unconscious life of organizations.* Westport, CT: Quorum.

Doherty, N., & Horsted, J. (1995, January 2). Helping survivors to stay on board. *People Management,* pp. 26-31.

Edell, J. A., & Burke, M. C. (1987). The power of feelings in understanding advertising effects. *Journal of Consumer Research, 14,* 421-433.

Edelmann, R. J. (1987). *The psychology of embarrassment.* New York: John Wiley.

Ehrlich, M. (1991). When placement people are displaced. *Journal of Career Planning and Employment, 52,* 71-74.

Ekman, P., Levenson, R. W., & Friesen, W. V. (1983). Autonomic nervous system activity distinguishes among emotions. *Science, 221,* 1208-1210.

Elmes, M. B., & Costello, M. (1992). Mystification and social drama: The hidden side of communication skills training. *Human Relations, 45,* 427-446.

Emler, N. (1994). Gossip, reputation, and social adaptation. In R. F. Goodman & A. Ben-Ze'ev (Eds.), *Good gossip* (pp. 117-138). Lawrence: University Press of Kansas.

Ferguson, T. J., & Crowley, S. L. (1997). Gender differences in the organization of guilt and shame. *Sex Roles, 37,* 19-44.

Ferguson, T. J., & Stegge, H. (1995). Emotional states and traits in children: The case of guilt and shame. In J. P. Tangney & K. W. Fischer (Eds.), *Self-conscious emotions: The psychology of shame, guilt, embarrassment, and pride* (pp. 174-197). New York: Guilford.

Ferguson, T. J., Stegge, H., & Damhuis, I. (1991). Children's understanding of guilt and shame. *Child Development, 62,* 827-840.

Fineman, S. (Ed.). (1993a). *Emotions in organizations.* Newbury Park, CA: Sage.

Fineman, S. (1993b). Organizations as emotional arenas. In S. Fineman (Ed.), *Emotions in organizations* (pp. 9-35). Newbury Park, CA: Sage.

Fischer, K. W., & Tangney, J. P. (1995). Self-conscious emotions and the affect revolution: Framework and overview. In J. P. Tangney & K. W. Fischer (Eds.), *Self-conscious emotions: The psychology of shame, guilt, embarrassment, and pride* (pp. 3-22). New York: Guilford.

Foss, S. K., & Griffin, C. (1992). A feminist perspective on rhetorical theory: Toward a clarification of boundaries. *Western Journal of Communication, 56,* 330-349.

Fredrickson, B. L., & Roberts, T.-A. (1997). Objectification theory: Toward understanding women's lived experiences and mental health risks. *Psychology of Women Quarterly, 21,* 173-206.

Frijda, N. H. (1986). *The emotions.* Cambridge: Cambridge University Press.

Frijda, N. H. (1994). The lex talionis: On vengeance. In S. H. M. van Goozen, N. E. van de Poll, & J. A. Sergeant (Eds.), *Emotions: Essays on emotion theory* (pp. 263-289). Hillsdale, NJ: Lawrence Erlbaum.

Frijda, N. H., Kuipers, P., ter Schure, E. (1989). Relations among emotion, appraisal, and emotional action readiness. *Journal of Personality and Social Psychology, 57,* 212-228.

Gabriel, Y. (1997). Meeting God: When organizational members come face to face with the supreme leader. *Human Relations, 50,* 315-342.

Gahr, E. (1997, March). Can shame tame cons? *Insight on the News, 13,* 38.

Garfinkel, H. (1956). Conditions of successful degradation ceremonies. *American Journal of Sociology, 61,* 420-424.

Gehm, T. L., & Scherer, K. R. (1988). Relating situational evaluation to emotion differentiation: Nonmetric analysis of cross-cultural questionnaire data. In K. R. Scherer (Ed.), *Facets of emotion: Recent research* (pp. 61-77). Hillsdale, NJ: Lawrence Erlbaum.

Geist, P., & Townsley, N. (1997, November). *"Swept under the rug" and other disappearing acts: Legitimate concerns for university's sexual harassment policy and procedures.* Paper presented at the annual meeting of the National Communication Association, Chicago.

Gemmill, G., & Oakley, J. (1992). Leadership: An alienating social myth? *Human Relations, 45,* 113-130.

Gherardi, S. (1995). *Gender, symbolism, and organizational cultures.* Thousand Oaks, CA: Sage.

Giddens, A. (1991). *Modernity and self-identity: Self and society in the late modern age.* Stanford, CA: Stanford University Press.

Gitterman, A., & Shulman, L. (Eds.). (1994). *Mutual aid groups, vulnerable populations, and the life cycle* (2nd ed.). New York: Columbia University Press.

Goleman, D. (1995). *Emotional intelligence.* New York: Bantam.

Gonzales, M. H., Manning, D. J., & Haugen, J. A. (1992). Explaining our sins: Factors influencing offender accounts and anticipated victim responses. *Journal of Personality and Social Psychology, 62,* 958-971.

Goodall, H. L., Jr., Wilson, G. L., & Waagen, C. L. (1986). The performance appraisal interview: An interpretive reassessment. *Quarterly Journal of Speech, 72,* 74-87.

Goodman, R. F., & Ben-Ze'ev, A. (Eds.). (1994). *Good gossip.* Lawrence: University Press of Kansas.

Gottman, J. M. (1994). *What predicts divorce?* Hillsdale, NJ: Lawrence Erlbaum.

Graham, S., Doubleday, C., & Guarino, P. A. (1984). The development of relations between perceived controllability and the emotions of pity, anger, and guilt. *Child Development, 55,* 561-565.

Grasmick, H. G., Blackwell, B. S., Bursik, R. J., Jr., & Mitchell, S. (1993). Changes in perceived threats of shame, embarrassment, and legal sanctions for interpersonal violence, 1982-1992. *Violence and Victims, 8,* 313-325.

Grasmick, H. G., & Bursik, R. J., Jr. (1990). Conscience, significant others, and rational choice: Extending the deterrence model. *Law and Society Review, 24,* 837-861.

Grasmick, H. G., Bursik, R. J., Jr., & Arneklev, B. (1993). Reduction in drunk driving as a response to increased threats of legal sanctions, shame, and embarrassment. *Criminology, 31,* 41-67.

Grasmick, H. G., Bursik, R. J., Jr., & Kinsey, K. A. (1991). Shame and embarrassment as deterrents to noncompliance with the law: The case of an antilittering campaign. *Environment and Behavior, 23,* 233-251.

Greenberg, J. S. (1995). Health care: First the heart, then the head. *Journal of Health Education, 26,* 214-223.

Greenspan, P. S. (1995). *Practical guilt: Moral dilemmas, emotions, and social norms.* New York: Oxford University Press.

Gregg, R. (1993). "Choice" as a double-edged sword: Information, guilt, and mother-blaming in a high-tech age. *Women and Health, 20,* 53-73.

Gutek, B. A., Cohen, A. G., & Konrad, A. M. (1990). Predicting sexual-social behavior at work: A contact hypothesis. *Academy of Management Journal, 33,* 560-577.

Gwartney-Gibbs, P. A., & Lach, D. H. (1994). Gender differences in clerical workers' disputes over tasks, interpersonal treatment, and emotion. *Human Relations 47,* 611-640.

Hafen, S. (1997, November). *Theorizing organizational gossip.* Paper presented at the annual meeting of the National Communication Association, Chicago.

Hagen, P. L. (1995). "Pure persuasion" and verbal irony. *Southern Communication Journal, 61,* 46-58.

Hargie, O., & Tourish, D. (1994). Communication skills training: Management manipulation or personal development. *Human Relations, 47,* 1377-1390.

Harris, P. (1989). *Children and emotion.* Oxford: Basil Blackwell.

Hartzell, G. N. (1992, April). Living with layoffs. *Executive Educator,* pp. 25-28.

Hochschild, A. R. (1983). *The managed heart: Commercialization of human feeling.* Berkeley: University of California Press.

Howard, G. R. (1993, September). Whites in multicultural education: Rethinking our role. *Phi Delta Kappan, 75,* 36-41.

Iggers, J. (1993, November-December). Innocence lost: Our complicated relationship with food. *Utne Reader, 60,* 54-60.

Izard, C. E. (1977). *Human emotions.* New York: Plenum.

Izard, C. E. (1991). *The psychology of emotions.* New York: Plenum.

James, W. (1984). What is an emotion? (Original work published 1884). In C. Calhoun & R. C. Solomon (Eds.), *What is an emotion?* (pp. 127-141). New York: Oxford University Press.

Jaspers, K. (1947). *The question of German guilt.* New York: Dial.

Johnson, S. M., & Greenberg, L. S. (1994). *The heart of the matter: Perspectives on emotion in marital therapy.* New York: Brunner/Mazel.

Jones, M. J. (1994). Speaking the unspoken: Parents of sexually victimized children. In A. Gitterman & L. Shulman (Eds.), *Mutual aid groups, vulnerable populations, and the life cycle* (2nd ed., pp. 239-265). New York: Columbia University Press.

Jones, W. H., Kugler, K., & Adams, P. (1995). You always hurt the one you love: Guilt and transgressions against relationship partners. In J. P. Tangney & K. W. Fischer (Eds.), *Self-conscious emotions: The psychology of shame, guilt, embarrassment, and pride* (pp. 301-321). New York: Guilford.

Karen, R. (1992, February). Shame. *Atlantic Monthly,* pp. 40-70.

Karp, H. P., & Sutton, N. (1993, July). Where diversity training goes wrong. *Training, 30,* 30-33.

Katz, J. (1988). *Seductions of crime.* New York: Basic Books.

Kaufman, G. (1992). *Shame: The power of caring* (3rd ed.). Rochester, VT: Schenkman.

Kaufman, G., & Raphael, L. (1996). *Coming out of shame: Transforming gay and lesbian lives.* New York: Doubleday.

Kellogg, N. D., & Huston, R. L. (1995). Unwanted sexual experiences in adolescents: Patterns of disclosure. *Clinical Pediatrics, 34,* 306-312.

Kets de Vries, M. F. R. (1991). *Organizations on the couch.* San Francisco: Jossey-Bass.

Kets de Vries, M. F. R. (1995). *Organizational paradoxes: Clinical approaches to management.* New York: Routledge.

Kets de Vries, M. F. R., & Balazs, K. (1997). The downside of downsizing. *Human Relations, 50,* 11-50.

Kets de Vries, M. F. R., & Miller, D. (1984). *The neurotic organization.* San Francisco: Jossey-Bass.

Kets de Vries, M. F. R., & Miller, D. (1987). *Unstable at the top: Inside the troubled organization.* New York: NAL.

Kirshbaum, H. (1991). Disability and humiliation. *Journal of Primary Prevention, 12,* 169-181.

Kitayama, S., Markus, H. R., & Matsumoto, H. (1995). Culture, self, and emotion: A cultural perspective on "self-conscious" emotions. In J. P. Tangney & K. W. Fischer (Eds.), *Self-conscious emotions: The psychology of shame, guilt, embarrassment, and pride* (pp. 439-464). New York: Guilford.

Kübler-Ross, E. (1969). *On death and dying.* New York: Macmillan.

Lakey, J. F. (1994). The profile and treatment of male adolescent sex offenders. *Adolescence, 29,* 755-761.

Lamb, L. (1992, July-August). For shame. *Utne Reader, 52,* 46-48.

Lansky, M. (1987). Shame and domestic violence. In D. L. Nathanson (Ed.), *The many faces of shame* (pp. 335-362). New York: Guilford.

Lapin, D. (1995, September 25). In praise of shame. *National Review, 47,* 87-89.

Lasch, C. (1984). *The minimal self: Psychic survival in troubled times.* New York: W. W. Norton.

Lasch, C. (1992, August 10). For shame: Why Americans should be wary of self-esteem. *New Republic, 207,* 29-35.

Lazarus, R. S. (1991). *Emotion and adaptation.* New York: Oxford University Press.

Lazear, E. P., & Kandel, E. (1992). Peer pressure and partnerships. *Journal of Political Economy, 100,* 801-817.

Lewis, H. B. (1971). *Shame and guilt in neurosis.* New York: International Universities Press.

Lewis, H. B. (1981). Shame and guilt in human nature. In S. Tuttman, C. Kaye, & M. Zimmerman (Eds.), *Object and self: A developmental approach* (pp. 235-265). New York: International Universities Press.

Lewis, H. B. (1987). Shame and the narcissistic personality. In D. L. Nathanson (Ed.), *The many faces of shame* (pp. 93-132). New York: Guilford.

Lewis, M. (1992). *Shame: The exposed self.* New York: Free Press.

Lewis, M. (1993). Self-conscious emotions: Embarrassment, pride, shame, and guilt. In M. Lewis & J. M. Haviland (Eds.), *Handbook of emotions* (pp. 563-573). New York: Guilford.

Liem, R. (1997). Shame and guilt among first- and second-generation Asian Americans and European Americans. *Journal of Cross-Cultural Psychology, 28,* 365-392.

Lindsay-Hartz, J. (1984). Contrasting experiences of shame and guilt. *American Behavioral Scientist, 27,* 689-704.

Lindsay-Hartz, J., de Rivera, J., & Mascolo, M. F. (1995). Differentiating guilt and shame and their effects on motivation. In J. P. Tangney & K. W. Fischer (Eds.), *Self-conscious emotions: The psychology of shame, guilt, embarrassment, and pride* (pp. 274-300). New York: Guilford.

Lisak, D. (1994). The psychological impact of sexual abuse: Content analysis of interviews with male survivors. *Journal of Traumatic Stress, 7,* 525-548.

Lopez, F. G., Gover, M. R., Leskela, J., Sauer, E. M., Schirmer, L., & Wyssmann, J. (1997). Attachment styles, shame, guilt, and collaborative problem-solving orientations. *Personal Relationships, 4,* 187-199.

Lukes, S. (1997). Humiliation and the politics of identity. *Social Research, 64,* 36-51.

Lynch, F. R. (1997). *The diversity machine: The drive to change the white male workplace.* New York: Free Press.

Mackey-Kallis, S., & Hahn, D. (1994). Who's to blame for America's drug problem? The search for scapegoats in the "war on drugs." *Communication Quarterly, 42,* 1-22.

Makkai, T., & Braithwaite, J. (1994a). The dialectics of corporate deterrence. *Journal of Research in Crime and Delinquency, 31,* 347-374.

Makkai, T., & Braithwaite, J. (1994b). Reintegrative shaming and compliance with regulatory standards. *Criminology, 32,* 361-385.

Malatesta-Magai, C., & Dorval, B. (1992). Language, affect, and social order. In M. R. Gunnar & M. Maratsos (Eds.), *Modularity and constraints in language and cognition: The Minnesota Symposia on Child Psychology* (Vol. 25, pp. 139-177). Hillsdale, NJ: Lawrence Erlbaum.

Manstead, A. S. R., & Tetlock, P. E. (1989). Cognitive appraisals and emotional experience: Further evidence. *Cognition and Emotion, 3,* 225-240.

March, J. G. (1994). *A primer on decision making: How decisions happen.* New York: Free Press.

Margalit, A. (1996). *The decent society* (N. Goldblum, Trans.). Cambridge, MA: Harvard University Press.

Markus, H. R., & Kitayama, S. (1991). Culture and the self: Implications for cognition, emotion, and motivation. *Psychological Review, 98,* 224-253.

Metts, S. (1997). Face and facework: Implications for the study of personal relationships. In S. Duck (Ed.), *Handbook of personal relationships* (2nd ed., pp. 373-390). West Sussex, UK: Wiley.

Miles, M. S., & Demi, A. S. (1991). A comparison of guilt in bereaved parents whose children died by suicide, accident, or chronic illness. *Omega, 24,* 203-215.

Miller, M. V., & Hoppe, S. K. (1994). Attributions for job termination and psychological distress. *Human Relations, 47,* 263-306.

Miller, R. S., & Leary, M. R. (1992). Social sources and interactive functions of emotion: The case of embarrassment. In M. S. Clark (Ed.), *Emotion and social behavior* (pp. 202-221). Newbury Park, CA: Sage.

Miller, R. S., & Tangney, J. P. (1994). Differentiating embarrassment and shame. *Journal of Social and Clinical Psychology, 13,* 273-287.

Miller, W. I. (1993). *Humiliation.* Ithaca, NY: Cornell University Press.

Moore, M. P. (1996). Rhetorical subterfuge and "the principles of perfection": Bob Packwood's response to sexual misconduct charges. *Western Journal of Communication, 60,* 1-20.

Morgan, G. (1986). *Images of organization.* Beverly Hills, CA: Sage.

Morrison, A. P. (1996). *The culture of shame.* New York: Ballantine.

Murphy, J. M. (1990). "A time of shame and sorrow": Robert E. Kennedy and the American Jeremiad. *Quarterly Journal of Speech, 76*, 401-414.

Nathanson, D. L. (1987a). Shaming systems in couples, families, and institutions. In D. L. Nathanson (Ed.), *The many faces of shame* (pp. 246-270). New York: Guilford.

Nathanson, D. L. (1987b). A timetable for shame. In D. L. Nathanson (Ed.), *The many faces of shame* (pp. 1-63). New York: Guilford.

Nathanson, D. L. (1992). *Shame and pride: Affect, sex, and the birth of the self.* New York: Norton.

Naziri, D., & Tzavaras, A. (1993). Mourning and guilt among Greek women having repeated abortions. *Omega, 26*, 137-144.

Neuberg, S. L., Smith, D. M., Hoffman, J. C., & Russell, F. J. (1994). When we observe stigmatized and "normal" individuals interacting: Stigma by association. *Personality and Social Psychology Bulletin, 20*, 196-209.

Niedenthal, P. M., Tangney, J. P., & Gavanski, I. (1994). "If only I weren't" versus "If only I hadn't": Distinguishing shame and guilt in counterfactual thinking. *Journal of Personality and Social Psychology, 67*, 585-596.

Noer, D. M. (1993). *Healing the wounds.* San Francisco: Jossey-Bass.

O'Keefe, D. J., & Figgé, M. (1997). A guilt-based explanation of the door-in-the-face influence strategy. *Human Communication Research, 24*, 64-81.

Oppedisano, J. (1997). Academics' shame: Our failure to confront sexual harassment. *National Women Studies Association Journal, 9*, 126-134.

Papa, M. J., Auwal, M. A., & Singhal, A. (1995). Dialectic of control and emancipation in organizing for social change: A multitheoretic study of the Grameen Bank in Bangladesh. *Communication Theory, 5*, 189-223.

Parker, G. (1993). Disability, caring, and marriage: The experience of younger couples when a partner is disabled after marriage. *British Journal of Social Work, 23*, 565-580.

Paternoster, R., & Simpson, S. (1996). Sanction threats and appeals to morality: Testing a rational choice of corporate crime. *Law and Society, 30*, 549-583.

Penelope, J., & Wolfe, S. J. (Eds.). (1995). *The original coming out stories.* Freedom, CA: Crossing.

Pinderhughes, E. (1989). *Understanding race, ethnicity, and power: The key to efficacy in clinical practice.* New York: Free Press.

Porter, J. F., Critelli, J. W., & Tang, C. S. K. (1992). Sexual and aggressive motives in sexually aggressive college males. *Archives of Sexual Behavior, 21*, 457-468.

Potter-Efron, R., & Potter-Efron, P. (1989). *Letting go of shame: Understanding how shame affects your life.* San Francisco: Harper & Row.

Pringle, R. (1988). *Secretaries talk* (2nd ed.). New York: Verso.

Pulakos, J. (1996). Family environment and shame: Is there a relationship? *Journal of Clinical Psychology, 52*, 617-623.

Putnam, L. L., & Mumby, D. K. (1993). *Organizations, emotion, and the myth of rationality.* In S. Fineman (Ed.), *Emotions in organizations* (pp. 36-57). Newbury Park, CA: Sage.

Quinton, A. (1997). Humiliation. *Social Research, 64*, 77-89.

Retzinger, S. M. (1991). *Violent emotions.* Newbury Park, CA: Sage.

Retzinger, S. M. (1995). Identifying shame and anger in discourse. *American Behavioral Scientist, 38*, 1104-1113.

Rimé, B., Finkenauer, C., Luminet, O., Zech, E., & Philippot, P. (1996). Social sharing of emotion: New evidence and new questions. In W. Stroebe & M. Hewstone (Eds.), *European review of social psychology* (Vol. 7). Chichester, UK: Wiley.

Ripstein, A. (1997). Responses to humiliation. *Social Research, 64*, 90-111.

Robinson, D. T., Smith-Lovin, L., & Tsoudis, O. (1994). Heinous crime or unfortunate accident? The effects of remorse and responses to mock criminal confessions. *Social Forces, 73*, 175-190.

Rodenbaugh, S. (1995, May-June). Better dead than unwed? Straight talk on the stigma of illegitimacy. *Utne Reader, 69*, 74-79.

Rodriguez, A., & Nicotera, A. M. (1997, November). *Graffiti as organizational communication: Sense-making and organizational culture.* Paper presented at the annual meeting of the National Communication Association, Chicago.

Roseman, I. J., Spindel, M. S., & Jose, P. E. (1990). Appraisals of emotion-eliciting events: Testing a theory of discrete emotions. *Journal of Personality and Social Psychology, 59,* 899-915.

Rosen, B., & Adams, J. S. (1974). Organizational cover-ups: Factors influencing the discipline of information gatekeepers. *Journal of Applied Social Psychology, 4,* 375-384.

Rosnow, R. L., & Fine, G. A. (1976). *Rumor and gossip: The social psychology of hearsay.* New York: Elsevier.

Rossiter, J. R., Percy, L., & Donovan, R. J. (1991). A better advertising planning grid. *Journal of Advertising Research, 31*(5), 11-21.

Rushing, W. A. (1995). *The AIDS epidemic: Social dimensions of an infectious disease.* Boulder, CO: Westview.

Rysman, A. (1977). How "gossip" became a woman. *Journal of Communication, 27,* 176-180.

Schachter, S., & Singer, J. (1962). Cognitive, social and physiological determinants of emotional state. *Psychological Review, 69,* 379-399.

Schaef, A. W., & Fassel, D. (1988). *The addictive organization.* San Francisco: Harper & Row.

Scheff, T. J. (1994). *Bloody revenge: Emotions, nationalism, and war.* Boulder, CO: Westview.

Scheff, T. J. (1995a). Conflict in family systems: The role of shame. In J. P. Tangney & K. W. Fischer (Eds.), *Self-conscious emotions: The psychology of shame, guilt, embarrassment, and pride* (pp. 393-412). New York: Guilford.

Scheff, T. J. (1995b). Shame and related emotions: An overview. *American Behavioral Scientist, 38,* 1053-1059.

Scheff, T. J., & Retzinger, S. M. (1991). *Emotions and violence.* Lexington, MA: Lexington.

Scheibel, D. (1994). Graffiti and "film school" culture: Displaying alienation. *Communication Monographs, 61,* 1-18.

Schick, F. (1997). On humiliation. *Social Research, 64,* 131-136.

Schneider, C. D. (1977). *Shame, exposure, and privacy.* Boston: Beacon.

Schneider, C. D. (1987). A mature sense of shame. In D. L. Nathanson (Ed.), *The many faces of shame* (pp. 194-213). New York: Guilford.

Schneiderman, S. (1995). *Saving face: America and the politics of shame.* New York: Knopf.

Schwartz, H. S. (1990). *Narcissistic processes and organizational decay.* New York: New York University Press.

Schwartz, H. S. (1993). Narcissistic emotion and university administration: An analysis of political correctness. In S. Fineman (Ed.), *Emotions in organizations* (pp. 190-215). Newbury Park, CA: Sage.

Searle, J. R. (1969). *Speech acts.* Cambridge: Cambridge University Press.

Secouler, L. M. (1992). Our elders: At high risk for humiliation. *Journal of Primary Prevention, 12,* 195-208.

Shaver, P., Schwartz, J., Kirson, D., & O'Connor, C. (1987). Emotion knowledge: Further explorations of a prototype approach. *Journal of Personality and Social Psychology, 52,* 1061-1086.

Shreve, B. W., & Kunkel, M. A. (1991). Self-psychology, shame, and adolescent suicide: Theoretical and practical implications. *Journal of Counseling and Development, 69,* 305-311.

Silverman, D. (1994). Describing sexual activities in HIV counseling: The cooperative management of the moral order. *Text, 14,* 427-453.

Skaine, R., & Skaine, J. C. (1996). Sexual harassment in education. In R. Skaine (Ed.), *Power and gender: Issues in sexual dominance and harassment* (pp. 242-306). Jefferson, NC: McFarland.

Smith, J. S. (1992). Humiliation, degradation, and the criminal justice system. *Journal of Primary Prevention, 12,* 209-222.

Solomon, R. C. (1989). The emotions of justice. *Social Justice Research, 3,* 345-374.

Solomon, R. C. (1990). *A passion for justice.* Reading, MA: Addison-Wesley.

Sowell, T. (1993, January 4). Right and wrong. *Forbes, 151,* 151-172.

Spacks, P. (1986). *Gossip.* New York: Knopf.

Stein, N. L., Trabasso, T., & Liwag, M. (1993). The representation and organization of emotional experience: Unfolding the emotion episode. In M. Lewis & J. M. Haviland (Eds.), *Handbook of emotions* (pp. 279-300). New York: Guilford.

Stewart, C. J. (1991). The ego function of protest songs: An implication of Gregg's theory of protest rhetoric. *Communication Studies, 42,* 240-253.

Stierlin, H. (1974). Shame and guilt in family relations. *Archives of General Psychiatry, 30,* 381-389.

Stoner, C. R., & Hartman, R. I. (1997). Organization therapy: Building survivor health and competitiveness. *SAM Advanced Management Journal, 62,* 25-32.

Swanson, G. I. (1993, June). The hall of shame. *Phi Delta Kappan, 74,* 796-798.

Swift, C. F. (1991). Section Two: Those at risk of humiliation . . . some issues in inter-gender humiliation. *Journal of Primary Prevention, 12,* 123-147.

Sykes, C. J. (1992). *A nation of victims: The decay of the American character.* New York: St. Martin's.

Tangney, J. P. (1990). Assessing individual differences in proneness to shame and guilt: Development of the self-conscious affect and attribution inventory. *Journal of Personality and Social Psychology, 59,* 102-111.

Tangney, J. P. (1991). Moral affect: The good, the bad, and the ugly. *Journal of Personality and Social Psychology, 61,* 598-607.

Tangney, J. P. (1992). Situational determinants of shame and guilt in young adulthood. *Personality and Social Psychology Bulletin, 18,* 199-205.

Tangney, J. P. (1995a). Recent advances in the empirical study of shame and guilt. *American Behavioral Scientist, 38,* 1132-1145.

Tangney, J. P. (1995b). Shame and guilt in interpersonal relationships. In J. P. Tangney & K. W. Fischer (Eds.), *Self-conscious emotions: The psychology of shame, guilt, embarrassment, and pride* (pp. 114-139). New York: Guilford.

Tangney, J. P. (1996). Conceptual and methodological issues in the assessment of shame and guilt. *Behavioral Research and Therapy, 34,* 741-754.

Tangney, J. P., Burggraf, S. A., & Wagner, P. E. (1995). Shame-proneness, guilt-proneness, and psychological symptoms. In J. P. Tangney & K. W. Fischer (Eds.), *Self-conscious emotions: The psychology of shame, guilt, embarrassment, and pride* (pp. 343-367). New York: Guilford.

Tangney, J. P., & Fischer, K. W. (Eds.). (1995). *Self-conscious emotions: The psychology of shame, guilt, embarrassment, and pride.* New York: Guilford.

Tangney, J. P., Miller, R. S., Flicker, L., & Barlow, D. H. (1996). Are shame, guilt, and embarrassment distinct emotions? *Journal of Personality and Social Psychology, 70,* 1256-1259.

Tangney, J. P., Wagner, P. E., Fletcher, C., & Gramzow, R. (1992). Shamed into anger? The relation of shame and guilt to anger and self-reported aggression. *Journal of Personality and Social Psychology, 62,* 669-675.

Tangney, J. P., Wagner, P. E., Hill-Barlow, D., Marschall, D. E., & Gramzow, R. (1996). Relation of shame and guilt to constructive versus destructive responses to anger across the lifespan. *Journal of Personality and Social Psychology, 70,* 797-809.

Tannen, D. (1990). *You just don't understand: Women and men in conversation.* New York: William Morrow.

Taylor, C., & Kleinke, C. L. (1992). Effects of severity of accident, history of drunk driving, intent, and remorse on judgments of a drunk driver. *Journal of Applied Social Psychology, 22,* 1641-1655.

Ting-Toomey, S. (1979, February). *Gossip as a communication construct.* Paper presented at the annual meeting of the Western Communication Association, Los Angeles.

Tisdale, S. (1993, November-December). The weight women carry. *Utne Reader 60,* 64-65.

Tomkins, S. S. (1963). *Affect, imagery, and consciousness: Vol. 2. The negative affects.* New York: Springer.

Turner, F. (1995). Shame, beauty, and the tragic view of history. *American Behavioral Scientist, 38,* 1060-1075.

Vangelisti, A. L., Daly, J. A., & Rudnick, J. R. (1991). Making people feel guilty in conversations: Techniques and correlates. *Human Communication Research, 18,* 3-39.

Vangelisti, A. L., & Sprague, R. J. (1998). Guilt and hurt: Similarities, distinctions, and conversational strategies. In P. A. Andersen & L. K. Guerrero (Eds.), *Handbook of communication and emotion: Research, theory, applications, and contexts* (pp. 123-154). San Diego, CA: Academic Press.

Victim justice. (1995, April). *New Republic, 212,* 9.

Villa-Vicencio, C. (1997). The burden of moral guilt: Its theological and political implications. *Journal of Church and State, 39,* 237-252.

Ware, N. D. (1992). Suffering and the social construction of illness: The delegitimization of illness experience in chronic fatigue syndrome. *Medical Anthropology Quarterly, 6,* 347-361.

Watson-Gegeo, K. A., & White, G. M. (1990). *Disentangling: Conflict discourse in Pacific societies.* Stanford, CA: Stanford University Press.

Wicker, F. W., Payne, G. C., & Morgan, R. D. (1983). Participant descriptions of guilt and shame. *Motivation and Emotion, 7,* 25-39.

Williams, C., & Bybee, J. (1994). What do children feel guilty about? Developmental and gender differences. *Developmental Psychology, 30,* 617-624.

Williams, K. R., Hawkins, R. (1989). The meaning of arrest for wife assault. *Criminology, 27,* 163-181.

Workman, T. (1996, November). *And the heads kept nodding: Politically correct resistance to diversity training.* Paper presented at the meeting of the Instructional Development Division, Speech Communication Association, San Diego, CA.

Wurmser, L. (1987). Shame: The veiled companion of narcissism. In D. L. Nathanson (Ed.), *The many faces of shame* (pp. 64-92). New York: Guilford.

Wurmser, L. (1995). *The mask of shame.* Northvale, NJ: Jason Aronson.

CHAPTER CONTENTS

2 Guilt and Social Influence

DANIEL J. O'KEEFE
University of Illinois, Urbana-Champaign

Research bearing on the role of guilt in social influence is reviewed in this chapter. Guilt is an emotion naturally suited to exploitation in the service of social influence, by virtue of its action-motivating aspects and its ability to be aroused by relationally significant others. Guilt can be a very powerful influence mechanism, as indicated by studies of guilt arousal in everyday life (where self-reports of behavioral change suggest that guilt commonly effects change), by studies of the relationship between transgressions and compliance (in which, a meta-analytic review reveals, relatively large effects of transgression on compliance are obtained under a variety of conditions), and by studies of hypocrisy-induction effects (which commonly are ascribed to dissonance but might equally well reflect guilt). However, guilt-based influence can fail quite dramatically; a meta-analysis of research on guilt-based appeals in persuasive messages reveals that, although more-explicit guilt appeals successfully arouse greater guilt than do less-explicit appeals, they are significantly less persuasive. Finally, recent research suggests that anticipated guilt feelings can play an important role in shaping conduct and hence may provide mechanisms of social influence.

T HE study of communicative social influence has commonly been dominated by views focused on "rational" or "logical" aspects of social influence (e.g., the aptly named theory of reasoned action; Fishbein & Ajzen, 1975). But students of persuasion have become increasingly interested in emotional facets of these communication processes (see, e.g., Cho & Stout, 1993; Dillard, 1993; Dillard & Kinney, 1994; Jorgensen, 1998; Kinder, 1994). Among various emotions that might be implicated in social-influence processes, the one that has received the most empirical and conceptual attention is fear. Thus, for example, fear appeals are commonly discussed in broad-scale summaries of persuasion-effects research. By contrast, such summaries rarely mention guilt as potentially having a role in social influence. Indeed, despite the quiet accumulation of a number of studies of the role of guilt in social influence, no general review of this literature has been undertaken.

Correspondence: Daniel J. O'Keefe, Department of Speech Communication, 244 Lincoln Hall, University of Illinois, 702 S. Wright Street, Urbana, IL 61801-3631; e-mail dokeefe@uiuc.edu

Communication Yearbook 23, pp. 67-101

This chapter summarizes and integrates several lines of research bearing on the role of guilt in social influence. First, the general nature of guilt is discussed, with particular attention to aspects of guilt relevant to social influence. Then four areas of social-influence research are reviewed, concerning guilt-based influence in interpersonal relationships, the impact of transgression on compliance, guilt appeals in persuasive messages, and hypocrisy induction. A final main section considers the role that anticipated feelings of guilt might play in social influence.

THE NATURE OF GUILT

Some background concerning the nature of guilt will be useful for understanding the roles that guilt might play in social influence. This section briefly discusses the nature of guilt, the experience of feeling guilty, and the interpersonal character of guilt.

The purpose of this initial section is to highlight some influence-relevant aspects of guilt. This review is specifically focused on research concerning guilt as a social-influence mechanism, and so I do not consider a variety of broader questions concerning guilt, such as the ontogenesis of guilt or details of guilt assessment procedures (for discussions of such aspects of guilt, see, e.g., Barrett, 1995; Ferguson & Crowley, 1997; Fischer & Tangney, 1995; Kugler & Jones, 1992; Tangney, 1995a). My interest here is less in providing a complete treatment of all aspects of guilt and more in identifying particular facets of guilt that are relevant to its roles in social-influence processes.

General Nature of Guilt

Guilt may be initially and briefly described as "an individual's unpleasant emotional state associated with possible objections to his or her actions, inaction, circumstances, or intentions" (Baumeister, Stillwell, & Heatherton, 1994, p. 245).[1] As even this brief characterization makes clear, guilt—by virtue of being connected to possible objections to one's conduct—is the sort of emotional state that might straightforwardly be aroused by another person (by another person's raising objections). That is to say, arousing guilt is the sort of thing a person might do rather more easily than (say) arousing sadness, precisely because guilt is connected to potential objections to one's conduct.

However, as Miceli (1992) has pointed out, there is something more involved in guilt than simply the recognition of possible objections to one's conduct. Miceli's analysis is cast in terms of the conditions under which guilt is likely to be aroused and identifies two initial "essential ingredients" for one person (A) to make someone else (B) feel guilty: "(1) To make B assume that he is responsible for a certain act or event x, i.e., that: (a) he caused x to happen either directly or indirectly; (b) his goal was to cause x, or at least (c) he had the power to avoid x but this was not his goal" and "(2) To make B assume a negative evaluation of harmfulness with regard to x and, more or less indirectly, to B himself as the perpetrator" (p. 82).

But these two conditions are not sufficient for guilt induction, because "B can acknowledge responsibility without feeling guilty" (p. 97). Hence Miceli suggests a third "crucial constituent of the sense of guilt: the thwarting of B's self-image" (p. 98). The reasoning here is that B can acknowledge responsibility, but experience no guilt, in circumstances in which the negative evaluation is not based on B's own standards. "B can objectively acknowledge his guilt (as regards others'—some person's, or group's—standards of evaluation) . . . but if he does not share those standards (values, norms), he will not come to translate the negative evaluation(s) into negative self-evaluations(s). And, if this translation fails to occur, B will not feel guilty" (p. 99). Hence guilt is a "self-judgment based on internal standards" (p. 99). Because B falls short of meeting B's own standards, B's self-image is correspondingly threatened.

Consistent with this general image, the sorts of circumstances that persons recall as being especially associated with feelings of guilt involve failures at duties (e.g., not studying enough), lying, stealing, neglecting others (e.g., not calling a friend for a long time), failing to maintain a diet or exercise plan, or cheating (Keltner & Buswell, 1996; Tangney, 1992). In all these situations, persons can be seen as having fallen short of their own standards.

In sum, guilt can be broadly understood as a negative emotional state associated with possible objections to one's conduct (action, inaction, and the like), where those objections are based in one's own standards. Thus guilt may be seen to arise from some (potential) inconsistency between the actor's conduct and the actor's standards.

The Experience of Feeling Guilty

In trying to distinguish various emotions, several studies have sought to identify the beliefs and feelings associated with different emotional states (guilt, anger, sadness, and so forth). Roseman, Wiest, and Swartz (1994) found that among the reactions distinctively associated with feelings of guilt were "thinking that you were in the wrong," "thinking that you shouldn't have done what you did," "feeling like undoing what you have done," "wanting to make up for what you've done wrong," and "wanting to be forgiven" (see p. 215). Tangney, Miller, Flicker, and Barlow (1996) found that persons asked to describe recalled guilt experiences commonly described themselves as wanting to make amends, feeling responsible, feeling as though they had violated some moral standard, and wishing they had acted differently. Niedenthal, Tangney, and Gavanski (1994), in focusing on shame and guilt particularly, found that persons "tended to undo shame situations by altering qualities of the self and to undo guilt situations by altering actions" (p. 585).

In the present context, what is notable about these findings is the apparent action-motivating force of guilt feelings. Whereas (for example) sadness seems not to evoke any particular motivations for conduct, guilt is plainly an emotion that motivates behavior. Making another person feel sad does not provide some manifest basis for shaping the person's conduct. But when a person is made to feel guilty, those guilt feelings do offer a basis for influencing the person's behavior. Thus the nature of guilt appears to make it an emotion particularly susceptible to being used in the service of social influence.

Interpersonal Character of Guilt

Baumeister, Stillwell, and Heatherton (1994, 1995a) have argued that guilt is an essentially social phenomenon, arising especially from interpersonal transactions. In this view, the "prototypical cause" of guilt is "the infliction of harm, loss, or distress on a relationship partner" (Baumeister et al., 1994, p. 245). This view does not claim that guilt arises only in the context of close relationships, but does suggest that guilt is strongest in the context of such relationships (for related ideas, see Tangney, 1995b; Vangelisti, Daly, & Rudnick, 1991; Vangelisti & Sprague, 1998).

In support of this emphasis, it might be noted that, compared to many other emotions (fear, frustration, etc.), guilt is especially likely to be experienced in interpersonal contexts, that is, in circumstances in which feelings of guilt are linked to one's relationship to or interaction with another person. For example, recalled guilt experiences are very commonly interpersonal ones (e.g., Baumeister, Reis, & Delespaul, 1995), and transgressions linked to interpersonal relationships are more closely tied to guilt than are nonrelational transgressions (Jones, Kugler, & Adams, 1995).

The point here is not that guilt arises only in interpersonal circumstances. People report feeling guilty for a variety of other reasons as well (e.g., failing to stick to a diet; see Baumeister, Reis, & Delespaul, 1995, p. 1264; Keltner & Buswell, 1996). What is of special interest for the present review is the attention that this interpersonal approach draws to the manifest ability that people—and particularly relational partners—have to make others feel guilty. Consider, by contrast, that people seem not to have quite such powers in the case of feelings such as frustration and anxiety. The relevant point is that such guilt-arousing capacity makes guilt a particularly suitable medium for the operation of social influence.

Guilt-Based Social Influence

The common general image of how guilt operates in social influence is easily stated: The influencing agent arouses guilt, which then motivates performance of the desired action. The sections that follow review four main lines of research that provide further illumination of this general process: the first concerns the use of guilt-based social influence in interpersonal relationships, the second examines the impact of committing transgressions on compliance, the third considers the use of guilt appeals in persuasive messages, and the last concerns induction of feelings of hypocrisy.

INTERPERSONAL GUILT-BASED SOCIAL INFLUENCE

Personal relationships provide a natural potential arena for the use of guilt induction as a mechanism of social influence. Such relationships create webs of obligations and expectations that, if not satisfied, obviously have guilt-arousing potential. Several studies have investigated the everyday occurrence of guilt, commonly through asking participants to recall and describe incidents in which they made others feel guilty or in which they were made to feel guilty by others. It might initially be noted that, as Vangelisti et al. (1991, p. 34) point out, participants in these studies have little apparent difficulty in recalling such incidents. This suggests that such guilt induction is in fact reasonably commonplace.

In everyday life, attempts to arouse guilt occur primarily in the context of close relationships. Baumeister, Stillwell, and Heatherton (1995b, Study 2) asked participants to describe either an incident in which they made someone feel guilty or an incident in which they were made to feel guilty by someone else; virtually all (93%) of the reported incidents involved close relationships. Similarly, Vangelisti et al. (1991) found that "attempts to inspire guilt happen predominantly among those who share some degree of intimacy" (p. 9; see also Baumeister, Stillwell, & Heatherton, 1995b, Study 1).

Even when no purposeful guilt elicitation occurs, guilt feelings are often connected to circumstances involving others. Baumeister, Reis, and Delespaul (1995, Study 2) asked participants to recall and describe the most recent incidents in which they experienced various emotions (guilt, frustration, anxiety, and so on). Guilt stories were more likely than stories about other emotions to be episodes in which other persons were involved, and indeed more than half the guilt stories involved partners in close relationships (as opposed to less than a third of the stories about other emotions). Relatedly, Jones et al. (1995) have provided some evidence suggesting that "what people typically feel guilty about are behaviors (both symbolic and real) that harm their relational partners" (p. 317).

As might be expected, when persons seek to arouse guilt in others, the overwhelmingly most common reported purpose is persuasion (Vangelisti et al., 1991, p. 13): Persons attempt to evoke guilt as a means of inducing others to alter their behavior (to stop engaging in some action, to undertake some new action, to refrain from some contemplated action, and so forth). Secondarily, persons report using guilt for purposes such as "venting frustration and anger" (Vangelisti et al., 1991, p. 17). As Baumeister, Stillwell, and Heatherton (1995a, p. 257) point out, guilt's use as a technique of social influence can serve to "equalize the balance of power" in a relationship, because it is a means of influence that is independent of formal or physical power (and hence is available to the otherwise less-powerful relationship partner).

There has been some limited work seeking to identify the means by which people try to make others feel guilt. Vangelisti et al. (1991, Studies 1 and 2) inductively derived a typology of linguistic guilt-eliciting techniques from respondents' descriptions of circumstances in which guilt was aroused and found this typology useful across varying samples of respondents (adults and college undergraduates). Among a dozen different guilt-eliciting techniques, the most commonly mentioned involved indicating that the other is not meeting some obligation that is part of the other's relationships, pointing out that the other's behavior does not reflect the other's knowledge of appropriate conduct, and displaying some sacrifice being made on the guilt inducer's part on behalf of the other (see p. 12). Vangelisti et al. (1991, Study 3) suggest that the different strategies can be seen to vary in the relative passivity of the guilt inducer (where the contrast is between active strategies, such as pointing out inequities, and passive ones, such as submissively acquiescing to the other's wishes), the directness of the technique (where the contrast is between direct techniques, such as explicitly pointing out a transgression, and indirect ones, such as hinting), and the focus of the technique (where the contrast is between techniques focused on the transgressor, such as emphasizing the transgressor's goals, and those focused on the guilt inducer, such as ones using the guilt inducer as a basis of comparison). (For related contrasts among guilt-induction methods, see Miceli, 1992.) In the context of interpersonal relations, each different technique "may generally be considered a variation on saying 'see how you are hurting me' " (Sommer & Baumeister, 1997, p. 43). More generally, all these strategies can be seen to involve drawing the person's attention to some way in which the person's conduct represents a transgression.

It is obviously difficult to obtain a realistic assessment of the persuasive success of guilt induction in interpersonal relationships. Baumeister, Stillwell, and Heatherton (1995b, Study 1, pp. 179-180) did find that descriptions of interpersonal incidents in which the participant experienced guilt were (compared with descriptions of nonguilt incidents) much more likely to mention that some lesson had been learned from the incident and to indicate that the participant's behavior had changed. As these researchers acknowledge, however, such data can indicate only that participants perceived guilt to have had an impact on their behavior (as opposed to showing that guilt in fact influenced their conduct). With respect to the secondary purpose identified by Vangelisti et al. (1991), that of venting anger and frustration, it is notable that Baumeister, Stillwell, and Heatherton (1995b, Study 2) found that persons describing incidents in which they induced guilt in others were more likely (than persons describing incidents in which another person made them feel guilty) to mention that the guilt inducer felt better afterward.

Interpersonal guilt-induction efforts appear to risk negative reactions from the target of influence. Baumeister, Stillwell, and Heatherton (1995b, Study 2) found that persons writing descriptions of incidents in which they were the target of guilt induction were more likely (than persons describing incidents in which they sought to induce guilt in others) to mention the target's resentment of the use of guilt. Indications of such resentment also appeared in Rubin and Shaffer's (1987) investigation, in which participants viewed a videotaped interpersonal conflict between two friends in which one person sought request compliance by evoking either guilt or altruism. Guilt-based influence attempts were judged more likely to evoke anger than were altruism-based attempts.

In sum, guilt arousal in everyday life appears to occur most commonly in the context of close relationships, with persuasion being its primary purpose. Such guilt-induction efforts give some sign of being effective means of influence (as indicated by self-reports of behavior change) but also commonly appear to create anger or resentment.

TRANSGRESSION AND COMPLIANCE

As noted earlier, guilt is an emotion with affiliated action motivations: Persons feeling guilty characteristically want to alter their actions, feel like wanting to make up for what they have done wrong, and so forth. The occurrence of such feelings leads quite naturally to a straightforward hypothesis: Persons who commit transgressions (and so presumably experience guilt) will be more likely (than persons who have not committed transgressions) to engage in helping behavior such as complying with requests.

This "transgression-compliance" hypothesis has been examined in a number of studies. For example, Konoske, Staple, and Graf (1979) had transgression-condition participants ostensibly upset a graduate student's carefully ordered computer cards. Subsequently, participants were asked by a confederate to make telephone calls to prospective participants. Participants who had committed the transgression volunteered to make significantly more calls than did participants in a nontransgression control condition.

This body of research has been discussed by a number of previous authors (e.g., Baumeister, Stillwell, & Heatherton, 1994; Brock, 1969; Freedman, 1970), but no prior treatment has reported a systematic literature search, and all were qualitative (narrative) reviews. For example, previous discussions have commonly treated nonsignificant effects as failures to replicate (e.g., Noel, 1973), but it remains to be seen whether a more careful quantitative review would underwrite such interpretations.

Thus a quantitative (meta-analytic) review of this research was undertaken to address the relationship of transgression to compliance (here understood specifically as helping behavior). The central question of interest was whether, as guilt-based reasoning would suggest, transgression produces dependably greater compliance than occurs in a nontransgression condition. Additionally, four potential moderating variables were considered: whether the transgression was accidental or purposeful, whether the compliance assessment involved presenting an explicit request or an opportunity for helping behavior, whether the request (or behavioral opportunity) was presented by the victim or by someone else, and whether the victim would benefit from compliance.

Methods

Identification of Relevant Investigations

Relevant research reports were located through personal knowledge of the literature, examination of previous review discussions, and inspection of reference lists in previously located reports. Additionally, searches were made through databases and document-retrieval services using such terms as "transgression and guilt," "transgression and compliance," "guilt and compliance," and "transgression and helping" as search bases; these searches covered material at least through June 1997 in PsycINFO, ERIC (Educational Resources Information Center), H. H. Wilson, Current Contents, CARL/Uncover (Colorado Association of Research Libraries), Medline, and Dissertation Abstracts Online.

To be included, an investigation had to satisfy four criteria. First, the study had to contain an experimental condition in which participants committed some apparent transgression (e.g., accidental infliction of harm) and an appropriate control condition in which no transgression occurred; transgressions included such actions as lying (e.g., McMillen, 1970), spilling another person's papers (e.g., Konecni, 1972), breaking another person's equipment (e.g., Wallace & Sadalla, 1966), and administering electric shocks (e.g., Carlsmith & Gross, 1969). Second, the study had to provide a subsequent opportunity to assess participants' compliance (e.g., consenting to some request). Third, the study had to provide appropriate quantitative information yielding a comparison between the experimental (transgression) and control (nontransgression) conditions with respect to compliance. Finally, the participants had to be adults (guilt is a self-conscious emotion, hence children might not be expected to experience the same guilt feelings from transgressions).

These criteria thus excluded studies in which no participant committed a transgression (Harvey & Enzle, 1981; McGraw, 1987; Riordan, James, & Dunaway, 1985), studies lacking suitable control conditions (Berscheid & Walster, 1967; Brock & Becker, 1966; Gromski & Nawrat, 1984; Hymoff, 1971; Keating & Brock, 1976; Kidd & Berkowitz, 1976, Experiment 2; Schallow, 1972), studies lacking assessment of posttransgression compliance (Roy, 1974), studies of children's transgressions (Silverman, 1967), and studies lacking appropriate quantitative information (McMillen & Austin, 1971; Silverman, Rivera, & Tedeschi, 1979).

Effect Size Measure

The outcome variable of interest was compliance (as assessed through such measures as acceptance of a request); the key contrast of interest was relative compliance in the transgression and nontransgression conditions. This effect size was expressed as a correlation, with positive correlations indicating greater compliance in the transgression condition. When multiple control conditions were available, the effect size was computed using the control condition that isolated the effects of the transgression. Whenever possible, multiple-factor designs were analyzed through reconstitution of the analyses such that individual-difference factors (but not, e.g., other experimental manipulations) were put back into the error term (following the suggestion of Johnson, 1989). Effect sizes were computed excluding conditions in which, between the transgression and the compliance assessment, some experimental manipulation was introduced with the prospect of altering the participants' guilt levels, moods, or the like; for example, the effect size for Riordan, Dunaway, Haas, James, and Kruger (1984) was based on the "inexcused" transgression condition, not the "excused" transgression condition, in which, following the transgression, the experimenter excused it as insignificant.

Some investigations provided multiple indices of compliance and hence multiple effect sizes. For example, Carlsmith and Gross's (1969, Experiment 1) research recorded both whether a participant was willing to make telephone calls for a requester and how many calls the participant volunteered to make. When multiple compliance indices were available, the separate effect sizes were averaged (using the r-to-z-to-r transformation procedure) to yield a single summary.

When a given investigation was reported in more than one outlet, it was treated as a single study and analyzed accordingly. The same research was reported (in whole or in part) in Noel (1971) and Noel (1973), recorded here under the latter; in Rawlings (1966), Rawlings (1968), and Rawlings (1970), recorded here under Rawlings (1968); and in Regan (1969) and Regan (1971), recorded here under the latter.

Independent (Moderator) Variables

Four variables were examined as possible moderators of the transgression-compliance effect. The first was whether the transgression was an (apparent) accident (for which the participant was seemingly responsible) or was some nonaccidental act. In some investigations, the transgression took the form of an apparent accident (such as upsetting a carefully arranged stack of cards; e.g., Cialdini, Darby, & Vincent, 1973); in others, the transgression was not an accident (as when participants were induced to lie; e.g., McMillen, 1970). The second variable was whether the compliance assessment involved the participant's responding to a direct request (such as being asked to volunteer for another experiment; e.g., Freedman, Wallington, & Bless, 1967) or involved the participant's being presented with an opportunity to help in the absence of an explicit request (such as encountering someone who has just spilled a stack of papers; e.g., Kidd & Berkowitz, 1976, Experiment 1). The third variable was the identity of the person making the request (or presenting the opportunity for helping); cases were distinguished on the basis of whether the request (or opportunity) was presented by the victim of the transgression or by someone else. The fourth variable concerned whether the victim would be a beneficiary of compliance. For example, where compliance with a request would amount to helping the victim do a task in which the victim was engaged (as when the victim asked for help in making phone calls; Carlsmith & Gross, 1969, Experiment 1), then the victim would qualify as a beneficiary of compliance.

The last two of these variables—whether the victim was the requester and whether the victim was a beneficiary—thus permitted distinguishing, for instance, cases in which compliance with a victim's request would directly help the victim (as when an experimenter who was the victim of the transgression asked the participant to volunteer for another study conducted by the experimenter; Wallace & Sadalla, 1966) from cases in which compliance with a victim's request would not so directly benefit the victim (as when an experimenter-victim asked the participant to volunteer for another study conducted by some other person; Riordan et al., 1984).

Analysis

The individual correlations (effect sizes) were initially transformed to Fisher's zs; the zs were analyzed using random-effects procedures described by Shadish and Haddock (1994), with results then transformed back to r. A random-effects analysis was employed in preference to a fixed-effects analysis because of an interest in generalizing across treatment implementations (for discussion, see Erez, Bloom, & Wells, 1996; Jackson, 1992, p. 123; Raudenbush, 1994; Shadish & Haddock, 1994). In a random-effects analysis, the confidence interval around an obtained mean effect size reflects not only the usual (human) sampling variation, but also between-studies variance. This has the effect of widening the confidence interval over what it would have been in a fixed-effects analysis (see Raudenbush, 1994, p. 306; Shadish & Haddock, 1994, p. 275).

Results

A total of 31 effect sizes were available, based on 1,342 participants. Details for each included case are contained in Table 2.1. Across these cases, the random-effects weighted mean correlation was .278 ($Q[30] = 35.4$, *ns*). The lower and upper bounds of the 95% confidence interval for this mean were .215 and .342, indicating a significantly positive overall effect of transgression on compliance.

Table 2.2 provides a summary of the results concerning the effects of the four potential moderating variables: whether the transgression was accidental or nonaccidental, whether the compliance assessment involved an explicit request or simply a behavioral opportunity, whether the request (or behavioral opportunity) was presented by the victim of the transgression or by someone else, and whether the victim would be a beneficiary of compliance.[2] As indicated in Table 2.2, there is no evidence that any of these factors influences the size of transgression-compliance effects. Under all these conditions, there is a dependably positive effect of transgression on compliance, and each subset of effect sizes is apparently homogeneous.

TABLE 2.1
Transgression-Compliance Cases

Study	r	n	Codings
Boster et al. (1998)	.272	60	2/1/2/2
Carlsmith & Gross (1969)			
Experiment 1	.404	40	2/1/1/1
Experiment 2, restitution	.311	20	2/1/1/1
Experiment 2, generalized guilt	.444	20	2/1/2/2
Cialdini, Darby, & Vincent (1973)	.219	15	1/1/2/2
Cunningham, Steinberg, & Grev (1980)			
Experiment 1	.346	30	1/2/2/2
Experiment 2	.180	80	1/1/2/2
Dietrich & Berkowitz (1997)	.467	30	2/2/2/2
Ellis (1979)	−.102	27	1/1/2/2
Freedman, Wallington, & Bless (1967)			
Experiment 1	.312	61	2/1/1/2
Experiment 2, relevant request	.100	32	1/1/2/1
Experiment 2, irrelevant request	.635	30	1/1/2/2
Experiment 3	.303	66	1/1/2/1
Kahwaty (1979)			
Experiment 1	.551	24	2/1/1/1
Experiment 2	.183	100	2/1/1/1
Katzev, Edelsack, Steinmetz, Walker, & Wright (1978)			
Experiment 1	.167	51	2/2/2/2
Experiment 2	.085	36	2/2/2/2
Kidd & Berkowitz (1976) Experiment 1	.474	20	2/2/2/2
Konecni (1972)			
restitution	.272	59	1/2/1/1
generalized guilt	.281	62	1/2/2/2
Konoske, Staple, & Graf (1979)	.257	60	1/1/2/2
McMillen (1970)	.191	32	2/1/1/1
McMillen (1971)	.548	22	2/1/1/1
McMillen, Jackson, & Austin (1974)	.437	50	2/1/1/1
Noel (1973)	.026	80	2/1/2/2
Rawlings (1968)	.444	20	2/2/2/2
Regan, Williams, & Sparling (1972)	.415	60	1/2/2/2
Regan (1971)	.237	27	2/1/2/2
Riordan, Dunaway, Haas, James, & Kruger (1984)	−.105	20	2/1/1/2
Shapiro (1991)	.187	69	2/1/2/2
Wallace & Sadalla (1966)	.387	39	2/1/1/1

NOTE: The coding judgments, in order, are as follows: nature of transgression (1 = accident, 2 = nonaccident), nature of compliance assessment (1 = request, 2 = behavioral opportunity), whether the request (behavioral opportunity) was presented by the victim (= 1) or by someone else (= 2), and whether the victim was (= 1) or was not (= 2) a beneficiary of compliance.

Discussion

General Effects

Plainly, transgressions can powerfully affect subsequent compliance. The observed mean effect ($r = .28$) is relatively large compared with other effect sizes in social-influence research. For example, the mean correlation between fear-appeal manipulations and behavior has been estimated as .10 (Boster & Mongeau, 1984) and .17 (Sutton, 1982), and that between fear-appeal manipulations and attitude as .21 (Boster & Mongeau, 1984) and .18 (Sutton, 1982). The mean compliance effect (expressed as a correlation) of the foot-in-the-door strategy has been reported as about .12 (Dillard, Hunter, & Burgoon, 1984, p. 471; Fern, Monroe, & Avila, 1986, p. 147), and that for the door-in-the-face strategy as about .10 (Dillard et al., 1984, p. 471; Fern et al., 1986, p. 150; O'Keefe & Hale, 1998).

Moreover, this transgression-compliance effect is apparently quite robust: It obtains no matter whether the transgression is accidental or purposeful, no matter whether the subsequent compliance involves a direct request or simply an opportunity to help, no matter whether the request (or opportunity to help) is presented by the victim or by someone else, and no matter whether compliance benefits the victim or not.[3] On its face, then, this research literature supports the expectation of a guilt-based analysis of transgression's effect on compliance: Transgression enhances compliance, presumably because of the guilt created by transgression.

Intervening Neutralizing Events

In some ways it may seem curious that transgression produces greater compliance independent of whether the person victimized by the transgression is helped by the act of compliance. What this might suggest is that dealing with feelings of guilt is most fundamentally not about some other-directed activity (e.g., restitution), but rather some self-directed activity.[4]

Some additional light may be shed on this aspect of the transgression-compliance effect if we consider those studies containing experimental variations in which some intervening event (between transgression and compliance) offers the prospect of alleviating or neutralizing negative feelings. For example, in the interval between the transgression and the compliance assessment in Kidd and Berkowitz's (1976, Experiment 1) investigation, some participants overheard (ostensibly accidentally) a humorous tape recording. The intervening event varies across these studies (as the event involves such things as bolstering the participant's self-esteem, having an opportunity to express one's feelings about one's conduct, having the victim excuse the transgression, and so on). But the common property of these intervening events is that each offers the possibility of reducing or nullifying any negative feelings engendered by transgression.

The comparison of interest in these studies is that between the usual no-transgression control condition (as above) and the transgression condition in which

TABLE 2.2
Transgression-Compliance: Summary of Results

	k	Mean r	95% CI	Q (df)	
All cases	31	.278	.215, .342	35.4	(30) *ns*
Accidental transgression	11	.279	.163, .396	12.9	(10) *ns*
Nonaccident	20	.274	.197, .352	22.4	(19) *ns*
Request made	22	.269	.185, .353	28.6	(21) *ns*
Behavioral opportunity presented	9	.309	.203, .415	6.0	(8) *ns*
Request/opportunity by victim	11	.318	.205, .431	10.7	(10) *ns*
Request/opportunity by nonvictim	20	.258	.179, .336	23.6	(19) *ns*
Victim benefits from compliance	11	.310	.218, .402	9.0	(10) *ns*
Victim does not benefit	20	.258	.172, .344	25.1	(19) *ns*

some such event intervened between the transgression and the compliance assessment. The question is whether the effect size under such conditions will be different from that observed previously (that is, in cases where no such event intervened).

Effect sizes are available for six such studies: Cialdini et al. (1973; $r = -.127$, $n = 16$), Dietrich and Berkowitz (1997; $r = -.467$, $n = 30$), Kidd and Berkowitz (1976, Experiment 1; $r = -.140$, $n = 20$), McMillen (1971; $r = .189$, $n = 22$), Regan (1971; $r = -.190$, $n = 28$), and Riordan et al. (1984; $r = .000$, $n = 20$). The random-effects weighted mean correlation across these cases is $-.159$ ($Q[5] = 6.1$, *ns*), which is not dependably different from zero (the 95% confidence interval is $-.339, .021$).

Plainly, the observed general effect of transgression on compliance is typically erased, and even potentially reversed, when an intervening event offers the prospect of neutralizing the negative feelings presumably engendered by transgression. Indeed, the observed general transgression-compliance effect (mean $r = .278$) is significantly different from that observed with an intervening positive event (mean $r = -.159$; the 95% confidence intervals do not overlap). This finding reinforces the idea that guilt feelings, even if stimulated by one's actions toward another, might be neutralized in ways other than compensatory action toward that other.

Guilt Assessment

One curious lacuna in the transgression-compliance literature is the lack of direct assessment of the putative intervening state of guilt. Although guilt has commonly been supposed to be the operative mediating state, most investigators have examined the effects of transgression on compliance without directly assessing guilt. However, in three cases in which guilt was assessed following experimental transgressions (and in which quantitative information was available), guilt was (perhaps unsurprisingly) found to be significantly greater among transgression-condition participants than among no-transgression-condition participants: Boster et al. (1998; $r = .337$, $n = 58$), Kahwaty (1979, Experiment 2; $r = .648$, $n = 100$), and Silverman et al. (1979, Experiment 2; $r = .271$, $n = 53$). The random-effects weighted mean correlation across these cases is .446 (the 95% confidence interval is .148, .745).

Moreover, the observed effects do recommend guilt as a naturally plausible explanation. Transgressions commonly make people feel guilty, as evidenced by the studies just mentioned and by self-reports of guilt-inducing circumstances (failure at duties, lying, and so on; Keltner & Buswell, 1996). Among the reactions associated with guilt are feeling that one is in the wrong, wanting to undo what one has done, wanting to be forgiven, and wanting to change one's conduct (Niedenthal et al., 1994; Roseman et al., 1994; Tangney et al., 1996). Compliance-helping behaviors of the sort assessed in the literature under review naturally provide a means of addressing these guilt-related feelings (notably, a predisposition to feel guilty is associated with greater prosocial volunteering behavior; Quiles & Bybee, 1997). In short, given the empirical evidence in hand, the most plausible account for the transgression-compliance effect involves guilt. At the same time, it will plainly be useful for future transgression-compliance studies to assess guilt explicitly.[5]

GUILT APPEALS IN PERSUASIVE MESSAGES

A number of studies have examined the effectiveness of guilt-based persuasive appeals. A guilt-based persuasive appeal characteristically has two parts: One is material designed to evoke some degree of guilt in the message receiver, and the other is the message's recommended viewpoint or action, which presumably might offer the prospect of guilt reduction. Thus, for example, a guilt appeal in a consumer advertisement might seek to make working parents feel guilty about neglecting their children, with the advertised product or service presented as providing a means of assuaging that guilt.

This research experimentally compares the persuasive effectiveness of messages that vary in the explicitness—intensity or directness—with which the messages attempt to evoke guilt in the receiver. This contrast is often glossed as one between a "high" (or "strong") guilt appeal and a "low" (or "weak") guilt appeal.

This contrast takes several different forms. Sometimes the low guilt appeal is simply the least explicit of several messages. For example, Zemach (1966) compared three messages concerning violations of civil rights. The "low-arousal" version "did not mention the responsibility of the reader," the "medium-arousal" version "argued that every citizen of America shared responsibility for the violations," and the "high-arousal" version addressed the reader personally with additional arguments aimed at arousing guilt (p. 9). In other studies, the low guilt appeal is a message that has something other than guilt as its explicit basis of justification. For example, Burnett (1989) compared a "guilt appeal" (a print advertisement clearly aimed at arousing guilt, headlined "Will you turn your back on the homeless?") with an "informational advertisement" (one emphasizing factual information about homelessness, headlined "Do you know the facts about the homeless?").

All these experimental realizations thus involve a common underlying dimension of message variation, namely, the explicitness with which the message attempts to create guilt. Hence the most useful general contrast—and a contrast available in all the studies reviewed here—is that between relatively more-explicit ("strong" or "high") and relatively less-explicit ("weak" or "low") guilt appeals, where this latter category includes appeals not apparently based on guilt.[6]

The general expectation is that these message variations will differ in persuasive effectiveness by virtue of their inducing differential levels of guilt. Thus in considering the research findings in this area, it will be important to distinguish (a) the relationship between guilt-appeal variations and persuasive outcomes from (b) the relationship between guilt-appeal variations and aroused guilt.

There has been no previous systematic review of this guilt-appeals research literature, and hence a meta-analytic review was undertaken. As tools for identifying and displaying the general structure of results among guilt-appeal studies, meta-analytic methods are especially helpful. Each investigation offers the prospect of contrasting the effect (on aroused guilt or on persuasive effectiveness) of some (relatively) inexplicit guilt appeal and that of some (relatively) more explicit guilt appeal. Even with a small number of studies, meta-analytic summaries can be useful because they minimize misinterpretations occasioned by an overemphasis on statistical significance.

Methods

Identification of Relevant Investigations

Relevant research reports were located through personal knowledge of the literature, examination of related papers, and inspection of reference lists in previously located reports. Additionally, searches were made through databases and document-retrieval services using terms such as "guilt appeal," "guilt and persuasion," and "guilt and compliance" as search bases; these searches covered material at least through May 1997 in PsycINFO, ERIC, H. H. Wilson, Current Contents, CARL/Uncover, Medline, and Dissertation Abstracts Online.

Two effects were of interest: the effect of variations in guilt-appeal explicitness on aroused guilt and the effect of variation in guilt-appeal explicitness on persuasive outcomes (e.g., attitude change, intention, behavior). Thus, to be included in the meta-analysis, an investigation had to provide appropriate quantitative information concerning at least one of these effects.[7]

Effect Size Measure

Effect sizes were obtained through the formation of a contrast between the least-explicit guilt appeal and any other (more-explicit) guilt appeals. Thus, for example, in a design with three levels of guilt appeal (low, medium, and high) distinguished by explicitness, the effect size reflected the comparison between the least-explicit appeal and the combination of the two more-explicit appeals.

Every effect was summarized using r as the effect size measure. Where more-explicit messages produced greater aroused guilt or persuasion, the sign was positive; where less-explicit messages produced greater guilt or persuasion, the sign was negative. When a given study contained multiple indices of an effect of interest (e.g., multiple indices of persuasion), these were averaged to yield a single summary effect, using the r-to-z-to-r transformation procedure, weighted by n. Whenever possible, multiple-factor designs were analyzed through the reconstitution of the analyses such that individual-difference factors (but not, e.g., other experimental manipulations) were put back into the error term (following the suggestion of Johnson, 1989).

Analysis

The individual correlations (effect sizes) were initially transformed to Fisher's zs; the zs were analyzed using random-effects procedures described by Shadish and Haddock (1994), with results then transformed back to r. A random-effects analysis was employed in preference to a fixed-effects analysis because of an interest in generalizing across messages.

Results

Guilt Appeals and Guilt Arousal

Concerning the relationship of guilt-appeal explicitness to aroused guilt, effect sizes were available for 9 cases, based on a total of 630 participants. The relevant cases (with r and n in parentheses) were Burnett (1989; .209, 74); Coulter and Pinto (1995; .719, 60); Dembroski and Pennebaker (1972, Study 1; .531, 41; and Study 2; .398, 27); Pinto and Priest (1991; .402, 46); Pinto and Worobetz (1992; .320, 57); Ruth and Faber (1988; .143, 154); Yinon, Bizman, Cohen, and Segev (1976; .797, 14); and Zemach (1966; .335, 157).[8]

Across these cases, the random-effects weighted mean correlation was .428 ($Q[8] = 33.8, p < .001$). The 95% confidence interval for this mean was .227, .628, indicating a significantly positive overall effect: More-explicit guilt appeals do indeed dependably arouse greater guilt than do less-explicit guilt appeals. Notably, despite the relatively small number of cases, and despite the use of a conservative analytic procedure that is very much influenced by the number of effect sizes available (the random-effects analysis), there is nevertheless a significantly positive mean effect.

Guilt Appeals and Persuasive Effects

Concerning the relationship of guilt-appeal explicitness to persuasive outcomes, effect sizes were available for 5 cases, based on a total of 323 participants. The relevant cases (with r and n in parentheses) were Coulter and Pinto (1995; $-.294$, 60), Dembroski and Pennebaker (1972, Study 1; $-.138$, 41; and Study 2; $-.332$, 27), Yinon et al. (1976; $-.451$, 90), and Zemach (1966; $-.074$, 105).[9]

Across these cases, the random-effects weighted mean correlation was $-.259$ ($Q[4] = 8.8$, ns). The 95% confidence interval for this mean was $-.126$, $-.392$, indicating a significantly negative overall effect: More-explicit guilt appeals were dependably less persuasive than were less-explicit guilt appeals. As with the effect of guilt-appeal variations on aroused guilt, the results are notable for the dependability of the observed mean effect, even given the small number of cases and the use of a random-effects analysis.

Discussion

More-explicit guilt appeals do arouse significantly more guilt than do less-explicit appeals (and do so rather powerfully), but are significantly less persuasive than their less-explicit counterparts. The observed effects on persuasive outcomes raise a natural question: Why are more-explicit guilt appeals not more persuasive, given that they arouse more guilt? This question becomes especially significant against the backdrop of two previously discussed findings. One is the finding that guilt is distinctively associated with feelings of wanting to change one's actions. The other is the previously discussed strong and general transgression-compliance effect. Taken together, these two findings suggest some powerfulness to guilt as a motivating force. And yet more-explicit guilt appeals, which do arouse greater guilt, do not produce correspondingly enhanced persuasive effects; in fact, those more-explicit appeals backfire.

One possible explanation is that the course of action advocated by the guilt-appeal messages is not seen as guilt reducing, and so is not accepted. In such a circumstance, a message might arouse considerable guilt but nevertheless fail to be persuasive concerning the advocated action. (The parallel with fear appeals might be instructive: A message could arouse fear but fail to be persuasive if the recommended course of action is insufficiently fear reducing.)

However, this account does not explain the consistently greater persuasive superiority of less-explicit guilt appeals. If this explanation were sound, one might expect that, on average, more-explicit guilt appeals would be neither more nor less persuasive than their less-explicit counterparts, because both sorts of appeal are accompanied by the same (putatively inadequate) recommendations. But in fact more-explicit guilt appeals are dependably less persuasive than less-explicit ones.

A second possible explanation is that more-explicit guilt appeals, even though successful in creating guilt, might also evoke other emotions that interfere with acceptance of the advocate's viewpoint. Specifically, more-explicit guilt appeals might evoke irritation, anger, annoyance, or similar negative reactions. Indeed, several studies have found that guilt-based appeals are capable of arousing emotions such as anger (Coulter, Cotte, & Moore, 1997; Coulter & Pinto, 1995; Englis, 1990; Pinto & Priest, 1991).

This explanation receives encouragement from studies of reactions to interpersonal guilt-based influence attempts. Baumeister, Stillwell, and Heatherton (1995b, Study 2) found that targets of guilt manipulation techniques often reported feelings of resentment about such manipulation. In Rubin and Shaffer's (1987) research, participants watched videotapes of influence attempts (requests) based on the elicitation of altruism or on the imposition of guilt. With altruism-based influence attempts (compared to guilt-based attempts), participants liked the influencing agents more, judged them less likely to evoke anger, and judged themselves more likely to comply with the request.

Thus one plausible account of why explicit guilt appeals backfire (with respect to persuasive effects) is that, although such appeals do create greater guilt, they also arouse other negative emotions. Receivers may resent comparatively explicit attempts at arousing guilt, perhaps believing that (for example) advertisers are not entitled to lodge such objections to their conduct (see, e.g., Coulter, Cotte, & Moore, 1999). Future research on guilt appeals might usefully be directed at clarifying the processes underlying the apparent persuasive failure of explicit guilt appeals.

A Curvilinear Relationship?

Some researchers have raised the possibility that there is a curvilinear relationship between the explicitness of guilt appeals and aroused guilt or persuasiveness (e.g., Pinto & Priest, 1991). The suggestion is that moderately explicit guilt appeals might successfully arouse greater guilt and be more persuasive than either more- or less-explicit appeals.

Empirical evidence concerning this hypothesis is limited. There are not many studies containing at least three levels of explicitness of guilt appeals, and of these, several do not provide sufficiently detailed quantitative information about effects (Bozinoff & Ghingold, 1983; Pinto & Worobetz, 1992). Nevertheless, it may be illuminating to examine the available contrasts between moderately explicit guilt appeals and the combination of higher- and lower-level appeals. If a curvilinear relationship obtains such that aroused guilt or persuasive success is greatest at intermediate levels of explicitness, such contrasts would presumably reveal it. In the following analyses, where moderately explicit messages produced greater aroused guilt or persuasion (compared with the combination of less- and more-explicit appeals), the correlation was given a positive sign.

Concerning the relationship of guilt-appeal explicitness to aroused guilt, effect sizes were available for 4 cases, based on a total of 277 participants. The relevant cases (with r and n in parentheses) were Coulter and Pinto (1995; .639, 60), Pinto and Priest (1991; .425, 46), Yinon et al. (1976; –.411, 14), and Zemach (1966; .010, 157). Across these cases, the random-effects weighted mean correlation was .225 ($Q[3] = 30.3, p < .001$). The 95% confidence interval for this mean was –.271, .722.

Concerning the relationship of guilt-appeal explicitness to persuasive outcomes, effect sizes were available for 3 cases, based on a total of 255 participants. The relevant cases (with r and n in parentheses) were Coulter and Pinto (1995; –.085, 60), Yinon et al. (1976; .425, 90), and Zemach (1966; .278, 105). Across these cases, the random-effects weighted mean correlation was .223 ($Q[2] = 10.1$, $p < .01$). The 95% confidence interval for this mean was –.087, .532.

Neither mean is significantly different from zero; even so, given the small number of cases, these means might lead one to entertain the possibility that in fact aroused guilt and persuasiveness are both greatest with moderately explicit guilt appeals. However, inspection of the individual cases suggests some complications for so simple a picture. Specifically, there is no study in which, compared to other appeals, a moderately explicit appeal both arouses substantially more guilt and is substantially more persuasive. Where the moderately explicit appeal arouses substantially greater guilt, it is, if anything, less persuasive than other appeals (Coulter & Pinto, 1995). In cases where the moderately explicit appeal is substantially more persuasive, it arouses guilt in amounts that are either indistinguishable from (Zemach, 1966) or substantially smaller than (Yinon et al., 1976) that aroused by other appeals; thus even when moderately explicit appeals are more persuasive, that greater persuasiveness appears not to derive from any enhanced guilt-arousing properties of the appeals.

In short, the supposition that moderately explicit appeals will yield both greater guilt and greater persuasion than other appeals remains to be supported. The extant evidence is sparse, and the question is surely worthy of further examination, but the research in hand does not appear encouraging. Indeed, taken together, the results from these two analyses (one comparing the least-explicit guilt appeal against all other appeals, the other contrasting moderately explicit appeals against all others) are consistent with the belief that guilt appeals—of whatever degree of explicitness—that successfully arouse guilt are unlikely also to enjoy persuasive success.[10]

HYPOCRISY INDUCTION

Hypocrisy, Dissonance, and Guilt

The research reviewed thus far has been work easily recognizable as concerning guilt-based social influence. But another line of research—not commonly treated as related to guilt-based processes—appears amenable to a guilt-based interpretation, namely, research on hypocrisy induction.

A number of recent studies have explored inducing hypocrisy as a means of influencing behavior. In these studies, hypocrisy-condition participants are led to advocate some position they already support but are reminded of their failure to act accordingly; this manipulation is expected to lead participants to alter their behaviors so as to be more consistent with their beliefs. For example, in Aronson, Fried, and Stone's (1991) study, hypocrisy-condition participants were reminded of (by being asked to describe fully) situations in which they had failed to use condoms; they then composed (and were videotaped delivering) short speeches advocating condom use (with the understanding that the tapes would be used as part of a high school-level AIDS prevention program). Such participants subsequently expressed significantly greater intentions to increase their use of condoms than did participants in a variety of control conditions (reminder only, speech only, and neither reminder nor speech). Similar effects have been obtained in a number of studies (Dickerson, Thibodeau, Aronson, & Miller, 1992; Fried & Aronson, 1995; Stone, Aronson, Crain, Winslow, & Fried, 1994).

This research is commonly treated as representing an application of cognitive dissonance theory (Festinger, 1957). "Dissonance is predicted in the condition that combines advocacy and saliency (hypocrisy condition), in which inconsistency between advocated personal standards and past inconsistent behaviors is strongest" (Fried & Aronson, 1995, p. 926). That is, the hypocrisy induction creates dissonance, which subsequently is reduced by the individual's altering behavior to make it more consonant with the relevant beliefs.

But an alternative guilt-based interpretation is presumably also plausible.[11] That is, hypocrisy-condition participants might well experience guilt as a result of having their inconsistency made so apparent to them. Indeed, inconsistency with one's own standards is a prototypical case of a guilt-inducing circumstance. A guilt-based analysis, like the dissonance-based interpretation, expects the greatest effects in a condition combining salience and advocacy (e.g., reminder plus speech) as opposed to conditions with only one of these manipulations, because the combination is likely to create the greatest guilt.[12]

Moreover, it is easy to see how Aronson et al.'s (1991) hypocrisy-condition participants could plausibly have had many of the beliefs and feelings characteristically associated with guilt: "I was wrong not to use condoms more often in the past," "I wish I had used condoms more often," "I shouldn't have failed to use condoms," and so forth. In fact, this is not entirely speculative: Aronson et al.'s hypocrisy-condition participants were more likely (than participants in other conditions) to judge their past use of condoms as insufficiently frequent (see p. 1637, esp. Fig. 1).

Plainly, given guilt feelings induced by awareness of one's hypocrisy, one natural avenue to guilt reduction is to alter one's behavior in ways that make one less hypocritical; that is precisely the effect observed in these studies.[13] Thus this hypocrisy-induction research might be understood as displaying the effects of guilt arousal and reduction, not dissonance arousal and reduction.

Other Dissonance Phenomena

Other aspects of dissonance-based research might also be amenable to guilt-based interpretation.[14] Consider, for example, classic dissonance research on induced ("forced") compliance—that is, a person's being led to act in ways contrary to his or her own beliefs (e.g., Festinger & Carlsmith, 1959). The common research concretization of induced compliance is counterattitudinal advocacy, in which a person is induced to advocate some viewpoint contrary to his or her own position. Such conduct is theorized to produce dissonance, which the person can reduce by changing his or her views to come into alignment with the advocated view.

The research findings attendant to counterattitudinal-advocacy situations are complex, and a number of limiting conditions appear to attach to the appearance of the effects predicted by dissonance theory. One common way of characterizing these conditions is to say that for dissonance effects to occur, persons must believe that some foreseeable, irrevocable aversive event will result from their advocacy, and that they freely chose to engage in the advocacy and hence are responsible for the aversive outcome (Cooper & Fazio, 1984; compare, e.g., Johnson, Kelly, & LeBlanc, 1995). But these seem also to identify circumstances under which feelings of guilt might well be aroused: If I am responsible for committing some act that I know in advance will produce some irreversible harm, I might well feel guilty about having done so (because such actions are presumably inconsistent with my beliefs about proper conduct). Such guilt feelings might be reduced by my coming to believe in the position advocated (thereby minimizing the inconsistency between belief and action). That is to say, one might wonder whether perhaps the attitudinal changes attendant to induced compliance reflect guilt-reduction efforts rather than dissonance-reduction efforts.

It is implausible to suppose that dissonance is nothing but guilt. For example, there appear to be at least some phenomena commonly treated as dissonance related that are difficult to encompass as guilt-based phenomena, such as selective exposure to information (e.g., Cotton, 1985; Frey, 1986). However, closer consideration of the relationship of dissonance and guilt does seem warranted. Surprisingly little attention has been given to this relationship: "Guilt" does not appear in the indices to Festinger's (1957) or other broad-scale treatments of dissonance (e.g., Abelson et al., 1968; Wicklund & Brehm, 1976), and general discussions of guilt do not mention dissonance (e.g., Fischer & Tangney, 1995; Lewis, 1993).[15]

Plainly, however, guilt and dissonance appear conceptually rather similar. One possible account of the relationship might be that dissonance is the actual motivating psychological state and guilt is a folk-psychological term applied to certain species of dissonance. In any event, the connections between phenomena apparently based in guilt (e.g., transgression-compliance) and phenomena apparently based in dissonance (e.g., hypocrisy induction) ought not be overlooked.[16]

More generally, it may be useful to consider that guilt-related processes may play some hitherto unnoticed roles in social influence. The general neglect of the role of emotion in social-influence research has in recent years been often remarked upon; we should not be surprised if familiar theoretical processes and research findings display new facets when reexamined with an eye attentive to emotion (see, e.g., O'Keefe & Figgé, 1997).

ANTICIPATED GUILT

The research reviewed thus far has emphasized the role of the experience of guilt feelings in shaping conduct. The underlying picture has been a guilt-arousal-and-reduction image in which aroused guilt leads to behavior that reduces guilt feelings. Approached from such a perspective, guilt-based social influence requires the creation of guilt—through the person's committing a transgression (as in transgression-compliance studies), through persuasive appeals that evoke guilt (as in guilt-appeals research), or through the person's being reminded of a past shortcoming/transgression (as in hypocrisy-induction studies). That is, the focus has been on the behavioral effects of aroused guilt.

This parallels the emphasis in studies of the behavioral impact of other emotions. Broadly speaking, the focus has been on how a given experienced emotion (fear, sadness, and so on) might influence behavior. For instance, studies of fear-appeal persuasive messages (which contain fear-arousing material and a recommended course of action meant to reduce the fear) address how message-induced feelings of fear might shape receptivity to the communicator's recommendations (see, e.g., Boster & Mongeau, 1984; Sutton, 1982).

But emotions might play a role in social influence in another way—namely, through anticipation of the emotional consequences of behavior. Indeed, a number of diverse studies suggest that conduct can be shaped by expectations about the feelings that will result from that conduct. One straightforward illustration is afforded by research on the relationship between media choices and mood. For example, there is evidence that people choose among entertainment offerings in ways suggestive of (perhaps not always conscious) expectations about likely emotional effects: Bored persons prefer arousing materials, whereas stressed persons prefer calming materials (for reviews and discussion, see Zillmann & Bryant, 1985, 1994). More broadly, uses-and-gratifications approaches to mass media (see, e.g., Rubin, 1994) happily accommodate the idea that one of the expected gratifications from media exposure might be the control of affective states (persons may expect to be put in a good mood by a comedy show, to be frightened by a horror movie, and so on).

As another example, anticipated regret appears to be capable of influencing decision making. Lechner, de Vries, and Offermans (1997) found that anticipated regret was the best predictor of mammography participation intentions among previous nonparticipants. Richard, van der Pligt, and de Vries (1995, 1996a; Richard, de Vries, & van der Pligt, 1998) found that prediction of intentions by the theory of planned behavior (Ajzen, 1991) could be significantly improved through the addition of assessments of anticipated regret and worry. Relatedly, Richard, van der Pligt, and de Vries (1996b) found significant increases in safe-sex intentions and behaviors as a result of interventions aimed at focusing attention on the negative postbehavioral feelings (such as regret) likely to result from unsafe sex. (For general discussions, see van der Pligt & de Vries, 1998; van der Pligt & Richard, 1994. For related research, see Bakker, Buunk, & Manstead, 1997; Janis & Mann, 1977, pp. 219-242; Josephs, Larrick, Steele, & Nisbett, 1992; Simonson, 1992.)[17]

Only recently has research on emotions come to attend at all closely to the role that anticipated feelings might play in shaping conduct. As Bagozzi, Baumgartner, and Pieters (1998) have pointed out, "Existing theories [of emotion] have not specified fully how anticipated emotions initiate volitional activities and goal directed behaviors" (p. 20).[18] Bagozzi et al. have sketched a model in which (inter alia) appraisals of the consequences of anticipated goal achievement (or failure) are hypothesized to lead to anticipated emotions, which in turn guide intentions, plans, and decisions. This model has received encouraging support in longitudinal studies of body weight regulation through diet and exercise (Bagozzi et al., 1998) and of salesperson behavior (Brown, Cron, & Slocum, 1997). The relevant general point is that an emerging body of research suggests that anticipated emotions can play a role in shaping behavior.

Turning to guilt specifically, it is easy enough to imagine how one's behavior might be influenced by expected feelings of guilt: "If I eat that piece of chocolate cake, I'll feel really guilty—so I guess I'll stick to my diet." Perhaps it is unsurprising that persons' estimates of how guilty they would feel if they were to engage in various health-risk behaviors are related to avoidance of those behaviors; people avoid the actions that they expect would make them feel guilty (Birkimer, Johnston, & Berry, 1993).

This invites reconsideration of how guilt-based social influence might operate. For example, guilt-based persuasive appeals need not actually arouse guilt; they could instead try to draw people's attention to the future feelings of guilt to be expected if the recommended course of action is not followed. In fact, guilt-based consumer advertising uses both advertisements that try to arouse guilt and advertisements drawing attention to anticipated guilt. Huhmann and Brotherton (1997) studied guilt-based appeals in a sampling of 48 issues of 24 popular magazines over a 2-year period. Most (62%) of the guilt appeals were "anticipatory" appeals, ones that "offer consumers an opportunity to avoid a transgression" (p. 37), as opposed to appeals meant to arouse actual guilt (either "reactive" appeals, which draw attention to some previous guilt-inducing conduct, or "existential" appeals, which draw attention to discrepancies between one's well-being and that of others).

Future work might usefully be directed at providing a careful explication of alternative means by which anticipated guilt might be aroused. Broadly speaking, however, one plausible general mechanism for evoking anticipated guilt might be to remind persons of their commitments or obligations. Such reminders may elicit thoughts of the guilt that would occur if the obligations went unfulfilled, and hence may spur obligation-consistent action. There is evidence that reminding people of a commitment they have made to perform a prosocial behavior (such as donating blood) can increase performance of that behavior (Ferrari, Barone, Jason, & Rose, 1985); anticipated guilt feelings provide one possible explanation for such effects.

Feelings of anticipated guilt do appear to be malleable for purposes of social influence. Surveys conducted before and after an antilittering media campaign in Oklahoma revealed a substantial increase in the proportion of respondents who agreed that they would feel guilty if they littered—and respondents were correspondingly less inclined to litter. Independent assessments confirmed that the campaign produced a large reduction in the amount of litter (Grasmick, Bursik, & Kinsey, 1991).

It may be worth emphasizing that anticipated guilt and actual guilt are distinct states. Indeed, in general, the anticipation of a given feeling and the experience of that feeling are distinguishable. A person who is feeling low and so (in the expectation of a brighter mood) is looking for a comedy on the video-rental shelves may be anticipating feelings of happiness from the contemplated action, but is not yet experiencing happiness. Similarly, a person anticipating feelings of guilt from a contemplated action is not yet experiencing guilt.

Thus it would seem to be unwise to treat anticipated feelings of guilt as identical to actual feelings of guilt, as some previous discussions have done. For example, Rawlings (1970, p. 164) treated "anticipatory guilt" and "reactive guilt" as otherwise identical uncomfortable states, distinguished only by the precipitating event (anticipated versus actual transgression). But the realization that guilt would be aroused by a contemplated transgression (i.e., the anticipation of possible guilt feelings) is plainly different from actual (aroused) guilt. Both states (the state of anticipating possible guilt if a given action is performed and the state of feeling guilty following a particular action) have the capacity to shape future behavior, but they clearly differ in other ways. For example, feeling guilty is associated with thoughts such as "I wish I hadn't done what I did" and "I wish I could make up for what I did" (Roseman et al., 1994; Tangney et al., 1996), but such thoughts could not be associated with contemplated future action (instead, the thoughts associated with anticipated guilt might be ones such as "If I do X I will wish I hadn't" and "If I do X I will feel guilty about having done so").[19]

Anticipated guilt and experienced (aroused) guilt might be related in complex ways. For example, the anticipation of future guilt might arouse current guilt feelings by serving as a reminder of past transgressions; a person who thinks, "I'll feel really guilty if I don't follow my diet" might also be led to think of past occasions on which he or she failed to follow the diet—and so be led to feel guilty about those past transgressions.[20] Conversely, reminders of past transgressions might both elicit actual guilt (about those transgressions) and encourage anticipatory guilt (when appropriate circumstances arise in the future). And the experience of guilt obviously provides a basis for the subsequent anticipation of guilt: A person who experiences guilt as a result of his or her behavior in a given circumstance might, when that circumstance arises again, be more likely to anticipate that certain behaviors will lead to guilt feelings.

In sum, anticipated feelings of guilt appear to be capable of playing important roles in shaping behavior and, correspondingly, may serve as mechanisms of social influence. Research and theorizing about the role of guilt in social influence have largely been dominated by a guilt-arousal-and-reduction model, in which social-influence efforts are seen as based on the creation of guilt feelings. It will be useful for future work to explore the social-influence potential of anticipated guilt as well; little is known about how anticipated guilt might be aroused or about the particulars of its effects (e.g., whether efforts at creating anticipated guilt can evoke the same negative reactions as are sometimes associated with guilt-arousal efforts).

CONCLUSION

The emotion of guilt might figure in behavior—and thereby be a focus of so-cial-influence efforts—in two broad ways: through the actual arousal of guilt or through anticipation of possible guilt feelings. The arousal of guilt can naturally be used in the service of social influence, because guilt is a state with built-in ac-tion-motivating aspects. There appear to be two abstract ways in which guilt can be aroused: by a person's committing some transgression or by a person's attention being drawn to some (past or ongoing) transgression. Although the experimental manipulations in transgression-compliance research and hypocrisy-induction re-search clearly involve such guilt-arousal mechanisms, neither line of work has yet given much systematic attention to assessing the guilt (or other emotions) that might arise from such manipulations.

Guilt arousal can apparently be a very powerful tool of social influence, as indi-cated by self-reports of behavioral change in interpersonal guilt-based influence attempts, by the large and robust transgression-compliance effect, and by the effects of hypocrisy inductions. But guilt arousal can also backfire quite dramati-cally, as indicated by research on guilt appeals in persuasive messages.

What is not yet clear is exactly how and why guilt arousal can boomerang in these ways. Guilt-arousal strategies apparently can sometimes also arouse anger and resentment (as indicated by studies of persuasive guilt appeals and by self-reports of interpersonal guilt-based influence events), but evidence is meager concerning the nature of the underlying mechanism, the particular circumstances or message features that might trigger negative reactions, and so on. Future research will want to devote attention to clarifying exactly how and why such effects arise.

One possibility worthy of exploration is that guilt can be aroused without accompanying anger (or resentment, reactance, and the like) only in circumstances in which guilt arousal appears unconnected with another person's purposeful social-influence efforts. That is, if one feels guilt because of an actual transgression (as in transgression-compliance research) or because one happens to be reminded of past transgressions (as in, ex hypothesi, hypocrisy-induction research), then perhaps the aroused guilt will be unlikely to be accompanied by anger and so will be more likely to make for behavioral change. But if one is led to feel guilty by virtue of another person's intentionally setting out to make one feel guilty as a means of influencing one's conduct (as in guilt-based consumer advertising or unsubtle interpersonal-relationship guilt-arousal techniques), then anger or reactance may overwhelm any behavioral effects of the aroused guilt.

The second broad way in which guilt might figure in behavior is through the anticipation of guilt. Broadly speaking, guilt anticipation would seem to be encouraged simply by the drawing of persons' attention to how they will feel if they pursue a given course of action. Anticipated guilt does appear to be malleable and capable of exerting some influence on behavior. But research evidence is sparse concerning the nature and effects of anticipated guilt. For example, there is little information about situations or factors that enhance the likelihood of such anticipated-guilt effects. There is also little evidence concerning how social-influence efforts might be constructed so as to make effective use of such anticipated feelings. And it is not clear whether, or under what circumstances, social-influence efforts based on anticipated guilt can evoke the same negative reactions that efforts based on aroused guilt apparently do.

Perhaps it is unsurprising that so many aspects of guilt-based social influence remain relatively unexplored. General theoretical treatments of social-influence processes have for many years emphasized "logical" or "rational" aspects of social influence; only recently has much attention been devoted to emotional facets of social influence, and even this attention has largely been focused on the emotion of fear. But the apparent power of the emotion of guilt recommends continuing research and theoretical attention.

NOTES

1. The kind of guilt that is of interest here is what might be thought of as ordinary guilt, as opposed to psychopathological guilt; as with many emotional states, guilt can develop in ways that threaten everyday functioning, but it is commonplace guilt that is the focus of this chapter (for a useful discussion, see Quiles & Bybee, 1997). Similarly, it is guilt feelings, not legal guilt (culpability), that is of concern here.

2. The nonsignificant value for Q in the overall analysis, indicating a failure to reject the null hypothesis of homogeneity among these effect sizes, might be taken to mean that examination of potential moderator variables would inevitably be fruitless. But, as Cook et al. (1992, pp. 313-314) and Hall and Rosenthal (1991, p. 440) point out, a nonsignificant heterogeneity test does not guarantee the absence of significant moderators at work with a set of effect sizes.

3. These conclusions must be tempered somewhat by the recognition that there may have been insufficient power to detect such moderator effects; on the other hand, the observed differences between the means are quite small. The largest observed difference between levels of a mod-

erator is that between requests (or behavioral opportunities) presented by the victim (mean r = .318) and those presented by a nonvictim (mean r = .258). These are mean rs, not rs, but a sense of the magnitude of this difference may be obtained using Cohen's (1988) q, an effect-size index for differences between correlations. This difference—the largest obtained—corresponds to q = .065; the other differences correspond to qs of .005, .044, and .057. Cohen labels a q of .10 a "small" difference, which suggests that the observed differences are quite small indeed. The point is that this is not a case in which large effects were nonsignificant because of low power.

4. Although space does not permit its careful exploration here, a similar view appears to be offered by Steele's (1988) work on self-affirmation processes, which suggests that threats to one's self-system can lead to acts of self-affirmation aimed not necessarily at coping with the particular threat at hand but rather at maintaining one's overall self-integrity. If guilt is taken to be one possible outcome of a challenge to self-integrity, the observed lack of effect for whether the victim of transgression is helped by compliance can be seen as consistent with Steele's analysis.

5. Actually, it will be useful for investigators to cast a broader net—to assess not only guilt but also other emotions that might compete with, or provide an explanation different from, guilt (e.g., anger, shame, embarrassment). Studies of fear appeals in persuasive messages have found it useful to examine not only fear but also other emotional reactions (see Dillard, Plotnick, Godbold, Freimuth, & Edgar, 1996; Stout & Sego, 1994); in general, examination of the roles played by emotion in communication might profitably consider multiple emotions simultaneously.

6. Because the topics used in this research area are (naturally enough) ones on which plausible guilt appeals might be constructed, any persuasive message (even one like Burnett's [1989] "informational" message) might be thought of as having the capacity to evoke guilt feelings. For present purposes, however, what is relevant is that the messages vary in the explicitness of the guilt appeal.

7. A third effect would naturally be of interest, namely, the relationship between aroused guilt and persuasive outcomes. But (somewhat surprisingly) research reports in this area rarely contain information concerning this relationship, thus preventing useful meta-analytic treatment.

8. Ruth and Faber's (1988) study was also reported in Ruth (1987). Bozinoff and Ghingold's (1983) research, also reported in Ghingold and Bozinoff (1981), was not included because of insufficient quantitative information. Haefner's (1956) dissertation was unavailable (through either interlibrary borrowing or UMI).

9. Insufficient quantitative information was available concerning Bozinoff and Ghingold's (1983) research, also reported in Ghingold and Bozinoff (1981); Burnett's (1989) study; and Ruth and Faber's (1988) study, also reported in Ruth (1987). Haefner's (1956) dissertation was unavailable (through either interlibrary borrowing or UMI). Pinto and Priest (1991) and Pinto and Worobetz (1992) did not include persuasion-outcome measures.

10. Indeed, only recently has there been any indication that greater message-evoked guilt might be associated with greater persuasiveness (Basil, Ridgway, Nakamoto, & Basil, 1998), although unhappily this research does not shed light on the message properties that might be associated with such effects.

11. Fried and Aronson (1995) claim to provide "independent evidence that hypocrisy is a form of cognitive dissonance arousal" (p. 925) by showing that when participants are given the opportunity to misattribute their arousal to plausible external factors, the effects of hypocrisy induction are reduced (paralleling the reduction of dissonance effects in induced-compliance studies when such misattribution is available, as in Zanna & Cooper, 1974). But such evidence can show only that there is some motivational state at work that is subject to attributional processes; this evidence cannot show that the relevant state is distinctively dissonance as opposed to guilt (or any other candidate).

12. Fried (1998, p. 146n1) suggests that the reminder alone can be sufficient to arouse the necessary dissonance. Notably, O'Malley and Andrews (1983) found that having persons recall and describe a situation in which they felt guilty—a manipulation akin to the "reminder" conditions in

hypocrisy-induction studies—can be sufficient to induce greater helping (compared to a neutral-mood induction condition).

13. An alternative means of dealing with such guilt feelings might be to denigrate the violated standards (e.g., by deciding that the standards are not important). Fried (1998) observed just such effects: Under conditions in which participants were identified with their transgressions (as opposed to being anonymous), participants reminded of past recycling transgressions did not adopt pro-recycling behaviors, but rather came to have less positive attitudes about the importance of recycling. For a general discussion of the cognitive devices available for mitigating guilt, see Miceli and Castelfranchi (1998).

14. Stice (1992) noted similarities between dissonance and guilt, but interprets these as suggesting that "dissonance is analogous to the feeling of guilt" (p. 75) and hence as underwriting a hypothesis that dissonance will be reduced by any methods effective in reducing guilt. The suggestion under consideration here is a stronger one.

15. One exception is Baumeister, Stillwell, and Heatherton's (1995b, pp. 190-191) brief discussion of the relationship of guilt and dissonance. The discussion notes some similarities between these authors' interpersonal view of guilt and some versions of dissonance theory, but is primarily focused on defending guilt-based explanations against possible dissonance-based alternatives. The suggestion here runs rather a different direction, as it contemplates reinterpreting dissonance phenomena as guilt based.

16. These connections might usefully be explored in the framework of Steele's (1988) self-affirmation model. Although Steele mentions guilt only briefly (see p. 283), guilt clearly can be one outcome of challenges to self-integrity. It remains to be seen whether Steele's analysis can successfully explain the accumulated findings of dissonance theory (for some discussion, see, e.g., Aronson, 1992; Steele & Liu, 1983; Steele & Spencer, 1992), but self-affirmation processes are plainly potentially relevant to a larger understanding of how guilt and dissonance might be related.

17. The relationship between regret and guilt deserves closer scrutiny. Much like guilt, regret is linked to perceived responsibility for the regretted outcome (e.g., Zeelenberg, van Dijk, & Manstead, 1998). When persons are asked to imagine "undoing" a regret-inducing event, they predominantly change their own actions (as opposed to changing aspects of the situation, which is more characteristic of disappointment-inducing events; Zeelenberg, van Dijk, van der Pligt, et al., 1998); a similar impulse is associated with undoing guilt-evoking circumstances (Niedenthal et al., 1994). Regret and guilt both appear to be associated with feelings of wanting to correct a mistake, wanting a second chance, and the like (Roseman et al., 1994; Zeelenberg, van Dijk, Manstead, & van der Pligt, 1998). If, as Zeelenberg, van Dijk, Manstead, and van der Pligt (1998) say, regret requires that "one not only has to perceive the outcome as negative, but one also has to realise that the unwanted outcome resulted from (or could have been prevented by) one's own behavior" (pp. 228-229), then perhaps guilt is a special case of regret in which the actor's personal standards are somehow violated (see Miceli, 1992).

18. Although existing theories of emotions have generally not attended to anticipated emotions, at least some work on decision making has recognized the role of anticipated feelings (e.g., Baron, 1992; Bell, 1982; Josephs et al., 1992; Loomes & Sugden, 1982, 1987).

19. Correspondingly, whereas Coulter et al. (1999) explicitly treat Huhmann and Brotherton's (1997) three kinds of guilt-related ads as all meant to "make the reader feel guilty" and to lead the reader to take action "to relieve the guilt feelings," the present analysis would underscore the difference between ads aimed at encouraging avoidance of future guilt (Huhmann & Brotherton's "anticipatory" appeals) and ads aimed at arousing guilt ("reactive" and "existential" appeals).

20. The anticipation of future guilt (from the contemplation of a possible future transgression) might be connected with current guilt feelings in another way: A person who contemplates a transgression might feel guilty about having done so—that is, about having even considered committing the transgression.

REFERENCES

Abelson, R. P., Aronson, E., McGuire, W. J., Newcomb, T. M., Rosenberg, M. J., & Tannenbaum, P. H. (Eds.). (1968). *Theories of cognitive consistency: A sourcebook.* Chicago: Rand McNally.

Ajzen, I. (1991). The theory of planned behavior. *Organizational Behavior and Human Decision Processes, 50,* 179-211.

Aronson, E. (1992). The return of the repressed: Dissonance theory makes a comeback. *Psychological Inquiry, 3,* 303-311.

Aronson, E., Fried, C., & Stone, J. (1991). Overcoming denial and increasing the intention to use condoms through the induction of hypocrisy. *American Journal of Public Health, 81,* 1636-1638.

Bagozzi, R. P., Baumgartner, H., & Pieters, R. (1998). Goal-directed emotions. *Cognition and Emotion, 12,* 1-26.

Bakker, A. B., Buunk, B. P., & Manstead, A. S. R. (1997). The moderating role of self-efficacy beliefs in the relationship between anticipated regret and condom use. *Journal of Applied Social Psychology, 27,* 2001-2014.

Baron, J. (1992). The effect of normative beliefs on anticipated emotions. *Journal of Personality and Social Psychology, 63,* 320-330.

Barrett, K. C. (1995). A functionalist approach to shame and guilt. In J. P. Tangney & K. W. Fischer (Eds.), *Self-conscious emotions: The psychology of shame, guilt, embarrassment, and pride* (pp. 25-63). New York: Guilford.

Basil, D. Z., Ridgway, N. M., Nakamoto, K., & Basil, M. D. (1998, February). *Charitable donations: The role of guilt, empathy, ad match, and donations.* Paper presented at the winter conference of the Society for Consumer Psychology, Austin, TX.

Baumeister, R. F., Reis, H. T., & Delespaul, P. A. E. G. (1995). Subjective and experiential correlates of guilt in daily life. *Personality and Social Psychology Bulletin, 21,* 1256-1268.

Baumeister, R. F., Stillwell, A. M., & Heatherton, T. F. (1994). Guilt: An interpersonal approach. *Psychological Bulletin, 115,* 243-267.

Baumeister, R. F., Stillwell, A. M., & Heatherton, T. F. (1995a). Interpersonal aspects of guilt: Evidence from narrative studies. In J. P. Tangney & K. W. Fischer (Eds.), *Self-conscious emotions: The psychology of shame, guilt, embarrassment, and pride* (pp. 255-273). New York: Guilford.

Baumeister, R. F., Stillwell, A. M., & Heatherton, T. F. (1995b). Personal narratives about guilt: Role in action control and interpersonal relationships. *Basic and Applied Social Psychology, 178,* 173-198.

Bell, D. E. (1982). Regret in decision making under uncertainty. *Operations Research, 30,* 961-981.

Berscheid, E., & Walster, E. (1967). When does a harm-doer compensate a victim? *Journal of Personality and Social Psychology, 6,* 435-441.

Birkimer, J. C., Johnston, P. L., & Berry, M. M. (1993). Guilt and help from friends: Variables related to healthy behavior. *Journal of Social Psychology, 133,* 683-692.

Boster, F. J., Mitchell, M. M., Lapinski, M. K., Cooper, H., Orrego, V., & Reinke, R. (1998, November). *The impact of guilt and type of compliance-gaining message on compliance.* Paper presented at the annual meeting of the National Communication Association, New York.

Boster, F. J., & Mongeau, P. (1984). Fear-arousing persuasive messages. In R. N. Bostrom (Ed.), *Communication yearbook 8* (pp. 330-375). Beverly Hills, CA: Sage.

Bozinoff, L., & Ghingold, M. (1983). Evaluating guilt arousing marketing communications. *Journal of Business Research, 11,* 243-255.

Brock, T. C. (1969). On interpreting the effects of transgression upon compliance. *Psychological Bulletin, 72,* 138-145.

Brock, T. C., & Becker, L. A. (1966). "Debriefing" and susceptibility to subsequent experimental manipulations. *Journal of Experimental Social Psychology, 2,* 314-323.

Brown, S. P., Cron, W. L., & Slocum, J. W., Jr. (1997). Effects of goal-directed emotions on salesperson volitions, behavior, and performance: A longitudinal study. *Journal of Marketing, 61*(1), 39-50.

Burnett, M. S. (1989). Guilt as an individual difference variable: Scale development and predictive validity assessment. *Dissertation Abstracts International, 50,* 1371A. (University Microfilms No.
AAG89-14988)

Carlsmith, J. M., & Gross, A. E. (1969). Some effects of guilt on compliance. *Journal of Personality
and Social Psychology, 11,* 232-239.

Cho, H., & Stout, P. A. (1993). An extended perspective on the role of emotion in advertising processing. In L. McAlister & M. L. Rothchild (Eds.), *Advances in consumer research* (Vol. 20,
pp. 692-697). Provo, UT: Association for Consumer Research.

Cialdini, R. B., Darby, B. L., & Vincent, J. E. (1973). Transgression and altruism: A case for hedonism. *Journal of Experimental Social Psychology, 9,* 502-516.

Cohen, J. (1988). *Statistical power analysis for the behavioral sciences* (2nd ed.). Hillsdale, NJ: Lawrence Erlbaum.

Cook, T. D., Cooper, H., Cordray, D. S., Hartmann, H., Hedges, L. V., Light, R. J., Louis, T. A., &
Mosteller, F. (1992). *Meta-analysis for explanation: A casebook.* New York: Russell Sage Foundation.

Cooper, J., & Fazio, R. H. (1984). A new look at dissonance theory. In L. Berkowitz (Ed.), *Advances in
experimental social psychology* (Vol. 17, pp. 229-266). New York: Academic Press.

Cotton, J. L. (1985). Cognitive dissonance in selective exposure. In D. Zillmann & J. Bryant (Eds.),
Selective exposure to communication (pp. 11-33). Hillsdale, NJ: Lawrence Erlbaum.

Coulter, R. H., Cotte, J., & Moore, M. L. (1997). Guilt appeals in advertising: Are you feeling guilty?
In D. T. LeClair & M. Hartline (Eds.), *1997 AMA Winter Educators' Conference: Marketing theory
and applications* (pp. 109-115). Chicago: American Marketing Association.

Coulter, R. H., Cotte, J., & Moore, M. L. (1999). Believe it or not: Persuasion, manipulation and credibility of guilt appeals. In L. Scott & E. J. Arnold (Eds.), *Advances in consumer research* (Vol. 26,
pp. 288-294). Provo, UT: Association for Consumer Research.

Coulter, R. H., & Pinto, M. B. (1995). Guilt appeals in advertising: What are their effects? *Journal of
Applied Psychology, 80,* 697-705.

Cunningham, M. R., Steinberg, J., & Grev, R. (1980). Wanting to and having to help: Separate motivations for positive mood and guilt-induced helping. *Journal of Personality and Social Psychology,
38,* 181-192.

Dembroski, T. M., & Pennebaker, J. W. (1972, April). *The effects of guilt-shame arousing communications on attitudes and behavior.* Paper presented at the annual meeting of the Southwestern Psychological Association, Oklahoma City. (ERIC Document Reproduction Service No. ED 072 361)

Dickerson, C. A., Thibodeau, R., Aronson, E., & Miller, D. (1992). Using cognitive dissonance to encourage water conservation. *Journal of Applied Social Psychology, 22,* 841-854.

Dietrich, D. M., & Berkowitz, L. (1997). Alleviation of dissonance by engaging in prosocial behavior
or receiving ego-enhancing feedback. *Journal of Social Behavior and Personality, 12,* 557-566.

Dillard, J. P. (1993). Persuasion past and present: Attitudes aren't what they used to be. *Communication Monographs, 60,* 90-97.

Dillard, J. P., Hunter, J. E., & Burgoon, M. (1984). Sequential-request strategies: Meta-analysis of
foot-in-the-door and door-in-the-face. *Human Communication Research, 10,* 461-488.

Dillard, J. P., & Kinney, T. A. (1994). Experiential and physiological responses to interpersonal influence. *Human Communication Research, 20,* 502-528.

Dillard, J. P., Plotnick, C. A., Godbold, L. C., Freimuth, V. S., & Edgar, T. (1996). The multiple affective outcomes of AIDS PSAs: Fear appeals do more than scare people. *Communication Research,
23,* 44-72.

Ellis, K. J. (1979). Personality and the transgression-altruism phenomenon. *Dissertation Abstracts
International, 40,* 1953-1954B. (University Microfilms No. 79-21461)

Englis, B. G. (1990). Consumer emotional reactions to television advertising and their effects on message recall. In S. J. Agres, J. A. Edell, & T. M. Dubitsky (Eds.), *Emotion in advertising: Theoretical
and practical explorations* (pp. 231-253). New York: Quorum.

Erez, A., Bloom, M. C., & Wells, M. T. (1996). Using random rather than fixed effects models in meta-analysis: Implications for situational specificity and validity generalization. *Personnel Psychology, 49,* 275-306.

Ferguson, T. J., & Crowley, S. L. (1997). Measure for measure: A multitrait-multimethod analysis of guilt and shame. *Journal of Personality Assessment, 69,* 425-441.

Fern, E. F., Monroe, K. B., & Avila, R. A. (1986). Effectiveness of multiple request strategies: A synthesis of research results. *Journal of Marketing Research, 23,* 144-152.

Ferrari, J. R., Barone, R. C., Jason, L. A., & Rose, T. (1985). The effects of a personal phone call prompt on blood donor commitment. *Journal of Community Psychology, 13,* 295-298.

Festinger, L. (1957). *A theory of cognitive dissonance.* Stanford, CA: Stanford University Press.

Festinger, L., & Carlsmith, J. M. (1959). Cognitive consequences of forced compliance. *Journal of Abnormal and Social Psychology, 58,* 203-210.

Fischer, K. W., & Tangney, J. P. (1995). Self-conscious emotions and the affect revolution: Framework and overview. In J. P. Tangney & K. W. Fischer (Eds.), *Self-conscious emotions: The psychology of shame, guilt, embarrassment, and pride* (pp. 3-22). New York: Guilford.

Fishbein, M., & Ajzen, I. (1975). *Belief, attitude, intention, and behavior: An introduction to theory and research.* Reading, MA: Addison-Wesley.

Freedman, J. L. (1970). Transgression, compliance, and guilt. In J. Macaulay & L. Berkowitz (Eds.), *Altruism and helping behavior* (pp. 155-161). New York: Academic Press.

Freedman, J. L., Wallington, S. A., & Bless, E. (1967). Compliance without pressure: The effect of guilt. *Journal of Personality and Social Psychology, 7,* 117-124.

Frey, D. (1986). Recent research on selective exposure to information. In L. Berkowitz (Ed.), *Advances in experimental social psychology* (Vol. 19, pp. 41-80). New York: Academic Press.

Fried, C. B. (1998). Hypocrisy and identification with transgressions: A case of undetected dissonance. *Basic and Applied Social Psychology, 20,* 145-154.

Fried, C. B., & Aronson, E. (1995). Hypocrisy, misattribution, and dissonance reduction. *Personality and Social Psychology Bulletin, 21,* 925-933.

Ghingold, M., & Bozinoff, L. (1981). Construct validation and empirical testing of guilt arousing marketing communications. In A. A. Mitchell (Ed.), *Advances in consumer research* (Vol. 9, pp. 210-214). St. Louis, MO: Association for Consumer Research.

Grasmick, H. G., Bursik, R. J., Jr., & Kinsey, K. A. (1991). Shame and embarrassment as deterrents to noncompliance with the law: The case of an antilittering campaign. *Environment and Behavior, 23,* 233-251.

Gromski, W., & Nawrat, R. (1984). Some determinants of perceived responsibility and guilt in a compliance situation. *Polish Psychological Bulletin, 15,* 235-244.

Haefner, D. P. (1956). *Some effects of guilt-arousing and fear-arousing persuasive communications on opinion change.* Unpublished doctoral dissertation, University of Rochester.

Hall, J. A., & Rosenthal, R. (1991). Testing for moderator variables in meta-analysis: Issues and methods. *Communication Monographs, 58,* 437-448.

Harvey, M. D., & Enzle, M. E. (1981). A cognitive model of social norms for understanding the transgression-helping effect. *Journal of Personality and Social Psychology, 41,* 866-875.

Huhmann, B. A., & Brotherton, T. P. (1997). A content analysis of guilt appeals in popular magazine advertisements. *Journal of Advertising, 26*(2), 35-45.

Hymoff, I. H. (1971). An experimental investigation of the relationship of Machiavellianism to guilt and compliance. *Dissertation Abstracts International, 32,* 1213-1214B. (University Microfilms No. 71-20269)

Jackson, S. (1992). *Message effects research: Principles of design and analysis.* New York: Guilford.

Janis, I. L., & Mann, L. (1977). *Decision making: A psychological analysis of conflict, choice, and commitment.* New York: Free Press.

Johnson, B. T. (1989). *DSTAT: Software for the meta-analytic review of research literatures.* Hillsdale, NJ: Lawrence Erlbaum.

Johnson, R. W., Kelly, R. J., & LeBlanc, B. A. (1995). Motivational basis of dissonance: Aversive consequences or inconsistency. *Personality and Social Psychology Bulletin, 21,* 850-855.

Jones, W. H., Kugler, K., & Adams, P. (1995). You always hurt the one you love: Guilt and transgressions against relationship partners. In J. P. Tangney & K. W. Fischer (Eds.), *Self-conscious emotions: The psychology of shame, guilt, embarrassment, and pride* (pp. 301-321). New York: Guilford.

Jorgensen, P. F. (1998). Affect, persuasion, and communication processes. In P. A. Andersen & L. K. Guerrero (Eds.), *Handbook of communication and emotion: Research, theory, applications, and contexts* (pp. 403-422). San Diego, CA: Academic Press.

Josephs, R. A., Larrick, R. P., Steele, C. M., & Nisbett, R. E. (1992). Protecting the self from the negative consequences of risky decisions. *Journal of Personality and Social Psychology, 62,* 26-37.

Kahwaty, R. C. (1979). Helping behavior as a consequence of undiscovered and discovered transgressions. *Dissertation Abstracts International, 39,* 4104-4105B. (University Microfilms No. 79-02548)

Katzev, R., Edelsack, L., Steinmetz, G., Walker, T., & Wright, R. (1978). The effect of reprimanding transgressions on subsequent helping behavior: Two field experiments. *Personality and Social Psychology Bulletin, 4,* 326-329.

Keating, J. P., & Brock, T. C. (1976). The effects of prior reward and punishment on subsequent reward and punishment: Guilt versus consistency. *Journal of Personality and Social Psychology, 34,* 327-333.

Keltner, D., & Buswell, B. N. (1996). Evidence for the distinctness of embarrassment, shame, and guilt: A study of recalled antecedents and facial expressions of emotion. *Cognition and Emotion, 10,* 155-172.

Kidd, R. F., & Berkowitz, L. (1976). Effect of dissonance arousal on helpfulness. *Journal of Personality and Social Psychology, 33,* 613-622.

Kinder, D. R. (1994). Reason and emotion in American political life. In R. C. Schank & E. Langer (Eds.), *Beliefs, reasoning, and decision making: Psycho-logic in honor of Bob Abelson* (pp. 277-314). Hillsdale, NJ: Lawrence Erlbaum.

Konecni, V. J. (1972). Some effects of guilt on compliance: A field replication. *Journal of Personality and Social Psychology, 23,* 30-32.

Konoske, P., Staple, S., & Graf, R. G. (1979). Compliant reactions to guilt: Self-esteem or self-punishment. *Journal of Social Psychology, 108,* 207-211.

Kugler, K., & Jones, W. H. (1992). On conceptualizing and assessing guilt. *Journal of Personality and Social Psychology, 62,* 318-327.

Lechner, L., de Vries, H., & Offermans, N. (1997). Participation in a breast cancer screening program: Influence of past behavior and determinants on future screening participation. *Preventive Medicine, 26,* 473-482.

Lewis, M. (1993). Self-conscious emotions: Embarrassment, pride, shame, and guilt. In M. Lewis & J. M. Haviland (Eds.), *Handbook of emotions* (pp. 563-573). New York: Guilford.

Loomes, G., & Sugden, R. (1982). Regret theory: An alternative theory of rational choice under uncertainty. *Economic Journal, 92,* 805-824.

Loomes, G., & Sugden, R. (1987). Testing for regret and disappointment in choice under uncertainty. *Economic Journal, 97*(Suppl.), 118-129.

McGraw, K. M. (1987). Guilt following transgression: An attribution of responsibility approach. *Journal of Personality and Social Psychology, 53,* 247-256.

McMillen, D. L. (1970). Transgression, fate control, and compliant behavior. *Psychonomic Science, 21,* 103-104.

McMillen, D. L. (1971). Transgression, self-image, and compliant behavior. *Journal of Personality and Social Psychology, 20,* 176-179.

McMillen, D. L., & Austin, J. B. (1971). Effect of positive feedback on compliance following transgression. *Psychonomic Science, 24,* 59-61.

McMillen, D. L., Jackson, J. A., & Austin, J. B. (1974). Effects of positive and negative requests on compliance following transgression. *Bulletin of the Psychonomic Society, 3,* 80-82.

Miceli, M. (1992). How to make someone feel guilty: Strategies of guilt inducement and their goals. *Journal for the Theory of Social Behavior, 22,* 81-104.

Miceli, M., & Castelfranchi, C. (1998). How to silence one's conscience: Cognitive defenses against the feeling of guilt. *Journal for the Theory of Social Behavior, 28,* 287-318.

Niedenthal, P. M., Tangney, J. P., & Gavanski, I. (1994). "If only I weren't" versus "If only I hadn't": Distinguishing shame and guilt in counterfactual thinking. *Journal of Personality and Social Psychology, 67,* 585-596.

Noel, R. C. (1971). Helping behavior as a consequence of a prior transgression. *Dissertation Abstracts International, 32,* 4109-4110A. (University Microfilms No. 72-3687)

Noel, R. C. (1973). Transgression-compliance: A failure to confirm. *Journal of Personality and Social Psychology, 27,* 151-153.

O'Keefe, D. J., & Figgé, M. (1997). A guilt-based explanation of the door-in-the-face influence strategy. *Human Communication Research, 24,* 64-81.

O'Keefe, D. J., & Hale, S. L. (1998). The door-in-the-face influence strategy: A random-effects meta-analytic review. In M. E. Roloff (Ed.), *Communication yearbook 21* (pp. 1-33). Thousand Oaks, CA: Sage.

O'Malley, M. N., & Andrews, L. (1983). The effect of mood and incentives on helping: Are there some things money can't buy? *Motivation and Emotion, 7,* 179-189.

Pinto, M. B., & Priest, S. (1991). Guilt appeals in advertising: An exploratory study. *Psychological Reports, 69,* 375-385.

Pinto, M. B., & Worobetz, N. D. (1992). Note on guilt appeals in advertising: Covariate effects of self-esteem and locus of control. *Psychological Reports, 70,* 19-22.

Quiles, Z. N., & Bybee, J. (1997). Chronic and predispositional guilt: Relations to mental health, prosocial behavior, and religiosity. *Journal of Personality Assessment, 69,* 104-126.

Raudenbush, S. W. (1994). Random effects models. In H. Cooper & L. V. Hedges (Eds.), *Handbook of research synthesis* (pp. 301-321). New York: Russell Sage Foundation.

Rawlings, E. I. (1966). An experimental study of some antecedent conditions affecting subsequent expressions of altruism. *Dissertation Abstracts International, 27,* 1294B. (University Microfilms No. AAG66-04581)

Rawlings, E. I. (1968). Witnessing harm to other: A reassessment of the role of guilt in altruistic behavior. *Journal of Personality and Social Psychology, 10,* 377-380.

Rawlings, E. I. (1970). Reactive guilt and anticipatory guilt in altruistic behavior. In J. Macaulay & L. Berkowitz (Eds.), *Altruism and helping behavior* (pp. 163-177). New York: Academic Press.

Regan, D. T., Williams, M., & Sparling, S. (1972). Voluntary expiation of guilt: A field experiment. *Journal of Personality and Social Psychology, 24,* 42-45.

Regan, J. W. (1969). Guilt, inequity and altruistic behavior. *Dissertation Abstracts International, 29,* 4106A. (University Microfilms No. AAG69-08248)

Regan, J. W. (1971). Guilt, perceived injustice, and altruistic behavior. *Journal of Personality and Social Psychology, 18,* 124-132.

Richard, R., de Vries, N. K., & van der Pligt, J. (1998). Anticipated regret and precautionary sexual behavior. *Journal of Applied Social Psychology, 28,* 1411-1428.

Richard, R., van der Pligt, J., & de Vries, N. K. (1995). Anticipated affective reactions and prevention of AIDS. *British Journal of Social Psychology, 34,* 9-21.

Richard, R., van der Pligt, J., & de Vries, N. K. (1996a). Anticipated affect and behavioral choice. *Basic and Applied Social Psychology, 18,* 111-129.

Richard, R., van der Pligt, J., & de Vries, N. K. (1996b). Anticipated regret and time perspective: Changing sexual risk-taking behavior. *Journal of Behavioral Decision Making, 9,* 185-199.

Riordan, C. A., Dunaway, F. A., Haas, P., James, M. K., & Kruger, D. (1984). Prosocial behavior following transgression: Evidence for intrapsychic and interpersonal motives. *Journal of Social Psychology, 124,* 51-55.

Riordan, C. A., James, M. K., & Dunaway, F. A. (1985). Interpersonal determinants of helping and the transgression-compliance relationship. *Journal of Social Psychology, 125,* 365-372.

Roseman, I. J., Wiest, C., & Swartz, T. S. (1994). Phenomenology, behaviors, and goals differentiate discrete emotions. *Journal of Personality and Social Psychology, 67,* 206-221.

Roy, R. E. (1974). Internal-external locus of control, resistance to temptation, and guilt after transgression. *Dissertation Abstracts International, 35,* 4153B. (University Microfilms No. 75-3444)

Rubin, A. M. (1994). Media uses and effects: A uses-and-gratifications perspective. In J. Bryant & D. Zillmann (Eds.), *Media effects: Advances in theory and research* (pp. 417-436). Hillsdale, NJ: Lawrence Erlbaum.

Rubin, J., & Shaffer, W. F. (1987). Some interpersonal effects of imposing guilt versus eliciting altruism. *Counseling and Values, 31,* 190-193.

Ruth, J. A. (1987). *The use of guilt advertising appeals as a means of facilitating prosocial behavior.* Unpublished master's thesis, University of Texas at Austin.

Ruth, J. A., & Faber, R. J. (1988). Guilt: An overlooked advertising appeal. In J. D. Leckenby (Ed.), *The proceedings of the 1988 conference of the American Academy of Advertising* (pp. 83-89). Austin, TX: American Academy of Advertising.

Schallow, J. R. (1972). Direct and displaced aggression, transgression compliance, and liking for one's victim in high- and low-guilt subjects. *Dissertation Abstracts International, 33,* 3929B. (University Microfilms No. 73-512)

Shadish, W. R., & Haddock, C. K. (1994). Combining estimates of effect size. In H. Cooper & L. V. Hedges (Eds.), *Handbook of research synthesis* (pp. 261-281). New York: Russell Sage Foundation.

Shapiro, J. S. (1991). The effects of self-esteem, self-esteem salience and transgression on helping. *Dissertation Abstracts International, 52,* 5581B. (University Microfilms No. AAG91-35689)

Silverman, I. W. (1967). Incidence of guilt reactions in children. *Journal of Personality and Social Psychology, 7,* 338-340.

Silverman, L. J., Rivera, A. N., & Tedeschi, J. T. (1979). Transgression-compliance: Guilt, negative affect, or impression management? *Journal of Social Psychology, 108,* 57-62.

Simonson, I. (1992). The influence of anticipating regret and responsibility on purchase decisions. *Journal of Consumer Research, 19,* 105-118.

Sommer, K. L., & Baumeister, R. F. (1997). Making someone feel guilty: Causes, strategies, and consequences. In R. M. Kowalski (Ed.), *Aversive interpersonal behaviors* (pp. 31-55). New York: Plenum.

Steele, C. M. (1988). The psychology of self-affirmation: Sustaining the integrity of the self. In L. Berkowitz (Ed.), *Advances in experimental social psychology* (Vol. 21, pp. 261-302). New York: Academic Press.

Steele, C. M., & Liu, T. J. (1983). Dissonance processes as self-affirmation. *Journal of Personality and Social Psychology, 45,* 5-19.

Steele, C. M., & Spencer, S. J. (1992). The primacy of self-integrity. *Psychological Inquiry, 3,* 345-346.

Stice, E. (1992). The similarities between cognitive dissonance and guilt: Confession as a relief of dissonance. *Current Psychology: Research and Reviews, 11,* 69-77.

Stone, J., Aronson, E., Crain, A. L., Winslow, M. P., & Fried, C. B. (1994). Inducing hypocrisy as a means of encouraging young adults to use condoms. *Personality and Social Psychology Bulletin, 20,* 116-128.

Stout, P. A., & Sego, T. (1994). Emotions elicited by threat appeals and their impact on persuasion. In K. W. King (Ed.), *Proceedings of the 1994 conference of the American Academy of Advertising* (pp. 8-16). Athens, GA: American Academy of Advertising.

Sutton, S. R. (1982). Fear-arousing communications: A critical examination of theory and research. In J. R. Eiser (Ed.), *Social psychology and behavioral medicine* (pp. 303-337). New York: John Wiley.

Tangney, J. P. (1992). Situational determinants of shame and guilt in young adulthood. *Personality and Social Psychology Bulletin, 18,* 199-205.

Tangney, J. P. (1995a). Recent advances in the empirical study of shame and guilt. *American Behavioral Scientist, 38,* 1132-1145.

Tangney, J. P. (1995b). Shame and guilt in interpersonal relationships. In J. P. Tangney & K. W. Fischer (Eds.), *Self-conscious emotions: The psychology of shame, guilt, embarrassment, and pride* (pp. 114-139). New York: Guilford.

Tangney, J. P., Miller, R. S., Flicker, L., & Barlow, D. H. (1996). Are shame, guilt, and embarrassment distinct emotions? *Journal of Personality and Social Psychology, 70,* 1256-1259.

van der Pligt, J., & de Vries, N. K. (1998). Expectancy-value models of health behaviour: The role of salience and anticipated affect. *Psychology and Health, 13,* 289-305.

van der Pligt, J., & Richard, R. (1994). Changing adolescents' sexual behaviour: Perceived risk, self-efficacy and anticipated regret. *Patient Education and Counseling, 23,* 187-196.

Vangelisti, A. L., Daly, J. A., & Rudnick, J. R. (1991). Making people feel guilty in conversations: Techniques and correlates. *Human Communication Research, 18,* 3-39.

Vangelisti, A. L., & Sprague, R. J. (1998). Guilt and hurt: Similarities, distinctions, and conversational strategies. In P. A. Andersen & L. K. Guerrero (Eds.), *Handbook of communication and emotion: Research, theory, applications, and contexts* (pp. 123-154). San Diego, CA: Academic Press.

Wallace, J., & Sadalla, E. (1966). Behavioral consequences of transgression: I. The effects of social recognition. *Journal of Experimental Research in Personality, 1,* 187-194.

Wicklund, R. A., & Brehm, J. W. (1976). *Perspectives on cognitive dissonance.* Hillsdale, NJ: Lawrence Erlbaum.

Yinon, Y., Bizman, A., Cohen, S., & Segev, J. (1976). Effects of guilt-arousal communications on volunteering to the civil guard: A field experiment. *Bulletin of the Psychonomic Society, 7,* 493-494.

Zanna, M. P., & Cooper, J. (1974). Dissonance and the pill: An attribution approach to studying the arousal properties of dissonance. *Journal of Personality and Social Psychology, 29,* 703-709.

Zeelenberg, M., van Dijk, W. W., & Manstead, A. S. R. (1998). Reconsidering the relation between regret and responsibility. *Organizational Behavior and Human Decision Processes, 74,* 254-272.

Zeelenberg, M., van Dijk, W. W., Manstead, A. S. R., & van der Pligt, J. (1998). The experience of regret and disappointment. *Cognition and Emotion, 12,* 221-230.

Zeelenberg, M., van Dijk, W. W., van der Pligt, J., Manstead, A. S. R., van Empelen, P., & Reinderman, D. (1998). Emotional reactions to the outcomes of decisions: The role of counterfactual thought in the experience of regret and disappointment. *Organizational Behavior and Human Decision Processes, 75,* 117-141.

Zemach, M. (1966). The effects of guilt-arousing communications on acceptance of recommendations. *Dissertation Abstracts, 27,* 255A. (University Microfilms No. AAG66-07691)

Zillmann, D., & Bryant, J. (1985). Affect, mood, and emotion as determinants of selective exposure. In D. Zillmann & J. Bryant (Eds.), *Selective exposure to communication* (pp. 157-190). Hillsdale, NJ: Lawrence Erlbaum.

Zillmann, D., & Bryant, J. (1994). Entertainment as media effect. In J. Bryant & D. Zillmann (Eds.), *Media effects: Advances in theory and research* (pp. 437-461). Hillsdale, NJ: Lawrence Erlbaum.

CHAPTER CONTENTS

3   Mood Management in the Context of Selective Exposure Theory

DOLF ZILLMANN
University of Alabama

In this chapter, the hedonistic premise of mood-management theory is examined and expanded to account for seemingly nonhedonistic choices of media content. Counterhedonistic message selection is considered in the context of selective-exposure theory. Informational utility is invoked as a choice-driving force that complements content selection. The confounded operation of hedonistic and informational choice determinants is detailed for various domains of communication. In particular, it is proposed that hedonistic motivation, as articulated in mood-management theory, dominates spontaneous entertainment choices, with nonhedonistic considerations being complementary to choice determination. The choice of educational and informational media content, in contrast, is thought to be dominated by considerations of informational utility, but also to entail noninformational anticipations. The integration of these and related choice determinants is emphasized for the development of comprehensive theories of selective exposure.

MOOD MANAGEMENT THROUGH
COMMUNICATION CHOICES

Mood-management theory is based on the premise that people, in their seemingly continual efforts at improving affective and emotional experience, follow a hedonistic impulsion toward pleasure maximization (Zillmann, 1988a, 1988b). Specifically, this theory posits that persons tend to arrange their stimulus environments so as to increase the likelihood that bad moods are short-lived and their experiential intensity is reduced, that good moods are prolonged and their experiential intensity is enhanced, and that bad moods are terminated and superseded by

Correspondence: Dolf Zillmann, College of Communication and Information Sciences, Office for Graduate Studies, 478 Reese Phifer Hall, University of Alabama, Tuscaloosa, AL 35487-0172; e-mail dzillman@icr.ua.edu

Communication Yearbook 23, pp.103-123

good moods of the highest possible experiential intensity. Focusing on such arrangements within the media environment, it can be considered to have been demonstrated that the indicated hedonistic objective is best served by selective exposure to material that (a) is excitationally opposite to prevailing states associated with noxiously experienced hypo- or hyperarousal, (b) has positive hedonic value above that of prevailing states, and (c) in hedonically negative states, has little or no semantic affinity with the prevailing states (see Fenigstein & Heyduk, 1985; Wakshlag, 1985; Zillmann, 1985, 1988b; Zillmann & Bryant, 1985, 1997; Zillmann & Wakshlag, 1985).

The merits of predictions derived from mood-management theory have been determined within a research paradigm that allows respondents to select messages for consumption, mostly from among entertaining but also from among informational and educational programming alternatives. Choices are exercised in hypothetical situations as well as under conditions of high ecological validity. The choices themselves serve as measures in the discernment of consumption motives. This, it should be noted, is in contrast to procedures, such as those defining the uses-and-gratifications approach, that attempt to explore motives through the assessment of respondents' introspection (e.g., Blumler & Katz, 1974; Rayburn, 1996; Rosengren, Wenner, & Palmgreen, 1985; Rubin, 1983). The selective-exposure paradigm (Zillmann & Bryant, 1985), of which mood-management theory is a part, avoids introspective assessments because they tend to reflect public discourse on motives rather than actual motives (see Zillmann & Bryant, 1997; Zillmann & Gan, 1997).

Using the selective-exposure methodology to evaluate the choice of exciting and unexciting programs as a function of noxious excitatory experience, for instance, Bryant and Zillmann (1984) placed respondents into a state of either boredom or stress and then provided them with the opportunity to watch television. Unbeknownst to the respondents, the investigators had arranged that only programs that had been preevaluated as either exciting or unexciting could be sampled. The respondents' secretly recorded viewing choices (in terms of accumulated time dedicated to content categories of interest) showed that bored viewers selected exciting over unexciting programs, whereas the viewers in acute stress selected unexciting over exciting ones. Without respondents' being able to articulate the reasons for their choices, their selections served excitatory homeostasis, as predicted, in that the return to normal levels of sympathetic excitedness was accelerated for both hypo- and hyperaroused persons.

Similarly conducted selective-exposure research gives evidence that viewers who sample entertaining programs seek to elude bad moods, such as being disappointed, depressed, frustrated, annoyed, or angry, by consuming comedy or engaging drama with an appeasing overall message (e.g., Helregel & Weaver, 1989; Meadowcroft & Zillmann, 1987; Zillmann, Schweitzer, & Mundorf, 1994; Zillmann & Wakshlag, 1985) and attempt to enhance normal and pleasant states through consumption of novel, exciting, and involving entertainment fare to which they have not habituated emotionally (e.g., Zillmann & Bryant, 1986).

An investigation on crime apprehension demonstrates perhaps most clearly that, in efforts at overcoming noxious experiential states, material with affinity to these states tends to be avoided, whereas material with little or no such affinity tends to be chosen (Wakshlag, Vial, & Tamborini, 1983). After respondents' fear of victimization was or was not made salient to them, they were asked to choose a drama from a set of crime dramas that differed with regard to the amount of featured violence and the justness of the resolution. It was observed that those who were acutely crime-apprehensive showed a stronger tendency than others to avoid drama dwelling on violence. These respondents also showed a stronger interest in drama holding the promise of featuring the triumph of justice in its resolution (see also Tamborini, Zillmann, & Bryant, 1984). It seems that in making such choices individuals tacitly understand that diversionary stimulation (i.e., exposure to programming with little or no semantic affinity to the prevailing experiential state) has a more beneficial effect than mulling over the conditions that foster bad moods or being continually reminded of these conditions (i.e., by exposure to material featuring related conditions and circumstances).

Nonexperimental research has produced further corroboration of mood management through specific and, at times, nonspecific choices of available media offerings. Anderson, Collins, Schmitt, and Jacobvitz (1996), for instance, conducted a massive behavior survey of television consumption in the family context. Specifically, these investigators assessed family stress levels and related them to television program choices. High stress levels proved to be associated with increased comedy viewing and decreased news consumption. This accords with mood-management theory in that comedy is considered programming with great absorption potential (see Bryant & Zillmann, 1977) and high positive hedonic valence—in short, programming with a high capacity for disrupting and alleviating bad moods. News programs, which are usually laden with reports of threatening events (e.g., Stone & Grusin, 1984), do not have this capacity and thus are likely to perpetuate bad moods based on troubling experiences. In addition, Anderson et al. observed that stressed women watched more game and variety programming. These women watched more television overall. The women also recognized themselves as "being addicted" to television. Stressed men were found to stare more than others into the tube, as if to force distraction on themselves.

This research relates to the work on conflict management, specifically to such management through media choices affecting mood improvements. Repetti (1989) conducted an investigation into the media behaviors of air-traffic controllers, whose profession is known for pronounced daily variation in stress levels. The controllers were observed in their homes after normal and highly stressful days at work. Acutely stressed controllers invariably attempted to watch television in order to calm down. When family circumstances allowed such diversionary stimulation, family life proceeded in comparatively tranquil fashion. When circumstances prevented this relaxation, friction with family members tended to escalate to aggravated conflict, often with destructive results. Rosenblatt and Cunningham (1976) have reported related observations.

All this is to say that a considerable amount of evidence indicates that people indeed use media offerings to manage moods in predictable ways. It also is to say that such mood management is not merely a matter of fostering potentially trivial amusements, amazements, pleasant titillations, and cheap thrills, but that the management of moods can have significant social consequences and even health benefits (e.g., Argyle, 1987; Haig, 1988; Zillmann, de Wied, King-Jablonski, & Jenzowsky, 1996; Zillmann, Rockwell, Schweitzer, & Sundar, 1993).

The evidence concerning mood management through communication choices is by no means monolithic, however, nor is mood-management theory all-encompassing. There are challenges in the pertinent findings, in fact, and my purpose in the remaining exposition is to address them by suggesting expansions to the choice paradigm under consideration. Contemplated expansions focus on the integration of apparently counterhedonistic motives as well as on motives that do not depend on the fickleness of transitory and transitional affective states. Consideration is also given to the influence of informational utility in the determination of selective exposure to media offerings.

SPONTANEOUS VERSUS TELIC HEDONISM

Parrott (1993) examined the research on the mood-behavior relationship and found a preponderance of work on the repair of negative moods (e.g., Clark & Isen, 1982; Morris & Reilly, 1987) and the maintenance of positive ones (e.g., Carlson, Charlin, & Miller, 1988; Clark & Isen, 1982). He observed that, in stark contrast, motives for inhibiting good moods and maintaining bad ones have received little attention and, essentially, have been left unexplored. Parrott sought to correct this neglect by compiling a seemingly exhaustive list of behavioral circumstances that appear to go, in his terms, "beyond hedonism"—or that might be construed as incidents of counterhedonistic behavior.

Mostly considering behaviors outside communication and selective-exposure issues, Parrott (1993) proposes four idiosyncratic motives for the inhibition of good moods: (a) prevention of bad fortune, should persons believe that excessive happiness causes such turns of events; (b) elimination of bad feelings about a good mood, should persons feel undeserving or guilty about the good mood; (c) building character, should persons believe self-denial to strengthen character; and (d) pursuit of spiritual betterment, should persons believe that indulgence in good moods implies undue involvement with insignificant matters. He also proposes four such motives for the maintenance of bad moods: (a) self-punishment and atonement for guilt, (b) preparation for or prevention of future bad fortune, (c) exploration of a negative worldview, and (d) prevention of worse moods.

Some of these suggestions may seem contrived. Others apply, no doubt, to mood management through communication exposure, especially through entertainment choices. Self-denial of mood improvement may prevent anyone who struggles with less-than-pleasant assignments from turning to more pleasant diversions.

Studying for a calculus exam, for instance, may be a trying experience. It might be tempting to watch a good movie or an exciting football game instead. Yielding to such temptations might improve mood momentarily, but surely it comes at a price: the anticipation and eventual materialization of a very bad mood at and after the examination. On the other hand, delayed positive mood may be anticipated as a result of tolerating a bad one for some time.

The logic here is very much that of forgoing immediate gratification in the interest of later gratification of potentially greater magnitude. Actually, with the likely exception of pathological pursuits, all of Parrott's suggestions are subject to this interpretation and thus do not pose a challenge to hedonism. His proposals help, however, to correct the erroneous impression that mood management is restricted to instant applications. Mood-affecting behavior choices are bound to engage anticipatory evaluations, and the anticipations in question may vary considerably in the time gap they span. At times, this gap may be trivial and negligible, with persons seeking mood improvement quasi-instantaneously. At other times, the denial of mood improvement and the associated acceptance of less-than-satisfactory moods might be of considerable duration. Such would seem to be the case, for instance, if a student in trouble decides to forgo movies and all sports events until after critical exams—or if a professor curtails similarly pleasant diversions for years in the interest of increased productivity and eventual academic glory.

The involvement of anticipatory considerations in individuals' making choices that affect mood is actually articulated in several theories. Scheier and Carver (1982), for example, have conceived of a "meta-mood experience" that entails the reflection of moods proper. This meta-mood experience would seem to serve hedonism in the long run, but allows violations in the short term. Additionally, in my three-factor theory of emotion, I have posited a monitoring function that ensures the appraisal of affect experienced and affect anticipated (Zillmann, 1983, 1996). Hedonistic strategies are thus put into a short as well as an extended time frame. These proposals are largely consistent with Lazarus's (1966; see also Lazarus & Folkman, 1987) conception of emotional coping, which distinguishes between immediate coping efforts directed at modifying the emotional state proper and potentially prolonged, elaborative efforts directed at controlling the evocation of such states at future times. Moreover, they are consistent with cognitive theories of telic self-regulation and self-control in hedonistic terms (e.g., Mischel, Cantor, & Feldman, 1996).

O'Neal and Taylor (1989) conducted a selective-exposure investigation that is suggestive of the merits of considering hedonism in an extended time frame. Acutely angry men were found to take an exceptionally strong interest in programs featuring hostility and violence, but only if they believed they would have an opportunity to retaliate against the person who had instigated their anger. When this person was of low status, enhanced consumption of the indicated fare was particularly strong. In comparison, equally angry men who believed that they would never meet their annoyer again showed little interest in violence-laden drama. They exhibited increased appetite for mood-improving comedy instead.

Such findings suggest that circumstances exist in which persons in a noxious affective state, anger in this case, seek to retain the experience. The adverse experience is apparently prolonged in the interest of future consummatory behavior believed to be of superior hedonic quality. For acutely angry men, the hedonistic objective is best served by "getting even" with someone who offended and provoked them, even if this is possible only after some delay. For them, genuine anger is not a laughing matter, and they avoid strong diversionary stimulation (achieved by exposure to material with little or no affinity to their experiential state) even though it might provide affective relief. Comedy in particular, with its belittlement of genuine emotions of the noxious variety, should hold little appeal for such men. Exposure to violent fare, in contrast, has stimulus-experience affinity and thus is likely, through frequent presentation of episodes of provocation and retaliation, to help sustain anger. For angry men who believe that they will be able to act on their anger, then, consumption of violence-laden programs has "emotional utility." For angry men who know that they are unable to act on their anger, the maintenance of anger serves no purpose. This sets them free, so to speak, to squelch their noxious experience in the most effective way possible under the circumstances, in this case by comedy consumption.

The experimental conditions that O'Neal and Taylor (1989) created did not allow respondents to avoid watching entertaining programs. Had a no-viewing choice been provided, acutely angry men may have avoided distraction by taking that option. Under conditions of minimal distraction, angry men (but not angry women) have, in fact, been observed mulling over abusive treatments that they have suffered. As a result, they retained and perpetuated their acute anger experience for considerable periods of time (e.g., Sapolsky, Stocking, & Zillmann, 1977), presumably in order to act out their anger as opportunities arise. An investigation by Christ and Medoff (1984) shows, in fact, that persons who have the option of not distracting themselves during intensely noxious states will refrain from watching television altogether. This suggests that persons who face genuine problems, problems that engage their emotions and that call for resolving action, are unlikely to make the choice to "escape from reality"—counter to what has been feared by many (e.g., Postman, 1985; van den Haag, 1960). Rather, mood management through communication choices offers itself as a remedy when immediate or somewhat delayed resolving action is not available and the maintenance of adverse emotions would be devoid of utility.

The indicated avoidance of diversionary stimulation during genuine, intensely experienced emotions suggests that, in general, persons are unlikely to seek to terminate noxious affect as long as the maintenance of that affect appears instrumental in helping to bring about a satisfactory resolution to the circumstances that caused the affect, be this by the removal of the instigating conditions or through some form of recompense. This limitation of mood management through communication choices has been pointed out earlier (e.g., Zillmann, 1988b). In fact, it has also been accepted that persons are unlikely to seek diversionary stimulation during intensely experienced euphoric states. Persons in these states should prefer to manage their moods by reveling in their states as long as they can—as resorting to distracting entertainments is likely to reduce their euphoria, thus amounting to a "step down."

It would seem to be prudent, then, to acknowledge that extreme emotional conditions exist in which persons fail to exercise the mood-modifying choices before them, despite the fact that these choices offer prompt relief from noxious states or enhancement of positive moods. Genuine emotions that demand immediate attention, especially in terms of action preparation, constitute such conditions. Enumeration of the discussed emotional circumstances under which persons may refrain from seeking mood improvement through communication choices should suffice in amending mood-management theory for the media context. Recognition of these empirically validated limiting conditions should serve the prediction of spontaneous mood management better than speculations about anticipated hedonistic closure in a large time frame. Predicting on grounds of empirical evidence that acutely angry persons who hope to act on their anger will refrain from watching comedy, for example, appears to be more prudent than predicting, in purely hypothetical terms, pleasure-denying comedy avoidance in the interest of "building character"—ultimately in the interest of delayed pleasures sanctioned within a personal hedonistic scheme. On the other hand, if genre aversions exist, because of self-censure or for any other reason, their empirical assessment obviously would assist the prediction of genre choices for the purpose of mood management.

Telic Hedonism and Emotional Preoccupation

Two conclusions can be drawn from the foregoing discussion. First, the telic pursuit of pleasure is capable of fostering the self-imposed denial of lesser immediately available pleasures. Noxious emotions may be retained in the interest of greater gratification upon resolution of those emotions. Moreover, gratifications may be critically evaluated and their desirability determined. Gratifications deemed superficial or otherwise inappropriate may then be avoided. In the interest of maximizing subjectively sanctioned gratifications, such self-imposed denial is likely to foster prolonged, enduring preferences.

Second, extreme emotional states entail state-focused cognitive preoccupation that halts the immediate pursuit of hedonistic objectives by unrelated means. During intensely experienced aversive states, diversionary stimulation would interfere with instrumental coping efforts and consequently tends to be avoided. During intensely experienced euphoria, diversionary stimulation would interfere with the maintenance of that desirable state and, hence, also tends to be avoided.

MOOD AND MANAGEMENT INTERACTIONS
WITH GENDER AND PERSONALITY

Research on mood management has consistently encountered considerable gender differences. Masters, Ford, and Arend (1983), for instance, found that bad moods prompted different needs for diversionary stimulation in 4- to 5-year-old boys compared with girls of the same ages. Medoff (1979) found stark gender differences in the consumption of comedy for male and female students in states of frustration and annoyance. Specifically, in accordance with mood-management considerations, frustrated and annoyed women were drawn to innocuous comedy at the expense of serious drama. Their male counterparts, in contrast, clearly avoided comedy, thereby challenging theoretical expectations. Biswas, Riffe, and Zillmann (1994) similarly observed that women in bad moods, compared with women in good moods, conformed with expectations in showing a clear preference for good news. Men, again challenging theory, showed no such preference and were drawn to bad news that could not help them as effectively as good news to diminish their noxious experience. Wells and Hakanen (1991), moreover, found that women appear to use music in better accordance with theoretical expectations than do men.

Such findings urge the consideration of gender in mood-management theorizing. It appears that boys and girls form gender-specific media preferences rather early, and that these preferences are largely retained throughout adolescence and adulthood. Collins-Standley, Gan, Yu, and Zillmann (1996), for instance, observed a partiality for violent and scary entertainments in 3-year-old boys. Their female counterparts exhibited a partiality for romantic tales. The indicated preferences were not evident at age 2, but emerged at age 3, and were clearly developed at age 4. The research findings of Hoffner and Haefner (1993), Oliver (1993), and Wright, Kunkel, Pinon, and Huston (1989) warrant similar conclusions. Regarding displays of agonistic events, boys were consistently observed to show more interest in them than girls. Luecke-Aleksa, Anderson, Collins, and Schmitt (1995) further observed that gender-constant 5-year-old boys were more strongly drawn to television programming intended for men, mostly action drama and sports, than were gender-preconstant boys of that age.

A gender gap has also been encountered in the consumption of sports programs (Sargent, Zillmann, & Weaver, 1998; Zillmann, 1995). Sports classifiable as combative (e.g., boxing, ice hockey, American football) and mechanized for speed (e.g., car racing) have proved to be the province of men. Sports classifiable as stylistic (e.g., diving, figure skating, gymnastics), in contrast, hold comparatively little appeal for men and define the domain of women's enthusiastic sports spectatorship. The combat versus beauty dichotomy for men and women, respectively, seems to span a great variety of cultures as well.

In predicting spontaneous choices among media offerings, it would be foolish to ignore such stable gender-specific consumption preferences. It is again the empirical securement of the indicated aversions and preferences whose integration in mood-management theory holds promise of improving predictive accuracy. Obviously, the more we know about gender-specific or trait-specific habits, the better we can eliminate available but inappropriate choices, and the more accurately we can delineate the most probable choice.

The consideration of traits extends the acceptance of gender influence to that of influence by individual differences in terms of personality. Personality characteristics are by definition neither short-lived nor situational. They are enduring, although not necessarily unchanging. The time-frame difference is usually expressed in the state-trait dichotomy. Traits, of which gender can be considered a special case, may be viewed as defining the undercurrent for state expression in situational terms. Mood management is obviously a state process. A transitory experience is enhanced or remedied. Traits, however, determine the extent to which circumstances induce euphoric and dysphoric states, and they further influence the ways of modifying these states. Strategies for the regulation of affect are a function of past experience that manifests itself in trait development and modification (see Salovey, Hsee, & Mayer, 1993). Strategies and habits for mood regulation through communication choices can be viewed in this context. Traits thus can be seen as exerting considerable influence on the evocation of states that then invoke trait-specific preferences for their regulation.

Research conducted on adolescent rebelliousness and music preferences illustrates the suggested processes. Whether a rebellious disposition develops because of constitutional factors (such as strong androgenization or similar conditions), experiential circumstances (such as a history of freedom-curtailing actions by parents and other persons in positions of authority), or the nature-nurture influences combined, defiantly assertive adolescents will on occasion enter into conflict and feel rebellious. These feelings of frustration and anger against authority cannot readily be expressed in consummatory responses, at least not with impunity. The commands of "oppressive" parents, teachers, and other caretakers cannot be ignored, and the persons in authority cannot be shoved aside in defiance without grievous repercussions. On the other hand, the adolescents' contempt is too genuine an affective experience to be squelched with exposure to a sweet love story, for example. In such a dilemma, adolescents may be expected to resort to the consumption of media fare that features others' defiance of authority. Rebellious music offers this type of material with themes like "smoking in the boys' room" and "we don't need no education." Visual embellishments of the music, such as depictions of parents thrown out the window and schoolhouses set ablaze, show the success of such defiance. The projection of others' successful defiance obviously does not solve the adolescents' immediate problems, but may nonetheless induce mood improvements by allowing the adolescents to feel allied with numerous others against a common enemy.

The available research evidence tends to support this interpretation. Bleich, Zillmann, and Weaver (1991) and Robinson, Weaver, and Zillmann (1996), for instance, observed that highly defiant adolescents were strongly drawn to rebellious music, whereas this music held comparatively little appeal for their nondefiant counterparts. In the investigation by Bleich et al., the selective consumption of music was assessed in ownership of recordings. It was assumed that the relative amount of owned recordings of rebellious music correlates with frequency of consumption. Such an assessment of selective exposure leaves open the question as to whether consumption occurred during periods of acute feelings of defiance—that is, during mood states in need of repair. The findings establish only that adolescents exhibiting rebelliousness as a trait own and are likely to consume defiant music disproportionally often, and that they enjoy this music more than alternative musical expressions.

Although these findings are entirely consistent with the notion that rebellious adolescents frequently enhance their mood by consumption of music with defiant themes (and in this sense manage their mood), the findings are at best suggestive of the usage of defiant musical themes in the management of bouts of acute rebelliousness. As only trait rebelliousness (not state rebelliousness) was measured and mood repair was not examined in situational terms, it can be argued that the demonstrated preference for rebellious musical themes by rebellious youths merely reflects a taste preference whose mood-management consequences may be rather trivial. Such a contention receives some support, in fact, from findings reported by Robinson et al. (1996). Their investigation involved assessments of psychoticism, neuroticism, and extraversion (see Eysenck & Eysenck, 1985) along with the measurement of rebelliousness. Although neuroticism and extraversion proved unrelated to musical taste, psychoticism was found to be linked to liking rebellious music. Specifically, persons scoring high on psychoticism showed the same preference as rebellious youths for defiant musical themes. Psychoticism is not uniquely linked to particular noxious mood experiences, however. Instead, it is indicative of callous dispositions, and it may be that these dispositions invite the enjoyment of material that dwells on hostility and deviance—or that these dispositions at least do not hamper enjoyment, as their absence might in adolescents scoring low on psychoticism.

The indicated ambiguity concerning media preferences by trait with regard to their service in mood repair applies to trait preferences generally. Research by Weaver (1991), for instance, has established associations between preferences for particular television genres and specific personality traits. Among other things, viewers comparatively high in neuroticism showed a particularly strong interest in news and educational programs while exhibiting relatively little interest in light-hearted comedy and action drama. Viewers comparatively high in psychoticism, in contrast, gave evidence of a particularly strong interest in action drama, especially in its most violent forms. Weaver, Brosius, and Mundorf (1993) carried this exploration of personality differences further by examining personality-defined preferences in different cultural contexts. In comparing the genre preferences of American and German audiences, for example, these investigators observed that the interest in tragedy declined as psychoticism increased. The interest in horror, on the other hand, increased with psychoticism. These relationships were observed for both American and German audiences. In contrast, the interest in sexually titillating comedy proved to be culture specific. The interest in such fare decreased for psychotically inclined German viewers. It increased, however, for American viewers with such inclination.

Exploring selective exposure to nonfictional events in the news, Sparks and Spirek (1988) observed differences as a function of environmental monitoring. These investigators classified respondents as "high monitors" who seek potentially distressing information in the interest of superior coping with similar actual events versus "low monitors" who avoid exposure to distressing information as a way of emotional coping (Miller, 1990). Consistent with these considerations, they found that high monitors watched more news about the *Challenger* disaster than did low monitors. In a related study with children, Hoffner and Haefner (1994) observed that children who felt especially vulnerable personally, and who, as a result, found news about human tragedy very disturbing, avoided news coverage of the Gulf War more than did other children.

In all these cases, specific media preferences translate into likely mood enhancement from consumption (i.e., an improvement over whatever state prevailed prior to consumption). However, the question of whether or not mood repair through consumption choices occurs in this context remains unaddressed and unresolved. The investigation of relationships between personality characteristics and media choices is, of course, important in its own right. It reveals selective-exposure patterns that are, by definition, relatively stable. It does not inform us, however, about situational uses of consumption that may serve mood repair as well as mood enhancement. In the continuing exploration of the suggested trait-state interactions concerning media preferences, it will be necessary to go beyond the assessment of choices by personality alone and to examine media choices as a joint function of both enduring traits and situationally determined moods.

Gender, Traits, and States

Various interactions among gender, aspects of personality, and transitory mood states are suggested. However, as these interactions remain unexplored, and it is currently not known under which conditions one or the other variable might exert dominant influence on selective exposure, only the likely effects of gender and traits can be indicated here:

1. Boys and men are markedly more strongly drawn than are girls and women to displays of acute conflict and, especially, overt agonistic behaviors. This exposure preference is evident in early childhood and persists through adolescence and adulthood.

2. Numerous personality variables influence selective exposure. Generally speaking, traits foster a preference for fictional and nonfictional media content that supports subjectively endorsed dispositions (e.g., rebelliousness) and avoidance of fictional and nonfictional media content that supports subjectively troubling dispositions (e.g., vulnerability).

3. Callousness diminishes the avoidance of distressing media content.

4. Saturation with specific media content, presumably because of excitatory habituation, diminishes the preference for that content.

5. Preference for, and avoidance of, media content may result from evaluative deliberation. Enduring aesthetic preference/avoidance is a case in point.

Regarding interactions, it can only be suggested that the effects of transitory moods that are emotionally compatible with particular dispositions (e.g., fear with vulnerability, anger with rebelliousness) are likely to combine in fostering the predicted preference or avoidance of media content. Analogously, such effects, if emotionally opposite and counteractive (e.g., anger and vulnerability, fear and rebelliousness) are likely to cancel each other out—at least to a degree.

WHEN MISERY LOVES COMPANY

Research on mood management through music consumption has encountered choice behavior that poses the strongest challenge yet to the proposal that all bad moods inspire efforts at mood repair, if not immediately, then after a relatively short delay (see Zillmann & Gan, 1997). Specifically, there appear to exist circumstances under which the maintenance of a noxious experience is preferred over its repair, despite the fact that the maintenance of the experience does not help to correct the inducing conditions, either by way of assisting revenge or atonement or by preventing the materialization of the experience in the future. This paradoxical case, reminiscent of the cynical contention that something can "hurt so good," concerns romantic unfulfillment or abandonment and the appeal of love-bemoaning music. American country music is laden with themes of unrequited love (e.g., I can't make you love me) and desertion (e.g., Come back to me), and it nonetheless, or perhaps because of the embrace of these themes, enjoys an enormous following. Adolescents' popular music is not far behind, however. Love-lamenting songs (e.g., "How could you leave me all alone?" in "I'm Crying," by Shanice) are enjoying the same popularity as love-celebrating songs (e.g., "Isn't it easy to see just how well we fit together," in "Good for Me," by Amy Grant). The undeniable appeal of the musical expression of hopeless yearning and heartless rejection is succinctly captured in Elton John's great hit focusing on the idea that "when every little hope is gone, sad songs say so much."

Gibson, Aust, Hoffman, and Zillmann (1995) conducted an investigation into the enjoyment of love-lamenting and love-celebrating music as a function of loneliness as a trait and found essentially no support for the proposal that love lamentation in life fosters appeal for love lamentation in music. The long-range experience of romantic loneliness (see Russell, Peplau, & Cutrona, 1980) proved to be inconsequential for the enjoyment of lamentation music. In contrast, the enjoyment of love-celebrating music was affected, but gender-specifically so. Lonely males found love-celebrating music particularly unenjoyable. Exposure to love-happy, jubilant others appears to be noxious for love-deprived men—akin to rubbing salt into their open wounds. Lonely females, on the other hand, enjoyed love-celebrating music more than did their romantically more successful counterparts. Romantic loneliness as a trait thus is a poor predictor of the enjoyment of music celebrating or lamenting love. The situation is strikingly different for romantic loneliness as a state—that is, for acute moods during unrequited love or after romantic rejection.

Gibson et al. (1995), working with high school students, examined adolescents' selections of love-lamenting and love-celebrating music under conditions of totally unrestricted choice. The teens were instructed to imagine themselves having just learned that their love for a person is reciprocated or that their romantic steady has abandoned them in favor of another partner. They were asked which of their recordings they were likely to listen to when getting home to the privacy of their own rooms. Their choices were coded for love-celebrating and love-lamenting content, as well as for content unrelated to love, by judges blind to the choice circumstances. The findings show that adolescents, both females and males, seek out music believed to maintain their moods, noxious or otherwise. Teens imagining being love-happy preferred love-celebrating music more than fourfold over alternative love music. Teens imagining being lovesick, in contrast, preferred love-lamenting music more than threefold over the alternatives. The latter preference is consistent with the argument that it may be distressing for love-distraught persons to see others happy in love, whereas it may be soothing to feel understood by similarly suffering others. The indicated preferences were found regardless of the degree of the teens' trait loneliness, suggesting that these preferences are situationally determined and potentially short-lived rather than a part of personality. It should be added that the reported affect-specific musical preferences were markedly stronger in female than in male teens.

Perhaps Elton John's aforementioned famous song hits on a solution to the paradox. When genuinely distraught, persons apparently attain some degree of comfort from witnessing others experiencing similar suffering and, in a sense, "share" their suffering with those others. In this state, witnessing the happiness of others can only foster envy (as suggested in the song of a dejected male: "Some guys [apparently the others] have all the luck" . . . with girls) and thus aggravate their feelings of misery. This selection tendency blocks, of course, mood repair through the consumption of hedonically opposite fare. Under the indicated choice-limiting conditions, then, the deliberate extension of bad moods without ulterior utility may not be as paradoxical as it appears at first glance. Still, the perpetuation of bad moods violates the hedonistic principle, unless it is assumed that (a) reactions such as feeling understood overwhelm feelings of misery and convert them to pleasantly experienced affect or (b) reactions of this kind at least neutralize feelings of misery—a result that other choices cannot readily bring about.

The indicated appeal of misery sharing is unlikely to be limited to the consumption of love music or of love as a theme. There is indication, for instance, that movies dwelling on romantic satisfaction are enjoyed less by romantically deprived adolescents than they are by romantically successful ones (Schweitzer, 1993). Whether this difference translates into romantic losers' avoidance of happy romantic films, along with their being disproportionally drawn to romantic tragedies, has by no means been established, however. Equally uncertain is whether nonromantic forms of experienced misery inspire (or deter) the selection of fictional and nonfictional expositions of similar misery. At present, it can only be acknowledged that in the choice of music for mood-management purposes, misery appears to love company. It also can be acknowledged that this hedonistic paradox still awaits a compelling explanation.

The discussed longing for being understood in one's misery might, of course, be considered a special case of the earlier stated proposition that the preferred material supports a subjectively endorsed disposition. Such argumentation leaves unexplained, however, why persons would want to endorse a disposition that demands the perpetuation of a noxious state. The dilemma seems resolvable only if one assumes that the satisfaction attained from eventually feeling understood outweighs the acceptance of an unnecessarily prolonged pensive mood.

INFORMATIONAL UTILITY
AND SELECTIVE EXPOSURE

Mares and Cantor (1992) have reported findings that seem to accord well with the misery-loves-company formula. These investigators determined the degree of experienced loneliness of elderly persons (assessed with a modified version of the Geriatric Depression Scale) and then had them evaluate the viewing desirability of various hedonically negative and hedonically positive programs. The pertinent programs were introduced as documentaries focusing on elderly persons. Three were said to feature an unhappy, lonely person, and three to feature a very happy, successful person. Two additional documentaries concerned self-help, in attaining fitness and in overcoming deafness; two more involved young protagonists in unpleasant or pleasant situations.

Lonely elderly viewers indicated a preference for seeing programs featuring unhappy persons. Their nonlonely counterparts indicated a preference for seeing programs featuring happy persons. It appears, then, that both unhappy and happy persons selected fare consistent with their condition—much in contrast to observations reported by Adams and McGuire (1986), who found it difficult to curtail a strong preference for comedy over serious drama in distraught elderly persons.

Mares and Cantor (1992) eventually exposed research participants to a documentary on a lonely man who, according to the narrator, exemplified one of the major problems facing elderly Americans, namely, loneliness. The protagonist described the death of his wife, his subsequent social isolation, and his inability to see much of his children. Suicide attempts and counseling were detailed by the narrator, who then generalized the man's plight. Another documentary featured a socially integrated man who lived happily with his wife, friends, and progeny. The narrator used him as an exemplar "that shatters the myth of problem-laden later years." Oddly, lonely elderly persons felt better after viewing the unhappy program than they did after the happy program, whereas nonlonely elderly persons felt better after seeing the happy program than they did after the unhappy one.

These findings relate to the much-debated problem of explaining the enjoyment of tragedy (see de Wied, Zillmann, & Ordman, 1994; Mills, 1993; Oliver, 1993).

Among numerous other rationales, a social-comparison process (Festinger, 1954) has been invoked to make sense of the apparent experience of pleasurable warmth from witnessing the suffering of others. Specifically, it has been argued that witnessing the despair of others that exceeds one's own will foster a comparison that yields comfort from the recognition that one's own situation is not all that bad—even that one is doing rather well. Such favorable comparison is possible only after one has witnessed others' misery. In the case of loneliness, only exposure to others' greater loneliness can provide it. Exposure to others' happiness, in contrast, is likely to evoke noxious feelings of envy. Moreover, socially integrated, happy people have no access to the pleasures of favorable self-comparison with persons in misery. They should suffer pleasure-diminishing empathic distress, even fearful apprehensions, when seeing less fortunate others.

To the extent that such comparative evaluative processes are operative, Mares and Cantor's (1992) findings concerning mood changes from program exposure can be considered explained. The selective-exposure findings may appear puzzling, but they also can be explained. If it is assumed that the elderly have a tacit understanding of their prospective affective reactions to the materials under consideration, could it be expected that, when suffering from loneliness, they prefer witnessing misery over happiness, and that when not lonely, they prefer witnessing happiness over misery? If so, the seemingly counterhedonistic decision of wanting to learn more about others' misery by persons feeling miserable themselves, as it is expected to provide some degree of relief and pleasure, would actually accord with hedonistic mood-management considerations.

It would seem prudent, however, to consider alternative explanations that may prove more parsimonious. An explanation of this kind can be developed from the recognition that the programs employed by Mares and Cantor were informational rather than entertaining. Elderly persons who suffer from loneliness may well have expected to learn from the documentaries about their problems, especially about ways to improve their own lot. This informational utility may have prompted their desire to see the program. For elderly persons who do not suffer from loneliness, such utility does not exist, setting them free to exercise a more directly hedonistic choice.

It is well-known that ailing persons tend to take an exceptionally strong interest in any information relating to ailments. They eagerly absorb any news concerning their own ongoing and feared illnesses. Such selective-exposure behavior is readily explained as the result of the utility, or potential utility, of the selected information (see Atkin, 1973, 1985; McGuire, 1974; Sears & Freedman, 1967). It would seem contrived to suggest that the behavior is fostered by a desire to persist in noxious apprehensions about illnesses.

Consideration of informational utility, then, explains the selective-exposure findings reported by Mares and Cantor. More important, however, informational utility should be recognized as an essential determinant of selective-exposure behavior whose operation is often confounded with that of other determinants, such as the hedonic valence of material.

Curiosity and Its Satisfaction

Sears and Freedman (1967) stress the practical usefulness of much media content and simply propose that "the greater the perceived utility of the information, the greater will be the subject's desire to be exposed to it" (p. 210). Atkin (1985) characterizes this kind of selection motive as "guidance-oriented selective exposure"—in contrast to "reinforcement-oriented selective exposure" aimed at dispositional support. He also emphasizes the availability of guidance-providing information in fictional as well as nonfictional media content, essentially pointing to the likely confounding in exposure motivation of his two selective-exposure dimensions.

Berlyne (1954), in a theory of epistemic curiosity, has conceptualized informational utility more formally as the curiosity-satisfying quality of information. He proposes that individuals who are confronted with uncertainty about a phenomenon experience a state of arousal that stimulates them to seek information capable of explaining the phenomenon. The stirring experience of curiosity then would be diminished and removed by the attainment of partly or fully satisfactory explanations. Berlyne acknowledges that the information search might entail random elements, but also likens the information search to problem solving in a structured fashion.

Information seeking in pursuit of answers to salient questions is undoubtedly an essential part of selective-exposure behavior. Those interested in gardening, for instance, are bound to have a multitude of questions that entice them to tune in to gardening shows. Analogously, those who try their hand at gourmet cooking will turn to cookbooks; those who love to tinker with cars, to automotive magazines. Less obviously, the fashion-conscious may be drawn to movies that feature pageantry, and immature daters to sitcoms that dwell on dating among peers. As has been suggested often enough (e.g., Atkin, 1985; Mendelsohn, 1966), individuals may learn useful things from such media exposure. What remains entirely uncertain, however, is the degree to which epistemic curiosity and guidance orientation may contribute to the indicated exposure—and how much of this information seeking derives from alternative motives, hedonism in particular. For instance, cooking programs are routinely seen by expert cooks who learn little, if anything, from the programs, but take immense pleasure from watching familiar rituals.

It should also be mentioned that much exposure-driving curiosity may be unrelated to uncertainty that demands resolution in terms of relevant explanation. It has been suggested that curiosity is often directed at imaginary phenomena such as threats, unfamiliar entities, and macabre happenings that cannot be of consequence to the lives of the attracted persons (Beer, 1984; Zillmann, 1998). Deep-rooted agonistic vigilance, mostly devoid of direct utility, has been invoked to account for selective-exposure behavior of this kind. So-called morbid curiosity is an aspect of this information-seeking behavior without problem-solving quality (Haskins, 1984). However, although the indicated type of curiosity is capable of shedding light on the appeal of fictional horror and nonfictional terror, it remains again unclear to what extent it contributes to the overall selective-exposure motivation. A confounding with hedonism cannot be ruled out—because even witnessing exceedingly morbid behavior, such as the public execution of a mass murderer, may be satisfying and sought out for that effect.

TOWARD THE INTEGRATION OF ELEMENTS OF SELECTIVE-EXPOSURE MOTIVATION

Despite the discussed difficulties concerning attempts to partition confoundedly operating elements of selective-exposure motivation, distinct domains for the dominant operation of either curiosity and informational utility versus hedonism and mood management are apparent. Generally speaking, it can be posited that informational utility is the dominant choice determinant for informational and educational messages, but that it is a secondary and potentially negligible choice determinant for entertaining presentations. Hedonism, on the other hand, must be regarded the dominant choice determinant for entertaining media content, and informational utility should be a secondary consideration. The primary objects of entertainment choices are, after all, mood repair and the attainment and enhancement of desirable moods. Mood management thus should remain the central paradigm for choices in the realm of media entertainment. However, those who derive choice predictions from mood-management theory are well advised to consider circumstances under which the influence of informational utility is likely to intrude and, in extreme cases, to foster counterhedonistic choices. Likewise, those who base predictions on considerations of the informational utility of messages ought to recognize the existence of circumstances under which the influence of informational utility is likely to be supplemented and on occasion overpowered by the hedonistic appeal of presentations.

Any advancement of comprehensive theory of selective exposure to media content will have to address the discussed composition of choice-motivating forces and integrate them into predictive paradigms. It might be necessary at first to construct specific paradigms for the distinct domains of communication, such as entertainment, education, and the news. But ultimately it will have to be determined to which degree the various motivating factors influence the choice of media content generally, either in complementary, additive fashion or interactively.

REFERENCES

Adams, E. R., & McGuire, F. A. (1986). Is laughter the best medicine? A study of the effects of humor on perceived pain and affect. *Activities, Adaptation, and Aging, 8,* 157-175.

Anderson, D. R., Collins, P. A., Schmitt, K. L., & Jacobvitz, R. S. (1996). Stressful life events and television viewing. *Communication Research, 23,* 243-260.

Argyle, M. (1987). *The psychology of happiness.* London: Methuen.

Atkin, C. K. (1973). Instrumental utilities and information seeking. In P. Clarke (Ed.), *New models for mass communication research* (pp. 205-242). Beverly Hills, CA: Sage.

Atkin, C. K. (1985). Informational utility and selective exposure to entertainment media. In D. Zillmann & J. Bryant (Eds.), *Selective exposure to communication* (pp. 63-91). Hillsdale, NJ: Lawrence Erlbaum.

Beer, C. (1984). Fearful curiosity in animals. In J. A. Crook, J. B. Haskins, & P. G. Ashdown (Eds.), *Morbid curiosity and the mass media: Proceedings of a symposium* (pp. 51-77). Knoxville: University of Tennessee/Gannett Foundation.

Berlyne, D. E. (1954). A theory of human curiosity. *British Journal of Psychology, 45,* 180-191.

Biswas, R., Riffe, D., & Zillmann, D. (1994). Mood influence on the appeal of bad news. *Journalism Quarterly, 71,* 689-696.

Bleich, S., Zillmann, D., & Weaver, J. (1991). Enjoyment and consumption of defiant rock music as a function of adolescent rebelliousness. *Journal of Broadcasting & Electronic Media, 35,* 351-366.

Blumler, J. G., & Katz, E. (Eds.). (1974). *The uses of mass communications: Current perspectives on gratifications research.* Beverly Hills, CA: Sage.

Bryant, J., & Zillmann, D. (1977). The mediating effect of the intervention potential of communications on displaced aggressiveness and retaliatory behavior. In B. D. Ruben (Ed.), *Communication yearbook 1* (pp. 291-306). New Brunswick, NJ: Transaction.

Bryant, J., & Zillmann, D. (1984). Using television to alleviate boredom and stress: Selective exposure as a function of induced excitational states. *Journal of Broadcasting, 28,* 1-20.

Carlson, M., Charlin, V., & Miller, N. (1988). Positive mood and helping behavior: A test of six hypotheses. *Journal of Personality and Social Psychology, 55,* 211-229.

Christ, W. G., & Medoff, N. J. (1984). Affective state and selective exposure to and use of television. *Journal of Broadcasting, 28,* 51-63.

Clark, M. S., & Isen, A. M. (1982). Toward understanding the relationship between feeling states and social behavior. In A. Hastorf & A. M. Isen (Eds.), *Cognitive social psychology* (pp. 73-108). New York: Elsevier North-Holland.

Collins-Standley, T., Gan, S., Yu, H. J., & Zillmann, D. (1996). Choice of romantic, violent, and scary fairy-tale books by preschool girls and boys. *Child Study Journal, 26,* 279-302.

de Wied, M., Zillmann, D., & Ordman, V. (1994). The role of empathic distress in the enjoyment of cinematic tragedy. *Poetics, 23,* 91-106.

Eysenck, H., & Eysenck, M. (1985). *Personality and individual differences: A natural science approach.* New York: Plenum.

Fenigstein, A., & Heyduk, R. G. (1985). Thought and action as determinants of media exposure. In D. Zillmann & J. Bryant (Eds.), *Selective exposure to communication* (pp. 113-139). Hillsdale, NJ: Lawrence Erlbaum.

Festinger, L. (1954). A theory of social comparison processes. *Human Relations, 7,* 117-140.

Gibson, R., Aust, C. F., Hoffman, K., & Zillmann, D. (1995, November). *Implications of adolescent loneliness for the enjoyment of love-lamenting and love-celebrating popular music.* Paper presented at the annual meeting of the Speech Communication Association, San Antonio, TX.

Haig, R. A. (1988). *The anatomy of humor: Biopsychosocial and therapeutic perspectives.* Springfield, IL: Charles C Thomas.

Haskins, J. B. (1984). Morbid curiosity and the mass media: A synergistic relationship. In J. A. Crook, J. B. Haskins, & P. G. Ashdown (Eds.), *Morbid curiosity and the mass media: Proceedings of a symposium* (pp. 1-44). Knoxville: University of Tennessee/Gannett Foundation.

Helregel, B. K., & Weaver, J. B. (1989). Mood-management during pregnancy through selective exposure to television. *Journal of Broadcasting & Electronic Media, 33,* 15-33.

Hoffner, C., & Haefner, M. J. (1993). Children's affective responses to news coverage of the war. In B. S. Greenberg & W. Gantz (Eds.), *Desert Storm and the mass media* (pp. 364-380). Cresskill, NJ: Hampton.

Hoffner, C., & Haefner, M. J. (1994). Children's news interest during the Gulf War: The role of negative affect. *Journal of Broadcasting & Electronic Media, 38,* 193-204.

Lazarus, R. S. (1966). *Psychological stress and the coping process.* New York: McGraw-Hill.

Lazarus, R. S., & Folkman, S. (1987). Transactional theory and research on emotions and coping. *European Journal of Personality, 1*(3), 141-169.

Luecke-Aleksa, D., Anderson, D. R., Collins, P. A., & Schmitt, K. L. (1995). Gender constancy and television viewing. *Developmental Psychology, 31,* 773-780.

Mares, M.-L., & Cantor, J. (1992). Elderly viewers' responses to televised portrayals of old age. *Communication Research, 19,* 459-478.

Masters, J. C., Ford, M. E., & Arend, R. A. (1983). Children's strategies for controlling affective responses to aversive social experience. *Motivation and Emotion, 7,* 103-116.

McGuire, W. (1974). Psychological motives and communication gratification. In J. G. Blumler & E. Katz (Eds.), *The uses of mass communications: Current perspectives on gratifications research* (pp. 167-196). Beverly Hills, CA: Sage.

Meadowcroft, J. M., & Zillmann, D. (1987). Women's comedy preferences during the menstrual cycle. *Communication Research, 14,* 204-218.

Medoff, N. J. (1979). *The avoidance of comedy by persons in a negative affective state: A further study in selective exposure.* Unpublished doctoral dissertation, Indiana University.

Mendelsohn, H. (1966). *Mass entertainment.* New Haven, CT: College & University Press.

Miller, S. M. (1990). To see or not to see: Cognitive informational styles in the coping process. In M. Rosenbaum (Ed.), *Learned resourcefulness: On coping skills, self-control, and adaptive behavior* (pp. 95-126). New York: Springer.

Mills, J. (1993). The appeal of tragedy: An attitude interpretation. *Basic and Applied Social Psychology, 14,* 255-271.

Mischel, W., Cantor, N., & Feldman, S. (1996). Principles of self-regulation: The nature of willpower and self-control. In E. T. Higgins & A. W. Kruglanski (Eds.), *Social psychology: Handbook of basic principles* (pp. 329-360). New York: Guilford.

Morris, W. N., & Reilly, N. P. (1987). Toward the self-regulation of mood: Theory and research. *Motivation and Emotion, 11,* 215-249.

Oliver, M. B. (1993). Exploring the paradox of the enjoyment of sad films. *Human Communication Research, 19,* 315-342.

O'Neal, E. C., & Taylor, S. L. (1989). Status of the provoker, opportunity to retaliate, and interest in video violence. *Aggressive Behavior, 15,* 171-180.

Parrott, W. G. (1993). Beyond hedonism: Motives for inhibiting good moods and for maintaining bad moods. In D. M. Wegner & J. W. Pennebaker (Eds.), *Handbook of mental control* (pp. 278-305). Englewood Cliffs, NJ: Prentice Hall.

Postman, N. (1985). *Amusing ourselves to death: Public discourse in the age of show business.* New York: Viking.

Rayburn, J. D., II. (1996). Uses and gratifications. In M. B. Salwen & D. W. Stacks (Eds.), *An integrated approach to communication theory and research* (pp. 145-163). Mahwah, NJ: Lawrence Erlbaum.

Repetti, R. L. (1989). Effects of daily workload on subsequent behavior during marital interaction: The roles of social withdrawal and spouse support. *Journal of Personality and Social Psychology, 57,* 651-659.

Robinson, T. O., Weaver, J. B., & Zillmann, D. (1996). Exploring the relation between personality and the appreciation of rock music. *Psychological Reports, 78,* 259-269.

Rosenblatt, P. C., & Cunningham, M. R. (1976). Television watching and family tensions. *Journal of Marriage and the Family, 38,* 105-111.

Rosengren, K. E., Wenner, L. A., & Palmgreen, P. (Eds.). (1985). *Media gratifications research: Current perspectives* (pp. 61-72). Beverly Hills, CA: Sage.

Rubin, A. M. (1983). Television uses and gratifications: The interactions of viewing patterns and motivations. *Journal of Broadcasting, 27,* 37-51.

Russell, D., Peplau, L. A., & Cutrona, C. E. (1980). The revised UCLA Loneliness Scale: Concurrent and discriminant validity evidence. *Journal of Personality and Social Psychology, 39,* 472-480.

Salovey, P., Hsee, C. K., & Mayer, J. D. (1993). Emotional intelligence and the self-regulation of affect. In D. M. Wegner & J. W. Pennebaker (Eds.), *Handbook of mental control* (pp. 258-277). Englewood Cliffs, NJ: Prentice Hall.

Sapolsky, B. S., Stocking, S. H., & Zillmann, D. (1977). Immediate vs. delayed retaliation in male and female adults. *Psychological Reports, 40,* 197-198.

Sargent, S. L., Zillmann, D., & Weaver, J. B. (1998). The gender gap in the enjoyment of televised sports. *Journal of Sport and Social Issues, 22*(1), 46-64.

Scheier, M. F., & Carver, C. S. (1982). Cognition, affect, and self-regulation. In M. S. Clark & S. T. Fiske (Eds.), *Affect and cognition: The 17th Annual Carnegie Symposium on Cognition* (pp. 157-183). Hillsdale, NJ: Lawrence Erlbaum.

Schweitzer, K. J. (1993). *Enjoyment of romantic films as a function of empathetic tendencies and satisfaction with romantic life.* Unpublished doctoral dissertation, University of Alabama.

Sears, D. O., & Freedman, J. L. (1967). Selective exposure to information: A critical review. *Public Opinion Quarterly, 31,* 194-213.

Sparks, G. G., & Spirek, M. M. (1988). Individual differences in coping with stressful mass media: An activation-arousal view. *Human Communication Research, 15,* 195-216.

Stone, G., & Grusin, E. (1984). Network television as a bad news bearer. *Journalism Quarterly, 61,* 517-523.

Tamborini, R., Zillmann, D., & Bryant, J. (1984). Fear and victimization: Exposure to television and perceptions of crime and fear. In R. N. Bostrom (Ed.), *Communication yearbook 8* (pp. 492-513). Beverly Hills, CA: Sage.

van den Haag, E. (1960, Spring). A dissent from the consensual society. *Daedalus,* pp. 315-324.

Wakshlag, J. (1985). Selective exposure to educational television. In D. Zillmann & J. Bryant (Eds.), *Selective exposure to communication* (pp. 191-201). Hillsdale, NJ: Lawrence Erlbaum.

Wakshlag, J., Vial, V., & Tamborini, R. (1983). Selecting crime drama and apprehension about crime. *Human Communication Research, 10,* 227-242.

Weaver, J. B. (1991). Exploring the links between personality and media preferences. *Personality and Individual Differences, 12,* 1293-1299.

Weaver, J. B., Brosius, H. B., & Mundorf, N. (1993). Personality and movie preferences: A comparison of American and German audiences. *Personality and Individual Differences, 14,* 307-315.

Wells, A., & Hakanen, E. A. (1991). The emotional use of popular music by adolescents. *Journalism Quarterly, 68,* 445-454.

Wright, J. C., Kunkel, D., Pinon, M., & Huston, A. C. (1989). How children reacted to televised coverage of the space shuttle disaster. *Journal of Communication, 39*(2), 27-45.

Zillmann, D. (1983). Transfer of excitation in emotional behavior. In J. T. Cacioppo & R. E. Petty (Eds.), *Social psychophysiology: A sourcebook* (pp. 215-240). New York: Guilford.

Zillmann, D. (1985). The experimental exploration of gratifications from media entertainment. In K. E. Rosengren, L. A. Wenner, & P. Palmgreen (Eds.), *Media gratifications research: Current perspectives* (pp. 225-239). Beverly Hills, CA: Sage.

Zillmann, D. (1988a). Mood management through communication choices. *American Behavioral Scientist, 31,* 327-340.

Zillmann, D. (1988b). Mood Management: Using entertainment to full advantage. In L. Donohew, H. E. Sypher, & E. T. Higgins (Eds.), *Communication, social cognition, and affect* (pp. 147-171). Hillsdale, NJ: Lawrence Erlbaum.

Zillmann, D. (1995). Sports and the media. In J. Mester (Ed.), *Images of sport in the world* (pp. 423-444). Cologne: German Sport University.

Zillmann, D. (1996). Sequential dependencies in emotional experience and behavior. In R. D. Kavanaugh, B. Zimmerberg, & S. Fein (Eds.), *Emotion: Interdisciplinary perspectives* (pp. 243-272). Mahwah, NJ: Lawrence Erlbaum.

Zillmann, D. (1998). The psychology of the appeal of portrayals of violence. In J. H. Goldstein (Ed.), *Why we watch: The attractions of violent entertainment* (pp. 179-211). New York: Oxford University Press.

Zillmann, D., & Bryant, J. (Eds.). (1985). *Selective exposure to communication.* Hillsdale, NJ: Lawrence Erlbaum.

Zillmann, D., & Bryant, J. (1986). Shifting preferences in pornography consumption. *Communication Research, 13,* 560-578.

Zillmann, D., & Bryant, J. (1997). Fernsehen. In B. Strauss (Ed.), *Zuschauer* (pp. 123-169). Göttingen, Germany: Hogrefe.

Zillmann, D., de Wied, M., King-Jablonski, C., & Jenzowsky, S. (1996). Drama-induced affect and pain sensitivity. *Psychosomatic Medicine, 58,* 333-341.

Zillmann, D., & Gan, S. (1997). Musical taste in adolescence. In D. J. Hargreaves & A. C. North (Eds.), *The social psychology of music* (pp. 161-187). Oxford: Oxford University Press.

Zillmann, D., Rockwell, S., Schweitzer, K., & Sundar, S. S. (1993). Does humor facilitate coping with physical discomfort? *Motivation and Emotion, 17,* 1-21.

Zillmann, D., Schweitzer, K. J., & Mundorf, N. (1994). Menstrual cycle variation of women's interest in erotica. *Archives of Sexual Behavior, 23,* 579-597.

Zillmann, D., & Wakshlag, J. (1985). Fear of victimization and the appeal of crime drama. In D. Zillmann & J. Bryant (Eds.), *Selective exposure to communication* (pp. 141-156). Hillsdale, NJ: Lawrence Erlbaum.

CHAPTER CONTENTS

4 Resistance to Interpersonal Requests: A Summary and Critique of Recent Research

DANETTE E. IFERT
West Virginia Wesleyan College

This chapter examines existing research on interpersonal influence by focusing on competing tensions between compliance with and resistance to interpersonal requests. Scholarship on compliance-resistance taxonomies, emotional responses to requests, and the role of obstacles in requesting, resistance, and responding is reviewed within the context of four theoretical perspectives: resource theory, politeness theory, attribution theory, and constructivism. The concluding section presents future research directions for compliance resistance in general and each of the four theoretical perspectives discussed.

W HEN individuals seek resources from others, compliance is assumed to be the expected outcome. Foa and Foa's (1972) resource theory supports this assumption by contending that people engage in interpersonal interactions with the goal of exchanging resources. Brown and Levinson's (1987) work on politeness presumes that refusal of a request is one of several speech acts that is inherently face threatening, and thus is likely to be an unwanted communicative response. The fact that individuals most often target intimates to fulfill requests (Rule, Bisanz, & Kohn, 1985; Shapiro, 1980) also suggests that people enter into request interactions with the expectation that their desired outcomes will be realized.

Despite a requester's desire and, often, presumption that compliance will be forthcoming, resistance does occur. Since McLaughlin, Cody, and Robey's (1980) initial study of compliance-resistance strategies, scholarship on resistance in interpersonal request situations has grown dramatically. My purpose in this review is to bring together the somewhat disconnected studies on compliance resistance

---

Correspondence: Danette E. Ifert, Department of Communication, West Virginia Wesleyan College, Buckhannon, WV 26201; e-mail ifert@wvwc.edu

Communication Yearbook 23, pp. 125-161

and to derive conclusions about the present state and future development of research on refusals of interpersonal requests. The following three sections are devoted to discussion of the importance of this research area, the scope of the present review, and the conceptual framework that guides this chapter.

IMPORTANCE OF THE RESEARCH AREA

The study of resistance in request interactions is important for several reasons. First, the development of research in the area has been piecemeal and, like the literature on compliance gaining (Kellermann & Cole, 1994), can be criticized for lacking a coherent theoretical base. The present review is intended to enable scholars to integrate research on resistance to requests and offers an explanatory framework to aid in our understanding of how and why people refuse the requests of others. Second, a large body of research exists that has not been reviewed previously; the review offered here will provide a useful tool both for those interested in studying refusals of requests and for those who simply wish an overview of the research area.

Third, refusals as responses to requests violate what conversation analysts have identified as a preference for agreement (Nofsinger, 1991). For instance, accounts are required when individuals refuse requests or engage in other unexpected behaviors (Read, 1992; Saeki & O'Keefe, 1994). Refusing a request often exposes the refuser to the requester's disdain, disappointment, or further persuasion attempts (Ifert & Roloff, 1996; Roloff & Janiszewski, 1989). That individuals do resist despite pressures to the contrary makes compliance resistance a phenomenon of interest.

Finally, understanding interpersonal compliance-resistance processes has very practical applications, as initial requests do not always result in compliance (Seibold, Cantrill, & Meyers, 1985, 1994). Becker (1982) found that children fail to comply with as many as 50% of peer requests. Ervin-Tripp, Guo, and Lampert (1990) found that children are successful in gaining compliance in an initial attempt only 37-51% of the time and that children often persist after refusal. Resistance to others' requests also influences interpersonal interaction patterns in classrooms (Burroughs, Kearney, & Plax, 1989), organizations (Roloff & Jordan, 1992) and intimate relationships (Roloff, Janiszewski, McGrath, Burns, & Manrai, 1988). Further, refusals are used positively to resist socially unacceptable behaviors such as smoking (Reardon, Sussman, & Flay, 1989) and drug or alcohol use (Alberts, Miller-Rassulo, & Hecht, 1991; Harrington, 1997; Hecht, Trost, Bator, & MacKinnon, 1997). From this research, it is clear that individuals often resist compliance attempts, so efforts to understand these interaction processes better may provide persons with methods of either overcoming opposition to their conversational requests or sustaining resistance when they wish to reject the solicitations of others. Although a wide variety of research could potentially be included in a review of compliance-resistance and compliance interactions, the present review is necessarily limited in order to facilitate understanding of the topics reviewed. The next section delineates the scope of this review.

SCOPE OF THE REVIEW

Although compliance-gaining attempts are typically precursors of compliance-resistance behaviors, this review focuses on how and why people resist influence attempts. Compliance gaining is discussed only in terms of how requesters attempt to overcome specific sources of resistance in formulating requests and how individuals respond to resistance. Such a limited focus is merited for at least two reasons. First, several comprehensive reviews of compliance-gaining research already exist (see Seibold et al., 1985, 1994; Wheeless, Barraclough, & Stewart, 1983). Context-specific reviews have also been published for areas such as influence within organizational settings (Barry & Watson, 1996) and responding to unwanted requests for sexual interaction (Edgar & Fitzpatrick, 1990; Metts & Spitzberg, 1996). As organizational influence and unwanted requests for sexual interaction have been the subject of recent comprehensive reviews, they are not included in the present chapter. Second, at a practical level, including both the compliance-gaining and compliance-resistance literatures in a single review would be unwieldy given the large number of studies published in both areas.

This review is also limited to influence appeals within interpersonal situations and does not include influence attempts aimed at mass audiences. Although mass messages are becoming more personalized, it remains rather difficult and expensive to tailor compliance-seeking or -resisting messages to individual audience members within a large group. Further, literature focusing on interpersonal influence assumes that, for the most part, a fairly intimate relationship exists between requester and request target (Rule et al., 1985; Shapiro, 1980). Interpersonal influence scholars also typically presuppose that maintenance or continuation of the relationship is an important constraint in the determination of what general strategies to enact and how to express messages (e.g., Besson, Roloff, & Paulson, 1998; Dillard, Segrin, & Harden, 1989; Kline & Floyd, 1990; Roloff et al., 1988). Saeki and O'Keefe (1994) assert that Brown and Levinson's (1987) politeness theory, a theoretical framework undergirding several compliance-resistance studies, assumes that interactants desire to continue relationships with request partners.

The importance of understanding influence attempts within interpersonal relationships is further elucidated by Alberts et al. (1991), who found from interviewing respondents in their teens and early 20s that drug offers from strangers were rare and were successfully refused, whereas half of all reported drug offers from friends were accepted. Alberts et al. observed that offers from friends accounted for 82% of all accepted drug offers, showing that focusing on resistance in interpersonal settings can have significant consequences. In attempts to influence mass audiences, individual interpersonal relationships are generally not as developed and maintenance thereof may not be as important as it is in the interpersonal settings examined in the literature reviewed here.

Only direct agent appeals are investigated within the scope of this review. Although researchers have examined situations in which compliance agents may be acting on behalf of organizations or other individuals (e.g., Saeki & O'Keefe, 1994), the research reviewed here emphasizes situations in which an individual makes a request on his or her own behalf and the influence attempt is resisted by another individual. Although interactions where a requester is acting on behalf of an organization are relatively common occurrences (e.g., sales interactions, requests to donate time or money to a cause), there may be additional group dynamics present in those interactions that are not significant factors in requests that an individual makes of another individual. Indeed, Besson et al. (1998) suggest that refusers who are expressing the desire of a group or organization may successfully diffuse responsibility for rejection, thereby distancing themselves from the refusal.

This review also concentrates on cognition and verbal behaviors to the exclusion of nonverbal behaviors. Although nonverbal messages are potentially important to interpersonal influence interactions (and will be discussed later, in the section on future directions for influence research), nonverbal cues simply have not been studied by those interested in compliance resistance, and thus data for such a review are unavailable.

The following section outlines the conceptual framework that undergirds this chapter and describes four theoretical perspectives utilized in existing compliance-resistance scholarship: resource theory, politeness theory, attribution theory, and constructivism.

CONCEPTUAL FRAMEWORK

Interpersonal influence interactions consist largely of two competing forces for request targets: forces for compliance and forces urging resistance. A primary force motivating individuals to comply with the requests of others is relational obligation (Roloff, 1987), as requesters most often seek out intimates as request targets (Rule et al., 1985; Shapiro, 1980). These request targets may explicitly recognize the obligation an individual has to assist an intimate (LaGaipa, 1977; Roloff et al., 1988) or may simply wish to maintain a fulfilling relationship. Kline and Floyd (1990) allude to these pressures for compliance when they write, "Effective refusals should not make the requester upset or angry but rather should preserve a desired relationship with the requester" (p. 455).

At the same time, obstacles to compliance represent the primary force motivating people to resist requests from others, as they reflect an individual's unwillingness or inability to comply with another's request. Obstacles to compliance have been defined as perceived barriers that cause request targets to resist compliance (Ifert & Roloff, 1998). Negotiating the tension between the competing forces of compliance and resistance becomes the central concern of the refuser. Refusers may negotiate this tension by withholding information about relevant obstacles (Folkes, 1982; Ifert & Roloff, 1994) or by engaging in politeness (Baxter, 1984; Ifert & Roloff, 1997; Lim & Bowers, 1991). Although this area has not yet been fully investigated by interpersonal influence researchers, it is also possible that refusers attempt to negotiate the tension between compliance and resistance by using deception (Burroughs et al., 1989), avoidance (Alberts et al., 1991; Burroughs et al., 1989; Kuczynski & Kochanska, 1990), and incompetent performance of a requested act.

The goal of requesters, by contrast, is to swing the balance toward compliance. Requesters have achieved this goal by engaging in persistence (Ifert & Roloff, 1996; Roloff et al., 1988; Roloff & Janiszewski, 1989; Wilson, Cruz, Marshall, & Rao, 1993) and by constructing specific messages designed to overcome obstacles (Ifert & Bearden, 1997; Ifert & Roloff, 1996). Requesters can use these strategies to elicit compliance in their construction of initial requests or in their continuing to seek compliance after initial resistance.

Several theoretical perspectives guiding existing scholarship in compliance resistance are concerned with varying aspects of this push-pull relationship between compliance and resistance. Four such theoretical perspectives are outlined below: resource theory, politeness theory, attribution theory, and constructivism. The summary of each theory is followed by discussion of an exemplar of compliance-resistance research grounded in that theoretical perspective.

Resource Theory

Foa and Foa's (1972) resource theory, a version of social exchange theory, provides one means of examining compliance resistance. Foa and Foa assert that interpersonal interactions are based on the exchange of resources such that individuals procure desired resources and give away resources that they possess in excess. Resources exchanged include love, status, information, goods, money, and services, and these resources vary in the degree to which they are concrete and the degree to which their sources are important. The appropriateness of the resources to be exchanged varies by situation. For example, it is typically inappropriate for an individual to respond to an offer of friendship with an offer of money. Foa and Foa arrange resources in a circular pattern: love-status-information-money-goods-services. They argue that resources are most readily exchanged for other resources that fall next to them in the circle and are less readily exchanged for resources positioned across the circle.

Roloff and Janiszewski (1989) apply Foa and Foa's (1972) resource theory to compliance resistance by suggesting that request interactions necessarily impose upon the request target, who either loses rewards directly or loses alternative opportunities to use resources. Different types of requests (e.g., borrowing an item with the expectation of returning it versus providing a service via a favor) entail different costs (e.g., time, energy, lost opportunities to use resources) and should therefore lead to varying request and resistance strategies. Indeed, Roloff and Janiszewski found differences between the kinds of messages college student respondents reported constructing to respond to borrowing requests and the messages they used to reject favor requests.

From the perspective of resource theory, negotiating the tension between compliance and resistance is a matter of costs and rewards for both requesters and request targets. Individuals will resist requests when the resources offered are of inappropriate type or when the costs associated with obtaining desired resources are high. Desires for compliance are present, however, because individuals seek to increase the resources, particularly scarce resources, they possess. Requests could be rewarding for both interactants, because at the same time a requester might gain access to goods or services, a request target could increase his or her status or enjoy relational rewards from the requester.

Politeness Theory

Brown and Levinson (1978, 1987) extend earlier work of Erving Goffman by proposing that politeness in language is governed by the desire to maintain "face." Assuming that persons are rational beings (meaning that they choose means that they perceive will lead to ends they seek to achieve), Brown and Levinson (1987) propose that persons possess positive and negative face; it is in the best interest of both interactants to uphold their own and their partner's face wants. They define positive face as "the positive consistent self-image or 'personality' (crucially including the desire that this self-image be appreciated and approved of) claimed by interactants" and negative face as "the basic claim to territories, personal preserves, rights to non-distraction—i.e. to freedom of action and freedom from imposition" (Brown & Levinson, 1987, p. 61).

Certain acts inherently present face threats (Brown & Levinson, 1987; Dillard & Kinney, 1994), such as requests, disagreements, challenges, and noncooperation in an activity. A person wishing to perform a face-threatening act has five alternative courses of action: performing the act without redress, performing the act while attending to positive face wants, performing the act and attending to negative face wants, performing the act "off record," and deciding not to perform the act. The choice of one of these methods is determined by the weight of the face threat posed, and Brown and Levinson (1987) assume that these courses of action, in the order listed, represent recognition of an increasingly greater face threat.

In applying politeness theory to request situations, Lim (1990) found that positive and negative face wants are often addressed in the same messages, meaning that both types of face threat can occur simultaneously (see Craig, Tracey, & Spisak, 1986). This finding is in contrast to Brown and Levinson's (1987) contention that positive and negative face should be examined separately. Lim and Bowers (1991) go further and suggest that Brown and Levinson focus on acts threatening negative face almost to the exclusion of acts that threaten positive face. Positive face, according to Lim and Bowers, is actually composed of two parts: a need to be included by others (fellowship face) and a need for one's abilities to be respected (competence face). These face needs are distinct such that positive face threats can be redressed only through positive politeness and negative face threats can be redressed only using negative politeness.

Face concerns represent a pull toward compliance (particularly in terms of fellowship and competence face) as well as a push away from compliance (in terms of the autonomy needs associated with negative face). As requesters seek compliance from targets most likely to possess the ability and willingness to comply (Rule et al., 1985; Shapiro, 1980), a target's expressed unwillingness to help a requester can threaten fellowship face. The target acknowledging inability to comply threatens the target's competence face needs because the requester expects the target to possess the necessary skills or resources to comply; otherwise, the requester would not have made the request. Concurrently, a request target's own desires for resource use (i.e., autonomy) work against compliance. The tension between these two forces is especially important if one agrees with Lim's (1990) assertion that positive and negative face concerns are present simultaneously, instead of separately, as Brown and Levinson (1987) have proposed. Interactants in influence situations thus are faced with the task of meeting needs for inclusion and competence while maintaining personal autonomy.

Attribution Theory

Weiner's (1972) attribution theory attempts to explain the causes for individuals' behavior. According to this theory, there are four antecedent conditions that may influence whether and to what degree of success a behavior is performed: effort, ability, task difficulty, and luck. Observers use situational cues and knowledge of these four antecedent conditions to determine which factors cause particular behaviors. Each of these antecedent conditions can be evaluated according to whether it reflects an internal or external locus of control and a high or low level of stability. For example, an individual's effort is seen as an internally controllable condition that can be relatively unstable over time. Conversely, task difficulty is seen as an external phenomenon (and therefore less controllable by the individual performing the action) that is likely to remain stable over time. Ability is inferred to be internally controlled but stable, whereas luck is viewed as externally controlled and unstable.

Within the compliance-resistance literature, Weiner's perspective has been applied to identification of the types of resistance messages that may be expressed in a request situation. Folkes (1982), using self-reports of college students, found that females rejecting date requests were more likely to express obstacles due to external forces and were more likely to suppress obstacles that reflected stable conditions personally associated with the requester (e.g., the requester is physically unattractive). In fact, impersonal obstacles represented nearly all of the *expressed* reasons for date rejection but accounted for only about half of all *unexpressed* reasons for rejection.

Within an attributional framework, the stress between compliance and resistance manifests itself in the causes assigned to behavior and subsequent perceptions of behavior by others. Take, for example, the case of a person who has an internal locus of control and who thus takes personal responsibility for the outcomes of his or her behavior. For an individual with an internal locus of control, admitting that external forces prevent his or her compliance may be damaging to self-concept. This would seem to be particularly true if the reason for resistance is stable (e.g., task difficulty) as opposed to unstable. In such a situation, compliance might represent the individual's faith in his or her own ability and/or effort to complete a task, whereas resistance might indicate the individual's lack of confidence in his or her ability and/or effort.

Constructivism

Constructivism is another theoretical perspective that has guided research in compliance resistance. Delia, O'Keefe, and O'Keefe (1982) assert that constructivism is an interpretative approach to communication whereby communication is a means of creating and reshaping reality. According to this perspective, biological and sociocultural factors work together to influence individuals' interpretations of events. Scholars in this tradition "hope to explain the ways in which social and situational factors and processes of development shape the cognitive processes of the individual and make possible the organization, control, and coordination of behavior" (Delia et al., 1982, p. 154). Interaction shapes a person's constructs, or mental representations of ideas, people, and events. Individual constructs are linked together to create construct systems, which enable people to assign meaning to both familiar and unfamiliar situations.

Although some constructivist research has focused on defining the nature of interpersonal construct systems (e.g., Hale & Delia, 1976), of greater relevance to students of compliance resistance is research examining the relationship between construct systems and strategic message choices during interaction. For example, O'Keefe and Delia (1979) found that the number of persuasive arguments generated is related to construct differentiation (i.e., the levels of distinction an individual can perceive among related constructs) and that level of justification used is influenced by construct abstractness. O'Keefe and Shepherd (1987) suggest that highly cognitively complex individuals use strategies that indicate recognition of and attempts to achieve multiple goals.

Given the idea presented above that compliance resistance involves competing forces for and against compliance, O'Keefe and Shepherd's (1987) research implies that highly cognitively complex individuals may be more adept than less-complex individuals at negotiating compliance-resistance interactions. The forces for and against compliance, then, must be interpreted through the individual's construct system. Highly differentiated individuals may be able to recognize and integrate the concerns of self and others, whereas less-differentiated individuals may be forced to resort to separating desires for resistance from compulsions to comply (O'Keefe & Delia, 1982).

The sections that follow present a review of the existing research on compliance resistance in interpersonal contexts, beginning with scholarship on the strategies used to resist compliance.

STRATEGIES USED TO RESIST COMPLIANCE

Like research on compliance gaining, early research on compliance resistance centered on the development of strategy lists or taxonomies. Each of the variety of classification schemes developed by researchers focuses on how individuals organize resistance messages, and the authors of these taxonomies assume that their classification schemes are related to the messages people enact during compliance resistance (Delia et al., 1982).

McLaughlin et al. (1980) describe the link between compliance gaining and compliance resisting as follows: "Strategies to resist compliance-gaining attempts may themselves be construed as compliance-gaining messages in which the 'target,' acting as an 'agent,' seeks to surmount various problems raised by her/his reluctance to comply" (p. 15). McLaughlin et al. provide a deductively based classification of resistance strategies based upon earlier work by Fitzpatrick and Winke (1979). Overt, straightforward statements of refusal to comply are classified as *nonnegotiation* messages, whereas manipulations of the identity of the target and/or agent constitute *identity-managing* strategies. *Justifying* strategies are defined as those statements in which targets explain that positive or negative outcomes will result from their fulfilling or refusing the request, and *negotiation* strategies occur when targets suggest alternative courses of action to those initially proposed by the requesters. McLaughlin et al.'s final category, *emotional appeal,* encompasses statements appealing to the affect of the requester (e.g., pleading). Results of this study, in which a sample of 230 college students responded to stimulus scenarios, indicated that the interaction of intimacy, relational consequences, and perceived right to resist the request predicted reported use of identity managing, justifying, negotiation, and nonnegotiation strategies; no significant relationship was found between the interaction of the predictor variables and the use of emotional appeals.

The McLaughlin et al. (1980) taxonomy has been revised and used by other researchers seeking to explain how individuals resist compliance. O'Hair, Cody, and O'Hair (1991) deleted McLaughlin et al.'s emotional appeal category, folding it into identity management, and divided identity management into two categories: positive identity management and negative identity management. O'Hair et al. discovered that message construction and strategy selection methodologies resulted in similar reports of negotiation, justifying, and positive identity strategies and speculated that selectionist methodologies may lead to underreporting of negatively valenced strategies. McQuillen, Higginbotham, and Cummings (1984) used the categories of negotiation, nonnegotiation, justifying, and identity managing in their study of developmental differences in the use of compliance-resistance strategies. After interviewing 118 children from first-, fourth-, and tenth-grade classes and asking them to respond to a variety of compliance scenarios, McQuillen et al. concluded that children use more justifying and identity managing and fewer nonnegotiation strategies as they get older and that the type of request (e.g., simple direct, incentive-based) and request agent (e.g., parent, sibling) influences the types of resistance strategies used.

Additional taxonomies have been developed for specific contexts. Burroughs et al. (1989) identified 19 strategies used by college students to resist influence attempts by teachers within classroom settings (see Table 4.1 for a list of these categories and their definitions). College students were provided with pro- or antisocial compliance-gaining messages from immediate or nonimmediate instructors and were asked to respond; responses to open-ended questions about how students would reply to the compliance-gaining message formed the basis for the 19 resistance strategies identified. The strategies include active and passive, constructive and destructive, and teacher-centered and student-centered behaviors. Teacher immediacy and type of compliance-gaining message were related to the reported frequency of use for resistance strategies.

Alberts et al. (1991) investigated adolescents' acceptance or refusal of drug offers and, based on interviews of 33 community college and high school students in their teens and early 20s, developed a four-category taxonomy of refusal strategies. Open-ended responses from the interviewees were coded into categories by two investigators. *Simple no* included situations in which the target refused the offer without additional explanation; *no with an explanation* included an explanation for refusal. *Deception* occurred when the refuser provided untrue reasons for refusal or pretended to engage in the requested behavior, and *leave* transpired when the refuser walked out on the situation. Hecht, Alberts, and Miller-Rassulo (1992) identified four resistance strategies college students reported using to refuse drug or alcohol offers: simple no, suggest alternative, statement of no desire, and statement of dislike. They found that the most frequently reported resistance strategies were statement of dislike and simple no. Harrington (1995) used focus groups and videotaped experimental interactions to develop a taxonomy of alcohol-resistance strategies with four categories: direct refusal, alternative, excuse, and explanation. Although the Alberts et al. (1991) taxonomy includes indirect strategies such as deception and leave, these studies by Alberts et al., Hecht et al., and Harrington are highly consistent in their inclusion of other strategy types.

Working with 2- and 3-year-olds and investigating the development of resistance strategies in children, Kuczynski, Kochanska, Radke-Yarrow, and Girnius-Brown (1987) identified four common resistance strategies derived from previous research: direct defiance, simple refusal, negotiation, and passive noncompliance. *Direct defiance* included poorly controlled anger and was assumed to be aversive to a requesting parent, and thus was classified as an unskillful strategy.

TABLE 4.1
Compliance-Resistance Categories Identified by Burroughs et al. (1989)

---

1. *Teacher advice:* Student offers advice or opinions to the teacher regarding ways to alter teacher behavior.

2. *Teacher blame:* Student criticizes or otherwise places blame on the teacher.

3. *Avoidance:* Student works to escape the notice of the teacher or otherwise evade the teacher.

4. *Reluctant compliance:* Student complies with the teacher's request but does not wish to do so. A student enacting this strategy is unlikely to confront the teacher directly but may harbor resentment toward the instructor and/or the course.

5. *Active resistance:* Student overtly refuses to comply with the teacher's request.

6. *Deception:* Student creates an illusion of compliance but is not really complying.

7. *Direct communication:* Student confronts the teacher directly with an explanation of noncompliance.

8. *Disruption:* Student interferes with the class and/or the teacher.

9. *Excuses:* Student provides self-oriented explanation for noncompliance.

10. *Ignoring the request:* Student behaves as though the request had not been made.

11. *Priorities:* Student explains noncompliance by noting that other priorities are more important.

12. *Challenge the basis of power:* Student confronts or questions the teacher's power in the class.

13. *Rally support:* Student attempts to gain the support of other students for resistance.

14. *Appeal to powerful others:* Student appeals to others who may have control or power over the teacher.

15. *Modeling behavior:* Student imitates teacher behavior.

16. *Modeling affect:* Student imitates teacher's affect or degree of involvement with the class.

17. *Hostile defensive:* Student makes aggressive statements that directly communicate noncompliance.

18. *Rebuttal:* Student refutes teacher's request using supporting evidence or reasoning.

19. *Revenge:* Student engages in overt, destructive response aimed at the teacher.

Passive noncompliance was defined as a nonresponse to a parental request, and *simple refusal* and *negotiation* were defined similarly to congruent categories in the typologies mentioned above. Using an observational method involving mothers and their 2- to 3-year-old children interacting in naturalistic laboratory settings, Kuczynski et al. found that simple refusal and negotiation were used more frequently by older children than by younger children, whereas use of passive noncompliance and direct defiance was less frequent in older than in younger children. Subsequent work by Kuczynski and Kochanska (1990) added excuses, bargains, and whining (defined as pleading tone of voice) to the typology of resistance strategies. Kuczynski and Kochanska observed the same children who participated in the Kuczynski et al. study at age 5 and found that use of passive noncompliance continued to decrease with age, that children who used unskillful forms of resistance (passive noncompliance and direct defiance) at an earlier age were likely to engage in similar strategies at age 5, and that children who used negotiation at ages

2 and 3 were more likely to use negotiation or bargaining at age 5. It should be noted that a child's resistance to parental requests is not necessarily construed as negative; in fact, use of skillful resistance strategies is viewed as a positive means of asserting the child's independence and autonomy (Kuczynski & Kochanska, 1990; Kuczynski et al., 1987). The findings that children use different resistance strategies at different developmental levels is further supported by the work of Lee, Levine, and Cambra (1997), who studied 420 fourth through eighth graders in Hawaii and found a positive relationship between age and students' reported likelihood of use of refusals (open expressions of unwillingness to comply) and comparisons (which included references to other teachers or students) in response to teacher requests for compliance. Plax, Kearney, Downs, and Stewart (1986) likewise focused on developmental differences in resistance strategies; they found that adult learners are more likely to use passive resistance strategies (e.g., avoidance, missing class, nonparticipation) than are students in elementary and secondary classrooms.

Although many typologies have been developed for specific contexts (Alberts et al., 1991; Burroughs et al., 1989; Harrington, 1995; Hecht et al., 1992; Kuczynski & Kochanska, 1990; Kuczynski et al., 1987), whereas the McLaughlin et al. (1980) taxonomy is designed to apply across settings, a number of similarities exist among the classification schemes. Several categories occur in more than one taxonomy, including deception (Alberts et al., 1991; Burroughs et al., 1989), withdrawal from the situation (Alberts et al., 1991; Burroughs et al., 1989), explanation (Alberts et al., 1991; Harrington, 1995; Hecht et al., 1992; McLaughlin et al., 1980), proposal of an alternative (Harrington, 1995; Hecht et al., 1992; Kuczynski & Kochanska, 1990; McLaughlin et al., 1980) and direct statement of no (Alberts et al., 1991; Burroughs et al., 1989; Harrington, 1995; Hecht et al., 1992; Kuczynski et al., 1987; McLaughlin et al., 1980).

These taxonomies also reflect the tension between compliance and resistance, as a number of specific strategies identified (e.g., McLaughlin et al.'s [1980] justifying; O'Hair et al.'s [1991] positive identity management; Alberts et al.'s [1991] no with explanation; Harrington's [1995] alternative) reflect the target's concern for own or partner's face needs. Providing an explanation or alternative may be one means of negotiating the tension between a sense of obligation to comply and a desire to resist. This idea is supported by findings that as children become older, they engage in more strategies that account for parents' face needs (such as negotiation and bargain) and fewer directly face-threatening strategies (such as passive noncompliance and direct defiance; Kuczynski & Kochanska, 1990; Kuczynski et al., 1987). Such an explanation is consistent with the constructivist notion that as individuals become more cognitively complex, they can more successfully manage complex interaction situations.

Differences also exist among the typologies, such as Burroughs et al.'s (1989) inclusion of nonverbal as well as verbal resistance behaviors. Some of the specific nonverbal resistance techniques identified include sitting in the back of the room as an avoidance technique and leaving the text at home as a technique of active resistance. Burroughs et al.'s inclusion of nonverbal strategies recognizes a heretofore unexamined aspect of resistance measures. It is uncertain, however, whether the nonverbal tactics that Burroughs et al. identify constitute an exhaustive list, whether nonverbal strategies may be context specific, or whether the tactics included are among the most common nonverbal resistance methods used.

A second difference among the taxonomies developed by Alberts et al. (1991), Burroughs et al. (1989), Harrington (1995), Hecht et al. (1992), Kuczynski and Kochanska (1990), and McLaughlin et al. (1980) is that the McLaughlin et al. classification scheme seems to include only prosocial strategies and omits the more negatively valenced strategies—such as deception, direct defiance, disruption, and hostile defensiveness—found in Alberts et al.'s, Burroughs et al.'s, and Kuczynski and Kochanska's typologies. Although McLaughlin et al. note less positive tactics as possible methods of enacting particular strategies (e.g., threat as a method of nonnegotiation), negative resistance methods are absent from their strategy definitions. Perhaps one reason for this difference is that McLaughlin et al. developed their strategy definitions deductively based upon the work of Fitzpatrick and Winke (1979), rather than by using inductively derived taxonomies, as did Alberts et al. and Burroughs et al. This explanation is consistent with O'Hair et al.'s (1991) suggestion that methodologies in which respondent reports are placed into preselected categories may be biased against the reporting of negative strategies. It should be noted that although the Harrington (1995) taxonomy also apparently ignores antisocial resistance strategies, that study did differentiate between instances of each strategy that accounted for the face needs of the requester and those that did not. Thus Harrington included in the analysis face-threatening acts that may be perceived as antisocial.

Whereas McLaughlin et al.'s (1980) typology tends toward overreliance on prosocial strategies, Burroughs et al.'s (1989) scheme seems to include a high number of negatively valenced strategies. One explanation is methodological, as McLaughlin et al. derived their taxonomy from existing literature, whereas Burroughs et al. allowed respondents to construct replies to influence situations and used those replies as the basis for developing taxonomic categories. A second possible explanation is that the Burroughs et al. typology is based upon a teacher-student relationship. It could be that such relationships are viewed, at least by the student respondents, as relatively short-term, even though they may be ongoing for a period of a semester or a year. The Alberts et al. (1991) and McLaughlin et al. taxonomies, by contrast, are based on reports of interactions within friendships and romantic relationships, which might reasonably be expected to last longer than teacher-student relationships. Similarly, although the Harrington (1995) and Hecht et al. (1992) taxonomies were not developed with highly intimate relationships in mind, they are based upon reports and observations of peer relationships, wherein the possibility of long-term relationships is more salient than in teacher-student relationships. The expectation of longer-term or more intimate relationships with peers, compared to relationships with teachers, may require greater attention to the competing forces of compliance and resistance and, as a result, more positively oriented strategies may be appropriate. By contrast, the short-term and relatively less intimate relationships expected between students and teachers may not lead the individuals involved to be especially concerned about the tension between compliance and resistance or to use a broad range of both positively and negatively valenced strategies, as there is not a strong relational bond to push a request target toward assent.

Evaluation of resistance strategies as positive or negative may also differ due to individualized cultural expectations. Kim, Shin, and Cai (1998) investigated requesting and re-requesting strategies selected by individuals who tended toward independence or interdependence. They define *independents* as individuals who are primarily concerned with maintaining a unique self and remaining true to that self, whereas *interdependents* are more concerned with the relationship between self and others and how self fits into the larger social system. Using a sample that included respondents from Korea, Hawaii, and the mainland United States, Kim et al. found that interdependent individuals reported they would be more likely to use hinting strategies, whereas independents reported greater likelihood of use for direct strategies; these findings held for both initial and second requests. Kim et al. also found that independents rated two of three request strategies as effective in initial requests, whereas interdependents rated two of the three strategies as effective in second requests. The researchers speculate from these results that independents may be open to a variety of strategies in approaching a request interaction and then narrow their strategies choices after refusal. Conversely, interdependents may enter a request situation with a relatively narrow list of possible strategies and may expand that list of strategies after refusal. Thus it remains clear that evaluation of strategies and use of specific resistance strategies may vary according to a number of individual, relational, and contextual factors.

Early research has identified several potential classification schemes for compliance-resistance strategies. While yielding insight into how people resist, these strategy lists also raise issues common in the compliance-gaining literature, including the relative validity of message construction and strategy selection methodologies and of deductively versus inductively derived classification schemes (Kellermann & Cole, 1994). Additionally, as is the case in the compliance-gaining literature or indeed any attempt to develop a typology of behaviors, finding a single, exhaustive classification of strategies is virtually impossible (Barry & Watson, 1996; Burgoon, 1994; Kellermann & Cole, 1994), particularly given Kellermann and Cole's (1994) observation that strategy lists are often developed at differing levels of abstraction, making integration difficult. Nevertheless, the taxonomies of compliance-resistance strategies summarized above provide a critical starting point for researchers interested in the ways people resist influence attempts.

One important strength of the research on compliance-resistance taxonomies is the focus on the messages themselves, which is sometimes overlooked in interpersonal influence research. As McQuillen et al. (1984) observe, "Targets do not resist situations; they resist specific compliance-gaining appeals generated within the context of specific situations" (p. 750). Several of the studies described above, including those by Burroughs et al. (1989) and McQuillen et al., provided influence targets with stimulus request statements upon which to base their responses. This recognition that compliance resistance occurs within situations and in response to specific messages has been an important underlying assumption for more recent research. The focus on individual messages of resistance and the interaction between a request and subsequent responses has also led, in part, to a scholarly shift from the strategies people use to refuse requests to the reasons underlying resistance. The next two sections address research areas concerned with reasons for resistance: emotional responses and specific obstacles that prevent compliance with a request.

EMOTIONAL RESPONSES
TO INFLUENCE ATTEMPTS

Recent work by Dillard and colleagues has focused on emotional responses associated with resistance (Dillard & Kinney, 1994; Dillard, Kinney, & Cruz, 1996). These investigations have been based in appraisal theories, which focus on how individual processing of stimuli determines emotions. If individuals perceive environmental events, they assess the degree of harm or benefit arising from the stimulus. If they deem the stimulus to be consistent with their goals or desires, positive emotion results; if they find the stimulus to be incongruent with their goals, negative emotion results (Dillard & Kinney, 1994). Dillard and Kinney (1994) tested models of emotional responses to requests based upon the explicitness and dominance of the request; this investigation utilized both self-reported and physiologically assessed (heart rate and skin conductance) measures of emotional response. Participants listened to audiotaped request scenarios and imagined themselves as influence targets before completing response measures. Although no consistent relationship was found between the predicted mediating variables, politeness and goal blockage, and emotional response, relationships were found between a third mediating variable, request legitimacy, and reports of surprise and anger. Dominance was negatively related to perceptions of politeness and request legitimacy and was positively related to perceptions of goal blockage.

In later work, Dillard et al. (1996) examined a larger range of cognitive appraisals that individuals might make about requests and found that valence (perceived pleasantness/unpleasantness), relevance (significance for individual's plans or activities), obstacle (extent to which request interferes with ongoing goals or plans), and legitimacy (degree to which stimulus is judged fair or equitable) were consistently related to emotional response across two studies using influence goals of gaining assistance and giving advice. The procedures used in this study were similar to those used by Dillard and Kinney (1994) except that respondents viewed videotaped request scenario materials instead of listening to audiotapes. As in the previous research, Dillard et al. (1996) found a positive relationship between message dominance and perceptions that the request constituted an obstacle and a negative relationship between perceptions of request legitimacy and dominance.

In contrast to other research reviewed here, emotional responses to requests do not necessarily require direct processing of the tension between compliance and resistance. Instead, how forces for compliance and resistance are resolved depends on the emotional responses generated by request statements. Thus a highly dominant message may be labeled by a request target as an illegitimate request and may result in an emotional response of anger. In such a case, resistance is more likely than compliance; in cases of extremely angry reactions, little if any inclination is likely to be shown toward compliance. Conversely, if the same dominant message is perceived by the target as legitimate, anger may be absent and the likelihood of compliance greater. Thus the individual's emotional response determines how he or she will balance pressures for compliance and resistance.

Although this line of research helps to elucidate the cognitive processes of those engaged in influence interactions and includes the often overlooked variable of emotional response, it has not yet addressed the effect of emotional responses on subsequent linguistic moves. For example, how do the linguistic responses to influence attempts differ when the emotional response is anger as opposed to surprise? This would seem to be a key question for understanding the relationship between emotional response and compliance or resistance. Research on the emotional responses to influence attempts may also be linked to nonverbal responses, an area that has been virtually ignored in previous research on compliance resistance (Dillard et al., 1996).

A second area of research that attempts to explain why people resist compliance focuses on obstacles preventing compliance. The following sections address the nature of obstacles and how obstacles influence the progression of influence interactions.

OBSTACLES PREVENTING COMPLIANCE

In order for individuals to enact compliance-resistance strategies or, indeed, for resistance to occur, there must exist some barrier or obstacle impeding compliance. Identifying obstacles to compliance is a necessary step for requesters in the creation of arguments and the achievement of influence goals (Clark & Delia,

1979). O'Keefe and Delia (1982) assert that the complexity of creating a request increases when persons anticipate obstacles preventing goal achievement; in a later article, they order persuasive messages hierarchically by the degree to which obstacles are "recognized and reconciled in messages" (O'Keefe & Delia, 1985, p. 69). The obstacle hypothesis goes even further by suggesting that message sources create requests that conquer the most likely source of resistance, or obstacle (Francik & Clark, 1985). Roloff and Jordan (1992) extend the importance of obstacles to the negotiation context by asserting that negotiation plans are composed of goals, obstacles to attaining those goals, and methods of overcoming obstacles. All of these scholars recognize the significance of obstacles in interpersonal request interactions. Whereas early attempts to define taxonomies of compliance-resistance strategies attempted to describe *how* individuals resisted requests, research on obstacles has focused on *why* people resist and how those obstacles influence the progression of influence interactions.

Classifying Obstacles

Before we can understand exactly how obstacles work in influencing the discourse of resistance, it is important that we determine what obstacles may exist. A number of researchers have attempted to define the types of obstacles that may impede compliance, and at least three taxonomies of obstacles have been proposed (Gibbs, 1987; Ifert & Roloff, 1994; Schwartz, 1992). Francik and Clark (1985) assert that two preconditions exist for compliance: willingness and ability. It would seem that failure to obtain either could constitute an obstacle to compliance. Common obstacles reflect an addressee's willingness, ability, and/or availability to comply (Gibbs, 1986).

Gibbs (1987) has presented six categories of obstacles derived from his earlier work on request forms (Gibbs, 1981). He identifies *possession* obstacles as those in which the request target does not have the resources or information requested and *permission* obstacles as those in which the request target is unable to give permission for the request to be fulfilled. *Ability* obstacles occur when a requestee does not have the capacity to comply. *State-of-the-world* obstacles transpire when the request target does not comprehend that a state of affairs in the world requires compliance, and *want/desire* obstacles indicate a failure by the requestee to recognize the requester's needs. Gibbs's final category is *imposition* obstacles, which include instances where a request target has prior commitments or is already engaging in activities that would preclude compliance.

A second taxonomy has been developed by Schwartz (1992), who has attempted to identify reasons friends refuse requests. Schwartz asked 69 college-age respondents to recall and describe situations in which they resisted or wished to resist complying with the request of a friend; their descriptions were subsequently used as the basis for a category scheme for obstacles. The 10 obstacles Schwartz defines are as follows: harmful for self/possessions, act is too costly, competing commitment, principle against, bad for other, other's prior actions violated trust, illegal/immoral, unreasonable request or expectation, third party, and self prefers not to.

Ifert and Roloff (1994) developed a seven-category typology derived in part from the work of Gibbs (1987); the obstacles in this taxonomy are possession, inadequate resources, imposition, inappropriate, no incentive, source responsibility, and recalcitrance. College-age volunteers were asked to respond to hypothetical interactions with a friend in two scenarios: borrowing class notes and requesting a favor of typing a paper. Participants' responses to these scenarios were coded into categories based initially on the work of Gibbs (1987); additional categories were created to account for statements that did not fit into Gibbs's categories. In the Ifert and Roloff typology, possession and imposition obstacles are defined in the same way as in Gibbs's work. Inadequate resources obstacles are defined as a speaker's indication that the requested resources are of poor quality, and inappropriate obstacles indicate that the request violates a rule or is otherwise improper. No incentive obstacles are defined as those for which there is no external motive to grant the request, and source responsibility obstacles show that the requester is obliged to take care of the request him- or herself. Recalcitrance obstacles indicate that the refuser simply does not wish to comply with the request.

Several similarities exist among the three category schemes described above. For example, Gibbs (1987) and Ifert and Roloff (1994) both identify a category called imposition, and Schwartz (1992) lists a category called competing commitment that is defined in a way roughly corresponding to imposition. Likewise, Schwartz's category called prefer not to and Ifert and Roloff's category of recalcitrance both focus on the desire of the requestee not to comply. These similarities and others among the schemes suggest that these taxonomies represent obstacles to compliance to some extent. However, as Table 4.2 illustrates, there appears to be substantial overlap between the Ifert and Roloff taxonomy and those of Gibbs and Schwartz, whereas there is little overlap between the Gibbs and Schwartz taxonomies.

An interesting point of difference among these three typologies is that Gibbs's categories are defined in a way that assumes the request target would assist the requester if he or she possessed the requisite skills or resources or understanding needed for compliance. Ifert and Roloff's and Schwartz's taxonomies do not seem to agree with this assumption, as each contains categories in which the obstacle is the result of something the requester has done (e.g., prior trust violation, inappropriate, source responsibility) or a decision made by a request target who is fully aware of the need for compliance (e.g., illegal/immoral, principle against, recalcitrance). The view of the rejecter presented by these two later typologies, then, is one of a person who can *choose* not to comply rather than of a person who refuses only because he or she lacks resources or understanding of the situation. Such an assumption is consistent with the idea that influence interactions involve competing forces for compliance and resistance, as it recognizes the potential for resistance even if a compliance target is capable of fulfilling a request.

Although these early attempts at classifying obstacles provide a basis for more recent work on conceptualizing the obstacle construct, these three classification schemes are largely based in theoretical speculation and provide limited evidence that people in actual conversations consider or even recognize the existence of such obstacles. Gibbs's (1987) taxonomy was derived from request forms in a prior study (Gibbs, 1981); Schwartz's (1992) categories were inductively derived from reports of refusals. Ifert and Roloff (1994) submitted exemplars of three obstacle categories (inadequate resources, imposition, and recalcitrance) to independent judges to see if exemplars from the same categories would be placed together. Results of this sorting task supported the categories identified, but only seven judges were used and only three of the seven categories in the classification scheme were tested in this manner.

All three of these attempts to identify obstacle categories share limitations aside from representational validity. The generalizability of these three typologies is restricted because Schwartz (1992) examined only obstacles occurring within friendships and Ifert and Roloff (1994) considered only obstacles between intimate and nonintimate peers. None of these attempts investigated obstacles preventing compliance within romantic relationships or in relationships such as service or employment encounters, where status differences may exist between requester and requestee. As taxonomies, each of these three classification schemes also fails to consider the possibility that obstacles may be multifaceted. Instead, obstacles are assumed to fit into discrete categories without consideration of the prospect that some obstacles may contain elements of more than one category.

Three more recent efforts at classifying obstacles improve upon the taxonomies discussed above by addressing representational validity concerns and by acknowledging the possibility that obstacles may be multifaceted. More important, all three attempt to provide theoretical frameworks to support obstacle types or dimensions. This marks a move away from seemingly random lists of strategies and toward meeting the challenge issued by those who have cited interpersonal influence research (Kellermann & Cole, 1994) and communication research in general (Berger, 1991) as being atheoretical. All three efforts—by Folkes (1982), Ifert and Roloff (1998), and Wilson et al. (1993)—use attributional frameworks to conceptualize obstacles.

Wilson et al. (1993) examined how obstacles vary on stability, locus (internal or external), and controllability in order to determine how obstacles influence subsequent discourse production. They selected obstacle exemplars from a pool of statements generated by respondents and asked another group of respondents to rate the exemplars on locus, controllability, and stability. These obstacle exemplars were used by confederates to refuse requesters in a subsequent study, in which requesters were asked to rate refusals on each of the three dimensions. Thus these researchers used two different groups of raters to assess the obstacle exemplars and found a high degree of correspondence in ratings of locus, controllability, and stability within and between the groups.

TABLE 4.2
Comparison of Obstacle Types

Gibbs (1987)	Schwartz (1992)	Ifert & Roloff (1994)
Possession		Possession
Permission		
Ability		Inadequate resources
State of the world		
Want/desire		
Imposition	Act is too costly; competing commitment	Imposition
	Harmful for self/possessions	
	Principle against; illegality/immorality	Inappropriate
	Unreasonable request	No incentive
	Bad for other; third party	
	Other's prior actions violated trust	
	Self prefers not to	Recalcitrance
		Source responsibility

Folkes (1982) classified date refusals according to their stability, controllability, and locus (personal or impersonal) and found that some types of obstacles are more commonly expressed than others. Ten independent judges from the same population as participants in Folkes's two studies rated obstacles to determine their placement on the three dimensions, so there is some support for the validity of the coded obstacles reported by Folkes.

Most recently, Ifert and Roloff (1998) used an attributional framework to suggest dimensions that might underlie various obstacle categories. First, 21 obstacle exemplars were generated from a group of statements identified in a pilot study. These exemplar statements were then presented to 130 individuals, who sorted the exemplars into groups. The results of the sorting task were subjected to cluster analysis, and support was found for the existence of six categories: possession, imposition, recalcitrance, inappropriateness (which combined the earlier categories of source responsibility and inappropriateness; Ifert & Roloff, 1994), no incentive, and postpone. Second, analysis of ratings of the obstacle exemplars by the same 130 individuals suggests that obstacle categories may vary along three dimensions: willingness-unwillingness, ability-inability, and focus on-focus away from requester. These three dimensions are grounded in attribution theory, as ability and willingness reflect two of Weiner's (1972) antecedent conditions for behavior: ability and effort. The focus on-focus away from requester dimension, the weakest dimension identified by Ifert and Roloff (1998), reflects the internality idea described by Weiner and used in research by Wilson et al. (1993) and Folkes (1982).

The studies by Folkes (1982), Ifert and Roloff (1998), and Wilson et al. (1993) noted above therefore provide evidence that the obstacle classification schemes generated by researchers are similar to evaluations of obstacles by naive participants. These studies also suggest that individual obstacles may vary along more than one conceptual dimension. Most important, however, these three studies represent attempts to find a theoretical basis, attribution theory, for obstacle classification schemes. Theoretical grounding is important because it can provide a means of both describing the characteristics of obstacles and ascertaining how persons respond to various barriers in request interactions. The following section addresses how individuals manage different types of obstacles in requests and refusals and how individuals respond to various expressed obstacles.

ADDRESSING OBSTACLES
IN REQUEST INTERACTIONS

Obstacles influence the progression of request interactions even before they are stated in refusals. Research has investigated how obstacles affect message construction during initial requests (Francik & Clark, 1985; Gibbs & Mueller, 1988), refusals (Folkes, 1982; Ifert & Roloff, 1994), and responses to refusals (Ifert & Roloff, 1996; Roloff & Janiszewski, 1989; Wilson et al., 1993).

Obstacles and Initial Requests

Scholarship on obstacles and requests has focused on the effects that obstacles have on how individuals construct requests and on evaluations of requests that take or fail to take obstacles into account. Delia, Kline, and Burleson (1979) have observed that requesters are able to deal in their initial requests with potential objections others might have by enacting advanced persuasive strategies. As Francik and Clark (1985) state more explicitly in their obstacle hypothesis, the obstacles that individuals expect to encounter influence how those individuals form requests. Francik and Clark conclude that persons deal with obstacles during the request phase in three ways: by designing indirect requests to overcome specific obstacles, by using general requests to overcome more general obstacles, or by approaching sensitive obstacles by indirectly testing out particular situations. One function of prerequests is to identify obstacles that may prevent compliance (Gibbs & Mueller, 1988; Jacobs & Jackson, 1983). For example, "Do you have a watch?" may serve to identify a potential obstacle to a subsequent request for the time, or "Did you see the Orioles' score from last night?" may help to determine whether a request target might reasonably be expected to possess desired information. Anticipated obstacles also influence the length of requests; Roloff et al. (1988) found that requesters created more elaborated messages only when they anticipated noncompliance or noncompliance had occurred.

Requests that address obstacles are evaluated favorably. Specifying obstacles within requests "allows speakers to ingratiate themselves with their listeners" (Gibbs, 1987, p. 187), presumably because specifying obstacles shows that the requesters have taken the targets' needs into consideration. People remember indirect requests that do not specify the obstacle present more than they remember indirect requests that do (Gibbs, 1987). This finding led Gibbs (1987) to conclude that requests that address obstacles are more conventional than those that do not. Gibbs further speculates that indirect requests are conventional because people have learned to associate particular obstacles with request situations.

Researchers have also investigated the perceived politeness with which various obstacles are stated in requests. Ervin-Tripp et al. (1990) discovered that requests addressing potential obstacles to compliance "are polite and reflect formal norms" (p. 316). Paulson and Roloff (1997) assert that the form and content of the request influence the way it is refused, so that requests that address unwillingness obstacles are perceived as more polite than those that address inability. Also, Paulson and Roloff found that requests incorporating specific obstacles were viewed as more polite than ambiguous requests. Presumably, requests that provide information about requesters' anticipated obstacles give guidance to refusers about potentially legitimate refusal forms. By formulating the request to allude to specific obstacles, the requester is, in effect, legitimating certain types of refusals while delegitimating others. These findings are consistent with Gibbs's (1986) assertion that mentioning conventional or socially appropriate but inactive obstacles allows speakers to ingratiate themselves with listeners.

Thus individuals take obstacles into account when forming initial requests (Francik & Clark, 1985), by creating prerequests (Francik & Clark, 1985; Gibbs & Mueller, 1988; Jacobs & Jackson, 1983) or by enacting elaborated request messages (Roloff et al., 1988). Addressing obstacles within a request also leads requesters to be perceived as polite (Ervin-Tripp et al., 1990; Paulson & Roloff, 1997) and may allow a requester to ingratiate him- or herself with a request target (Gibbs, 1987). From this scholarship, we may conclude that one way for a requester to address conflicting forces for and against compliance is to use the request form itself or prerequests to convey concern for an interaction partner, or, in cases where compliance would be difficult or impossible, the requester might avoid making the request altogether. This type of approach may invoke reciprocity norms such that, because the requester has taken into account potential concerns of the request target, the target has some obligation to comply. In this manner, requesters make resistance more difficult and shift the balance of pressure toward compliance.

Despite the insights provided by existing research, scholarship on the role of obstacles in formulating requests has failed to address at least two important issues. First, researchers have seemed to assume for the most part that requesters are equally sensitive to obstacles and are able to adapt requests to address obstacles. Interpersonal influence research has shown that there are differences in the types of persuasive strategies used by individuals of differing ages (Clark & Delia, 1976; Delia & Clark, 1977; Kuczynski & Kochanska, 1990; McQuillen et al., 1984), and research on communication competence among adults reflects the fact that not all individuals possess equal levels of knowledge or skill (Spitzberg, 1994). Kline and Floyd (1990) applied a constructivist framework to examine refusal content and found that cognitively differentiated individuals produced refusals that considered the other person's perspective and were more complex than refusals created by less cognitively differentiated individuals. Researchers have not, however, fully researched cognitive or other differences that might influence how well a person can anticipate and/or adapt requests to the presence of obstacles. Second, although existing research has addressed such issues as request comprehension (Francik & Clark, 1985; Gibbs, 1987) and politeness (Ervin-Tripp et al., 1990; Paulson & Roloff, 1997), it has not assessed whether requests that address obstacles are more successful in forestalling resistance than requests that do not. Given that the ultimate goal of any request, from the requester's viewpoint, is compliance, knowing whether and when consideration of obstacles leads to greater compliance is a fundamental question for influence scholars.

Obstacles and Refusals

Although obstacles may influence creation and perception of requests, they exert perhaps their greatest influence in request interactions by the way they are stated by targets in refusals. Research indicates that some obstacles are more likely to be stated than others during refusals. Folkes (1982), for example, notes a discrepancy between publicly stated and privately held reasons for refusing date requests. She found that the reasons publicly stated for refusal tended to be impersonal, uncontrollable, and unstable. Among those rejecting dates, however, Folkes found that 90% of stated obstacles were unstable, compared with 53% of unstated obstacles; 9% of stated obstacles were classified as personal and stable, but 40% of unstated obstacles were personal and stable. Ifert and Roloff (1994) found that inability obstacles are more frequently expressed than are unwillingness obstacles. Further, Ifert and Roloff found that as intimacy increases, a greater number of inability obstacles than unwillingness obstacles are expected to be present; this relationship did not hold, however, for obstacles actually expressed within the discourse of refusals. The results of these studies by Folkes and by Ifert and Roloff provide support for an attributional approach toward obstacles by contributing evidence that although obstacles that reflect personally on the requester or that reflect a refuser's lack of desire to comply may present barriers to compliance, such obstacles are not always stated in refusal messages. These findings also tie into politeness theory, as personally reflective obstacles, especially stable ones, might also be expected to threaten competence face. Stating and concealing obstacles, viewed from either theoretical perspective, also illustrate how individuals manage the competing desires to resist and pressures to comply. Refusers may thus express reasons for noncompliance or may, in fact, comply with requests, but the actual reasons for refusal may remain unexpressed.

Although existing research on expression and suppression of obstacles lends insight into refusal construction, important questions remain to be answered. One of these involves how requesters respond to obstacles that are unstated but that are likely to be preventing compliance. How, for example, does a date requester respond if the refuser's dislike of the requester is suspected but is not the stated reason for refusal? Ifert and Roloff (1994) have mentioned this problem as a direction for continuing research, but scholars have not pursued the issue. A related issue concerns the refuser's response when stated obstacles are overcome by a requester but unstated reasons for noncompliance remain. The refuser may be forced to comply because the stated obstacle has been conquered, even though reasons for noncompliance still exist. Continuing with the dating example, a requester might successfully thwart an obstacle of "I have another obligation" by suggesting an alternative time or activity. The refuser is then faced with pressure to comply even if unstated reasons for noncompliance still exist. Alternatively, the refuser may elect to resist by stating additional obstacles and thereby risk threats to the requester's (e.g., by expressing obstacles that reflect personal characteristics of the requester) or the refuser's (e.g., by admitting that the initially expressed obstacles were not the real barriers to compliance and thus acknowledging deception) face needs.

Research has shown that certain types of obstacles are more likely to be expressed in refusals, whereas others, even when present, may remain unexpressed. Those obstacles that are expressed can influence subsequent conversational moves by both requester and refuser. The next subsection summarizes the research on responses to obstacles.

Responses to Obstacles

Obstacles stated in both requests and refusals can affect the way influence interactions proceed by affecting the linguistic content of responses to refusal. Roloff and Janiszewski (1989) found that when respondents were provided with request scenarios and given an opportunity to express how they would respond, responses to refusals of borrowing requests included more forgiving statements and more continued persuasion statements as intimacy increased, whereas in favor situations, greater intimacy was associated with additional clauses explaining the need for compliance. Refusals of favor requests also generated more forgiving responses in intimate than in nonintimate relationships. Roloff et al. (1988) found that refusals from intimates evoked less forgiving and more attempts at further persuasion, as intimacy was positively related to persuasion and negatively associated with forgiveness. DeTurck (1985) observed that requesters relied more on negative persuasion strategies after refusal than during an initial request. Examining requests to consume alcohol, Harrington (1997) found that direct refusals resulted

in more simple offers as follow-up persistence strategies, whereas refusals including excuses prompted minimization of negative consequences by the requester.

Negotiating the tension between pressures to comply and desires to refuse has
been addressed in terms of refusal politeness in response to general obstacles.
Besson et al. (1998) note, "When turning down a date, a refusal must be clear and
persuasive enough so as to terminate the influence attempt but must also be sufficiently face sensitive so as not to offend the requester" (p. 186); these researchers
found that females rejecting date requests reported responding with face-support-
ing messages, including counteroffers, expressions of future interest, apologies,
and expressions of appreciation for the request. Even refusers who did not desire
further interaction with their requesters included apologies, statements of appreciation, and concerns for the requesters' feelings with their direct refusals.

The type of obstacle expressed has also been found to influence subsequent discourse. Wilson et al. (1993) used an experimental model in which 50 undergraduates telephoned confederates who had ostensibly failed to fulfill a research commitment. Confederates gave one of several preselected refusal types and the
undergraduate participants attempted to persuade the confederates to fulfill their
obligations. Results showed that unstable obstacles led to greater persistence and
denials of the validity of the obstacle than did stable obstacles. Requesters also
failed to address the obstacle directly when it was internal, controllable, and stable
as opposed to external, uncontrollable, and unstable. Ifert and Roloff (1996), using
hypothetical request scenarios, found that requesters reported being more persistent when facing unwillingness than inability obstacles and that unwillingness
obstacles prompted less forgiving, more inquiries, and more attempts at further
persuasion. This finding is consistent with an attributional perspective, as ability
obstacles are likely to represent more stable barriers than unwillingness obstacles,
and thus requesters may not expend the effort to overcome stable and potentially
unconquerable obstacles. This also ties into politeness theory, as persisting in the
face of inability obstacles challenges the competence face of the refuser. Obstacles
also influence the rational or emotional content of responses to refusal, with
inability obstacles prompting more rational than emotional responses (Ifert &
Bearden, 1997). Metts, Cupach, and Imahori (1992) found that sexual rejection
messages indicating that the refuser was not ready to engage in sexual activity
were less face threatening and more comfortable than messages specifying that the
refuser was not sexually attracted to the requester. The content of the rejection
messages also influenced the requester's expectations of the possibility of future
sexual activity.

The studies noted above thus show that responses to refusals are affected by
both the type of request situation and the type of obstacle stated in refusal. The
reluctance of requesters to attack internal, stable, and controllable obstacles (Wilson et al., 1993) and the greater effort expended to respond to unwillingness compared with inability obstacles (Ifert & Roloff, 1996) indicate that concerns aside
from influence, such as relational development or identity management (Dillard et

al., 1989), may be important to influence interactions. From the research reviewed above, it seems that refusers may mitigate these often competing goals by deciding whether to persist and by selecting linguistic responses that not only take into account their own desire to resist but also acknowledge, at least indirectly, the pressures urging compliance. Continuing research on responses to refusals can further examine the impact of multiple or competing goals on the composition of response messages.

Researchers investigating resistance to interpersonal requests have examined how people go about defying others' influence attempts by identifying the strategies used to resist compliance in general (McLaughlin et al., 1980) and specific (Alberts et al., 1991; Burroughs et al., 1989; Kuczynski et al., 1987) contexts. Emotional responses to requests have also been investigated (Dillard & Kinney, 1994; Dillard et al., 1996) and may provide an explanatory framework for future research examining how emotional responses influence subsequent moves in influence interactions. Scholars have also cataloged the obstacles determining why individuals resist (Gibbs, 1987; Ifert & Roloff, 1998; Schwartz, 1992; Wilson et al., 1993) and have described some of the ways in which obstacles can influence request production (Francik & Clark, 1985; Gibbs & Mueller, 1988), refusal statements (Besson et al., 1998; Folkes, 1982; Ifert & Roloff, 1994), and responses to refusals (Roloff & Janiszewski, 1989; Wilson et al., 1993). Although researchers have provided useful information about interpersonal influence processes, additional questions remain to be answered by those interested in compliance resistance. In the next section, I propose several potentially fruitful directions for future research.

DIRECTIONS FOR FUTURE RESEARCH

Given the present state of compliance-resistance research, several directions may be useful for continuing inquiries into refusals. In this section I first discuss some general directions for researchers interested in negotiating the tension between compliance and resistance and then address some specific directions for research from each of the four theoretical perspectives discussed throughout this chapter: resource theory, politeness theory, attribution theory, and constructivism.

General Directions

Researchers have largely ignored the success of resistance efforts. Although substantial energy has been expended, for example, to identify the types of obstacles that may prevent compliance and to determine how requesters respond to such obstacles, little research has addressed whether particular types of obstacles are more difficult to surmount than others or are more likely to result in disengagement by a requester. Although Folkes (1982) has suggested that some obstacles remain unexpressed because they might threaten the face needs of one or both interactants, it is also possible that some obstacles are stated or unstated because they may be more successful in ending the interaction and lessening persistence by the requester.

Second, scholars should investigate the implications of resistance, especially continuing or repeated resistance, on relationship development. Lewis and Gallois (1984) found that refusing friends were perceived to have lower social skills and were more hurtful than refusing strangers. Resistance may legitimately be viewed as a source of conflict in a relationship, and thus relational partners may elect to deal with resistance in several ways. Resistance may lead to increasing verbal aggression, as suggested by deTurck's (1985) finding that compliance-gaining strategies become more punishment oriented as resistance continues and Ifert and Long's (1990) finding that manipulation and threat are used more often in attempts to gain compliance after initial and repeated refusals. Verbal aggression has been linked to physical abuse, embarrassment, and other forms of relational damage (Infante, Trebing, Shepherd, & Seeds, 1984). Research exploring the role that stating or withholding specific obstacles plays in defusing verbal aggression or investigating more positive techniques for responding to refusals could have positive implications for interpersonal relationships. Emotional responses to influence attempts (Dillard & Kinney, 1994; Dillard et al., 1996) might also be relevant to our understanding of what kinds of refusals are more or less likely to lead to verbal or physical aggression.

Beyond simple verbal aggression, in their work examining parental responses to child noncompliance in abusive and nonabusive parent-child relationships, Oldershaw, Walters, and Hall (1986) found that children of abusive mothers were significantly more noncompliant (53% noncompliance in a laboratory study) than were children of nonabusive mothers (22% noncompliance). Further, abusive mothers responded to noncompliance with more power-assertive control strategies, more negative affect, and no positive affect when compared with nonabusive mothers. Although Oldershaw et al. note that the use of negative strategies by abusive mothers may be a result of their interacting with difficult children, it is clear that the communication strategies used by parents and even young children can contribute to negative outcomes. Although training a small child to engage in positive strategies may be rather difficult, continuing research could certainly examine how parents could be instructed in effective compliance techniques and responses to children's refusals to comply. The benefits of such instruction may be long-term, as Kochanska (1997) speculates that a positively valenced, reciprocal relationship between parent and child may be useful for negotiating the child's need for autonomy and the parent's need for compliance, both with young children and with older adolescents.

Moreover, development of a child's competent interaction behaviors is hindered by ineffective role models. Oldershaw et al. (1986) observe that abusive mothers

COMMUNICATION YEARBOOK 23

respond to child compliance with negative messages nearly as often as they respond with positive messages. Given such inconsistent reinforcement patterns, it is not surprising that children of abusive mothers are more noncompliant than their peers with nonabusive mothers. In a follow-up to their earlier studies, Kuczynski and Kochanska (1995) discovered that oppositional, noncompliant children (defined in this study as children using passive noncompliance and direct defiance strategies) received fewer proactive demands, fewer requests to assist in their own physical care, and "fewer pressures for competent behavior" (p. 625) than did their nonoppositional peers. Thus noncompliant children not only have ineffective role models but are given fewer opportunities to engage in competent interpersonal behaviors, and thus are less likely to develop effective strategies for engaging in relationships with others.

Ongoing resistance to a request may also result in the development of taboo topics that are off-limits for discussion within a relationship (Baxter & Wilmot, 1985). Existing research on taboo topics indicates that subjects are often declared taboo in relationships because discussion of those topics may cause relational damage or because relational partners have determined that the other will not change his or her mind (Baxter & Wilmot, 1985; Roloff & Cloven, 1994). Roloff and Ifert (1998) found that long-standing disagreements between dating partners were associated with explicit agreements to declare a topic taboo and with reported frequency of both symbolic and physical aggression. Processes of request resistance and persistence may have serious long-term relational consequences.

A third promising area of inquiry for those interested in pursuing compliance resistance involves the role that nonverbal behaviors play in refusals. As noted above, requesters may respond differently to refusals phrased in more or less polite ways. Similarly, the nonverbal cues—particularly vocalic, facial, and kinesic cues—that accompany verbal messages can influence subsequent responses to refusals. If, for example, a refuser says to a cat-sitting request, "I'd be uncomfortable doing it because I'm not really a cat person" while conveying hostile nonverbals, the reaction of the requester and the success of the refusal might be different from those in a situation where the refuser conveys more empathic nonverbal cues. Refusals may also occur without any explicit verbal messages, as suggested by Burroughs et al.'s (1989) resistance strategy of avoidance, Alberts et al.'s (1991) leaving strategy, and Kim et al.'s (1998) silence strategy. Other than limited mention in taxonomies such as those noted above, nonverbal resistance methods have been largely ignored by communication scholars. McQuillen et al. (1984) note that compliance resistance occurs within situations and in response to specific verbal messages; it would also seem that compliance-resistance messages occur within specific nonverbal contexts and that nonverbal messages may influence how resistance is enacted and perceived. In striking the sometimes delicate balance between compliance and resistance, it may be that individuals use nonverbal cues of empathy and support in conjunction with more direct verbal messages to negotiate both resistance and relational goals successfully.

Finally, scholars may want to examine forms of resistance other than refusals. Although refusal may be the most common form of compliance resistance, there may be situations in which role expectations or status differences between requester and refuser preclude overt refusal of requests but where resistance still exists. It is plausible that resistance may take other forms, including, but certainly not limited to, nonverbal messages (Burroughs et al., 1989), procrastination, noncompliance with other tasks (Trethewey, 1997), and incompetent performance of the requested behavior. Kuczynski and Kochanska's (1990) passive resistance strategy, in which a person simply ignores a request, has likewise been disregarded by researchers outside the context of small children and their parents. Kim et al. (1998) call for further examination of silence as a request strategy; it would seem that silence may also form a basis of resistance and should be investigated more fully as such. These resistance forms, particularly procrastination and incompetent performance, may be even more effective in thwarting future requests than direct, overt refusal. Alternative forms of resistance have not received attention from compliance-resistance scholars, but such acts, which can occur during or after the request interaction, are methods of resistance that can influence the success of current and future influence interactions.

Directions Grounded in Resource Theory

Although the ideas of resource exchange and costs have been included in the conceptual framework of compliance resistance, resistance researchers have largely ignored the relationships among resources outlined by Foa and Foa (1972). Appropriate resources for exchange vary by situation, and adjoining resources in a circular arrangement (love-status-information-money-goods-services) are more appropriately exchanged than are resources positioned across the circle from each other. Continuing scholarship on resistance might examine whether resistance is often the result of an inappropriate exchange request and whether offering an alternative exchange of appropriate resources could be a means of overcoming resistance. For example, if one requests a favor from a friend by offering to exchange money for services, offense and rejection may occur. Perhaps this rejection could be thwarted by an alternative resource offer of love or status. Overcoming obstacles, from this perspective, would simply be a matter of facilitating the exchange of appropriate resources instead of inappropriate ones.

Continuing research might also explore the nature of costs to compliance. Although obstacles, as barriers preventing compliance, are costs in a sense, researchers might also examine competing costs, such as relational damage, missed alternative opportunities, and loss of autonomy, to see how costs and rewards interact to promote and sustain or to overcome resistance. To continue with the above example, a friend who requests a favor for services in exchange for increased affection (a seemingly appropriate exchange of resources) might be thwarted by costs such as lost autonomy or the potential loss of other relationships.

Investigation of this type of research question would provide additional insight into how individuals negotiate the tensions between acquiescence and refusal.

Directions Grounded in Politeness Theory

A question related to the success of various obstacles noted previously is the way in which obstacles are expressed. Politeness has been examined in compliance-gaining research (Baxter, 1984), but it would seem that particular obstacles could be expressed more or less politely and that the level of politeness might influence a refusal's success. For example, a person unwilling to comply with a request to take care of a friend's cat might say, "I despise cats and don't want to do it" or "I'd be uncomfortable doing it because I'm not really a cat person." The second would generally be considered a more polite response, and continuing research could address the relative success of such messages both in terms of maintaining relationships and in terms of successful resistance. Such an approach is consistent with that advocated by Besson et al. (1998). Harrington (1995) found that requesters who received face-supportive resistance messages rated refusers as more attractive and expressed greater satisfaction with their relationships with the refusers than did those who did not receive face-supportive messages. Even more interesting to examine are those situations in which less polite refusals are more successful, as might be the case with extremely persistent or other specific types of requesters or requests.

Researchers might also investigate how obstacles that are often unexpressed (e.g., highly personal or unwillingness obstacles) may be expressed politely. One possible explanation for refusers' tendency to withhold such obstacles (Ifert & Roloff, 1996; Wilson et al., 1993) is that they lack the skill to express these difficult obstacles without damaging the face needs or relationship of the interactants involved. Scholarship examining methods of expressing such obstacles in a socially acceptable manner could enable refusers to expand their repertoires of resistance strategies and to express their true reasons for noncompliance. Brown and Levinson (1987) note that some requests can be made indirectly, so that they are "off record." It would be interesting to examine whether the same is true for refusals. Even indirect refusals may be "on record" by necessity. Although a request can be ignored, so that it remains off record, a refusal that is ignored still leaves an unanswered request. Using highly indirect refusals may lead requesters to perceive compliance only to find later that compliance is not forthcoming and may place refusers in the position of having to justify inaction in other ways.

Directions Grounded
in Attribution Theory

Existing research investigating compliance resistance from an attributional perspective (Folkes, 1982; Ifert & Roloff, 1998; Wilson et al., 1993) has focused on the general dimensions of stability and locus of control that distinguish among

Weiner's (1972) antecedent conditions for behavior or on two of the antecedent behaviors themselves, effort and ability. Although luck, as an external and unstable cause of behavior, is difficult to control, it does seem reasonable that continuing research from an attributional perspective should include task difficulty in its models of compliance resistance. Although Roloff and Janiszewski (1989) did not employ attribution theory as a basis for their investigation, they did include the idea of task difficulty (which they defined as degree of imposition associated with compliance) in their study. These authors manipulated request type and relational intimacy as determinants of the degree of imposition associated with a request and found that the form of an initial request depended on request type and intimacy; responses to rejection also varied by request type and intimacy.

Studies of compliance resistance that have employed attributional frameworks (Folkes, 1982; Ifert & Roloff, 1998; Wilson et al., 1993) have not taken into account the difficulty of the compliance task for the compliance target. It would seem that the difficulty of a request situation, particularly the difficulty of managing strong forces for compliance and strong desires for resistance, would influence the types and linguistic structures of refusals stated. Task difficulty could influence perceptions of ability and willingness obstacles such that ability could be seen as a legitimate obstacle when task difficulty is high but willingness may be perceived as a more serious obstacle when task difficulty is low. Future research might examine how people respond to different types of obstacles (e.g., ability and willingness) when task difficulty varies and whether specific response strategies are more effective in overcoming obstacles depending on task difficulty.

Additionally, it seems that resistance is primarily a refuser's act proposing a reason or cause for noncompliance, whereas persistence is a requester's act that challenges the refuser's reasons or causes, often by providing additional reasons the target should comply. From an attributional perspective, examining how requester and refuser negotiate this interaction of reasons and counterreasons may provide insight into the processes individuals use to develop attributions about others' behaviors.

Directions Grounded in Constructivism

One issue that could be addressed from a constructivist perspective is how people express and respond to multiple obstacles. As constructivism is concerned with how individuals organize information and select communication strategies (Delia et al., 1982), how individuals cognitively organize and behaviorally respond to multiple obstacles could appropriately be examined from a constructivist viewpoint.

The fact that expressed and unexpressed obstacles may be present in influence situations (Folkes, 1982; Ifert & Roloff, 1994) suggests that multiple obstacles may be preventing compliance with a single request. When multiple obstacles are stated or inferred to be present by a requester, how does the requestee respond?

Requesters may approach response hierarchically by attempting to overcome what they perceive as the most important obstacles first. Alternatively, they may attempt to create generalized messages that address several obstacles at once. Constructivist thought would suggest that people with differing levels of cognitive complexity and different construct systems would respond differently to multiple obstacles and, in fact, may be differentially able to identify whether and what kind of unstated obstacles exist. Current research has largely ignored this issue, and it would seem to be an important area for increasing our understanding of individuals' responses to resistance.

A related concern is how individuals deal with multifaceted obstacles. The studies by Folkes (1982), Ifert and Roloff (1998) and Wilson et al. (1993) discussed above suggest that a single obstacle may vary along several dimensions. Now that dimensional frameworks for interpreting obstacles have been identified (Ifert & Roloff, 1998; Wilson et al., 1993), researchers can begin to explore, for example, how obstacles that reflect a low level of willingness to comply but a high degree of ability differ from obstacles that reflect low levels of both willingness and ability to accede. Obstacles differing in their dimensional placement may be expressed differently, may be more or less successful as resistance tools, and may be responded to in different ways even though they share some characteristics, such as a low level of ability to fulfill the request. Again, from the constructivist perspective, it might be assumed that highly cognitively complex individuals can use obstacles that vary in their dimensional placement more readily than can their less cognitively complex counterparts, but such ideas remain to be tested.

CONCLUSION

Regardless of the theoretical perspective employed, continuing research on interpersonal influence interactions needs to examine how individuals negotiate the tension between pressures to comply and desires to resist. The research reviewed in this chapter plays an important role in providing basic knowledge about resistance strategies, emotional responses to requests, and obstacles. Future research needs to extend this basic knowledge by testing competing theoretical explanations for how people interact in influence situations. The theoretical perspectives discussed throughout this chapter that underlie much of the existing scholarship on resistance are potentially fruitful bases for future study, as each is capable of integrating forces both for and against compliance. Not all studies that test competing theories yield clear conclusions (e.g., Dillard & Kinney's [1994] test of politeness versus cognitive appraisal theory in explaining emotional responses to requests), but such studies are necessary to advance our understanding of resistance processes by supporting or disconfirming potential explanatory frameworks.

It is also possible that a single theoretical perspective may be insufficient to explain resistance. There is, for example, significant overlap between attribution theory and politeness theory in some studies of resistance (e.g., Folkes, 1982). It could be that complex resistance phenomena require explanations that are more sophisticated than a single theory.

Regardless of the theoretical approach employed, however, future inquiry should provide additional insight into how the competing forces of compliance and resistance are negotiated in everyday interpersonal relationships. The directions for further research proposed here, although not the only possibilities, can furnish researchers with some starting points for ongoing attempts to understand requests and refusals.

REFERENCES

Alberts, J. K., Miller-Rassulo, M. A., & Hecht, M. L. (1991). A typology of drug resistance strategies. *Journal of Applied Communication Research, 19,* 129-151.

Barry, B., & Watson, M. R. (1996). Communication aspects of dyadic social influence in organizations: A review and integration of conceptual and empirical developments. In B. R. Burleson (Ed.), *Communication yearbook 19* (pp. 269-317). Thousand Oaks, CA: Sage.

Baxter, L. A. (1984). An investigation of compliance-gaining as politeness. *Human Communication Research, 10,* 427-456.

Baxter, L. A., & Wilmot, W. W. (1985). Taboo topics in close relationships. *Journal of Social and Personal Relationships, 2,* 253-269.

Becker, J. A. (1982). Children's strategic use of requests to mark and manipulate social status. In S. Kuczaj II (Ed.), *Language development: Vol. 2. Language, thought, and culture* (pp. 1-36). Hillsdale, NJ: Lawrence Erlbaum.

Berger, C. R. (1991). Communication theories and other curios. *Communication Monographs, 58,* 101-113.

Besson, A. L., Roloff, M. E., & Paulson, G. D. (1998). Preserving face in refusal situations. *Communication Research, 25,* 183-199.

Brown, P., & Levinson, S. C. (1978). Universals in language usage: Politeness phenomena. In E. N. Goody (Ed.), *Questions and politeness: Strategies in social interaction* (pp. 56-289). Cambridge: Cambridge University Press.

Brown, P., & Levinson, S. C. (1987). *Politeness: Some universals in language use.* Cambridge: Cambridge University Press.

Burgoon, M. (1994). Paths II: The garden variety. *Communication Theory, 4,* 81-92.

Burroughs, N. F., Kearney, P., & Plax, T. G. (1989). Compliance-resisting in the college classroom. *Communication Education, 38,* 214-229.

Clark, R. A., & Delia, J. G. (1976). The development of functional persuasive skills in childhood and early adolescence. *Child Development, 47,* 1-10.

Clark, R. A., & Delia, J. G. (1979). Topoi and rhetorical competence. *Quarterly Journal of Speech, 65,* 187-206.

Craig, R. T., Tracey, K., & Spisak, F. (1986). The discourse of requests: Assessment of a politeness approach. *Human Communication Research, 12,* 437-468.

Delia, J. G., & Clark, R. A. (1977). Cognitive complexity, social perception, and the development of listener-adapted communication in six-, eight-, ten-, and twelve-year-old boys. *Communication Monographs, 44,* 326-345.

Delia, J. G., Kline, S. L., & Burleson, B. R. (1979). The development of persuasive communication strategies in kindergartners through twelfth-graders. *Communication Monographs, 46,* 241-256.

Delia, J. G., O'Keefe, B. J., & O'Keefe, D. J. (1982). The constructivist approach to communication. In F. E. X. Dance (Ed.), *Human communication theory* (pp. 147-191). New York: Harper & Row.

deTurck, M. A. (1985). A transactional analysis of compliance-gaining behavior: Effects of noncompliance, relational contexts, and actors' gender. *Human Communication Research, 12,* 54-78.

Dillard, J. P., & Kinney, T. A. (1994). Experiential and physiological responses to interpersonal influence. *Human Communication Research, 20,* 502-528.

Dillard, J. P., Kinney, T. A., & Cruz, M. G. (1996). Influence, appraisals, and emotions in close relationships. *Communication Monographs, 63,* 105-130.

Dillard, J. P., Segrin, C., & Harden, J. M. (1989). Primary and secondary goals in the production of interpersonal influence messages. *Communication Monographs, 56,* 19-38.

Edgar, T., & Fitzpatrick, M. A. (1990). Communicating sexual desire: Message tactics for having and avoiding intercourse. In J. P. Dillard (Ed.), *Seeking compliance: The production of interpersonal influence messages* (pp. 107-122). Scottsdale, AZ: Gorsuch Scarisbrick.

Ervin-Tripp, S., Guo, J., & Lampert, M. (1990). Politeness and persuasion in children's control acts. *Journal of Pragmatics, 14,* 307-331.

Fitzpatrick, M. A., & Winke, J. (1979). You always hurt the one you love: Strategies and tactics in interpersonal conflict. *Communication Quarterly, 27,* 3-11.

Foa, U. G., & Foa, E. B. (1972). Resource exchange: Toward a structural theory of interpersonal communication. In A. W. Seigman & B. Pope (Eds.), *Studies in dyadic communication* (pp. 291-325). New York: Pergamon.

Folkes, V. S. (1982). Communicating the reasons for social rejection. *Journal of Experimental Social Psychology, 18,* 235-252.

Francik, E. P., & Clark, H. H. (1985). How to make requests that overcome obstacles to compliance. *Journal of Memory and Language, 24,* 560-568.

Gibbs, R. W., Jr. (1981). Your wish is my command: Convention and context in interpreting indirect requests. *Journal of Verbal Learning and Verbal Behavior, 20,* 431-444.

Gibbs, R. W., Jr. (1986). What makes some indirect speech acts conventional? *Journal of Memory and Language, 25,* 181-196.

Gibbs, R. W., Jr. (1987). Memory for requests in conversation revisited. *American Journal of Psychology, 100,* 179-191.

Gibbs, R. W., Jr., & Mueller, R. A. G. (1988). Conversational sequences and preferences for indirect speech acts. *Discourse Processes, 11,* 101-116.

Hale, C. L., & Delia, J. G. (1976). Cognitive complexity and social perspective-taking. *Communication Monographs, 43,* 195-203.

Harrington, N. G. (1995). The effects of college students' alcohol resistance strategies. *Health Communication, 7,* 371-391.

Harrington, N. G. (1997). Strategies used by college students to persuade peers to drink. *Southern Communication Journal, 62,* 229-242.

Hecht, M., Alberts, J. K., & Miller-Rassulo, M. A. (1992). Resistance to drug offers among college students. *International Journal of the Addictions, 27,* 995-1017.

Hecht, M., Trost, M. R., Bator, R. J., & MacKinnon, D. (1997). Ethnicity and sex similarities and differences in drug resistance. *Journal of Applied Communication Research, 25,* 75-97.

Ifert, D. E., & Bearden, L. (1997). The use of rational, emotional, and combination appeals to respond to rejected requests. *Communication Research Reports, 14,* 65-73.

Ifert, D. E., & Long, K. M. (1990, April). *Differences in compliance-gaining strategies during successive attempts.* Paper presented at the annual meeting of the Eastern Communication Association, Philadelphia.

Ifert, D. E., & Roloff, M. E. (1994). Anticipated obstacles to compliance: Predicting their presence and expression. *Communication Studies, 45,* 120-130.

Ifert, D. E., & Roloff, M. E. (1996). Responding to rejected requests: Persistence and response type as functions of obstacles to compliance. *Journal of Language and Social Psychology, 15,* 40-58.

Ifert, D. E., & Roloff, M. E. (1997, November). *Threats to the face needs of requesters: Differences among obstacles to compliance and influences on responses to refusals.* Paper presented at the annual meeting of the Speech Communication Association, Chicago.

Ifert, D. E., & Roloff, M. E. (1998). Understanding obstacles preventing compliance: Conceptualization and classification. *Communication Research, 25,* 131-153.

Infante, D. A., Trebing, J. D., Shepherd, P. E., & Seeds, D. E. (1984). The relationship of argumentativeness to verbal aggression. *Southern Speech Communication Journal, 50,* 67-77.

Jacobs, S., & Jackson, S. (1983). Strategy and structure in conversational influence attempts. *Communication Monographs, 50,* 285-304.

Kellermann, K., & Cole, T. (1994). Classifying compliance-gaining messages: Taxonomic disorder and strategic confusion. *Communication Theory, 4,* 3-60.

Kim, M.-S., Shin, H. C., & Cai, D. (1998). The influence of cultural orientations on the preferred forms of requesting and rerequesting. *Communication Monographs, 65,* 47-66.

Kline, S. L., & Floyd, C. H. (1990). On the art of saying no: The influence of social cognitive development on messages of refusal. *Western Journal of Speech Communication, 54,* 454-472.

Kochanska, G. (1997). Mutually responsive orientation between mothers and their young children: Implications for early socialization. *Child Development, 68,* 94-112.

Kuczynski, L., & Kochanska, G. (1990). Development of children's noncompliance strategies from toddlerhood to age 5. *Developmental Psychology, 26,* 398-408.

Kuczynski, L., & Kochanska, G. (1995). Function and content of maternal demands: Developmental significance of early demands for competent action. *Child Development, 66,* 616-628.

Kuczynski, L., Kochanska, G., Radke-Yarrow, M., & Girnius-Brown, O. (1987). A developmental interpretation of young children's noncompliance. *Developmental Psychology, 23,* 799-806.

LaGaipa, J. (1977). Testing a multidimensional approach to friendship. In S. Duck (Ed.), *Theory and practice in interpersonal attraction* (pp. 250-270). New York: Academic Press.

Lee, C. R., Levine, T. R., & Cambra, R. (1997). Resisting compliance in the multicultural classroom. *Communication Education, 46,* 29-43.

Lewis, P. N., & Gallois, C. (1984). Disagreements, refusals, or negative feelings: Perceptions of negatively asserted messages from friends and strangers. *Behavior Therapy, 15,* 353-368.

Lim, T. (1990). Politeness behavior in social situations. In J. P. Dillard (Ed.), *Seeking compliance: The production of interpersonal influence messages* (pp. 75-86). Scottsdale, AZ: Gorsuch Scarisbrick.

Lim, T., & Bowers, J. W. (1991). Facework: Solidarity, approbation, and tact. *Human Communication Research, 17,* 415-450.

McLaughlin, M. L., Cody, M. J., & Robey, C. S. (1980). Situational influences on the selection of strategies to resist compliance-gaining attempts. *Human Communication Research, 7,* 14-36.

McQuillen, J. S., Higginbotham, D. C., & Cummings, M. C. (1984). Compliance-resisting behaviors: The effects of age, agent, and types of request. In R. N. Bostrom (Ed.), *Communication yearbook 8* (pp. 747-763). Beverly Hills, CA: Sage.

Metts, S., Cupach, W. R., & Imahori, T. T. (1992). Perceptions of sexual compliance-resisting messages in three types of cross-sex relationships. *Western Journal of Communication, 56,* 1-17.

Metts, S., & Spitzberg, B. H. (1996). Sexual communication in interpersonal contexts: A script-based approach. In B. R. Burleson (Ed.), *Communication yearbook 19* (pp. 49-91). Thousand Oaks, CA: Sage.

Nofsinger, R. (1991). *Everyday conversation.* Newbury Park, CA: Sage.

O'Hair, M. J., Cody, M. J., & O'Hair, H. D. (1991). The impact of situational dimensions on compliance-resisting strategies: A comparison of methods. *Communication Quarterly, 39,* 226-240.

O'Keefe, B. J., & Delia, J. G. (1979). Construct comprehensiveness and cognitive complexity as predictors of the number and strategic adaptation of arguments and appeals in a persuasive message. *Communication Monographs, 46,* 231-240.

O'Keefe, B. J., & Delia, J. G. (1982). Impression formation and message production. In M. E. Roloff & C. R. Berger (Eds.), *Social cognition and communication* (pp. 33-72). Beverly Hills, CA: Sage.

O'Keefe, B. J., & Delia, J. G. (1985). Psychological and interactional dimensions of communicative development. In H. Giles & R. N. St. Clair (Eds.), *Recent advances in language, communication, and social psychology* (pp. 41-85). Hillsdale, NJ: Lawrence Erlbaum.

O'Keefe, B. J., & Shepherd, G. J. (1987). The pursuit of multiple objectives in face-to-face persuasive interactions: Effects of construct differentiation on message organization. *Communication Monographs, 54*, 396-419.

Oldershaw, L., Walters, G. C., & Hall, D. K. (1986). Control strategies and noncompliance in abusive mother-child dyads: An observational study. *Child Psychology, 57*, 722-732.

Paulson, G. D., & Roloff, M. E. (1997). The effect of request form and content on constructing obstacles to compliance. *Communication Research, 24*, 261-290.

Plax, T. G., Kearney, P. Downs, T. M., & Stewart, R. A. (1986). College student resistance toward teachers' use of selective control strategies. *Communication Research Reports, 3*, 20-27.

Read, S. J. (1992). Constructing accounts: The role of explanatory coherence. In M. L. McLaughlin, M. J. Cody, & S. J. Read (Eds.), *Explaining one's self to others: Reason-giving in a social context* (pp. 3-21). Hillsdale, NJ: Lawrence Erlbaum.

Reardon, K. K., Sussman, S., & Flay, B. R. (1989). Are we marketing the right message: Can kids "just say 'no' " to smoking? *Communication Monographs, 56*, 306-324.

Roloff, M. E. (1987). Communication and reciprocity within intimate relationships. In M. E. Roloff & G. R. Miller (Eds.), *Interpersonal processes: New directions in communication research* (pp. 11-38). Newbury Park, CA: Sage.

Roloff, M. E., & Cloven, D. H. (1994, November). *Conditions under which relational commitment leads to conflict avoidance.* Paper presented at the annual meeting of the Speech Communication Association, New Orleans.

Roloff, M. E., & Ifert, D. E. (1998). Antecedents and consequences of explicit agreements declaring a topic taboo in dating relationships. *Personal Relationships, 5*, 191-205.

Roloff, M. E., & Janiszewski, C. A. (1989). Overcoming obstacles to interpersonal compliance: A principle of message construction. *Human Communication Research, 16*, 33-61.

Roloff, M. E., Janiszewski, C. A., McGrath, M. A., Burns, C. S., & Manrai, L. A. (1988). Acquiring resources from intimates: When obligation substitutes for persuasion. *Human Communication Research, 14*, 364-396.

Roloff, M. E., & Jordan, J. M. (1992). Achieving negotiation goals: The "fruits and foibles" of planning ahead. In L. L. Putnam & M. E. Roloff (Eds.), *Communication and negotiation* (pp. 21-45). Newbury Park, CA: Sage.

Rule, B. G., Bisanz, G. L., & Kohn, M. (1985). Anatomy of a persuasion schema: Targets, goals, and strategies. *Journal of Personality and Social Psychology, 48*, 1127-1140.

Saeki, M., & O'Keefe, B. J. (1994). Refusals and rejections: Designing messages to serve multiple goals. *Human Communication Research, 21*, 67-102.

Schwartz, L. A. (1992, October). *The answer is "no": An exploration of refusals in friendship.* Paper presented at the annual meeting of the Speech Communication Association, Chicago.

Seibold, D. R., Cantrill, J. G., & Meyers, R. A. (1985). Communication and interpersonal influence. In M. L. Knapp & G. R. Miller (Eds.), *Handbook of interpersonal communication* (pp. 551-615). Beverly Hills, CA: Sage.

Seibold, D. R., Cantrill, J. G., & Meyers, R. A. (1994). Communication and interpersonal influence. In M. L. Knapp & G. R. Miller (Eds.), *Handbook of interpersonal communication* (2nd ed., pp. 542-588). Thousand Oaks, CA: Sage.

Shapiro, E. G. (1980). Is seeking help from a friend like seeking help from a stranger? *Social Psychology Quarterly, 43*, 259-263.

Spitzberg, B. H. (1994). The dark side of (in)competence. In W. R. Cupach & B. H. Spitzberg (Eds.), *The dark side of interpersonal communication* (pp. 25-49). Hillsdale, NJ: Lawrence Erlbaum.

Trethewey, A. (1997). Resistance, identity, and empowerment: A postmodern feminist analysis of clients in a human service organization. *Communication Monographs, 64*, 281-301.

Weiner, B. (1972). *Theories of motivation: From mechanism to cognition.* Chicago: Rand McNally.

Wheeless, L. R., Barraclough, R., & Stewart, R. A. (1983). Compliance-gaining and power in persuasion. In R. N. Bostrom (Ed.), *Communication yearbook 7* (pp. 105-145). Beverly Hills, CA: Sage.

Wilson, S. R., Cruz, M. G., Marshall, L. J., & Rao, N. (1993). An attributional analysis of compliance-gaining interactions. *Communication Monographs, 60,* 1-22.

CHAPTER CONTENTS

5 Sexual Harassment Research: Integration, Reformulation, and Implications for Mitigation Efforts

LAURA L. JANSMA
University of California, Santa Barbara

The purposes of this essay are (a) to review existing academic research and integrate it with legal and organizational approaches to sexual harassment in the workplace and (b) to establish a framework from which to develop theoretically coherent and empirically testable techniques for reducing workplace sexual harassment. The essay begins with an overview of the development of sexual harassment as a workplace problem, followed by a summary and critique of legal, organizational, and academic conceptualizations of sexual harassment. Six areas of empirical research are reviewed: (a) studies of sexual harassment prevalence, correlates, and outcomes; (b) typologies of sexually harassing behaviors; (c) factors that contribute to perceptions regarding sexual harassment; (d) assessments of the proclivity to sexually harass; (e) responses to sexual harassment; and (f) strategies to combat sexual harassment. Sexual harassment is reconceptualized as a multidimensional phenomenon in which formal power and perceived perpetrator intent moderate behavioral manifestations of sexual harassment and its perceived severity. This framework offers general guidelines from which specific strategies can be generated and against which existing tactics can be evaluated.

S EXUAL harassment is widely understood to be unwelcome sexual conduct that unreasonably and negatively affects individuals' employment conditions and productivity (Crocker, 1983; Frazier, Cochran, & Olson, 1995; Hotelling, 1991a). As recently as 1970, the formal term *sexual harassment* did not exist (Brewer & Berk, 1982; Fitzgerald, 1993b; MacKinnon, 1979), yet in little more than two decades the media, legal decisions, and research reports have collectively transformed what was formerly a working woman's private dilemma into

AUTHOR'S NOTE: I would like to thank Edward Donnerstein, Tony Mulac, Dale Kunkel, Paula Rudolph, and David Seibold for their comments on earlier drafts of this work, and for their continued support.

Correspondence: Laura L. Jansma, Jansma Associates, P.O. Box 30043, Santa Barbara, CA 93130-0043; e-mail lljansma@impulse.net

Communication Yearbook 23, pp. 163-225

a workplace concern of women and men, a legal matter, and a social science construct (Brewer & Berk, 1982; Fitzgerald, 1993b, MacKinnon, 1979; O'Donohue, 1997; Weeks, Boles, Garbin, & Blaunt, 1985; Wood, 1992).

While American judicial systems and organizations have attempted to curtail sexual harassment, scholarly researchers have focused more on the structure and implications of the phenomenon (Keyton & Rhodes, 1994) than on curtailment techniques. As a result, a paradox exists. Organizations, motivated by legal concerns (Keyton, 1996), are implementing "solutions" to the problem of sexual harassment that are grounded in neither theoretically coherent explanations of sexual harassment nor empirically validated methods for controlling it (Grundmann, O'Donohue, & Peterson, 1997; Moyer & Nath, 1998). At the same time, scholars are pursuing investigations of a "problem" that organizations already are "solving," while their investigations contribute only indirectly to the practical resolution of sexual harassment.

This comprehensive review and ensuing reformulation are responsive to the need for an academic foundation from which intervention efforts can proceed. Several assumptions undergird this essay. First, existing conceptualizations and empirical studies of sexual harassment offer multiple insights into sexual harassment, and this literature is valuable on its own terms. Second, social science investigations, and communication research in particular, have the potential to improve sexual harassment mitigation efforts by (a) determining the effectiveness of existing interventions, (b) offering impetuses for improving current curtailment efforts, and (c) providing direction for future efforts based upon theoretical and empirical analyses of abatement strategies.

The third assumption guiding this review is that mitigation research will benefit from the integration of academic, legal, and organizational understandings of sexual harassment. Only when such integration has taken place will researchers and practitioners be able to generate theoretically valid curtailment procedures that are understood easily by organizational members and are readily applicable to the daily workplace interactions in which sexual harassment is situated. Fourth, current conceptualizations and experimentations do not synthesize the multiple understandings of this complex issue either within academicians' approaches or among academic, legal, and organizational perspectives. As a result, they do not furnish an adequate framework from which to develop efficacious mitigation strategies. Hence my dual purposes in this essay are (a) to review and integrate existing academic research in a manner that is compatible with legal and organizational approaches to sexual harassment and (b) to establish a framework from which may be developed theoretically coherent and empirically testable orientations for reducing sexual harassment in the workplace.

Two primary characteristics of the literature to date warrant note here. First, academic treatments often neglect to consider sexual harassment on the level at which the problem is manifested on a daily basis—the *communicative* interaction between individuals, most often between women and men. Second, researchers have tended to overlook the *multidimensional* nature of sexual harassment, which is inherent in the various conceptualizations of sexual harassment and in the diverse data-based findings to be reviewed and integrated in this essay.[1] In particular, conceptual approaches to sexual harassment and empirical research have often failed to treat explicitly the effects of formal *power differentials* and *perpetrator intentionality* on the types and perceived seriousness of sexual harassment and on harasser, harassed, and third-party interpretations of potentially harassing interaction. I will argue that these two variables are intrinsic to sexual harassment, and thus each requires attention in curtailment efforts. The integrative reformulation that I propose in this analysis treats these issues as foundational.

This essay in organized in four sections. First, the development of sexual harassment as a social problem is outlined. The second section contains a summary and critique of legal, organizational, and academic conceptualizations of sexual harassment in the workplace. In the third section, six areas of *empirical* research are surveyed: (a) studies of sexual harassment prevalence, its outcomes, and correlates; (b) typologies of sexually harassing behaviors; (c) factors that contribute to perceptions of sexual harassment and its severity; (d) assessments of proclivities to sexually harass; (e) responses to sexual harassment; and (f) strategies to combat sexual harassment. The fourth section offers a reconceptualization of sexual harassment that incorporates the dimensions of *formal power* and *perpetrator intent* as variables that moderate *behavioral manifestations* of sexual harassment and its *perceived severity.* This framework rests upon communicative aspects of sexual harassment that are explicit or implied within legal, organizational, and academic contexts. It offers general guidelines from which specific strategies can be generated and against which existing tactics can be evaluated.

EMERGENCE OF SEXUAL HARASSMENT AS A SOCIAL PROBLEM

Spawned by media attention, the issue of sexual harassment has emerged from contemporary concerns surrounding gender discrimination rather than from theoretical or empirical foundations (Brewer & Berk, 1982; Livingston, 1982; Weeks et al., 1985). These public origins are the bases for lay understandings, government legislation, and organizational interventions designed to curtail sexual harassment that have developed concurrently with, but often separately from, academic research. This section provides a review of the emergence of the issue of sexual harassment as a public concern, a legal issue, and an organizational problem.

From Private Issue to Public Concern

Termed the "hidden issue" by the Project on the Status and Education of Women in 1978 (Hotelling, 1991a), sexual harassment typically had been viewed as a skeleton in the working woman's closet. Victims remained silent, assuming at least partial responsibility for their plight and seeing little recourse (Hotelling, 1991a).

Similarly, organizations dealt with incidents quietly, avoiding publicity or escalation of the problem. Thus sexual harassment was typically a *private* concern of female employees (Weeks et al., 1985), with early accounts dating to the 1700s (Fitzgerald, 1993b).

Although passage of the Civil Rights Act in 1964 declared harassment on the basis of sex to be a violation of Americans' constitutional rights (U.S. Merit Services Protection Board [USMSPB], 1988), concern surrounding sexual harassment did not surface until the 1970s, as a result of media coverage and policy makers' involvement with the issue. For example, *Redbook* published a questionnaire in 1976 titled "How Do You Handle Sex on the Job?" increasing women's awareness that this "private" problem is shared, to some degree, by most professional women (Safran, 1976). Other researchers trace the emergence of the issue in greater detail than I can offer here (e.g., Weeks et al., 1985).

As awareness increased, the problem shifted from a victims' issue to one shared by government as well. U.S. Senate subcommittee hearings investigated the problem and, guided by Title VII of the Civil Rights Act, sexual harassment was declared a special case of sexual discrimination, punishable by federal law (Livingston, 1982; U.S. Office of Personnel Management [USOPM], 1980a). The U.S. Office of Personnel Management (1980a) issued a policy defining sexual harassment and prohibiting its practice, and several state governments followed suit by creating redress under common tort law (Conte, 1997; Sigler & Johnson, 1986). Integral to these outcomes was the legal decree that organizations are responsible for the sexual harassment of their employees (Conte, 1997). The issue of sexual harassment, once something organizations could ignore, thus became a legal concern for American companies.

Although sexual harassment was salient for activists and corporate America by the 1980s, the general public had no reason to grasp the issue's breadth or complexity fully until it became a major media focus in the following decade. Publicity surrounding chief neurosurgeon Dr. Frances Conley's resignation from the Stanford University School of Medicine in the summer of 1990—prompted by claims of sexual harassment over the course of her highly successful 25-year career at Stanford—garnered public attention. A major media event followed in October 1991 with the U.S. Senate hearings on the confirmation of Clarence Thomas's appointment to the Supreme Court, during which he was accused of sexually harassing Anita Hill. Daily news coverage of the sexual harassment issue thus entered America's living rooms. The following year the public was still solidifying its beliefs and opinions: A *U.S. News & World Report* survey indicated that the proportion of men who believed Clarence Thomas's account dropped from 69% in 1991 to 44% by early 1992 (Borger, Gest, & Thornton, 1992).

Interest in sexual harassment continued to accelerate with coverage of a gauntlet-style sexual assault of female peers by 200 men at the U.S. Navy's 1991 Tailhook convention, followed by the Navy's investigation and the Defense Department's official report, released at a press conference in September 1992.

Charges of sexual harassment against President Bill Clinton, and a record number of four pending U.S. Supreme Court cases in 1998 heightened awareness further. Today, daily news reports include charges against, analyses, and investigations of both women and men at all levels of organizations in the public and private sector, as well as substantial financial settlements (e.g., Armour & Mauro, 1998; Goodman, 1998). The largest settlement to date, $9.8 million, was granted in a case against Astra Pharmaceutical Corporation, whose top executives engaged in both quid pro quo and hostile environment harassment (Rubin & Peres, 1998).

For organizations, the public's recognition of sexual harassment as widespread and a legal offense transformed what was a minor concern in the 1980s into a serious threat requiring immediate intervention in the 1990s. Within a week of the Hill-Thomas hearings, the number of calls to the National Association of Working Women's hot line tripled (Galen, Weber, & Cuneo, 1991). On October 11, 1991, while Professor Hill was testifying on national television, the chief executive and chair of AT&T was broadcasting to corporate employees the company's strict prohibition against and penalties for sexual harassment (Strom, 1991). Similarly, as the media reported Lieutenant Coughlin's accusations and her dissatisfaction with the Navy's investigation of the Tailhook incident, naval officials had already instituted fleetwide "zero tolerance" sexual harassment training programs. In the course of less than 20 years, sexual harassment shifted from a working woman's private issue to a public issue, a government concern, and a bona fide workplace problem.

Social Science and Sexual Harassment Mitigation

As awareness of sexual harassment has increased, so have reports of incidents. Since the first formal case in 1974, annual reports of sexual harassment have continued to rise. In the year following the Hill-Thomas hearings, the number of cases of sexual harassment filed with the U.S. Equal Employment Opportunity Commission (USEEOC) doubled—from 6,000 to 12,000 (Schweikhart, 1995). By 1997, such cases numbered nearly 16,000, and $49.5 million in damages had been awarded (Rubin & Peres, 1998). Widespread concern and reports of increases in workplace sexual harassment have created the need for a viable approach to remediation (Fitzgerald & Shullman, 1993; Schweikhart, 1995; Webb, 1992).

The swift and extensive implementation of workplace interventions attests to organizations' commitment to reducing sexual harassment. However, scholars, whose research is needed to inform organizational efforts, are still in the early stages of investigating sexual harassment mitigation. Some 20 years of academic research into this phenomenon offers definitions, correlates, and responses to sexual harassment, but virtually no empirically tested solutions to this societal problem (Grundmann et al., 1997). This is not to minimize the value of research thus far, but to draw attention to three issues that provide a warrant for academic study that develops and assesses general strategies and specific tactics for combating sexual harassment. First, as noted above, organizational interventions have risen in response to legal and social demand rather than based on social scientific intervention research (see Fitzgerald, Gelfand, & Drasgow, 1995). Second, as a result, organizational efforts to combat sexual harassment may have little theoretical or empirical grounding and virtually no empirical validation. Finally, new applied research that is readily applicable to sexual harassment mitigation in daily workplace interactions is imperative. Kazoleas (1997), a human resources manager at the Mitsubishi plant that recently faced one of the largest sexual harassment lawsuits ever brought, has called for academic researchers to "provide a practical application of theory to the practitioner in a manner that is easily retrieved and available for use" (p. 4). It is my intent to contribute to that end in this essay by reviewing the knowledge of sexual harassment that is commonly agreed upon by legal, lay, and academic experts.

CONCEPTUALIZATIONS OF
SEXUAL HARASSMENT

Conceptual understandings and working definitions of sexual harassment vary across legal, organizational, and academic research perspectives, each of which will be noted here briefly. For additional discussion of conceptualizations, see Fitzgerald, Swan, and Magley's (1997) distinctions between the legal concept and the personal experience of sexual harassment. Important to any analysis of these approaches is the fact that all three assume that women and men coexist in work-oriented environments customarily dominated by men. All three also presuppose the existence of sex differences and sex role socialization that prescribe and enforce different behavioral norms for women and men. Hence one can be a victim of sexual harassment only in a work-oriented environment and because of one's sex. A final supposition is that sexual harassment is manifested during interaction between one or more offenders and one or more victims. Yet determinations of whether sexual harassment has transpired often are made from three perspectives—the circumstances are subject to interpretation by the harasser, the harassed, and third parties, such as judges and managers, external to the principal interactants.

In addition to these assumptions, a distinction is made here between sexual harassment and sexism, concepts closely related to sexual harassment and sex roles. Sexism is the unnecessary and extreme adherence to gender roles or sexual roles in nonsexual situations (Albee, 1983; American Psychological Association, 1994). Because strict conformance to sexual roles, such as treating women as sex objects, is offensive and unwanted in many work-related situations, sexual harassment is a form of sexism. However, although frequently discriminatory, sexism in the workplace is not necessarily sexual harassment. Sexism may manifest itself in the form of inequities between sexes, such as unequal pay, without being sexual in nature.

Legal Perspectives

Legal definitions are integral to the conceptualization of sexual harassment, first, because either directly or indirectly (as interpreted and reported by the mass media), legal definitions of sexual harassment are a basis for third parties' (e.g., coworkers', managers', judges', and juries') understandings of the issue. Ultimately it is these third parties who decide whether sexual harassment has transpired in the eyes of the law, the organization, and the general public. Second, legal definitions of sexual harassment, as interpreted and presented by the mass media and organizational trainers, are integral to conceptualizations of sexual harassment because they are a primary basis for the understandings held by members of the American workforce. As such, they are the foundations from which sexual harassers and their targets operate in the workforce. Finally, because (a) legal definitions may be assumed to be a primary basis for both offenders' and victims' understandings of the issue and (b) perpetrators and victims may ultimately be judged by legal definitions, intervention efforts that attempt to reach offenders and/or harassed persons will benefit from consonance with legal definitions.

Legally, sexual harassment is a subcategory of sexual discrimination under Title VII of the 1964 Equal Rights Amendment, which states: "All employees and applicants for employment should receive fair and equitable treatment in all aspects of personnel management without regard to political affiliation, race, color, religion, national origin, sex, marital status, age, or handicapping condition" (U.S. Opportunity Commission, 1980, p. 182). The Civil Service Reform Act prohibits such discrimination as a personnel practice (USMSPB, 1988). Sexual harassment was defined expressly by the U.S. Equal Employment Opportunity Commission guidelines and declared unlawful on November 10, 1980 (USMSPB, 1988). The purpose of the definition is to guide judgments of whether sexual harassment has occurred. Defining harassment as a "form of employee misconduct" and as a "prohibited personnel practice" (USOPM, 1980a, p. 8) frames the issue on an organizational level. It also describes sexual harassment on the level of individual behavior by clearly acknowledging the interactive nature of sexual harassment—specifying both the conduct and intent of the source as well as its detrimental effect on the recipient.

> Unwelcome sexual advances, requests for sexual favors, and other verbal or physical conduct of a sexual nature constitute sexual harassment when: (1) submission to such conduct is made either explicitly or implicitly a term of condition of instruction, employment, (2) submission to or rejection of such conduct by an individual is used as the basis for employment decisions affecting such individuals, or (3) such conduct has the purpose or effect of unreasonably interfering with an individual's work performance or of creating an intimidating, hostile, or offensive working environment. (USOPM, 1980a, p. 8)

The first two elements of this definition describe *quid pro quo harassment,* considered the more blatant and more easily recognizable of the two forms (Cohen,

1987; MacKinnon, 1979). Quid quo pro, meaning "this for that," imposes a sexual exchange of favors from employees in return for employment opportunities granted by management. The third element in the USEEOC definition describes *hostile environment harassment* (Cohen, 1987; MacKinnon, 1979), the second major category of sexual harassment. This form of sexual harassment can be more subtle and thus more difficult to identify than quid pro quo harassment (Gilsdorf, 1990; Woerner & Oswald, 1990). Rather than an exchange of favors, it involves a pattern of unwanted, sexually oriented experiences that can accumulate over time and may originate from more than one source, including coworkers, management, and/or their employees (Linenberger, 1983). Because other researchers offer detailed reviews of legal decisions and their implications (e.g., Conte, 1997; Keyton, 1996; Paetzold & O'Leary-Kelly, 1996; Riger, 1992), I will not provide further discussion of these matters here.

Organizational Perspectives

In keeping with legal and public mandates outlined previously, organizations tend to view sexual harassment pragmatically, framing it as an economic threat (Weeks et al., 1985). From an institutional perspective, sexual harassment is a basis for government regulations that impose economic burdens, most directly in the form of financial settlements (Garvey, 1986; Gilsdorf, 1990; Schafran, 1991; Zedeck & Casio, 1984). The legal responsibilities borne by organizations also cause them to incur expenses for the development of sexual harassment policies, training programs designed to protect the organizations from litigation, internal investigations of complaints, and the like (Wagner, 1992). Additionally, sexual harassment poses indirect economic costs associated with decreased employee morale, turnover, and blemished corporate image (Wagner, 1992). Organizational attempts to combat sexual harassment are driven largely by the need to reduce liabilities and costs (Culbertson & Rosenfeld, 1993; Grundmann et al., 1997).

Congruent with legal approaches, organizations attempt to define sexual harassment for purposes of evaluating whether or not it has occurred and, if so, what consequences should follow. Hence organizations may identify potentially harassing behaviors in order to enable the monitoring of those behaviors by managers and supervisors, and in order that certain behaviors may be interpreted as forms of employee misconduct. Organizations also may "manage" sexual harassment of their employees in much the same way they deal with costly health-related issues, such as illness or alcoholism—providing counseling and helping employees cope with the outcomes of their experiences.[2]

Academic Research Perspectives

In contrast to organizations' pragmatic approach, a variety of theoretical perspectives are evident in academic conceptualizations of sexual harassment, with most tied to researchers' disciplinary roots. As a result, each approach privileges selected aspects of the issue but does not treat other salient features. Explorations of sexual harassment have been generated primarily by social psychologists, with recent contributions from communication researchers. Except in the context of reviews, academics have had little opportunity to integrate their findings fully with others' work. Similarly, although academic research often overlaps with legal or organizational treatments of sexual harassment, consistencies across these arenas seldom are articulated. One potential advantage of a comprehensive review is that it can serve to elucidate implicit but otherwise unspecified connections across research conceptualizations, operationalizations, and empirical investigations. In the following review I attempt to achieve that end by (a) drawing explicit attention to the roles of power imbalances and perpetrator intent in shaping forms of, and responses to, harassment; (b) underscoring and defining the multidimensional nature of sexual harassment that is congruent with other conceptualizations; and (c) suggesting that mitigation efforts should be guided by that multidimensional framework.

Sexual harassment research foci vary from broad-based theoretical perspectives to narrowly defined empirical studies. A macro approach may explain that power, not sexuality, is the driving impetus behind sexual harassment (Hoffman, 1986; Stringer, Remick, Salisbury, & Ginorio, 1990). Early theorists emphasized the purpose and outcomes of power abuse as endemic to sexual harassment (e.g., Backhouse & Cohen, 1981; Farley, 1978; MacKinnon, 1979). For example, Farley (1978) paints a picture of sexual harassment that is similar to rape. Some conceive of sexual harassment as an extension of sex discrimination, a "pattern of interpersonal behavior that functions at the social structural level to reinforce and perpetuate the subordination of women as a class" (Hoffman, 1986, p. 107). Sexual harassment in the workplace often is framed as a carryover of cultural sex roles, in which men have more power than do women (e.g., Brewer & Berk, 1982; Gutek, 1985; Hemming, 1985). Gutek's (1985) theory of "sex role spillover" suggests that men are socialized as sexual aggressors and women as targets of men's advances and that these roles conflict with women's work roles. Spanning these broad theoretical approaches is the assumption that power, usually within sex roles and economic relationships, is the key motivator for sexually harassing behavior (Fitzgerald, 1993a; Gutek & Morasch, 1982). Stockdale (1996) and Leeser and O'Donohue (1997) offer cogent theoretical discussions of the role of power in sexual harassment. For more detailed reviews of theoretical approaches that address the causes of sexual harassment, see Grundmann et al. (1997) and Keyton (1996).

Although power is at the core of sexual harassment (Gutek & Morasch, 1982; MacKinnon, 1979; Pryor, 1987; Tangri, Burt, & Johnson, 1982), broad-based perspectives cannot examine (a) power relationships on an interpersonal level, (b) why these socialized roles are evident in some relationships and not in others, or (c) why certain individuals are more likely than others in similar situations to become involved in sexual harassment. Nor do they customarily address cases in which counterstereotypic harassment occurs (e.g., men being sexually harassed by women or same-sex harassment).

In contrast to broad-based theorists, empirical researchers tend to emphasize the role of the individual. They may examine behaviors of harassers, such as leering, sexual comments, or sexual coercion (e.g., Frazier et al., 1995; Gruber, 1992), and attitudes and traits indicative of individuals who are more likely than others to sexually harass or who are more tolerant of sexual harassment—such as acceptance of violence against women (e.g., Bingham & Burleson, 1996; Pryor, 1987). They may assess harassers' awareness of their own behavior (e.g., Bargh & Raymond, 1995) or develop victim profiles (e.g., Gruber & Bjorn, 1986). Taken individually, these studies offer limited insight regarding the relationship between the harasser and the harassed, their communication patterns, or how these patterns differ from those in nonharassing interactions. However, taken together, individual-level studies reveal patterns of interaction with power imbalances in which harassers have greater power (informal or formal) than their victims. This collective pattern is essential to the framework for conceptualizing sexual harassment for purposes of mitigation that I will propose in the final section of this essay.

A limited amount of research concentrates directly on the communicative interaction between source and recipient. Brewer (1982) draws upon social psychology literature regarding attributions in social-influence situations involving power. She explains that, during interaction, the higher-status individual is likely to be motivated by interpersonal attraction and will communicate based upon internal attributions about the lower-status person, such as personal interest, rather than external attributions, such as role behavior. Power clearly plays a part in this relational-level analysis, as it does in the broad conceptualizations reviewed above, but is explained on the level of interpersonal communication—the level at which sexual harassment transpires.

Fiske and Glick (1995) also focus on the interactive nature of the relationship between harasser and harassed. These researchers suggest that ambivalent harasser motives combined with gender stereotyping of women and occupations determine manifest forms of sexual harassment. This study highlights the multidimensional quality of sexual harassment, which often is not articulated. This multidimensional treatment of sexual harassment—that is, not whether or not it transpires, but what factors contribute to its various forms—is consistent with the reconceptualization of sexual harassment proposed in this essay.

Communication scholars are inclined to focus on the language and behavioral choices of sources and victims of harassment and the outcomes of these choices (e.g., Bingham, 1994; Kreps, 1993). From a communicative perspective, sexual harassment is symbolically constructed through individual interpretations of experiences, and it is manifested in interpersonal interactions. For example, Clair (1993) suggests that victims of sexual harassment perpetuate its existence through their compliance with status quo interpretations of their experiences. Taylor and Conrad (1992) interpret victims' accounts of their sexual harassment experiences as politically regulated by organizational meanings and practices. Bing and Lombardo (1997) contribute to the threefold interpretation in their analyses of judicial, initiator, and victim frames. The concept of power surfaces in interpretative research as maintenance of the status quo. In a relationally based analysis, Hickson, Grierson, and Linder (1991) conceptualize sexual harassment as an asynchronous communication interaction, describing misinterpretation of source and recipient goals as the primary basis for sexual harassment. Their analysis, like Brewer's (1982) social-influence model, provides an interactive interpretation of the process of sexual harassment that is central to the reformulation I will offer later in this essay.

Although these eclectic approaches have sharpened our current understanding of sexual harassment, it is appropriate to evaluate the course of research conducted to date and to consider how this course may best be directed toward a goal of curtailing sexual harassment. The following critique specifies that in order to inform organizational intervention efforts, academic approaches can and should be reconciled with the legally driven approaches to sexual harassment that are familiar to organizations and to the general workforce.

Critique of Academic Conceptualizations

Sexual harassment is an interactive process involving at least two persons and sexual behavior that is "unwelcome" (USEEOC, 1980). It is this "unwelcome" aspect, determined by the recipient, that distinguishes sexual harassment from a consensual sexual relationship (Gilsdorf, 1990). The same sexually oriented conduct that may be acceptable, even appreciated, when directed toward one person may constitute sexual harassment if it is directed toward another. Likewise, identical behaviors from different sources may or may not be sexual harassment.

Despite the crucial role of the recipient in defining sexual harassment, few social scientific studies approach sexual harassment as an interactive process (Pryor, 1985). The focus is usually on the behaviors of the source, rather than on the relationship between source and recipient, the interpretation of potentially harassing behaviors by the recipient (Keyton & Rhodes, 1994; Konsky, Kang, & Woods, 1992), or what factors may affect the recipient's determination of whether sexual behaviors are unwanted. Most researchers implicitly acknowledge two aspects of the sexual harassment specified by legal definitions: the behaviors of the harasser and the effect of this conduct from the harassee's perspective. However, the most widely shared explicit conception is the description of sexual harassment as a specific behavior or a combination of behavioral acts by a perpetrator (Dziech & Weiner, 1984; Frazier et al., 1995). For example, Sandler (1990) describes sexual harassment as encompassing a wide variety of behaviors ranging from sexual innuendoes under the guise of humor to coercive sexual relations. Vance (1981) quips, "More than a wink, yet less than a seduction" (p. 30). Cammaert (1985) enumerates behaviors such as "repeated and unwanted sexual advances, looks, jokes, innuendoes, leering, ogling, 'accidentally' brushing against a woman's breast, a 'friendly' pat, a squeeze, a pinch, an arm around a person" (p. 388). The acts included in these definitions vary—predominantly in terms of severity and/or whether gender discrimination, which is not sexual, is included—but the focus is behavioral.

Overemphasis on source behavior can impede accurate understanding of sexual harassment. First, it causes situations to appear similar on a behavioral level, when they may be different on a psychological or relational level. Second, it overlooks variables that potentially moderate harassment, such as the source's power, intent, and awareness. Third, it assumes artificial points regarding the time at which harassment begins and ends. Fourth, it encourages greater focus on perpetrator behavior than on the effects of this behavior on the target. Perhaps most salient for intervention efforts, it emphasizes determining whether an offender is guilty of sexual harassment, rather than managing or improving the relationship between the offender and the victim. Without more knowledge regarding the interactive nature of sexual harassment, such as that offered by Brewer (1982) and Hickson et al. (1991), understanding of sexual harassment can be (a) incomplete, and hence portray the process inaccurately, and (b) decontextualized, thus subject to misinterpretation. As a result, mitigation efforts grounded in knowledge of source behavior rather than interaction may be misguided. Even if effective, such efforts may address only part of the problem.

A related limitation of social science conceptualizations is that they tend to oversimplify a complex issue (Fiske & Glick, 1995; Pryor & Day, 1988) by defining sexual harassment as a unidimensional rather than a multidimensional construct (Brewer, 1982). As a consequence, these conceptualizations do not (a) incorporate all forms of sexual harassment; (b) establish conceptual differences among forms of sexual harassment; (c) address sexual harassment on an interpersonal level as well as a societal level; (d) consider the three-part determinations of sexual harassment that result from harasser, harassed, and third-party interpretations; or (e) address how conceptual understandings relate to legal and lay definitions that are the primary bases for the public's understanding of sexual harassment.

Treating sexual harassment unidimensionally when it is a more complex phenomenon may restrict the development of efficacious mitigation strategies in three ways. First, a homogeneous conceptualization does not anticipate antecedent conditions or varying levels of key dimensions that moderate forms of harassment. Thus some academic conceptualizations may encourage harassers, victims, and third parties to view sexual coercion from a manager as equivalent to a pattern of sexist jokes from a coworker—both simply as sexual harassment. In contrast, legal definitions distinguish types of harassment—specifically quid pro quo from hostile environment harassment—based, in part, upon the formal power of the perpetrator in relation to the victim.

Second, a unidimensional conceptualization of sexual harassment fosters unidimensional solutions that cannot adequately address a problem that is conceptualized so diversely (ranging from unintentional misinterpretation to the systematic subjugation of women), manifested so disparately (ranging from sexual innuendoes to sexual coercion), and affects differentially a spectrum of organizational members. Without adequate conceptualization of the complex nature of sexual harassment, mitigation strategies may be overly simplistic, and thus unrealistic and ineffective.

A third restrictive trend evident in scholarly conceptualizations is that many researchers treat sexual harassment as a women's issue, leading to assumptions that women are the only victims and men the only perpetrators. Although sexual harassment is most frequently directed toward working women, there are other reasons researchers might take this approach. The women's movement was a primary force in bringing sexual harassment into the public spotlight (MacKinnon, 1979; Weeks et al., 1985). Similarly, feminist researchers who conceptualize sexual harassment as male domination of women have been paramount in the development of academic research on this issue (Fitzgerald, 1993a). However, it is unclear whether the phenomenon is inherently gender based or whether gender is conflated with a predominance of male power in the workplace. Assumptions that sexual harassment is gender based may be premature or erroneous absent more complete data from work environments in which women have more organizational power than do men. Furthermore, this assumption may drive investigative and mitigation efforts toward biased conclusions that are not generalizable to women's sexual harassment of men or to same-sex sexual harassment. A recent U.S. Supreme Court decision recognizing same-sex harassment underscores this concern (Greenburg, 1998; *Oncale v. Sundowner Offshore Services,* 1998).

The foregoing review and critique of academic conceptualizations of sexual harassment has highlighted major contributions to the understanding of the phenomenon—most notably, the role of power as inherent in sexual harassment. It also has delineated three limitations—focus on source behavior, unidimensionality of sexual harassment construct, and gender bias—that may restrict or misguide mitigation research efforts. The eclectic conceptualizations in academic research provide a solid body of work from which future investigations might be leveraged, and in the critique above I have called for a corresponding foundation for mitigation research. Imperative for intervention efforts is an integrated, multidimensional framework that is theoretically commensurate with other models and from which key concepts can be operationalized and tested empirically.

EMPIRICAL RESEARCH ON SEXUAL HARASSMENT

This section presents a comprehensive review of empirical research concerning sexual harassment in the workplace. The review is organized into six areas: (a) studies of sexual harassment prevalence, its outcomes, and correlates; (b) typologies of sexually harassing behaviors; (c) factors that contribute to perceptions regarding sexual harassment; (d) assessments of the proclivity to sexually harass; (e) responses to sexual harassment; and (f) strategies to combat sexual harassment. Although nearly all of the studies reviewed are driven by the behavior-oriented perspective described in the preceding section, it will be apparent that these lines of research are relatively independent of one another. I will argue that levels of perpetrator power and intentionality play key roles in helping us to understand the occurrence and behavioral forms of, as well as the seriousness of and responses to, sexual harassment.

Sexual Harassment Prevalence and Correlates

Incidence

Originally driven by feminist efforts to establish sexual harassment as a social problem, prevalence research focuses on the frequency with which sexual harassment occurs, costs incurred by victims and organizations, and demographic characteristics of victims and perpetrators. This type of research is characteristic of the initial stages of any research, which, as Brewer and Berk (1982) state, require validation of the problem's existence and lay the groundwork for future exploration. In general, research into the prevalence of sexual harassment has relied on self-report questionnaires that ask respondents to describe their own experiences of sexual harassment or sexually harassing behaviors (Collins & Blodgett, 1981; Crosthwaite & Swanton, 1986; Farley, 1978; USMSPB, 1981). For example, Cammaert (1985) administered questionnaires to 800 undergraduate and 200 graduate women. Participants then reported the frequency with which they had experienced sexually inappropriate behaviors, as well as the strategies they had used to handle these situations.

Although findings vary greatly, an overview of the research suggests that approximately 40-50% of women and 5-10% of men have been victims of sexual harassment in the workplace (Dziech & Weiner, 1984; Fitzgerald, 1993b; MacKinnon, 1979; Sandler, 1990). In the most comprehensive study to date, conducted by the U.S. Merit Systems Protective Board (1981), 10,648 government workers were surveyed, and 42% of working women and 15% of working men in that sample reported sexually harassing experiences. An update of this survey produced virtually identical statistics (USMSPB, 1988). The majority of all sexual harassment comes from coworkers, but nearly half is perpetrated by those in positions of authority over the targets (Collins & Blodgett, 1981; Fitzgerald, 1993b; Sandler, 1990; USMSPB, 1981, 1988).

Surveys have found consistently that, of the two legally defined forms of offense, hostile environment harassment is more common than quid pro quo harassment (Dziech & Weiner, 1984; Sandler, 1990; USMSPB, 1981). Gruber (1992) suggests that surveys tend to focus on incidents of more serious harassment and exclude reports of minor incidents that can contribute to hostile environment. Hence the incidence of sexual harassment, and especially less serious harassment, may be underreported.

Intrinsic in prevalence research is the question of harm. Victims of sexual harassment suffer physical, emotional, and psychological stress (Crull, 1982), and organizations incur financial losses due to litigation, internal investigations, decreased productivity, and turnover (Frierson, 1989; Garvey, 1986; Wagner, 1992). The USMSPB (1988) assessed the monetary loss to the U.S. government between May 1985 and May 1987 to be $267 million in terms of job turnover, sick leave, and reduced productivity. Victims' salary losses were estimated at $9.9 million.

Measurement Issues in Prevalence Research

Investigation into the pervasiveness of sexual harassment yields mixed results depending upon (a) how sexual harassment is measured, (b) the willingness of participants to label what they have experienced as sexual harassment, and (c) the type of setting in which the survey is conducted (Fitzgerald, 1993a; Hotelling, 1991b). With regard to the first issue, a major reason for the widespread variation in reports of prevalence of sexual harassment is that researchers' definitions differ among themselves and also differ from survey respondents' definitions of harassment. For example, some researchers define sexual harassment for their respondents behaviorally, and include less serious behaviors such as sexist comments in their definitions (Fitzgerald et al., 1988). Other researchers are more conservative in their definitions, and still others offer no definitions, leaving respondents to determine what constitutes sexual harassment. Such variation in methods makes valid comparisons of incidence across studies difficult (Gruber, 1992) and conclusions speculative (Lees-Haley, Lees-Haley, Price, & Williams, 1994).

A second measurement consideration, and one related to the definitional issues evident in survey research on sexual harassment, is that respondents are commonly asked to accept or to apply the label of "sexual harassment" to incidents they have experienced. This method requires each participant to "make a subjective judgment as to whether or not she had been harassed" (Fitzgerald et al., 1988, p. 157). Thus prevalence is confounded with participants' willingness to label incidents as sexual harassment. Researchers' tendency to ask participants to label situations dichotomously—as either harassment or not harassment—conforms with legal and organizational interpretations of the issue, which often necessitate decisions about whether or not harassment has taken place. However, this emphasis on labeling is problematic because victims often are unwilling to use the term *sexual harassment* even in severe cases. For example, Walker, Erickson, and Woolsey (1987) found that many of the same respondents who answered no when asked whether they ever had been victims of harassment answered yes when asked if they had been victims of a variety of sexually harassing actions. Similarly, Jaschik and Fretz (1991) found that only 3% of women who viewed a video of a clearly sexually harassing incident labeled the behavior as such. Instead, they used terms such as *inappropriate, offensive,* and *unprofessional.* These findings lend further credence to claims that sexual harassment may be underreported. Fitzgerald, Gelfand, and Drasgow (1995) offer the Sexual Experiences Questionnaire (SEQ), which attempts to overcome this pitfall by describing situations, such as "repeated requests for drinks, dinner, despite rejection," and "attempts to stroke or fondle," rather than asking respondents explicitly whether they have experienced sexual harassment.

Third, research into the prevalence of sexual harassment has spanned several contexts. Most studies have focused on academic settings and on students in particular (e.g., Cammaert, 1985), making generalizations to the greater U.S. population difficult. Nonstudent populations that have been investigated include military and nonmilitary federal employees and members of professions that are traditionally male (such as law; Rosenberg, Perlstadt, & Phillips, 1993), traditionally female (such as nursing; Dan, Pinsof, & Riggs, 1995), or gender integrated. Findings regarding the prevalence of sexual harassment have varied depending on context and across studies within contexts. For example, the incidence of sexual harassment in blue-collar settings has been reported to be both greater than and equivalent to that in white-collar work environments (Gutek & O'Connor, 1995).

Correlates of Sexual Harassment Derived From Prevalence Research

As an outgrowth of attempts to establish a nationwide estimate of the frequency of sexual harassment, analyses of demographic and organizational factors reveal correlates of sexual harassment that offer a richer understanding of the phenomenon. These comparative analyses reveal that sexual harassment is not a universal or a unidimensional phenomenon that occurs in the same manner, or with the same frequency, across all levels and types of organizations. Nor are all employees equally likely to be victims or perpetrators of sexual harassment. Systematic differences in occurrences of workplace sexual harassment are outlined below.

Research on the prevalence of sexual harassment has led to the discovery of some factors concerning profiles of persons who are more likely than others *to be harassed.* At least 90% of persons who have been harassed are women—most often, single women (Neibuhr & Boyles, 1991; Terpstra & Baker, 1989). Although physical attractiveness appears to have little impact in this regard, age is a factor (USMSPB, 1981)—women 30 years old and younger are more frequent victims. Lesbians, gays, and African American women are singled out more often as targets (Gruber & Bjorn, 1986; Schneider, 1982; Shoop & Edwards, 1994). Oaks and Landrum-Brown (1997) argue that women from Asian cultures may be particularly subject to sexual harassment in the United States because they often are taught to "obey men and to defer to their judgment unquestionably" (p. 218) and because of stereotypes that characterize these women as exotic, submissive, and demure.

Characteristics of individuals who are most likely *to harass* also have been examined. Some researchers profile the harasser as a "lecher" (Dziech & Weiner, 1984), and Coles (1986) and Hemming (1985) have found that the harasser is usually male and older than the victim. Both coworkers and supervisors are likely candidates (USMSPB, 1981). Identifying personality traits of actual harassers would be a highly sensitive and thus difficult task, and no researcher to date has attempted this challenge. Studies that have attempted to identify personal attributes of persons with a proclivity to sexually harass are reviewed later in this essay.

Perhaps the most marked conclusion that can be drawn from comparisons of prevalence research across contexts is that the incidence of sexual harassment is higher in sex-segregated (traditionally female or traditionally male) occupations than in sex-integrated fields. This is true especially with regard to the harassment of women. Women are harassed more when they work in traditionally female vocations than when they work in sex-integrated occupations (Gutek & Morasch, 1982; Neibuhr & Boyles, 1991). For example, female nurses report higher-than-average amounts of harassment from male patients and from male doctors (Grieco, 1987). Women also are harassed more when they attempt to break into traditionally male occupations (Spann, 1990). Some 70% of female "gender pioneers" (those who are among the first of their sex in their fields) in the military report having experienced sexual harassment (Neibuhr & Boyles, 1991; Wood, 1992). Women who represent a highly visible minority within their work areas are subject to frequent and severe harassment (Terpstra & Baker, 1989).

As is evident in this review, research on the prevalence of sexual harassment offers some insights regarding the harassed, potential harassers, and the contexts in which sexual harassment is most prevalent as well as about incidence. In the following critique, I note some of the limitations of prevalence research.

Critique of Prevalence Research

Although estimates are only approximate, the research reviewed above on the prevalence and correlates of sexual harassment clearly establishes sexual harassment as a widespread problem in the workplace. Valid assessment and longitudinal monitoring of the problem are limited by methodological issues that, taken collectively, provide inadequate estimates of the incidence of sexual harassment in the workplace (for further critiques, see Arvey & Cavanaugh, 1995; Gruber, 1992). The common technique of dichotomously labeling sexual harassment (a) fails to ascertain which types of behaviors are unwanted or why; (b) fails to explore the nature of the interaction between recipient and source of the potentially harassing behaviors; (c) restricts the ability to reconcile findings with legal definitions and organizational conceptions, because it does not sufficiently differentiate between forms of sexual harassment, such as quid pro quo and hostile environment; and (d) does little to clarify whether the interaction is intimidating, hostile, offensive, or interfering—outcomes specified by the USEEOC definition. Moreover, labeling sexual harassment as a unidimensional, concretely identifiable phenomenon may promote misunderstandings or resentments in the workplace, because individuals disagree over what constitutes sexual harassment. It also may draw attention away from the improvement of workplace climate and relationships.

An additional limitation of prevalence research is that the aspect of sexual harassment that causes it to be "unwelcome," when compared to consensual sexually oriented encounters, is virtually unexplored (Keyton & Rhodes, 1994). We need this information if we are to explain how (a) the same behaviors from two different individuals can be differentially determined by the same target to be sexual harassment, and (b) how the same behaviors from the same person can be sexually harassing to one target and not to another.

Finally, much prevalence research appears to be driven by a feminist ideological inclination that seeks to establish sexual harassment as a social problem that disadvantages women in the workplace. Evidence of this inclination can be found in (a) convenience samples that frequently include only female participants, rather than randomly selected samples that are more representative of the total workforce, and (b) reliance upon women's interpretations of what constitutes sexual harassment to conceptualize the phenomenon. Prevalence research does little to tap the interactive nature of sexual harassment, in part because survey research rarely includes the perspectives of the harasser. Hence we do not know whether the offender views sexual harassment as such, and on what these judgments are based. Although these kinds of data are sensitive, and therefore can be difficult to gather, self-reports of potentially harassing behaviors are needed to clarify these actions from the perpetrator perspective and to illuminate differences among types of harassers and forms of harassment.

Sexual Harassment Typologies

A second major area of investigation, sexual harassment typologies, is driven by the behaviorally oriented conceptualizations discussed previously and, as such, focuses on identifying and classifying types of sexually harassing behaviors. Typological research may be considered an extension of attempts to define sexual harassment by delineating harassing behaviors and an extension of prevalence research that distills types of sexually harassing encounters. Typically, in typological research survey respondents are asked to recall incidents of sexual harassment and to describe the types of behaviors involved (e.g., Collins & Blodgett, 1981; Gruber & Bjorn, 1986; Lafontaine & Tredeau, 1986). From these accounts, researchers identify specific categories of harassment—such as sexual advances, sexual bribery, abusive language, and pressure for sexual favors—which they often place along a continuum of severity. The numbers of categories specified range from two to seven. Gruber (1992) details three main categories of harassment in his meta-analysis of sexual harassment typologies: verbal requests, verbal comments, and nonverbal displays. Some typologies can be highly detailed. For example, Cammaert (1985) outlines three ways in which touch can be sexually harassing: blatantly, accidentally, and covertly. Sexual comments and sexual posturing are reported as the most frequently occurring forms of sexual harassment (Gruber, 1992). Fitzgerald's popularly accepted typology includes nonsexual harassment that reflects sex discrimination, rather than sexual harassment as defined by the legal, organizational, and academic conceptualizations reviewed earlier (for a summary and comparison of approaches to contextualizing sexual harassment, see Fitzgerald et al., 1997).

Critique of Sexual Harassment Typologies

Typological research remains in the elementary stages. There appears to be little agreement among researchers regarding categories of harassment, making comparisons among these studies difficult. Unfortunately, typologies derived academically do not coincide with the legal definitions of sexual harassment that are applied in the workplace (Gruber, 1992). Many include gender harassment of a nonsexual nature (e.g., Fitzgerald & Hesson-McInnes, 1989), but few survey studies have assessed sexually harassing behaviors that readily correspond to quid pro quo or hostile environment sexual harassment. As a point of illustration, Gruber (1992) notes that sexual bribery, the most basic form of quid pro quo harassment, is rarely included in typological analyses. Thus it is difficult to reconcile this research with applied intervention efforts based on legal definitions of sexual harassment (quid pro quo and hostile environment). Perhaps the most pertinent finding from typological studies for mitigation efforts is that sexual comments and sexual posturing are reported as the most frequent forms of sexual harassment.[3]

Perceptual Determinants of Sexual Harassment

A third and especially diverse area of sexual harassment research assesses (a) factors that affect observers' perceptions of what constitutes sexual harassment and its degree of severity and (b) factors that influence attributions about harassers and targets of harassment. Developed concurrently with prevalence surveys, studies in this area offer a broader perspective than do the behaviorally oriented approaches reviewed thus far. Collectively, this research provides empirically based definitions of sexual harassment that offer insight into the roles of the harasser, the harassed, and third parties involved in sexual harassment.

Research in this area typically involves respondents' use of Likert-type scales to indicate their degree of agreement or disagreement that particular behaviors constitute sexual harassment (e.g., Reilly, Carpenter, Dull, & Bartlett, 1982; Thomann & Wiener, 1987; Weber-Burdin & Rossi, 1982). Compared with the dichotomous labeling frequently employed in prevalence research, this method allows participants more latitude in making determinations of sexual harassment. Potentially harassing behaviors are stated in brief phrases or developed in vignettes. Scenarios, which vary widely across studies, represent perceptual, attributional, and situational factors that affect respondents' judgments (Fitzgerald & Ormerod, 1991; Gutek, Morasch, & Cohen, 1983; Kenig & Ryan, 1986). It is reasonable to assume that elements that affect perceptions of sexual harassment interact with one another, and in some cases cancel or increase the effects of other factors (Pryor & Day, 1988). For purposes of clarity, however, I will outline the perceptual determinants of sexual harassment that have been examined to date separately in the following discussion before I address the implications of their interaction.

Victim Role

Characteristics of targets, such as physical appearance, affect observers' perceptions regarding sexual harassment, including the likelihood that targets will be harassed, their responsibility for harassment incidents, and the severity of their sexually harassing experiences. Women who respond negatively to sexual overtures may be more likely to be seen as harassed than those who do not (Jones & Remland, 1992). Workman and Johnson (1991) found that both female and male college students rated a woman wearing moderate or heavy makeup as more likely to be sexually harassed than the same woman wearing no makeup. Similarly, Pryor and Day (1988) discovered that respondents judged behaviors toward a woman who attempted to dress in a sexy manner as less harassing than the same behaviors toward a woman who did not; the respondents also judged the "sexy" woman to be more to blame for her own harassment. According to the attribution perspective, clothing may reflect sexual intentions, suggesting that a woman who dresses provocatively may be seen as more to blame if she is harassed (Pryor & Day, 1988). Because cosmetics are associated with sexual attractiveness and femininity (Workman & Johnson, 1991), they also may contribute to attribution of blame toward the target.

Harasser Role

A consequential finding regarding perceptions of what constitutes sexual harassment focuses on the intentions of the harasser. Although intent may not be ascertainable, even by the perpetrator, observers make attributions regarding perpetrator intent (Pryor, 1985) and base judgments on these attributions. Perceived perpetrator intentionality increases the likelihood that certain behaviors/situations will be judged as harassment (Pryor & Day, 1988). For example, sexual innuendoes meant to be flattering may be less likely to be perceived as harassing than innuendoes intended to intimidate. The importance of this issue will become evident later in this essay, when I discuss perpetrator intentionality in detail.

The reputation and pattern of past behavior exhibited by the potential harasser also influences judgments concerning sexual harassment. Women and men appear to rely on reputation to help them decide whether an individual is guilty of sexual harassment (Reilly et al., 1982; Thomann & Wiener, 1987). For instance, belief that a potential perpetrator had been involved in multiple occurrences increased the likelihood that respondents would rate the behavior as sexual harassment, attribute more responsibility to the alleged harasser, and recommend more severe punishment (Gruber, Smith, & Kauppinen-Toropainen, 1996; Thomann & Wiener, 1987). In contrast, positive attributions—those lowering likelihood of blame—have resulted when perpetrators showed remorse by offering apologies for their behavior (Hunter & McClelland, 1991). Attribution theory has been applied to explain variance across potential harassers by comparing the consistency, distinctiveness, and consensus of information in a given scenario (Jensen & Gutek, 1982; Pryor & Day, 1988). An initiator who repeatedly behaves in a sexual or hostile manner toward the target (consistency), who directs similar behaviors toward others (consensus), and whose behaviors are different from others (distinctiveness) is more likely to be seen as a harasser (Pryor, 1985).

Women appear less likely to judge the same scenario as sexual harassment when the perpetrator is attractive and single (Konda, 1994). Littler-Bishop, Seidler-Feller, and Opaluch (1982) offer a social exchange explanation for findings of this nature. For example, they found that female flight attendants perceived sexual advances from airline pilots as more acceptable than similar overtures from airplane cleaning staff. Littler-Bishop et al. conclude that this is because women are less likely to consider behavior to be sexually harassing if it emanates from a desirable potential mate. Pilots, who are of higher status than cleaning crew members, may be viewed as mediators of social rewards.

Victim-Harasser Relationship

Situational factors, such as interpersonal relationships, may affect perceptions of whether or not a target has been harassed. Pryor (1985) found that when a target of harassment had a history of an intimate relationship with the harassed, observers were less likely to judge the situation as sexual harassment. Reilly et al. (1982) also determined that a past relationship between the potential harasser and the target decreased the likelihood of observers' labeling the potential harasser's behavior as sexual harassment.

Power has been investigated in more detail than have some other aspects of sexual harassment. Consistent with legal definitions and with prevalence research, studies on perceptions of sexual harassment have found that formal power is not necessary for sexual harassment to be perceived. Other forms of power—such as age, interpersonal power, or physical power—may play important roles when formal power is not salient (Gruber & Bjorn, 1986; Gutek & Morasch, 1982; Riger, 1992). Surveys indicate that formal power differentials intensify the threat of harassment: The higher the formal status of the initiator, the more serious and threatening the situation is judged to be (Collins & Blodgett, 1981; Gutek et al., 1983; Popovich, Licata, Nokovich, Martelli, & Zoloty, 1986; Reilly et al., 1982; Tata, 1993; USMSPB, 1981). Consistent with legal approaches, which find harassment from supervisors to be more serious, targets have judged supervisors' harassment to be more severe than that involving coworkers (Gruber & Bjorn, 1986). Solomon and Williams (1997) found that sex, power, and message explicitness interacted such that male supervisors who used explicit sexual messages were perceived as most harassing.

Tata (1993) provides a framework for examining the relationship between the dimension of power and different forms of sexual harassment. She discovered that the harasser's formal power level interacted with types of harassment in affecting observers' perceptions of sexual harassment. Power increased the perceived seriousness of lesser forms of harassment, such as gender harassment and seductive behavior, but did not affect judgments regarding more blatant offenses, such as sexual bribery, sexual coercion, and sexual assault. Apparently the more serious forms of sexual harassment are considered egregious regardless of power level, but the less severe forms are more variable, suggesting systematic differences among forms of sexual harassment. This interaction effect is foundational to the multidimensional framework for conceptualizing sexual harassment that I offer later in this essay.

Perceiver Characteristics

Perceptions regarding sexual harassment are affected not only by the roles of the actors involved, but by demographic, attitudinal, and individual characteristics of the perceivers of harassment. Occasional perceptual differences between African Americans and Anglo-American men have been detected in judgments of seriousness of sexual harassment. For example, Sigler and Johnson (1986) found that female and male African Americans, as well as Anglo-American women, were more likely than Anglo-American men to endorse criminalization of severe harassment.

Some researchers have investigated whether the perceiver's locus of control affects perception regarding sexual harassment. Individuals who feel more in control of situations (high internal locus of control) may be less likely to consider behaviors from an external source to be sexually harassing. This assumption appears to hold true for men more than for women. Booth-Butterfield (1989) determined that men with high external locus of control were more likely than men with high internal locus of control to perceive behaviors/situations as sexual harassment. Women showed no differences on this variable. However, Booth-Butterfield did not assess the effects of internal or external locus of control on level of severity or on different forms of sexual harassment, such as blatant versus subtle or quid pro quo versus hostile environment.

Sex and Sex Roles

The most notable and consistent independent variable that affects perceptions about sexual harassment is biological sex. Women and men differ in their judgments about sexual harassment (Baker, Terpstra, & Larntz, 1990; Booth-Butterfield, 1989; Gutek & O'Connor, 1995; Jones, Remland, & Brunner, 1987; Riger, 1992; Terpstra & Baker, 1986; Workman & Johnson, 1991). Men are more likely to believe that accounts of sexual harassment in the workplace are exaggerated (Collins & Blodgett, 1981). Women perceive a wider range of behaviors as sexually harassing and harmful, whereas men perceive a wider range of behaviors to be innocuous or flattering (Gutek et al., 1983; Powell, 1986; Pryor, 1985). Women also perceive a greater difference between harassing and immediate behaviors, and consider harassing behaviors to be more inappropriate (Mongeau,

1993). Terpstra and Baker (1986) found that 25% of the women in their sample, and only 12% of the men, considered coarse language to be sexually harassing. Women generally perceive less aggressive sexual behaviors, such as leering and sexual innuendoes, to be more harassing than do men (Jones et al., 1987). Although women and men agree that physical behavior is more serious (Gill, 1993) and therefore more likely to be perceived as harassment than is verbal behavior, Gutek (1985) discovered that only 59% of the men in her sample, as opposed to 84% of the women, considered sexual touching to be sexual harassment.

A sex-related variable, gender role identity, also affects perceptions of sexual harassment. Less-traditional sex role attitudes correlate with a higher likelihood of labeling behaviors as sexual harassment and of reporting occurrences of sexual harassment. As a point of illustration, Powell (1986) found that masculine women were more likely than masculine men to perceive selected behaviors/situations to be sexual harassment. Androgynous individuals, when compared with sex-typed individuals, tested similarly. A closely related study revealed that respondents with liberal attitudes toward women were more likely to perceive behaviors as harassing than were those with conservative attitudes toward women (Baker et al., 1990). Similarly, office workers with feminist attitudes were most likely to report having experienced sexual harassment (Pryor & Day, 1988). Women with high self-esteem and traditional sex role beliefs are more tolerant of sexual harassment and less aware of its negative consequences than are others (Malovich & Stake, 1990). Women with more traditional attitudes also hold women more responsible for sexual harassment (Jensen & Gutek, 1982).

In sum, it appears that women are more likely than men to perceive and to report sexual harassment. However, women and men who are more androgynous and less traditional in their sex roles may be least tolerant of sexual harassment. Although sex differences are detected more frequently, it is unclear whether biological sex or sex role identity is more influential in judgments regarding sexual harassment.

Some researchers have applied attribution theory to explain gender differences regarding sexual harassment (Terpstra & Baker, 1987; Workman & Johnson, 1991). For example, Workman and Johnson (1991) contend that men approach the issue from a perpetrator perspective, given that the overwhelming majority of harassers are men. Accordingly, men are more likely than women to blame the victim for the harassment and to see the victim as provoking harassment.

Although gender differences are the strongest and most consistent findings across studies, they vary in magnitude across contexts and demographic variables. For example, gender differences in judgments regarding sexual harassment are less distinct among professionals than among college students (Booth-Butterfield, 1989; Terpstra & Baker, 1987). Such gender differences are also less common in gender-integrated work environments than in gender-segregated contexts (Konrad & Gutek, 1986). Men who work in gender-integrated environments, and those who have been in the workforce for longer periods of time, tend to perceive a wider range of behaviors as sexually harassing and to consider harassing behaviors as less appropriate than do men who work in gender-segregated environments and those who have been in the workforce for shorter periods.

Critique of Perceptual Determinants Research

This body of research offers diverse and abundant insights into the everyday attributions made by workforce employees who constitute harassers, harassed, and third parties. The rich understanding of sexual harassment offered by research in this area may be enhanced in the future through the addition of (a) variables that delineate forms and levels of severity of sexual harassment (as seen in Tata, 1993), (b) factors that differentiate forms of perpetrator power, and (c) more consistent assessment of sex role differences in addition to sex differences. For example, Workman and Johnson's (1991) attributional analysis of gender differences suggests that men approach the issue from a perpetrator perspective, and therefore are more likely than women to blame the victim for the harassment and to judge the victim as likely to provoke harassment. In light of the findings reviewed above regarding the influence of sex and sex role attitudes on judgments of victim blame (in which both women and men who hold traditional sex role attitudes are more likely to blame the victim), Workman and Johnson's attributional analysis has two shortcomings that reduce its explanatory value. First, identification with the perpetrator seems a more appropriate explanation for men who hold traditional sex role attitudes than for all men, particularly androgynous men. Traditional men are more likely than androgynous men to blame the victim and to see situations as less sexually harassing. Second, men's identification with the perpetrator does not explain why women who hold more traditional sex role attitudes place greater blame on victims than do androgynous women. An assessment of sex role in addition to sex might shed some light on this issue.

Research examining the role of the victim in affecting perceptions of sexual harassment has revealed that certain aspects of the victim's physical appearance, such as heavy use of cosmetics and attempts to dress in a sexy manner, increase perceptions of victim blame and likelihood of being harassed. Analyses of factors that contribute to victim appearance, and whether they correlate with sexual harassment, are needed to determine whether attributions made by observers are consistent with fact. Are women who wear sexy clothing and heavier makeup harassed more frequently or more severely than other women? If so, and if physical appearance correlates with the likelihood of actually being harassed, then this information may help inform other areas of research, such as perpetrator motivation and prevention efforts.

Implications of Perceptual Determinants of Sexual Harassment

Research regarding factors that affect determinations of sexual harassment proffers a reconceptualization of sexual harassment as a phenomenon that is moderated not only by the power relationship between harasser and harassed but by other relational dimensions as well. Some of these dimensions include (a) the severity of sources' behaviors; (b) target characteristics, such as physical appearance; (c) harasser characteristics, including intent, past behaviors, and attractiveness; (d) perceiver characteristics, such as sex, sex role attitudes, and race; and (e) locus of control. The effects of some of these factors are clearer when interpreted in combination with other moderating factors. For example, the interaction between formal power and the perceived severity of harassment and the relationship between perceiver sex and perceived intentionality may yield implications for our understanding of sexual harassment that are not evident when each of these factors is treated separately. I discuss below some potential relationships among factors.

Research indicates that observers are more likely to rate a potential male harasser's behavior as sexual harassment if they believe he has been involved in multiple occurrences of sexual harassment (Gruber et al., 1996; Thomann & Wiener, 1987). The USMSPB (1981) survey found that perpetrators frequently reported multiple occurrences of harassing others—lending credence to observers' attributions regarding multiple harassment. Studies of multiple occurrences also have the potential to tap perceived perpetrator intent—that is, are the behaviors of harassers who are involved in multiple cases of sexual harassment more likely to be viewed as intentionally harassing their victims?

Although abundant studies have established that higher power differentials lead to greater perceived severity of harassment (see Gruber et al., 1996), only one study has tested for interaction effects between power differentials and types of harassment (Tata, 1993). Consistent with previous research, Tata (1993) found that greater power increased the perceived seriousness of less severe forms of sexual harassment. However, additional knowledge regarding the relationship between power and perceived severity was uncovered when types of sexual harassment were treated separately rather than combined as if they constituted a single entity. Tata determined that power did not affect observers' judgments regarding more blatant types of sexual harassment such as sexual bribery, sexual advances, and sexual coercion. Thus, as Pryor and Day (1988) contend, more serious forms of harassment are less open to ambiguity than are less serious forms of harassment. This interaction effect suggests the following three implications for the study of sexual harassment for purposes of mitigation.

First, if less serious forms of sexual harassment are obscure to observers, they are less likely to be clear to the interactants in a potentially harassing situation. This ambiguity may contribute to mutual misinterpretation of messages—referred to as "asynchronous communication" in research by Hickson et al. (1991). Hence ambiguity regarding less serious forms of sexual behavior in the workplace may contribute to *unintentional* sexual harassment. Second, Tata's (1993) findings indicate that individuals do not regard sexual harassment as unidimensional, but perceive distinctions among types of harassment. This research adds richness to the study of sexual harassment by recognizing multidimensionality rather than assigning homogeneity to the phenomenon. Third, the interaction between formal power and type of harassment further emphasizes multidimensionality. Conceptualizations of sexual harassment that highlight dimensions of power and forms of harassment may encourage testing for interaction effects through a factorial design. Interaction effects give more information regarding the structure of a phenomenon than do main effects (Singleton, Straits, Straits, & McAllister, 1988). By extension, these designs could produce a basis for diverse curtailment strategies.

A third general category of findings, the discovery of sex differences in perceptions of what constitutes sexual harassment, is not surprising. We know that women are victims and men are perpetrators of sexual harassment in the overwhelming majority of cases. Therefore, as the phenomenon of sexual harassment is investigated, we would anticipate finding sex differences. The fact that women and men hold different conceptions of what constitutes sexual harassment, as well as which types of sexually oriented situations are unwanted, has two implications for sexual harassment mitigation. First, because the perceptions of women and men differ with regard to the nature and severity of sexual harassment, they also may differ with regard to the effectiveness of specific tactics for ending sexual harassment. Second, disagreement between women and men regarding whether certain interactions are innocuous or unwanted undoubtedly leads to some harassment of women by men. Such situations call into question the intentionality of men's sexual harassment of women. A related line of research on sex differences regarding perceptions of sexual intent (Abbey, 1982; Abbey, Cozzerelli, McLaughlin, & Harnish, 1987; Saal, 1996) supports the conclusion that, at times, women and men interpret potentially sexual interactions and behaviors differently. Abbey (1982) discovered that men perceive friendly behaviors as more sexual than do women. Similarly, Sigal, Gibbs, Adams, and Derfler (1988) found that in ambiguous situations depicted on film, men were more likely than women to perceive interactions as sexual. Workman and Johnson (1991) also conclude that "men may view certain appearance cues as a sign of sexual interest or consent" (p. 763). Thus it appears that men may be sexually harassing women unintentionally in some cases because they have misinterpreted friendly actions as sexual cues. This understanding of sexual harassment also is consistent with Hickson et al.'s (1991) analysis of sexual harassment as an asynchronous communication relationship, and it warrants further investigation. In light of Tata's (1993) finding that more ambiguity surrounds less severe forms of sexual harassment, less blatant harassment may be due in part to perceptual differences between women and men—is it therefore unintentional? If so, then strategies for dealing with unintentional sexual harassment may require clarification of perceptual differences. It is just as reasonable to assume that other, more intentionally malicious, behaviors conceivably require different mitigation strategies—such as legal recourse.

Men's Proclivity to Sexually Harass

A fourth highly specific area of research attempts to identify men with a proclivity to sexually harass women. A few cautions must precede the discussion of this literature. First, the studies reviewed reflect the behavioral intentions of participants only; the findings cannot be used to make predictions regarding the intentions, behaviors, or traits of actual harassers. Second, for a summary of relevant research that reviews the limitations of using dispositions and attitudes to predict behaviors, see Eagly and Chaiken (1993). Finally, because the studies reviewed below assess behavioral intentions, they examine only purposeful sexual harassment, not the type of unintended miscommunication described by Hickson et al. (1991) and discussed above.

Pryor (1987) has developed the Likelihood to Sexually Harass (LSH) scale, which focuses on quid pro quo sexual harassment. In his investigations, Pryor placed men in a series of scenarios in which they controlled the rewards or punishments for an attractive woman. The men reported their likelihood to sexually harass in each of the scenarios (which included the proviso that they would be immune to reprisal). Pryor and his colleagues discovered that men who reported a likelihood to sexually harass women in the quid pro quo situations also endorsed traditional male sex role stereotypes (on Thompson & Pleck's [1986] scale), found it difficult to assume others' perspectives, scored high on measures of authoritarianism (Pryor, LaVite, & Stoller, 1993), and preferred dominance and manipulation strategies when attempting to influence women (Pryor & Stoller, 1994). Social sexual behavior was also measured. The LSH predicted men who, when placed in a position of authority over a female confederate in a laboratory setting, engaged in more sexual touching and bodily contact with the woman than did their colleagues (Pryor, 1987). High LSH scorers also were more likely to model the sexual behaviors of a confederate (Pryor et al., 1993).

In a similar line of study, Bingham and Burleson (1996) developed a scale that taps a broader range of sexually harassing behaviors than does Pryor's LSH and is not limited to harassment of attractive women. The Sexual Harassment Proclivity Index (SHPI) addresses quid pro quo harassment and "intrusive harassment" (sexual advances). Compared with other men, those who reported a likelihood to engage in either form of harassment ranked higher on Pryor's LSH scale (1987), were more tolerant of sexual harassment (on Lott, Reilly, & Howard's [1982] scale), were more accepting of rape myths (on Burt's [1980] scale), and showed lower levels of dating competence. Men who reported a likelihood to engage in quid pro quo harassment also reported a higher tolerance of violence toward women (on Burt's scale) than did other men.

Bargh and Raymond (1995) investigated the schematic processes of men who reported a likelihood to engage in quid pro quo harassment of women (according to Pryor's LSH scale) or to sexually exploit women. They conclude that these men cognitively link power and sexuality, such that when they are in positions of power over women, sexual thoughts come to their minds automatically. These men likely attribute their sexually oriented behavior toward women to sexual attraction, not power, and do not perceive their conduct to be an inappropriate use of power.

A strength and a limitation of the above-noted proclivity assessments is that the SHPI and the LSH focus on men who profess intentions to harass. Neither identifies individuals who are likely to harass unintentionally or those who may contribute to hostile environment harassment (except in terms of sexual advances). Further research is needed to distinguish among types of potential harassers and to differentiate them from those who are unlikely to sexually harass and from actual harassers.

Responses to Sexual Harassment

The fifth area of empirical research to be reviewed examines how people respond to sexually harassing situations. Although not abundant, this research has proceeded more rapidly toward in-depth understanding of sexual harassment curtailment than have the areas of research discussed thus far. Initially, scholars attempted to establish only a typology of target responses to sexual harassment. More recent research has laid the groundwork for mitigation efforts by delineating responses to specific forms of harassment, the perceived effectiveness of types of responses, and the reactions of observers to responses from both accuser and accused. Most important for a multidimensional understanding of the issue, several researchers have found that disparate outcomes may result from varied forms of sexual harassment and may be moderated by interpersonal and/or situational factors.

Early research in this area employed surveys in which participants were asked to select from predetermined categories of formal or informal reactions those that best conformed to their actual responses to sexual harassment they had experienced personally (e.g., Crull, 1982; USMSPB, 1981). More recent studies have used open-ended questions, delivered through either interpersonal interviews or written questionnaires; respondents have been asked to recount their actual responses to sexually harassing situations they have experienced or to give their reactions to situations laid out in fictional vignettes (Gruber & Bjorn, 1986; Gutek, 1985; Terpstra & Baker, 1989). Responses have been categorized according to reaction types. Whereas Fitzgerald and Hesson-McInnes (1989) employed factor analysis to distinguish categories of sexual harassment responses, most other researchers have used more subjective methods of analysis.

In one noteworthy investigation, Terpstra and Baker (1989) asked 286 female and male college students and working women to document how they would respond to 18 randomly ordered scenarios. The replies generated more than 5,000 responses, which were then categorized into 10 primary reaction types. Although such studies are too diverse to produce a single valid typology of responses to sexual harassment (Baker et al., 1990), some of the most frequently enumerated categories include behaviorally focused responses such as ignoring, joking, leaving the job, direct confrontation, and external or internal reporting (Baker et al., 1990; Gruber & Bjorn, 1986; Gutek, 1985; Terpstra & Baker, 1989; USMSPB, 1981). The most frequently reported response to sexual harassment is avoidance (Gutek, 1985; Sandroff, 1992; Terpstra & Baker, 1986). Responses to sexual harassment vary along dimensions such as directness or passivity (Gruber & Bjorn, 1986) and can be moderated by sex of target, situational factors (such as organizational climate), and personal factors (such as self-esteem) (Knapp, Faley, Ekeberg, & DuBois, 1997; Terpstra & Baker, 1989). Yount (1997) supplies an account of three diverse strategies employed by female coal miners. The women responded to men's sexual conduct by being ladylike, flirtatious, or tomboyish.

Factors That Moderate Behavioral Responses

Just as women and men hold different perceptions of what constitutes harassment and experience sexual harassment with different frequency, they also report different reactions to sexually harassing situations (Gutek, 1985; USMSPB, 1988). The USMSPB (1981) study, which assessed responses of more than 10,000 sexually harassed women and men, found that women were more likely than men to avoid a harasser, to tell the harasser to stop, and to report the situation. Conversely, men were more likely to comply with the harassment. Dunn, Cody, and Haynie (1996) discovered that, in response to hypothetical situations in which they were victims of harassment, women reported a greater tendency to document incidents, to refer the situation to others, to propose training, and to comfort the accused, whereas men were more likely than women to warn the harasser to stop. Terpstra and Baker (1989) found that men were more likely to report that they would leave the field or respond physically to sexual harassment.

In an extension of Terpstra and Baker's 1989 study, Baker et al. (1990) found that gender differences in responses to sexual harassment interacted with the severity of the situation. Women's reactions, more than men's, varied according to the women's perceptions of the seriousness of the incident. In overt cases involving fondling, rape, or quid pro quo propositioning, significantly more male than female participants claimed that they would leave the field, report the incident, or react physically, whereas in reaction to more minor offensive behavior, such as coarse language, off-color jokes, or gestures, more women than men anticipated using passive responses, such as ignoring the behavior or avoiding the target. Among nearly 2,000 Canadian working women, severity of harassment was found to be a strong predictor of assertive versus nonassertive responses (Gruber & Smith, 1995). These women responded more assertively to more severe harassment, but less so when the harasser had supervisory power.

Passive responses to sexual harassment appear to be frequent among women with little organizational power. Gruber and Bjorn (1986) evaluated the passivity versus assertiveness of the actual responses recalled by 150 blue-collar women. They report that women in low-status or low-skilled jobs (a) responded in a powerless manner compared with high-status, high-power peers; (b) were more limited in their responses than were less frequently targeted groups of respondents; and (c) responded more passively to advances from their supervisors than to sexual harassment from peers. Lower organizational power was the strongest predictor of women's use of passive responses to sexual harassment when compared with other factors such as sociocultural or individual variables. For example, women of higher sociocultural status but in low-status, unskilled professions responded similarly to African American women, young women, and unmarried women—all of whom are of lower sociocultural status and are more frequent targets of sexual harassment.

Among women in blue-collar positions, Gruber and Bjorn (1986) found that those with high self-esteem responded more assertively to sexual harassment than did women with low self-esteem. Although causality is not easily determined from the data, Gruber and Bjorn speculate that sexual harassment lowers self-esteem, thus decreasing women's ability to respond in an assertive manner. However, self-esteem does not appear to influence responses in all sexually harassing situations. Baker et al. (1990) tested the responses of 144 women and men to 18 scenarios and discovered that self-esteem did not affect respondents' reactions.

Internal versus external locus of control also has been examined as a potential moderating variable (Booth-Butterfield, 1989). For example, Baker et al. (1990) found that respondents with high internal locus of control were more likely to respond assertively than passively to a sexually harassing situation that involved rape. However, there is no evidence to suggest that locus of control affects the nature of targets' responses to other forms of sexual harassment.

Knapp et al. (1997) have reviewed targets' behavioral responses to sexual harassment. Drawing upon both whistle-blowing and stress/coping research, they offer a theoretical model of potential determinants of victim responses. They propose that antecedent conditions, such as power, organizational characteristics, and individual characteristics, interact with predictor variables, such as severity of harassment, outcome expectancy, and level of distress, to moderate the ways in which targets respond.

Nonbehavioral Responses

Unfortunately, only a few studies have examined target responses in nonbehavioral terms. Participants' affective responses to actual or fictional experiences offer a more in-depth view of sexual harassment than do behavioral responses alone. For example, Lee and Heppner (1991) sorted the perceptual reactions of 133 supervisors and managers to potentially harassing behaviors into the four categories specified by the USEEOC (1980): interference, hostility, intimidation, and offensiveness. They discovered that offensiveness and intimidation were key elements in determining respondents' feelings of harassment.

Clair (1993) analyzed women's latent responses to sexual harassment by interviewing working women who had experienced sexual harassment and then examining their accounts through a framing perspective. Clair discovered that the women most frequently employed trivialization and denotative hesitancy as framing devices to describe their experiences. As they recounted episodes of sexual harassment, they joked or otherwise made light of the events (trivialization), and/or they were unwilling or unable to label their experiences as "sexual harassment" (denotative hesitancy). Clair presents the use of framing devices that trivialize or fail to identify sexual harassment as a hegemonic means of supporting its existence. When victims trivialize or deny the severity of their sexual harassment experiences, they encourage others to do the same, reducing the perceived negative effects of such harassment and therefore its importance as a problem.

Observer Evaluations of Responses

A final approach to the study of responses to sexual harassment examines how observers react to the interactants in sexually harassing situations. Dunn et al. (1996) tested how respondents reacted to an accused male's denial, evasion, or acceptance of responsibility for his actions. They found that the accused was rated as more competent, likable, dedicated, and credible when he accepted responsibility rather than denying or evading it. Hunter and McClelland (1991) found that the perceived seriousness of sexual harassment increased when harassers offered justifications for their actions and decreased when harassers apologized.

Critique and Implications of Research on Responses to Sexual Harassment

Studies of responses to sexual harassment have been relatively infrequent compared with research into prevalence or perceptual determinants of sexual harassment, but they offer a great deal of insight into sexual harassment and, by extension, potential for its curtailment. The contributions from this line of research are varied, ranging from typologies of targets' behavioral responses to observers' perceptions of harassers and targets based upon their accounts.

Treating sexual harassment as a multidimensional phenomenon, research into responses to sexual harassment recognizes that different forms of harassment elicit different reactions, which, in turn, are moderated by interpersonal and/or situational factors. For example, Lee and Heppner (1991) claim that targets may feel easily intimidated under specific conditions or in certain work environments, and they may feel offended in others. This approach has implications for the future study of sexual harassment. First, because the USEEOC (1980) defines sexual harassment as interfering, intimidating, hostile, and/or offensive sexual conduct in the workplace, academics' attention to these aspects of sexual harassment promotes consistency between legal and academic arenas. As a result, organizational trainers and other lay practitioners—who frequently rely on the USEEOC definition—will find academic research employing these terms to be more easily interpretable. Second, as an alternative to the traditional dichotomous labeling approach, prevalence research could utilize these four dimensions instead of, or in conjunction with, the label of *sexual harassment* in surveys designed to establish the frequency and correlates of this behavior. Finally, this approach raises new questions regarding relationships among dimensions of sexual harassment. For example, which situational or dispositional factors best determine whether a target of sexual harassment will respond in an assertive or a passive manner?

Consistent with the findings of the literature reviewed above, which reveals that formal power moderates perceptions of sexual harassment and its severity, response research demonstrates that power moderates how victims react in situations of sexual harassment. Formal organizational power appears to be a stronger indicator of type of response to sexual harassment than does self-esteem, locus of control, or sociocultural status. The relationship between formal power and type of response is not entirely clear, however, and requires further investigation across diverse populations. Gruber and Bjorn's (1986) finding that lower organizational power is indicative of passive responses to sexual harassment may imply that women who are harassed by their supervisors will respond more passively because they hold low organizational power, relative to the supervisors. Expectations of passivity are consistent with empirical findings that a victim is unlikely to report sexual harassment if the perpetrator is a supervisor or manager (e.g., Hotelling, 1991a). However, other research suggests an alternative hypothesis. Both legal decisions and academic research have concluded that sexual harassment from management is perceived by both women and men to be more severe than harassment from coworkers (Gutek et al., 1983; Reilly et al., 1982; Tata, 1993; USMSPB, 1981). Terpstra and Baker (1989) found that women responded more assertively to more severe types of sexual harassment. Other researchers also claim that more severe sexual harassment is more likely to be reported (e.g., Jones & Remland, 1992). Therefore, one might anticipate that women will perceive harassment from management to be more serious and will respond to it more assertively, or at least more actively. These ostensibly conflicting conclusions require further investigation in order to determine whether organizational power or perceived severity is the more important determinant of the assertiveness of women's responses to sexual harassment and whether other factors, such as perceived perpetrator intent, affect women's responses.

Sex role attitudes, which have been shown to affect perceptions of sexual harassment, also may shed light upon the question of whether and in what ways a perpetrator's formal power moderates victim responses. Gruber and Bjorn (1986) found that women with more liberal attitudes toward women were more likely to employ assertive responses to sexual harassment. Congruent with this finding, Malovich and Stake (1990) observed that women and men with less traditional sex role attitudes were more likely to perceive situations as sexual harassment. If nontraditional women perceive particular situations as more harassing, then it is possible that they would react more strongly—employing assertive rather than passive responses.

Among other variables that warrant attention in conjunction with responses to sexual harassment is self-esteem. Discussions of self-esteem and sexual harassment suggest a potentially reciprocal relationship between the two, and that self-esteem may influence how targets respond to harassers. Gruber and Bjorn (1986) speculate that sexual harassment lowers self-esteem, thus decreasing women's ability to respond in an assertive manner. Although Baker et al. (1990) found no support for the claim that victims' levels of self-esteem affect their responses, the variable has surfaced frequently in other sexual harassment research. Victim accounts have indicated repeatedly that being sexually harassed can lower self-esteem (Coles, 1986; "Our Stories," 1992; Sumrall & Taylor, 1992), and women with low self-esteem are more aware of the negative consequences of sexual harassment than are others (Malovich & Stake, 1990).

If sexual harassment induces low self-esteem in targets, and low self-esteem elicits passive responses from women, then passivity would be a commonly expected response to sexual harassment. This is indeed the case. Passivity, in the form of avoidance, is the most frequent type of response from women (Gutek, 1985; Sandroff, 1992; Terpstra & Baker, 1986), particularly when they are facing less blatant forms of harassment (Baker et al., 1990). On the other hand, it also is possible that women with lower self-esteem may be more frequent targets of sexual harassment because of their lower interpersonal power. In a departure from the popular behavioral focus, Clair (1993), Dunn et al. (1996), and Hunter and McClelland (1991) offer a wider perspective than previously offered and contribute to a more complete understanding of sexual harassment. This broader approach highlights the potential effects that sexual harassment has on third parties, such as relational partners, other organizational employees, and court judges. By increasing our understanding of third-party interpretations, we may better comprehend investigative decision-making processes and outcomes regarding sexual harassment in the workplace.

Perhaps the most compelling questions raised, but left unanswered, by research into responses to sexual harassment concern how target responses affect harassers, whether any of the known target responses are effective in curtailing sexual harassment, and, if so, what factors moderate their effectiveness. The following section presents a review of the literature on recommendations for and assessments of sexual harassment curtailment efforts.

EMPIRICAL RESEARCH ON
SEXUAL HARASSMENT INTERVENTIONS

Although the research reviewed thus far offers insights into the nature and dimensions of sexual harassment and, by extension, lays a foundation for mitigation efforts, it offers no specific solutions to the problem. The final area of research to be reviewed is solution oriented, centering on methods for handling sexual harassment on societal, organizational, and interpersonal levels. Academic researchers offer recommendations for curtailment of harassment, but typically only as part of a broader research focus. These recommendations differ from the responses to sexual harassment reviewed above in that they are anticipatory methods of dealing with sexual harassment, rather than reactions from victims. Furthermore, these recommendations frequently parallel researchers' disciplinary roots and, consequently, their conceptualizations of sexual harassment. Hence, as with attempts to establish and explain sexual harassment as a social problem, efforts to curtail harassment have been based primarily upon a unidimensional, behavior-oriented approach, and they often fail to integrate academic, legal, and organizational perspectives.

Societal-Level Interventions

Researchers who study sexual harassment as a societal phenomenon often advocate *government policy efforts* combined with *educational efforts*—for women and men—as the most expedient means of curtailing sexual harassment (e.g., Fitzgerald, 1993b). They encourage government agencies to recognize a broader range of incidents as sexual harassment, promote greater liability for harassers and their employers, and award damages to victims of sexual harassment. This approach attempts to protect victims of sexual harassment and to provide them with recourse under the law. Among other benefits, educational efforts inform potential harassers of the deleterious effects their actions may have on others and the potential legal ramifications of their behaviors, in an attempt to modify their workplace interactions accordingly. Many researchers also recommend gender integration of the workplace as the most efficacious long-term strategy, arguing that because sexual harassment is based in sex differences, reducing sex differences in the work environment will reduce sexual harassment (e.g., Fitzgerald, 1993b; Gutek & Morasch, 1982). These broad approaches are indirect, attempting to reach harassers and targets but with no means of identifying their audiences and addressing them directly.

In keeping with, and perhaps in response to, these three broad-based approaches, laws have changed, sexual harassment education has increased, and organizations have become more gender integrated. Recommendations, interpretations, and applications of government regulations have expanded since the first case of sexual harassment was tried before a federal court in 1974 (e.g., Conte, 1997; Keyton, 1996; Woerner & Oswald, 1990). For example, the "reasonable woman" standard is a more liberal interpretation of the law than was the original "reasonable person" standard, and a 1998 U.S. Supreme Court decision expanded the definition of sexual harassment to include same-sex harassment (Greenburg, 1998; *Oncale v. Sundowner Offshore Services,* 1998). It is possible, even probable, that changes in government policy such as these have had the kinds of mitigating effects on sexual harassment that academics and activists advocate.

Also consistent with societal-level recommendations, efforts toward educating the public with regard to sexual harassment currently are being implemented. Mass-media attention (discussed in the beginning of this essay) and organizational training programs (discussed in the next subsection) have increased organizational members' knowledge of sexual harassment over the past several years. In accordance with the aim of these strategies, knowledge of what is and is not appropriate workplace behavior may have lowered the incidence of sexual harassment. Finally, in keeping with broad-based intervention strategies, the workplace has become more gender integrated than when sexual harassment first was declared unlawful.

Unfortunately, the effects of these three phenomena are difficult to measure collectively and ostensibly impossible to disentangle. As a result, virtually no theoretical or empirical analyses of these societal recommendations have been conducted. In short, we have no evidence as to whether the overall level of sexual harassment is beginning to decline.

Organizational-Level Interventions

As I have noted at the beginning of this essay, there are several reasons American corporations take steps to prevent and reduce sexual harassment. As a result of government actions, employers are liable for the occurrence of sexual harassment within their organizations unless they have taken reasonable measures to prevent it (Garvey, 1986). Increasingly stringent federal regulations now hold employers potentially liable for sexual harassment even when they are not aware of its occurrence (Garvey, 1986), which acts as an impetus for many employers to attempt to reduce sexual harassment (Grundmann et al., 1997; Keyton, 1996). Employers who want to reduce costs associated with turnover and decreased productivity also may attempt to prevent sexual harassment among their employees (Garvey, 1986; Gilsdorf, 1990; Schafran, 1991; Zedeck & Casio, 1984). Those who are concerned about their organizations' public images may be more motivated to reduce sexual harassment than are those who are less concerned. Finally, as a result of increased knowledge with regard to the issue and their legal rights surrounding it, employees may place individual or collective demands on employers to reduce sexual harassment in the work environment.

Frequently, the responsibility for determining and implementing organizational strategies to combat sexual harassment falls upon equal employment officers or human resources personnel (Keyton, 1996; Weeks et al., 1985). Some organizations attempt to control sexual harassment by making such control a supervisory responsibility, treating it similarly to tardiness or other unacceptable personnel practices (USEEOC, 1980). In these cases, high incidence of sexual harassment within a department may lead to negative performance evaluations for the departmental supervisor or manager. This treatment of sexual harassment can enable the tracking of its prevalence within specific departments and in the company as a whole.

Organizations employ a variety of strategies in their attempts to reduce the incidence of sexual harassment. These range from simply posting the Equal Employment Opportunity Commission's guidelines regarding sexual harassment to careful screening of potential employees and the creation of task forces to monitor the issue. One of the earliest and still most frequently enacted strategies is the creation of a companywide sexual harassment policy and a corresponding effort to make the policy known to employees (Sandler, 1990; Wagner, 1992). In this relatively passive manner, employers endeavor to inform employees that sexual harassment is illegal and therefore not acceptable conduct within the organization. Because this simple act reduces employer liability (Riger, 1992), many organizations may be content with this understated approach. No empirical evidence suggests that the creation and circulation of a sexual harassment policy actually reduces or contributes to the curtailment of the incidence or severity of sexual harassment (Grundmann et al., 1997). However, these efforts are consonant with academic researchers' recommendations to educate women and men as to the illegality of sexual harassment, and may represent a first step toward that goal.

A more *active* strategy, one implemented frequently within government organizations and adopted increasingly in the private sector, involves intervention programs in which some or all employees are educated about sexual harassment (Webb, 1992). This strategy also parallels the education and awareness approach touted by academics (e.g., Fitzgerald, 1993a, 1993b). These programs minimally include legal definitions and explanations of different forms of sexual harassment (Sandler, 1990; Wagner, 1992; Webb, 1992). They also may incorporate information about costs to the organization, company policies regarding sexual harassment, and recommended procedures for filing complaints within the organization. Approaches to sexual harassment training proposed by social scientists (e.g., Berryman-Fink, 1993; Fitzgerald, 1993a; Hickson et al., 1991; Sandler, 1990), government agencies (e.g., Lebrato, 1986; Pearman & Lebrato, 1984; USOPM, 1980b), and lay practitioners (e.g., Franklin, Moglen, Zatlin-Boring, Angress, 1981; Learning International, 1982; Petrocelli & Repa, 1994; Wagner, 1992; Webb, 1992) tend to advocate three primary elements: (a) training to increase awareness, (b) formal policies prohibiting sexual harassment, and (c) complaint procedures that are easily accessible to victims. The focus of many early intervention programs was on the illegality of sexual harassment, how to recognize its occurrence, women's right to be free from it, and, in some programs, men's responsibility to change their behavior (e.g., Borah, 1991; Clair, 1993; Rose, 1992). In order to address organizations' legal responsibilities, training programs tend to define sexual harassment according to the USEEOC definition. Many attempt to elucidate the issue further through specific behavior-oriented examples. When compared with many areas of research reviewed in this essay, these core elements of sexual harassment training programs are highly consistent across legal, organizational, and academic arenas. However, individual programs differ considerably in terms of defining sexual harassment in behavioral terms, assignment of responsibility to perpetrators versus victims (or men versus women), examples used, and so forth.

More *comprehensive* intervention programs include the aforementioned elements but also may focus on prevention through *organizational and interpersonal actions.* For example, some lay practitioners recommend conducting personnel interviews and audits, holding meetings, and forming task groups to deal with sexual harassment (e.g., Wagner, 1992). These actions may be intended to show management support for curtailment of sexual harassment (Webb, 1992) or to empower women (Lebrato, 1986). Some interventions have included sensitivity training, especially for men in the workplace, and assertive communication skills training (discussed in the following subsection), directed primarily toward women.

Empirical assessments of organizational-level strategies to reduce sexual harassment are rare (Grundmann et al., 1997). In one of the few, Beauvais (1986) found increases in the overall knowledge of 53 student-peer advisers concerning the nature of sexual harassment, its prevalence, and its illegality after the subjects had participated in a 2-hour sexual harassment education seminar. Men's knowledge increased more than did women's. Moyer and Nath (1998), who assessed two types of training efforts, also found that men were affected more than women. Written training exercises increased male students' expertise in identifying sexual harassment, whereas women's expert knowledge did not change. However, viewing a sexual harassment training video increased both female and male college students' tendency to perceive sexual harassment in written scenarios about male-female interactions. Both studies found that, prior to training, women were more knowledgeable about sexual harassment than were men.

These investigations provide a foundation for future efforts to evaluate organizational training programs and suggest that such programs may differentially affect participants. However, it remains unclear whether these and other training programs increase only knowledge of and perceptions about the phenomenon or whether they also affect participants' subsequent *attitudes* and *behaviors*. Although lay practitioners occasionally report successful organizational-level interventions, their evaluations are not based upon valid scientific assessments of attitudinal or behavioral effects. A common indicator of the "success" of a sexual harassment intervention program is an increase in the number of reported cases following implementation of the program (e.g., Rose, 1992).

Thus it is not possible to ascertain whether current educational training efforts achieve the desired outcomes, create a boomerang effect, or produce other unforeseen consequences (Rowe, 1996). As a point of illustration, one organization reported that two male employees were so distressed after attending the company's sexual harassment training program that they resigned (M. Chapman, personal communication, February 17, 1994). Despite the face validity offered by consistency among academic, organizational, and government recommendations for sexual harassment training programs, these approaches lack any theoretical basis and empirical support.

Interpersonal-Level Interventions

Interpersonal-level strategies for combating sexual harassment are directed primarily toward potential targets of sexual harassment. The most frequently advocated interpersonal-level strategy for harassment targets is the use of assertive communication techniques (Bingham, 1988; Blalock, 1995; Booth-Butterfield,

1986). Recommended by academics and lay practitioners, this strategy is integral to, for example, the U.S. Navy sexual harassment training program. *Assertiveness* can be defined as the direct expression of one's feelings, preferences, needs, and opinions in a way that is neither threatening nor punishing to another and does not involve undue anxiety or fear for the communicator (Bingham, 1991; Carr-Ruffino, 1993; Lange & Jakubowski, 1976; Smith, 1983; for a more detailed explication of assertive communication, see Jansma, 1997).

Researchers have begun to assess the efficacy of assertive communication as a strategy to combat sexual harassment; however, the term *assertiveness* is used inconsistently throughout the literature. Many conceive of assertiveness as occupying the center of a continuum between passivity and aggressiveness (Bingham, 1988), but assertiveness also has been conceptualized as the opposite of passivity. When researchers such as Gruber and Bjorn (1986) and Baker et al. (1990) refer to respondents' strategies as assertive, they include aggressive strategies as well. Lay practitioners who consider assertiveness as a strategy to combat sexual harassment hold similarly diverse interpretations of what assertiveness means (Burley-Allen, 1995; Carr-Ruffino, 1993; LeMon, 1990). Hence when researchers and lay practitioners advocate assertiveness as a sexual harassment intervention strategy, they are sometimes proposing related responses as well, such as aggressiveness. Underlying all recommendations of this sort, however, is the idea that a target of sexual harassment should respond in an active, rather than passive, manner. This usually includes directly confronting the source of the harassment.

Scant research has addressed the efficacy of interpersonal-level interventions. Bingham and Burleson (1991) assessed the potential effectiveness of verbal interpersonal strategies designed to achieve a variety of communication goals. When 577 undergraduate students rated the efficacy of these strategies for stopping sexual harassment, none was judged to be effective. Bingham and Scherer (1993) found that targets who confronted their harassers were more satisfied with the outcomes. One theoretical and empirical assessment of the efficacy of passive, assertive, and aggressive responses to men's unintentional sexual harassment of women found that employees from 54 organizations rated assertive communication as the most effective of the three in terms of stopping the harassment and in terms of satisfaction with themselves (Jansma, 1997). However, they felt that assertive responses might be more harmful to their relationships than would passive responses.

LePoire, Burgoon, and Parrott (1992) offer an interpersonal-level strategy that differs conceptually from most in that it is directed toward potential sexual harassers and is theoretically driven. They suggest that supervisors who are concerned about unintentionally harassing employees should learn to interpret avoidance cues that indicate an invasion of employee privacy. Furthermore, they recommend that supervisors use the knowledge gained from these cues to guide their future behavior toward employees. LePoire et al. report no data concerning the efficacy of their recommendations, however.

Multilevel Interventions

In one of the few theoretically based analyses of sexual harassment intervention strategies that has been conducted, Grundmann et al. (1997) present a survey of implications from several perspectives. Drawing upon a model of sexual abuse, they suggest a four-factor approach to sexual harassment that integrates aspects of other theoretical perspectives. Designed to change the preconditions of sexual harassment, their multilevel approach to sexual harassment intervention involves (a) reducing motivational factors, such as power, sexist beliefs, and anger toward women; (b) increasing internal inhibitors, including respect for others' rights, empathy, and outcome expectancies; (c) increasing external motivators, which involve situational factors at societal, organizational, and immediate levels; and (d) increasing target role in active reduction. One element of this model has been tested empirically. External inhibitors, such as a work environment that is professional, is intolerant of sexist behavior, and makes employees aware of grievance procedures, were found to decrease women's likelihood of experiencing harassment (Grundmann & O'Donohue, in press). This perspective is consistent with the multidimensional framework for mitigation efforts offered in the final section of this essay, and is discussed further in that section. (See also Rowe, 1996, for a discussion of a systems approach to creating a reporting structure and complaint procedure.)

Critique and Implications of Sexual Harassment Intervention Efforts

As is evident from the preceding review, a plethora of social scientific research has been devoted to the incidence of sexual harassment and its correlates, as well as to factors that affect perceptions of harassment. In contrast, research regarding potential strategies for curtailing sexual harassment has been relatively sparse and rarely presented as a focus in and of itself. When social scientists offer recommendations for combating sexual harassment, they often present those recommendations merely as "implications" of research that addresses other aspects of sexual harassment.

Despite the paucity of direct efforts from social science, and perhaps in response to media attention (as discussed earlier), all of the recommended intervention strategies reviewed above are being implemented to some degree. Societal-level efforts to curtail sexual harassment are in place and often assume forms that are advocated by academics and activists. Certainly government regulations, educational efforts, and workplace integration are multiplying. Similarly, organizational-level interventions are common. In a 1994 survey by the Society for Human Resource Management, more than 95% of 292 workers indicated that their organizations had written sexual harassment policies, and more than 70% reported that their corporations had instituted educational training programs. Whether organizational members are using interpersonal-level strategies, such as assertive communication, and whether the use of these strategies has increased in recent years remains uncertain. This question needs to be addressed by future research that examines responses to sexual harassment. However, the more important issue to be answered by intervention research is whether and which of these strategies (on any level) is reducing sexual harassment and decreasing tolerance for it. By extension, which interventions work best for which types of sexual harassment and what factors moderate the effectiveness of each?

Mitigation research on a *societal level* might employ public opinion polls to ascertain the effects of government regulation, public education, and workplace integration. For example, researchers could replicate opinion polls first administered during the Hill-Thomas era in order to discern the degree of change or stability in societal beliefs and attitudes over the past several years. Tied to such investigations might be surveys tracking the origins of public beliefs, attitudes, and behaviors, attempting to trace them to media exposure, personal experiences, and so forth. Researchers could also assess the depth, breadth, tone, quantity, and accuracy of fictional and nonfictional mass-media messages regarding sexual harassment in general as well as specific cases. Following content analyses, the effects of such depictions might be investigated. Although the data involved would be sensitive, information regarding the past and current workplace conduct of elected officials and their staff members also could offer some insight into society's tolerance for sexual harassment.

Ideally, *organizational-level* interventions would begin by basing their efforts in the theoretical and empirical foundations presented in this and other essays (e.g., Grundmann et al., 1997). Absent theoretical grounding and empirical assessment, the benefits of lay practitioners' sexual harassment training programs are speculative. Assumptions that these interventions are reducing sexual harassment are premature—and perhaps misguided. As a point of comparison, an empirical evaluation of a rape prevention program conducted in high schools revealed a boomerang effect for some male participants—the program intensified rather than reduced their beliefs in certain rape myths (Filotas, 1993). However strong the theoretical foundations, it is imperative that researchers undertake data-based assessments of the effects of sexual harassment prevention efforts. A multilevel analysis, such as advocated by Kirkpatrick (1987), would provide a meaningful evaluation of an organizational intervention. With a foundation of rigorous empirical assessments of organizational interventions, researchers can begin to guide lay practitioners toward efficacious training programs and help them to defend against potentially negative outcomes.

Theoretical and empirical assessment of *interpersonal-level* strategies is in its infancy. Certainly, examining assertive communication and knowledge gain are logical first steps. However, assessments must build upon and reach beyond these early attempts to evaluate communication strategies to encompass conflict management and other relational-level approaches. Ultimately, combinations of several levels of interventions might be assessed—such as Grundmann et al. (1997) suggest.

Merging Social Science and Practitioner Interventions

"After decades of research, we really are not sure about what, if anything, works to educate people about sexual harassment, . . . reduce incidents of sexual harassment and help people cope with harassment" (Pryor & McKinney, 1995, p. 605). Regardless of their effects on participants, sexual harassment intervention programs (a) satisfy organizations' legal obligation to make good-faith efforts toward preventing sexual harassment and (b) provide financial gain for practitioners, and thereby (c) create a mutually satisfying, homeostatic relationship between organizations and lay practitioners. Without impetus from an outside force, there is no reason to expect change in this system (Handy, 1993; Katz & Kahn, 1966). This challenge falls to academic research.

Social science involvement in the area of sexual harassment intervention could benefit mitigation efforts in three ways. First, social scientists could determine whether existing organizational efforts are *effective*, based upon assessment of the outcomes of sexual harassment intervention programs that are currently implemented in organizations. Second, social scientific advancement in the area of sexual harassment intervention could provide an impetus for improvement of existing intervention strategies, if warranted. Finally, academic researchers could provide direction for future efforts to combat sexual harassment, based upon theoretical foundations and empirical assessment of sexual harassment intervention strategies. The following, and final, section focuses on this third goal.

MULTIDIMENSIONAL RECONCEPTUALIZATION OF SEXUAL HARASSMENT: IMPLICATIONS FOR MITIGATION

The preceding review of literature has integrated legal, organizational, and academic perspectives in a manner intended to deepen understanding of the problem of sexual harassment and to clarify its complex, multidimensional nature. In this essay, I have argued (a) that the most essential information regarding sexual harassment is that which is common to all three areas and (b) that mitigation efforts should be grounded in that common foundation. Core to that foundation, the preceding review has revealed that the work of legal entities, laypersons, and academics collectively leads to the following six conclusions. First, and most obvious, sexual conduct that unreasonably interferes with work performance or creates an intimidating, hostile, or offensive work environment constitutes sexual harassment. Second, in the relationship between the offender and the harassed, the perpetrator has greater power—which is often, but not necessarily, formal organizational power. Third, potentially harassing incidents and specific behaviors that constitute sexual harassment vary in degree of severity. Fourth, the perpetrator's formal power moderates severity of sexual harassment and its two primary categories, quid pro quo and hostile environment. Fifth, the perceived intentions of the perpetrator moderate severity of sexual harassment. Finally, perceptions regarding sexual harassment, its severity, perpetrator power, and perpetrator intent are subject to differing interpretations from the harasser, the harassed, and third parties. The following discussion extends these conclusions. Drawing upon this integrated foundation of knowledge, the framework offered in the following section is designed to strengthen the conceptual bases and guide the study of sexual harassment curtailment.[4] The roles of formal power and perpetrator intent are explicated and framed as key dimensions that moderate the perceived seriousness of sexual harassment and its two primary categories, quid pro quo and hostile environment.

Power as a Dimension of Sexual Harassment

Power is a primary dimension of sexual harassment, as attested by (a) researchers' consensus that power is integral to sexual harassment (Crocker, 1983; Dziech & Weiner, 1984; Sandler, 1990; Walker et al., 1987), (b) conceptualizations of sexual harassment as a use or abuse of power (Bargh & Raymond, 1995; Farley, 1978; MacKinnon, 1979), (c) the deleterious effects targets suffer as a result of harassers' influence, and (d) legal categories of sexual harassment—quid pro quo and hostile environment—based upon different power relationships. Power is the influence of one person over another stemming from an organizational role, an interpersonal relationship, or an individual characteristic (Berger, 1994; Ragins & Sundstrom, 1989). Because all forms of power are not alike, it is important to understand the relationships among forms of power based on two assumptions that are implicit in the power literature (Ragins & Sundstrom, 1989). First, power is additive. Various forms of power (resources, expertise, status, referral, capabilities) can accumulate to create greater overall power. Second, a deficit in one form of power may be compensated for with another form (French & Raven, 1959).

An imbalance of power must exist between harasser and harassed for sexual harassment to occur, such that the harasser has greater power than the target and thus the ability to influence the harassed (Crocker, 1983; Dziech & Weiner, 1984; MacKinnon, 1979; Sandler, 1990; Walker et al., 1987). Understanding sexual harassment as a power relationship of perpetrator over target has implications for efforts to mitigate sexual harassment. Because a *power imbalance* in which the harasser has more power than the harassed is necessary for sexual harassment to transpire, a *balance of power* has the potential to inhibit sexual harassment. At the most fundamental level, *increasing the power of targets* relative to harassers' power may be the primary function of efforts to mitigate sexual harassment. This is precisely the rationale for educating prospective targets with regard to their legal rights—it offers them a form of power by providing a strategy for preventing and redressing the interference, intimidation, offensiveness, and/or hostility that create a hostile environment and the discriminatory conditions of employment that constitute quid pro quo harassment.

The additive and compensatory qualities of power have implications for the power relationship between potential sexual harassers and targets as well as for mitigation efforts. Because different forms of power cumulate and interact, a power imbalance between harasser and harassed may be equalized by the target's acquisition of (a) the same type of power held by the potential harasser or (b) different forms of power, creating a compensatory effect. For example, a harasser often has formal positional power over a target. This potential imbalance of power may be compensated for by the target's interpersonal power and/or knowledge and/or assertion of legal rights. Thus, regardless of its form, power employed by the target, if it can equal that of the perpetrator, can potentially inhibit sexual harassment.

Formal organizational power is a useful conceptual lens through which to view the power imbalance present in sexual harassment and its mitigation. As sociologists have proposed (Blau, 1964; Kanter, 1977; Thompson, 1967), formal positional power affords control of resources related to employment conditions, such as advancement, compensation, and placement. This enables those in power to leverage employment resources for personal advantage, such as sexual favors. Although able to engage in sexual harassment, those who do not hold formal organizational power do not possess the same capacity to trade employment resources for sexual favors. For example, coworkers may have the power to exchange some resources (such as information) for sexual favors, but they do not control more potentially vital resources, such as salary and advancement.

The two legally defined forms of sexual harassment, quid pro quo and hostile environment, may be differentially characterized by the formal positional power relationship between the harasser and harassed. A harasser must have the ability to offer or withhold resources in order to exchange those resources for sexual favors. Thus, consistent with the legal definition of sexual harassment, the existence of formal organizational power or control of resources is a necessary antecedent condition for quid pro quo harassment, which involves sexual bribery. Conversely, quid pro quo seldom occurs when the perpetrator does not have formal power over the source, because without the control of employment opportunities (such as salary, job description, promotion, location) the perpetrator does not have resources to reward (or punish) the target's compliance (or noncompliance).

In contrast, formal power is not essential to the creation of a sexually hostile environment that includes all other forms of harassment (such as sexual advances, teasing, and nonverbal cues) that have the intent or effect of unreasonably interfering with work performance or creating an intimidating, hostile, or offensive workplace. The type of influence necessary to create hostile environment harassment may be formal or informal power. It may stem as easily from seniority, majority, age, gender, or physical attributes as from supervisory privilege. Thus the dimension of formal power moderates fundamental differences between quid pro quo and hostile environment harassment.

As is evident in legal rulings, and in the empirical investigations reviewed in this essay, formal power moderates the perceived severity of sexual harassment, such that sexually harassing behaviors from supervisors are viewed as more severe than are the same behaviors from coworkers. Empirical studies also indicate that (a) formal organizational power can elicit conciliatory strategies from subordinate employees (Gruber & Bjorn, 1986), (b) conciliatory behavior from those in lower power may be *misinterpreted* by those with formal power as affiliative behavior (Hickson et al., 1991), and (c) these conditions can foster unintentional sexual harassment. As a pivotal dimension from which to frame sexual harassment intervention efforts, formal organizational power also is an appealing variable because it can be measured conveniently and is readily understood by persons in the workforce. As such, it addresses concerns regarding academic operationalizations, meaningfulness to laypersons, and consistency with legal interpretations.

Perpetrator Intent as a Dimension of Sexual Harassment

A second dimension, the concept of perpetrator intentionality, has been raised throughout this review and integration. In this reconceptualization of sexual harassment, perpetrator intent moderates (a) behavioral forms of sexual harassment, such that intentionality is a likely antecedent for some types of sexual harassment (e.g., quid pro quo) but is not necessary for other types (e.g., hostile environment), and (b) perceived severity of sexual harassment, such that beliefs of malicious perpetrator intention increase perceptions of severity. Motley (1986) describes intention as a goal "one might have to transmit a message for eventual interpretation by a receiver" (p. 5). Intentionality also may be defined as the creation of goals as desired outcomes of a situation, and is rooted in actors' attitudes and subjective norms (Eagly & Chaiken, 1993). Considerable research on compliance gaining and persuasion rests on the assumption that communicators identify their goals, analyze targets and situations, and intentionally select strategies to maximize their desired outcomes (Berger, 1994; Knapp, Miller, & Fudge, 1994). In contrast to goal-oriented approaches, research on mindless activity suggests that many communication behaviors take place without any forethought as to goals (e.g., Langer, 1978), especially when behavior is habitual, as a result of repeated experiences with the same situation. Furthermore, some communication theories preclude intention, suggesting that behaviors affect others regardless of communicator intent (Dance, 1970). Hence it appears that some communicative behavior is intentional and some is not.

Bowers and Bradac (1982) assert that communication researchers do not distinguish between intent and attributions of intent. For this essay, such a distinction is not functional, because actual intentions may never be known in their entirety, even by the communicator. Similarly, the intentions of a sexual harasser may not be known, but are subject to interpretation. Targets and various third parties draw conclusions about perpetrator intent that can differ widely from perpetrators' self-attributions. Perceived malicious intent increases the likelihood that behaviors/situations will be judged as harassment (Pryor & Day, 1988).

The legal definition of sexual harassment states that sexual conduct having the *purpose or effect* of interfering with an employee's work environment is sexual harassment (USEEOC, 1980). Hence sexual harassment may be, but need not be, purposeful. Thus sexual conduct can be unintentional yet still be harassment if it has the effect of interfering with work environment. By default, sexual harassment that is not unintentional may be considered intentional harassment. In this analysis, the term *intentional sexual harassment* refers to sexual harassment that appears to have the purpose of unreasonably interfering with another's work performance or of creating an intimidating, hostile, or offensive work environment. One may argue that individuals would not intentionally sexually harass others, particularly with knowledge of the penalties imposed by organizations and the courts. One view of intentional sexual harassment may be to liken it to certain hate crimes, date rape, or hazing rituals, in which individuals break the law with little fear of discovery and reprisal. Men may be motivated to commit sexual offenses against women for several reasons, including power needs, sexist beliefs, or anger toward women (Grundmann et al., 1997). Pryor and Whalen (1997) discuss sexual exploitation, misogyny, and homo-anathema as motivators for harassment. Alternatively, persons might engage knowingly in sexual conduct that unreasonably interferes with, intimidates, or offends others without realizing that their behaviors could be interpreted as sexual harassment.

Distinct dynamics with respect to perpetrator intent may be operating in various types of sexual harassment. For example, the dimension of perpetrator intent may moderate the two types of harassment defined by the Equal Employment Opportunity Commission. Quid pro quo harassment most likely is an intentional act, because it involves an exchange of specific behaviors (sexual favors for employment conditions). Pryor's research has identified men who profess a willingness to harass women intentionally in a quid pro quo manner (e.g., Pryor et al., 1993; Pryor & Stoller, 1994). For such an unwelcome arrangement to transpire, both parties require awareness of its conditions. Under certain conditions, hazing rituals and blatant forms of harassment also are likely to be intentional, especially if designed to produce observable responses from the targets. In contrast, hostile environment harassment may be either intentional or unintentional. Sexual banter and joking may be forms of friendly behaviors, with no malice intended. Additionally, some of men's sexually oriented behavior toward women may be due to misinterpretations of women's friendly behaviors (i.e., mistaking them for sexual behaviors) and thus result in unintentional sexual harassment. Ambiguity surrounding what constitutes less serious forms of harassment may contribute to asynchronous communication and thus result in unintentional harassment.

In light of these issues surrounding perpetrator intent, it appears that harasser intentionality is vital to the investigation of sexual harassment for several reasons. First, harasser intentionality has received only scattered attention in previous research. Thus existing conceptualizations of sexual harassment may be neglecting a dimension that is central to the phenomenon. Pryor and Day (1988) address intention directly, concluding that perceived negative intent increases perceptions of harassment. Hickson et al. (1991), who frame some sexual harassment as asynchronous communication, raise the specter of misunderstanding. This conceptualization is more readily applicable to unintentional sexual harassment than to intentional sexual harassment. Similarly, Hunter and McClelland (1991) speak indirectly to judgments of perpetrator intent. They discovered that sexual harassment was considered more severe when harassers offered justifications for their actions and less serious when harassers apologized. It is possible that harassers' justifications may lead to judgments of perceived intent, whereas their apologies may foster perceptions of unintentional harassment. In contrast, tools for assessing individuals' propensity to sexually harass, such as Pryor's (1987) LSH and Bingham and Burleson's (1996) SHPI, assume that sexual harassment is intentional—participants proclaim a willingness to abuse their power in order to obtain sexual favors.

Second, perpetrators who intentionally harass may be differentially motivated or otherwise systematically different from unintentional offenders. As noted above, Lafontaine and Tredeau (1986) and Pryor (see Pryor, Giedd, & Williams, 1995) have concluded that those who are inclined to seek and to use power in their interpersonal, work-oriented relationships are more inclined to sexually harass women in a quid pro manner. Finally, a more complete understanding of the effects of perpetrator intent on sexual harassment may permit intervention strategies to address both intentional and unintentional sexual harassment more effectively. Distinct types of strategies for curtailing harassment may be needed for addressing the two kinds of cases. It stands to reason that an individual who intentionally coerces another to perform sexual favors in return for career opportunities may not respond to the same tactics that would discourage one who unintentionally offends someone by continually using sexually graphic language or gestures in everyday workplace conversation. Conversely, if existing conceptualizations of sexual harassment fail to recognize differences between intentional and unintentional sexual harassment, then the theoretical foundations from which strategies to combat sexual harassment are derived are likely to be inadequate. Intervention strategies derived from inaccurate foundations are likely to be ineffective.

Role of Perceived Severity

A third dimension that surfaces throughout legal, organizational, and academic understandings of sexual harassment is perceived severity. The critical review and integration of these perspectives indicates that perceived severity is moderated by behavioral manifestation of sexual harassment, power differential between source and recipient, and perceived perpetrator intentionality. Forms of sexual harassment involving physical contact are perceived as more severe than is verbal sexual harassment. Quid pro quo sexual harassment is perceived as more severe than is hostile environment harassment. Formal power of the harasser over the harassed increases perceived severity. Gruber et al. (1996) summarize attributions of greater severity in terms of five moderating factors: (a) formal power of the perpetrator; (b) greater frequency, duration, or repetition; (c) personal and direct; (d) hostile, offensive, and aversive; and (e) threatening and intimidating. As noted above, perceived perpetrator intentionality also increases the perceived severity of sexual harassment such that sexual harassment that is thought to be a misunderstanding is perceived as less severe.

Multidimensional Framework for
Sexual Harassment Mitigation Efforts

In keeping with the multidimensional reconceptualization outlined above, the framework presented in Figure 5.1 proposes that conditions dictated by the power relationship between the harasser and harassed, and by the perceived intentions of the harasser, moderate the behavioral form and perceived severity of sexual harassment. For example, formal organizational power and perpetrator intent are logical antecedent conditions for quid pro quo sexual harassment (Quadrant 2). A source must have the ability to offer employment resources in exchange for sexual favors and thus must hold formal power over the target. Furthermore, as outlined in the discussion above, because quid pro quo harassment is an exchange of behaviors, actors must be aware of the explicit or implicit intent. In contrast, neither formal organizational power nor perpetrator intent is a necessary antecedent condition for hostile environment harassment (Quadrants 1, 3, and 4). However, the existence of formal power and intentionality does not preclude hostile environment harassment. Hence the combination of formal power and perpetrator intent may result in either hostile environment sexual harassment or quid pro quo harassment (Quadrant 2).

The interactive nature of sexual harassment is embedded in the framework via the target's role of determining "unwelcomeness" of the source's behavior (rather than defining sexual harassment according to source behavior only) and in the formal power of the source relative to the target. This framework also assumes, as the literature implies but frequently conflates, three separate perspectives from which sexual harassment may be determined: those of the harassed, the harasser, and third parties (such as coworkers, managers, spouses, judges, and juries). From the harassed's perspective, sexual harassment is established through the recipient's interpretation of communicative messages sent by the source, which, in turn, are moderated by the source's level of formal power. The receiver also determines that the situation (a) is sexual, (b) is unwelcome, (c) has the intent or effect of interfering with the receiver's employment functions, and (d) is severe enough to warrant

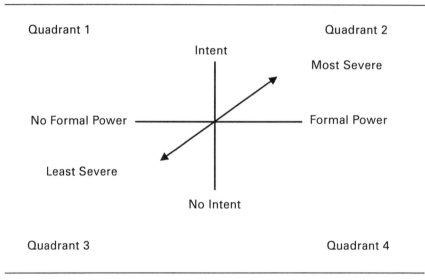

Quadrant 1   Quadrant 2

Quadrant 3   Quadrant 4

Figure 5.1. A Multidimensional Framework for Conceptualizing Sexual Harassment: Type of Harassment and Degree of Severity as Functions of Perpetrator's Formal Power and Perceived Intentionality

further attention. Observers of sexual behavior that is directed toward others also may be victims of sexual harassment. Determination of sexual harassment from the offender's perspective is structurally identical to determination from the harassed's perspective. However, the harasser's interpretations regarding each component may vary substantially from the target's interpretations. In terms of the model, a manager's questionable conduct may be interpreted as unintentionally offensive by the manager (Quadrant 4) but as intentionally intimidating and offensive by the manager's employee (Quadrant 2).

Ultimately, third-party interpretations determine both formal organizational and legal decisions regarding whether sexual harassment has transpired and may influence victims' perceptions as well. Third parties, such as significant others, coworkers, supervisors, human resource personnel, attorneys, and judges, make attributions regarding the behaviors of the perpetrator and their effects on the victims. Third-party judgments of sexual harassment may be derived from the harasser's and the harassed's accounts of communicative interaction, through the witnessing of behavioral interaction that is potentially harassing, or a combination of these. These assessments are moderated by the third parties' knowledge or beliefs about the formal power of the harasser relative to the target.

As is evident from the foregoing discussion, the framework proposed in Figure 5.1 reconceptualizes sexual harassment as a gender-neutral communicative process, subject to interpretation by source and recipient, that resides within a larger context created by organizational power and is subject to third-party interpretation. I have argued in this essay that curtailment efforts must spring from an integrated understanding of the phenomenon of sexual harassment that addresses its multidimensional nature. The dimensions articulated in this framework, and their relationships, offer useful guidelines from which specific strategies can be generated and against which existing tactics can be evaluated for the four conditions specified. Theoretically driven mitigation efforts can be grounded in the two primary dimensions that moderate types of sexual harassment: formal power and perpetrator intent. I discuss each of these briefly next in order to illustrate the program of mitigation research that I am advocating.

Formal Power Dimension

When the perpetrator holds formal organizational power over the harassed, the victim-harasser relationship poses a unique set of issues. As one nurse explained to a researcher: "If it's some creep on the street, it's no problem for me. Or if it's a peer it's no problem for me. But if it's an authority figure, it's awful. It still is for me . . . as assertive as I think I am . . . it's still hard when it's someone who's an authority figure" (quoted in Dan et al., 1995, p. 574). Attempts to curtail sexual harassment from a supervisor or manager must be considered in terms of power imbalance. Potential bodies of research may include, but are not limited to, (a) characteristics typical of employer-employee relationships and (b) communication and bases of power. Jablin (1979) offers the landmark review of the superior-subordinate communication literature, and others have built upon this research to include superiors' compliance-gaining strategies (e.g., Fairhurst, Green, & Snavely, 1984). In their analysis of gender conflicts within the supervisory relationship, Waldron, Foreman, and Miller (1993) shed light on how women typically deal with male supervisors. Additionally, French and Raven's (1959) five traditional bases of power and Wheeless, Barraclough, and Stewart's (1983) communication-centered bases of power provide foundations from which to understand the employer-employee relationship and to balance the formal power of the employer, as suggested in the previous discussion of power.

Studies of the superior-subordinate relationship suggest that interpersonal interactions and face-to-face communications between employer and employee are more limited than those between coworkers, are most often task related, and are typically initiated by the person in power. Such communication is more concise than that between coworkers, and formal as opposed to casual. When communication is initiated by person with lower power, it may not be reciprocated. Employees may be expected to understand and interpret communicative messages from managers or supervisors in less time and with less verbiage than is typical in coworker communication. In addition to evaluating employees' performance in terms of specific job-related skills, managers or supervisors may judge employees' attitudes, cooperativeness, appearance, and other bona fide occupational qualifications. Because of this dependency relationship, and subject to the above-noted constraints, employees may feel a greater level of pressure and a greater desire to please when interacting with managers or supervisors than when communicating with coworkers. Paetzold and O'Leary-Kelly (1996) found that women reported they had "gone along" with physical advances from their supervisors for fear that refusals would negatively affect the working relationship. Strategies designed to prevent or combat sexual harassment from those with formal organizational power must consider these pressures as well as other factors that limit employees' abilities to make immediate and accurate assessments of inappropriate sexual conduct, to decide how to respond, and to communicate their responses effectively.

Formal complaint procedures may serve this purpose, especially if combined with the promise of potential punitive action, such as is often available through legal proceedings or within organizations. Researchers can analyze complaint procedures and their outcomes theoretically to assess whether these increase employees' power with respect to that of managers or supervisors. Some authors have suggested that internal complaint procedures are awkward, and that outcomes may be arbitrary (e.g., Rowe, 1996, critiques complaint procedures from a systems perspective). In such cases, employees' interpersonal power may be reduced rather than increased, lowering their level of power overall rather than increasing it. When an employee's complaint is heard by a team of organizational members that is diverse in terms of race, gender, and organizational positions, this may increase the employee's feeling of power. However, if no punishment accompanies a determination of perpetrator guilt, then the employee gains no punitive power.

Communication approaches to mitigation also can be generated and evaluated in terms of superior-subordinate communication. One approach may be to clarify whether the sexual conduct is based upon a role relationship or an interpersonal relationship. In this approach, assertive communication skills may help the employee determine whether the manager's or supervisor's sexual conduct was toward the employee as a subordinate or as an individual (outside of the role of the working relationship). Once the roles are clarified, the unwanted sexual attention may be combated more appropriately.

Perpetrator Intent Dimension

The second dimension that distinguishes types of sexual harassment—perpetrator intent—also can guide the general approaches and more specific strategies and tactics employed to mitigate sexual harassment. Although the true intent of an action may never be known, even to the initiator, perceptions of intent guide judgments of how to interpret and respond to potential sexual harassment.

When sexual harassment is unintentional, a harasser may be more likely to want to repair the relationship, because the harm was not purposeful. Given the likelihood that such harassment is a form of miscommunication, and not intentionally abusive, one might assess the effectiveness of passive, assertive, and aggressive responses to such harassment. In investigating this issue, one could begin by assessing the perceived effectiveness of various responses among organizational members at various levels and then determine the receptivity of organizational members to the preferred responses. Continuing investigations could evaluate the outcomes of actually using such responses.

When sexual harassment is deliberate, the perpetrator is less likely to repair the damaged relationship. Victims of deliberate harassment have reported that their harassers have intimidated them with "Your word versus mine" or "So what?" when confronted with the illegality of the situation or their moral wrongdoing (Sumrall & Taylor, 1992). Obviously, simply asking such a perpetrator to stop (an assertive response) will be far less effective than in cases of unintentional harassment. However, theoretical efforts to end intentional harassment could begin with Grundmann et al.'s (1997) four-factor approach to changing the preconditions of sexual harassment. According to the model, harassment may be deterred by (a) reducing motivation to harass, (b) increasing internal inhibitors, (c) increasing external inhibitors, and (d) increasing victim resistance. A deliberate harasser may be motivated to sexually harass due to anger toward women, deviant sexual arousal, or adversarial sex role beliefs, among other reasons. An intentional harasser is likely to demonstrate little internal inhibition—showing little concern for the welfare of the victim. These are areas that eventually may be changed through societal efforts or through a program directed toward the specific harasser, but over which a target can exert little control. Therefore, the external situational factors and victim role become more important in curbing this type of harassment. Grundmann et al. suggest that external facilitators and inhibitors can operate on three levels: sociocultural, organizational, and immediate (interpersonal). They also have discovered that a professional environment that is intolerant of sexist behavior, obscene language, alcohol, inappropriate displays of emotion, and so on, and one in which employees are aware of grievance procedures, can act as an external inhibitor of sexual harassment. Finally, Grundmann et al.'s model calls for women to take an active role in reducing their likelihood of being harassed—such as by projecting a powerful image.

Interactions of Power and Intention

The framework in Figure 5.1 proposes that combinations of perpetrator power and intentionality create four unique conditions that require separate attention in terms of mitigation approaches. Hazing rituals are a clear example of intentional sexual harassment from peers (Quadrant 1). This type of activity often is directed toward women in traditionally male occupations (Boggs, 1998; Yount, 1991). Mitigation efforts for these situations can be understood in terms of the intentional harassment conditions described above.

Intentional sexual harassment also may come from a supervisor or manager. Quid pro quo harassment is a clear illustration of intentional harassment from a person with formal power (Quadrant 2). As described earlier, quid pro quo harassment, which involves attempts to trade employment privileges for sexual favors, is likely to be a deliberate act because it requires (a) awareness of the conditions of exchange and (b) the formal power to control employment resources. This form of harassment is considered the most serious, and thus would most likely require a combination of approaches—those for conditions of formal power and those for intentional harassment. That is, both (a) the external inhibitors and an active role on the part of the target and (b) punitive power and relief from pressure and constraints may be needed to deal with these cases.

Considered the least severe form of sexual harassment, and the most ambiguous, is unintentional harassment from peers (Quadrant 3). Often this type of sexual harassment is based in miscommunication and is an outcome of misunderstanding more than abuse. In such conditions, interpersonal-level strategies that keep the indiscretion between the interactants, rather than reporting it to others, may be most appropriate. Here, assertive communication appears to be most applicable (see Jansma, 1997), but this warrants further investigation.

Somewhere between the unintentional misunderstanding among coworkers and the deliberate attempt at sexual bribery by an employer lies the difficulty of dealing with unintentional sexual harassment of an employee by a supervisor or manager (Quadrant 4). Issues concerning employer-employee relationships surface even when managers are well-intentioned. Thus one must consider the issue of power when attempting to clarify misunderstandings between an employee and a supervisor or manager. Although assertive communication might be advocated, it is reasonable to assume that an employee would find speaking in an assertive manner to a supervisor with regard to that person's sexual conduct to be more intimidating than speaking with a coworker concerning the same issue. And, as the research indicates, few victims of sexual harassment approach even their harassing coworkers in an assertive manner.

Certainly not all potential applications of this multidimensional framework can be discussed here. I offer the suggestions above in order to stimulate further exploration of the proposed conceptual differences among forms of sexual harassment as well as the appropriate assessment of the efficacy of intervention efforts. One practical use of this framework would be for researchers to view the mitigation efforts proposed by others through this conceptual lens and determine the appropriateness of each strategy for the type of sexual harassment depicted by each quadrant of the model.

CONCLUSION

Sexual harassment is an interpersonal issue that negatively affects work environments and primarily affects women as targets of men's unwanted sexual conduct. In this essay I have argued that social science contributions to sexual harassment intervention strategies are necessary, and that in order to reduce sexual harassment in the workplace measurably, social science developments must be conjoined with legal and organizational efforts. The past 20 years of research—fueled by media attention to this issue and case law concerning it—have increased awareness of and knowledge about sexual harassment. I have reviewed the literature based upon academic, legal, and organizational conceptualizations of sexual harassment and have examined related empirical studies: (a) emergence of sexual harassment as a social and legal problem, (b) theoretical conceptualizations of sexual harassment, (c) aspects of sexual harassment that have been studied by social scientists, and (d) implications of research for integrated understandings of sexual harassment and as a basis for its mitigation. In response to Keyton's (1996) call to integrate "the individual, relational, organizational, and societal factors that enable harassment" (p. 146), this reconceptualization suggests that the dimensions of formal power and perpetrator intent may moderate such factors on any level.

In this essay I have integrated legal, organizational, and academic theoretical and empirical understandings of sexual harassment and have proposed reformulations that emphasize the communicative relationship and the multidimensional nature of sexual harassment. The final product of this reconceptualization, a multidimensional model of sexual harassment, offers a framework for viewing sexual harassment as a communicative process, subject to interpretation by source and recipient, that resides within a larger context created by organizational power, source intentions, and behavioral manifestations, and that also is subject to third-party interpretation. It can be an effective foundation from which researchers can theoretically develop and empirically assess sexual harassment mitigation strategies.

However, current research leaves several questions unanswered and invites exploration of new foci of study in this area. Research is needed to analyze theoretically and to test empirically the potential for various strategies to combat intentional versus unintentional sexual harassment. In my own work, I have built upon the foundation laid in this essay by focusing on one form of sexual harassment (unintentional sexual harassment) and by assessing the potential for one type of communication strategy (assertive communication) to mitigate unintentional sexual harassment in the workplace (Jansma, 1997). Further study is needed to pursue potential gender differences in defining intentional versus unintentional sexual harassment. Moreover, future research should consider (a) the potential for various mitigation strategies to combat intentional versus unintentional sexual harassment and (b) the influence of formal power on strategy efficacy.

NOTES

1. The term *multidimensional* may be understood best in contrast to *unidimensional*. A unidimensional conceptualization of sexual harassment is binary—either it exists or it does not.

This conceptualization is useful in determining the guilt versus innocence of the accused. It also may be validating to the victim to label his or her experience as sexual harassment. However, a deeper understanding of sexual harassment can be gained through the acknowledgment of the threefold perspective from which sexual harassment is interpreted (harasser, harassed, and third parties) and the identification of different forms that it takes (e.g., quid pro quo or hostile environment, or the variety of typological characterizations produced by researchers). Furthermore, a deeper understanding of sexual harassment requires analysis of its levels of severity. For example, courts consider harassment from a supervisor or manager to be more severe than the same conduct from a coworker. The complexity inherent in interpretations, forms, and severity of harassment are what I refer to as *multidimensionality*. For one example of a multidimensional treatment of sexual harassment, see Fitzgerald, Hulin, and Drasgow (1995). The multidimensional nature of sexual harassment suggests that it is not feasible for individual studies to address all forms of sexual harassment or interpretations by source, victims, and third parties. What is feasible in a single study is to acknowledge which aspects of sexual harassment are addressed and which are not.

2. This pattern has become evident in my personal communication and organizational consulting experience, as well as in that of a number of my colleagues.

3. These behaviors do not fall into the category of quid pro quo harassment because no trade of favors is specified. They may be categorized more accurately as indicative of hostile environment or may be considered as a separate category similar to what Bingham and Burleson (1996) term "intrusive harassment." Hence the finding that sexual comments and sexual posturing are the most frequently occurring forms of sexual harassment is consistent with findings generated by prevalence research—hostile environment harassment is more common than quid pro quo harassment (Cammaert, 1985; MacKinnon, 1979; USMSPB, 1981).

4. An ethical/legal issue regarding sexual harassment research within organizations warrants consideration. Any data collected from organizations may be subject to examination or used as evidence. Documentation of prevalent sexual harassment could pose potential harm to the organization. Researchers and consultants interested in collecting such data may be wise to request some assurance that the organization will take proactive steps to reduce sexual harassment.

REFERENCES

Abbey, A. (1982). Sex differences in attributions of friendly behavior: Do males misperceive females' friendliness? *Journal of Personality and Social Psychology, 42,* 830-838.

Abbey, A., Cozzerelli, C., McLaughlin, K., & Harnish, R. (1987). The effects of clothing and sex dyad composition on perceptions of sexual intent: Do women and men evaluate these cues differently? *Journal of Applied Social Psychology, 17,* 108-126.

Albee, G. (1983). The prevention of sexism. *Professional Psychology, 12,* 20-28.

American Psychological Association. (1994). *Publication manual of the American Psychological Association* (4th ed.). Washington, DC: Author.

Armour, S, & Mauro, T. (1998, April 3-5). Arkansas judge's ruling clouds already confusing issue. *USA Today,* pp. 1-2.

Arvey, R. D., & Cavanaugh, M. A. (1995). Using surveys to assess the prevalence of sexual harassment: Some methodological problems. *Journal of Social Issues, 51*(1), 39-52.

Backhouse, C., & Cohen, L. (1981). *Sexual harassment on the job: How to avoid the working woman's nightmare.* Englewood Cliffs, NJ: Prentice Hall.

Baker, D. D., Terpstra, D. E., & Larntz, K. (1990). The influence of individual characteristics and severity of harassing behavior on reactions to sexual harassment. *Sex Roles, 22,* 305-325.

Bargh, J. A., & Raymond, P. (1995). The naive misuse of power: Nonconscious sources of sexual harassment. *Journal of Social Issues, 51*(1), 85-96.

Beauvais, K. (1986). Workshops to combat sexual harassment: A case study of changing attitudes. *Signs, 12,* 130-145.

Berger, C. R. (1994). Power, dominance, and social interaction. In M. L. Knapp & G. R. Miller (Eds.), *Handbook of interpersonal communication* (2nd ed., pp. 450-507). Thousand Oaks, CA: Sage.

Berryman-Fink, C. (1993). Preventing sexual harassment through male-female communication training. In G. L. Kreps (Ed.), *Sexual harassment: Communication implications* (pp. 267-280). Cresskill, NJ: Hampton.

Bing, J. M., & Lombardo, L. X. (1997). Talking past each other about sexual harassment: An exploration of frames for understanding. *Discourse and Society, 8,* 293-311.

Bingham, S. G. (1988). *Interpersonal responses to sexual harassment.* Unpublished doctoral dissertation, Purdue University.

Bingham, S. G. (1991). Communication strategies for managing sexual harassment in organizations: Understanding message options and their effects. *Journal of Applied Communication Research, 19,* 88-115.

Bingham, S. G. (Ed.). (1994). *Conceptualizing sexual harassment as discursive practice.* Westport, CT: Praeger.

Bingham, S. G., & Burleson, B. R. (1991). Multiple effects of messages with multiple goals: Some perceived outcomes of responses to sexual harassment. *Human Communication Research, 16,* 184-216.

Bingham, S. G., & Burleson, B. R. (1996). The development of the sexual harassment proclivity scale: Construct validation and relationship to communication competence. *Communication Quarterly, 44,* 308-325.

Bingham, S. G., & Scherer, L. L. (1993). Factors associated with responses to sexual harassment and satisfaction with outcome. *Sex Roles, 29,* 239-269.

Blalock, J. (1995). *Getting along without getting in trouble.* Dubuque, IA: Kendall/Hunt.

Blau, M. (1964). *Exchange and power in social life.* New York: John Wiley.

Boggs, C. (1998). *Equal employment opportunity, communication accommodation climate and the gender structuration of organizations: Development and test of a model for understanding the dynamics of male resistance to workplace gender integration.* Unpublished doctoral dissertation, University of California, Santa Barbara.

Booth-Butterfield, M. (1986). Recognizing and communicating in harassment-prone organizational climates. *Women's Studies in Communication, 9,* 42-51.

Booth-Butterfield, M. (1989). Perception of harassing communication as a function of locus of control, work force participation, and gender. *Communication Quarterly, 37,* 262-275.

Borah, F. (1991, October). *Prevention of sexual harassment.* Training program presented to the Department of Communication, University of California, Santa Barbara.

Borger, G., Gest, T., & Thornton, J. (1992, January 17). The untold story. *U.S. News & World Report, 113,* 28-37.

Bowers, J. W., & Bradac, J. J. (1982). Issues in communication theory: A metatheoretical analysis. In M. Burgoon (Ed.), *Communication yearbook 5* (pp. 1-28). New Brunswick, NJ: Transaction.

Brewer, M. B. (1982). Further beyond nine to five: An integration and future directions. *Journal of Social Issues, 38*(4), 149-158.

Brewer, M. B., & Berk, R. A. (1982). Beyond nine to five: Introduction. *Journal of Social Issues, 38*(4), 1-4.

Burley-Allen, M. (1995). *Managing assertively: How to improve your people skills* (2nd ed.). New York: John Wiley.

Burt, M. R. (1980). Cultural myths and supports for rape. *Journal of Personality and Social Psychology, 38,* 217-230.

218

COMMUNICATION YEARBOOK 23

Cammaert, L. P. (1985). How widespread is sexual harassment on campus? *International Journal of Women's Studies, 8,* 388-397.

Carr-Ruffino, N. (1993). *The promotable woman.* Belmont, CA: Wadsworth.

Clair, R. P. (1993). The use of framing devices to sequester organizational narratives: Hegemony and harassment. *Communication Monographs, 60,* 113-136.

Cohen, C. R. (1987). Legal dilemmas in sexual harassment cases. *Labor Law Journal, 38,* 681-689.

Coles, F. S. (1986). Forced to quit: Sexual harassment complaints and agency response. *Sex Roles, 14,* 81-95.

Collins, E. G. C., & Blodgett, T. B. (1981). Sexual harassment . . . some see it . . . some won't. *Harvard Business Review, 59*(4), 76-96.

Conte, A. (1997). Legal theories of sexual harassment. In W. O'Donohue (Ed.), *Sexual harassment theory, research, and treatment* (pp. 50-83). Boston: Allyn & Bacon.

Crocker, P. L. (1983). An analysis of university definitions of sexual harassment. *Signs, 12,* 696-707.

Crosthwaite, J., & Swanton, C. (1986). On the nature of sexual harassment. *Australian Journal of Philosophy, 64,* 91-106.

Crull, P. (1982). Stress effects of sexual harassment on the job: Implications for counseling. *American Journal of Orthopsychiatry, 52,* 539-544.

Culbertson, A. L., & Rosenfeld, P. (1993). Understanding sexual harassment through organizational surveys. In P. Rosenfeld, J. E. Edwards, & M. D. Thomas (Eds.), *Improving organizational surveys: New directions, methods, and applications* (pp. 164-187). Newbury Park, CA: Sage.

Dan, A. J., Pinsof, D. A., & Riggs, L. L. (1995). Sexual harassment as an occupational hazard in nursing. In G. L. Kreps (Ed.), *Sexual harassment: Communication implications* (pp. 563-580). Cresskill, NJ: Hampton.

Dance, F. E. X. (1970). The "concept" of communication. *Journal of Communication, 20,* 201-210.

Dunn, D., Cody, M. J., & Haynie, B. F. (1996, February). *Accounting for alleged sexual harassment: Account credibility and public images of accuser and accused.* Paper presented at the annual meeting of the Western States Communication Association, Pasadena, CA.

Dziech, B. W., & Weiner, L. (1984). *The lecherous professor: Sexual harassment on campus.* Boston: Beacon.

Eagly, A. H., & Chaiken, S. (1993). *The psychology of attitudes.* Ft. Worth, TX: Harcourt Brace Jovanovich.

Fairhurst, G. T., Green, S. G., & Snavely, B. K. (1984). Managerial control and discipline: Whips and chains. In R. N. Bostrom (Ed.), *Communication yearbook 8* (pp. 558-593). Beverly Hills, CA: Sage.

Farley, L. (1978). *Sexual shakedown.* New York: McGraw-Hill.

Filotas, D. Y. (1993). *Adolescents' rape attitudes: Effectiveness of rape prevention education in high school classrooms.* Unpublished master's thesis, University of California, Santa Barbara.

Fiske, S. T., & Glick, P. (1995). Ambivalence and stereotypes cause sexual harassment: A theory with implications for organizational change. *Journal of Social Issues, 51*(1), 97-115.

Fitzgerald, L. F. (1993a). *The last great open secret: The sexual harassment of women in the workplace and academia* (Proceedings of the Science and Public Policy Seminar). Washington, DC: Federation of Behavioral, Psychological and Cognitive Sciences.

Fitzgerald, L. F. (1993b). Sexual harassment: Violence against women in the workplace. *American Psychologist, 48,* 1070-1076.

Fitzgerald, L. F., Gelfand, M. J., & Drasgow, F. (1995). Measuring sexual harassment: Theoretical and psychometric advances. *Basic and Applied Psychology, 17,* 425-445.

Fitzgerald, L. F., & Hesson-McInnes, M. (1989). The dimensions of sexual harassment: A structural analysis. *Journal of Vocational Behavior, 35,* 309-326.

Fitzgerald, L. F., Hulin, C. L., & Drasgow, F. (1995). The antecedents and consequences of sexual harassment in organizations: An integrated model. In G. P. Keita & J. J. Hurell, Jr. (Eds.), *Job stress in a changing workforce: Investigating gender, diversity, and family issues* (pp. 55-73). Washington, DC: American Psychological Association.

Fitzgerald, L. F., & Ormerod, A. J. (1991). Perceptions of sexual harassment: The influence of gender and academic context. *Psychology of Women Quarterly, 15,* 281-294.

Fitzgerald, L. F., & Shullman, S. L. (1993). Sexual harassment: A research analysis and agenda for the 1990's. *Journal of Vocational Behavior, 42,* 5-27.

Fitzgerald, L. F., Shullman, S. L., Bailey, N., Richards, M., Swecker, J., Gold, Y., Ormerod, M., & Weitzman, L. (1988). The incidence and dimensions of sexual harassment in academia and the workplace. *Journal of Vocational Behavior, 32,* 152-175.

Fitzgerald, L. F., Swan, S., & Magley, V. J. (1997). But was it really sexual harassment? Legal, behavioral and psychological definitions of the workplace victimization of women. In W. O'Donohue (Ed.), *Sexual harassment theory, research, and treatment* (pp. 5-28). Boston: Allyn & Bacon.

Franklin, P., Moglen, H., Zatlin-Boring, P., & Angress, R. (1981). *Sexual and gender harassment in the academy.* New York: Modern Language Association of America.

Frazier, P. A., Cochran, C. C., & Olson, A. M. (1995). Social science research on lay definitions of sexual harassment. *Journal of Social Issues, 51*(1), 21-37.

French, J. R. P., & Raven, B. (1959). The bases of social power. In D. Cartwright (Ed.), *Studies in social power* (pp. 150-167). Ann Arbor: University of Michigan, Institute for Social Research.

Frierson, J. G. (1989). Reduce the costs of sexual harassment. *Personnel Journal, 68*(11), 79-85.

Galen, M., Weber, J., & Cuneo, A. Z. (1991, October 28). Out of the shadows: The Thomas hearings force business to confront an ugly reality. *Business Week, 3236,* 30-31.

Garvey, M. S. (1986). Labor relations: The high cost of sexual harassment suits. *Personnel Journal, 65*(1), 75-78, 80.

Gill, M. J. (1993). Academic sexual harassment: Perceptions of behaviors. In G. L. Kreps (Ed.), *Sexual harassment: Communication implications* (pp. 149-169). Cresskill, NJ: Hampton.

Gilsdorf, J. W. (1990). Sexual harassment as a liability issue in communication. *Bulletin of the Association for Business Communication, 53,* 68-75.

Goodman, E. (1998, April 28). Double standard: Sorting out sexual harassment. *Santa Barbara News Press,* p. A9.

Greenburg, J. C. (1998, March 24). Liability at crux of sex harassment case. *Chicago Tribune,* pp. 1, 16.

Grieco, A. (1987). Scope and nature of sexual harassment in nursing. *Journal of Sex Research, 23,* 261-266.

Gruber, J. E. (1992). A typology of personal and environmental sexual harassment: Research and policy implications for the 1990's. *Sex Roles, 26,* 447-464.

Gruber, J. E., & Bjorn, L. (1986). Women's responses to sexual harassment: An analysis of sociocultural, organizational, and personal resource models. *Social Science Quarterly, 67,* 814-826.

Gruber, J. E., Smith, M. D. (1995). Women's responses to sexual harassment: A multivariate analysis. *Basic and Applied Psychology, 17,* 543-562.

Gruber, J. E., Smith, M. D., & Kauppinen-Toropainen, K. (1996). Sexual harassment types and severity: Linking research and policy. In M. S. Stockdale (Ed.), *Sexual harassment in the workplace: Perspectives, frontiers, and response strategies* (pp. 151-173). Thousand Oaks, CA: Sage.

Grundmann, E., & O'Donohue, W. (in press). Sexual harassment: Identifying risk factors. *Archives of Sexual Behavior.*

Grundmann, E., O'Donohue, W., & Peterson, S. H. (1997). The prevention of sexual harassment. In W. O'Donohue (Ed.), *Sexual harassment theory, research, and treatment* (pp. 175-184). Boston: Allyn & Bacon.

Gutek, B. A. (1985). *Sex in the workplace: The impact of sexual behavior and harassment on women, men, and organizations.* San Francisco: Jossey-Bass.

Gutek, B. A., & Morasch, B. (1982). Sex-ratios, sex-role spillover, and sexual harassment of women at work. *Journal of Social Issues, 38*(4), 55-74.

Gutek, B. A., Morasch, B., & Cohen, A. G. (1983). Interpreting social-sexual behavior in a work setting. *Journal of Vocational Behavior, 22*, 33-48.

Gutek, B. A., & O'Connor, M. (1995). The empirical basis for the reasonable woman standard. *Journal of Social Issues, 51*(1), 151-166.

Handy, C. (1993). *Understanding organizations.* New York: Oxford University Press.

Hemming, H. (1985). Women in a man's world: Sexual harassment. *Human Relations, 38*, 67-79.

Hickson, M., Grierson, R. D., & Linder, B. C. (1991). A communication perspective on sexual harassment: Affiliative nonverbal behaviors in asynchronous relationships. *Communication Quarterly, 39*, 111-118.

Hoffman, F. L. (1986). Sexual harassment in academia: Feminist theory and institutional practice. *Harvard Educational Review, 56*(2), 105-121.

Hotelling, K. (1991a). Sexual harassment: A problem shielded by silence. *Journal of Counseling and Development, 69*, 497-501.

Hotelling, K. (1991b). Special feature: Sexual harassment. *Journal of Counseling and Development, 69*, 495-496.

Hunter, C., & McClelland, K. (1991). Honoring accounts for sexual harassment: A factorial survey analysis. *Sex Roles, 24*, 725-751.

Jablin, F. M. (1979). Superior-subordinate communication: The state of the art. *Psychological Bulletin, 86*, 1201-1222.

Jansma, L. L. (1997, May). *Assertive communication as a strategy to mitigate men's unintentional sexual harassment of women: A multiple goals approach.* Paper presented at the annual meeting of the International Communication Association, Montreal.

Jaschik, M. L., & Fretz, B. R. (1991). Women's perceptions and labeling of sexual harassment. *Sex Roles, 25*, 19-23.

Jensen, I. W., & Gutek, B. A. (1982). Attributions and assignment of responsibility in sexual harassment. *Journal of Social Issues, 38*(4), 121-136.

Jones, T. S., & Remland, M. S. (1992). Sources of variability in perceptions of and responses to sexual harassment. *Sex Roles, 27*, 121-142.

Jones, T. S., Remland, M. S., & Brunner, C. C. (1987). Effects of employment relationship, response of recipient, and sex of rater on perceptions of sexual harassment. *Perceptual and Motor Skills, 65*, 55-63.

Kanter, R. M. (1977). *Men and women of the corporation.* New York: Basic Books.

Katz, D., & Kahn, R. L. (1966). *The social psychology of organizations.* New York: John Wiley.

Kazoleas, D. (1997, April). *The human resources practitioner's contributions to theory development.* Paper presented at the annual meeting of the Central States Communication Association, St. Louis, MO.

Kenig, S., & Ryan, J. (1986). Sex differences in levels of tolerance and attribution of blame for sexual harassment on a university campus. *Sex Roles, 15*, 535-549.

Keyton, J. (1996). Sexual harassment: A multidisciplinary synthesis and critique. In B. R. Burleson (Ed.), *Communication yearbook 19* (pp. 93-155). Thousand Oaks, CA: Sage.

Keyton, J., & Rhodes, S. C. (1994, November). *Alternative perspectives on sexual harassment.* Paper presented at the annual meeting of the Speech Communication Association, New Orleans.

Kirkpatrick, D. L. (1987). *Training and development handbook* (3rd ed.). New York: McGraw-Hill.

Knapp, D. E., Faley, R. H., Ekeberg, S. E., & DuBois, C. L. Z. (1997). Determinants of target responses to sexual harassment: A conceptual framework. *Academy of Management Review, 22*, 687-729.

Knapp, M. L., Miller, G. R., & Fudge, K. (1994). Background and current trends in the study of interpersonal communication. In M. L. Knapp & G. R. Miller (Eds.), *Handbook of interpersonal communication* (2nd ed., pp. 3-20). Thousand Oaks, CA: Sage.

Konda, V. (1994, September). Sexual harassment: The attractiveness factor. *Psychology Today,*
pp. 16-17.

Konrad, A. M., & Gutek, B. A. (1986). Impact of work experiences on attitudes toward sexual harassment. *Administrative Science Quarterly, 31,* 422-438.

Konsky, C., Kang, J., & Woods, A. M. (1992, November). *Communication strategies in instances of
workplace sexual harassment.* Paper presented at the annual meeting of the Speech Communication Association, Chicago.

Kreps, G. L. (Ed.). (1993). *Sexual harassment: Communication implications.* Cresskill, NJ:
Hampton.

Lafontaine, E., & Tredeau, L. (1986). The frequency, sources, and correlates of sexual harassment
among women in traditional male occupations. *Sex Roles, 15,* 433-441.

Lange, A. J., & Jakubowski, P. (1976). *Responsible and assertive behavior: Cognitive/behavioral
procedures for trainers.* Champaign, IL: Research Press.

Langer, E. (1978). Rethinking the role of thought in social interaction. In J. Harvey, W. J. Ickes, & R. F.
Kidd (Eds.), *New directions in attribution research* (Vol. 1, pp. 35-58). Hillsdale, NJ: Lawrence
Erlbaum.

Learning International. (1982). *Sexual harassment awareness program: Participant's manual.* Stam-
ford, CT: Xerox Corporation.

Lebrato, M. T. (Ed.). (1986). *Help yourself: A manual for dealing with sexual harassment.* Sacramento: California Commission on the Status of Women.

Lee, L. A., & Heppner, P. P. (1991). The development and evaluation of a sexual harassment inventory.
Journal of Counseling and Development, 69, 512-517.

Leeser, J., & O'Donohue, W. (1997). Normative issues in defining sexual harassment. In W.
O'Donohue (Ed.), *Sexual harassment theory, research, and treatment* (pp. 29-49). Boston: Allyn &
Bacon.

Lees-Haley, P. R., Lees-Haley, C. E., Price, J. R., & Williams, C. W. (1994). A sexual harass-
ment-emotional distress rating scale. *American Journal of Forensic Psychology, 12,* 39-54.

LeMon, C. (1990). *Assertiveness: Get what you want without being pushy.* Shawnee Mission, KS: National Press.

LePoire, B. A., Burgoon, J. K., & Parrott, R. (1992). Status and privacy restoring communication in
the workplace. *Journal of Applied Communication Research, 20,* 419-436.

Linenberger, P. (1983). What behavior constitutes sexual harassment? *Labor Law Journal, 34,*
238-247.

Littler-Bishop, S., Seidler-Feller, D., & Opaluch, R. E. (1982). Sexual harassment in the workplace as
a function of initiator's status: The case of airline personnel. *Journal of Social Issues, 38*(4),
137-148.

Livingston, J. A. (1982). Responses to sexual harassment on the job: Legal, organizational, and individual actions. *Journal of Social Issues, 38*(4), 5-22.

Lott, B., Reilly, M. E., & Howard, D. R. (1982). Sexual assault and harassment: A campus community
case study. *Signs, 8,* 296-319.

MacKinnon, C. (1979). *Sexual harassment of working women: A case of sex discrimination.* New Haven, CT: Yale University Press.

Malovich, N. J., & Stake, J. E. (1990). Sexual harassment on campus: Individual differences in attitudes and beliefs. *Psychology of Women Quarterly, 14,* 63-81.

Mongeau, P. A. (1993, February). *Student evaluations of instructor immediacy and sexually harassing
behaviors.* Paper presented at the annual meeting of the Western States Communication Association, Albuquerque, NM.

Motley, M. T. (1986). Consciousness and intentionality in communication: A preliminary model and methodological approaches. *Western Journal of Speech Communication, 50,* 3-23.

Moyer, R. S., & Nath, A. (1998). Some effects of brief training interventions on perceptions of sexual harassment. *Journal of Social Psychology, 128,* 333-356.

Neibuhr, R. R., & Boyles, W. R. (1991). Sexual harassment of military personnel: An examination of power differentials. *International Journal of Intercultural Relations, 15,* 445-457.

Oaks, R., & Landrum-Brown, J. (1997). Cross-cultural issues and influences. In B. R. Sandler & R. J. Shoop (Eds.), *Sexual harassment on campus: A guide for administrators, faculty, and students* (pp. 214-233). Needham Heights, MA: Allyn & Bacon.

O'Donohue, W. (Ed.). (1997). *Sexual harassment theory, research, and treatment.* Boston: Allyn & Bacon.

Oncale v. Sundowner Offshore Services, 118 S. Ct. 998 (1998).

"Our stories": Communication professionals' narratives of sexual harassment. (1992). *Journal of Applied Communication Research, 20,* 363-400.

Paetzold, R. L., & O'Leary-Kelly, A. M. (1996). The implications of U.S. Supreme Court and circuit court decisions for hostile environment sexual harassment cases. In M. S. Stockdale (Ed.), *Sexual harassment in the workplace: Perspectives, frontiers, and response strategies* (pp. 85-104). Thousand Oaks, CA: Sage.

Pearman, M. I., & Lebrato, M. T. (1984). *Sexual harassment in employment investigator's guidebook.* Sacramento: California Personnel Board.

Petrocelli, W., & Repa, B. K. (1994). *Sexual harassment on the job: A step by step guide for working women* (2nd ed.). Berkeley, CA: Nolo.

Popovich, P. M., Licata, B. J., Nokovich, D., Martelli, T., & Zoloty, S. (1986). Assessing the incidence and perceptions of sexual harassment behaviors among American undergraduates. *Journal of Psychology, 120,* 387-396.

Powell, G. N. (1986). Effects of sex role identity and sex on definitions of sexual harassment. *Sex Roles, 14,* 9-19.

Pryor, J. B. (1985). The lay person's understanding of sexual harassment. *Sex Roles, 13,* 273-286.

Pryor, J. B. (1987). Sexual harassment proclivities in men. *Sex Roles, 17,* 269-290.

Pryor, J. B., & Day, J. D. (1988). Interpretations of sexual harassment: An attributional analysis. *Sex Roles, 18,* 405-417.

Pryor, J. B., Giedd, J. L., & Williams, K. B. (1995). A social psychological model for predicting sexual harassment. *Journal of Social Issues, 51*(1), 69-84.

Pryor, J. B., LaVite, C. M., & Stoller, L. M. (1993). A social psychological analysis of sexual harassment: The person/situation interaction. *Journal of Vocational Behavior, 42,* 68-83.

Pryor, J. B., & McKinney, K. (1995). Research on sexual harassment: Lingering issues and future directions. *Basic and Applied Social Psychology, 17,* 605-611.

Pryor, J. B., & Stoller, L. M. (1994). Sexual cognition processes in men who are high in the likelihood to sexual harass: Evidence for a sexuality/dominance schema. *Personality and Social Psychology Bulletin, 10,* 163-169.

Pryor, J. B., & Whalen, N. J. (1997). A typology of sexual harassment: Characteristics of harassers and the social circumstances under which sexual harassment occurs. In W. O'Donohue (Ed.), *Sexual harassment theory, research, and treatment* (pp. 129-151). Boston: Allyn & Bacon.

Ragins, B. R., & Sundstrom, E. (1989). Gender and power in organizations: A longitudinal perspective. *Psychological Bulletin, 105,* 51-88.

Reilly, T., Carpenter, S., Dull, V., & Bartlett, K. (1982). The factorial survey: An approach to defining sexual harassment on campus. *Journal of Social Issues, 38*(4), 99-110.

Riger, S. (1992). Gender dilemmas in sexual harassment policies and procedures. In E. Wall (Ed.), *Sexual harassment: Confrontations and decisions* (pp. 197-215). Buffalo, NY: Prometheus.

Rose, S. (1992, May 15). *Sexual harassment.* Panel presented at the Women's Day Conference, Santa Barbara, CA.

Rosenberg, J., Perlstadt, H., & Phillips, W. R. F. (1993). Now that we are here: Discrimination, disparagement, and harassment at work and the experience of women lawyers. *Gender & Society, 7,* 415-433.

Rowe, M. P. (1996). Dealing with sexual harassment: A systems approach. In M. S. Stockdale (Ed.), *Sexual harassment in the workplace: Perspectives, frontiers, and response strategies* (pp. 241-271). Thousand Oaks, CA: Sage.

Rubin, B. M., & Peres, J. (1998, April 3). Jones vs. Clinton: The ruling's aftermath: Workplace on edge over harassment. *Chicago Tribune,* pp. 1, 24.

Saal, F. E. (1996). Men's misperceptions of women's interpersonal behaviors and sexual harassment. In M. S. Stockdale (Ed.), *Sexual harassment in the workplace: Perspectives, frontiers, and response strategies* (pp. 67-84). Thousand Oaks, CA: Sage.

Safran, C. (1976, November). What men do to women on the job: A shocking look at sexual harassment. *Redbook, 149,* 217-224.

Sandler, B. (1990). Sexual harassment: A new issue for institutions. *Initiatives, 52,* 5-10.

Sandroff, R. (1992, June). Sexual harassment: The inside story. *Working Woman, 78,* 47-52.

Schafran, L. H. (1991, October 13). The harsh lessons on Professor Hill. *New York Times Forum,* p. D3.

Schneider, B. E. (1982). Consciousness about sexual harassment among heterosexual and lesbian women workers. *Journal of Social Issues, 38*(4), 75-98.

Schweikhart, G. (1995, Fall). Sexual harassment: How to ensure it doesn't happen and how to deal with it when it inevitably does. *Business News, 113,* 30-36.

Shoop, R. J., & Edwards, D. L. (1994). *How to stop sexual harassment in our schools.* Boston: Allyn & Bacon.

Sigal, J., Gibbs, M., Adams, B., & Derfler, R. (1988). The effect of romantic and nonromantic films on perceptions of female friendly and seductive behavior. *Sex Roles, 19,* 545-554.

Sigler, R., & Johnson, I. M. (1986). Public perceptions of the need for criminalization of sexual harassment. *Journal of Criminal Justice, 14,* 229-237.

Singleton, R., Jr., Straits, B. C., Straits, M. M., & McAllister, R. J. (1988). *Approaches to social science research.* New York: Oxford University Press.

Smith, M. J. (1983). *When I say "no" I feel guilty.* New York: Bantam.

Society for Human Resource Management. (1994, June 26). *Sexual harassment remains a workplace problem but most employers have policies in place, SHRM survey finds* [Brochure]. Alexandria, VA: Author.

Solomon, D. H., & Williams, M. L. M. (1997). Perceptions of social-sexual communication at work as sexually harassing. *Management Communication Quarterly, 11,* 147-184.

Spann, J. (1990). Dealing effectively with sexual harassment: Some practical lessons from one city's experience. *Public Personnel Management, 19*(1), 53-60.

Stockdale, M. S. (1996). What we know and what we need to learn about sexual harassment. In M. S. Stockdale (Ed.), *Sexual harassment in the workplace: Perspectives, frontiers, and response strategies* (pp. 3-28). Thousand Oaks, CA: Sage.

Stringer, D. M., Remick, H., Salisbury, J., & Ginorio, A. B. (1990). The power and reasons behind sexual harassment: An employer's guide to solutions. *Public Personnel Management, 19,* 43-52.

Strom, S. (1991, October 20). Harassment rules often not pushed. *New York Times,* pp. 1, 22.

Sumrall, A. C., & Taylor, D. (Eds.). (1992). *Sexual harassment: Women speak out.* Freedom, CA: Crossing.

Tangri, S. S., Burt, M. R., & Johnson, L. B. (1982). Sexual harassment at work: Three explanatory models. *Journal of Social Issues, 38*(4), 35-54.

Tata, J. (1993). The structure and phenomenon of sexual harassment: Impact of category of sexually harassing behavior, gender, and hierarchical level. *Journal of Applied Social Psychology, 23,* 199-211.

Taylor, B., & Conrad, C. (1992). Narratives of sexual harassment: Organizational dimensions. *Journal of Applied Communication Research, 20,* 401-418.

Terpstra, D. E., & Baker, D. D. (1986). A framework for the study of sexual harassment. *Basic and Applied Social Psychology, 7,* 17-34.

Terpstra, D. E., & Baker, D. D. (1987). A hierarchy of sexual harassment. *Journal of Psychology, 121,* 599-605.

Terpstra, D. E., & Baker, D. D. (1989). The identification and classification of reactions to sexual harassment. *Journal of Organizational Behavior, 10,* 1-14.

Thomann, D. A., & Wiener, R. L. (1987). Physical and psychological causality as determinants of culpability in sexual harassment. *Sex Roles, 17,* 573-591.

Thompson, E. H., Jr., & Pleck, J. H. (1986). The structure of male role norms. *American Behavioral Scientist, 29,* 531-543.

Thompson, M. E. (1967). *Organizations in action.* New York: McGraw-Hill.

U.S. Equal Employment Opportunity Commission (USEEOC). (1980). Discrimination because of sex under Title VII of the 1964 Civil Rights Act as amended: Adoption of interim guidelines—sexual harassment. *Federal Register, 45,* 25024-25025.

U.S. Merit Services Protection Board (USMSPB). (1981). *Sexual harassment in the federal workplace: Is it a problem?* Washington, DC: Government Printing Office.

U.S. Merit Systems Protection Board (USMSPB). (1988). *Sexual harassment in the federal government: An update.* Washington, DC: Government Printing Office.

U.S. Office of Personnel Management (USOPM). (1980a). *Workshop on sexual harassment: Participant materials.* Washington, DC: Government Printing Office.

U.S. Office of Personnel Management (USOPM). (1980b). *Workshop on sexual harassment: Trainer's manual.* Washington, DC: Government Printing Office.

U.S. Opportunity Commission. (1980, November 10). *Final amendment to guidelines on discrimination because of sex under Title VII of the Civil Rights Act of 1964, as amended, 29 CFR Part 1604,* Federal Register 45 (pp. 181-190). Washington, DC: Government Printing Office.

Vance, S. M. (1981). Sexual harassment of women students. In R. H. Stein & M. C. Baca (Eds.), *Professional ethics in university administration* (pp. 29-40). San Francisco: Jossey-Bass.

Wagner, E. J. (1992). *Sexual harassment in the workplace.* New York: AMACOM.

Waldron, V. R., Foreman, C., & Miller, R. (1993). Managing gender conflicts in the supervisory relationship: Relationship-definition tactics used by women and men. In G. L. Kreps (Ed.), *Sexual harassment: Communication implications* (pp. 234-256). Cresskill, NJ: Hampton.

Walker, G., Erickson, L., & Woolsey, L. (1987). Sexual harassment: Ethical research and clinical implications in the academic setting. *International Journal of Women's Studies, 8,* 424-426.

Webb, S. L. (1992). *Step forward: Sexual harassment in the workplace—What you need to know.* New York: Mastermedia.

Weber-Burdin, E., & Rossi, P. H. (1982). Defining sexual harassment on campus: A replication and extension. *Journal of Social Issues, 38*(4), 111-120.

Weeks, E. L., Boles, J. M., Garbin, A. P., & Blaunt, J. (1985). The transformation of sexual harassment from a private trouble into a public issue. *Sociological Inquiry, 56,* 432-455.

Wheeless, L. R., Barraclough, R., & Stewart, R. (1983). Compliance-gaining and power in persuasion. In R. N. Bostrom (Ed.), *Communication yearbook 7* (pp. 105-145). Beverly Hills, CA: Sage.

Woerner, W. L., & Oswald, S. L. (1990). Sexual harassment in the workplace: A view through the eyes of the courts. *Labor Law Journal, 41,* 786-793.

Wood, J. T. (1992). Telling our stories: Narratives as a basis for theorizing sexual harassment. *Journal of Applied Communication Research, 20,* 349-362.

Workman, J. E., & Johnson, K. K. P. (1991). The role of cosmetics in attributions about sexual harassment. *Sex Roles, 24,* 759-769.

Yount, K. R. (1991). Ladies, flirts, and tomboys: Strategies for managing sexual harassment in an underground coal mine. *Journal of Contemporary Ethnography, 19,* 396-422.

Zedeck, S., & Casio, W. F. (1984). Psychological issues in personnel decisions. *Annual Psychological Review, 35,* 461-518.

CHAPTER CONTENTS

6 A Multicultural View of Conflict Management Styles: Review and Critical Synthesis

MIN-SUN KIM
TRUMAN LEUNG
University of Hawaii at Manoa

This chapter reviews the literature on conflict management and critically analyzes it from a cultural point of view. Cross-cultural conflict style theorists have accepted Blake and Mouton's (1964) two-dimensional framework without due caution, and they invariably cite that framework as the basis for their own work. Given the general assumption of the desirability of direct confrontation of conflicts, it is not surprising that researchers have conceptualized avoidance styles as reflective of low concern for self as well as for the other. This assumption is taken so much for granted in individualist cultures that it has rarely been stated explicitly. The individualist assumption that overt conflict resolution is better than avoidance has led to a focus on only certain aspects of conflict resolution and has resulted in ignorance about, or misinterpretation of, alternative conflict management styles. The authors propose a framework for explaining why people of different cultural identities tend to approach and manage conflict situations differently. The model suggests that interdependents' tendency to avoid conflict can be explained by their desire to preserve relational harmony and their motivation to save others' face. Furthermore, the authors suggest that bicultural individuals are likely to be more flexible and effective than culture-typed individuals (individualist or collectivist) in dealing with conflict situations. The review concludes with suggestions for avenues for future research and some practical implications.

> The person who raises his/her voice first has already lost.
>
> *Japanese expression*

> The bigger a**h*le wins.
>
> *American expression*

AUTHOR'S NOTE: The first draft of this chapter was completed during Min-Sun Kim's sabbatical to the Department of Communication, Michigan State University in fall 1997. She would like to express her gratitude to the faculty for making her sabbatical possible.

Correspondence: Min-Sun Kim, Department of Speech, George Hall 331, University of Hawaii at Manoa, Honolulu, HI 96822; e-mail kmin@hawaii.edu

Communication Yearbook 23, pp. 227-269

CONFLICT is an all-pervasive and inevitable human experience (Roloff, 1987). Conflict resolution skill is an important component in the maintenance of virtually all interpersonal relationships. Problems of cross-cultural conflict are particularly acute in today's world. The growth in foreign travel for business, study, and pleasure, the migration of people seeking work in other countries, and the expansion of international trade have all naturally led to increased contacts across national and ethnic borders, together with severe communication problems and conflict situations (Ross, 1993).

Cross-cultural conflict is a topic with a growing body of literature. There have been numerous cross-cultural comparison studies of different conflict management strategies, most utilizing a "national culture" approach (e.g., Cushman & King, 1985; Hofstede, 1980, 1991; Kumagai & Straus, 1983; Lee & Rogan, 1991; Nomura & Barnlund, 1983; Ohbuchi & Takahashi, 1994; Rossi & Todd-Mancillas, 1985; Wolfson & Norden, 1984). Many studies have sought to describe the differences in styles used by members of different cultures. However, others have begun to test theory-based hypotheses in attempts not only to describe but to understand the differences in conflict handling between cultures (e.g., Chiu & Kosinski, 1994; Chua & Gudykunst, 1987; Kim & Hunter, 1995; Kim & Kitani, 1998; Leung, 1987, 1988; Miyahara, Kim, Shin, & Yoon, 1998; Sanders, Congalton, Wiseman, Gass, & Du, 1992; Ting-Toomey et al., 1991; Trubisky, Ting-Toomey, & Lin, 1991).

Although cross-cultural research on styles of handling interpersonal conflict has gained increased attention recently, two major limitations exist. First, individualism-collectivism has been used as the primary dimension of cultural variability in a number of cross-cultural studies on conflict-handling styles (e.g., Chua & Gudykunst, 1987; Lee & Rogan, 1991; Leung, 1987; Leung & Iwawaki, 1988; Ting-Toomey et al., 1991; Trubisky et al., 1991). These studies have operationalized culture in terms of the participants' nationalities; that is, they have generalized Hofstede's (1980) classification of certain countries as being either individualist or collectivist to the individualism/collectivism of their samples. In other words, the researchers have assumed that all persons in their samples from certain cultures or nations exhibit the same level of individualism or collectivism. However, individual variation within groups can be substantial (Gudykunst et al., 1996; Kim et al., 1996; Markus & Kitayama, 1991; Smith & Bond, 1994).

As Ting-Toomey (1988) states, "The dimension of individualism-collectivism . . . [has] been used as a starting point to aid in the theorizing process of conflict face-negotiation" (p. 232). Although the individualism and collectivism dimensions have been found to be a useful means of differentiating clusters of culture, a solid theory of intercultural communication should be based on individual- as well as culture-level analyses. Given the complexities of the influence of culture on conflict behavior, it is necessary to find relevant intervening variables in order to understand what it is in culture that accounts for cultural differences. Surely, the

of the world into "individualist" and "collectivist" cultures is a broad-brush sim-
plification that deserves a more systematic and detailed examination (see
Gudykunst et al., 1996; Kashima et al., 1995; Kim et al., 1996; Schwartz, 1990;
Singelis & Brown, 1995).

The method of comparing findings in different cultures has frequently been
used to examine the impact of culture on conflict management behaviors.
Although useful in evaluating whether cross-cultural differences exist, this is far
less helpful in explaining why culture has an effect. Several major cultural dimensions (e.g., individualism and collectivism, masculinity and femininity) emerge
from the literature as high-order psychological concepts that can help explain
cross-cultural differences in behavior over a wide range of situations. In many
cases, a broad concept is invoked to explain major aspects of the behavior of an
entire cultural population. However, high-level concepts such as individualism
and collectivism tend to be loosely defined. It is also difficult to ascertain their
validity, because the delimitations of these broad concepts (i.e., the boundaries
between aspects of behavior that are covered by the concept and those that are not)
remain unclear.

It should be noted that the construct of self-construal is *not* intended to replace
individualism and collectivism. Rather, self-construal as part of individual-level
cultural dimensions provides a convenient vehicle for exploring some of the potential pitfalls of the culture-level variables, so that we might understand more precisely the processes by which culture influences behavior. However, this is not
meant to imply that high-level concepts (e.g., individualism versus collectivism)
are invalid dimensions. Rather, this approach shows that we may achieve a more
parsimonious and precise explanation (of the kinds of cross-cultural differences
ascribed to cultural variability dimensions) by resorting to certain mediating variables.

Gaines et al. (1997) attest that "certain potentially erroneous assumptions
regarding individuals' personal and social identities seem to have been made. . . .
One such assumption is that individuals (and, for that matter, entire nations) can be
depicted accurately as either individualistic or collectivistic—an assumption that
may reflect the bias of the United States and other Western nations toward
dichotomization of constructs" (pp. 1460-1461). More recently, researchers have
been supportive of an individual-level approach to theorizing about cross-cultural
differences. Through an individual-level approach, stereotypical cultural distinctions can be eliminated and within-culture variations can be accounted for. Hence
we will examine cultural self-concept through independent and interdependent
self-construals.

To understand the effects of national culture, it is necessary to specify the psychological variables that distinguish people who are from different cultures. One
dimension that has emerged in a variety of conceptual analyses pertains to how
individuals define themselves and their relationships with other people. It has been

well documented that how an individual views his or her relationship to others is affected by that person's culture's individualist and collectivist tendencies. In certain cultures, such as the United States, the core of self-concept tends to be based on the person's "unique configuration of internal attributes (e.g., traits, abilities, motives, and values)" (Markus & Kitayama, 1991, p. 224). In other cultures, such as the People's Republic of China, individuals' self-concepts tend to be defined primarily on the basis of their relationships with other people constituting their in-groups (Brockner & Chen, 1996).

Following this line of reasoning, Markus and Kitayama (1991) have proposed independent and interdependent self-construals—constructs that parallel individualism and collectivism, respectively. In struggles to define the self, however, self-identification is often dichotomized as either individualist or collectivist. Cross-cultural research on the self has also commonly classified the self as either individualist (the self as a bounded and unique object) or collectivist (the self as an ensembled object, merged into the common life of the group) (Sampson, 1988; Triandis, 1988). The point is that some individuals may simultaneously maintain high independent as well as high interdependent self-construals. As people struggle to come to terms with cultural pluralism, there is growing recognition of identity challenges in the lives of bicultural and multicultural individuals and their potential communication patterns. At present, however, there is a paucity of research on the potential effectiveness of bicultural individuals in their communication behavior.

Another main limitation of the past research on cross-cultural conflict styles stems from confusion regarding conceptualizations of conflict management styles. The majority of this research has relied on conflict typologies that were created in the U.S. context, and the generalizability of these typologies to intercultural contexts is unclear. In typical studies of cross-cultural conflict styles, researchers have relied heavily on either three or five styles of conflict inventories, which are based on two dimensions, variously called *concern for production and concern for people* or *concern for self and concern for others* (Blake & Mouton, 1964; Brown, Yelsma, & Keller, 1981; Thomas, 1976). The conceptualization of conflict styles based on these two dimensions may not be generalizable across cultures. For instance, whereas past researchers in interpersonal and organizational conflict have tended to conceptualize the avoidance style as reflective of both low concern for self and low concern for the other (e.g., Canary & Spitzberg, 1987; Putnam & Wilson, 1982; Rahim, 1983), the use of an avoidance style in collectivist cultures seems to be associated positively with the other-face concern dimension (see Kim & Hunter, 1995; Ting-Toomey, 1989; Weldon & Jehn, 1995). Such validity problems indicate that the dimensions used to conceptualize and operationalize styles in the U.S. context may not be the generative mechanisms of behavioral choices in different cultures.

In this chapter we review and critically analyze the conflict literature from a cultural point of view. The remainder of the chapter is organized as follows. First, we review the literature on cross-cultural conflict management. We follow this review with an analysis of the conceptual difficulties and individualist biases in the past conflict typologies with respect to cultural assumptions. We then introduce the concepts of individual-level culture dimensions (i.e., independent and interdependent self-construals). Finally, we integrate this information into a general model of ethnocultural conflict styles that explains why individuals with different cultural orientations would prefer one set of conflict styles over another in different situations. We also consider the implications of the model for future research and training.

RESEARCH ON CROSS-CULTURAL
CONFLICT MANAGEMENT

Defining Conflict Resolution Styles

Conflict researchers have proffered a plethora of different definitions of conflict. Simons (1972) defines conflict as a state of social relationship in which incompatible interests between two or more parties give rise to a struggle between them. Ting-Toomey (1985) calls conflict a form of intense interpersonal and/or intrapersonal dissonance (tension or antagonism) between two or more interdependent parties based on incompatible goals, needs, desires, values, beliefs, and/or attitudes. Schneer and Chanin (1987) view conflict as a natural phenomenon involving individual perceptions of a continuous process between two or more interacting parties with incompatible goals, ideas, values, behaviors, or emotions. Thomas (1976) considers dyadic conflict as a *process* that includes the perceptions, emotions, behaviors, and outcomes of two parties—when one party perceives that the other has frustrated, or is about to frustrate, some concern of the first party. For the purposes of this review, we limit the domain of conflict to interpersonal conflict. Thus we define conflict as a communicative exchange between at least two interdependent parties who have different, opposite, or incompatible opinions and goals and who perceive that the other is interfering in the achievement of his or her goals (Hocker & Wilmot, 1995; Lulofs, 1993; Putnam & Wilson, 1982; Ting-Toomey, 1988).

When in conflict, individuals often demonstrate preferences for certain communication styles (Roloff, 1987). Nadler, Nadler, and Broome (1985) state that "communication is the means by which conflict receives a social definition, the instrument through which influence in conflict is exercised, and the vehicle by which partisans or third parties may prevent, manage or resolve conflict" (p. 90). Because much conflict is managed through verbal means, individuals' general communication patterns should influence conflict management styles as well.

Conflict management styles are viewed as patterned responses to conflict situations through diverse communication strategies (Ting-Toomey et al., 1991). Conflict management does not necessarily mean the resolution of conflict. Rather, it should be viewed as an ongoing process of handling conflict interactions. Intercultural conflict research has used different terms for conflict management styles: conflict *handling/management/resolution styles/strategies/behaviors/ modes/orientations.* Virtually every investigation of intercultural, interpersonal conflict has focused on identifying the styles of conflict management (as manifested by scores on conflict style scales), rather than on the parties' actual communicative practices. According to Putnam and Poole (1987), "In most studies, perceptions of message behaviors is substituted for the actual communication of a style" (p. 556). Thus conflict management styles in this review denote the perceptions of appropriate conflict management behaviors rather than actual communicative strategy choices.

General Findings on Cross-Cultural
Conflict Management Behaviors

Conflict, as part of interpersonal interactions, occurs in specific cultural settings. Ross (1993) stresses that viewing conflict as a cultural behavior helps explain why disputes over seemingly similar issues can be handled so dissimilarly in different cultures. The notion that the East and the West differ in many traditional values, beliefs, and behavioral patterns is hardly new, and there is a large literature documenting cultural differences in conflict styles.

Research on conflict management across cultures clearly indicates that there are differences in conflict styles in individualist and collectivist cultures. Using data collected from international students studying in the United States, Chua and Gudykunst (1987) found that members of low-context cultures used solution orientations more than did members of high-context cultures, whereas members of high-context cultures used nonconfrontation more than did members of low-context cultures. Bond, Leung, Wan, and Giacalone (1985) found that Chinese respondents (members of a low individualist culture) were more likely to advise an executive to meet with an insulter and the target of the insult separately so that conflict between the two could be avoided. North Americans (members of a high individualist culture), on the other hand, more frequently advised a joint meeting, so the problem between the insulter and the target could be openly resolved. Also consistent with this research are findings from studies on conflict resolution styles of Mexicans (members of a low individualist culture) and Anglo-Americans (Kagan, Knight, & Martinez-Romero, 1982; Kagan & Madsen, 1971; Madsen, 1971; McGinn, Harburg, & Ginsburg, 1973). These studies revealed that Mexican participants tend to use more passive, avoidance strategies, whereas Anglo-Americans tend to use more active, confrontational strategies.

In testing for differences between African American and Euro-American conflict styles, Ting-Toomey (1986) found that African American participants tended to use more controlling style strategies than did Euro-American participants, and that Euro-American participants tended to use more solution-oriented style strategies than did African American participants. Tang and Kirkbride (1986) also report cultural differences in conflict-handling orientations in the Hong Kong civil service between local Chinese and expatriate British executives. The results of their study clearly suggest significant differences in conflict-handling preferences, with the Chinese executives favoring the less assertive compromising and avoiding behaviors as their dominant orientations and their British counterparts preferring the more assertive collaborating and competing orientations. In a subsequent extension study, Kirkbride, Tang, and Westwood (1991) gathered data from 981 Hong Kong Chinese respondents between 1986 and 1987 using Thomas and Kilmann's (1978) Management of Differences Exercise (MODE) instrument. Overall, these results reveal that Chinese cultural values and cognitive orientations have influenced the Chinese people to preserve overt harmony by avoiding confrontation and by adopting a nonassertive approach to conflict resolution.

Lee and Rogan (1991) found that whereas Korean study participants tended to use solution-oriented conflict strategies, North American participants tended to use either controlling or avoidance strategies. Although the finding on the use of competitive, controlling strategies by North Americans has been supported by this research, the finding on avoidance strategies is surprising. Lee and Rogan speculate that this finding may be due to the fact that their U.S. data were obtained in the southern region of the country, wherein group cohesion is relatively higher than in other parts of the United States. Also, Sue and Kitano (1973) found that the Asian American families in their study were more conforming and cohesive than their Caucasian counterparts. Nomura and Barnlund (1983) found that the Japanese in their sample preferred passive forms of criticism, whereas North Americans preferred active forms. Further, Leung and Iwawaki (1988; see also Leung, 1988) observed that members of individualist cultures in their sample tended to use a direct conflict communication style and solution-orientation style, whereas members of collectivist cultures tended to use an indirect conflict communication style and an avoidant style. In addition, collectivists displayed stronger preference for conflict mediation and bargaining procedures than did individualists (Leung, 1987).

Ting-Toomey et al. (1991) employed Rahim's (1983) Organizational Conflict Inventory-II (ROCI-II) to test face-negotiation theory. *Face* is defined as the claimed sense of self-image in a relational situation (Ting-Toomey, 1988). Ting-Toomey (1988) explains the differences in conflict management styles in individualist and collectivist cultures using the concept of facework. According to Ting-Toomey, individualists tend to value autonomy face needs and self-concern face needs, whereas collectivists emphasize approval face needs and other-concern or mutual-concern face needs. Ting-Toomey et al. (1991) predicted that in conflict interactions, the self-concern face would be expressed through the use of direct face-negotiation strategies and controlling face mode, whereas the other-concern need would be expressed through the use of indirect face-negotiation strategies and the affiliative smoothing face mode. In relating the face set with the conflict set, they found that other-face contributed most strongly to integrating, avoiding, and compromising styles, and that self-face contributed most strongly to dominating styles.

The findings reported in the cross-cultural conflict literature point to a picture of collectivists as persons who value harmonious interpersonal relationships with others (Cathcart & Cathcart, 1976; De Vos, 1975), prefer indirect styles of dealing with conflict (Chua & Gudykunst, 1987; Cushman & King, 1985; Hofstede, 1991; Ohbuchi & Takahashi, 1994; Ting-Toomey, 1988), and show concern for face saving (Nomura & Barnlund, 1983; Sueda & Wiseman, 1992). Most comparative analyses of conflict management behavior, however, have contrasted groups such as Japanese ("collectivists") and Americans ("individualists"). One exception is Leung, Au, Fernandez-Dols, and Iwawaki's (1992) study of procedural justice, which contrasted two collectivist societies: Japan from the East and Spain from the West. In another rare exception, Gire and Carment (1993) analyzed the differences in procedural preferences between students from Nigeria (a non-Asian collectivist society) and Canada (an individualist society). The results were not in line with those of previous research. Not only did Canadian participants show a clear preference for negotiation, but Nigerian participants showed almost equal preference for both negotiation and arbitration.

The subtle but important differences in cultural attributes among varying Eastern "collectivist" cultures (e.g., Japanese and Koreans) have often been distorted or simply overlooked. Recently, Miyahara et al. (1998) explored how Japanese and Koreans may differ in their preferences for conflict management styles, focusing on the importance attached to conversational constraints in conflict situations. Their main findings indicate that Koreans are more collectivist in conflict communication styles than are Japanese. Specifically, Miyahara et al.'s results seem to suggest different processes of conflict management in the two cultures, with Japanese focusing on clarity constraint (conveying the message clearly and efficiently) more than Koreans and Koreans focusing on social relations constraints (avoiding imposition to the hearer or loss of face by the hearer) more than Japanese.

Critique

In the studies conducted to date, researchers have primarily used the dimension of individualism-collectivism in theorizing the process of conflict management styles across different cultural groups. Typically, the general conclusions go like this: Members of individualist cultures prefer direct conflict styles, whereas members of collectivist cultures prefer indirect conflict styles. Although these characterizations of conflict behaviors along the dimension of collectivism-individualism appear to be sound and reasonable, many authors have criticized the use of broad cultural variability dimensions because of their lack of explanatory power (see Gudykunst et al., 1996; Kim, 1995; Kim et al., 1996; Kim & Sharkey, 1995; Schwartz, 1990; Singelis & Brown, 1995). Researchers who have examined intercultural conflict resolutions often have failed to examine individual-level cultural dimensions. Despite the popularity of individualism and collectivism as major cultural dimensions, the psychological validity of these dimensions is not well established.

Another important issue is related to the very notion of expecting differences in conflict management preferences on the basis of the individualism-collectivism dichotomy. Generally, the two values have been presumed to function as bipolar opposites. However, as Schwartz (1990) indicates in his critique, the individualism-collectivism dichotomy sometimes influences people to overlook values that inherently serve both individual and collective interests: It disregards values that foster the goals of collectivities other than the in-group, and it promotes the erroneous assumption that individualist and collectivist values form coherent syndromes that are always in polar opposition.

Finally, mixed empirical findings reveal the confusion regarding conceptualizations of different conflict styles. Although findings on the use of competitive, controlling strategies by individualists (North American participants) have been consistently supported, findings on integrating and compromising styles have been contradictory or mixed (see Ting-Toomey et al., 1991; Trubisky et al., 1991). Furthermore, in relating the face set (self- versus other-face) with the conflict set, no clear evidence has been found for the relationship between self-face maintenance and integrating conflict styles (Ting-Toomey et al., 1991). Perhaps we know less about measuring cross-cultural conflict styles and about cross-cultural conflict management styles, strategies, and behaviors than the wealth of measurement devices would suggest. In the following section, we present a brief history of the development of typologies of conflict styles and then discuss the individualist bias in conceptualizations of past conflict management typologies.

CONFLICT MANAGEMENT TYPOLOGIES

People handle interpersonal conflicts with various styles of behavior. There have been many attempts to measure interpersonal conflict management styles (Kilmann & Thomas, 1975; Putnam & Wilson, 1982; Rahim, 1983; Rusbult & Zembrodt, 1983; Sillars, 1980; Sillars, Coletti, Parry, & Rogers, 1982). Beginning with Blake and his associates, five proposed conflict styles were organized on a two-dimensional grid (Blake & Mouton, 1964; Blake, Shepard, & Mouton, 1964). These styles and dimensions have been renamed several times, and several instruments have been devised to measure the styles. Work on the five-style scheme of conflict handling has been conducted by several different researchers and teams of researchers, including Lawrence and Lorsch (1967), Hall (1986), Thomas (1976; Kilmann & Thomas, 1977; Thomas & Kilmann, 1978), and Rahim and Bonoma (1979; Rahim, 1983). One of the most popular models developed has been Rahim and Bonoma's (1979); their model consists of two orthogonal dimensions (i.e., concern for self and concern for others) and five styles (i.e., integrating, obliging, dominating, avoiding, and compromising). The five styles result from the combination of the two dimensions. Accordingly, it has been asserted that the *integrating* style results from high concern for both self and others; the *obliging* style results from low concern for self and high concern for others; the *dominating* style results from high concern for self and low concern for others; the *avoiding* style results from low concern for both self and others; and the *compromising* style results from intermediate concern for both self and others.

Thomas and Kilmann's (1978) MODE has also been a popular instrument among researchers conducting conflict management studies. Kilmann and Thomas (1975) classified five conflict styles: competing, collaborating, compromising, avoiding, and accommodating. These styles are reflections of the two underlying cognitive/affective dimensions: assertiveness (attempting to satisfy one's own concerns) and cooperation (attempting to satisfy the other person's concerns). As interpreted by Thomas (1976), *competing* is a power-oriented mode in which one pursues one's own concerns at the other person's expense in a manner that is both assertive and uncooperative. *Collaborating* is an assertive and cooperative approach in which one party attempts to work with the other party in an effort to find an integrative and mutually satisfying solution. *Avoiding* occurs when one is unassertive and yet uncooperative. Interests are not articulated, and the conflict is postponed to resurface at a later stage. *Accommodating* represents a mix of cooperation and unassertiveness and occurs when one neglects one's own concerns in order to satisfy the concerns of the other party. *Compromising* represents an intermediate position in terms of both assertiveness and cooperation and a situation in which both parties satisfy at least some of their concerns. We shall argue later that conceptions of avoiding vary cross-culturally.

Although a couple of studies do support the construct validity of a five-style scheme (Rahim, 1983) and two dimensions (Ruble & Thomas, 1976), several other studies have found support for only three styles. Several factor analyses of Lawrence and Lorsch's (1967) instrument have resulted in three rather than five factors (Fry, Kidron, Osborn, & Trafton, 1980). In the same way, Putnam and Wilson's (1982) factor analysis of a pool of items designed to tap Blake and Mouton's (1964) five styles revealed only three factors, which they named the nonconfrontation (avoidance and soothing strategies), solution-oriented (problem-solving and compromising strategies), and control (forcing strategies) conflict strategies. Comstock and Strzyzewski (1990) used the integrative, distributive, and avoidance conflict strategies in their content analysis of family conflict on prime-time television programs. These three styles are approximately parallel to the three basic strategies found by Sillars (1980) in roommate conflicts: passive and indirect, distributive, and integrative strategies.

In Kim and Hunter's (1995) study of individuals from a variety of ethnic backgrounds, only three discrete dimensions of conflict styles emerged: compromising/integrating, obliging/avoiding, and dominating. Kim and Hunter found the integrating and compromising styles to be highly correlated with each other; they found the same for the obliging and avoiding styles. The similarity between compromising and integrating styles may stem from the fact that both styles aim for an acceptable solution; in the compromising approach the conflicting parties settle for the middle ground, and in the integrating approach the parties focus on an inte-grative or creative solution (see Putnam & Wilson, 1982). The reason that the obliging and avoiding styles formed one factor may stem from the fact that both strategies partly involve "giving in" to the other's wishes. Conceptually, the three factors resemble Horney's (1945) typology of moving away from (nonconfronta-tion), moving toward (solution orientation), and moving against (control) the opposing party.

Rahim (1986) makes the claim that due to greater work experience, experienced employees can distinguish among the five styles (i.e., integrating, obliging, domi-nating, avoiding, and compromising), whereas inexperienced employees and stu-dents cannot. However, even his own conceptual definitions of obliging and avoid-ing seem to have confounding similarities. Obligers, he says, attempt to play down the differences. At the same time, he describes avoiders as those who refuse to acknowledge publicly the existence of a conflict. Both styles seem to describe the same basic behavior of trying to smooth over or suppress the conflict.

Filley and House (1969) outline another set of three methods of conflict man-agement: the win-lose method, the lose-lose method, and the win-win method. In the win-lose method, one party will lose in the conflict and the other will win. Filley and House claim that in the lose-lose situation, many people employ avoid-ance techniques rather than personally confront the other party. Their last style of conflict, win-win, ultimately leads to both parties winning in the situation. It is called win-win because a final solution is reached that is acceptable to both parties.

In investigating conflict resolution skills among children from two private Roman Catholic schools in California, Bryant (1992) noted three strategies for responding to conflict situations: (a) anger retaliation strategy (exploding in anger in response to a classmate's expressing anger), (b) withdrawal/avoidance strategy (withdrawing and avoiding a classmate as a response to the classmate's expression of anger), and (c) calm discussion strategy (remaining calm and talking in response to a classmate's expression of anger until the problem is resolved and both people feel okay about each other). Bryant found that rejected children were viewed as more likely to use the withdrawal/avoidance strategy than were children in other groups (e.g., popular, average).

In examining cross-cultural conflict resolution styles between parents and ado-lescents, Rosenthal, Demetriou, and Efklides (1989) found that behaviors in con-flict situations seemed to be of three types: emotional expression of hostility (e.g., become physically aggressive, raise voice, or yell), rational discussion of the situa-tion (e.g., carefully explain, talk things through), and, for mothers and adolescents but not fathers, avoidance of confrontation (e.g., become quiet or withdrawn, refuse to discuss the matter).

According to Canary and Spitzberg (1989), behaviors during conflict manage-ment fall into three distinctive categories: integrative, distributive, and avoidant. Integrative communication promotes relational objectives, in contrast to distribu-tive tactics, which pursue individual goals to the exclusion of the partner's goals, and avoidant tactics, which attempt to avert direct conflict. Canary and Spitzberg found that integrative tactics had the greatest impact on competence perceptions. Distributive and avoidant strategies affected competence perceptions negatively. Using the three-style typology, Sillars (1980) examined the relationship between attributions concerning the locus of causality and responsibility for conflict and individuals' conflict styles with their roommates. The data from this study showed that attributions of responsibility to the roommate increased the use of avoidance and distributive conflict strategies and decreased the use of integrative strategies.

Volkema and Bergmann (1989) argue that both the three- and five-style schemes were originally developed for research into conflict within organizations, and thus they represent only behaviors that might typically be used with task-related conflict issues, disregarding relationally applicable ones. In their study of conflict strategies used between same- and opposite-sex friends, Fitzpatrick and Winke (1979) hypothesized five styles: manipulation, nonnegotiation, emotional appeal, personal rejection, and empathic understanding. Sternberg and Soriano (1984) have proposed seven styles that might be used in interpersonal, interorganizational, and international conflicts: accept situation, wait-and-see, undermine esteem, economic action, step down, physical action, and third-party intervention.

In an attempt to examine more emotional aspects of interpersonal conflict styles in work settings, Volkema and Bergmann (1989) used the following 21 conflict behaviors taken from Roloff's (1976) Modes of Conflict Resolution instrument: sabotage the person's work; throw things; push, strike, or punch the person; cry; try to get even; take a drink or pill and forget about it; try to get the person to leave their job or the company; leave my job (resign); ask for a transfer; shout at the person; use my authority to settle the issue; form alliances with other people in the organization; don't talk to the person; go to this person's supervisor or someone higher in the organization; talk behind the person's back; avoid the person; try to convince the person; discuss the conflict with people outside of work; listen carefully to the person; discuss the conflict with coworkers; discuss the issue with the person. Nicotera (1993) devised an eight-style, three-dimensional scheme (attention to one's own view, attention to the other's view, emotional/relational valence): assertive, consolidation, evasive, accommodating, aggressive, begrudging, estranged, and patronizing. Ohbuchi and Takahashi (1994; see also Fablo & Peplau, 1980; Ohbuchi & Yamamoto, 1990) organized many interpersonal conflict tactics into five basic styles: direct bilateral, direct unilateral, indirect bilateral, indirect unilateral, and avoidance.

The exit-voice-loyalty-neglect typology (Rusbult & Zembrodt, 1983) has been recognized in conflict studies in close relationships (Healey & Bell, 1990; Metts & Cupach, 1990). Each of the four modes represents a behavior derived from two dimensions: active-passive and constructive-destructive. Using the exit-voice-loyalty-neglect typology, Metts and Cupach (1990) examined the relationships among dysfunctional relationship beliefs, satisfaction, and four problem-solving responses (exit, voice, loyalty, and neglect). The data from their research suggest that the voice strategy is positively related and exit and neglect strategies are negatively related to relational satisfaction. Also, those who believe that disagreement is destructive are more likely to use exit and neglect, avoiding giving voice to their problems.

Critique

In their critique of past research, Weldon and Jehn (1995) question whether traditional measures and constructs used in the literature on conflict styles can be generalized. Specifically, they argue that the shortcomings of past research derive from the fact that the researchers adopted dimensions, styles, and measures of conflict management behavior developed in Western, individualist countries. They assert that a direct comparison of conflict styles would produce a misleading understanding of cross-cultural differences, because conflict styles may have different meanings in collectivist and individualist societies. Their critique centers on three methodological issues. First, most researchers do not explore the nomological nets to test for universal meaning of conflict styles; they simply assume the conflict styles to be etics. A few researchers have examined correlations between the variables under study (Lee & Rogan, 1991; Ting-Toomey et al., 1991), which, in the absence of nomological nets, can provide some information about the meaning of the constructs. In Lee and Rogan's (1991) and Ting-Toomey et al.'s (1991) studies, the correlations differed across cultures, casting doubt on the implicit assumption of universal meaning. Second, similar factor structures of conflict styles may not necessarily indicate that the styles have the same meaning and that the measures are valid across cultures. Factors composed of similar items may have different meanings in different cultures. Third, culture-specific, emic conflict styles have rarely been considered. Using Thomas and Kilmann's (1978; Kilmann & Thomas, 1977) MODE instrument, Jehn and Weldon (1992) rejected the assumption of universal meaning after intracultural factor analyses (among managers in the United States and the People's Republic of China) produced different factor structures. They then treated the obtained factors as emic conflict styles. Although this approach avoids problems created when styles are assumed to be etics, it falls short as a study of emics, because the Western questionnaire used in this study did not include items measuring concepts peculiar to Chinese culture (see Weldon & Jehn, 1995). Ironically, although most conflict styles theorists have been profoundly influenced by the two-dimensional managerial grid, the factor structures of the instruments developed have been disparate, inconsistent, or unclear. Conflict categories have been located within dimensional structures that are researcher defined and researcher salient (see Nicotera, 1993, for further discussion on this issue). Although the two-dimensional conceptualization may be useful for the operationalization of conflict styles in the U.S. context, it is unwise for researchers to impose it at the conceptual level. In the following section, we will argue that the individualist ideology in mainstream American society has led researchers to assume that confrontation is more desirable than avoidance.

A CRITIQUE OF CONCEPTUALIZATIONS OF
CONFLICT RESOLUTION INVENTORIES

As we have noted, popular conflict management scales (e.g., Rahim, 1983; Thomas & Kilmann, 1978) have relied heavily on Blake and Mouton's (1964) conceptualization of conflict management, which yields a five-style configuration based on self- versus other-concern. Although researchers vary in their terms, they generally have assumed a two-dimensional scheme. Regardless of whether one assumes five styles (e.g., Hall, 1986; Rahim, 1983; Thomas & Kilmann, 1978) or four styles (leaving out "compromise"; e.g., Pruitt & Rubin, 1986), or whether one collapses the number of styles to three (e.g., Canary & Spitzberg, 1987; Putnam & Wilson, 1982; Sillars, 1980), the styles are still influenced by the two assumed dimensions. Conflict styles based on the two assumed dimensions have been adopted frequently by communication researchers (Brown et al., 1981; Cahn, 1985; Canary & Spitzberg, 1987; Chua & Gudykunst, 1987; Kabanoff, 1987; Putnam & Wilson, 1982; Sillars, 1980; Sillars et al., 1982; Ting-Toomey, 1988; Trubisky et al., 1991).

Several other models also assume two dimensions: Hall (1986) distinguishes between concern for personal goals and concern for relationships. Pruitt and Rubin (1986) also characterize the dimensions in terms of concern for one's own outcome and concern for the other's outcome. Thomas (1976) interprets the five-category scheme as combining two independent dimensions: cooperation, or attempting to satisfy the other party's concerns, and assertiveness, or attempting to satisfy one's own concerns. Brown et al. (1981) propose two dimensions for distinguishing conflict styles: feelings (positive or negative) and task energy (high expenditure or low expenditure). Similarly, conflict styles are broken down into two dimensions of assertiveness and cooperativeness (Chusmir & Mills, 1989). Assertiveness involves the desire to fulfill the needs of the individual resolving conflict. The cooperativeness dimension involves fulfilling the needs of others.

The models relying on Blake and Mouton's (1964) work conceptualize avoiding (or withdrawal style) as negative and/or destructive. According to Rahim (1983), avoiding styles reflect "low concern for self" and "low concern for others." Putnam and Wilson (1982) also consider avoidance or nonconfrontation as a "lose-lose" style. Thomas (1976) interprets avoiding as "unassertive" and "uncooperative." Brown et al. (1981) claim that withdrawing action means "negative feelings" and "low task energy." The flavor of these scales is that confrontation is more desirable than avoidance. Nicotera (1993) highlights possible logical flaws in existing taxonomic structures of conflict strategies. In the three-dimensional model (other's view, own view, and emotional/relational valence) *inductively* derived from the data set, Nicotera for instance distinguishes "evasive" (which is not disruptive to personal relations) from "estranged" (which is disruptive to personal relations).

Traditionally, within the U.S. context, it has been argued that "covert, or hidden, conflict also is destructive in that it leaves issues unresolved and may result in psychological and/or physical estrangement" (Comstock & Buller, 1991, p. 48). Galvin and Brommel (1986) claim that most conflict that is avoided leaves nagging tensions unresolved, creates a climate ripe for future overt destructive conflict, and fosters separation among family members. Furthermore, it has been argued that when people use integrative conflict strategies, constructive outcomes result, whereas use of avoidance strategies results in destructive outcomes (see Comstock & Buller, 1991). According to Filley and House (1969), in the lose-lose conflict situation, people are more likely to employ avoidance technique than to personally confront the other party. In the context of children's conflict resolution skills, Bryant (1992) asserts that both anger/retaliation and withdrawal/avoidance are potentially disruptive to social relationships.

Likewise, the work in this area has been biased by the individualist assumption that confrontation is more desirable than avoidance, which limits a full understanding of the conflict phenomenon. Hsieh, Shybut, and Lotsof (1969) capture the essence of the individualist ideology in describing mainstream American culture as "a culture that emphasizes the uniqueness, independence, and self-reliance of each individual" (p. 122). Among other things, U.S. culture places a high value on the ideology of "openness" in conflict resolution. Given the general assumption of the desirability of direct confrontation of conflicts, it is not surprising that researchers have conceptualized avoidance styles as reflective of low concern for self as well as low concern for others. This assumption is taken so much for granted in individualist cultures that it has rarely been stated explicitly. Similarly, some researchers who consider argument (direct confrontation of matter) to be a beneficial and prosocial mode of conflict resolution also view avoidance as less socially acceptable (e.g., Infante, Trebing, Shepherd, & Seeds, 1984; Rancer, Baukus, & Infante, 1985). Because of an individualist bias, researchers have overlooked the potentially positive attributes of conflict avoidance and suppression. Furthermore, they have ignored the dialectic between conflict avoidance and confrontation and the complexity of avoidance as a conflict management strategy.

Cross-cultural conflict style theorists have accepted Blake and Mouton's (1964) two-dimensional framework without due caution, and they invariably cite that framework as the basis for their own work. Avoidance of conflict can help the individual to control emotion, and may at times also allow the passive expression of discontentment without the dangers of a direct challenge. Just as messages of silence (extreme forms of indirectness) might be evaluated differently within different relationship contexts (see Tannen, 1985), avoidance (or withdrawal) strategies can be seen as positive or negative by members of different cultural orientations (as measured against what is expected in those contexts). In individualist contexts, a "demand to interact" appears to characterize much of dyadic communication—there is a built-in assumption that when people are engaged in focused conversation, it is their responsibility to keep verbal communication active. Silence or avoidant conflict styles might, at times, represent a threat to this responsibility. Specifically, just like inferences regarding silences, avoidance of conflicts among interdependents can be seen as negative politeness—being nice to others

by not imposing (see Tannen, 1985, for similar arguments regarding cultural differences in perceptions of silence). Avoidance among independents may be seen
as the failure of positive politeness—the need to be involved with others. This can
occur in any culture but seems to be the unmarked case in cultures that may be
characterized as relatively individualist.

The benefits for an interdependent of using avoidance strategies come from
being understood without putting one's meaning on record, so that understanding
is seen not as the result of putting meaning into words, but rather as the greater
understanding of shared perspective, expectations, and intimacy. Likewise,
although past studies in interpersonal and organizational conflict have tended to
conceptualize the avoidance style as reflective of low concern for both self and
other (e.g., Canary & Spitzberg, 1987; Rahim, 1983), the use of avoiding style in
collectivist cultures seems to be associated positively with the other-face concern
dimension. The findings of Kim and Hunter's (1995) study clarify the issues
regarding conceptualizations of conflict styles. Kim and Hunter found a significant direct link between independence and dominating conflict styles. Expectedly,
self-face concern directly influenced dominating style and "other-face concern"
influenced the four nonforcing conflict management styles (i.e., obliging/avoiding
and integrating/compromising).

In a similar vein, Van de Vliert and Kabanoff (1990) and Van de Vliert and Prein
(1989) have taken issue with the two-dimensional models and have shown how
plots of relationships among the five styles do not fit the predicted quadrants in the
original Blake and Mouton model. By reanalyzing data from six studies of managers, Van de Vliert and Kabanoff (1990) assessed the construct validity of the two
best-known self-report instruments for measuring the five conflict styles originally defined in Blake and Mouton's (1964) managerial grid (Rahim, 1983;
Thomas & Kilmann, 1978). Both instruments (MODE and ROCI) more or less
failed to discriminate between avoiding and accommodating. Furthermore, compromising did not occupy a midpoint position. Van de Vliert and Prein (1989)
found that dominating or forcing is isolated from the other four styles. The four
styles clustered in the same related quadrants.

Similar to these findings, Trubisky et al. (1991) found that members of a collectivist culture used higher levels of compromising and integrating styles to handle
conflict than did members of an individualist culture. And in Ting-Toomey et al.'s
(1991) study, opposite to their predictions, members of collectivist cultures opted
for integrating styles more than did members of individualist cultures. Overall, the
evidence suggests that members of individualist cultures tend to prefer direct
(dominating) conflict communication styles. Conversely, members of collectivist
cultures tend to prefer obliging, compromising, integrating, and conflict-avoiding
styles. The latter four styles tend to emphasize the value for passive compliance to
a certain degree and for maintaining relational harmony in conflict interactions
(see Trubisky et al., 1991).

Because of the difficulties noted above with the existing conceptualizations and
the methodological shortcomings of conflict style typologies, we want to begin to

develop a more adequate explanation of conflict style use based on cross-cultural differences in self-construal. In the following section, we discuss the relationship between construals of self and styles of interpersonal communication, including conflict resolution.

A MULTICULTURAL VIEW OF CONFLICT RESOLUTION STYLES: FOCUSING ON CULTURAL IDENTITY

Content of Self in Different Cultures: Independent and Interdependent Construals of Self

Our self-conceptions influence how we communicate with others and our choices (conscious and unconscious) of those with whom we form relationships. The self can be construed, framed, or conceptualized in different ways. Triandis (1989) suggests that collectivist cultures encourage the development of many cognitions that refer to a group or collective, thus increasing the chances that individuals will sample these cognitions frequently. On the other hand, individualist cultures nurture the growth of cognitions that refer to the individual's traits and states.

Recent findings from Kitayama, Markus, Matsumoto, and Norasakkunkit's (1997) research indicate that the historical environment of a given culture may influence the psychological processes of the individuals living within that culture. According to Roberts and Helson (1997), from the 1950s to the 1970s Americans turned away from defining themselves in terms of formal roles, social norms, and broad social values and turned toward their inner feelings and traits. Thus Americans are relatively likely to engage in self-enhancing communication, because the Western historical context has paved the way for increased individualism.

By contrast, Asian cultures do not emphasize the explicit separation of each individual. Rather, these cultures are organized according to meanings and practices that promote the fundamental connectedness among individuals within significant relationships (e.g., family, workplace, and classroom). The self is made meaningful in reference to those social relations of which the self is a participating part. Those of this cultural orientation may be motivated to adjust to and fit themselves into meaningful social relationships. Kitayama et al.'s (1997) findings suggest that in order for one to achieve the cultural task of fitting in, it is important for one to identify consensual standards of excellence shared in a relationship, or in the society in general, and to engage in self-criticism by identifying those shortcomings, deficits, or problems that prevent one from meeting such standards.

Even though many aspects of culture affect a person's self-image, our focus in this review is on what people "believe about the relationship between the self and *others* and, especially, the degree to which they see themselves as *separate* from others or as *connected* with others" (Markus & Kitayama, 1991, p. 226). An expanding body of literature on the cultural self-concept has revealed that a limited focus on culture-level generalizations is no longer adequate for the study of intercultural communication (e.g., Cross & Markus, 1991; Kim et al., 1996; Kim, Sharkey, & Singelis, 1994; Kitayama et al., 1997; Markus & Kitayama, 1991; Singelis & Brown, 1995).

Until recently, social psychological theories of the self have focused on the individuated self-concept—the person's sense of unique identity differentiated from others. Cross-cultural perspectives, however, have brought a renewed interest in the social aspects of the self and the extent to which individuals define themselves in terms of their relationships to others and to social groups (Brewer & Gardner, 1996; Kim, 1999; Kitayama et al., 1997; Markus & Kitayama, 1991). Independent and interdependent construals of self are among the most important self-schemata for distinguishing culture. Markus and Kitayama (1991) propose that whereas the self-system is the complete configuration of self-schemata (e.g., including those of gender, race, religion, social class, and developmental history; Markus & Wurf, 1987), independent and interdependent construals of self are among the most general and overarching self-schemata in an individual's self-system. Based on an extensive review of cross-cultural literature, Markus and Kitayama (1991) argue that these two construals of self may influence cognition, emotion, and motivation more powerfully than previously thought. These two images of self were originally conceptualized as reflecting the emphasis on connectedness and relations often found in "non-Western" cultures (interdependent) and the separateness and uniqueness of the individual stressed in the "West" (independent).

According to Markus and Kitayama (1991, 1994), the main difference between the two kinds of self-construal is found in the belief a person holds regarding how the self is related to others. Those with highly developed independent construals see themselves as separate from others; those with highly developed interdependent construals see themselves as connected with others. These beliefs of separateness and connectedness differentiate the two self-construals. The normative imperative of independent cultures is to achieve independence and self-actualization. A goal of social maturity in this view is to be self-sufficient—not to be dependent on anyone. Those of this view also strive to know themselves and to express their own unique strengths. In contrast, the normative imperative of interdependent individuals is to maintain "interdependence" with significant others. To be mature in this view is to be able to control or suppress internally one's opinions, emotions, or goals in deference to normative behaviors specific to the current social context.

Both selves have self-schemata in relation to others (Markus & Kitayama, 1991). In other words, significant others are important to both selves. The independent self is responsive to the social environment in that others serve to appraise or confirm the expression or assertion of the internal attributes of the self. Self-schemata in relation to others are important as a means to realize the goal of the independent self to distinguish the self from others. Whereas the core of the independent self is its internal attributes, the core of the interdependent self is its relationships with significant others. The interdependent self may have knowledge about its internal attributes, but this knowledge is not as important as knowledge in relation to others. As such, for the interdependent self, relationships are not simply means to achieve individual goals, as they may be for independent selves, but rather are end goals in themselves. These interdependent relationships are also reciprocal, in that one strives to realize significant others' goals while passively monitoring the tacit agreement that the significant others will make reciprocal contributions toward one's own goals. Although these concepts are not new, the interdependent self-construal provides a more indigenous conceptualization of what has often been seen by Westerners as a "group orientation" (Singelis, 1994). We should make it clear that interdependent selves do not indiscriminately attend to the needs, desires, and goals of all others, but only to those of significant others who are included within the membership of their in-groups (Markus & Kitayama, 1991).

Cultural differences in self-construal have been well established by recent studies (Gudykunst et al., 1996; Kashima et al., 1995; Kim et al., 1996). Singelis (1994; Singelis & Brown, 1995) developed a measure that taps the independent and interdependent dimensions of the self and found that in Hawaii, participants from Asian backgrounds were both more interdependent and less independent relative to those with European backgrounds. Bochner (1994) found that Malaysian self-construals were more interdependent and less independent than Australian and British self-construals. Recent studies have also shown that the degree of independent and interdependent construal of self systematically affects the perceived importance of "conversational constraints" within cultures as well as across different cultural groups (Kim et al., 1994, 1996; Kim & Sharkey, 1995).

In addition, a number of researchers have recently noted that individualism and collectivism are likely to be separate dimensions rather than the polar opposites of a single dimension (Kâgitçibasi & Berry, 1989; Kim et al., 1996; Oyserman, 1993). Elements of both worldviews may exist at the cultural and individual levels. For instance, Oyserman (1993) explored some aspects of the subjective experience of individualism and collectivism among Arabs and Jews, groups that simultaneously emphasize both worldviews. The data support the speculation that individualism and collectivism are distinct dimensions; Arabs and Jews both endorsed elements of individualism and collectivism. For instance, in Israel, individuals adhere to an amalgam of individualist and collectivist perspectives on personhood and the self.

In the following subsection, we first consider the preferred conflict management styles of culture-typed individuals (i.e., independents and interdependents) and then, going beyond the culture-typed styles of behaviors, we examine the implications of bi- or multiculturalism for conflict management behaviors.

Cultural Orientations and Preferred
Conflict-Handling Methods

We need to reconsider the motivations that may underlie conflict avoidance and confrontation. Among high independents, individuals' control of their own autonomy, freedom, and individual boundaries is of paramount importance to sense of respect and ego. The independent's self-image (compared with that of the interdependent) places a higher priority on maintaining independence and asserting individual needs and goals. It is the individual's responsibility to "say what's on his or her mind" if he or she expects to be attended to or understood (Markus & Kitayama, 1991). The independent's communicative actions will tend to be more self-focused and more self-expressive. In general, conflict among high independents is viewed as functional when it provides an open opportunity for solving problematic issues. On the other hand, high interdependents may view conflict as primarily dysfunctional, interpersonally embarrassing, and distressing, and as a forum for potential humiliation and loss of face (Ting-Toomey, 1994).

Recently, Kim, Shin, and Cai (1998), in a study of participants from Korea, Hawaii, and the mainland United States, found that the higher a person's independent cultural orientations, the less prone he or she would be to remain silent in both first- and the second-attempt requests. Thus for a person oriented toward the independent construal of self, the general tone of social interaction may concern the expression of his or her own needs and rights. Therefore, independent self-construal may systematically increase the importance of the *self-face need* in guiding choices of conflict strategies.

It has been suggested that in the "West," persons may focus on "open" communication, believing that open discussion is the best way to deal with problems with partners. Ting-Toomey (1991) contends that the norms and rules of intimacy expression and communication are differently perceived across cultures; for example, American couples openly discuss the partners' intimate issues, whereas Japanese couples tend to use indirect communication modes in managing intimate issues and problems. Ting-Toomey states that collectivists tend to use the "flight" or "exit" approach to manage relational issues in romantic conflict situations. She suggests that collectivists tend to control revealing their own feelings and voicing their opinions to their partners. On the other hand, she suggests, people from individualist cultures (those who emphasize an independent self-construal) would tend to use the "voice" approach to deal with relational conflict issues. That is, they would probably engage in a greater degree of overt argument and disagreement when conflict occurs. The control style consists basically of behaviors that have been variously called dominating (Rahim, 1983), competing (Thomas, 1976), distributive (Comstock & Strzyzewski, 1990), and equitable (Leung, 1988).

Markus and Kitayama (1991) posit that a normative imperative for members of interdependent cultures is internal self-control of private desires, emotions, or opinions that do not conform to those of the collective. In fact, to assert one's own agenda without regard for others would be considered immature in such cultures.

Cahn (1985) argues that such collectivist needs lead people in collectivist cultures (who predominantly emphasize interdependent construal of self) to use nonconfrontational communication modes in conflict or problem situations. Lebra (1984) describes several tendencies of collectivist behavior in conflict situations that can be characterized as emphasis on interdependent self-construals: (a) anticipatory management, or the use of management to prevent a conflict before it happens; (b) negative communication, which refers to the expression of conflict emotions in a negative manner (such as the expression of anger or frustration by noncommunication, such as ignorance and silence); (c) situational code switching, which refers to the pretense of being harmonious in other people's presence even though two parties in conflict are actually avoiding each other; (d) triadic management or displacement, which refers to the management of conflict situations between two parties by using a third party or go-between; and (e) self-aggression, which refers to the tendency to direct accusations against oneself (intropunitive behavior).

It can be assumed that individuals with a highly developed interdependent self-construal are unlikely to express negative emotions, such as anger, to confront each other, and to engage in open discussion in conflict situations. They may even avoid reactions to their relational problems that can potentially cause further conflict. Among interdependents, the stress is not so much on the individual and his or her interests as it is on the maintenance of the collectivity and the continuation of "harmonious" relationships. In general, conflict is viewed as damaging to social face and relational harmony and should be avoided as much as possible (Ting-Toomey, 1994). These ideas, as applied to face-maintenance dimensions, would mean that individuals with an interdependent self-view have, as an overall goal, the desire to avoid loss of face and to be accepted by in-group members, which strengthens their preference for *other-face needs* for achieving conflict goals. The requirement is to "read" the other's mind, and thus to know what the other is thinking or feeling (Kim et al., 1994). Interdependents' value patterns associated with relational harmony and "saving the other's face" will likely lead them to avoid conflict and to seek "harmony"-maintaining compromises (see Ho, 1976; Kirkbride et al., 1991).

In the past, self-face maintenance was predicted to be associated strongly with variates dominated by the dominating and integrating styles (Ting-Toomey et al., 1991). Furthermore, members of individualist cultures were predicted typically to prefer dominating and integrating (solution-oriented) styles. Although findings on the use of competitive, controlling styles by individualists have been consistently supported by cross-cultural conflict studies, no clear evidence has been found concerning integrating and compromising styles. Overall, recent evidence lends strong support for the relationship between "integrating/compromising" styles and "avoiding/obliging" styles on the one hand and other-face maintenance on the other (Kim & Hunter, 1995). Even though both integrating and compromising styles in the context of Rahim's (1983) scale reflect both high self-concern and high other-concern, both styles seem to be strongly associated with other-face concern. Furthermore, although researchers examining interpersonal and organizational conflict have tended to conceptualize the avoidance style as reflective of low concern for both self and other, the avoiding style has been found to be strongly associated with other-face concern (Kim & Hunter, 1995; Ting-Toomey et al., 1991; Trubisky et al., 1991).

Overall, the other-face need seems to be expressed through the use of indirect strategies (obliging, compromising, and avoiding styles) of conflict interaction. Obliging, compromising, and avoiding styles reflect the need to satisfy other-concern and other-face needs. Integrative style emphasizes the importance of mutual face needs and the creative search for a possible conflict solution that will be acceptable to both parties. Therefore, as the mutual face-maintenance dimension, the integrating style is also more likely to be affected by other-face need. In sum, we suggest that interdependents are less openly assertive in conflict situations due to their heightened sensitivity to others' face needs. Thus they naturally adopt high compromising and avoiding behaviors and show a relatively low preference for competing and assertive postures. The interdependents' imperative toward group-mindedness, relationship-centeredness, and the need to maintain interpersonal equilibrium may militate against the adoption of open confrontation and overtly competitive styles of behavior (Kirkbride et al., 1991). Avoiding and compromising styles may serve to dilute antagonisms that might otherwise surface in the immediate situation. The fear of shame as a result of damaging or ruffling the social fabric or damaging someone else's face would also lead interdependents to avoid assertive or direct styles of handling conflicts. All these arguments suggest a likely preference among high interdependents for saving the other's face in conflict management. It may seem better to avoid the possibility of damaging the other's face by engaging in avoidance behavior.

Situational Influences

According to Triandis (1989), each self has different probabilities of being sampled in different kinds of social/cultural environments. He discusses sampling in terms of a universe of units to be sampled and the probability of a unit's being sampled. Within certain cultural environments, the activation of certain types of units (i.e., self-schemata) is encouraged. With each activation, adjacent and similar units increase in salience. In this manner, during the process of socialization/maturation or enculturation, the salience of units normative in the social environment are cultivated into prominence. The subjective experience of individualism or collectivism is clearly culturally and situationally rooted. Cultures may also vary in the situations in which collectivism is cued. Some cultures may prime in-group cooperation across many contexts and individual competition in few contexts. Other cultures may set individual competition as the norm, with in-group cooperation rarely being primed (Oyserman, 1993). The self is viewed as dynamic, having the ability to sample different self-schemata as appropriate to different situations

(Markus & Wurf, 1987). Nevertheless, among people of higher independent self-construals, behavior that changes with the situation is more likely to be framed as waffling, hypocritical, or even pathological than as flexible or responsive.[1]

According to Markus and Kitayama (1998), the good, authentic, or genuine personality in Western literature is one in which the attributes are unified or integrated into a system or a whole with strong boundaries, that is stable over time, and that can resist influence from others and situations. Others are typically cast as part of the situational context, which should not have much influence on person factors. The idea of a bounded individual who is separate from others and who should not be unduly influenced by them also leads to a powerful consistency ethic in which the good or authentic self is the same relatively unchanging self across different situations. On the other hand, selves in interdependent cultural contexts are, for the most part, constructed in a relatively context-specific fashion (Markus & Kitayama, 1998). Selves in Asian cultures are mainly context dependent, perhaps because they are integrated with and experienced within social roles, positions, and relationships. This mode of personality organization is distinct from the Western mode, where the person is constructed to be coherent, stable, and consistent being organized by an assortment of *essences* or traitlike attributes (Markus & Kitayama, 1998).

Based on the conventional findings concerning individualism and collectivism, one might assume that independent selves would always be direct, whereas interdependent selves would always be indirect. This, however, would be an overly simplistic assumption. Virtually all previous research on conflict style preference has utilized self-benefit situations. Boster and Stiff (1984) found that people will exert greater persuasive effort on issues that benefit the target. Such persuasive effort may even extend to the use of very direct and distributive tactics. The use of forceful strategies, in this case, may be less vulnerable to relational disruption when both parties understand that the intent is for the target's own good. Cody et al. (1985) found that their subjects used distributive tactics more frequently and face maintenance tactics less frequently when the personal benefits were few. This effect seems to hinge upon relational stability or security—that is, the interdependence of the relationship.

Markus and Kitayama (1991) describe interdependent selves as having flexible and variable structure, the self-schemata of which can vary in salience according to the social context in order to attend appropriately to the needs, desires, and goals of the significant other(s) with whom the selves are currently interacting. Furthermore, interdependent construals are defined by intimate and reciprocal relationships with specific others. Interdependents within these relationships may be careful to behave in an other-face-saving manner when they confront self-benefit conflict issues. However, interdependent individuals, more so than independent individuals, may become direct and persistent when trying to confront stubborn friends or family members for their own good. Therefore, to the degree that in-group relationships are secure and stable, it seems reasonable to expect that in other-benefit conflicts, more so than in self-benefit conflict situations, interdependent selves will prefer using styles that are direct and/or confrontational.

The preferential use of conflict styles among people of different cultural orientations may also depend on the situational variable of whether they are dealing with in-group or out-group interactants. Attempts have been made to find interactions among relational distance, conflict styles, and self/other perception (Lee & Rogan, 1991; Leung, 1987, 1988). Although Leung's (1987) first attempt to find the in-group/out-group distinction did not yield any significant effects for the in-group/out-group variable, his second attempt (1988) did produce a partial effect with regard to the avoidance style. Leung (1988) found that Chinese participants in his study, more so than American participants, used avoiding more with friends and less with strangers. Leung has suggested that future research should use core in-group members (i.e., best friends or family) in the manipulation of the in-group condition in order to elicit a stronger effect.

The existence of ethnocentrism—otherwise known as in-group bias (i.e., the positive evaluation of the in-group relative to the out-group)—has been well documented at the group level (Boski, 1988). Platow, McClintock, and Liebrand (1990) claim that laboratory participants have been commonly observed to allocate more resources arbitrarily to in-group members than to out-group members. Also, many individualism-collectivism researchers hold that allocentrics (i.e., members of collectivist cultures) seem to be highly cooperative with in-group members but generally distrustful, uncooperative, manipulative, and even exploitative with out-group members (Leung & Bond, 1984; Triandis, 1972; Triandis & Vassiliou, 1972).

There are clear differences in conflict management styles among interdependent individuals, depending on whether they are communicating with in-group or out-group members. Research indicates that collectivists draw clear distinctions between in-group and out-group, whereas independents do not draw such clear distinctions. Specifically, interdependent selves attend to the needs, desires, and goals of in-group members with whom they have reciprocal and equitable relationships. On the other hand, interdependents do not treat out-group members with any special regard; Markus and Kitayama (1991) maintain that out-group members "are treated quite differently [than in-group members] and are unlikely to experience either the advantages or disadvantages of interdependence" (p. 229). Because the very nature of the interdependent self is founded upon the maintenance of reciprocal relationships with significant others (i.e., in-group members), interdependent selves may make sharp in-group versus out-group distinctions (Markus & Kitayama, 1991; Triandis, 1989).

On the other hand, independent selves' behaviors are much less contingent on those of others. Although independents are selective in their associations with others, they do not make severe distinctions in the degrees to which they attend to the needs, goals, and desires of in-group members as opposed to out-group members

(Markus & Kitayama, 1991). Consequently, interdependents would be more concerned with relational maintenance and cooperation than would independents when dealing with in-group members rather than out-group members.

The Dynamic Self-Concept

To this point, our review and discussion have focused on preferred conflict management styles of "culture-typed" individuals. The conceptualization of a culturally embedded sense of self can lead to the dangerous dichotomization of individuals as either independent or interdependent. Although most prior attempts to measure individualism-collectivism have assumed it to be a single bipolar dimension (Triandis, McCusker, & Hui, 1990), the two aspects of self can coexist. Instead of a person's being either independent or interdependent in self-orientation, he or she might exhibit both orientations; that is, a person may simultaneously maintain high independent and high interdependent construals or low independent and low interdependent construals.

The trend toward viewing the self-concept as including social as well as personal identities is laudable. However, certain erroneous assumptions seem to have been made regarding individuals' personal and social identities. One such assumption is the Aristotelian categorization of A and not-A. If you are individualist (independent), you cannot be collectivist (interdependent). You are at one end or another of a linear measure, or occasionally in between. Nevertheless, categories A and not-A are mutually exclusive. Every increment of individualism necessarily reduces your collectivism, and vice versa (for further discussion on this issue, see Hampden-Turner & Trompenaars, 1997). For instance, Hofstede (1980) identified the constructs of individualism and collectivism as opposite poles of a value dimension that differentiates world cultures. Most prior work on cultural dimensions has presumed, implicitly or explicitly, that cultural categories are linear and exclusive.

Similarly, there has been a tendency among researchers to treat self-construals (as individual-level correlates of individualism and collectivism) as bipolar opposites. The main issue concerns the dimensionality of these constructs. Are interdependence and independence bipolar opposites (one dimension) or distinct constructs (two dimensions) (see Rhee, Uleman, & Lee, 1996)? Two distinct models have guided thinking about this question: a linear, bipolar model and a two-dimensional model. In the linear model, self-concept is conceptualized along a continuum from strong independent orientation at one extreme to strong interdependent orientation at the other. The assumption underlying this model is that a stronger identification with one requires a weakening of identification with the other (see Figure 6.1).

Some scholars have suggested that individuals can possess both orientations (Kâgitçibasi, 1987; Kashima, 1987; Sinha & Tripathi, 1994), and recent empirical work at the individual level supports the multidimensional conception of col-

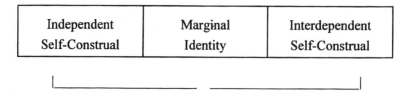

Figure 6.1. Unidimensional Model of Self-Construals

lectivism and individualism (Cross, 1995; Gudykunst et al., 1996; Kim et al., 1996; Rhee et al., 1996; Singelis, 1994). It appears that independent and interdependent self-construals are unrelated to one another, not bipolar opposites, as their verbal labels might imply. Schwartz (1990) has noted that viewing collectivism and individualism as bipolar opposites obscures important differences among types of individualism and types of collectivism.

Bicultural identity is conceptually incompatible with the unidimensional model of self-construals. In the unidimensional model, bicultural individuals are "forced" to occupy a space between the two cultural poles, suggesting marginal competence and sensitivity in both cultures. Similar to the unidimensional model of acculturation, the unidimensional model of cultural identity is still popular with most researchers. A graphic representation of the two-dimensional model is shown in Figure 6.2. In the unidimensional model, movement away from the independent pole necessarily brings one closer to the interdependent pole. In contrast, this alternative model suggests that there are not merely two extremes, but at least four possible distinct cultural orientations (see Berry & Kim, 1988, for a similar model applied to acculturation). A high score on both dimensions is indicative of bicultural identity; a low score on both dimensions suggests marginal identity. A high score on only one dimension indicates culture-typed identity (either independent or interdependent).

A vital step in the development of effective partnerships among people involves moving away from the assumptions of the linear model of cultural identity. Our goal in the next subsection is to develop an understanding of the nature of bicultural identity and conflict management styles. Due to lack of research in this area, however, our discussion of biculturalism is speculative in nature. Nevertheless, we are able to identify several characteristics that, we hypothesize, are central to communication competence in conflict situations.

Bicultural Identities: Will Bicultural Individuals
Fare Better in Conflict Situations?

There is a growing awareness of the identity challenges and communication patterns in the lives of bicultural and multicultural persons. Looking around the

Independence

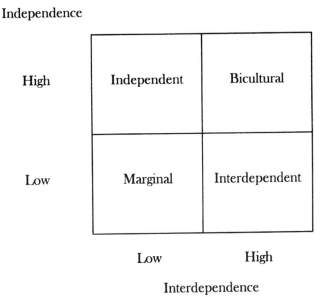

Figure 6.2. Two-Dimensional Model of Self-Construals

United States in the 1990s alone, multicultural people are evident everywhere. Whether through immigration, sojourning, marriage, adoption, or birth, a wide range of people are actively carrying the frames of reference of two or more cultures (see Bennett, 1993).

Recent findings lend credence to the view that individualism and collectivism are essentially independent perspectives (see Kim et al., 1996; Triandis, 1989). According to Markus and Kitayama (1991), on the average, relatively more individuals in Western cultures than in non-Western cultures hold independent self-construals. Within a given culture, however, individuals vary in the extent to which they are "typical" and construe the self in the "typical" way. Thus not all people who are part of an individualist culture possess primarily independent self-construals, nor do all those who are part of a collectivist culture possess primarily interdependent self-construals. Cross and Markus (1991) found support for two dimensions of self in their study of stress and coping behavior among North American and East Asian exchange students. East Asian students who viewed the interdependent or collective aspects of the self as less important, and had developed the independent aspects of the self, reported less stress. When asked to indicate the importance of the independent and interdependent facets of the self, the East Asian exchange students placed much more importance on the interdependent dimension of the self than did the American students, but importance scores on the independent dimension did not differ between the groups. So the Asian exchange students appeared to have developed internal, private, autonomous self-systems while continuing to retain the interdependent aspects of the self.

Cross (1995) has found empirical support for the existence of the dual construal of self. Certain individuals, whom Cross calls biculturals, were found to have both highly developed independent and highly developed interdependent self-construals, the possession of which enabled these biculturals to cope better, with less stress, in cultural environments foreign to their own. In separate studies, Kim and her associates found that self-construals were indeed separate dimensions (Kim et al., 1994, 1996; Kim & Hunter, 1995). Kim et al. (1996) grouped respondents into four types of culture orientation: bicultural (high development of both independent and interdependent construals), independent (high development of independent but underdevelopment of interdependent construals), interdependent (high development of interdependent but underdevelopment of independent construals), and marginal (underdevelopment of both construals). There was a significant main effect of cultural orientation, with bicultural individuals expressing the highest level of overall conversational concern, followed by interdependent, then independent, and, finally, marginal individuals expressing the lowest level of concern. Such findings imply a tendency for bicultural and interdependent individuals to be more adaptive than independent or marginal individuals in intercultural conversational settings.

Several authors have noted the additive element of biculturality or multi-culturality, suggesting that the acculturation process need not substitute new cultural values for old. Rather, acculturation may add new behaviors that allow for cultural frame-of-reference shifting (Dyal & Dyal, 1981). Saltzman's (1986) "150 percent person" represents just such a culturally expanded individual. Bennett (1993) asserts that two potential responses to living on cultural margins are *constructive marginality* and *encapsulated marginality*. The encapsulated ("trapped") marginal is a person who is buffeted by conflicting cultural loyalties and unable to construct a unified identity. In contrast, by maintaining control of choice and construction of boundaries, a person may become a constructive marginal ("bicultural"). A constructive marginal is a person who is able to construct context intentionally and consciously for the purpose of creating his or her own identity.

The model of acculturation described by Berry and Kim (1988) posits four modes that are based on an individual's willingness and ability to change, add, and/or retain cultural identity. In many senses, this can be understood as a process of adjusting self-identity (or not). An individual who assimilates will replace his or her self-image with the self-view prevalent in the culture in which the individual wishes to belong (*assimilation*). A person who integrates (from either a collectivist or an individualist culture) may develop an independent self (or interdependent self) in addition to his or her original self-concept—the *bicultural. Separation* is the result of a choice to retain the original self in lieu of assimilation or integration.

Finally, *marginalization* may be the result of a degradation of the original self without its replacement by the new self-image, thus leaving the individual "marginal," without any well-defined sense of self. The point is that some individuals may simultaneously maintain high independent as well as high interdependent self-construals.

The usefulness of a bicultural self-perspective has been noted by several authors (Bennett, 1993; Kim et al., 1996; Oyserman, 1993). A person who simultaneously maintains high independent and high interdependent self-construals (i.e., who is bicultural) may be able to modify his or her behavior appropriately and successfully when moving from one culture to another. This notion of adaptability seems to coincide with the "rhetorically sensitive person" (Hart & Burks, 1972), who tries to accept role taking as part of the human condition, attempts to avoid stylized verbal behavior, and is characteristically willing to undergo the strain of *adaptation*. Similarly, individuals with high independent as well as high interdependent self-construals may be well aware of "appropriate" styles of conflict management and show high flexibility for behavioral adaptation. This vision of people as multifaceted also seems to coincide with such concepts as the "universal person" (Walsh, 1973), the "multicultural person" (Adler, 1987), and the "international person" (Lutzker, 1960). Adler (1987), for example, explains the unique characteristics of the multicultural person as neither totally a part of nor totally apart from his or her culture. Such a person may be capable of reconciling the conflicts posed by competing conflict management styles and achieving a high level of communication competence. He or she may be better able than others to make deliberate choices in specific situations and to maintain a dynamic balance between avoidance and confrontation rather than being bound by culturally imposed emphases on conflict management behaviors.

Because bicultural individuals may identify to a high degree with both independent and interdependent characteristics, they may be free from cultural pressures to restrict their strategy choices to stereotypic roles. Thus bicultural individuals are more likely than marginal, or culture-typed, individuals to display conversational adaptability across different conflict situations. A certain level of adherence to self-concern is as essential for the successful achievement of interactional balance as the maintenance of good interpersonal relationships, whereas the exact patterns of resolving this conflict may depend on other factors, such as the importance of primary goals, relational outcome values, and nature of the situation.

The above discussion is summarized in Table 6.1. Bi- or multicultural individuals come to a deeper understanding and appreciation of their cultural identities. This culmination may require resolution or coming to terms with two or more extremes of cultural identifications. Bi- or multicultural identity development may continue in cycles that involve further exploration or rethinking of the role or meaning of one's cultural identity and corresponding conflict management styles.

SUMMARY AND CONCLUSION

In view of the growing interconnectedness of societies and economies around the world, human civilization is now entering an age of intercultural mixing on a scale not previously witnessed. As a result, the possibility for conflict—often substantial within cultures—is even more probable between members of different cultures. Research that is aimed at a better understanding of the ways in which people prefer to handle interpersonal conflicts, and how those preferences vary according to cultural and other variables, has begun and should be continued. Knowledge about such conflict-related behavioral tendencies might help in the development of strategies for interpersonal, intercultural conflict resolution or prevention.

We began this chapter with a review of cross-cultural studies on conflict management behaviors and their popularly adopted typologies of conflict management. Blake and Mouton's (1964) two-dimensional framework has been accepted without due caution among cross-cultural conflict management style theorists, who invariably cite the framework as the basis for their own work. We believe that under scrutiny, this two-dimensional model of conflict management proves inadequate to be applied cross-culturally. We have attempted to demonstrate how the individualist orientation of American culture has led researchers to assume that confrontation is more desirable than avoidance. However, this assumption is faulty and is the result of scholars' neglect of the dialectic between confrontation and avoidance. Certainly, knowledge concerning the motivations behind different conflict styles is one important tool for expanding our understanding of conflict phenomena.

In sum, this review of conflict styles implies the need for a reformulation of theories in this and related areas. Errors in conceptualization and interpretation of results have been engendered by the individualist bias of work in this area. As our review suggests, interdependents' tendency to avoid conflict can be explained by their desire to preserve relational harmony and their motivation to save other's face. The individualist assumption that overt conflict resolution is more desirable than covert conflict has led to the discovery of only certain facts about conflict resolution and has resulted in ignorance about, or misinterpretation of, other conflict management styles. Based on our examination of the literature to date, we have proposed a multicultural framework of conflict styles that attempts to explain systematically why individuals of different cultural identities tend to approach and manage conflict situations differently.

Because of the difficulties with existing conceptualizations of conflict styles, future research should give special attention to the development of an instrument that will more validly assess the five modes—particularly by minimizing the ethnocentric conceptualizations of the styles. Unless such an instrument can be developed, further research in the field of conflict management will be severely limited, because most substantive findings will be subject to alternative explanations. The multicultural framework of conflict management behavior highlights possible logical flaws in existing taxonomic structures of conflict strategy styles.

TABLE 6.1
Paradigms in Cultural Identity and Conflict Management Styles

Representation of Identity	Interdependent Self-Construal	Independent Self-Construal	Bicultural or Multicultural Identity
Identity	culture-typed identity; identity as a given		identity as choice, seeking to understand meaning of cultural identity for oneself
Development	preencounter, unexamined cultural identity, lack of interest or concern regarding cultural identity		cultural identity achieved through awareness
Important features	hierarchical status, and social roles	individual, abilities, thoughts	familiarity with, and competence in, more than one culture
Tasks	fulfilling culturally mandated tasks; preference for values of dominant culture		self-awareness of culturally mandated tasks and choice making
Basis of self-esteem	following cultural heritage and being an ideal member of a culture		understanding of multiple perspectives, respect for cultural differences
Conflict management styles	culturally patterned conflict management behavior		dynamic code switching, wider repertoire of conflict strategies and styles

This model will allow for richer insights into conflict behavior, upon which intercultural theory building may build.

In the mainstream U.S. context, open controversy has been considered normal (Folger & Poole, 1984) and beneficial for decision making (Tjosvold & Johnson, 1978). Furthermore, conflict suppression has been viewed as causing misunderstanding, lack of innovativeness, resentment, and long-term conflict escalation. According to Roloff (1987), conflict suppression or avoidance provides necessary stability for individual and coordinated action, but it may also have negative effects. As Roloff rightly points out, minimal research has focused on this seemingly necessary balance between conflict avoidance and confrontation. Researchers, therefore, need to reconceptualize the notion of conflict and refine measures of it. We must note in this context the technical problems of alternative conflict questionnaires. Some measurements of conflict styles include sets of culture-specific proverbs (e.g., Lawrence & Lorsch, 1967); this format is unlikely to work among diverse ethnic groups. Some measures ignore the role of communication as a way to handle disagreement (e.g., Sternberg & Soriano, 1984) or use only a single item for each style that simply asks subjects to rank-order five statements (Blake & Mouton, 1964). Some measures use forced-choice questions (Kilmann & Thomas, 1977). Even a few instruments developed from communication-based items are not situationally based (e.g., Brown et al., 1981) or exclusively focused on organizational setting (e.g., Putnam & Wilson, 1982).

Furthermore, future research should examine conflict styles other than "the usual suspects." Covert or overt revenge by way of slander or sabotage is not covered by current conflict style models. Nicotera (1993), in her inductive investigation of conflict behavior, found several behaviors resulting from anger (aggression, begrudging, estranging, and patronizing) that were not effectively distinguished by the existing conflict style models. Also, personal rejection (i.e., the berating of the interactant's personal traits) has not been covered adequately. There is room for improvement regarding the comprehensiveness of conflict style scales. Tests of construct and predictive validity, as well as perhaps test-retest reliability and response distortion, would be helpful for the evaluation of instruments' effectiveness in future conflict style research.

Researchers also need to consider emic conflict styles. Emics are culture-specific aspects of a phenomenon that are necessary to an understanding of the culture's indigenous conception of that phenomenon. Therefore, conflict researchers must search for emic styles not included in Western theories of conflict management behavior (see Weldon & Jehn, 1995). When a theory and questionnaire are transported across cultures, emic (culture-specific) constructs important to an understanding of the phenomenon in other cultures are not included. Thus we need to search for emic conflict management styles to produce a complete understanding of how conflict is managed in other cultures.

Another problem arises because the cross-cultural studies on conflict resolution have mostly used Asian samples (e.g., Lee & Rogan, 1991; Leung, 1987; Trubisky et al., 1991), in spite of the fact that some value orientations exist that are unique to Asian cultures. For example, the Confucian work dynamism value has been identified as a separate and almost exclusively Asian value (Chinese Culture Connection, 1987), yet it is quite possible that this value, operating alone or interacting with collectivism or some other value, may be responsible for the obtained preference pattern (see Gire & Carment, 1993). Furthermore, observers of Asian cultures have emphasized sensitivity to and use of nonverbal communication as a means of facilitating indirect communication in those cultures (e.g., Bond, 1986; Doi, 1973; Okabe, 1983). Theoretically, harmonious conflict resolution should be enhanced by an increase in attention to, and perception of, emotional (nonverbal) messages. Obviously, more research work is called for in this important area.

Future research must take into consideration that individualism and collectivism appear to constitute a dialectic. That is, individualism and collectivism exist in all cultures, and individuals hold both individualist and collectivist values. This position is consistent with Schwartz's (1990) contention that individualist and collectivist values are not necessarily incompatible; they can coexist. This idea is compatible with several recent discussions of individualism and collectivism. If individualism-collectivism is a dialectic at both the cultural and individual levels, as it appears, then it is critical that future research hypotheses involve very specific predictions regarding the linkages between various aspects of individualism-collectivism and individuals' behavior (Gudykunst, Guzley, & Ota, 1993). A universally applicable theory should concern itself with individual-level as well as cultural-level issues (see Gudykunst et al., 1996; Kim, 1995; Kim et al., 1994). Because self-concept provides a link between the norms and values of a culture and the everyday behavior of individuals, it is a promising means of explaining conflict styles in different cultures. The notion of self-concept brings broad cultural variability dimensions to the individual level. The nature of divergent self-systems permits us to specify more fully the precise role of the self in mediating the effect of culture-level individualism and collectivism on conflict management styles.

Future theoretical development should also focus on investigating the combined effects of context (e.g., self- versus other-benefit, in-group versus out-group situations) and individual-level cultural dimensions. This review suggests that conflict management choices are culturally and situationally dependent; that is, the interplay of the individual and the context is a critically important interaction to be accounted for in the assessment of conflict styles (King & Miles, 1990). According to Ting-Toomey (1989), context includes components such as situational and relational contexts (*relational context* refers to the influence of family or friendship networks). An individual's self-system depends heavily on the context in which an encounter takes place. How a person constructs and presents a "self" in a relationship is, to a large degree, situation dependent (see Triandis, 1989). Specifically, future research should examine the effects of various situational and psychological variables—such as social status, power difference, conflict size, relationship type, emotional intensity, moral constraints, and perceived effectiveness of style—on preference for conflict style. In addition, intercultural researchers should examine the following factors suggested by Nadler et al. (1985): beliefs about conflict (i.e., whether it is good, bad, or neutral), expectations for resolutions (e.g., satisfaction of all needs, mutual acceptability of outcome, or cessation of open confrontation), beliefs regarding fairness of resolutions (i.e., how they depend on equality, equity, or responsibility), perspectives on time (e.g., monochronic versus polychronic, preoccupation with schedules), and decision-making styles (e.g., those based on deductive logic, inductive logic, consensus building, emotional appeals, and intuition, and participatory versus authoritative decision making). Overall, researchers need to develop theoretical assumptions concerning why some situational contingencies may affect cross-cultural conflict management styles.

Several other issues also need to be addressed in future studies of conflict communication. Researchers need to ascertain the degree to which one can generalize self-reported preference for a conflict style in hypothetical situations to actual probability of its use in real conflict situations. As some critics of styles research have suggested, scores on even the most sophisticated style measures cannot be assumed to predict communication strategies in conflict situations (Donohue, 1981; Putnam & Poole, 1987). Conrad (1991) found that even initial strategic choices deviated in important ways from some styles scores, and the pattern of deviation changed with subsequent strategic choices. However, the pattern of deviation was not as simple as some critics suggest. Scores on some styles are less predictive of communicative actions than are others. Thus the degree of deviation may depend on the interrelationships among a host of factors and on the characteristics of specific styles. For instance, in an emotionally charged conflict situation, interactants will likely not take the time to decide rationally from a set of conflict styles they would prefer most. Although it is convenient to study conflict behavior in hypothetical situations, perhaps conflict researchers should reexamine the usefulness of their self-reported data. Overall, the lengthy tradition of focusing on conflict styles in isolation from communicative strategies should be revised in fundamental ways.

Heretofore, the study of conflict-handling styles has mostly concerned itself with preferences for conflict styles to be used to initiate conflict interactions. However, our understanding of conflict styles will greatly improve once we can understand how the use of certain styles affects preference for style later in the interaction. Researchers should examine preference for conflict style at every stage in the conflict situation. As Ohbuchi and Takahashi (1994) point out, an important decision at the very beginning is whether to let the other party know of the existence of the conflict issue. Future research should specify the factors that influence this overt versus covert decision and how that decision influences preference for conflict style at the beginning of the conflict interaction. Research should then examine how interactants' preferences for conflict styles vary according to the style used by the other party at each successive exchange in the interaction. Escalating emotions can be a factor (e.g., initial users of integrating may switch to dominating if the other party has been dominating). The perceived effectiveness of conflict styles, both of those used on the other party and of those used by the other party, should be examined for their influence on successive style use (e.g., whether one believes the other party is capable of and willing to carry out a threat).

Implications

People's abilities to resolve social conflicts successfully depend in large measure on their being able to predict accurately the effectiveness of conflict management strategies. The consequences described by such much-abused terms as *communication breakdown* and *cross-cultural miscommunication* (Coupland, Giles, & Wiemann, 1991) can often be attributed to different perceptions regarding choices of conflict tactics. For instance, communication breakdown in conflict situations typically occurs because interactants disagree about the effectiveness or social appropriateness of one another's conflict strategies. Individuals' beliefs about the appropriateness of particular conflict strategies are apt to affect the conflict tactics and strategies they choose and the inferences they make about their own and others' conflict-handling behavior. The review we have presented in this chapter implies that differing cultural orientations may cause people to have drastically different ideas about what constitute appropriate conflict strategies or tactics.

Miller and Steinberg (1975) distinguish between pseudoconflicts and simple conflicts. Simple conflicts stem from incompatible goals, whereas pseudoconflicts arise from communicative misunderstanding between parties. Given that intercultural communication is generally characterized by many ostensible differences between interactants, such as different expectations, the potential for pseudoconflicts is greater in intercultural relationships than in intracultural ones (see Lee & Rogan, 1991). Similarly, it is often not the content of conflict that creates tensions or frictions; rather, it is cultural style that creates uncertainty and anxiety in the conflict encounter situation (Ting-Toomey, 1988).

In this era of multicultural societies, cultural diversity has to be recognized, understood, and used appropriately in organizations and interpersonal settings. Most theoreticians and researchers have created an ethnocentric, Western bias toward championing the independent self (see Sampson, 1988). Extending this conceptualization of self portrays avoidance of conflict as a negative and destructive tendency of an individual that needs to be "corrected" through counseling or clinical help. In a broader context, communication avoidance (e.g., lack of verbal assertiveness) has been associated with "deficiency." It is easy to find explicit references in the literature to the view that communication approach is more desirable than communication avoidance (e.g., Rancer et al., 1985; Richmond & McCroskey, 1995). People with avoidant communication tendencies have been described as suffering from general anxiety, having low tolerance for ambiguity, lacking self-control, not being adventurous, lacking emotional maturity, being introverted, having low self-esteem, not being innovative, having low tolerance for disagreement, and not being assertive (for a review, see Richmond & McCroskey, 1995). The association of these constructs with communication avoidance misrepresents the sources of communication avoidance solely as defects or inadequacies. The value placed on direct conflict management styles in individualist cultures is not shared by many other cultures. Different conflict management styles are generated by differing concepts of self, which in part stem from differing cultural contexts.

The prevailing factor of cultural variability in intercultural communication research during the past decade has been the perception of self as either individualist or collectivist. In a multicultural society, the development of a bicultural or expanded self may be viewed as an asset, because such a perspective necessarily diminishes rigid culture-typed behaviors. Consciousness of one's own cultural identity has been called a state of "dynamic betweenness" (Yoshikawa, 1988). The suggestion here is of continual and comfortable movement between cultural identities such that an integrated, multicultural existence is maintained and conscious, deliberate choice making of conflict management strategies prevails. This awareness of living on the margins of at least two cultures eliminates a person's being overly dependent upon a single culture for identity ("culture typed"). Rather, bicultural individuals tend to be constructive in dealings with culturally diverse others. Thus, increasingly, bicultural identity will be recognized as a resource to be harnessed for professional or social advantage. At present, however, there is a paucity of research on the potential effectiveness of bicultural individuals in their communication behavior.

Given that cross-cultural interactions are burgeoning, there has never been more need for knowledge about conflict styles in different cultures (Ting-Toomey, 1988). Theories on cross-cultural conflict styles are still in their infancy. Continuous conceptual refinement and diverse means of testing theories should yield a deeper understanding of cross-cultural conflict communication processes. We hope that the ideas presented here are sufficiently thought-provoking to stimulate related research by other scholars.

NOTE

1. The measure of "overall" self-construal may not predict behavior in specific situations if individuals activate different self-construals in different situations. To predict communication in a specific situation and model the exact functioning of self-construals, the self-construal measure would have to be adapted to the specific situation. As of now, situation-specific measures of self-construals do not exist. Thus it is an open question whether individuals do in fact change their self-construals depending on context. For example, might a "collectivist" activate interdependent self-construals with in-group members but use independent self-construals with out-group members? Although we are aware of this issue, our discussion of situational influences is based on the general assumption that people with high scores on overall measures of interdependent self-construals may be more sensitive to situational context than people with high scores on overall measures of independent self-construals.

REFERENCES

Adler, P. S. (1987). Beyond cultural identity: Reflections on cultural and multicultural man. In L. A. Samovar & R. E. Porter (Eds.), *Intercultural communication: A reader* (5th ed.). Belmont, CA: Wadsworth.

Bennett, J. M. (1993). Cultural marginality: Identity issues in intercultural training. In M. Paige (Ed.), *Education for the intercultural experience* (pp. 109-135). Yarmouth, ME: Intercultural Press.

Berry, J. W., & Kim, U. (1988). Acculturation and mental health. In P. R. Dasen, J. W. Berry, & N. Sartorius (Eds.), *Health and cross-cultural psychology* (pp. 207-236). New York: Academic Press.

Blake, R. R., & Mouton, J. S. (1964). *The managerial grid.* Houston, TX: Gulf.

Blake, R. R., Shepard, H. A., & Mouton, J. S. (1964). *Managing intergroup conflict in industry.* Houston, TX: Gulf.

Bochner, S. (1994). Cross-cultural differences in the self concept: A test of Hofstede's individualism/collectivism distinction. *Journal of Cross-Cultural Psychology, 25,* 273-283.

Bond, M. H. (Ed.). (1986). *The psychology of the Chinese people.* Hong Kong: Oxford University Press.

Bond, M. H., Leung, K., Wan, K. C., & Giacalone, R. A. (1985). How are responses to verbal insult related to cultural collectivism and power distance? *Journal of Cross-Cultural Psychology, 16,* 111-127.

Boski, P. (1988). Cross-cultural studies of person-perception: Effects of ingroup/outgroup membership and ethnic schemata. *Journal of Cross-Cultural Psychology, 19,* 287-328.

Boster, F. J., & Stiff, J. B. (1984). Compliance-gaining message selection behavior. *Human Communication Research, 10,* 539-556.

Brewer, M. B., & Gardner, W. (1996). Who is this "we"? Levels of collective identity and self-representations. *Journal of Personality and Social Psychology, 71,* 83-93.

Brockner, J., & Chen, Y.-R. (1996). The moderating roles of self-esteem and self-construal in reaction to a threat to the self: Evidence from the People's Republic of China and the United States. *Journal of Personality and Social Psychology, 71,* 603-615.

Brown, C. T., Yelsma, P., & Keller, P. W. (1981). Communication-conflict predisposition: Development of a theory and an instrument. *Human Relations, 34,* 1103-1117.

Bryant, B. K. (1992). Conflict resolution strategies in relation to children's peer relations. *Journal of Applied Developmental Psychology, 13,* 35-50.

Cahn, D. D. (1985). Communication competence in the resolution of intercultural conflict. *World Communication, 14,* 85-94.

Canary, D., & Spitzberg, B. H. (1987). Appropriateness and effectiveness perceptions of conflict strategies. *Human Communication Research, 14,* 93-118.

Canary, D., & Spitzberg, B. H. (1989). A model of perceived competence of conflict strategies. *Human Communication Research, 15,* 630-649.

Cathcart, D., & Cathcart, R. (1976). A Japanese social experience and concept of groups. In L. A. Samovar & R. E. Porter (Eds.), *Intercultural communication: A reader* (2nd ed., pp. 58-66). Belmont, CA: Wadsworth.

Chinese Culture Connection. (1987). Chinese values and the search for culture-free dimensions. *Journal of Cross-Cultural Psychology, 18,* 143-164.

Chiu, R. K., & Kosinski, F. A. (1994). Is Chinese conflict-handling behavior influenced by Chinese values? *Social Behavior and Personality, 22,* 81-90.

Chua, E., & Gudykunst, W. B. (1987). Conflict resolution styles in low- and high-context cultures. *Communication Research Reports, 5,* 32-37.

Chusmir, L., & Mills, J. (1989). Gender differences in conflict resolution styles of managers: At work and at home. *Sex Roles, 20,* 149-162.

Cody, M. J., Greene, J. O., Marston, P. J., O'Hair, H. D., Baaske, K. T., & Schneider, M. J. (1985). Situation perception and message strategy selection. In M. L. McLaughlin (Ed.), *Communication yearbook 9* (pp. 390-420). Beverly Hills, CA: Sage.

Comstock, J., & Buller, D. B. (1991). Conflict strategies adolescents use with their parents: Testing the cognitive communicator characteristics model. *Journal of Language and Social Psychology, 10,* 47-59.

Comstock, J., & Strzyzewski, K. (1990). Interpersonal interaction on television: Family conflict jealousy on primetime. *Journal of Broadcasting & Electronic Media, 34,* 263-282.

Conrad, C. (1991). Communication in conflict: Style-strategy relationships. *Communication Monographs, 58,* 135-155.

Coupland, N., Giles, H., & Wiemann, J. M. (Eds.). (1991). *"Miscommunication" and problematic talk.* Newbury Park, CA: Sage.

Cross, S. E. (1995). Self-construals, coping, and stress in cross-cultural adaptation. *Journal of Cross-Cultural Psychology, 6,* 673-697.

Cross, S. E., & Markus, H. R. (1991, July). *Cultural adaptation and the self: Self-construal, coping, and stress.* Paper presented at the 99th Annual Meeting of the American Psychological Association, San Francisco.

Cushman, D. P., & King, S. S. (1985). National and organizational cultures in conflict resolution: Japan, the United States, and Yugoslavia. In W. B. Gudykunst, L. P. Stewart, & S. Ting-Toomey (Eds.), *Communication, culture, and organizational processes* (pp. 114-133). Beverly Hills, CA: Sage.

De Vos, G. (1975). Apprenticeship and paternalism. In E. G. Vogel (Ed.), *Modern Japanese organization and decision-making* (pp. 228-248). Tokyo: Charles E. Tuttle.

Doi, L. T. (1973). The Japanese patterns of communication and the concept of *amae. Quarterly Journal of Speech, 59,* 180-185.

Donohue, W. A. (1981). Analyzing negotiation tactics. *Human Communication Research, 7,* 273-287.

Dyal, J. A., & Dyal, R. Y. (1981). Acculturation, stress and coping: Some implications for research and education. *International Journal of Intercultural Relations, 5,* 301-328.

Fablo, T., & Peplau, L. A. (1980). Power strategies in intimate relationships. *Journal of Personality and Social Psychology, 38,* 618-628.

Filley, A. C., & House, R. J. (1969). *Managerial process and organizational behavior.* Glenview, IL: Scott, Foresman.

Fitzpatrick, M. A., & Winke, J. (1979). You always hurt the one you love: Strategies and tactics in interpersonal conflict. *Communication Quarterly, 27,* 3-11.

Folger, P., & Poole, M. S. (1984). *Working through conflict: A communication perspective.* Glenview, IL: Scott, Foresman.

Fry, L. W., Kidron, A. G., Osborn, R. N., & Trafton, R. S. (1980). A constructive replication of the Lawrence and Lorsch conflict resolution methodology. *Journal of Management, 6,* 7-19.

Gaines, S. O., Jr., Marelich, W. D., Bledsoe, K. L., Steers, W. N., Henderson, M. C., Granrose, C. S., Barajas, L., Hicks, D., Lyde, M., Takahashi, Y., Yum, N., Rios, D. I., Garcia, B. F., Farris, K. R., & Page, M. S. (1997). Links between race/ethnicity and cultural values as mediated by racial/ethnic identity and moderated by gender. *Journal of Personality and Social Psychology, 72,* 1460-1476.

Galvin, K. M., & Brommel, B. J. (1986). *Family communication: Cohesion and change.* Glenview, IL: Scott, Foresman.

Gire, J. T., & Carment, D. W. (1993). Dealing with disputes: The influence of individualism-collectivism. *Journal of Social Psychology, 133,* 81-95.

Gudykunst, W. B., Guzley, R. M., & Ota, H. (1993). Issue for future research on communication in Japan and the United States. In W. B. Gudykunst (Ed.), *Communication in Japan and the United States* (pp. 291-322). Albany: State University of New York Press.

Gudykunst, W. B., Matsumoto, Y., Ting-Toomey, S., Nishida, T., Kim, K., & Heyman, S. (1996). The influence of cultural individualism-collectivism, self-construals, and individual values on communication styles across cultures. *Human Communication Research, 22,* 510-543.

Hall, J. (1986). *Conflict management survey: A survey of one's characteristic reaction to and handling of conflicts between himself and others.* Conroe, TX: Teleometrics.

Hampden-Turner, C., & Trompenaars, F. (1997). Response to Geert Hofstede. *International Journal of Intercultural Relations, 21,* 149-156.

Hart, R. P., & Burks, D. M. (1972). Rhetorical sensitivity and social interaction. *Speech Monographs, 39,* 75-91.

Healey, J. G., & Bell, R. A. (1990). Assessing alternative responses to conflict in friendship. In D. D. Cody (Ed.), *Intimates in conflict: A communication perspective* (pp. 25-48). Hillsdale, NJ: Lawrence Erlbaum.

Ho, D. Y. F. (1976). On the concept of face. *American Journal of Psychology, 81,* 867-884.

Hocker, J. L., & Wilmot, W. W. (1995). *Interpersonal conflict.* Madison, WI: Brown & Benchmark.

Hofstede, G. (1980). *Culture's consequences: International differences in work-related values.* Beverly Hills, CA: Sage.

Hofstede, G. (1991). *Cultures and organizations: Software of the mind.* London: McGraw-Hill.

Horney, K. (1945). *Our inner conflicts.* New York: W. W. Norton.

Hsieh, T. T., Shybut, J., & Lotsof, E. J. (1969). Internal versus external control and ethnic group membership. *Journal of Consulting and Clinical Psychology, 33,* 122-124.

Infante, D. A., Trebing, J. D., Shepherd, P. E., & Seeds, D. E. (1984). The relationship of argumentativeness to verbal aggression. *Southern Speech Communication Journal, 50,* 67-77.

Jehn, K., & Weldon, E. (1992, August). *A comparative study of managerial attitudes toward conflict in the United States and the People's Republic of China: Issues of theory and management.* Paper presented at the annual meeting of the Academy of Management, Las Vegas.

Kabanoff, B. (1987). Predictive validity of the MODE Conflict Instrument. *Journal of Applied Psychology, 72,* 160-163.

Kagan, S., Knight, G., & Martinez-Romero, S. (1982). Culture and the development of conflict resolution style. *Journal of Cross-Cultural Psychology, 13,* 43-59.

Kagan, S., & Madsen, M. (1971). Cooperation and competition of Mexican, Mexican American, and Anglo American children of two ages under four instructional sets. *Developmental Psychology, 5,* 32-39.

Kâgitçibasi, Ç. (1987). Individual and group loyalties: Are they possible? In Ç. Kâgitçibasi (Ed.), *Growth and progress in cross-cultural psychology* (pp. 94-103). Lisse, Netherlands: Swets & Zeitlinger.

Kâgitçibasi, Ç., & Berry, J. W. (1989). Cross-cultural psychology: Current research and trends. *Annual Review of Psychology, 40,* 493-531.

Kashima, Y. (1987). Conceptions of person: Implications in individualism-collectivism research. In Ç. Kâgitçibasi (Ed.), *Growth and progress in cross-cultural psychology* (pp. 104-112). Lisse, Netherlands: Swets & Zeitlinger.

Kashima, Y., Yamaguchi, S., Kim, U., Choi, S.-C., Gelfand, M. J., & Yuki, M. (1995). Culture, gender, and self: A perspective from individualism-collectivism research. *Journal of Personality and Social Psychology, 69,* 925-937.

Kilmann, R. H., & Thomas, K. W. (1975). Interpersonal conflict-handling behaviors reflections of Jungian personality dimensions. *Psychological Report, 37,* 971-980.

Kilmann, R. H., & Thomas, K. W. (1977). Developing a forced-choice measure of conflict-handling behavior: The "MODE" instrument. *Educational and Psychological Measurement, 37,* 309-325.

Kim, M.-S. (1994). Cross-cultural comparisons of the perceived importance of conversational constraints. *Human Communication Research, 21,* 128-151.

Kim, M.-S. (1995). Toward a theory of conversational constraints: Focusing on individual-level dimensions of culture. In R. L. Wiseman (Ed.), *Intercultural communication theory* (pp. 148-169). Thousand Oaks, CA: Sage.

Kim, M.-S. (1999). Cross-cultural perspectives on motivations of verbal communication: Review, critique,and a theoretical framework. In M. Roloff (Ed.), *Communication yearbook 22* (pp. 51-89). Thousand Oaks, CA: Sage.

Kim, M.-S., & Hunter, J. E. (1995, November). *A test of a cultural model of conflict styles.* Paper presented at the annual meeting of the Speech Communication Association, San Antonio, TX.

Kim, M.-S., Hunter, J. E., Miyahara, A., Horvath, A., Bresnahan, M., & Yoon, H.-J. (1996). Individual- vs. culture-level dimensions of individualism and collectivism: Effects on preferred conversational styles. *Communication Monographs, 63,* 29-49.

Kim, M.-S., & Kitani, K. (1998). Conflict management styles of Asian- and Caucasian-Americans in romantic relationships in Hawaii. *Journal of Asian Pacific Communication, 8,* 51-68.

Kim, M.-S., & Sharkey, W. F. (1995). Independent and interdependent construals of self: Explaining cultural patterns of interpersonal communication in multi-cultural organizational settings. *Communication Quarterly, 43,* 20-38.

Kim, M.-S., Sharkey, W. F., & Singelis, T. M. (1994). The relationship between individuals' self-construals and perceived importance of interactive constraints. *International Journal of Intercultural Relations, 18,* 117-140.

Kim, M.-S., Shin, H. C., & Cai, D. (1998). The influence of cultural orientations on the preferred forms of requesting and rerequesting. *Communication Monographs, 65,* 47-66.

King, W. C., & Miles, E. W. (1990). What we know—and don't know—about measuring conflict: An examination of the ROCI-II and the OCCI conflict instruments. *Management Communication Quarterly, 4,* 222-243.

Kirkbride, P. S., Tang, S. F., & Westwood, R. I. (1991). Chinese conflict preferences and negotiating behavior: Cultural and psychological influences. *Organization Studies, 12,* 365-386.

Kitayama, S., Markus, H. R., Matsumoto, H., & Norasakkunkit, V. (1997). Individual and collective processes in the construction of the self: Self-enhancement in the United States and self-criticism in Japan. *Journal of Personality and Social Psychology, 72,* 1245-1267.

Kumagai, F., & Straus, M. A. (1983). Conflict resolution tactics in Japan, India, and the USA. *Journal of Comparative Family Studies, 14,* 377-387.

Lawrence, P. R., & Lorsch, J. W. (1967). *Organization and environment: Managing differentiation and integration.* Cambridge, MA: Harvard University Press.

Lebra, S. L. (1984). Nonconfrontational strategies for management of interpersonal conflict. In E. S. Krauss, T. P. Rohlem, & P. G. Steinhoff (Eds.), *Conflict in Japan* (pp. 41-60). Honolulu: University of Hawaii Press.

Lee, H., & Rogan, R. (1991). A cross-cultural comparison of organizational conflict management behaviors. *International Journal of Conflict Management, 2,* 181-199.

Leung, K. (1987). Some determinants of reactions to procedural models for conflict resolution: A cross-national study. *Journal of Personality and Social Psychology, 53,* 898-908.

Leung, K. (1988). Some determinants of conflict avoidance. *Journal of Cross-Cultural Psychology, 19,* 125-136.

Leung, K., Au, Y., Fernandez-Dols, J. M., & Iwawaki, S. (1992). Preference for method of conflict processing in collectivist cultures. *International Journal of Psychology, 27,* 195-209.

Leung, K., & Bond, M. H. (1984). The impact of cultural collectivism on reward allocation. *Journal of Personality and Social Psychology, 47,* 793-804.

Leung, K., & Iwawaki, S. (1988). Cultural collectivism and distributive behavior. *Journal of Cross-Cultural Psychology, 19,* 35-49.

Lulofs, R. S. (1993). *Conflict: From theory to action.* Scottsdale, AZ: Gorsuch Scarisbrick.

Lutzker, D. (1960). Internationalism as a predictor of cooperative behavior. *Journal of Conflict Resolution, 4,* 426-430.

Madsen, M. C. (1971). Developmental and cross-cultural differences in the cooperation and competitive behavior of young children. *Journal of Cross-Cultural Psychology, 2,* 365-371.

Markus, H. R., & Kitayama, S. (1991). Culture and the self: Implications for cognition, emotion, and motivation. *Psychological Review, 98,* 224-252.

Markus, H. R., & Kitayama, S. (1994). A collective fear of the collective: Implications for selves and theories of selves. *Personality and Social Psychology, 20,* 568-579.

Markus, H. R., & Kitayama, S. (1998). The cultural psychology of personality. *Journal of Cross-Cultural Psychology, 29,* 63-87.

Markus, H. R., & Wurf, E. (1987). The dynamic self-concept: A social psychological perspective. *Annual Review of Psychology, 38,* 299-337.

McGinn, N. F., Harburg, E., & Ginsburg, G. P. (1973). Responses to interpersonal conflict by middle-class males in Guadalajara and Michigan. In F. E. Jandt (Ed.), *Conflict resolution through communication* (pp. 105-120). New York: Harper & Row.

Metts, S., & Cupach, W. R. (1990). The influence of relationship belief and problem-solving responses on satisfaction in romantic relationships. *Human Communication Research, 17,* 170-185.

Miller, G. R., & Steinberg, M. (1975). *Between people: A new analysis of interpersonal communication.* Chicago: Science Research Associates.

Miyahara, A., Kim, M.-S., Shin, H. C., & Yoon, K. (1998). Conflict styles among "collectivist" cultures: A comparison between Japanese and Koreans. *International Journal of Intercultural Relations, 22,* 505-525.

Nadler, L. B., Nadler, M. K., & Broome, B. (1985). Culture and the management of conflict situations. In W. B. Gudykunst & S. Ting-Toomey (Eds.), *Communication, culture, and organization processes* (pp. 87-113). Beverly Hills, CA: Sage.

Nicotera, A. M. (1993). Beyond two dimensions: A grounded theory model of conflict-handling behavior. *Management Communication Quarterly, 6,* 282-306.

Nomura, N., & Barnlund, D. C. (1983). Patterns of interpersonal criticism in Japan and the United States. *International Journal of Intercultural Relations, 7,* 1-18.

Ohbuchi, K., & Takahashi, Y. (1994). Cultural styles of conflict management in Japanese and Americans: Passivity, covertness, and effectiveness of strategies. *Journal of Applied Social Psychology, 24,* 1345-1366.

Ohbuchi, K., & Yamamoto, I. (1990). Power strategies of Japanese children in interpersonal conflict: Effects of age, gender, and target upon their use. *Journal of Genetic Psychology, 151,* 349-360.

Okabe, R. (1983). Cultural assumptions of East and West: Japan and the United States. In W. B. Gudykunst (Ed.), *Intercultural communication theory* (pp. 21-44). Beverly Hills, CA: Sage.

Oyserman, D. (1993). The lens of personhood: Viewing the self and others in a multicultural society. *Journal of Personality and Social Psychology, 65,* 993-1009.

Platow, M. J., McClintock, C. G., & Liebrand, W. B. G. (1990). Predicting intergroup fairness and ingroup bias in the minimal group paradigm. *European Journal of Social Psychology, 20,* 221-239.

Pruitt, D. G., Rubin, J. Z. (1986). *Social conflict: Escalation, stalemate, and settlement.* New York: Random House.

Putnam, L. L., & Poole, M. S. (1987). Conflict and negotiation. In F. Jablin, L. L. Putnam, K. Roberts, & L. Porter (Eds.), *Handbook of organizational communication* (pp. 549-599). Newbury Park, CA: Sage.

Putnam, L. L., & Wilson, C. E. (1982). Communication strategies in organizational conflicts: Reliability and validity of a measurement. In M. Burgoon (Ed.), *Communication yearbook 6* (pp. 629-652). Beverly Hills, CA: Sage.

Rahim, M. A. (1983). A measure of styles of handling interpersonal conflict. *Academy of Management Journal, 26,* 368-376.

Rahim, M. A. (1986). *Managing conflict in organizations.* New York: Praeger.

Rahim, M. A., & Bonoma, T. V. (1979). Managing organizational conflict: A model for diagnosis and intervention. *Psychological Reports, 44,* 1323-1344.

Rancer, A. S., Baukus, R. A., & Infante, D. A. (1985). Relations between argumentativeness and belief structures about arguing. *Communication Education, 34,* 37-47.

Rhee, E., Uleman, J. S., & Lee, H. K. (1996). Variations in collectivism and individualism by ingroup and culture: Confirmatory factor analyses. *Journal of Personality and Social Psychology, 71,* 1037-1054.

Richmond, V. P., & McCroskey, J. C. (1995). *Communication: Apprehension, avoidance, and effectiveness.* Scottsdale, AZ: Gorsuch Scarisbrick.

Roberts, B. W., & Helson, R. (1997). Changes in culture, changes in personality: The influence of individualism in a longitudinal study of women. *Journal of Personality and Social Psychology, 72,* 641-651.

Roloff, M. E. (1976). Communication strategies, relationships, and relational changes. In G. R. Miller (Ed.), *Explorations in interpersonal communication* (pp. 173-196). Beverly Hills, CA: Sage.

Roloff, M. E. (1987). Communication and conflict. In C. R. Berger & S. H. Chaffee (Eds.), *Handbook of communication science* (pp. 484-534). Newbury Park, CA, Sage.

Rosenthal, D. A., Demetriou, A., & Efklides, A. (1989). A cross-national study of the influence of culture on conflict between parents and adolescents. *International Journal of Behavioral Development, 12,* 207-219.

Ross, H. M. (1993). *The culture of conflict: Interpretations and interests in comparative perspective.* New Haven, CT: Yale University Press.

Rossi, A. M., & Todd-Mancillas, W. R. (1985). A comparison of managerial communication strategies between Brazilian and American women. *Communication Research Reports, 2,* 128-134.

Ruble, T. L., & Thomas, K. W. (1976). Support for a two-dimensional model of conflict behavior. *Organizational Behavior and Human Performance, 16,* 143-155.

Rusbult, C. E., & Zembrodt, I. M. (1983). Responses to dissatisfaction on romantic involvements: A multidimensional scaling analysis. *Journal of Experimental Social Psychology, 19,* 274-293.

Saltzman, C. E. (1986). One hundred and fifty percent persons: Models for orienting international students. In R. M. Paige (Ed.), *Cross-cultural orientation: New conceptualizations and applications* (pp. 247-268). Lanham, MD: University Press of America.

Sampson, E. E. (1988). The debate on individualism: Indigenous psychologies of the individual and their role in personal and societal functioning. *American Psychologist, 43,* 15-22.

Sanders, J. A., Congalton, J. K., Wiseman, R. L., Gass, R. H., & Du, R. (1992, November). *A cross-cultural analysis of compliance gaining: China and the United States.* Paper presented at the annual meeting of the Speech Communication Association, Chicago.

Schneer, J. A., & Chanin, M. N. (1987). Manifest needs as personality predispositions to conflict-handling behavior. *Human Relations, 40,* 575-590.

Schwartz, S. H. (1990). Individualism-collectivism: Critique and proposed refinements. *Journal of Cross-Cultural Psychology, 21,* 139-157.

Sillars, A. L. (1980). Attribution and communication in roommate conflict. *Communication Monographs, 47,* 180-200.

Sillars, A. L., Coletti, S. F., Parry, D., & Rogers, M. A. (1982). Coding verbal conflict tactics: Nonverbal and perceptual correlates of the "avoidance-distributive-integrative" distinction. *Human Communication Research, 9,* 83-95.

Simons, H. W. (1972). Persuasion in social conflicts: A critique of prevailing conceptions and a framework for future research. *Speech Monographs, 39,* 227-247.

Singelis, T. M. (1994). The measurement of independent and interdependent self-construals. *Personality and Social Psychology Bulletin, 20,* 580-591.

Singelis, T. M., & Brown, W. J. (1995). Culture, self, and collectivist communication: Linking culture to individual behavior. *Human Communication Research, 21,* 354-389.

Sinha, D., & Tripathi, R. C. (1994). Individualism in a collectivist culture: A case of coexistence of opposites. In U. Kim, H. C. Triandis, C. Kâgitçibasi, S.-C. Choi, & G. Yoon (Eds.), *Individualism and collectivism: Theory, method, and applications* (pp. 123-136). Thousand Oaks, CA: Sage.

Smith, P. B., & Bond, M. H. (1994). *Social psychology across cultures: Analysis and perspectives.* Boston: Allyn & Bacon.

Sternberg, R. J., & Soriano, L. J. (1984). Styles of conflict resolution. *Journal of Personality and Social Psychology, 47,* 115-126.

Sue, S., & Kitano, H. (1973). Stereotypes as a measure of success. *Journal of Social Issues, 29*(2), 83-98.

Sueda, H., & Wiseman, R. L. (1992). Embarrassment remediation in Japan and the United States. *International Journal of Intercultural Relations, 16,* 159-173.

Tang, S. F. Y., & Kirkbride, P. S. (1986). Developing conflict management skills in Hong Kong: An analysis of some cross-cultural implications. *Management Education and Development, 17,* 287-301.

Tannen, D. (1985). Silence: Anything but. In D. Tannen & M. Saville-Troike (Eds.), *Perspectives on silence* (pp. 93-111). Norwood, NJ: Ablex.

Thomas, K. W. (1976). Conflict and conflict management. In M. Dunnette (Ed.), *Handbook of industrial and organizational psychology* (pp. 889-935). Chicago: Rand McNally.

Thomas, K. W., & Kilmann, R. H. (1978). Comparison of four instruments measuring conflict behavior. *Psychological Reports, 42,* 1139-1145.

Ting-Toomey, S. (1985). Toward a theory of conflict and culture. In W. B. Gudykunst, L. P. Stewart, & S. Ting-Toomey (Eds.), *Communication, culture, and organizational processes* (pp. 71-86). Beverly Hills, CA: Sage.

Ting-Toomey, S. (1986). Conflict communication styles in black and white subjective cultures. In Y. Y. Kim (Ed.), *Interethnic communication: Current research* (pp. 75-88). Beverly Hills, CA: Sage.

Ting-Toomey, S. (1988). Intercultural conflict styles: A face-negotiation theory. In Y. Y. Kim & W. B. Gudykunst (Eds.), *Theories in intercultural communication* (pp. 213-235). Newbury Park, CA: Sage.

Ting-Toomey, S. (1989). Identity and interpersonal bonding. In M. K. Asante & W. B. Gudykunst (Eds.), *Handbook of international and intercultural communication* (pp. 163-185). Newbury Park, CA: Sage.

Ting-Toomey, S. (1991). Intimacy expressions in three cultures: France, Japan, and the United States. *International Journal of Intercultural Relations, 15,* 29-46.

Ting-Toomey, S. (1994). Managing intercultural conflicts effectively. In L. A. Samovar & R. E. Porter (Eds.), *Intercultural communication: A reader* (pp. 360-372). Belmont, CA: Wadsworth.

Ting-Toomey, S., Gao, G., Trubisky, P., Yang, Z., Kim, H. S., Lin, S. L., & Nishida, T. (1991). Culture, face maintenance, and styles of handling interpersonal conflict: A study in five cultures. *International Journal of Conflict Management, 2,* 275-296.

Tjosvold, D., & Johnson, D. W. (1978). Controversy within a cooperative or competitive context and cognitive perspective-taking. *Contemporary Educational Psychology, 3,* 376-386.

Triandis, H. C. (1972). *The analysis of subjective culture.* New York: John Wiley.

Triandis, H. C. (1988). Collectivism vs. individualism: A reconceptualization of a basic concept in cross-cultural psychology. In C. Bagley & G. K. Verma (Eds.), *Cross-cultural studies of personality, attitudes and cognition* (pp. 60-95). London: Macmillan.

Triandis, H. C. (1989). The self and social behavior in differing cultural contexts. *Psychological Review, 96,* 506-520.

Triandis, H. C., McCusker, C., & Hui, C. H. (1990). Multimethod probes of individualism and collectivism. *Journal of Personality and Social Psychology, 59,* 1006-1020.

Triandis, H. C., & Vassiliou, V. (1972). A comparative analysis of subjective culture. In H. C. Triandis (Ed.), *The analysis of subjective culture* (pp. 299-335). New York: John Wiley.

Trubisky, P., Ting-Toomey, S., & Lin, S. L. (1991). The influence of individualism-collectivism and self-monitoring on conflict styles. *International Journal of Intercultural Relations, 15,* 65-84.

Van de Vliert, E., & Kabanoff, B. (1990). Toward theory-based measures of conflict management. *Academy of Management Journal, 33,* 199-209.

Van de Vliert, E., & Prein, H. C. M. (1989). The difference in the meaning of forcing in the conflict management of actors and observers. In M. A. Rahim (Ed.), *Managing conflict: An interdisciplinary approach* (pp. 51-70). New York: Praeger.

Volkema, R. J., & Bergmann, T. J. (1989). Interpersonal conflict at work: An analysis of behavioral responses. *Human Relations, 42,* 757-770.

Walsh, J. E. (1973). *Intercultural education in the community of man.* Honolulu: University of Hawaii Press.

Weldon, E., & Jehn, K. A. (1995). Examining cross-cultural differences in conflict management behavior: A strategy for future research. *International Journal of Conflict Management, 6,* 387-403.

Wolfson, K., & Norden, M. (1984). Measuring responses to filmed interpersonal conflict. In W. B. Gudykunst & Y. Y. Kim (Eds.), *Methods for intercultural communication research* (pp. 155-166). Beverly Hills, CA: Sage.

Yoshikawa, M. J. (1988). Cross-cultural adaptation and perceptual development. In Y. Y. Kim & W. B. Gudykunst (Eds.), *Cross-cultural adaptation: Current approaches.* Newbury Park, CA: Sage.

CHAPTER CONTENTS

7 More Than Meets the Eye: An Exploration of Literature Related to the Mass Media's Role in Encouraging Changes in Body Image

RONALD BISHOP
Drexel University

Until recently, there has been little research on the mediated messages that may help fuel Americans' obsession with losing weight. This chapter is an interdisciplinary look at the impact of the mass media on body image. Bringing together work from the fields of psychology, psychiatry, and sociology, this review explores seminal body-image research and then looks critically at communication research that tries to link consumption of media messages with body-image deterioration. The chapter concludes with the suggestion that researchers study mass-media messages and their effects on body image with a new array of methodological tools, including ethnography and diaries.

AMERICANS, particularly American women, hate their bodies. We spend more than $30 billion a year on diet products and weight-loss regimens (Haney, 1991). At any given time, almost 50 million of us are dieting. Fitness centers are filled to capacity. A great deal of information about dieting and fitness comes to us from the mass media, particularly from television. This information takes two forms: messages that directly endorse dieting and thinness (e.g., commercials for fitness centers, weight-loss products, and "lite" foods) and messages that show being thin in a positive light. But until recently, there has been little research on the mediated messages that may help fuel our obsession with losing weight. In much of the research that has been done, scholars have focused on finding a causal relationship between positive portrayals of thinness and deterioration in body image. In fact, it has become popular to blame the media for our dissatisfaction with our bodies. However, medical literature and new treatments for eating

Correspondence: Ronald Bishop, 5032 MacAlister Hall, Drexel University, 33rd and Chestnut Streets, Philadelphia, PA 19104; e-mail bishoprc@post.drexel.edu

Communication Yearbook 23, pp. 271-303

disorders (Claude-Pierre, 1997) tell us that changes and distortions in body image constitute a much more complicated issue. Blame is too readily placed on mediated messages; there has been little exploration of the cultural framework in which they occur or the cultural values they embody. Researchers have added mediated messages to the list of causes of eating disorders without exploring the relationships among those causes or assessing how individuals interact with and use these messages. Their focus should be "the central role that cultural images play in women's problems with food, eating, and body image" (Bordo, 1998, p. 116). Instead of casting positive images of thinness as simply the "trigger" for body-image distortion, communication researchers should recognize that these disorders "need to be understood not as individual psychopathology, but as social pathology" (Bordo, 1998, p. 116). The next step, then, is to explore the values that these images project and how individuals internalize those values. In short, we must devise ways to explore the meaning of what Bordo (1993) calls "the ideal of slenderness" (p. 46). Communication researchers must look at this ideal as a "cultural formation that expresses ideals, anxieties, and social changes much deeper than the merely aesthetic" (p. 46). Only then can we truly determine what leads so many of us to paint such distorted pictures of our bodies.

As a backdrop for future study, this chapter offers an interdisciplinary look at the impact of the mass media on body image. In this review, I bring together work from the fields of psychology, psychiatry, and sociology to explore seminal body-image research, and then look critically at communication research that tries to link consumption of media messages with body-image deterioration. The following section presents some theoretical background on body image and eating disorders.

THEORETICAL AND HISTORICAL FOUNDATIONS

Paul Schilder (1950) defines body image as "the picture of our own body which we form in our mind" and "the way in which the body appears to ourselves" (p. 1). Body image is not a "mere perception"; it is "an organized model" that "modifies the impressions produced by incoming sensory impulses" (p. 1). More important, Schilder argues that an individual's body image "expand[s] beyond the body" and that there exists a strong sense of community or closeness between an individual's body image and the body images held by his or her peers. For Schilder, the body is the focal point of personality, teeming with "emotions, feelings, tendencies, and thoughts" (p. 1). Recall Mead's (1934) claim that we construct our sense of self from our perceptions of how others see us. Thrown into this mix are our desires for self-expression and to be part of a social network. For Mead, body image might best be described as an interactional defense mechanism, expressed or withdrawn depending on an individual's confidence in the ability to interact. Our fascination with dieting, to follow Schilder's reasoning, does not come from a desire for self-improvement. We are unhappy with our ability to interact in a social network, a network where preoccupation with thinness is a condition for entry. For some

Americans, genuine interaction depends on the ability to speak proudly about efforts to, and success in, losing weight. Americans have only grown stronger in their belief that losing weight is the first step on the path to social and spiritual renewal, according to historian Hillel Schwartz (1986). In his "who's who" of diet product makers, Schwartz analyzes how we have become convinced that weight and appearance "reveal something desperately true" about ourselves. Fear of fat and the desire to diet are social constructs "so fundamental to our notions of company, beauty, mortality, and power" that they trickle down to our children, "who share the styles of our bodies which have become the measure of our lives" (p. 302).

Chief among the illusions fostered by the diet industry is the idea that the desire to diet and weight-loss success will bring an individual closer to friends and family members. Ironically, although the ritual of dieting is "universal," it divides us, localizing those who partake in it. Flawed interaction forces us to diet alone; we then bring the results to the interactional table, looking for acceptance. Thus mediated messages that promote dieting, along with family and peer relationships, are the most important forces in Lewin's (1951) "field" for our discussion, forces that pull with varying degrees of strength. Placing value on mediated portrayals of thinness presents an interesting tie-in with symbolic interactionism (Mead, 1934). Dieters look at the ideal body image—a product, to a large extent, of television's fascination with thin, fit characters—as a sort of "generalized other." Interaction with generalized others allows us to develop a sense of appropriate behavior. Through interaction with others, Mead (1934) argues, we stockpile behaviors for later use. If an individual with low self-esteem interacts with a disproportionately large number of individuals who believe thinness is a manifestation of positive behavior and who denigrate others' appearance, that individual would be guided by their opinions, according to Mead.

The Myth of Community

The desire to diet may stem from self-inspection, but realization of the desire occurs in a public forum. As Schwartz (1986) argues in his work on the cultural history of dieting, few of us would be secure in our desire to lose weight unless we did it publicly. The tendency to conform is stronger when adoption of a particular behavior is made public. We might argue, then, that television, although viewed privately or in small groups, is publicly discussed and its behavioral cues publicly adopted. It may be that individuals are motivated to diet by peers and parents who see the same idealized depictions of thinness. Whenever it begins, the tendency to diet touches on the notions of "normative" and "informational" social influence. The latter drives individuals to act in the "correct" manner, whereas the former motivates individuals to seek the approval of others for their actions. Together, these influences drive us toward preoccupation with establishing and maintaining a workable social image. The fact that eating disorders are often played out through interaction indicates that the desire to be thin is built on a foundation of seeking acceptance. Social images—the images that others have of us—are more important for individuals who suffer from eating disorders than are their own self-images and self-concepts. As Schwartz explains, "Our bodies and our foods are as much social constructs as they are proteins, carbohydrates, and fats" (p. 338). Schwartz's comment brings us back to Mead, who contends that an individual's regulation of his or her behavior begins with observing others.

What makes dieting and television conceptually compatible is the myth of community that both purvey. Television claims that it can experientially connect millions of people; dieting, as Schwartz (1986) explains, is a battle of universal proportions, pitting all of us against demon fat. But, as Schwartz notes, dieting "discriminates" and "localizes" (p. 15). Dieting is portrayed as a prerequisite of membership in "common humanity," a membership not available to those who refuse to join in the battle by not dieting or being satisfied with weight and appearance, a truly iconoclastic gesture in today's society. Television is also adept at masking the rigor required to lose weight. Television—both in programs and in commercials—hides the true nature of dieting under "positive terminology," linking dieting to fitness and health and to psychological well-being (Macdonald, 1995).

The effort to convince more of us to join the quest for the perfect body has become more difficult for the makers of weight-related products, thanks to the 1990 decision of the Federal Trade Commission (FTC) to pursue charges of false advertising against the country's leading diet companies. In advertising their products, these companies have always moved along both the "central" and "peripheral" paths of persuasion posited by Petty and Cacioppo (1986). Diet products and regimens have typically nudged consumers down the central path with claims about how dieting will bring them closer to their families and expedite the realization of their dreams—things very salient to most of us. Positive portrayals of thinness in television programming, news stories, and even magazine ads for products unrelated to dieting allow companies that make weight-related products to cover the peripheral path to message processing. An episode of *Baywatch,* for example, probably does not provoke a lot of thought about the merits of weight-loss products, but it certainly promotes thinness as a desirable attribute. With the FTC's intervention, the claims in advertising have changed somewhat: Nutritional value has replaced rapid weight loss as the key claim in much current advertising for weight-loss products. But the promised nutritional value is still linked to "getting the most out of life"—something salient that may move individuals to pay attention to the argument and seek more information about the product. The connection between weight-related product advertising and weight consciousness has yet to be explored.

Men, Women, and Weight Loss

Conditions for entry into the social network discussed earlier have always been different for men and women. In the 18th century, as Schwartz (1986) explains, men who set out to lose weight embarked on "a romance, an unburdening, a freeing up, a moral athleticism" (p. 17). But for women, dieting always has been ritual bordering on drudgery, an ascetic regimen performed to battle "waste, fat and fatigue." According to Schwartz, campaigns for diet products have been constructed on this line of reasoning. Advertising messages aimed at men "have been framed as adventures, romances that will provoke an immediate change in the world: physical prowess, political action, business success" (p. 18). Advertising aimed at women, on the other hand, has revolved around "rituals of watchfulness in response to external threats" (p. 18), including peer and parental pressure. By the Jacksonian era, Schwartz notes, Americans had come to regard obesity as a moral cancer. "We are decided admirers of leanness," announced one newspaper from the period. "Our greatest characters are usually little, attenuated men; stomachless, meager, lean and lath-like beings, who have spiritualized themselves by keeping matter in due subordination to mind" (quoted in Schwartz, 1986, pp. 38-39). In the 19th and early 20th centuries, staying in shape became more of a social duty, according to Macdonald (1995). Americans' staying healthy improved the nation's chances of staying economically competitive. Since that time, however, a number of factors—improvements in public health and in birth control, better sports and leisure facilities—have changed the nature of this duty from public to private (Macdonald, 1995). Through exercise and diet, men try to stave off age; women, on the other hand, try to maintain their appearance. "Where beauty, in the Victorian ideal, was seen as attainable through spiritual purity," Macdonald argues, "it is now more actively to be worked for in the aerobics class" (p. 202). The relationship between appearance and health hides, for most dieters, the role that genetics play in creating the body.

Seid (1989) contends that the battle to be thin may not be worth fighting, at least not as a means of maintaining health. Thanks to the urgings of diet product manufacturers and the willing cooperation of many doctors, Americans see obesity—not the health problems caused by obesity—as a perfidious disease, despite the fact that the majority of dieters are in no danger of becoming obese. Americans are repeatedly confronted with messages equating weight gain with moral sin, caused by lapses in judgment. Each year, scores of television and newspaper stories warn Americans about the dangers of cholesterol and high-fat diets. We give credence to these misconceptions through our predisposition to see heavy people as being lazier, slower, and less mature than thin people, and as lacking moral and spiritual strength. Seid asserts that, for many of us, thinness has become a reflection of character and moral strength. Ironically, despite our desire to "have it all," we are faced with our own "suspicion of surplus." Many diet commercials promise us "great taste, without the guilt"—or the ability to have our cake and eat it, too.

More important, thinness and dieting are often portrayed as a kind of currency for social interaction. We often begin and sustain conversations by talking about how much weight an acquaintance or coworker has lost—or gained. As Macdonald (1995) argues, the desire to lose weight, wherever it originates, "is part of a positive discourse about responding to a challenge, making the most of yourself, and feeling good" (p. 202).

CHILDREN, ADOLESCENTS, AND BODY IMAGE

When do we begin to think about dieting? According to Staffieri (1967), it is during the period between 6 and 9 years of age that children begin to recognize the social and interactive utility of body image. Children in Staffieri's study used positive and negative body types to discriminate among peers, associating with children who matched their somatic ideal and shunning those who did not. Pediatricians later came across a characteristic they labeled "fear of fat." Children between 9 and 17 years old were found to be subjecting themselves to restrictive diets that had stunted their growth and sexual development. Tendency to diet correlated strongly with the family's preoccupation with dieting. These children "simply feared fat," believing that "it would make them less attractive and shorten their lives" (Schwartz, 1986, p. 301). It is still unclear, however, whether this fear of fat foreshadows the development of eating disorders in children (Richards, Casper, & Larson, 1990).

Nevertheless, the fear for some is quite strong. Distorted body perceptions and extreme concerns about weight are common in junior high school girls. Fueling this fear for some young people are their relationships with peers and parents. Larson (1975) argues that adolescents place these relationships into a "salience hierarchy" that reflects their influence on attitudes and behavior. There are differences of opinion about how to explain and predict evolution of this characteristic. Some researchers advocate a "grade-level" approach, arguing that as children move into adolescence, they become more attached to their peers and look to the peer branch of the social network for behavioral guidance. Only with peers can an adolescent make sense of feeling lost between childhood and adulthood. "It is with peers . . . that the adolescent is able to develop a sense of identity, power, belonging, and security" (Larson, 1975, p. 292). Adolescents are influenced only by those individuals who can help them reach their goals.

The Situational Hypothesis

Larson (1975) endorses a "situational" hypothesis in which influence is evenly divided between peers and parents: Parents exert more influence when a young person is contemplating a decision with long-term ramifications, but young persons tend to rely on peers "when the decision involves current status and identity needs" (p. 292). Adolescents rarely consider the ramifications of prolonged dieting, Larson contends; they view weight loss as a means to achieve a degree of status and to establish an identity.

Costanzo (1975) takes Larson's argument a step further, suggesting that conformity explains the nature of adolescents' relationships. Costanzo first defines "social conformity" as a "consequence of the child's generalized level of resistance to deviation from group standards" (p. 310). Costanzo detects an unmistakable movement by adolescents into closer contact with their peers as they get older. The peer group becomes the standard against which a young person measures him- or herself. "The stronger the individual's identification with the peer group," Costanzo claims, "the greater the probability that he will value the peer group's attributes more positively than his own" (p. 321).

More recent research has revealed that the pressure to be thin may begin at a very young age. Although Richards et al. (1990) found that concern about weight is not a major concern before a child moves into adolescence, Taylor et al. (1998) found that the importance that peers put on weight was a strong predictor of concern with weight for two groups of girls, one from elementary school and the other from middle school. In their study of 483 students in the fifth through ninth grades, Richards et al. found that preoccupation with food began for girls in the fifth and sixth grades and intensified when they went through puberty. These authors assert that continued concern through eighth and ninth grades is an indication of more serious emotional distress, and that such distress may put a young girl at risk for an eating disorder (p. 207). Communication researchers should take a cue from Richards et al.'s use of the experience sampling method in their study. Respondents were paged at random times during a weeklong period, and they crafted written reports about their state of mind at those times. It would be interesting to know whether mediated messages were included in these descriptions.

Questions in the instrument that Taylor et al. (1998) used to measure peer influence were designed to assess how much respondents changed their eating habits when they were around boys, whether they thought their weight had anything to do with other children liking them, how much they had been teased about their weight, and whether teasing had any impact on how much they liked themselves. Taylor et al. also found that pressure from parents was not a strong predictor of weight concern, a finding that contradicts much of the literature on eating disorders. Johnson, Stuckey, Lewis, and Schwartz (1982) and Strober and Humphrey (1987) note that families of anorexics are often controlling and overprotective, and they often deny the existence of conflict. Families of bulimics are chaotic, disengaged, and neglectful.

Peer Pressure

Crandall (1988) notes that pressure from peers in a social group is a key element in the development of eating disorders. Crandall found that group norms governed binge-eating behavior in two college sororities. In one of the sororities, a student was more popular if she binged a great deal. In the other sorority, a student's popularity depended on whether she binged "the right amount" (p. 588). These students were motivated, Crandall argues, "to imitate or model attitudes or behaviors that are important, characteristic, or definitional to the social group." If the group plays a key role in the life of an individual, and the behavior is central to the group, "the greater the pressure toward uniformity and the more likely that members of the group will imitate each others' behavior" (p. 590).

WHEN DIETING TURNS
INTO AN EATING DISORDER

If the seeds of eating disorders are planted through peer-driven excessive concern with weight, their growth is nurtured in the family. Ironically, however, health professionals have only recently incorporated the role of the family into the treatment of eating disorders. Minuchin, Rosman, and Baker (1978) note that many doctors who treat anorexics and bulimics now apply a "systems model" built on "observation of how and to what extent interpersonal transactions govern each family member's range of behavior" (p. 20). Doctors previously viewed anorexic patients as the "passive targets" of the effects of psychosomaticism. Minuchin et al. sum up the epistemological shift: "The psychological unit is not the individual. It is the individual in his social context" (p. 21). As mentioned earlier, communication researchers have yet to probe "social context" as an aspect of the relationship between mediated messages that endorse thinness and changes in body image.

Minuchin et al.'s (1978) work also touches on the psychosomatic behavior of children suffering from eating disorders. These authors argue that "certain types of family organization are closely related to the development and maintenance of psychosomatic syndromes in children" and that their psychosomatic symptoms "play an important role in maintaining the family's homeostasis" (p. 20). If a family's behavioral routine includes psychosomatic behavior by a child, that routine would be disrupted by a change in the child's behavior. Similarly, if a child were to rebel against a parent's scolding about weight loss, the family's relationships would be threatened.

McLorg and Taub (1987) have developed a valuable three-stage model to describe how an eating disorder takes control of an adolescent. They base their model on informal interviews with participants and a 2-year observation of an eating disorders self-help group, which allowed them to examine the meanings these individuals attach to anorexia and bulimia. In the first stage of the model, "conforming behavior," the adolescent conforms to cultural norms—for our purposes, thinness and fitness—and is pointed toward the eating-disordered behavior by positive thinness messages. In the second stage, called "primary deviance," the individual experiences some of the purported fruits of the behavioral change. The adolescent is lauded by peers and parents for his or her diligence in trying to lose weight. In this stage, persuasive messages reinforce the desire to continue the behavior that yields positive interaction. Finally, the adolescent enters into the "secondary deviance" stage, where he or she becomes defined by the eating disorder. The simple behavioral adjustments made in the earlier stages overtake the individual, thanks to reinforcement by peers and family members and, as the studies reviewed in a later section argue, in response to positive dieting messages from the media. Sadly, peers and family members define the individual by the eating disorder. "He could help himself if he wanted to" and "She could gain weight if she really tried" replace the reinforcing comments heard before the onset of the disorder, McLorg and Taub note. Their three-stage model is particularly valuable because it gives researchers a clear picture of where the adolescent's consumption and usage of mediated information may fit into the eating disorder puzzle.

Impact of Family Relationships

Scalf-McIver and Thompson (1989) found that the individuals in their sample suffering from bulimia typically experienced "inconsistency" with one or both parents. Bulimic behavior was related directly to a lack of expressed affection in relationships with parents. These authors also found that the degree of support and commitment (consistency) from parents tailed off as bulimic symptoms worsened. Further, lack of commitment and support from family members was the best predictor of subjects' dissatisfaction with appearance.

But there is disagreement as to how much influence a strained family relationship has on body image and the tendency to diet. Wertheim et al. (1992) found that adolescents who diet and those who try to lose a great deal of weight do so independent of family issues. However, these authors recognize that "those girls who diet despite being thin and those who have gone beyond experimentation and crash diet, vomit, or use other extreme methods on a regular basis report greater psychological distress and lesser perceived emotional bonding in the family" (p. 158). Respondents in their study who frequently used extreme weight-loss behaviors (EWLBs) had lower self-esteem, were more depressed, reported less family cohesion, and felt their fathers cared less than did respondents who used EWLBs less frequently. As noted earlier, Wertheim et al. found that family-related variables did not predict weight-loss behaviors in all females. Only when heavier girls were removed from the sample or when the authors examined the EWLB groups did these variables become predictive.

Other researchers have reached different conclusions about the origins of eating-disordered behavior (Dykens & Garrard, 1986; Humphrey, 1989). Anorexics typically deal with a facade of nurturing and affection from parents that hides the parents' indifference to and lack of understanding about the anorexics' condition. Scalf-McIver and Thompson (1989) found that the family relationships of the bulimics in their study were usually hostile and marked by the inconsistent expression of affection. Minuchin et al. (1978) claim that anorexia nervosa reflects "familial dysfunction" brought on by an anorexic's physical vulnerability, the anorexic's "enmeshment" in family conflicts, and a family structure marked by, among other characteristics, rigidity, overprotection, and the inability to resolve conflicts. In anorexic families, individuals typically lack autonomy and interact in rigid patterns. There is low tolerance for conflict. Most of the time, family members simply withdraw from conflicts rather than face them.

It should be noted that Wertheim et al. (1992) did not ask how much respondents and their parents and other family members talked about dieting, or how these talks made them feel. Indeed, Shugar and Krueger (1995) report that anorexics in their study improved if their families adopted a communication style that expresses aggression rather than suppressing it. Huon (1994) found that negative attitudes about the body can be modified successfully through group discussion. In presenting his conclusions, Huon argues that researchers have placed too much emphasis on the consequences of eating disorders and not enough on preventing them. In an earlier study, Huon (1988) found that group discussion made young women more aware of the pressure they put on one another. He divided 24 psychology students into four groups. Two groups talked about strategies that would bring about change for women their age and the barriers standing in the way of change. In the first of two hour-long discussions, the groups focused on developing a positive body image; in the second, they talked about giving up dieting. Before and after the group discussions, respondents completed a modified Positive and Negative Affect Scale (PANAS; Watson, Clark, & Tellegen, 1988), indicating how they felt about their bodies, their weight and shapes, and their eating habits. Huon also asked respondents to indicate the likelihood of their going on a diet in the future. He found that when respondents had talked about strategies to help other young women develop positive body images, the positive affect scores increased. There was no increase for respondents who had discussed barriers to change. According to Huon, respondents felt empowered when they talked about strategies to achieve a better body image. In contrast, talking about issues such as the media's encouragement of thinness and society's general attitude toward heavy people made respondents angry. Of the 12 respondents who talked about strategies, 7 became less preoccupied with their weight; 5 said that it was less likely (after the study) that they would begin dieting in the next 12 months.

Shugar and Krueger (1995) followed Minuchin et al.'s (1978) lead in examining confrontation, hostility, and aggressiveness in anorexics' interactions with their families. They hypothesized (a) that families of anorexics suppress hostility and aggression; (b) that after undergoing therapy, these families would move from covert to overt aggression; (c) that weight gain and improved eating attitudes are related to changes in family communication style; and (d) that dysfunctional family patterns "promote and perpetuate" anorexic behavior in young anorexics. Taking part in the study were 15 families with anorexic daughters. All regularly attended therapy and agreed to allow the researchers to videotape a series (12-14) of 60-minute sessions conducted by a therapist. Family aggression was rated using a 15-item scale that classified aggressive behavior as covert, indirect, or overt. Four child and adolescent psychiatrists rated the interaction in the videotapes. Shugar and Krueger subsequently measured weight gains and changes in respondents' attitudes toward their bodies. They found that all respondents gained weight and showed improvement in scores on the Eating Attitude Test (EAT). Further, the number of interactions for all families grew from 138 in the beginning phase to 250 in the middle phase to 324 in the end stage. Daughters in families whose members expressed aggression in all phases of the therapy gained the most weight and showed the most improvement in their eating attitudes.

To motivate anorexics to be more expressive, therapists must often probe what appear to be normal family relationships. Humphrey (1992) asserts that families of anorexic children typically are not dissatisfied with "the ways their families operate" and that anorexic families seem to be less unhappy and less poorly adjusted on self-ratings than nonanorexic families. However, Humphrey notes, these self-ratings clearly conflict with behavioral observations of anorexic families, indicating that they are in denial about and idealize their family situations. Parents of anorexic girls are often extremely affectionate, but they also try to control their daughters and to negate their daughters' identities.

Driven to Succeed

One thing on which most researchers agree is that individuals who suffer from eating disorders are typically driven to succeed, whether at a job or in school. At first glance, this simply means that parents of eating-disordered adolescents want them to succeed. In many cases, however, the push to succeed comes at the expense of other emotions—love, support, and commitment. As a result, eating-disordered adolescents often set unattainable standards of performance for themselves. When they fail to meet these standards, they look for a part of their lives they can control—in many cases, that is their weight. Thus an anorexic's lack of self-esteem and constant self-criticism become "entangled" with controlling weight through starvation (Palmer, 1988). A degree of entanglement, Palmer (1988) notes, occurs in many individuals: "Appearance and body size and shape are issues which may be of considerable importance, particularly to young women, in determining the individual's degree of self-esteem" (p. 41). Anorexics always feel as if they are about to lose control of these factors, and that if they consume even small amounts of food, their weight will mushroom. Palmer argues that anorexia nervosa and bulimia are the most radical manifestations of what he calls a "slimming philosophy," which exaggerates the ease with which we can change our weight and how much this influences the shape of our bodies. Palmer notes that it is particularly dangerous when anorexics believe that they have failed in their attempts to lose weight. They come to believe that they have not tried hard enough, or that they have not used the right techniques. They see their "fatness" as a misfortune and a failure.

In exploring why eating disorders are more prevalent among women than among men, Hsu (1989) posits three factors that precede the development of anorexia nervosa or bulimia: (a) adolescent turmoil, which Hsu defines as "an interruption of peaceful growth which resembles . . . a variety of other emotional upsets and upheavals" (p. 397); (b) poor self-concept and body concept stemming from sexual maturation; and (c) identity confusion, marked by "a heightened sense of ineffectiveness, interpersonal distrust, and lack of interceptive awareness" (p. 400). According to Hsu, a depressed person is more likely to go on a diet. Physical attractiveness is the barometer many of us use to evaluate our peers; we simply make the criteria more difficult for women to meet.

Physical and emotional changes that occur during puberty can damage a young female's self-confidence. Played out against our society's fascination with thinness, puberty drives some young women to be thin. Because women rely more than men do on social experiences to create self-concepts, Hsu (1989) argues, the thinness ideal creates a conflict. In addition, girls tend to define themselves in terms of how successful they are in attracting the opposite sex. Women who pursue careers run into the same confusion, Hsu notes: They fear a lack of femininity and interpersonal rejection. Fear of professional success is found more often in women who defy traditional sex roles by striking out on a career path. According to Hsu, women develop eating disorders when they cannot reconcile these conflicts. Role confusion drives women to "seek refuge" in dieting.

One Step From an Eating Disorder

One of the issues that divides scholars and medical professionals who study eating disorders is the existence of a group of individuals whose persistent tendency to diet may foreshadow a descent into eating disorders. Scalf-McIver and Thompson (1989) have explored this "subclinical" population, building on an idea from Kagan and Squires (1985). Scalf-McIver and Thompson found a "moderate relationship" between the level of family dysfunction and the presence of bulimic symptoms. Kagan and Squires had discovered that "normal weight females who eat compulsively perceive their families as uncohesive" (Scalf-McIver & Thompson, 1989, p. 467). As the bulimia worsens, the degree of commitment and support from family members decreases. Scalf-McIver and Thompson built their study by observing respondents rather than by relying on self-reports. They suggest that if researchers are going to use self-reports, they should start gathering data about family relationships while subjects are at a young age, to eliminate the bias of "retrospective recall." Dysfunctional families, these authors observe, may put more emphasis on food- and body-related behaviors because of family members' feelings of lack of support and their inability to express themselves. In families that exhibit these characteristics, the media—particularly television—may bridge the interaction gap. Future researchers should adapt Scalf-McIver and Thompson's methodology—combining observations of respondents with self-report measures—to study the influence of mediated messages on body image (a point I will take up later).

There has been a great deal of disagreement about the existence of a subclinical population, as well as about whether anorexia nervosa is the extreme point on a behavioral continuum, preceded by a period of extreme weight consciousness. Garner and Garfinkel (1979) discovered an "overrepresentation" of anorexia nervosa in professions (ballet, for example) where there is intense pressure to diet. However, they also found many individuals who exhibited many of the disorder's symptoms but did not meet a "rigorous diagnostic standard." Other theorists cite "fundamental differences in the psychopathology" between anorexia nervosa and milder expression of symptoms (Crisp, 1980). For anorexics, dieting is a regression "to a prepubertal body shape and hormonal status in an attempt to escape the conflicts of adolescence" (Crisp, 1980, p. 256). Such intensity is typically not found in the "subclinical" population. Mild expressions of anorexic symptoms are not associated with psychosocial impairment. This work underscores the importance "of a multidimensional evaluation of psychopathology in those suspected of having eating disorders" (Crisp, 1980, p. 264). Mild cases of anorexia nervosa "must be evaluated in psychological as well as behavioral or dieting terms, since the meaning or motivation behind the anorexic's dieting may be different in essential ways from that of the extreme dieter" (Crisp, 1980, p. 264).

Thus anorexia nervosa and bulimia are best understood as multidimensional disorders with origins in dysfunctional peer and family relationships. Those who have researched the connection between mass-media messages and body image have built much of their work on the hypothesis that mediated messages are the "trigger" that moves an individual into an eating disorder. However, such a claim has to date served only to move the fields apart. Medical professionals insist that although the media may play a role in bringing about eating disorders, underlying psychological factors such as damaged self-esteem and strained family relationships are usually the true causes; communication scholars argue that it is mediated messages that trigger body-image dissatisfaction. Ironically, much of the communication literature reviewed here seems to argue that these messages have direct effects on individuals. Bordo (1993) advocates studying eating disorders against a cultural backdrop: "In positing culture as a 'contributory' factor and families as the 'real' cause they forget that families do not exist outside cultural time and space" (p. 117). Clearly, the media play a role in shaping body image; it is not, however, the preeminent role. Nor is it simply one item on a laundry list of factors that shape body image. As a group, the media are one cultural force—part of the backdrop against which our body images are played out. Mediated messages are perhaps the most obvious of these forces, but they still are part of a larger picture. The time is right for a research approach that embraces this point of view. To determine accurately how the media affect body image, researchers must look at how individuals navigate, internalize, and make use of weight-loss information provided by the media. The media do not trigger body-image disturbances; they reflect them, and provide clues as to how they develop. The next sections provide a two-part review of research into the relationship between these messages and body-image dissatisfaction.

THE MASS MEDIA
AND THE "THIN IDEAL"

A number of researchers argue that mediated messages about the benefits of dieting and about being thin produce body-image dissatisfaction in some individuals in several ways: by portraying thinness in a positive light in programming and in product advertisements, by emphasizing fitness in exercise programs that air on a variety of channels, by promoting (in ads) the consumption of "light" and "fat-free" foods, and by promoting treatments and products that will help individuals attain the "ideal body" (Harrison & Cantor, 1996; Irving, 1990; Stice, Schupak-Neuberg, Shaw, & Stein, 1994; Stice & Shaw, 1994). Thus it should be no surprise to learn that the television series *Baywatch,* which chronicles the exploits of a group of lifeguards with seemingly perfect bodies, is the most-watched program in the world. But *Baywatch* is only one of the most obvious examples of the media's fondness for fitness and thinness. Characters in television programs are usually thin; further, they often talk about dieting and wanting to lose weight. Moreover, advertisements for a variety of products show thin individuals achieving success by acquiring "status" items. These ads do not specifically promote dieting or diet products, but research has revealed that individuals relate to the appearance of the characters (Myers & Biocca, 1992).

Heavy people, on the other hand, typically appear in television programs as the butt of jokes or as comedic foils. On *The Drew Carey Show,* for example, the main character's weight drives much of the comedy. Kathy Kinney's character, Mimi, is also overweight; Kinney plays Mimi as a foul-mouthed, angry individual with a penchant for garish makeup. Further, heavy people rarely appear in product advertisements; when they do appear, it is for comedic effect, or as the "before" images in commercials for weight-loss products. The editors of *Mode* magazine might argue that their new publication is designed to eliminate some of this bias through its focus on the "plus-size" woman, but their idea of "plus-size" is women who wear a size 14—or the average American woman.

Thinness and dieting are promoted in television and print advertisements for a range of appetite suppressants (Dexatrim, Fibre Trim), prepackaged diet foods (NutriSystem, Ultra Slim-Fast), and weight-loss regimens (Jenny Craig, Weight Watchers). "Watching what we eat"—a step removed from dieting—is promoted in commercials for the growing list of "light" and "fat-free" products. As I have noted briefly above, the thematic focus in commercials for diet and weight-loss products has shifted from rapid weight loss to promises that products have high nutritional value and that they are the result of scientific research (Bishop, 1997). This change was not voluntary; the Federal Trade Commission in 1990 filed actions against many of the top diet product makers, challenging their claims about product effectiveness. To settle the suits, the product makers agreed to provide more thorough substantiation of the claims made in their ads. But in making the changes ordered by the FTC, the product makers have hitched their stylistic wagon to the nation's obsession with fitness (Bishop, 1997). Thanks at least in part to the FTC, however, dieters have learned that a combination of dieting and exercise—not fad diets—will give them the "ideal body." Why they want the ideal body has yet to be explored, and it is still unclear whether those wanting to lose weight have simply traded one obsession for another.

Wiseman, Gray, Mosimann, and Ahrens (1992) note that the number of articles related to diet and exercise in the most popular women's magazines (*Harper's Bazaar, Vogue, Ladies' Home Journal, Good Housekeeping, Woman's Day,*

McCall's) increased steadily as a percentage of all articles published in these magazines from the late 1950s to 1988. These authors also found that the number of exercise articles in women's magazines has surpassed the number of diet articles, suggesting that the media are following the fitness and diet industries as they move away from endorsing diet alone for individuals who want to lose weight to a more sensible combination of diet and exercise. Andersen and DiDomenico (1992) discovered that women's magazines publish a little more than 10 times more ads and articles endorsing weight loss than do men's magazines. Fitness industry pioneers Jack LaLanne and Richard Simmons have been joined by Jake (FitTV) and Kiana (ESPN). Infomercials sell scores of sometimes effective, sometimes useless weight-loss products. One of the newer cable programming channels, FitTV, airs nothing but fitness-related programs.

Defenders of the media would argue that more attention has been paid to eating disorders in the past two decades. Many celebrities, including Princess Diana, singer Karen Carpenter, and actress Tracey Gold, have had their stories of suffering told in the public arena. Moreover, eating disorders are a popular talk-show topic. However, the proportion of articles about eating disorders in women's magazines (compared with total articles) continues to be alarmingly low, possibly because dieting is such a prevalent feature in so many of the articles and ads that appear in these publications, and because diet product makers buy a significant amount of ad space.

Efforts by the medical community to promote awareness of eating disorders have been hampered by public disagreement about how many young men and women suffer from anorexia nervosa and bulimia. In her best-selling book *The Beauty Myth,* Naomi Wolf (1991) claims that 15% of all college-age women suffer from eating disorders. Wolf also contends that 150,000 American women die of anorexia nervosa each year, a claim she bases on information supplied by the American Anorexia and Bulimia Association. Sommers (1994), however, contends that Wolf exaggerates the number of eating disorder-related deaths. According to Sommers's sources, only 54 women died of anorexia nervosa in 1991, 67 in 1988, and 101 in 1983. This disagreement, however, should not deflect attention from the problems so many of us have with our bodies. Killen et al. (1986) found that 11% of the 15-year-old girls in their study vomited to control their weight. Another 8% used diet pills, and 7% used laxatives. Cash and Henry (1995) note that more than half of American women say they are dissatisfied with their appearance, and one-third have negative body images.

News organizations pay a great deal of attention to medical advances in the treatment of obesity, a condition that affects one-third of all adult Americans and 21% of American adolescents between the ages of 12 and 19 (Lentini, 1995). In April 1996, the U.S. Food and Drug Administration (FDA) approved a combination of the appetite suppressants fenfluramine and phentermine for retail sale as a treatment for obesity. Fenfluramine had been available since 1973, but did not become popular with dieters until researchers found that phentermine offset the fatigue experienced by many fenfluramine users (Cowley & Springen, 1997).

Pharmaceutical giant Wyeth-Ayerst sold the diet drug combination under the name Redux.

To their credit, many journalists discussed the drug's side effects and warned that casual dieters should not use it. It is sad and ironic that millions of Americans disregarded this information and sought Redux prescriptions. News organizations turned a more critical eye on the diet industry when Wyeth-Ayerst announced in September 1997 that it was taking Redux off the market at the FDA's request. To date, however, there has been no systematic exploration of news media coverage of the release and demise of Redux. The company faces a growing number of claims from users that the drug leaves waxy deposits on a user's heart valves and is known to cause pulmonary hypertension and brain damage.

Without Redux, some dieters headed back to behavior modification-based diet programs such as those offered by Jenny Craig and Weight Watchers. One would think that upon hearing of the dangers of Redux, individuals who want to lose only a few pounds might have reexamined their motives for dieting. Perhaps some have, but the diet industry certainly has not given them much time to do so. Doctors employed by NutriSystem, for example, are now prescribing phen-Pro, a combination of phentermine and Prozac, for their patients. Other drug makers are "racing to get other obesity treatments into the market" (Cowley & Springen, 1997).

Why, if these products are so dangerous, do consumers buy them? Communication scholars have only begun to tackle this question. As I have noted above, the last step before an eating disorder appears to be a predisposition for eating-disordered behavior, shaped by dysfunctional peer and parental relationships and triggered, the studies reviewed in the next section argue, by the behavioral cues found in mediated images of dieting and thinness in television programming (Myers & Biocca, 1992) and in television commercials. It may be that individuals' desire to look like characters seen on television and in magazines damages their ability to use and make sense of information about how to reach this goal. But information about new diet drugs and commercials for diet products do not, as some researchers argue, act as the catalyst for weight consciousness. Communication scholars must explore and operationalize the cultural context in which weight consciousness develops. They must examine the impact of mediated messages about thinness as it relates to the meaning that being thin has for so many of us. Going on a diet is not an unthinking response to commercials for diet products or to television programs that feature thin people. It is not, as will be discussed, a function of how much television an individual watches (Melcher, Walkosz, Burgoon, & Chen, 1997). It is likely that individuals compare their bodies to those they see on television and struggle to measure up, but there is disagreement as to whether individuals internalize these comparisons. Irving (1990) contends that individuals rank media as the strongest source of pressure to be thin; however, Stice et al. (1994) found that media exposure did not lead individuals to internalize the ideal-body stereotype promoted by the media. As Bordo (1993) notes, the blame for poor body image is too readily placed on the media, advertising agencies, and the fashion industry. Researchers approach these institutions as "a whimsical, capricious enemy, capable of indoctrinating and tyrannizing passive and impressionable young girls by means of whatever imagery it arbitrarily decide[s] to promote that season" (p. 46). As I have noted above, it is still up to researchers in all of the fields concerned with this issue to develop a better understanding of why obsession with thinness, a psychopathology, has become such a dominant cultural ideal and how that ideal shapes the entire lives of weight-conscious individuals.

MEDIATED MESSAGES: THE "TRIGGER" FOR EATING DISORDERS?

Many researchers argue that internalization of the thin ideal encourages body dissatisfaction in some individuals and may be a partial cause of eating disorders (Katzman & Wolchik, 1984; Kendler et al., 1991; Post & Crowther, 1985; Stice & Shaw, 1994). To be sure, the ideal body type for women is thinner now than at any point in history (Hesse-Biber, 1989, p. 81). As Striegel-Moore, Silberstein, and Rodin (1986) note, girls learn at a young age "that being attractive is intricately interwoven with pleasing and serving others, and, in turn, will secure their love" (p. 249). The mass media, particularly television, teach girls "a singular feminine ideal of thinness, beauty, and youth, set against a world in which men are more competent and also more diverse in appearance" (p. 249). As noted earlier, scholars have yet to delve into why this ideal is important to the young women who allegedly aspire to it, nor have they tried to assess how individuals derive meaning from messages imbued with the ideal. For some time, researchers have pointed to a strong relationship between the "thin ideal" and escalating rates of body-image distortion and eating disorders, but have done little to explore the link or to explain why thinness is such a dominant cultural ideal.

In a cultivation-based analysis, Tan (1979) found that female high school students exposed to a series of 15 commercials for beauty products felt that it was more important to be beautiful in order to be popular with men than did students in a control group that saw a block of neutral commercials. Respondents who watched the beauty product commercials said that being beautiful was more important to them than did individuals who saw the neutral commercials. Respondents who saw the beauty product commercials were better able to remember the products and their brand names than were respondents in the neutral-commercial group. Tan's study was the first to explore beauty commercials, and its experimental design was different from most cultivation studies. Investigating themes in commercials and how these themes affect viewers' conceptions provides "a more complete picture" of television's cultivation effects, Tan argues (p. 284). However, she acknowledges that "audience perceptions of social reality are more likely to be affected after repeated media exposure over a period of time" (p. 284). Tan's task was to establish the internal validity of cultivation analysis, but she admitted that "it remains unclear whether the media cause audience perceptions of social reality" or "attract people with certain patterns of social reality perceptions" (p. 284).

As the following discussion will reveal, Tan's concerns have not been sufficiently addressed.

Other researchers have been content to perform content analyses of thinness-related messages. Garner, Garfinkel, Schwartz, and Thompson (1980), for example, found that contestants in the Miss America pageant and women posing for *Playboy* centerfolds became thinner during the period 1960-1979. Silverstein, Perdue, Peterson, and Kelly (1986) found that more than 69% of the female characters in television programs sampled for their study were rated as thin, compared with 17.5% of male characters. They also discovered that women are exposed to more thinness-related messages than are men: They found 63 advertisements for diet foods in the 48 issues of women's magazines (*Family Circle, Ladies' Home Journal, Redbook, Woman's Day*) they examined, and only 1 diet product ad in 48 issues of four leading men's magazines (*Field and Stream, Playboy, Popular Mechanics, Sports Illustrated*). Furthermore, they discovered that women, compared with men, are exposed to a dramatically higher number of ads for food: Whereas the women's magazines they examined featured 226 articles on food, the men's magazines featured only 10. Thus women receive conflicting messages about food; in advertisements for Nabisco SnackWell's cookies, for example, women are seen fervently pursuing the product. Compare this to messages that endorse the thinness ideal. But again, the important factor is not how many messages we see; it is how we internalize those messages—and why cultural institutions put so much emphasis on them.

Lakoff and Scherr (1984) argue that we see television performers and models in magazines "as realistic representations of what people look like," despite the fact that they have makeup artists and personal trainers at their disposal (quoted in Striegel-Moore et al., 1986, p. 256). This "look," Lakoff and Scherr claim, is "rapidly and widely disseminated, so that the public receives a uniform picture of beauty" (quoted in Striegel-Moore et al., 1986, p. 256). Hesse-Biber (1989) reports that this "look" has a great deal of impact on the self-perceptions of women. Hesse-Biber developed a measure that allowed the women in her sample to compare their perceptions of weight with a weight chart provided by a local diet center (she calls this the "cultural model"). She contrasted these self-perceptions with the self-perceptions of a group of women whose perceptions of their weight agreed with medically desired figures derived from the Metropolitan Life Insurance Company's desirable weight charts. Most of the women in Hesse-Biber's sample followed the cultural model of ideal weight.

To get a better idea of changes in the standards for female attractiveness, Silverstein, Perdue, Peterson, and Kelly (1986) charted changes in the bodies of models photographed for *Ladies' Home Journal* and *Vogue*. Sampling photos every 4 years since the magazines' inceptions, they found that the bust-to-waist ratios of the models dropped precipitously from about 1910 to 1925, rose slightly into the 1940s, then dropped again through the 1960s and 1970s. The authors assert that this shrinking standard of attractiveness "may have played a role in producing the recent outbreak of eating disorders among women" (p. 529). They also examined photos of well-known actresses from 1932 to 1979 to see if the standard of attractiveness they portrayed had become less curvaceous. Bust-to-waist ratios revealed that these actresses had indeed become thinner and less curvaceous between the 1930s and 1970s. In their conclusion, Silverstein et al. acknowledge that their study does not establish that the media cause women to become dissatisfied with their bodies, nor did they calculate the media's influence on body dissatisfaction compared with other factors. They do claim, however, that the popularity of an extremely thin attractiveness standard leads to eating disorders. Silverstein, Peterson, and Perdue (1986) contend that in the 1920s, there was an epidemic of eating disorders; during this period, they argue, models appearing in women's magazines were as thin as they were when their 1986 study was completed.

A Step Forward: Social Comparison Theory

Irving (1990) took a step forward by studying the effect of the thin ideal on the self-esteem and body images of women who exhibited varying levels of bulimic symptoms. Irving applied Festinger's (1954) social comparison theory, which claims that we evaluate ourselves through comparison with others. "Given a range of comparison persons," Irving argues, "individuals will choose to compare themselves to others who are similar on a specified ability or opinions" (p. 231). Miller (1982) asserts that attractiveness is usually a salient factor in social comparison. In the studies reviewed below, comparisons were made with members of groups to which respondents did not belong. They may have shared social characteristics—young women may have been the same ages as models or television personalities, for instance—but there was no social interaction (Merton, 1957). Goethals (1986) draws a distinction between sought and unsought comparison. It is difficult for us, he contends, to see an accomplished person and not compare ourselves to that person. The media encourage us to make unsought comparisons. Like Irving, Rachins (1991) has applied Festinger's ideas, arguing that we compare ourselves to the idealized characters in product advertisements. These images, Rachins found, raise the comparison standard for physical attractiveness (p. 71). Festinger's theory is also the basis for work by Melcher et al. (1997) in which they found that men and women who asserted that television characters are attractive reported more agreement with American culture's current attractiveness ideal.

Irving (1990) asked more than 900 female psychology students to complete the BULIT, a 36-item test designed to detect symptoms of bulimia. Of these 900, 162 women took part in the study. They were grouped according to the degree of bulimic symptoms they exhibited. The first group looked at slides of thin fashion models, the second group was exposed to slides of models of average weight, and the third group looked at slides of overweight models. A control group saw no slides. The slides of the thin models were taken from the magazines *Elle* and *Glamour* and from the fashion catalog *Avon Fashions*. A professional photographer took the photos of the average women used in the study, and Irving took the photos of the overweight women from a Spiegel catalog for plus-size women.

Told that they were participating in a study of successful advertising, respondents were asked to rate the credibility, trustworthiness, and persuasiveness of the women appearing in the slides. They were later asked to complete three questionnaires designed to measure pressure to be thin felt from family, peers, and the media; self-esteem; and body esteem. Irving (1990) found that an increasing level of bulimic symptoms was related to greater pressure to be thin. The media—the most "distant" source in the study—exerted more pressure to be thin than did peers or parents (p. 236). Irving notes that the "media may be the strongest proponent of the thin standard of beauty. It makes sense that peers, also under the influence of the current standard of beauty, are the next largest source of pressure" (p. 239). Family members exert the least pressure, according to Irving, "because their standards of beauty have relaxed as they have accommodated their own bodily changes" (p. 239). Moreover, older individuals "may also remain under the influence of a previous, more curvaceous standard of beauty" (p. 239).

Irving's study did not confirm her hypothesis that respondents who exhibited a high degree of bulimic symptoms would report lower self-evaluations in response to the thin model slides than would respondents reporting a low degree of bulimic symptoms. Irving suggests that bulimics may be too far gone to be affected by the thin ideal. Respondents with a high degree of symptoms reported more pressure to be thin from the media than from their families or peers. Irving acknowledges that it is not clear whether this finding stems from environmental differences, because individuals with severe bulimic symptoms "are surrounded by more food-conscious peers, family, and media" (p. 239), or from individual differences seen in responses to the same stimulus. Ironically, the sizes of the models in the slides had no relationship to how sexually attractive respondents felt. Respondents may have seen the models as "similar" to themselves in terms of sexual attractiveness and "dissimilar" in terms of weight-related attractiveness, Irving argues (p. 239). Bulimic symptoms, Irving contends, "may be particularly related to dissatisfaction with one's sexual attractiveness" (p. 240). Women who have severe bulimia "may sacrifice their physical strength to maintain or lose weight" (p. 240).

Internalization and Gender Role Endorsement

In two more-recent studies, researchers have examined the impact of the thin ideal on women who show no symptoms of eating disorders. Stice et al. (1994) argue that internalization of the thin ideal, gender role endorsement, and body satisfaction mediate the relationship between exposure to mediated portrayals of the thin ideal and eating disorder symptomatology. Unrealistic body weight goals created by internalization of the thin ideal produce greater body dissatisfaction, Stice et al. claim. Internalizing the thin ideal may lead to an eating disorder: "Even if a woman is satisfied with her body, she may engage in disordered eating behavior to maintain a low weight" (p. 836). Stice et al. also argue that seeing these images leads women to internalize gender roles. Although researchers have found a relationship between media use and gender role endorsement, Stice et al. hypothesized that endorsement would not predict eating pathology, because the stereotypes at issue "focus more on social roles than body dimensions" (p. 837). Further, researchers have yet to link gender role endorsement and eating pathology conclusively (Katzman & Wolchik, 1984). As a result, Stice et al. hypothesized that gender role endorsement would have an effect on eating pathology through the internalization of the ideal body stereotype. Finally, they hypothesized that the media's overemphasis on dieting would predict eating pathology, gender role endorsement, and ideal body stereotype internalization.

Stice et al. (1994) measured media exposure by asking their 238 female respondents to indicate the number of health and fitness, beauty and fashion, and entertainment, arts, and gossip magazines they had seen in the previous month as well as the number of hours they spent watching television comedies, dramas, and game shows. Respondents also completed instruments designed to measure gender role endorsement (the Attitudes Toward Women Scale; Spence, Helmreich, & Strapp, 1973; and the Attitudes Toward the Male Role Scale; Doyle & Moore, 1978), ideal-body stereotype internalization, body dissatisfaction (a subscale of the Eating Disorders Inventory; Garner, Olmsted, & Polivy, 1983), and eating disorder symptomatology (the Eating Attitudes Test; Garner, Olmsted, Bohr, & Garfinkel, 1982).

Stice et al. found significant direct effects of media exposure on eating disorder symptomatology ($r = .30, p < .001$) and gender role endorsement ($r = .21, p < .05$). Gender role endorsement was related to internalization of the ideal-body stereotype ($r = .37, p = .001$), and internalization predicted body dissatisfaction ($r = .17$, $p = .05$), although this relationship was not particularly strong. Moreover, no significant relationship was found between media exposure and ideal-body stereotype internalization ($r = -.08$) or between ideal-body stereotype internalization and eating disorder symptoms ($r = .06$).

Stice et al. also found support for the notion that exposure to the thin ideal is related to eating pathology. In addition, they found that internalization of the thin ideal at least partially mediated the effects of seeing the ideal body images presented by the media. They attribute their study's failure to support a direct link between media exposure and ideal-body stereotype internalization to the fact that "other socialization agents, such as family and peers, play a larger role in promoting the thin ideal" (p. 839). They acknowledge that the study's reliance on self-report data—a recurring problem in many of the studies reviewed here—was problematic, and that asking respondents to recall the amount of media consumed was imprecise. Further, they made no attempt to assess the level of bulimic symptoms before the treatment. Such a measure would have provided a point of comparison.

Stice and Shaw (1994) revisited the methodology used by Irving (1990) to try to assess the adverse effects of the thin ideal on women. One group of respondents ($n = 157$) viewed full-body pictures of thin models taken from *Cosmopolitan* magazine and contained in a binder. A second group looked at photos of women of average weight, which the authors collected from a magazine for plus-size women. A control group looked at photos with no people in them. Recall that Irving (1990) used slides of thin, average, and overweight models.

After looking at the photos, respondents completed a mood scale designed to assess their affective state. Depression, happiness, shame, guilt, confidence, anxiety, and stress were assessed using 5-point scales that ranged from *not at all* to *extremely*. Respondents also completed the Beck Depression Inventory (BDI; Beck & Steer, 1991) as well as instruments designed to assess body stereotype endorsement, body dissatisfaction, and bulimic symptomatology. Stice and Shaw also asked respondents to rate the average attractiveness of the women in the photos on a 7-point Likert scale ranging from *not at all attractive* to *extremely attractive*. Women in the photos used in the thin condition were judged more attractive than were the women in the photos used in the average-weight condition.

Stice and Shaw performed multiple regression analyses to get a clearer picture of the effect of exposure to the thin ideal. Each of the nine criterion variables (depressed, happy, shameful, guilty, confident, anxious, stressed, body dissatisfaction, thin ideal stereotype) was regressed on two dummy-coded vectors designated to represent experimental effects, after age, parental education, and body mass. Stice and Shaw found that the individuals who looked at the photos of the thin models felt more depression, unhappiness, shame, guilt, and stress and less confidence than did individuals who looked at the photos of average-weight models. Respondents in the thin condition also felt more dissatisfaction with their bodies than did respondents in the average-weight condition. Further, depression (β = .18), shame (β = .14), stress (β = .19), and guilt (β = .20) were found to be positively associated with bulimic symptomatology. Confidence (β = −.37) and happiness (β = −.28) were negatively related with bulimic symptomatology.

Stice and Shaw (1994) conclude that seeing the thin ideal leads individuals to feel depressed, shameful, guilty, unhappy, unconfident, and dissatisfied with their bodies. These results are limited, they acknowledge, but promising. However, Stice and Shaw found no effect of exposure to "the ideal body" on internalization of the thin ideal. They argue that women internalize this ideal when they are young, and might not be influenced during a brief experiment. They also discovered that almost all of the factors they measured predicted bulimic symptomatology. This research broke new ground by uncovering relationships of shame, guilt, and confidence to bulimic symptomatology. Most previous research in this area had focused on depression.

Based on their findings, Stice and Shaw suggest that negative affect results when we see the ideal body on television or in magazines. This may trigger binge eating in individuals predisposed to bulimia. Stice and Shaw propose a second path: from exposure to the thin ideal to body dissatisfaction to eating-disordered behavior. However, they chart this path without taking into account the influence of peers and parents, as other researchers have done.

None of the studies reviewed above addresses the claim made by Striegel-Moore et al. (1986) that not only do the media present the thin ideal, they present and endorse the means to attain it, "including how to diet, purge, and engage in other disregulating behavior" (p. 256). One best-selling diet book has even endorsed a form of bulimia, instructing individuals to counteract binges by eating large amounts of fruit in order to cause diarrhea (Mazel, 1981). Further, the studies reviewed were based on one-time or short-term exposure to mediated images. Respondents were not given the chance to reflect on the texts.

Self-Schemata and Social Learning Theory

Myers and Biocca (1992) argue that there is a causal relationship between television's portrayals of the ideal body and distortion of self-perceived body size by young women, but they do so against a more social backdrop. A recurring element in their work is the notion of the "self-schema," defined as "a person's construction of those traits that make the person distinctive and constitute the sense of 'me' " (p. 115). We build self-schemata from our observations of our own behaviors, reactions of others to those behaviors, and "social cues that suggest which attributes of the self are the most important" (p. 115).

Television advertising and programming, Myers and Biocca contend, highlight a number of these social cues, including what constitutes a desirable body image. They argue that for a young woman, body image is constructed from four models: (a) the socially represented ideal body, (b) the young woman's internalized ideal body, (c) the young woman's present body image, and (d) the young woman's objective body shape. Myers and Biocca's most important contention is that the "socially represented ideal body" is taken from cultural ideals of beauty. The primary source of these ideals is the mass media—specifically, television advertising and programming. Myers and Biocca also recognize that an individual's body image is partially a product of peer and family relationships.

Instead of focusing on the motivation to diet, Myers and Biocca (1992) hypothesized that thinness portrayals in television advertising and programming play an indirect role in prompting individuals to distort their body images. The role begins with the media's influence on the development in young women of the internalized ideal body. Myers and Biocca also posited that exposure to body-image commercials and body-image programming would create "a greater gap and tension" between a young woman's internalized ideal body and her objective body shape, as measured by increases in body size overestimations. Body-image programming is programming built around "the display, viewing, and explicit concentration" on ideal body representations, such as the spokesmodel segments of the nationally syndicated program *Star Search*. In body-image commercials, female bodies are used "in a decorative fashion, whether they do or do not relate to an intrinsic property of the product being sold" (Myers & Biocca, 1992, p. 119).

One of the commercials Myers and Biocca used in their study featured women in bathing suits selling Coors beer. A sample comprising 76 male and female university students watched videotapes crafted to resemble actual television programs. The videotapes included body-image programming and body-image commercials. After watching the tapes, participants went to one of two rooms equipped

with body-image detection devices. The devices allowed each individual to estimate his or her body shape by changing the widths of three bands of light representing the individual's chest, waist, and hips. All three measurements were projected at the same time. The researchers found that watching body-image
programming led participants to overestimate their body size to a lesser degree
than did participants in neutral-image and control groups. They also found a
decrease in body overestimation following exposure to body-image commercials.
Viewing body-image commercials significantly affected participants' perceptions
of their waists and hips.

Myers and Biocca also discovered that watching body-image commercials
caused lower levels of depression in respondents. No differences were found in
levels of depression between body-image programming and neutral-image programming used in the study. These findings confirmed those of earlier studies in
which young women were found to tend to overestimate their body size. More
important, however, is Myers and Biocca's conclusion that a woman's body image
is elastic, because it can be changed by the woman's watching even 30 minutes of
television. Television messages revolving around the "ideal female body" caused
women in the study first to think about their bodies and then to experience fluctuations in their body images. The body-image commercials used by Myers and
Biocca purportedly made the young women in the study feel thinner than they
actually were.

Interestingly, Myers and Biocca found that participants actually felt better about
themselves after watching the body-image commercials—an indication, they
claimed, that participants "imagined themselves in the ideal body presented by
advertising." Body-image programming, on the other hand, did not successfully
sell "an agenda of personal change" or present images of a brighter, thinner future.
Myers and Biocca also conclude that body-image disturbance is a two-stage phenomenon. First, individuals "generate, absorb, or reinforce" a representation of the
ideal body, a representation found frequently in television programs and commercials. After the ad's effect dissipates and the individuals realize that the body ideal
is unattainable, they may reject their body shapes—the second stage of
body-image disturbance.

In their examination of the relationship between mediated messages and eating
disorders, Harrison and Cantor (1996) argue that individuals, primarily women,
model their thinness-related behavior after what they see on television and in magazines. Through modeling (Bandura, 1977), individuals acquire the ideal of a thin
body and become motivated to diet and, perhaps, to engage in eating-disordered
behavior. Mediated messages help to form both the linkages between peer and
family factors that may cause an individual to think about dieting and a pattern of
action—going on the diet.

Harrison and Cantor (1996) focused on two factors from Bandura's (1977)
social learning model, *prevalence* and *incentives,* arguing that we are more likely
to model our behaviors on "events" that we see frequently. They note that television and magazines abound with diet- and thinness-related images that serve as a

source of incentives for engaging in the modeled behavior. We go on diets and/or try to lose weight to achieve rewards put before us by peers, parents, and the media. If a figure we see on television is rewarded for losing weight, we may feel that we will be similarly rewarded, Harrison and Cantor (and Bandura) claim. They also explain the difference between direct and inferential links that join the media and modeled behavior. In direct modeling, an individual sees a behavior and repeats it. Inferential modeling, Harrison and Cantor explain, occurs when the act and the result—dieting and being thin—are not linked. In the television programs used in their study, dieting is often not shown as the reason the characters in the programs are thin. The same cannot be said for the women's magazines they mention. In such magazines, women see images of thinness and read scores of articles that explain how to achieve these images. Harrison and Cantor predicted that individuals who watched a great deal of television and read many magazines would more likely suffer from "disordered eating" and would be more dissatisfied with their bodies. Further, they hypothesized that individuals who consumed a great deal of television and magazines would exhibit a higher "drive for thinness," as defined by Garner (1991), than individuals who consumed smaller amounts of television and magazines.

Harrison and Cantor (1996) asked participants to complete a questionnaire that measured how much television they watched on an average weekday, an average Saturday, and an average Sunday, and how often they watched the programs *Beverly Hills 90210, Melrose Place, Seinfeld, Northern Exposure, Designing Women,* and *Roseanne.* These shows were chosen because they represent a range of body types. *Beverly Hills 90210* and *Melrose Place* were designated "thin" shows because most of their female main characters are thin. *Seinfeld* and *Northern Exposure* were designated "average" shows because the main female characters have average bodies, and *Roseanne* and *Designing Women* were designated "heavy" shows because their lead characters are heavy. Harrison and Cantor asked their respondents to indicate the numbers of issues of magazines they read each month in these categories: health/fitness, beauty/fashion, entertainment/gossip, news/current events, and men's/entertainment. From this information, the researchers created a magazine reading index. Respondents then completed the Eating Attitudes Test (Garner & Garfinkel, 1979) and five of eight subscales found in the Eating Disorders Inventory (Garner et al., 1983).

Harrison and Cantor found that media consumption was positively related to eating-disordered behavior in women for magazines, but not for television. EAT scores were highly correlated with reading fitness magazines ($r = .30, p < .001$) and fashion magazines ($r = .17, p < .05$). The researchers performed a multiple regression analysis on the respondents' EAT scores, using as predictors reading fitness, fashion, gossip, and news magazines, and found that reading fitness magazines significantly predicted EAT scores. The relationship remained strong even when interest in dieting and interest in fitness were partialed out.

As for television, Harrison and Cantor found no support for their idea that watching shows with thin main characters is related to eating-disordered behavior.

However, they did find that watching television was a significant predictor of body dissatisfaction and a fairly significant predictor of the drive for thinness. Magazine reading did not significantly predict body dissatisfaction, but did significantly predict drive for thinness.

Based on their findings, Harrison and Cantor claim that the relationship between magazine reading and eating disorder symptomatology is stronger than the relationship between television viewing and eating disorder symptomatology, and that respondents who logged the highest EAT scores were much more interested in fitness and dieting than were respondents who scored low on the EAT. They suggest that consumption of messages that depict and promote thinness may nurture eating disorders, which in turn causes a growing interest in these media.

There are a few problems with Harrison and Cantor's approach, however. First, the researchers did not attempt to assess how the respondents used the information they received in these messages. Further, they seemingly investigate these issues in a vacuum, without first assessing the role of peer and family pressure in encouraging the development of eating disorders in individuals. In addition, they excerpted images of characters rather than allowing respondents to watch real-time or taped segments of the programs in which the characters appear. But even if respondents did see taped segments of the programs, viewing shows whose main characters are thin does not promote eating disorders, as Harrison and Cantor suggest. In most cases of anorexia nervosa or bulimia, there are peer- or parent-induced feelings of inadequacy that may be activated or confirmed by the eating-disordered individuals' being exposed to positive thinness messages. Harrison and Cantor did not try to find out why individuals attend to this information, what kinds of information they find valuable, or whether the information triggers connections with other parts of their lives, such as their relationships with peers and parents. And although it is interesting to explore individuals' feelings about television characters, it might have been even more helpful to examine the reactions of the respondents to the situations in which thin and heavy characters found themselves. We may see that Maggie in *Northern Exposure* is thin, but how is her thinness related to the story? Does the fact that she is thin help her to achieve some things and miss out on others? Is she shown dieting or watching her weight? Harrison and Cantor could have addressed these issues by simply comparing the numbers of times thin and heavy characters engage in certain "status" behaviors (earning a great deal of money, having many possessions) and examining when the characters talk about weight or engage in eating-related behaviors, including dieting and watching their weight. The key, however, is trying to assess how respondents give meaning to the information.

There is also an unexplored difference in the impacts of images of thin characters on body image and messages specifically designed to promote weight loss, such as commercials for diet products. It could be argued that images of happy, productive thin people simply help create the backdrop for weight consciousness; commercials may give individuals the tools with which they can color that backdrop.

Finally, Taylor et al. (1998) found that it is the importance that peers place on weight that most strongly predicts concern with weight. Two groups of young girls, one from elementary school and the other from middle school, made up Taylor et al.'s sample. The instrument the researchers used assessed a variety of factors, including how much importance peers place on weight, how much respondents were teased about their weight, the impact of being teased, parental concern with thinness, how much respondents were bothered by changes in their bodies, and how much they tried to look like girls and women they saw in magazines and on TV. Only one media-related question was included. A multivariate stepwise regression revealed that the importance that peers placed on weight and on eating was most strongly related to concern about weight for the elementary school girls. Peer influence, body mass index, and trying to look like girls and women on TV entered a model that accounted for 57% of the variance in respondents' weight concerns. For the middle school sample, mediated messages were even less important. Peer influence again was the strongest predictor, followed by self-confidence, body mass index, and trying to look like girls and women on TV and in magazines. Again, the researchers included no measure of how the respondents used or internalized the mediated messages.

CONCLUSIONS

Researchers talk a great deal about how culture defines attractiveness, yet the research reviewed here reveals little about the cultural basis of the connection between exposure to the mass media and changes in body image. This review reveals that researchers are dancing around the real issue: How do individuals internalize positive information about thinness and dieting? How do they give meaning to programs like *Baywatch,* on which the entire cast is fit and thin, and to commercials for diet products and workout regimens? To date, researchers have focused on finding a definitive link between mediated messages and deterioration in body image; images of thin people have been taken from the media and studied out of context. The next step is to develop a model that accurately reflects how our culture's fascination with thinness, encouraged by the media, colors the family and peer relationships that in turn shape how we feel about our bodies.

A similar gap is developing in research on new treatments for eating disorders. Claude-Pierre (1997) contends that the anorexic's struggle is not really about weight or being thin. Anorexics subordinate their needs and desires "by learning society's values and what [they] must do to live up to them" (p. 55). They try to please others before themselves. They feel a strong sense of responsibility for everything that goes on around them. The drive to perfection comes not from a sense of superiority; anorexics struggle "to prove their worth to others because they lack an internal sense of self" (p. 53). It could be argued, then, that weight consciousness is not always about weight, either. But the studies reviewed here reveal that scholars studying body image and the media have focused incorrectly on whether messages affect how individuals feel about their weight and appearance; they should be focusing on how the information precipitates weight consciousness. The factors that precipitate an eating disorder—a smothering family, unkind peers, mediated images of thinness—are not the real issue, Claude-Pierre claims; instead, it is "one's attitude toward and perception of the issues that brings on the manifestation of the condition" (p. 19). Thus, to understand the role of the media in shaping people's body images, communication researchers must turn their attention to these attitudes, especially if they are going to continue to contend that mediated images have a deleterious effect on healthy body images. Researchers must investigate what individuals think about the images they see and how they interact with messages that endorse thinness.

Clearly, this kind of approach begins with the influence of peers and parents. Researchers should determine, for example, if individuals who are exposed to information about thinness while they are alone place more or less value on it than they do when they are exposed to the same information in the presence of parents or peers. In most of the studies reviewed here, researchers have exposed respondents to media images and then noted any changes in the respondents' body images and self-concepts. It would be more revealing for researchers to allow respondents to experience images and messages in real-life "media" settings—while watching television programs or thumbing through magazines. The researchers could then have respondents talk about the texts or simply explore with them their thoughts about what they have seen. Researchers could accomplish this by using a talk-aloud protocol, by holding a series of lengthy interviews with respondents, or by asking respondents to keep diaries with a special focus on how they use sources of information about body image.

Studies using diaries would allow researchers to develop a more coherent model of the changing influence of the media on body image. In such studies, children and teenagers in a range of adjoining age groups would keep diaries for a 3- or 6-month period. To support the data obtained from the diaries, and to ensure that peer and parental relationships are included in the model, the researcher would observe the same subjects in their daily activities for a predetermined period. The researcher would look for weight-related behaviors and any discussion of what precipitated them. Thus the researcher would be able to determine, with reasonable accuracy, whether the respondents are putting information taken from the media to any use. Variations on this design could include day- or weeklong ethnographic sessions or the use of the experience sampling method cited earlier (Richards et al., 1990). Here, the researcher could keep a "running tab" of thinness and dieting references and could assess the cultural origins of these comments. I have created such a diary design to study lunchtime conversation at an elementary or middle school.

Such an approach would go a long way toward recognizing that the pressure to be thin must be approached "not as individual psychopathology, but as social pathology" (Bordo, 1998, p. 116). The images used in the studies reviewed here have already created cultural benchmarks for weight and for appearance. The cat, as it were, is out of the bag. We now need to find out why individuals "no longer have the luxury of a distinction between what's required of a fashion model and what's required of them" (Bordo, 1998, p. 116). Pressure from peers, perfectionistic or indifferent families, and mediated images that endorse thinness are interrelated. Scholars must develop methods that will enable them to explore the causes of body image dissatisfaction "in cultural time and space" (Bordo, 1998, p. 117). How is the value that society places on being thin communicated to children? Images of thin people in television programs and in magazine advertisements are only one way to get this message across. Researchers must also recognize that for many, weight consciousness is normative behavior. There is a crying need to find out why this has happened as well as for well-reasoned attempts to correct it.

Researchers in all of the fields touched on here could then develop ways to use the media and mediated messages to promote a more realistic view of the body among children and adolescents. Riva, Melis, and Bolzoni (1997) have moved in this direction with their development of a virtual reality model for treating body-image disturbances that has produced an increase in the body satisfaction of experiment participants. This is a step forward from the information-based models at the heart of most eating disorder prevention programs in place in high schools and universities. Mann et al. (1997) found, for example, that a group of freshman college students who attended an eating disorder prevention program showed more symptoms of eating disorders than a group of students who did not attend the program. The program featured talks from classmates who had recovered from eating disorders. Mann et al. contend that the program may have inadvertently normalized eating disorders in its attempt to reduce the stigma surrounding them. Such a finding shows the danger of studying any aspect of our obsession with weight outside of its cultural context.

REFERENCES

Andersen, A. E., & DiDomenico, L. (1992). Diet vs. shape content of popular male and female magazines: A dose-response relationship to the incidence of eating disorders? *International Journal of Eating Disorders, 11,* 283-287.

Bandura, A. (1977). *Social learning theory.* Englewood Cliffs, NJ: Prentice Hall.

Beck, A. T., & Steer, R. A. (1991). Screening for adolescent depression: A comparison of depression scales. *Journal of the American Academy of Child and Adolescent Psychiatry, 30,* 58-66.

Bishop, R. (1997, May). *A wolf in sheep's clothing: Narrative style changes in commercials for diet and weight loss products from 1990 to present.* Paper presented at the annual meeting of the International Communication Association, Montreal.

Bordo, S. (1993). *Unbearable weight: Feminism, Western culture, and the body.* Berkeley: University of California Press.

Bordo, S. (1998). *Twilight zones: The hidden life of cultural images from Plato to OJ.* Berkeley: University of California Press.

Cash, T. F., & Henry, P. E. (1995). Women's body images: The results of a national survey in the U.S.A. *Sex Roles, 33,* 19-27.

Claude-Pierre, P. (1997). *The secret language of eating disorders.* New York: Times Books.

Costanzo, P. (1975). Conformity development as a function of self-blame. In J. J. Goner (Ed.), *Contemporary issues in adolescent development* (pp. 309-322). New York: Harper & Row.

Cowley, G., & Springen, K. (1997, September 29). After Fen-Phen. *Newsweek* [On-line]. Available Internet: http://www.newsweek.com/nwsrv/issue/13_97b/printed/us/md0113.htm

Crandall, C. (1988). Social contagion of binge eating. *Journal of Personality and Social Psychology, 55,* 588-598.

Crisp, A. H. (1980). *Anorexia nervosa: Let me be.* London: Academic Press.

Doyle, J., & Moore, R. (1978). Attitudes toward the Male Role Scale: An objective instrument to measure attitudes toward the male's role in society. *Catalog of Selected Documents in Psychology, 8,* 35.

Dykens, E., & Gerrard, M. (1986). Psychological profiles of purging bulimics, repeat dieters, and controls. *Journal of Consulting and Clinical Psychology, 54,* 283-288.

Festinger, L. (1954). A theory of social comparison processes. *Human Relations, 7,* 117-140.

Garner, D. M. (1991). *Eating Disorder Inventory 2: Professional manual.* Odessa, FL: Psychological Assessment Resources.

Garner, D. M., & Garfinkel, P. E. (1979). The Eating Attitudes Test: An index of the symptoms of anorexia nervosa. *Psychological Medicine, 9,* 273-279.

Garner, D. M., Garfinkel, P. E., Schwartz, D., & Thompson, M. (1980). Cultural expectations of thinness in women. *Psychological Reports, 47,* 483-491.

Garner, D. M., Olmsted, M. P., Bohr, Y., & Garfinkel, P. E. (1982). The Eating Attitudes Test: Psychometric features and clinical correlates. *Psychological Medicine, 12,* 871-878.

Garner, D. M., Olmsted, M. P., & Polivy, J. (1983). The Eating Disorder Inventory: A measure of cognitive-behavioral dimensions of anorexia nervosa and bulimia. In P. Darby, P. E. Garfinkel, D. M. Garner, & D. Coscina (Eds.), *Anorexia nervosa: Recent developments in research* (pp. 173-184). New York: Alan R. Liss.

Goethals, G. (1986). Social comparison theory: Psychology from the lost and found. *Personality and Social Psychology Bulletin, 12,* 261-278.

Haney, D. (1991, June 27). Warning for dieters. *Philadelphia Inquirer,* pp. 1, 8.

Harrison, K., & Cantor, J. (1996). The relationship between media consumption and eating disorders. *Journal of Communication, 46*(1), 40-68.

Hesse-Biber, S. (1989). Eating patterns and disorders in a college population: Are college women's eating problems a new phenomenon? *Sex Roles, 20*(11-12), 71-89.

Hsu, G. (1989). The gender gap in eating disorders: Why are the eating disorders more common among women? *Clinical Psychology Review, 9,* 393-407.

Humphrey, L. (1989). Observed family interactions among subtypes of eating disorders using structural analysis of social behavior. *Journal of Consulting and Clinical Psychology, 57,* 206-214.

Humphrey, L. (1992). Family relationships. In K. Halmi (Ed.), *Psychobiology and treatment of anorexia nervosa and bulimia nervosa* (pp. 263-284). Washington, DC: American Psychiatric Press.

Huon, G. F. (1988). Towards the prevention of eating disorders. In D. Hardoff & E. Chiger (Eds.), *Eating disorders in adolescents and young adults* (pp. 447-454). London: Freund.

Huon, G. F. (1994). Towards the prevention of dieting-induced disorders: Modifying negative food- and body-related attitudes. *International Journal of Eating Disorders, 16,* 395-399.

Irving, L. (1990). Mirror images: Effects of the standard of beauty on the self- and body-esteem of women exhibiting varying levels of bulimic symptoms. *Journal of Social and Clinical Psychology, 9*, 230-242.

Johnson, C. L., Stuckey, M. R., Lewis, L. D., & Schwartz, D. M. (1982). Bulimia: A descriptive survey of 316 cases. *International Journal of Eating Disorders, 2*, 3-16.

Kagan, D. M., & Squires, R. L. (1985). Family cohesion, family adaptability, and eating behaviors among college students. *International Journal of Eating Disorders, 4*, 267-280.

Katzman, M., & Wolchik, S. (1984). Bulimia and binge eating in college women: A comparison of personality and behavioral characteristics. *Journal of Consulting and Clinical Psychology, 52*, 423-428.

Kendler, K. S., MacLean, C., Neale, M., Kessler, R., Heath, A., & Eaves, L. (1991). The genetic epidemiology of bulimia nervosa. *American Journal of Psychiatry, 148*, 1627-1637.

Killen, J. D., Taylor, C. D., Telch, M. J., Saylor, K. E., Maron, D. J., & Robinson, T. R. (1986). Self-induced vomiting and laxative and diuretic use among teenagers: Precursors of the binge-purge syndrome? *Journal of the American Medical Association, 255*, 1447-1449.

Lakoff, R. T., & Scherr, R. L. (1984). *Face value: The politics of beauty.* Boston: Routledge & Kegan Paul.

Larson, L. (1975). The relative influence of parent-adolescent affect in predicting the salience hierarchy among youth. In J. J. Conger (Ed.), *Contemporary issues in adolescent development* (pp. 291-308). New York: Harper & Row.

Lentini, C. (1995, August 21). Weighing the ideal. *Philadelphia Inquirer,* pp. G1, G4.

Lewin, K. (1951). *Field theory in social science.* New York: Harper & Row.

Macdonald, M. (1995). *Representing women: Myths of femininity in the popular media.* New York: St. Martin's.

Mann, T., Hoeksema, S., Huang, K., Burgard, D., Wright, A., & Hanson, K. (1997). Are two interventions worse than none? Primary and secondary preventions of eating disorders in college females. *Health Psychology, 16*, 215-225.

Mazel, J. (1981). *The Beverly Hills diet.* New York: Macmillan.

McLorg, P., & Taub, D. (1987). Anorexia nervosa and bulimia: The development of deviant identities. *Deviant Behavior, 8*, 177-189.

Mead, G. H. (1934). *Mind, self, and society: From the standpoint of a social behaviorist* (C. W. Morris, Ed.). Chicago: University of Chicago Press.

Melcher, C., Walkosz, B., Burgoon, M., & Chen, X. (1997, May). *The weigh it is II: Men's and women's comparisons to people on television.* Paper presented at the annual meeting of the International Communication Association, Montreal.

Merton, R. (1957). *Social theory and social structure.* Glencoe, IL: Free Press.

Miller, C. T. (1982). The role of performance-related similarity in social comparison of abilities: A test of the related attributes hypothesis. *Journal of Experimental Social Psychology, 18*, 513-523.

Minuchin, S., Rosman, B., & Baker, L. (1978). *Psychosomatic families: Anorexia nervosa in context.* Cambridge, MA: Harvard University Press.

Myers, P., & Biocca, F. (1992). The elastic body image: The effect of television advertising and programming on body image distortions in young women. *Journal of Communication, 42*(3), 108-132.

Palmer, R. L. (1988). *Anorexia nervosa: A guide for sufferers and their families.* London: Penguin.

Petty, R. E., & Cacioppo, J. T. (1986). The elaboration likelihood model of persuasion. In L. Berkowitz (Ed.), *Advances in experimental social psychology* (Vol. 19, pp. 123-205). New York: Academic Press.

Post, G., & Crowther, J. H. (1985). Variables that discriminate bulimic from nonbulimic adolescent females. *Journal of Youth and Adolescence, 14*, 85-98.

Rachins, M. (1991). Social comparison and the idealized images of advertising. *Journal of Consumer Research, 18,* 71-83.

Richards, M. H., Casper, R. C., & Larson, R. (1990). Weight and eating concerns among pre- and young adolescent boys and girls. *Journal of Adolescent Health Care, 11,* 203-209.

Riva, G., Melis, L., & Bolzoni, M. (1997). Treating body-image disturbances. *Communications of the ACM, 40,* 69-71.

Seid, R. P. (1989). *Never too thin: Why women are at war with their bodies.* Englewood Cliffs, NJ: Prentice Hall.

Scalf-McIver, L., & Thompson, J. K. (1989). Family correlates of bulimic characteristics in college females. *Journal of Clinical Psychology, 45,* 467-472.

Schilder, P. (1950). *The image and appearance of the human body.* New York: International Universities Press.

Schwartz, H. (1986). *Never satisfied: A cultural history of diets, fantasies, and fat.* New York: Free Press.

Shugar, G., & Krueger, S. (1995). Aggressive family communication, weight gain, and improved eating attitudes during systemic family therapy for anorexia nervosa. *International Journal of Eating Disorders, 17,* 23-31.

Silverstein, B., Perdue, L., Peterson, B., & Kelly, E. (1986). The role of the mass media in promoting a thin standard of bodily attractiveness for women. *Sex Roles, 14,* 519-532.

Silverstein, B., Peterson, B., & Perdue, L. (1986). Some correlates of the thin standard of bodily attractiveness for women. *International Journal of Eating Disorders, 5,* 895-905.

Sommers, C. H. (1994). *Who stole feminism? How women have betrayed women.* New York: Simon & Schuster.

Spence, J., Helmreich, R., & Strapp, J. (1973). A short version of the Attitudes Toward Women Scale. *Bulletin of the Psychonomic Society, 2,* 219-220.

Staffieri, R. (1967). A study of social stereotype of body image in children. *Journal of Personality and Social Psychology, 7,* 101-104.

Stice, E., Schupak-Neuberg, E., Shaw, H. E., & Stein, R. J. (1994). Relation of media exposure to eating disorder symptomatology: An examination of mediating mechanisms. *Journal of Abnormal Psychology, 103,* 836-840.

Stice, E., & Shaw, H. E. (1994). Adverse effects of the media-portrayed thin ideal on women and linkages to bulimic symptomatology. *Journal of Social and Clinical Psychology, 13,* 288-308.

Striegel-Moore, R. H., Silberstein, L. R., & Rodin, J. (1986). Toward an understanding of risk factors for bulimia. *American Psychologist, 41,* 246-263.

Strober, M., & Humphrey, L. (1987). Familial contributions to the aetiology and cause of anorexia nervosa and bulimia. *Journal of Consulting and Clinical Psychology, 55,* 654-659.

Tan, A. (1979). TV beauty ads and role expectations of adolescent female viewers. *Journalism Quarterly, 56,* 283-288.

Taylor, C. B., Sharpe, T., Shisslak, C., Bryson, S., Estes, L., Gray, N., McKnight, K. M., Crago, M., Kraemer, H., & Killen, J. (1998). Factors associated with weight concern in adolescent girls. *International Journal of Eating Disorders, 24,* 31-42.

Watson, D., Clark, L., & Tellegen, A. (1988). Development and validation of brief measures of positive and negative affect: The PANAS scales. *Journal of Personality and Social Psychology, 54,* 1063-1070.

Wertheim, E., Paxton, S., Maude, D., Szmukler, G., Gibbons, K., & Hiller, L. (1992). Psychosocial predictors of weight loss behaviors and binge eating in adolescent girls and boys. *International Journal of Eating Disorders, 12,* 151-160.

Wiseman, C., Gray, J., Mosimann, J., & Ahrens, A. (1992). Cultural expectations of thinness in women: An update. *International Journal of Eating Disorders, 11,* 85-89.

Wolf, N. (1991). *The beauty myth.* New York: Doubleday.

Wooley, S., & Wooley, O. W. (1982). The Beverly Hills eating disorder: The mass marketing of anorexia nervosa. *International Journal of Eating Disorders, 1,* 57-69.

CHAPTER CONTENTS

8 Current Research Programs on Relational Maintenance Behaviors

DANIEL J. CANARY
ELAINE D. ZELLEY
Pennsylvania State University

This chapter addresses how communication theoretically functions to maintain personal relationships. In particular, four sustained lines of research are reviewed that specify how communication helps to maintain ongoing heterosexual, romantic involvements. A synthesis of the research programs leads the authors to believe that communication can operate as an independent, mediating, or dependent factor. In other words, the chapter highlights some specific ways in which communication behavior both affects and reflects the nature of people's personal relationships.

I N the foreword to *Explorations in Interpersonal Communication*, G. R. Miller (1976) wrote that a "symbiotic" link exists between interpersonal communication and relationship development, such that one cannot discuss one topic without mentioning the other (p. 15). Certainly Miller's observation has been reflected in the research on interpersonal communication published in the past three decades, as chronicled in articles (e.g., Burgoon & Hale's [1984] extensive review of "fundamental topoi" of relational communication), scholarly books (e.g., Duck's [1994] examination of the way communication constitutes relationships), textbooks (e.g., Knapp & Vangelisti's [1992] emphasis on relational development and decay), and journals (e.g., the *Journal of Social and Personal Relationships,* whose list of editorial board members reveals a sizable proportion of human communication scholars).

The symbiotic link between interpersonal communication and relational development can naturally obscure the differences between communication processes and relationship properties. Some scholars have sought to specify the boundaries between relating and relationships (e.g., Cappella, 1987). In addition, the lion's

---

AUTHORS' NOTE: We wish to thank Michael Roloff and two anonymous reviewers for their helpful suggestions regarding this chapter.

Correspondence: Daniel J. Canary, Hugh Downs School of Human Communication, Arizona State University, Tempe, AZ 85287-1205; e-mail dan.canary@asu.edu

share of research examining the communication-relationship link over the past 30 years has focused on types of communication that people use to escalate or de-escalate their personal involvements, for instance, self-disclosure (e.g., Altman & Taylor, 1973) and relational initiation and termination strategies (e.g., Baxter & Philpot, 1982). Although the field's focus on the communication-relationship link has not been universal, it has prompted some scholars to question the presumption that forms of communication such as self-disclosure work largely in the service of developing relationships (e.g., Parks, 1982). In addition, the issue of how communication functions to *maintain* ongoing personal relationships has been treated as a secondary concern.

With Ayres's (1983) work seeking to uncover communicative strategies that keep a relationship stable at a particular level of intimacy, communication scholars began to focus their attention on message behaviors that clearly function to maintain personal relationships. Scholars took it as a given that people spend more time maintaining their relationships than in creating or dissolving them; hence we should muster the same concerted effort to examine how communication functions in that potentially longer, more commonly experienced span of time (Duck, 1988). Since the mid-1980s, and in increasing numbers, researchers have examined links between relating and relationships in terms of maintenance strategies and activities (e.g., Baxter & Simon, 1993; Bell, Daly, & Gonzalez, 1987; Canary & Stafford, 1992; Dindia, 1994; Dindia & Baxter, 1987; Ragsdale, 1996; Shea & Pearson, 1986; Stafford & Canary, 1991; Waldron, 1991).

Definitions of relational maintenance vary. Dindia and Canary (1993) specify that relational maintenance is conceptualized in four broad ways: (a) keeping a relationship stable, in existence; (b) keeping a relationship in a satisfactory condition; (c) retaining a desired level of a relational feature, such as intimacy and commitment; and (d) repairing a relationship that has seen tough times. As we note later, those adopting a dialectical view argue that change inheres in relationships and that other terms (e.g., *sustainment*) should be used instead of *maintenance* (Montgomery, 1993; Rawlins, 1994). Given the broad scope implicated in these definitions, researchers who examine the communication-relationship link in terms of maintenance activities risk the indictment that they (a) cannot possibly circumscribe the many ways that communication functions to maintain relationships or (b) assume too much variation is explained by communicative behaviors that ostensibly function for maintenance purposes. On the first point, we believe that the term *maintenance* indicates an important, albeit broad and complex, set of phenomena that necessarily implicate communicative processes at work. As with any other broadly defined topic, one must rely on the relevance-determining nature of theory to provide focus. On the second point, we hold that both communicative and noncommunicative activities work to maintain relationships. Accordingly, one task of communication scholars is to articulate how the most salient communication behaviors combine or collide with noncommunicative features to maintain personal relationships.

To demonstrate how researchers have accomplished the above two tasks, we review below four programs of research that represent three alternative approaches to the study of communication and relational maintenance: social exchange, interactional, and dialectical. Of all social exchange orientations, interdependence theory and equity theory provide the framework for two programs of research specifically concerned with relational maintenance processes and outcomes. Next, the interactional approach (as labeled by Gottman, 1979) focuses on conversational behavior as a means to understand relational stability—that is, how communicative patterns reflect stable marriages versus unstable ones. Finally, as the newest of the three to be applied to interpersonal communication, the dialectical approach attends to contradictory but mutually necessary requirements of relational life, for instance, the tensions embedded in the interdependence-autonomy dialectic. As we indicate, this approach has focused on relational maintenance as change, especially on the ways that people manage ongoing fluctuations between opposing facets of relationships.

We do not attempt to represent all of the literature on communication and relational maintenance. Our objective in this review is to reflect how various sustained programs of research bring insight to the way communication functions to maintain ongoing, personal involvements. Thus, for instance, we do not examine research on maintaining superior-subordinate work relationships, group member maintenance behaviors, or social, nonintimate relationships. Nor do we review the literature that delineates relational maintenance strategies, because this literature does not consistently reflect the progression of theoretically based research programs (see Dindia, 1994, for a clear review of maintenance strategies).

As we show in the following sections, the role of communication in maintaining personal relationships differs in fundamental ways among programs of research. For each program of research, we first present its basic assumptions and then offer our assessment. Following the review of each program, we conclude with a few suggestions regarding the direction of this domain of inquiry.

SOCIAL EXCHANGE AND
RELATIONAL MAINTENANCE

Social exchange as a theoretical net contains several approaches to the study of interpersonal communication and relationships (for a review, see Roloff, 1981). Whereas virtually all social exchange theories have informed interpersonal communication in general, interdependence theory as outlined by Rusbult and colleagues in the "investment model" (e.g., Rusbult, 1987; Rusbult, Drigotas, & Verette, 1994) and equity theory as utilized by Canary and Stafford (1992, 1993, 1994, 1997) have delineated the role of communication in maintaining relationships.

Adapting Interdependence Theory:
Rusbult's Investment Model

Kelley and Thibaut (1978; Kelley, 1979) provide the formulations of interdependence theory. In brief, this theory holds that people find relationships satisfying when they are rewarding relative to existing standards (i.e., comparison levels, or CL) and stable when they match well against alternative partners or activities (i.e., comparison levels for alternatives, or CLalt). Accordingly, people determine rewards against costs by using CL and CLalt as frames of reference. For instance, one might be involved in a wonderful relationship but remain dissatisfied due to a previous involvement that one now idealizes; or one might be in a dissatisfying relationship but depend on it because desirable and feasible alternatives do not appear on the horizon. Interdependence theory also stresses that people control each other in terms of their unilateral or bilateral dependence (Kelley, 1979). Areas of control include individual reactions (i.e., reflexive control), behaviors (i.e., behavioral control), and outcomes (i.e., fate control). Accordingly, a relationship can be characterized in terms of whether one person dominates the other (i.e., unilateral reflexive control, unilateral behavioral control, and/or unilateral fate control) or the relationship is mutually defined in terms of its interdependence (i.e., bilateral reflexive control, bilateral behavioral control, and bilateral fate control). Thus interdependence theory explains the nature and structure of people's reliance on each other.

Rusbult and colleagues have extended interdependence theory to the area of relational maintenance with the investment model (Rusbult, 1987; Rusbult & Buunk, 1993; Rusbult et al., 1994). The heart of the investment model is the individual's *commitment level,* where *commitment* references the extent to which a person wants to remain in the relationship and has feelings of attachment. Indeed, Rusbult et al. (1994) call commitment "macromotive," insofar as a person's commitment level theoretically filters the effects of interdependence on maintenance processes. In other words, the investment model holds that (a) people assess a relationship in terms of its rewards and costs (i.e., comparison levels, such as a previous partner), quality of alternatives (e.g., number of potentials in the field of eligibles, new career), and investments already made (e.g., time, effort, mutual friends). (b) These three factors then determine how committed an individual is. As one might anticipate, higher levels of satisfaction and investment and lower levels of desired alternatives are said to associate positively with commitment. (c) Commitment level then affects maintenance activities. Figure 8.1 summarizes the investment model's description of maintenance processes.

According to Rusbult et al. (1994), maintenance activities involve the following factors: decision to remain with one's partner, tendencies to accommodate, derogation of alternatives, willingness to sacrifice, and perceived superiority of one's relationship. By definition, decision to remain reflects one's commitment. Tendencies to accommodate are the positive minus negative responses that partners employ during relational trouble, and they most directly implicate communicative

Interdependence Factors   Mediating Factor   Maintenance Activities

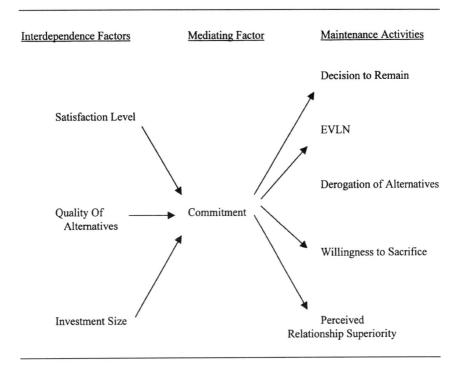

Figure 8.1. Investment Model of Relationship Maintenance
SOURCE: Rusbult et al. (1994, p. 124). Reprinted by permission of Caryl Rusbult.

responses. Responses to relational problems—exit, voice, loyalty, and neglect—vary according to their activity versus passivity as well as valence (constructive versus destructive): *exit* is active and destructive, *voice* is active and constructive, *loyalty* is passive and constructive, and *neglect* is passive and destructive. Exit behaviors include threatening the partner, intimidating the partner, and leaving; voice entails the use of disclosure and discussion; loyalty involves waiting and hoping for things to improve; and neglect behaviors include stonewalling and avoidance of the partner. Thus the sum of accommodating behaviors can be reflected in voice and loyalty minus neglect and exit responses.

As one might expect, commitment is positively associated with tendencies to accommodate one's partner in terms of loyalty and voice, and commitment is negatively associated with exit and neglect (e.g., Rusbult, 1983; Rusbult, Johnson, & Morrow, 1986; Rusbult, Verette, Whitney, Slovick, & Lipkus, 1991). In addition, willingness to sacrifice on behalf of the partner has been found to be most positively linked to one's commitment. For instance, in a series of six studies, commitment predicted an average 28% of the variance in such activities as forfeiting one's personally important activities for the partner, engaging in undesirable activities for the sake of the relationship, and increasing one's rate of stair-stepping to earn money for the partner (Van Lange et al., 1997).

Tendencies to accommodate the partner are also affected by features that constitute commitment (Rusbult, 1987). For instance, neglect is likely to be used when satisfaction, investment, and alternatives are low, whereas exit is more likely to be used when satisfaction and investment are low but alternatives are high. Likewise, the use of voice is likely when satisfaction, investment, and alternatives are high, whereas loyalty is a preferred response in relationships marked by high satisfaction and investment but low alternatives. Moreover, connections to individual-difference factors, such as psychological sex and self-esteem, are thought to be mediated by the relational factors of satisfaction, investment, and availability of alternatives (Rusbult et al., 1991, p. 57). For example, perspective taking (i.e., ability to understand the partner from the partner's point of view) theoretically increases accommodation behaviors only to the extent that it also links positively to satisfaction and investments (or associates negatively with viable alternatives) (Rusbult et al., 1991).

An important process-related element in Rusbult's model concerns the manner in which "transformation of motivation" occurs (i.e., the desire to behave in a competitive manner is replaced by a cooperative orientation). Transformation of motivation is critical when the rewards and costs of interdependent parties conflict; Rusbult and colleagues emphasize situations wherein one person behaves poorly so as to affect the partner in a negative manner and the partner can respond in like manner (which would result in a similar but negative outcome matrix for both people) or in a more relationally proactive manner (which reflects the transformation of motivation) (Yovetich & Rusbult, 1994). Studies show (a) that people are more likely to engage in more destructive ways when they do not consider the effects on or potential outcomes for their partners or relationships (Yovetich & Rusbult, 1994), (b) that highly interdependent partners are more likely to transform their motivation to accommodate (Rusbult et al., 1991), but (c) that people require more time to consider constructive (versus destructive) responses to their partners' negative behaviors (Yovetich & Rusbult, 1994). These findings indicate that the transformation of motivation to respond in positive ways to partner negativity requires thoughtfulness and is more likely to occur in long-term, committed relationships.

Research also indicates that people engage in psychological distortion to enhance their relationships when commitment level is high (Rusbult & Buunk, 1993; Rusbult et al., 1994). That is, people devalue third-party alternatives, especially when the third party is attractive and commitment is high. As mentioned, committed people appear more willing to sacrifice self-interest for the sake of the partner. Also, committed individuals tend to perceive their relationship as superior to others of its kind (Rusbult et al., 1994). In other words, a committed person is more likely to believe that a current relationship is better than other entanglements.

Assessment of the Investment Model

Rusbult's development of the investment model represents an important contribution to the study of communication and relational maintenance. Both the presentation and adaptation of Kelley and Thibaut's (1978) interdependence theory reflect the assumptions of social exchange thinking and provide clear extensions to communicative behavior. Although Rusbult's exit-voice-loyalty-neglect (EVLN) typology is derived from organizational literature, it appears appropriate to the study of personal relationships. It is also important to note that Rusbult specifies psychological processes (e.g., derogation of alternatives) that combine with communicative strategies to keep relationships intact.

Although the investment model has been largely accepted by communication scholars (e.g., Metts & Cupach, 1990), not all research has supported its predictions. Assessing the effects of relational factors (i.e., satisfaction, alternatives, and commitment) on the satisfaction of 30 dating couples, Sacher and Fine (1996) did not find support for the investment model. They found that relationship satisfaction and quality of alternatives did predict commitment for both male and female partners when measured contemporaneously, but they did not find significant associations between commitment (measured at T1) and relational satisfaction measured 6 months later (T2). Sacher and Fine did find that a female lack of alternatives at T1 (and to a lesser extent male satisfaction at T1) predicted couple satisfaction at T2. However, we should note that Sacher and Fine did not assess investment size nor any of the maintenance activities, including the interaction behaviors of exit, voice, loyalty, and neglect. Accordingly, they did not test how maintenance activities at T1 might affect relational factors (including investment size) at T2.

As we have mentioned, commitment is central to the investment model. Rusbult et al. (1991) have provided evidence that commitment largely mediates the associations between relational factors and accommodating behaviors (voice and loyalty minus exit and neglect). Using regression analyses, Rusbult et al. found that most of the unique variance in accommodation was due to commitment, with only 17 of 54 residual effects significant or marginal. However, using path analysis, they found that a few individual-difference factors had direct effects (i.e., effects beyond those mediated by commitment) as well as indirect effects on accommodation behaviors. Specifically, partner perspective taking (i.e., taking the role of one's partner), psychological femininity, and centrality of the relationship to one's identity all directly affected accommodation (in addition to affecting accommodation indirectly through commitment). Moreover, Rusbult et al. (1991) found that a higher comparison level was *positively* associated with commitment; they interpret this finding to reflect a "self-fulfilling effect: People who expect a lot out of their relationships appear to behave in ways that confirm those expectations" (p. 74). An alternative interpretation is that people who have high comparison levels have tested prototypes for building satisfying relationships; that is, people with positive relational histories have learned how to develop and maintain satisfactory involvements. Regardless, this last finding suggests that the role of comparison levels in predicting commitment needs rethinking.

Other research efforts that use Rusbult's concepts have reported mixed results as well. For example, in an examination of the chilling effect (i.e., withholding irritations), Cloven and Roloff (1993) predicted that people low in commitment and alternatives would withhold complaints when dealing with an aggressive partner. But they found that people low in commitment and alternatives voiced more irritations than did their counterparts, possibly because "these individuals do not seem to value their assets very highly; perhaps as a consequence, they are not concerned about the negative repercussions of confronting powerful partners" (p. 214).

Finally, EVLN behaviors apply most to responses to relational problems and partner misbehavior. As responses to problematic events, the EVLN typology probably does not exhaust the garden-variety attempts at maintenance that have been located in other research (for a review, see Dindia, 1994). These would include such activities as sharing activities, acting positive and cheerful, and discussion about the future. Sprecher, Metts, Burleson, Hatfield, and Thompson (1995), for example, examined the manner in which three domains of expressiveness (companionship, supportiveness, and sexual expressiveness) are linked to commitment. They found moderate to strong associations between these domains and commitment (rs = .28 to .56), and satisfaction largely mediated the effects of these three domains on commitment (i.e., satisfaction appeared to be directly related to commitment, consistent with Rusbult's model). The point is that such expressive behaviors probably act as "intrinsic investments in the relationship" (Sprecher et al., 1995, p. 205) that increase one's satisfaction and commitment to the partner.

In brief, Rusbult's investment model predicts that satisfaction, investment, and stability lead to commitment, which in turn predicts relational maintenance activities. Accommodation tendencies (EVLN) and psychological distortions represent maintenance activities, so Rusbult's theory provides the language to combine and perhaps compare the efficacy of communicative and psychological mechanisms to maintain relationships. In its focus on partner's interdependence, the investment model presumes that interdependence in the form of satisfaction, investments, and alternatives sufficiently predicts commitment, which then affects maintenance processes. In this manner, commitment is conceptualized as an internal mediating factor and maintenance behaviors are conceptualized as outcomes. As we see in the discussion of the next program born from a social exchange approach, satisfaction may not be enough to predict maintenance activities, and commitment can be viewed as a consequence rather than as an antecedent of communicative behavior.

Equity and Relational Maintenance Strategies

Equity theory has long served interpersonal communication scholars seeking to explain people's use of relational communicative strategies (e.g., Cody's [1982] study of relational termination strategies). Equity is based on the *principle of distributive justice,* which holds that rewards should be distributed according to who provides the most inputs into the dyadic or group system (Deutsch, 1985). The "equity formula" indicates that equitable relationships exist when the ratios of outcomes to inputs are the same for both partners: When the outcome/input ratios are the same, then the relationship is equitable; when one person has a greater outcome/input ratio than his or her partner, that person is *overbenefited*; when one person experiences a lower outcome/input ratio compared to the partner, that person is *underbenefited.* As with other social exchange approaches, equity theory holds that people attempt to maximize their rewards and reduce their costs. However, according to equity theory, people do so in a fair manner, and they seek to restore equity in cases where the relationship has become inequitable (for reviews, see Hatfield, Traupmann, Sprecher, Utne, & Hay, 1985; Roloff, 1981; Van Yperen & Buunk, 1990).

The most satisfying relationships, theoretically, are those in which partners obtain desired rewards *and* enjoy equitable outcomes, versus partners in under- or overbenefited involvements (Hatfield et al., 1985). Overbenefited people (versus equitably treated people) are less content due to their disenchantment and guilt, whereas underbenefited people are the least content of all because they do not have the rewards that their overbenefited partners obtain (Hatfield et al., 1985). Sprecher (1986) assessed partners' reactions to being overbenefited and underbenefited. She found that neither overbenefitedness nor underbenefitedness was desirable, but being underbenefited was more dramatically associated with negative emotions, such as hostility, anger, depression, and sadness.

In the face of inequity, and especially when underbenefited, people take steps to restore equity (Hatfield et al., 1985). Adams (1965) has suggested some of the methods that people use to restore equity (see also Walster [Hatfield], Berscheid, & Walster, 1983). Adams indicates that an underbenefited person can restore equity, for instance, by decreasing own inputs (e.g., stop cooking dinner every night), increasing own outcomes (e.g., going out with friends), changing the partner's behavior to increase his or her inputs (e.g., persuading the partner to shop for groceries and to cook more), psychologically distorting the inequity (e.g., changing the bases of evaluation from one's partner to one's unhappy friends), punishing the partner (e.g., having an affair), or "leaving the field" (e.g., separation). Adams argues that simply not providing inputs is the most efficient way to resolve one's underbenefitedness, that psychological distortions are difficult to sustain over time, and that punishing the partner and leaving the field constitute radical and perhaps desperate measures to restore equity.

Equity theory provides the language for inferring a necessary bridge between one partner's inputs and the other partner's outcomes: In a two-person system, the inputs offered by one person to the relationship function simultaneously as outcomes for the other person (Davidson, Balswick, & Halverson, 1983; Michaels, Edwards, & Acock, 1984; Van Yperen & Buunk, 1990). This point is important to the extent that equity might match equality (i.e., both people receiving identical outcomes regardless of inputs). However, because equity is perceived, one partner might not interpret the other's attempts at maintaining the relationship as an outcome for the first partner (e.g., one person's cleaning the house is not interpreted as a favor but as his or her performing a [past due] obligation to clean up his or her own messes).

Canary and Stafford (1992, 1993, 1994, 1997; Stafford & Canary, 1991) adopted equity theory in conceptualizing relational maintenance strategies as inputs that one offers as well as outcomes that one receives. Stafford and Canary (1991) first derived a taxonomy of maintenance behaviors based on the maintenance literature and open-ended essays on how married people maintain their marriages to their satisfaction. Factor analyzing the results, Stafford and Canary found five maintenance strategies: *positivity,* or acting cheerful when not, avoiding criticism, and the like; *openness,* or directly discussing the nature of the relationship; *assurances,* or persuading the partner of one's love, as well as providing commitment and comfort when needed; *networks,* or relying on friends and family members; and *sharing tasks,* or doing one's fair share of the work that needs to be done. It is important to note that these factors were not theoretically derived, so they represent maintenance strategies in a more generic sense. For example, Burleson and Samter's (1994) research shows that providing comfort represents an important skill in maintaining friendships, apart from an equity formulation.

Canary and Stafford (1992, 1993) have argued and found that people in equitable involvements offer maintenance strategies the most, as opposed to people who perceive their situation as overbenefited or underbenefited. In their 1992 study, they found that wives' reports of equity (i.e., relationships that were grouped according to the wives' reports of equity, using difference scores from the Marital Comparison Level Index, or MCLI) differentially predicted both wives' and husbands' reports of partners' positivity (acting happy when not), openness (directly discussing the relationship), assurances (comforting the partner), and social networks (inclusion of friends and family). On the other hand, husbands' reports of equity affected perceptions of the partner sharing tasks (doing chores) to maintain the relationship, in addition to positivity and assurances. In addition, self-reported inequity combined with perceptions of partners' maintenance strategies to affect important relationship characteristics, such as commitment.

Canary and Stafford (1993, 1994) have presented other theoretical propositions that extend this foundation to maintenance activities. These include the notion that maintenance strategies vary according to the type of relationship (i.e., friends, lovers, relatives, and so on) and the development of the relationship (Canary, Stafford, Hause, & Wallace, 1993). For example, Stafford and Canary (1991) found that partners in the most affectionate stages (i.e., engaged, seriously dating) perceived more openness than did married partners or people who were casually dating. In addition, Canary and Stafford (1993, 1994) have argued that noninteractive processes (e.g., personality factors, such as locus of control for problem solving) complement interactive processes (maintenance strategies) to bring about desired relational characteristics. In addition, equity predicts relational maintenance activities, and these, in turn, lead to relational characteristics including commitment, control mutuality, and liking. Canary and Stafford's view of commitment is identical to Rusbult's, although they do not view commitment as an internal mediating factor. *Control mutuality* refers to the extent to which both partners agree about who has the right to influence the other (Morton et al., 1976), and it resembles Kelley's (1979) notion of bilaterality of control. *Liking* refers to one partner's admiration of the other, as reflected in Rubin's (1973) conceptualization of the term. Figure 8.2 summarizes Canary and Stafford's model of relational maintenance.

Assessment of the Equity Model of Maintenance

The equity model of maintenance as presented by Canary and Stafford assumes that people are aware of inputs and outcomes and that relational maintenance strategies are considered in the equation. Not all scholars agree. Some people are said to adopt a communal orientation, in lieu of one that is mindful of inputs and outcomes (Mills & Clark, 1982). A communal approach is often seen as more functional than an equity approach. For instance, Van Lange et al. (1997) argue that transformation of motivation cannot be explained by rules such as the principle of distributive justice: "Thus it seems likely that partners' concerns derive from considerations other than justice—considerations that encompass genuine concern for the well-being of a relationship or partner and that may be embodied in such motives as commitment or in processes involving merged identity or communal orientation" (p. 1390). The point that people consider more than their own rewards and costs (i.e., that they undergo transformation of motivation) is well taken. At the same time, equity theorists would hold that inequitable arrangements wear on the parties over time and lead to relational disenchantment and (perhaps) dissolution. In addition, intimate partners develop more sophisticated modes of exchange over time that evade the tit-for-tat reconciliation implied by those who argue that relationships should be more communal (see Roloff, 1978).

Stafford and Canary (1991) hold that relational characteristics can function as predictors of maintenance behaviors in a recursive manner. In other words, relational outcomes can serve as predictors of future maintenance activities. However, in a longitudinal test of this proposition using partial cross-lagged panel correlations, Canary, Semic, and Stafford (1996) found that married partners' maintenance behaviors and relational outcomes did not predict each other over time; relational outcomes at T1 did not predict maintenance behaviors at T2 (a month later) or T3 (a month following T2), nor did maintenance behaviors at T1 predict relational characteristics at T2 or T3. Nor did the T2 relational factors predict the T3 maintenance behaviors. Instead, maintenance behaviors and relational outcomes were uniquely correlated only when measured at the same time. The authors interpret this pattern of results as support for the construct validity of their proactive maintenance strategies, because it appears that the effects of maintenance activities last only so long and then diminish, as one might expect "maintenance" behav-

Antecedent Conditions ———▶	Maintenance Activities ———▶	Relational Outcomes
Equity	Positivity (+)	Commitment
Underbenefited (-)	Openness (+/-)	Control Mutuality
Equitably Treated (+)	Assurances (+)	Liking
Overbenefited (-)	Social Networks (+)	
Relational Type/History	Sharing Tasks (+)	
Personality Factors		

Figure 8.2. Canary and Stafford's Model
SOURCE: Canary and Stafford (1994).

iors to do. Still, the reciprocal causal link between maintenance strategies and relational characteristics was not supported.

Questioning the utility of the equity model, Ragsdale (1996) claims that Canary and Stafford's (1992) results are ambiguous to the extent that each of the univariate tests did not reveal significant findings that supported the multivariate tests (apparently assuming that each univariate test must reflect the multivariate test). Ragsdale holds that interdependence theory, versus equity theory, could predict the five maintenance strategies of positivity, openness, assurances, tasks, and networks. More specifically, Ragsdale argues that satisfaction, defined in terms of interdependence theory, is sufficient to predict maintenance behavior, but that equity apart from satisfaction is an insufficient explanation. We should observe here that presuming that equity excludes satisfaction does not reflect equity theory accurately.

Ragsdale (1996) found no multivariate or univariate support for his argument when testing the linear associations between the Marital Comparison Level Index and maintenance strategy use. Unfortunately, Ragsdale did not explore the curvilinear relationship between the MCLI and maintenance strategies, which Canary and Stafford (1992) had done in uncovering significant links between outcomes/inputs and maintenance activities. Hence Ragsdale did not test alternative hypotheses derived from interdependence and equity theories.

In a direct comparison of interdependence and equity theory predictions, Canary and Stafford (1997) found more support for equity theory. When controlling for partners' responses using MANCOVA, Canary and Stafford found that maintenance behaviors were predicted by underbenefited, equitable, and over-benefited groups but not by high, moderate, and low interdependence groups; equitably treated individuals (versus underbenefited people) were most likely to perceive their partners' use of maintenance behaviors. However, using regression techniques (and again controlling for partner responses), Canary and Stafford found support for both interdependence and equity. That is, use of maintenance behaviors was predicted by a lack of underbenefitedness and a lack of overbene-fitedness, in addition to one's satisfaction as measured by the MCLI. Given Canary and Stafford's direct comparison, we believe that support for the general equity proposition remains intact—that is, people are most content in relationships that are rewarding *and* equitable.

In sum, two programs of research regarding relational maintenance processes have been derived from social exchange theory. Again, these two programs do not fully represent the rich and diverse research on interpersonal communication from a social exchange paradigm; nevertheless, they qualify as programmatic efforts on the topic of relational maintenance and communicative behaviors.

These two programs share a few similarities. For instance, both programs view social exchange factors as antecedents to maintenance activities. In Rusbult's investment model, maintenance behaviors are treated as dependent variables that are directly predicted by commitment and indirectly predicted by satisfaction (comparison level), previous investments, and alternatives. In Canary and Stafford's model, maintenance strategies constitute endogenous variables that are directly affected by (in)equity; the maintenance strategies then are said to affect relationship characteristics. Additionally, the two programs rely on some measure of costs. Rusbult calls these "investments" and Canary and Stafford reference these as "inputs."

These two programs also differ. Perhaps most important, Rusbult and associates view commitment as macromotive, whereas Canary and Stafford view commit-ment as an outcome of maintenance activities. In addition, Rusbult has chosen to derive destructive responses, which she subtracts from the constructive responses to obtain a measure of accommodation. As mentioned, Canary and Stafford derived their taxonomy of maintenance behaviors from other literature on rela-tional maintenance and from open-ended comments about behaviors used for maintenance purposes (Stafford & Canary, 1991), and accordingly have focused virtually all of their efforts on proactive and constructive maintenance strategies. Thus Canary and Stafford's research on the connection between equity and rela-tional maintenance ignores some of the negative, although probably less com-monly used, maintenance behaviors that have been reported elsewhere (e.g., Canary et al., 1993; Roloff & Cloven, 1994).

Additionally, and as one might anticipate, the assumption of distributive justice (i.e., social systems should have similar reward/cost ratios) separates these two models. Rusbult and colleagues hold that the transformation of motivation to behave in a constructive fashion in response to partner negativity is a revealing and critically important element of relational maintenance, and this transformation cannot be explained by close adherence to fairness.

INTERACTION AS THE BASIS OF RELATIONAL MAINTENANCE: GOTTMAN'S ASSESSMENT OF RELATIONAL STABILITY

Emphasizing an interactional perspective, Gottman (1994) has compiled his views on how communication affects relational stability. The term *interactional* refers to the manner in which the exchange of messages defines a relationship, most typically in order to separate functional from dysfunctional systems (Gottman, 1979). Such an approach is certainly not unique to Gottman (e.g., Courtright, Millar, & Rogers-Millar, 1979; Margolin & Wampold, 1981; Revenstorf, Hahlweg, Schindler, & Vogel, 1984; Ting-Toomey, 1983). However, the concentrated effort to examine the communication-relationship link in terms of specifying maintenance processes is perhaps unique to Gottman. As the following material indicates, Gottman's model informs relational maintenance processes by indicating what partners should *not* do perhaps more than what they should do to sustain a marriage.

Gottman's Causal Model of Relational Conflict

Gottman's theory reflects a causal process model that specifies alternative paths that satisfied versus dissatisfied married partners take. Gottman (1994) argues that marital partners' negative behavior causes a shift in perceptions of each other that lead to unfavorable beliefs about each other. Gottman further structures his theory on the framework of the "cascade model," where first one observes a "decline in marital satisfaction, which leads to consideration of separation or divorce, which leads to separation, which leads to divorce" (p. 88). The question concerns what might initially lead to the perceptual shifts, and the answer stresses how people use various negative and positive messages in conflict and how their partners respond cognitively and physiologically.

As Gottman (1994) has reviewed, negative message behavior (e.g., sarcasm, accusations, defensiveness) is more predictive of relational stability than is positive behavior (e.g., offering and seeking disclosure, humor). Additionally, the ratio of positive messages to negative messages indicates the extent to which partners remain in "balance"; satisfied couples have a 5:1 positive-to-negative ratio, whereas dissatisfied couples have a 1:1 positive-to-negative ratio. According to Gottman, negative conflict behaviors lead to emotional reactions that he calls *flooding*, or feelings of being "surprised, overwhelmed, and disorganized by your partner's expression of negative emotions" (p. 21). Four negative behaviors—which Gottman calls the Four Horsemen of the Apocalypse—are particularly corrosive and are hypothesized to occur in a general sequence: initial complaining/

criticizing, which leads to contempt, which leads to defensiveness, which leads to stonewalling (p. 415). These negative behaviors lead to an extreme experience of flooding that Gottman calls *diffuse physiological arousal,* which is indicated by increased blood pressure, heart rate, and perspiration, as well as other "fight versus flight" symptoms (Gottman, 1990, 1994; Levenson & Gottman, 1983, 1985).

Not only do dissatisfied (versus satisfied) couples engage in more negative behaviors, they also tend to reciprocate those behaviors for longer periods of time (e.g., Gottman, 1979; Margolin & Wampold, 1981; Ting-Toomey, 1983). The reason for the longer reciprocation of negative messages and emotions between partners in dissatisfied marriages is again explained by individual physiological responses to negativity. Gottman and colleagues have argued that negative messages become "absorbing," such that unhappy partners tend to focus more on the negative features of a message, whereas happy partners tend to focus more on the implied request for repair that might be contained in a negative message (Gottman, 1994; Levenson, Carstensen, & Gottman, 1994; Levenson & Gottman, 1983, 1985). For instance, the criticism "You watch too much TV" can be interpreted as a personal attack or as a request for attention. Dissatisfied partners would likely use the former interpretation, whereas satisfied partners would rely on the latter interpretation and attempt to rectify the situation. As Gottman (1994) argues: "The response to the negativity continues for long chains of reciprocated negative affect in dissatisfied marriages. Negativity as an absorbing state implies that all these social processes [e.g., functional use of metacommunication] have less of a chance of working, because what people attend to and respond to is the negativity" (p. 64).

Gottman (1982) has identified several patterns of negative reciprocity. These include exchanging complaints (i.e., complaint-countercomplaint), reciprocation of negative metacommunication, reflections of negative mind reading, and proposal-counterproposal without any acknowledgment of the initial proposal. Other patterns of negative reciprocity have also been uncovered (e.g., Christensen & Heavey, 1990; Revenstorf et al., 1984; Ting-Toomey, 1983). Gottman and Levenson (1992; see also Gottman, 1994; Levenson & Gottman, 1983, 1985) have shown that partners reciprocate negative physiology that coincides with their negative behavior. The reciprocation of negative physiological responses is called *physiological linkage.*

At a critical juncture, partners begin to interpret each other's negative behaviors as stemming from global, stable, internal, and blameworthy causes versus specific, unstable, external, and praiseworthy causes (see also Fincham, Bradbury, & Scott, 1990). Readers familiar with attribution theory will recognize that the dimension of *globality* refers to how many issues an explanation covers; *stability* refers to an enduring trait of the individual; and *internality refers* to a property of the communicator. Accordingly, one partner interprets the other partner's complaints, criticisms, and defensiveness as arising from permanent features of the partner that pervade several areas of the relationship (e.g., "inconsiderate" explains why he or she is perpetually late, never writes, does not cook, does not vote), and such interpretations prompt the first partner to question his or her feelings for other (Fincham et al., 1990). These reactions coincide with other research on how dissatisfied (versus satisfied) couples defensively interpret their partners' complaints. For example, Alberts (1988) found that dissatisfied couples (versus satisfied couples) were more likely to use and reciprocate complaints about the personal characteristics of the partner. The perceptual shift from benign to hostile attributions reflects "an abrupt flip in the perception of [one's own] well being. . . . This is the initial catastrophic change" (Gottman, 1994, p. 335).

According to Gottman (1994), a person perceives his or her partner's conflict messages in one of two ways—in a benign (neutral or positive) manner or in a self-defensive manner, which is a natural response to negative messages. In terms of the self-defensive mode, two common reactions stem from the partner's negativity (especially criticisms/complaints, contempt, defensiveness, and stonewalling): "(a) hurt, disappointment, and perceived attack, the 'innocent victim' perception in which a person is in a stance of warding off perceived attack, or (b) hurt, disappointment, and 'righteous indignation,' in which a person is in the mode of rehearsing retaliation" (p. 412). Continued negativity and perceptual reactions of these types establish a "set point" that positive, prosocial behaviors cannot budge. The negative behaviors cause one to feel flooded and to make harsh (global and stable) attributions for partner behaviors, which leads to distance and isolation, recasting the history of the marriage, and dissolution. Satisfied couples, on the other hand, "balance" negative behaviors with positive ones and experience a sense of well-being. The phases of Gottman's model are presented in Figure 8.3.

In summary, then, partners' negative behaviors and reciprocation of negative messages corrode the relationship. Negative conflict behaviors produce diffuse physiological arousal and negative physiological linkage to the partner. In a self-protective move, one begins to assign global, stable, and internal explanations to the partner's negative behavior. These assessments lead one to question one's satisfaction and, eventually, one's desire to maintain the marriage.

Assessment of Gottman's Model

It is difficult to think of a more concerted effort to bridge communication behaviors to relational outcomes. By this assertion, we mean that Gottman's (1994) summary work reveals precision in measuring actual message behavior between spouses and linking these behaviors to relational dissolution years later. In addition, the creation of techniques to measure and to analyze various features of messages and their impacts, such as verbal messages (CISS codes), nonverbal cues, responses to one's previous messages, and physiological responses to messages over time, allows for empirical support of the theory.

Gottman clearly depends on interaction as the means by which people maintain their marriages. Indeed, as a corollary to his theory, Gottman (1994) has developed

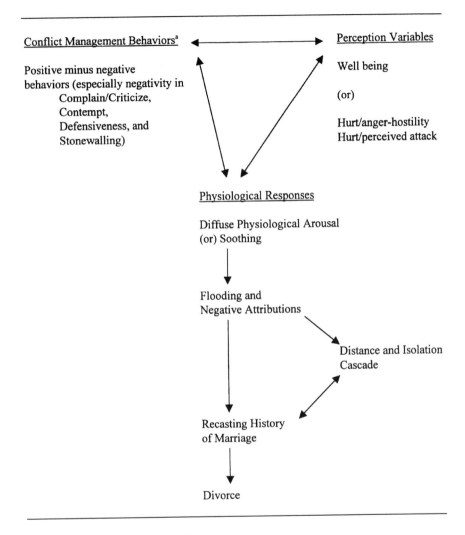

Figure 8.3. Gottman's Model of Dissolution
SOURCE: Adapted from Gottman (1994, p. 370), by permission of Lawrence Erlbaum and Associates.
a. Gottman also references these as "flow" variables.

three couple types that resemble Fitzpatrick's (1988) couple types; however, Gottman's types are derived entirely from the way they manage conflict discussions. Stressing interaction between spouses, Gottman pinpoints corrosive communicative behaviors. Accordingly, he provides concrete ways to maintain marriage as a means to prevent the cascade to isolation from gaining momentum, which he calls "minimal marital therapy" (Gottman, 1994, pp. 430-440).

Gottman does appear to overreach his results at times. This is most apparent when he makes inferences about sex differences when no tests for such differences have been performed (e.g., Gottman & Carrere, 1994). Prescriptions regarding sex differences cannot rely on tests that are not consistently performed. Moreover, and based on these presumed sex differences, Gottman appears to hold husbands (versus wives) more responsible for maintenance activities; that is, advice regarding who should pay attention more to the partner's needs speaks to changes in husbands more than in wives (e.g., husbands should not avoid conflict and should seek to help more in sharing tasks).

In addition, Gottman (1994) might stress too much the findings from a study conducted by Gottman and Krokoff (1989). Specifically, Gottman and Krokoff found wife contempt and anger to be negatively associated with marital satisfaction when these were assessed at the same time. But these same incidents of wife contempt and anger were positively associated with wife satisfaction measured 3 years later. Gottman (1994) interprets these findings as support for the view that one should welcome expressions of anger for their long-term benefit (e.g., p. 414). Two reservations come to mind with regard to this prescription. First, this is the only study to find that one person's intemperate behavior associates with positive relational functioning years later, and as such should be viewed with caution. Second, it is possible that the positive correlation with increased satisfaction reflects an artifactual relationship. Because anger and lower satisfaction were positively correlated at T1, increases in satisfaction at T2 might also reflect wife anger at T1. In other words, increases in satisfaction would have to include and thereby reflect that angry wives' low satisfaction scores at T1 would probably be higher at T2.

Finally, Gottman (1994) has offered several hypotheses to explain certain results (e.g., sex differences stem from different forms of play). Although the hypotheses are intriguing, they do not add to the model in making coherent links among factors. Despite these reservations, Gottman's work is foundational for scholars wanting to connect communicative behaviors and responses to relational outcomes. Its attention to micro-level analyses of communication and associations with perceptions and physiological reactions are in many ways models for how researchers should assess ties between communicative patterns and relationship properties (Cappella, 1987).

A DIALECTICAL APPROACH
TO RELATIONAL MAINTENANCE

Although relatively new as applied to interpersonal communication, the dialectical perspective of Baxter and others serves as a thorough approach to relational communication inquiry, particularly within the domain of relational maintenance (Baxter, 1988, 1990, 1993, 1994; Baxter & Montgomery, 1996; Baxter & Simon, 1993; Baxter & Widenmann, 1993). In this section we seek to address a dialectical view of relational maintenance by offering a conceptual framework that explains maintenance dialectically and by presenting our assessment of this approach.

Dialectics as Fundamental to Relating

Opposing tensions might be a fact of life—love and hate, peace and war, birth and death. According to Baxter (1990), such mutually negating, opposing tendencies are equally abundant within personal relationships, such that within a relationship, partners seek both autonomy *and* connection, predictability *and* novelty, openness *and* closedness. Despite the potential abundance of such contradictions, much of the research on relational maintenance has ignored these inherent tensions, favoring logic, functionalism, or formal cause as an appropriate means of explaining and predicting human behavior (Ball, 1979). Although cause/effect as well as either/or theories can and often do offer relational insight, such models can be indicted for significant limitations within the realm of communication and relationships, because social interaction does not follow a logical pattern (Ball, 1979).

Unlike the causal models reviewed above, a dialectical approach posits that people *spiral* between communicative behaviors. Different from a linear or cyclical approach, a spiraling model suggests that relationships often experience redundancy (as opposed to linear cause/effect or cyclical repetition) with similar situations. Further, because people and their relationships also are moving forward in time, elements of context and situation inherently change each experience so that none is repeated exactly. In essence, people act and *re*act while spiraling forward and reshaping reality.

A dialectical perspective attempts to explain the notion that relationships are dynamic processes faced with the continuous management of opposing tendencies, specifically focusing on the question of how relationships operate in the midst of partners' being drawn together as well as pushed apart. The dialectical perspective also holds that a relational entity cannot exist without the fluctuating interplay between its contradictory parts. Whereas other approaches to relational communication, for instance, have tried to isolate these parts, such separation prevents a comprehensive understanding of the whole (Rawlins, 1989).

Dialectical reasoning is not new. Marx, Freud, and Malthus recognized dialectical methods as means of discussing tensions and contradictions within a capitalist economy, social hierarchy, and population growth, respectively (Ball, 1979). Social theorist Mikhail Bakhtin (1981) further extended and reshaped the Marxist idea of dialectic to coin "dialogism," an understanding of what he called "a contradiction-ridden, tension-filled unity of two embattled tendencies" (p. 272). Bakhtin went on to label these tendencies *centripetal* and *centrifugal,* such that the former seeks to draw together and the latter seeks to differentiate. Additionally, Bakhtin specified that these contradictory tendencies are most apparently played out within the communicative behaviors (i.e., "dialogue") established within a given relationship.

Although Bakhtin's focus of dialogism was not personal relationships, Baxter and colleagues (Baxter, 1988, 1990, 1993, 1994; Baxter & Montgomery, 1996; Baxter & Simon, 1993; Baxter & Widenmann, 1993), as well as others (Altman, Vinsel, & Brown, 1981; Cissna, Cox, & Bochner, 1990; Goldsmith, 1990; Maines, 1989; Rawlins, 1989), have adapted a sociological dialectical perspective to the study of interpersonal communication. Because Baxter's understanding of a dialectical perspective has been most readily and systematically applied to relational maintenance, it is important to understand her conceptualization of dialectical relating.

Baxter and Montgomery (1996) view relational dialectics as a perspective, or metatheory, which is a series of assumptions rather than a theory or a hierarchical list of axioms and arguments. Extending Bakhtin's centripetal/centrifugal thinking as well as Cornforth's (1968) and Baxter's (1988) premises of contradiction and process, Baxter and Montgomery (1996; see also Rawlins, 1989) have identified four key assumptions of a dialectical perspective: contradiction, change, praxis, and totality.

Contradiction. A dialectical perspective assumes that interdependent but opposing tensions or contradictions occur regularly within personal relationships, thereby pulling people together and pushing them apart. Significantly, in order to have a contradiction, two opposite poles must exist, but the experience of both poles cannot occur simultaneously. Thus a dialectical contradiction involves interdependent, mutually negative tendencies that cannot be fulfilled completely at the same time (Cornforth, 1968). It is important to note that *contradiction* in the dialectical sense carries no negative association; rather, these tensions are necessary within "healthy" relationships because realization of each opposing pole is necessary to some degree. Notably, although opposition is necessary, it is not enough to support the notion of contradiction without a sense of dynamic interdependence (Baxter & Montgomery, 1996). Applied relationally, partners experience a dynamic current of ebb and flow and thus move between opposing tendencies while trying to fulfill the demands of each pole. As such, relational contradictions are inherent, dynamic, and necessary.

Baxter (1993) has located three primary points of contradiction that are most visible within interpersonal relationships: integration/separation, stability/ change, and expression/privacy. Bakhtin's centripetal/centrifugal influence is visible in that Baxter's primary points of contradiction serve either to unite or to differentiate, with the recognition that both needs are legitimate and relationally essential. Notably, each of the three points of contradiction may be manifested internally within the relationship as well as externally between the relational pair and social others (Ball, 1979). Figure 8.4 presents the dialectical tensions that are external and internal to the relationship (Baxter, 1994).

Change. As with the presence of unified opposites or contradictions, the concept of change is also inherent to a dialectical perspective of relationships. Change, however, also implies the presence of periods of stability (Baxter & Montgomery, 1996). Notably, contradictions act as agents of change, such that if pole A is being fulfilled, pole B is, by nature of opposition, left unfulfilled, thereby creating a tension that leads to the desire for fulfillment of the latter pole. Because both poles cannot be addressed completely at once, tension and change always exist to some degree.

Praxis. The third assumption for relational dialectic involves praxis, the idea that "people are at once actors and objects of their own actions" (Baxter & Montgomery, 1996, p. 12). Simply put, the concept of praxis identifies people as "proactive" and able to make choices about their social behaviors. At the same time, the concept of praxis presumes that humans are also "reactive" to their situations. Only people can realize contradictions; however, these very contradictions create boundaries that cause humans to react. The dialectical perspective, therefore, holds that this proactive/reactive response to contradiction and change mutually influences behavior.

Totality. The concept of totality suggests that one can understand concepts, events, and situations only when they are related or linked with other concepts, events, and situations. As Baxter and Montgomery (1996) state, totality is a "way to think about the world as a process of relations or interdependencies" (p. 15). Thus social life cannot be examined successfully within a vacuum because no such interaction naturally occurs this way; all relationships and interactions are interrelated, overlapping, and mutually evolving. A dialectical perspective attempts to study relationships in such a fashion by attending to the contexts from which aspects of contradiction and change have arisen.

In terms of relational maintenance, we should stress that a dialectical outlook assumes that change, contradiction, and interdependent tensions inhere in relationships (Baxter, 1988, 1990, 1993, 1994; Baxter & Montgomery, 1996; Montgomery, 1993; Rawlins, 1989, 1994). Accordingly, relational partners periodically feel a pull or tension between opposing poles and thus fluctuate between spiraling intervals of satisfaction and dissatisfaction. Thus at least one popular definition—that maintenance involves keeping a relationship in a specific condition or state (Dindia & Canary, 1993)—appears contrary to a dialectical perspective (Montgomery, 1993; Rawlins, 1994).

A dialectical point of view differs radically from other approaches to relational maintenance. Montgomery (1993) argues that studies employing a dialectical approach to relational maintenance offer a more holistic conceptualization of relationships. Thus people should find "maintenance," defined as achieving and keeping a desired state, impossible to achieve in the face of continuous contradiction, change, and tension. It is important to note that in studying the phenomenon of

	Dialectic of Integration/ Separation	Dialectic of Stability/ Change	Dialectic of Expression/ Privacy
Internal Manifesta- tions	Connection/ Autonomy	Predictability /Novelty	Openness/ Closedness
External Manifesta- tions	Inclusion/ Seclusion	Convention- ality/ Uniqueness	Revelation/ Concealment

Figure 8.4. Summary of Internal and External Dialectical Contradictions
SOURCE: Baxter (1994, p. 240). Reprinted by permission of Leslie Baxter.

continuing relationships, researchers should give consideration to contradiction, change, and tension, because these variables affect the means by which couples choose and react to relational maintenance strategies. In this light, *relational maintenance* is an oxymoron. Montgomery (1993) argues that the term *maintenance* seems to counter dialectical thinking because it denotes change as an anomaly rather than as an inherent construct. She suggests that maintenance, when viewed dialectically, be described as relational *sustainment.* We concur with her in principle; however, we will continue to refer to the term *maintenance* as a scientific construct that varies according to the scholars who define it.

Support for a Dialectical Approach
to Relational Maintenance

In every theoretical approach, the researcher must describe the phenomenon under investigation. Researchers applying a dialectical framework have accomplished this goal in the area of interpersonal communication and relational maintenance by identifying dialectics in operation and how people respond to these dialectics. Persons within a relationship are said to experience three central contradictions: autonomy/connectedness, openness/closedness, and predictability/novelty (Baxter, 1988). Although one of the first to study and describe central tensions systematically, Baxter (1988) was not the first to recognize the possibility of dialectical dilemmas in social relating. Altman et al.'s (1981) revision of social penetration theory (Altman & Taylor, 1973) advanced a theoretic understanding of both the openness/closedness and the stability/change dialectics. Altman et al. described openness/closedness, in particular, in terms of privacy or boundary regulation whereby individuals exercise control over the extent to which others may permeate their environment. They contended that the dominance of either openness or closedness is temporary, with individuals fluctuating between the two poles in efforts to adapt situationally.

To continue a relationship, however, partners must somehow manage dialectical tensions. Baxter (1988) has reported four primary strategies used by partners to manage these contradictions: selection (of one pole over another), separation (through either cyclic alternation or topical segmentation), neutralization (through either moderation or disqualification), and reframing (or redefining the problem in terms of dialectical thinking). In a subsequent study, Baxter (1990) discovered that separation, through both topical segmentation and cyclic alternation, exists as the most frequently used strategy to manage relational tensions. According to topical segmentation, couples cope with relational tensions by separating either activities or content into one pole or another. For example, a couple might decide that Tuesday is "guys'/gals' night out," when each partner socializes separately with friends, and Friday is the couple's "date night," which they spend together, thereby separating autonomy with an activity from connectedness with an activity. According to cyclic alternation, partners will cycle between spending time together and time apart, for instance, but not necessarily based upon certain activities. Interestingly, Baxter (1990) found that couples underutilize more advanced and possibly more satisfactory strategies, such as reframing the tension so that it no longer functions as a contradiction, which suggests that couples do not necessarily understand the flux of relational tensions and are therefore unable to cope most effectively with them.

Baxter and Simon (1993) examined how perceived use of maintenance strategies influences relational satisfaction during perceived dialectical "moments" of contradiction. Specifically, they noted that the maintenance strategies of contact, romance, and avoidance operate in specific ways to transition a relationship "toward dialectical equilibrium." Further, their findings suggest that an abundance of autonomy, closeness, and predictability exist as typical problems or tensions for couples.

An emerging area of study embodying the dialectical framework is that of relational rejuvenation. Specifically, rejuvenation focuses on how relational partners work to *improve* their relationships in the midst of dialectical tensions. As Montgomery (1993) posits, ongoing "relationships are constantly changing, for the better or for the worse or for neither, and, therefore, partners are constantly making adjustments that serve to sustain the relationship through flux" (p. 216). Building on Montgomery's notion of change as inherent in relationships, Wilmot and Stevens (1994) suggest that *regressive spirals* exist as commonplace in most relational partnerships. Thus relationships often experience degrees of deterioration as a result of ongoing misunderstandings, conflict, and discord. In other words, even in a healthy, ongoing relationship, periods of deterioration often result from unavoidable dynamic tensions. Efforts to rejuvenate relationships, then, serve as vehicles that promote close relationships to renewed heights of improved quality after they have slipped into periods of dissatisfaction.

The first researchers to explore rejuvenation behaviors, Wilmot and Stevens (1994), investigated the dialectical manifestation of rejuvenation strategies. Using an open-ended interview technique, they identified three categories of events that typified partners' decline phase across relationship types (friendship, kinship, or romantic partnership): (a) relational issues, (b) escalation events, and (c) influences external to the dyad. Further, they discovered that when asked what partners did to rejuvenate a declining relationship, the most common responses were as follows: (a) change behaviors, (b) have a "Big Relationship Talk," (c) make gestures of reconciliation, (d) reassess the importance of the relationship, (e) accept or forgive the other, and (f) seek third-party help. Wilmot and Stevens's findings comport with a dialectical framework. For example, if a partner attributes a decline in the relationship to a relational issue, such as a reduction of interaction or involvement (perhaps due to job stress or the like), a tension between autonomy and connection is created such that too much autonomy is present. To balance this tension, then, one strategy would be for the partners to change behaviors by spending more time together (e.g., making a date or taking a weekend away together). Reviewing Wilmot and Stevens's findings, each rejuvenation strategy appears to balance at least one of the decline events noted. Clearly, a partner who described relationship decline as a result of a lack of involvement would not want to reverse the situation by "taking time apart," as such a strategy would not balance the autonomy/connection tension. However, the person who reported that too much dependence on each other signaled decline may want to give "the other more *space*" (Wilmot & Stevens, 1994, p. 111) to balance the autonomy/connection tension.

Recalling the three primary tensions offered by Baxter (1993; integration/separation, stability/change, and expression/privacy) and the subsequent internal and external manifestations (that is, internally within a dyad and externally between the dyad and others), we note that the vast majority of dialectical research has focused on internal contradictions (i.e., tensions between relational partners). In one exception, Baxter and Widenmann (1993) examined college-age romantic partners' decisions to reveal or not reveal the status of their romantic relationship to others, thus examining the external dialectical tension of revelation/concealment (see Figure 8.1). This study illuminates the complexities that exist not only within a relationship, but between the relational pair and others.

Assessment of the Dialectical Approach

As stated earlier, the dialectical approach is relatively new to the study of interpersonal relationships. Although substantial research has been undertaken in the past decade to help define and support the perspective, we should know more about relational maintenance from a contradiction-laden and tension-ridden viewpoint. This area is virtually unexplored; empirical work has yet to examine the possible interplay and interaction among internal contradictions or between internal and external contradictions. Tensions among internal contradictions as well as between internal and external contradictions may exist, thereby creating metatensions that need to be addressed and managed relationally. Although not explicitly stated, Cissna et al.'s (1990) study of parental relationships within the stepfamily appears to involve both internal and external aspects of Baxter's (1993) expression/privacy contradiction. Specifically, Cissna et al.'s investigation focused on the metacommunicative tensions between marital and parental relationships. Analysis revealed that the partners in couples who had remarried were able to talk to each other about their own relationship development and problems with relative ease (internal expression, or openness), but had great difficulty in disclosing the same types of relational information with the children in their newly "blended" families (external privacy, or concealment). Cissna et al. note that "the quality of life in the stepfamily may depend on how the tension between [the marital and parental relationships within the stepfamily] is managed" (p. 56). Clearly, more work needs to look at the interplay between internal and external contradictions as well as how possible metatensions are managed and the consequences thereof.

Additionally, a shortage of research exists that dialectically investigates maintenance behaviors outside of close, personal relationships such as friendships (e.g., Maines, 1989; Rawlins, 1989, 1994), kinships (e.g., Cissna et al., 1990), and romantic involvements (e.g., Baxter & Simon, 1993; Baxter & Widenmann, 1993; Goldsmith, 1990). It may be time to apply a dialectical framework to areas other than these types of close relationships. For example, one recent study examined the interaction between staff and clients in shelters for battered women (Stairs & Stamp, 1997). This investigation illuminates the need for a dialectical examination of the construct of "power" and, as a result, emphasizes a dialectic of emancipation/control.

Similarly, one might wonder at the exhaustiveness of dialectical tensions that are said to be in force. Baxter (1990) has admitted the possibility that there are more than three primary contradictions. Rawlins (1989), for example, has suggested a temporal contradiction. As Stairs and Stamp (1997) note, a dialectic of emancipation/control exists in superior/subordinate types of relationships. Identification of other dialectical contradictions would ultimately change and expand the parameters of the current perspective. At the same time, such expansion could serve as a useful heuristic.

Finally, current methods that are used to investigate dialectical tensions appear static in light of the perspective's emphasis on change. The complexity and dynamic nature of the approach seem to outstrip the methods currently employed, which are typically pencil-and-paper recollections of strategies used in the past. Although this indictment is not unique to the dialectical framework, questionnaire data are problematic from a construct-validity standpoint. Approaches to obtaining information on dialectical tensions need to be more sophisticated in order to capture the fluctuations between tensions and partners' responses to such fluctuations.

In sum, the dialectical perspective offers several heuristic advantages for the study of relational maintenance. Specifically, the notion of both changing and contradictory tensions as inherent to relationships gives the notion of relational *maintenance* a new twist—one that perhaps speaks more holistically to a relationship's macro existence, or "the big picture," rather than to more micro, daily events and behaviors. Although this spiraling model has value, the potential for abuse of the perspective must not be underestimated. Particularly because dialectical thinking is just that—a perspective without firmly grounded laws and axioms—it may become easy to throw nearly any research question into the mix and explain away relational conflict via "tensions," "contradictions," and "inherent change." To do so would be a mistake and a grave misrepresentation of the framework.

CONCLUSIONS AND CONCERNS REGARDING COMMUNICATION AND RELATIONAL MAINTENANCE

Several conclusions regarding the four approaches we have reviewed appear to be in order. As is so often the case, the conclusions we have derived from the literature suggest new ways for research to be conducted. We also realize that many of the following statements may be summarized as a cynical outlook on the nature of the research. On the contrary, we believe that research on the topic of relational maintenance behaviors has progressed very quickly in recent years and that a new generation of studies will offer exciting findings and theoretical refinements.

First, the preceding review indicates that the link between communication and relational maintenance is punctuated differently by each of the four programs examined. Gottman considers communication as *antecedent* to whether or not a marriage remains satisfying and stable. Couples who do not know how to balance their negative affect with positivity have met the conditions for the cascade model to predict eventual dissolution. On the other hand, Rusbult regards communication (i.e., EVLN) as an *outcome* of commitment, which itself is previously predicted by interdependence factors (i.e., comparison-level satisfaction, investments, and alternatives). However, one might consider positive expressions as one form of investments (Sprecher et al., 1995). Canary and Stafford conceptualize maintenance strategies as *mediating* the link between perceived equity and relational outcomes, including commitment. Making the issue more complex, Rusbult and Canary and Stafford have stated that their final outcome factors have the potential for affecting their initial independent variables over time. Moreover, the dialectical approach would appear to eschew such linear composites and instead direct attention to how tensions are managed in particular "moments" of dialectical shifts. In brief, the research on communication and relational maintenance does not consistently locate where relating or relationship processes begin and end.

Second, what qualifies as maintenance behavior varies according to each approach we have reviewed. Rusbult and colleagues have examined responses to relational problems using the EVLN typology. Canary and Stafford (1992; Stafford & Canary, 1991) focus on prosocial and constructive communicative strategies that people use to maintain their personal involvements. Gottman (1994) examines conflict messages that couples use when engaged in problem-solving discussion. Finally, Baxter and colleagues have stressed responses to dialectical tensions in addition to maintenance strategies (e.g., Baxter & Dindia, 1990; Baxter & Simon, 1993).

Such variation in delineating the constitutive features of *maintenance communication* implies one or more of the following interpretations: (a) Processes attendant to maintenance activities are numerous and resist clear definition and categorization, (b) some programs are less focused on maintenance than they are on other processes, and/or (c) the programs we have reviewed hold clearly alternative points of view with regard to how couples maintain their relationships. Each of these opinions has merit, although we believe that the relevance-determining nature of theory accounts for the most variance, qualitatively speaking, in the types of communicative behavior studied. In this manner it is no surprise, for example, that Gottman (1994) emphasizes conflict management from an interactional perspective because, in his words, "nearly all the research on marital interaction has involved the observation of conflict resolution" (p. 66). Other justifications for probing particular kinds of communicative behavior that involves maintenance can be found in Rusbult (1987), Stafford and Canary (1991), and Baxter (1990).

Third, and nevertheless, a synthesis of the approaches above indicates that one partner's accommodation to the other in communicative behavior is essential (Rusbult et al., 1994). In other words, negative comments must be balanced with positive comments (Gottman, 1994), which no doubt include positivity, assurances, openness, and other constructive messages (Stafford & Canary, 1991). Partners who learn how to accommodate communicatively to each other no doubt promote desirable relational features, such as commitment and liking, and they also prevent against unkind attributions that function as redoubts against partner attacks. In addition, positive accommodation stops the reciprocation of negative affect and emotional reactivity. It is not immediately clear how one partner's positive accommodation to the other partner's negativity is reflected in response to dialectical tensions. However, from a dialectical point of view, one must believe that some dialectical responses in general have a prorelational effect.

Unfortunately, certain couples do maintain their relationships using negative messages, and the parties have a difficult time restructuring their interactions to change those relationships (Gottman, 1994). It appears instructive to explore more completely troubled involvements for their interaction patterns. Along these lines, Roloff and Cloven (1994) assessed the literature regarding *transgressed relationships,* or relationships that entail violations of important behaviors or rules. They uncovered five relational maintenance approaches: (a) retribution (e.g., be unfaithful to a violator), (b) reformulation (e.g., change rule to accommodate partner), (c) prevention (e.g., avoid talking to an abusive husband), (d) minimization (e.g., minimize hurt to self, accept blame), and (e) relational justification (e.g., justify abuse by calling it a sign of love). Likewise, dialectical tensions that occur in dysfunctional or terminating relationships should be explored. For example, Sabourin and Stamp (1995) examined dialectical tensions in abusive and nonabusive families. By comparing negative (dysfunctional) maintenance patterns to positive (functional) maintenance patterns, we should be better able to predict the critical turning points, in a communicative sense, that in many cases establish and perpetuate the trajectories of relationships. It appears critical to determine which communicative behaviors most dramatically alter relationally enhancing attributions to relationally debasing attributions that lead to isolation and withdrawal (Gottman, 1994).

Fourth, the review also shows that communicative behavior complements non-communicative/nonsymbolic behavior to maintain relationships. Rusbult's investment model suggests that people engage in accommodating, positive ways to a partner's poor behavior or relational problem *and* partake in psychological distortion. Canary and Stafford have examined personality characteristics as well as such strategies as sharing activities and sharing tasks (Canary & Stafford, 1993; Canary et al., 1993). Gottman (1994) hypothesizes that people approach conflict in different ways, in part to match genetic features. The manner in which symbolic attempts to maintain relationships work with other personal characteristics of relational partners needs much more investigation. We need to know more about how interactive and noninteractive processes work together to maintain relationships. This concern also questions the impact of message behavior on relationships that have acquired a sense of stability.

Perhaps most relevant to this point, the programs of research we have reviewed in this chapter suggest that partners must somehow engage in communicative behavior in order for the relationship to be maintained. However, Attridge (1994) has presented the countervailing view that it is difficult to disengage from relationships due to external constraints (e.g., legal agreement, economic dependence) as well as internal constraints (e.g., the extent to which one's personal identity includes one's partner). Attridge argues that one can maintain a marriage by explicitly or implicitly reminding the partner of existing constraints. Attridge's arguments (and evidence) suggest that relational maintenance strategies, including responses to dialectical tensions, do not operate apart from the social structures that bind people together.

Fifth, almost all of the research on communication and relational maintenance has focused on North American friends or lovers. One exception is the work of Yum and Canary (1997), who found that South Korean participants self-reported *less* use of positivity, openness, assurances, sharing tasks, and social networks than did U.S. participants. In addition, the correlations between maintenance strategy use and relational outcomes were weaker for South Koreans relative to their North American counterparts. These results indicate that maintenance behaviors have less powerful effects on relational outcomes in Korea. More important, these findings suggest that some concepts that provide the foundation for relational maintenance research, such as commitment, may be less relevant in other cultures. Likewise, Goldsmith (1990) has recognized that, at present, the dialectical perspective is bound by culture. It may be possible that dialectical tensions that are primary in North America are experienced less in other cultures (e.g., autonomy versus interdependence). Cross-cultural and intercultural research on relational maintenance messages and relational outcomes needs to be conducted, with researchers keeping in mind the critical cultural features that frame relationships.

Sixth, the issue of whether relational maintenance activities and relational characteristics, such as liking and satisfaction, reciprocally affect each other remains largely unanswered, although both of the social exchange programs claim reciprocal causation. The problem of specifying the precise manner in which communicative behaviors and relational features are reciprocally connected typifies much of the research on relational maintenance. In other words, researchers hypothesize in very general ways that a reciprocal causal relationship exists between communication and relationships in lieu of articulating the mechanisms that would lead one back to the beginning of a linear causal model. Although scholars might argue for reciprocal causality between maintenance behaviors and relational features, the research on this issue is quite limited. In addition, Canary et al. (1996) found no support for the assumption of reciprocal causality.

In our view, the problem of reciprocal causality does not disappear when we discuss dialectical theory; rather, it becomes more acute. If we want to research how people respond to dialectical tensions, then we need to find ways to measure such moments and subsequent responses to determine their effects on sustaining relationships. For the most part, the research reflects a static image beneath a dynamic title. Regardless, and for the moment, we only wish to indicate that limited testing exists regarding how maintenance strategies connect to relational features over time, despite the centrality of the claim to our understanding of the link between communication and relationships.

Finally, although we have reviewed the approaches discussed above as discrete and mutually exclusive, it appears that they might be combined in meaningful ways (although one would need to provide justification for doing so). For example, thinking of maintenance processes in terms of dialectical thinking and social exchange theory could prove insightful. Reframing or somehow balancing relational tensions such that they are no longer viewed as problematic may be viewed as a reward. Conversely, the inability to manage dialectical tensions may be viewed as a cost. In addition, equity theory focuses on a *micro* explanation of behaviors within relational maintenance, whereas the dialectical perspective offers more of a *macro* explanation of tensions and contradictions. That is, considerations of equity and how to resolve it appear to be bound by time and context more than the fluid nature of dialectical tensions. Thus it may be possible to view the two viewpoints as complementary, rather than as mutually exclusive. For instance, one person may believe that he is investing more time in the household and, accordingly, that he deserves attention and companionship. His partner, however, may identify the home as a refuge for contemplation and relaxation that are best experienced alone. Such relational dilemmas present issues that equity and dialectical theoretical perspectives can inform. Altering the levels of analysis might allow researchers to see the interplay among various theories and may serve as a useful investigative framework.

In conclusion, we do not wish to diminish the gains that have been made concerning the links between communication and relational maintenance. These gains have been acquired in a relatively brief span of time and have emphasized theoretical understandings on the topic. The opportunity to expand our understanding of how communication connects to relationships should increase with serious consideration of the issues we present above. Certainly we have the theoretical and methodological tools available to undertake such a discussion.

REFERENCES

Adams, J. (1965). Inequity in social exchange. In L. Berkowitz (Ed.), *Advances in experimental social psychology* (Vol. 2, pp. 267-299). New York: Academic Press.

Alberts, J. K. (1988). An analysis of couples' conversational complaints. *Communication Monographs, 55,* 184-197.

Altman, I., & Taylor, D. (1973). *Social penetration: The development of interpersonal relationships.* Austin, TX: Holt, Rinehart & Winston.

Altman, I., Vinsel, A., & Brown, M. (1981). Dialectical conceptions in social psychology: An application to social penetration theory and privacy regulation. In L. Berkowitz (Ed.), *Advances in experimental social psychology* (Vol. 14, pp. 107-160). New York: Academic Press.

Attridge, M. (1994). Barriers to dissolution of romantic relationships. In D. J. Canary & L. Stafford (Eds.), *Communication and relational maintenance* (pp. 141-164). San Diego, CA: Academic Press.

Ayres, J. (1983). Strategies to maintain relationships: Their identification and perceived usage. *Communication Quarterly, 31,* 62-67.

Bakhtin, M. M. (1981). *The dialogic imagination: Four essays* (M. Holquist, Ed.; M. Holquist & C. Emerson, Trans.). Austin: University of Texas Press.

Ball, R. A. (1979). The dialectical method: Its application to social theory. *Social Forces, 57,* 785-798.

Baxter, L. A. (1988). A dialectical perspective on communication strategies in relationship development. In S. Duck (Ed.), *Handbook of personal relationships: Theory, research and interventions* (pp. 257-273). New York: John Wiley.

Baxter, L. A. (1990). Dialectical contradictions in relationship development. *Journal of Social and Personal Relationships, 7,* 69-88.

Baxter, L. A. (1993). The social side of personal relationships: A dialectical perspective. In S. Duck (Ed.), *Understanding relationship processes* (pp. 139-165). Newbury Park, CA: Sage.

Baxter, L. A. (1994). A dialogic approach to relationship maintenance. In D. J. Canary & L. Stafford (Eds.), *Communication and relational maintenance* (pp. 233-251). San Diego, CA: Academic Press.

Baxter, L. A., & Dindia, K. (1990). Marital partners' perception of marital maintenance strategies. *Journal of Social and Personal Relationships, 7,* 187-208.

Baxter, L. A., & Montgomery, B. M. (1996). *Relating: Dialogues and dialectics.* New York: Guilford.

Baxter, L. A., & Philpot, J. (1982). Attribution-based strategies for initiating and terminating relationships. *Communication Quarterly, 30,* 217-224.

Baxter, L. A., & Simon, E. P. (1993). Relationship maintenance strategies and dialectical contradictions in personal relationships. *Journal of Social and Personal Relationships, 10,* 225-242.

Baxter, L. A., & Widenmann, S. (1993). Revealing and not revealing the status of romantic relationships to social networks. *Journal of Social and Personal Relationships, 10,* 321-337.

Bell, R. A., Daly, J. A., & Gonzalez, C. (1987). Affinity-maintenance in marriage and its relationship to women's marital satisfaction. *Journal of Marriage and the Family, 49,* 445-454.

Burgoon, J. K., & Hale, J. L. (1984). The fundamental topoi of relational communication. *Communication Monographs, 51,* 193-214.

Burleson, B. R., & Samter, W. (1994). A social skills approach to relationship maintenance: How individual differences in communication affect the achievement of relationship functions. In D. J. Canary & L. Stafford (Eds.), *Communication and relational maintenance* (pp. 61-90). San Diego, CA: Academic Press.

Canary, D. J., Semic, B. A., & Stafford, L. (1996, June). *Continuity of maintenance strategies and their associations with relational characteristics: A longitudinal test.* Paper presented at the meeting of the International Network on Personal Relationships, Seattle, WA.

Canary, D. J., & Stafford, L. (1992). Relational maintenance strategies and equity in marriage. *Communication Monographs, 59,* 243-267.

Canary, D. J., & Stafford, L. (1993). Preservation of relational characteristics: Maintenance strategies, equity, and locus of control. In P. J. Kalbfleisch (Ed.), *Interpersonal communication: Evolving interpersonal relationships* (pp. 237-259). Hillsdale, NJ: Lawrence Erlbaum.

Canary, D. J., & Stafford, L. (1994). Maintaining relationships through strategic and routine interaction. In D. J. Canary & L. Stafford (Eds.), *Communication and relational maintenance* (pp. 3-22). San Diego, CA: Academic Press.

Canary, D. J., & Stafford, L. (1997, July). *Equity and interdependence predictions of relational maintenance strategy use.* Paper presented at the meeting of the International Network on Personal Relationships, Miami University, Oxford, OH.

Canary, D. J., Stafford, L., Hause, K., & Wallace, L. (1993). An inductive analysis of relational maintenance strategies: A comparison among lovers, relatives, friends, and others. *Communication Research Reports, 10,* 5-14.

Cappella, J. N. (1987). Interpersonal communication: Definitions and fundamental questions. In C. R. Berger & S. H. Chaffee (Eds.), *Handbook of communication science* (pp. 184-238). Newbury Park, CA: Sage.

Christensen, A., & Heavey, C. L. (1990). Gender and social structure in the demand/withdrawal pattern of marital conflict. *Journal of Personality and Social Psychology, 59,* 73-81.

Cissna, K. N., Cox, D. E., & Bochner, A. P. (1990). The dialectic of marital and parental relationships within the stepfamily. *Communication Monographs, 57,* 44-61.

Cloven, D. H., & Roloff, M. E. (1993). The chilling effect of aggressive potential on the expression of complaints in intimate relationships. *Communication Monographs, 60,* 199-219.

Cody, M. J. (1982). A typology of disengagement strategies and an examination of the roles intimacy, reactions to inequity, and relational problems play in strategy selection. *Communication Monographs, 49,* 148-170.

Cornforth, M. (1968). *Materialism and the dialectical method.* New York: International.

Courtright, F. A., Millar, F. E., & Rogers-Millar, L. E. (1979). Domineeringness and dominance: Replication and extension. *Communication Monographs, 46,* 179-192.

Davidson, B., Balswick, J., & Halverson, C. (1983). Affective self-disclosure and marital adjustment. *Social Psychology Quarterly, 45,* 177-181.

Deutsch, M. (1985). *Distributive justice: A social-psychological perspective.* New Haven, CT: Yale University Press.

Dindia, K. (1994). A multiphasic view of relationship maintenance strategies. In D. J. Canary & L. Stafford (Eds.), *Communication and relational maintenance* (pp. 91-114). San Diego, CA: Academic Press.

Dindia, K., & Baxter, L. A. (1987). Strategies for maintaining and repairing marital relationships. *Journal of Social and Personal Relationships, 4,* 143-158.

Dindia, K., & Canary, D. J. (1993). Definitions and theoretical perspectives on maintaining relationships. *Journal of Social and Personal Relationships, 10,* 163-173.

Duck, S. (1988). *Relating to others.* Chicago: Dorsey.

Duck, S. (1994). *Meaningful relationships: Talking, sense, and relating.* Thousand Oaks, CA: Sage.

Fincham, F. D., Bradbury, T. N., & Scott, C. K. (1990). Cognition in marriage. In F. D. Fincham & T. N. Bradbury (Eds.), *The psychology of marriage: Basic issues and applications* (pp. 118-149). New York: Guilford.

Fitzpatrick, M. A. (1988). *Between husbands and wives: Communication in marriage.* Newbury Park, CA: Sage.

Goldsmith, D. (1990). A dialectic perspective on the expression of autonomy and connection in romantic relationships. *Western Journal of Speech Communication, 54,* 537-556.

Gottman, J. M. (1979). *Marital interaction: Experimental investigations.* New York: Academic Press.

Gottman, J. M. (1982). Emotional responsiveness in marital conversations. *Journal of Communication, 32,* 108-120.

Gottman, J. M. (1990). Finding the laws of personal relationships. In I. E. Sigel & G. H. Brody (Eds.), *Methods of family research: Biographies of research projects I. Normal families* (pp. 249-263). Hillsdale, NJ: Lawrence Erlbaum.

Gottman, J. M. (1994). *What predicts divorce? The relationship between marital processes and marital outcomes.* Hillsdale, NJ: Lawrence Erlbaum.

Gottman, J. M., & Carrere, S. (1994). Why can't men and women get along? Developmental roots and marital inequities. In D. J. Canary & L. Stafford (Eds.), *Communication and relational maintenance* (pp. 203-229). San Diego, CA: Academic Press.

Gottman, J. M., & Krokoff, L. J. (1989). Marital interaction and marital satisfaction: A longitudinal view. *Journal of Consulting and Clinical Psychology, 57,* 47-52.

Gottman, J. M., & Levenson, R. W. (1992). Marital processes predictive of later dissolution: Behavior, physiology, and health. *Journal of Personality and Social Psychology, 63,* 221-233.

Hatfield, E., Traupmann, J., Sprecher, S., Utne, M., & Hay, M. (1985). Equity in close relationships. In W. Ickes (Ed.), *Compatible and incompatible relationships* (pp. 91-117). New York: Springer-Verlag.

Kelley, H. H. (1979). *Personal relationships: Their structures and processes.* Hillsdale, NJ: Lawrence Erlbaum.

Kelley, H. H., & Thibaut, J. W. (1978). *Interpersonal relations: A theory of interdependence.* New York: John Wiley.

Knapp, M. L., & Vangelisti, A. (1992). *Interpersonal communication and human relationships* (2nd ed.). Needham Heights, MA: Allyn & Bacon.

Levenson, R. W., Carstensen, L. L., & Gottman, J. M. (1994). The influence of age and gender on affect, physiology, and their interrelations: A study of long-term marriages. *Journal of Personality and Social Psychology, 45,* 587-597.

Levenson, R. W., & Gottman, J. M. (1983). Marital interaction: Physiological linkage and affective predictors of change in relationship satisfaction. *Journal of Personality and Social Psychology, 45,* 587-597.

Levenson, R. W., & Gottman, J. M. (1985). Physiological and affective predictors of change in relationship satisfaction. *Journal of Personality and Social Psychology, 49,* 85-94.

Maines, D. R. (1989). Further dialectics: Strangers, friends, and historical transformations. In J. A. Anderson (Ed.), *Communication yearbook 12* (pp. 190-202). Newbury Park, CA: Sage.

Margolin, G., & Wampold, B. E. (1981). Sequential analysis of conflict and accord in distressed and nondistressed marital partners. *Journal of Consulting and Clinical Psychology, 49,* 554-567.

Metts, S., & Cupach, W. R. (1990). The influence of relationship beliefs and problem-solving responses on satisfaction in romantic relationships. *Human Communication Research, 17,* 170-185.

Michaels, J. W., Edwards, J. N., & Acock, A. C. (1984). Satisfaction in intimate relationships as a function of inequality, inequity, and outcomes. *Social Psychology Quarterly, 47,* 347-357.

Miller, G. R. (1976). Foreword. In G. R. Miller (Ed.), *Explorations in interpersonal communication* (pp. 9-16). Beverly Hills, CA: Sage.

Mills, J., & Clark, M. S. (1982). Exchange and communal relationships. In L. Wheeler (Ed.), *Review of personality and social psychology* (pp. 121-144). Beverly Hills, CA: Sage.

Montgomery, B. M. (1993). Relationship maintenance versus relationship change: A dialectical dilemma. *Journal of Social and Personal Relationships, 10,* 205-223.

Morton, T. C., Alexander, J. F., & Altman, I. (1976). Communication and relationship definition. In G. R. Miller (Ed.), *Explorations in interpersonal communication* (pp. 105-126). Beverly Hills, CA: Sage.

Parks, M. (1982). Ideology in interpersonal communication: Off the couch and into the real world. In M. Burgoon (Ed.), *Communication yearbook 6* (pp. 79-107). Beverly Hills, CA: Sage.

Ragsdale, J. D. (1996). Gender, satisfaction level, and the use of relational maintenance strategies in marriage. *Communication Monographs, 63,* 354-369.

Rawlins, W. K. (1989). A dialectical analysis of the tensions, functions, and strategic challenges of communication in young adult friendships. In J. A. Anderson (Ed.), *Communication yearbook 12* (pp. 157-189). Newbury Park, CA: Sage.

Rawlins, W. K. (1994). Being there and growing apart: Sustaining friendships during adulthood. In D. J. Canary & L. Stafford (Eds.), *Communication and relational maintenance* (pp. 275-294). San Diego, CA: Academic Press.

Revenstorf, D., Hahlweg, K., Schindler, L., & Vogel, B. (1984). Interaction analysis of marital conflict. In K. Hahlweg & N. S. Jacobson (Eds.), *Marital interaction: Analysis and modification* (pp. 159-181). New York: Guilford.

Roloff, M. E. (1978). Communication and reciprocity within intimate relationships. In M. E. Roloff & G. R. Miller (Eds.), *Interpersonal processes: New directions in communication research* (pp. 11-38). Beverly Hills, CA: Sage.

Roloff, M. E. (1981). *Interpersonal communication: The social exchange approach.* Beverly Hills, CA: Sage.

Roloff, M. E., & Cloven, D. H. (1994). When partners transgress: Maintaining violated relationships. In D. J. Canary & L. Stafford (Eds.), *Communication and relational maintenance* (pp. 23-43). San Diego, CA: Academic Press.

Rubin, Z. (1973). *Liking and loving.* New York: Holt, Rinehart & Winston.

Rusbult, C. E. (1983). A longitudinal test of the investment model: The development (and deterioration) of satisfaction and commitment in heterosexual involvements. *Journal of Personality and Social Psychology, 45,* 101-117.

Rusbult, C. E. (1987). Responses to dissatisfaction in close relationships: The exit-voice-loyalty-neglect model. In D. Perlman & S. Duck (Eds.), *Intimate relationships: Development, dynamics, and deterioration* (pp. 209-237). Newbury Park, CA: Sage.

Rusbult, C. E., & Buunk, B. (1993). Commitment processes in close relationships: An interdependence analysis. *Journal of Social and Personal Relationships, 10,* 175-204.

Rusbult, C. E., Drigotas, S. M., & Verette, J. (1994). The investment model: An interdependence analysis of commitment processes and relationship maintenance phenomena. In D. J. Canary & L. Stafford (Eds.), *Communication and relational maintenance* (pp. 115-139). San Diego, CA: Academic Press.

Rusbult, C. E., Johnson, D. J., & Morrow, G. D. (1986). Predicting satisfaction and commitment in adult romantic involvements: An assessment of the generalizability of the investment model. *Social Psychology Quarterly, 94,* 81-89.

Rusbult, C. E., Verette, J., Whitney, G. A., Slovik, L. F., & Lipkus, L. (1991). Accommodation processes in close relationships: Theory and preliminary evidence. *Journal of Personality and Social Psychology, 60,* 53-78.

Sabourin, T. C., & Stamp, G. H. (1995). Communication and the experience of dialectical tensions in family life: An examination of abusive and nonabusive families. *Communication Monographs, 62,* 211-239.

Sacher, J. A., & Fine, M. A. (1996). Predicting relationship status and satisfaction after six months among dating couples. *Journal of Marriage and the Family, 58,* 21-32.

Shea, B. C., & Pearson, J. C. (1986). The effects of relationship type, partner intent, and gender on the selection of relationship maintenance strategies. *Communication Monographs, 53,* 354-364.

Sprecher, S. (1986). The relation between equity and emotions in close relationships. *Social Psychology Bulletin, 49,* 309-321.

Sprecher, S., Metts, S., Burleson, B. R., Hatfield, E., & Thompson, A. (1995). Domains of expressive interaction in intimate relationships. *Family Relations, 44,* 203-210.

Stafford, L., & Canary, D. J. (1991). Maintenance strategies and romantic relationship type, gender, and relational characteristics. *Journal of Social and Personal Relationships, 8,* 217-242.

Stairs, M. E., & Stamp, G. H. (1997, November). *The empowerment dilemma: The dialectic of emancipation and control in staff/client interaction at shelters for battered women.* Paper presented at the annual meeting of the National Communication Association, Chicago.

Ting-Toomey, S. (1983). An analysis of verbal communication patterns in high and low marital adjustment groups. *Human Communication Research, 9,* 306-319.

Van Lange, P. A. M., Rusbult, C. E., Drigotas, S. M., Arriaga, X. B., Witcher, B. S., & Cox, C. L. (1997). Willingness to sacrifice in close relationships. *Journal of Personality and Social Psychology, 72,* 1373-1395.

Van Yperen, N. W., & Buunk, B. (1990). A longitudinal study of equity and satisfaction in intimate relationships. *European Journal of Social Psychology, 20,* 287-309.

Waldron, V. R. (1991). Achieving communication goals in superior-subordinate relationships: The multi-functionality of upward maintenance tactics. *Communication Monographs, 28,* 289-306.

Walster (Hatfield), E., Berscheid, E., & Walster, G. W. (1983). New directions in equity research. *Journal of Personality and Social Psychology, 25,* 151-176.

Wilmot, W. W., & Stevens, D. C. (1994). Relationship rejuvenation: Arresting decline in personal relationships. In R. L. Conville (Ed.), *Uses of structure in communication studies* (pp. 103-124). Westport, CT: Praeger.

Yovetich, N. A., & Rusbult, C. E. (1994). Accommodative behaviors in close relationships: Exploring transformation of motivation. *Journal of Experimental Social Psychology, 30,* 138-164.

Yum, Y.-O., & Canary, D. J. (1997, July). *Maintenance behaviors, relational characteristics, and culture: A comparison between the U.S. and South Korea.* Paper presented at the meeting of the International Network on Personal Relationships, Miami University, Oxford, OH.

CHAPTER CONTENTS

9 Structuration Theory in Small Group Communication: A Review and Agenda for Future Research

BRYAN SEYFARTH
University of Minnesota at Minneapolis-St. Paul

Due to its rich theoretical grounding and some insightful empirical work, structuration theory has been identified as one of the most influential small group communication theories to develop during the 1980s. However, as the discipline enters the twilight of the 1990s, it becomes important to reevaluate the progress of situated approaches to structuration theory and to identify key issues that these approaches currently face. Consequently, this essay reviews four situated approaches to structuration theory—the multiple-sequence model of small group decision development, the distribution of valence model of group influence, an area that examines "arguments as structures," and adaptive structuration theory—and raises some questions regarding these approaches in order to point out some of the potential hurdles that researchers in this area must overcome. The first part of this essay introduces the principles that have generally guided M. Scott Poole and his colleagues' application of the theory and reviews the areas in small group communication research that Poole and his colleagues have examined from a structurational perspective. Next, it focuses on two key issues that Poole, Seibold, and McPhee (1996) believe good structurational theories must address and provides an in-depth analysis of how well Poole and his colleagues have been able to address them. The closing section identifies two key implications of these issues for future research in the area.

THE theory of structuration, originally outlined by social theorist Anthony Giddens (1979, 1984, 1993), has been proposed as a metatheory with great explanatory power for a variety of phenomena in communication research. Researchers have argued that structuration provides a framework that may lead to the resolution of two key dilemmas in current social scientific research: the "structure::action" dilemma and the "stability::instability" dilemma (see Poole, Seibold, & McPhee, 1985; Van de Ven & Poole, 1988). In other words, the theory provides an explanation of social phenomena that accounts for (a) the impact of social struc-

---

Correspondence: Bryan Seyfarth, Cogos Consulting, Inc., 450 Harriet Avenue, Shoreview, MN 55126-3918; e-mail Bryan_Seyfarth@cogos.com

Communication Yearbook 23, pp. 341-379

ture *and* human action as well as (b) the maintenance of social stability and the processes that generate social change.

One of the most comprehensive applications of Giddens's theory to empirical work in the social sciences has been initiated by Poole, Seibold, and McPhee (1985, 1986, 1996), who have used the theory to account for a variety of phenomena within the context of small group decision making. This group of researchers introduced structuration theory into the field of communication in 1980 (McPhee & Poole, 1980; Poole, 1980a; Seibold, Poole, & McPhee, 1980) in response to a perceived lack of theoretical work, not only in the subdiscipline of small group communication (see Cragan & Wright, 1980) but more broadly in the field of communication itself (see Budd, 1977). Since that introduction, they have used structuration to explain a number of group processes from their early work (Poole, McPhee, & Seibold, 1982), which was designed to explain how communication processes affect group outcomes, to their most recent study (DeSanctis & Poole, 1994), which accounts for the ways new communication technologies affect group decision-making processes. Due to its rich theoretical grounding and some insightful empirical work, structuration theory has been identified as one of the most influential small group communication theories to develop during the 1980s (Cragan & Wright, 1990).

As the discipline enters the twilight of the 1990s, it becomes important to reevaluate the progress of situated approaches to structuration theory and to identify key issues that these approaches currently face. Consequently, in this chapter I review these situated approaches to structuration theory and raise some questions regarding these approaches to point out some of the potential hurdles that researchers in this area must overcome.[1] The first part of the essay introduces the principles that have generally guided Poole and his colleagues' application of the theory and reviews the four areas in small group communication research that these researchers have examined from a structurational perspective. Next, I focus on two key issues that Poole et al. (1996) believe good structurational theories must address and provide an in-depth analysis of how well Poole and his colleagues have been able to address them. Finally, in the closing section I identify two key implications of these issues for future research in the area.

BACKGROUND ON STRUCTURATION THEORY

Structuration theory was first proposed by Giddens (1979) as a means of recasting the classical sociological "question of order" in the following form: How are social systems produced and reproduced across space and time? In his book *The Constitution of Society* (1984), Giddens proceeds in a manner that is characteristic of almost all of his work: He systematically dissects a variety of sociological arguments that have characterized previous theorizing and then uses the remains of these arguments to construct his own theory, which deals with these shortcomings. For example, in his 1984 work, Giddens provides an analysis of the structural-functionalist viewpoint attributed to Talcott Parsons. He notes that despite repeated references to notions of "voluntarism," Parsons actually viewed society and its normative structures as being largely deterministic in respect to the lives and thoughts of human actors. In the positivist tradition of Auguste Comte and Emile Durkheim, Parsons posited that objective and empirical methods could be used to "measure" society and to produce lawlike statements that would explain, predict, and control social life.

Giddens responds by stating that "there are no universal laws in the social sciences, and there will not be any—not, first and foremost, because methods of empirical testing and validation are somewhat inadequate but because . . . the causal conditions involved in generalizations about human social conduct are inherently unstable in respect to the very knowledge (or beliefs) that actors have about the circumstances of their own action" (p. xxxii). In his extended introductory argument, Giddens notes that the goals of social science should not necessarily (or even primarily) be to formulate the types of generalizations that are made in the natural sciences. The reason for this is that there is a mutual interpretative interplay between social scientists and "lay actors," or those people whose activities compose the very subject matter of social science.[2]

Giddens (1984) also warns against taking an alternative approach in hermeneutic or phenomenological theories: "By attacking objectivism—and structural sociology—those influenced by hermeneutics or phenomenology were able to lay bare major shortcomings of those views. But they in turn veered sharply towards subjectivism. The conceptual divide between subject and social object yawned as widely as ever" (p. xx). The essence of Giddens's argument is that although these questions appear to be epistemological, one cannot answer them without revising ontological assumptions as well; in fact, in many ways his theory is an attempt to redefine the nature of social science itself. Giddens characterizes the basic domain of the social sciences as "neither the experience of the individual actor, nor the existence of any form of societal totality, but social practices ordered across space and time" (p. 2). Giddens's goal is to escape from the dualism of objectivity and subjectivity by reconceptualizing it as a duality—one he calls the "duality of structure."

Here lies the central argument in the theory of structuration. Giddens (1984) begins by distinguishing between two primary terms, *structures* and *systems,* which are presented in the theorem of the duality of structure. First, he describes structures as "rules and resources, recursively implicated in the reproduction of social systems" (p. 377). Structure is what allows for the " 'binding' of time-space" (p. 17) and thus the creation of social systems. Giddens's definition of *structure* is broad and significantly different from the way structural sociologists use the term. Whereas structural and functional theorists are typically concerned with operationalizing and measuring the "structures" that hold society together, Giddens denies the fundamental role usually given to such structures in determining social life. He notes that social systems "do not have 'structures' [in the way that structuralists and functionalists use the term] but rather exhibit 'structural properties' and that structure exists . . . only in its instantiations in such practices and as memory traces orienting the conduct of knowledgeable human agents" (p. 17).

Giddens (1984) defines his second primary term, *system,* as "reproduced relations between actors or collectivities, organized as regular social practices" (p. 25). This is where structures are recursively implicated as the "situated activity of human agents, reproduced across time and space" (p. 25). Implicit in this observation is Giddens's conceptualization of the human agent as continually engaged in reflexive action with the world. He contends that "human agents . . . have, as an inherent aspect of what they do, the capacity to understand what they do while they do it. . . . [But] this reflexivity operates only partly on a discursive level. What agents know about what they do, and why they do it—their knowledgeability as agents—is largely carried in practical consciousness" (p. xxiii). This relates to what Giddens calls the three levels of consciousness that define human actors: *discursive consciousness,* or the ability of actors to give reasons (discursively) for their behavior or actions; *practical consciousness,* which is what actors know about the conditions of their own actions, but do not express discursively due to its routine nature; and *unconscious motive,* which is similar to traditional definitions of the repressed unconscious.

How do structures and systems relate to each other? Giddens (1984) fuses the two concepts by suggesting:

> Analyzing the structuration of social systems means studying the modes in which such systems, grounded in the knowledgeable activities of situated actors who draw upon rules and resources in the diversity of action contexts, are produced and reproduced in interaction. . . . [Thus] the constitution of agents and structures are not two independently given sets of phenomena, a dualism, but represent a duality. According to the notion of the *duality of structure,* the structural properties of social systems are both the medium and the outcome of the practices they recursively organize. (p. 26; emphasis added)

Thus, rather than siding with the functionalist viewpoint, which takes societal "structures" as the prime causal force in society, or with interpretivists, who focus on the actor as the prime causal force in society, Giddens stakes out a middle ground that allows for an interaction of both to occur in the process of creating the social system. Giddens's theory implies that although we have the power to construct our own reality (e.g., Berger & Luckmann, 1967), we usually draw on building blocks already present in society (i.e., structures) to construct that reality.

This process of structuration also addresses not only the structure::action debate in sociology (and in other disciplines) but the stability::instability debate. Because structuration posits a process in which knowledgeable agents continually implicate structures in the production and reproduction of social systems, this implies that in the examination of such systems, any *observed* stability comes from the stability of an underlying process in which agents continually reproduce certain structures in a like manner. Moreover, as Poole et al. (1985) note, "Since structure is *produced* by human actors, it is continuously open to change by the play of human creativity" (p. 76). Therefore, depending on the active (but not unlimited) choices of human agents that are situated within a flow of social activity, the very mechanism that produces stability may also produce instability. This allows for a healthy balance between perspectives, such as institutional theory (see DiMaggio & Powell, 1991; Meyer & Rowan, 1977), which emphasizes stability, and perspectives such as Weick's (1979) theory of organizing, which emphasizes instability.[3]

POOLE AND HIS COLLEAGUES' SITUATED VERSIONS OF STRUCTURATION THEORY

In their applications of structuration theory to the small group context, Poole and his colleagues consistently draw a central distinction that directly parallels Giddens's use of the terms *system* and *structure*.[4] Specifically, they define a system as "a social entity, such as a group, pursuing various practices which give rise to observable patterns of relations" (Poole et al., 1996, p. 117), whereas structures are "the rules and resources which [group members] use to generate and sustain the system.... The nature of structures and the relations between structure and system are represented in the concept of *structuration,* which refers to *the process by which systems* [e.g., small group processes] *are produced and reproduced through members' use of rules and resources* [i.e., structures]" (p. 117).

These rules and resources generate and maintain small group processes, and Poole and his colleagues assume that the key to understanding group practices is to analyze those structures that underlie them. Also following Giddens, Poole et al. (1996) note that structures are *dualities.* Not only are they the medium of action, they are also the outcome of action:

> They are the medium of action because members draw on structures to interact. They are [the outcome of action] because rules and resources exist only by virtue of being used in a practice. Whenever a structure is employed, the activity reproduces it by invoking it and confirming it as a meaningful basis for action. So when a group takes a vote, it is employing the rules behind voting to act, but—more than this—it is reminding itself that these rules exist, working out a way of using these rules, perhaps creating a special version of them. In short, by voting the group is producing and reproducing the rules for present and future use. (p. 117)

Poole et al. (1996) also present an interpretation of Giddens's work that explains the forces that influence structurational processes. They believe these may be placed in two broad classes. First, there are factors that limit group members' ability to control action, including (a) the necessary temporal ordering of action; (b) contextual features, such as historical precedents and situational factors that shape action; (c) the differential distribution of knowledge and resources among group members; and (d) the "unintended consequences" of actions. This last factor refers to the fact that due to the complexity of social systems, leaders and other group members are not able to see the full consequences of their actions. Poole et al. (1996) offer an example of such a process: "[A] group leader who wins a point despite opposition from group members may not realize that he or she is undermining the leadership role's power by encouraging opposing members to build defensive coalitions. The consequences of action can 'loop back' in a variety of ways to alter group actions (Masuch, 1985)" (p. 121).

The second broad class of factors that influence structurational processes (again, based on Giddens's writings) includes dynamics through which different structural features mediate and interact with one another. Poole et al. (1996) explain this by noting several key points. First, "many characteristics of groups . . . are typically the result of larger scale social processes, such as the design of the group by an organization" (p. 121). Second, groups are always struggling to maintain their boundaries in the face of recurrent and multiple outside demands on the group. Finally, "group processes themselves, no less than language and thought processes, are properties of social systems, learned throughout one's life" (p. 121). Thus a continuing concern of structuration theory is the study of *appropriation,* which is how small groups adopt structural features from larger institutions and develop situated versions of these structures as they go about their day-to-day work.

Although Poole and his colleagues have used structuration theory to explain a variety of phenomena, ranging from organizational climate to organizational structure to organizational change, there are four areas in which they have elaborated the theory most explicitly: (a) as a rationale to explain the multiple-sequence model of small group decision development (see Poole & Doelger, 1986); (b) in the distribution of valence model of group influence, which is designed to explain the relationship between communication and group decision outcomes (see Poole et al., 1982); (c) as a theoretical framework to guide the study of argumentation in group processes (see Seibold, McPhee, Poole, Tanita, & Canary, 1981); and (d) in the advancement of adaptive structuration theory, which explains the effects that new communication technologies have on small group decision processes (see Poole & DeSanctis, 1990). Each of these areas is reviewed in turn below. Although at this point the primary purpose of this section is to describe the core concepts and findings that characterize each of these approaches, this discussion also sets the stage for the critiques of these approaches offered later in this essay.

The Multiple-Sequence Model of Small Group Decision Development

Poole's work with the multiple-sequence model (MSM) began with his dissertation (Poole, 1980b), which laid out the basic assumptions that underlie the approach and provided initial evidence for the model. Initially, this work was undertaken as a simple challenge to traditional models of decision development (e.g., Bales & Strodtbeck, 1951; Fisher, 1970), most of which posited that decision development is best characterized by a *unitary* sequence of stages (although there have been exceptions; see Mintzberg, Raisinghani, & Theoret, 1976; Nutt, 1984). Poole set out to demonstrate that unitary models tell only part of the story; although it is true that decision-making groups do sometimes follow a unitary sequence, his early research yielded more support for a multiple-sequence model, in which there are a multitude of paths that a small group might take as it progresses through the decision-making process (Poole, 1981, 1983a; for the most recent version of this finding, see Poole & Holmes, 1995). However, this led to another question: What causes a group to take one path over another? Poole (1983b) answered this by establishing a contingency theory of decision development that explains differences in group decision paths in terms of two panels of variables: *group structure* characteristics (e.g., group size, conflict history, and cohesiveness) and *task* characteristics (e.g., novelty, openness, and goal clarity). Later studies provided a basis for additional theoretical elaboration and strong evidence to support such a contingency model, which usually explained more than 60% of the variance in the nature of the decision path (Poole & Roth, 1989a, 1989b).

Although Poole outlined the MSM in 1983, it was not until later that the structurational grounding of the model became more explicit. Two articles described how structuration theory explains *why* phases occur as they do (Poole, 1985; Poole & Doelger, 1986)—or, more accurately, how structuration theory provides the "generative mechanism" (Harré & Madden, 1975) for the multiple-sequence model. The key to his explanation lies in the idea that group members use phase models to *actively structure* their decisions. Poole and Roth (1989a) summarize this logic:

> Group members attempt to adapt their activities to [various contingencies] so as to make the most effective decision possible. One of the "tools" they use in this adaptive process are idealized, normative models of decision-making such as those portrayed in unitary phase models. These models—part of the cultural stock of "common sense" knowledge every competent member of society has—organize the group's behavior in a general way. They serve as frames that help members to make sense of their actions and to plan future moves. (p. 327)

In other words, unitary phase models may be considered *structures* that group members use to generate the resulting *system* of small group interaction. However, these structures are not the only factors that influence the pattern of small group interaction; there are a variety of constraints that hold as well, as summarized in the panels of contingency variables noted earlier (i.e., group structure variables and task variables).

Poole and his colleagues are a bit more specific in describing the rules and resources that group members use to structure decision processes. One of the key structures they highlight is explicitly cognitive—something they call a *task representation*. Drawing on the work of Abric (1971), Poole and Baldwin (1996) describe task representations as "mental models of how the task should be done [that are] made up of a substantive representation of the nature of the task and a decision logic specifying how the group should make decisions" (p. 226; see also Poole & Doelger, 1986). Moreover, task representations have two interdependent components: (a) a theory of the formal requirements of decision making (what Poole, 1985, calls a *decision logic*) and (b) an "agenda" of the particular issues the group must address. Whereas the agenda component of the task representation is unique to each decision situation, decision logics are more general schemes that members use to orient their groups.

Poole (1985) outlines four common (but not comprehensive) decision logics that characterize many decision-making processes: (a) an *assumed consensus* logic, in which members assume that they agree on basic values and on the nature of the decision task and, therefore, attempt to find a solution quickly and then work it out in detail; (b) a *political* logic, in which members assume that decision making is a process of winning adherents for their own favored alternatives; (c) a *rational* logic, in which members attempt to make the best possible decision in the technical sense; and (d) a *reactive* logic, which is really not a logic at all, given that members have no expectations about the decision-making process and look to others to guide their way through the decision.

Poole points out that task representations also exist on a different and non-cognitive plane—these are what he calls *collective* task representations, or social products and properties of a group's discourse. All other things being equal, this collective representation (not the individual task representations) is the core generative mechanism that drives a group's choice of a decision path. Poole calls this a *steering mechanism* that gives rise to the observed phases in a decision-making process. However, this mechanism is not the only force that determines the final decision path. Two things may interfere with the group's ability to work out a decision: the contingency variables discussed earlier and disagreements among members regarding the collective task representation.[5]

The Distribution of Valence
Model of Group Influence

Poole and his colleagues' first explicit application of structuration theory to empirical research came with the establishment of their distribution of valence model (DVM) of group influence, which was an early attempt to provide evidence for the value of the structurational approach. This approach is premised on the structurational notion that "the factors that determine social action exist *only* in the stream of ongoing interaction" (Poole et al., 1982, p. 3). Poole et al. explain this initially counterintuitive notion by noting that " 'external' factors only have bearing on action in so far as they are produced and reproduced by group members using them in interaction. Even seemingly stable factors such as a majority decision scheme of the group's task are mediated by interaction" (p. 3). This suggests that the way in which small group researchers have previously approached the study of small group communication is slightly flawed. They have tended to focus primarily on how *input* variables have affected small group outcomes, rather than on how those input variables are first *reproduced* in the process of group interaction and then how the reproduction of those variables affects group outcomes.

To improve this methodological and theoretical shortsightedness, Poole et al. (1982) recommended that communication researchers turn this traditional strategy on its head by following a three-step research strategy. First, researchers should select *interactional* variables that directly mirror noninteractional variables traditionally used in small group research; second, they should construct congruent models that measure the effects of both the interactional and the noninteractional variables on the dependent variable of interest (which are usually decision outcomes); finally, they should compare the two models in terms of strength and immediacy to determine their ability to predict and explain small group processes. Poole et al. believed that "if the external factors are produced and reproduced in interaction, as the theory of structuration asserts, then interactional factors should be more powerful and immediate factors; if the opposite is true, the external factors should predominate" (p. 3). Thus positive results for the interactional variables would provide not only support for structuration theory, but also an additional rationale for the value of a communication-centered emphasis for small group theory.

This is exactly the approach used in studies of the DVM. The DVM was designed to counteract previous approaches to the prediction of group decision outcomes. Poole et al. (1982) conducted a study designed to provide the strongest test of this approach. They contrasted Davis's (1973) classic social decision schemes (SDS) model against the more communication-based DVM. As Poole and others (e.g., Hewes, 1986) argue, the SDS model effectively throws down the gauntlet to the entire discipline of small group communication, because it is able to predict (quite accurately) the outcomes of decision processes based only on knowledge of (a) the preinteraction dispositions of the participants and (b) a decision rule that Davis derives deductively—both of which are *input* variables.

Poole et al. (1982) note that the core difference between the SDS model and the DVM is that the DVM is based on dispositions expressed in the process of interaction rather than on norms that guide interaction. "The [DVM] assumes that preferences change and emerge through the mutual influence of members, whereas the SDS model assumes that prediscussion preferences are not affected by interaction, which serves primarily as a channel for the operation of powerful decision norms" (p. 5). In light of this distinction and the core similarity between the SDS model and the DVM, Poole and his colleagues posited that the DVM is the minimal interactional analogue to the SDS model; therefore, a test comparing the two approaches should allow for researchers to evaluate the relative strengths of both.

Generally, the results of the test that Poole et al. (1982) report support the hypothesis that the interaction process mediates the effects of initial member preferences on the final decision outcome. The DVM was slightly more accurate than the SDS model in predicting decision outcomes. In fact, the results support a model in which members' predispositions do not have a strong direct effect on group decisions (although they do have a small indirect effect); rather, social decision schemes have a strong direct effect on the distribution of valence during decision processes, and this valence distribution then has a strong direct effect on group decisions. As such, this study does provide some degree of validation for this general assumption of structuration theory (Poole et al., 1986).

Unfortunately, as Hewes (1986) later argued, these results do not tell us as much about the value of communication-centered approaches as Poole and his colleagues originally intended.[6] The reason for this, according to Hewes, is that the results have little to say about the value of interaction processes as forces that affect outcomes *in and of themselves.* If interaction only mediates the relationship between input variables and outcomes and does not have a strong impact on decision outcomes *independent of* inputs (or in statistical interaction with them), then this test still confirms the input variables as the primary explanation for decision outcomes. Hewes (1986) argues that, at the very best, the sole contribution of the DVM is to reduce the standard error of the estimate of those preinteraction dispositions, and notes, "Given Davis's comparatively casual measurement of pre-interaction dispositions, it would be no wonder that the DVM's predictions are slightly more accurate due to improved measurement alone" (p. 273). Therefore, although the results of this attempt to test the structurational model are generally supportive of structurational assumptions, their meaning for the subdiscipline of small group communication is ultimately ambiguous. The study provides some evidence for the role of communication process in mediating the effects of input variables upon group outcomes, but questions remain about the value of the interaction process as a relevant variable in and of itself.[7]

Arguments as Structures

The next application of structuration theory to decision-making research comes from work that David Seibold and his colleagues have undertaken to study group argumentation and the way that arguments are used to structure the practice of small group decision-making processes (e.g., Canary, Brossman, & Seibold, 1987; Meyers & Seibold, 1990; Seibold & Meyers, 1986; Seibold et al., 1981)—an area that I refer to as *arguments as structures* research for shorthand purposes. Although this area is not as well developed as the other three discussed here, the work to date is worth discussing in light of the arguments advanced later in this essay.

Initially, work in this area followed directly from early work done with the DVM; however, Seibold and his colleagues hoped to take a more complex view of argument than the perspective advanced in the DVM. Specifically, they argued that the conception of communication that underlay the DVM research was so basic that it understated the complexities of communication. By focusing only on the positive and negative valences of the communication acts, scholars ignored deeper levels of the communication, including "the logic of the expressed argument and the force of strategic interpersonal influence" (Seibold et al., 1981, p. 666). Therefore, Seibold et al. hoped to develop the notions they had outlined earlier (see Seibold et al., 1980, pp. 13-15), which entailed analysis of arguments at deeper levels. These deeper levels included (a) the argument expressed (i.e., the reasons behind the valenced comment) and (b) the strategy chosen (i.e., how those reasons are linked to their chosen audiences).

Seibold et al. (1981) also offered some additional theoretical rationales to provide the foundation for their analysis. They posited that the process of group argument "can be viewed as a *system* of interaction (in Giddens's sense) that is produced by members engaging in advancing *arguables,* or utterances that are potentially disagreeable to other members" (Seibold, Canary, & Ratledge, 1983, p. 17). Members advance arguables by drawing on *structures* (i.e., rules and resources); in turn, the types of structures on which they are able to draw are conditioned by the system of interaction itself. Therefore, the notion of the duality of structure is again present in this framework, because "arguments are produced in use, but reproduced through use; they are both medium and outcome of interaction" (Meyers & Seibold, 1990, p. 285).

To examine these ideas in an empirical setting, Seibold et al. (1981) constructed a series of coding systems to perform a qualitative analysis of the argumentation processes that characterize group decision making. Later studies refined this system (Canary, Ratledge, & Seibold, 1982; Ratledge, 1986; Seibold et al., 1983). Eventually, Canary, Brossman, Sillars, and LoVette (1987) defined four major classes of arguments, which have been summarized as follows by Poole et al. (1996): "(1) simple arguments, (2) compound arguments which combine or embed simple ones, (3) eroded arguments which fail to develop, and (4) convergent arguments which combine elements of several members' arguments and are sometimes produced in a 'tag team' fashion by several members" (p. 128). Additionally, Seibold et al. (1981) noted that the key structures that seem to be appropriated routinely in this decision process are either majority influence structures or structures that implicated relative power or status of members.[8]

Perhaps the most valuable aspect of this line of research in light of the arguments I will make later in this chapter is that it represents a good initial attempt to theorize explicitly about cognitive aspects of structurational processes. In a review of their work in this area, Meyers and Seibold (1990) contend that argumentation research can be placed in two categories: the cognitive-informational (CI) and the social-interactional (SI). The CI approach "focuses primarily upon the arguer, and views both the process of arguing and the resultant arguments as relatively fixed and stable" (p. 269), whereas SI approaches implicitly or explicitly treat argument as "a jointly produced, socially governed, interactive activity. Their focus is primarily upon the social unit, and the process of arguing and resultant arguments are seen as emergent, creative, and transformational" (p. 269). On its own, Meyers and Seibold posit, neither kind of approach is capable of providing a complete description of group argument practices; therefore, there is a need for a theory that can subsume both within the *same* perspective. Enter structuration theory.

Meyers and Seibold (1990) demonstrate the value of their approach by critiquing the CI-based persuasive arguments theory (PAT) perspective on group argument from an SI standpoint and then use their critique to provide additional rationale for a structurational view of group argument. The cognitive aspects of the perspective they spell out are as follows. First, they believe that "a structurational view of argument is not interested in cognitive responses as singular predictive mechanisms, but instead as potential knowledge structures that inform, enhance, or constrain argumentative interaction. It seeks to understand how individuals use these resources to produce argument and, subsequently, how these resources are reproduced in those practices" (p. 286).

Moreover, they distinguish between two types of "cognitive" rules and resources—those that are collectively shared and those that are unique to individual arguers. *Collectively shared* cognitive rules and resources are ones that all members of a small group discussion share—for example, conceptual knowledge about what an argument *is,* how arguments should proceed, what kinds of statements make for "good" arguments, how arguments differ from other conversational activities, or what sets of *standard arguments* (in PAT terminology) characterize certain decision problems. On the other hand, *individually held* cognitive rules and resources are unique to individuals (although Meyers & Seibold, 1990, contend that even these rules and resources have their primary basis in socially derived knowledge structures). In this respect, Meyers and Seibold agree with Poole and Doelger (1986), who believe that these rules and resources are of at least two types: (a) individual interpretations of the task or (b) individual interpretations of how the argument should proceed (see the preceding discussion of the MSM regarding task representations).

Meyers and Seibold (1990) close their discussion regarding cognitive rules and resources by noting: "In short, from a structurational view, the study of individual cognitive arguments . . . apart from the interactive context in which they function is incomplete. Similarly, the investigation of members' interactive arguments without studying their bases in collectively shared resources paints only half a picture. Study of the production and reproduction of both these elements is imperative" (p. 291). Such a sentiment is exactly in line with the thrust of this project, which is designed to construct a balance between the social and the cognitive foundations of group activity.

Adaptive Structuration Theory

Perhaps the most important application of structuration theory by Poole and his colleagues is their recent construction of adaptive structuration theory (AST; Poole & DeSanctis, 1990, 1992; DeSanctis & Poole, 1994). AST is a situated version of structuration theory that has been used to explain how the structures present in communication technology are appropriated during group processes. This program of research has involved the study of small decision-making groups that use a new form of communication technology called group decision support systems

(GDSSs). Poole and DeSanctis have focused on two areas in this research: They have tried to identify structures or structural features that come into play during decision-making processes, and they have tried to identify the role that those structures play in the process and how they are used.

In examining structures in the technological context (or, in other words, in examining technology as a structure), Poole and DeSanctis (1990) found it was necessary to describe two important characteristics of such structures: First, such structures have a *spirit,* reflected in the general goals and attitudes the technology aims to promote; second, they also have *structural features* actually built into the technology. A feature is "the specific rule or resource that operates in the group, whereas the *spirit* is the principle of coherence that holds a set of rules and resources together. Obviously, features are designed to promote a certain spirit. However, features are functionally independent of spirit and may be used in ways contrary to it by some groups" (p. 179).

A key question that AST raises is how groups appropriate structures not only from the larger society (e.g., what are the rules of parliamentary procedure?) but from the structural features built into a GDSS itself. It is Poole and DeSanctis's (1992) general hypothesis that groups that appropriate the structures of the GDSS in a stable manner will have more predictable outcomes than those that do not. This will be marked by (a) faithful or ironic use of the system (Is it consistent with the intended *spirit* of the technology?), (b) attitudes toward structure (Are members comfortable with the system, and do they respect it?), and (c) the level of consensus that exists regarding how to use the system.

With these assumptions defined, Poole and DeSanctis (1992) initiated research on decision-making groups and GDSSs. They recorded group interaction processes and then applied a unique coding system to the groups' communication to develop a typology of "appropriation moves." This innovative scheme is based on classical Elizabethan theories of rhetorical tropes and served to identify "moves" that group members could use to appropriate a structure. Although this scheme is complicated (it is organized into nine general categories and a total of 31 potential subcategories), it deserves some elaboration here because it is an outstanding initial attempt to describe and classify structuration processes systematically.[9]

The nine categories that Poole and DeSanctis (1992; see also DeSanctis & Poole, 1994) constructed to analyze the group decision-making process are outlined in Table 9.1. Although they constructed these to deal specifically with the appropriation of their GDSS system, the scheme is general enough to serve also as a model for any type of appropriation process, because none of the "types" or "subtypes" in the classification system deals directly with a GDSS per se. For example, their code "6a: Constraint-definition" involves explaining the meaning of a structure and how it should be used. A simple hypothetical example of a statement by a group member that might fit this code would be as follows: "Member 2: 'The voting tool on the GDSS is for allowing us to vote anonymously; however, the rules in the GDSS manual say that we shouldn't use the tool until after we have discussed the issue a little bit.' " This type of example is quite intuitive, as it gets at exactly

TABLE 9.1
Summary of Types and Subtypes of Structuring (Appropriation) Moves

Type	Subtype	Definition
1. Direct appropriation	a. explicit	openly use and refer to the structure
	b. implicit	use without referring to the structure (e.g., typing)
	c. bid	suggest use of the structure
2. Substitution	a. part	use part of the structure instead of the whole
	b. related	use a similar structure in place of structure at hand
	c. unrelated[a]	use an opposing structure in place of structure at hand
3. Combination	a. composition	combine structures in a way consistent with their spirit
	b. paradox[a]	combine contrary structures with no acknowledgment that they are contrary
	c. corrective	use one structure as a corrective for a perceived deficiency in another
4. Enlargement	a. positive	note the similarity between the structure and another structure via positive allusion or metaphor
	b. negative	note the similarity between the structure and another structure via negative allusion or metaphor
5. Contrast	a. contrary	express the structure by noting what it is not—that is, in terms of contrasting structure
	b. favored	compare structures and favor one over others
	c. none favored	compare structures and favor none over others
	d. criticism	criticize the structure, but without an explicit contrast
6. Constraint	a. definition	explain meaning of a structure and how it should be used
	b. command	give directions/order others to use the structure
	c. diagnosis	comment on how the structure is working, either positive (+) or negative (−)
	d. ordering	specify the order in which structures should be used
	e. queries	ask questions about the structure's meaning/how to use it
	f. closure	show how use of a structure has been completed
	g. status report	state what has been or is being done with the structure
	h. status request	question what has been or is being done with the structure
7. Affirmation	a. agreement	agree with an appropriation of the structure
	b. bid agree	ask others to agree with the appropriation of a structure
	c. agree to reject	others agree with a bid to reject appropriation of structure
	d. compliment	note an advantage of the structure
8. Negation	a. reject	disagree or otherwise directly reject the appropriation
	b. indirect	reject appropriation of the structure by ignoring it, such as ignoring another's bid to use it
	c. bid reject	suggest or ask others to reject use of the structure
9. Neutrality	—	express uncertainty/neutrality toward use of the structure

SOURCE: Adapted from DeSanctis and Poole (1994, p. 135).
a. These are ironic appropriations; all others are faithful appropriations.

what Poole and DeSanctis are trying to study in their research—how technology is *actually* used by a group in a situated setting.

However, this code might also apply to the following statement: "Member 3: 'The agenda says that we should analyze the problem first. This means coming up with a formal problem statement that we all agree with.' " In other words, this scheme may be used to study a GDSS, an agenda, or a variety of other "structures" that may enter into a decision-making process, including a judge's instructions to a jury (see Hastie & Pennington, 1991), a mission statement established by a corporate board of directors (see Seyfarth, 1996), and goals provided to a work team (see Locke & Latham, 1990). This generality is perhaps one of the greatest strengths of Poole and DeSanctis's scheme.

After coding the interaction, Poole and DeSanctis created a timeline of appropriation moves on the types of structures used in the groups. According to Poole et al. (1996), "This enabled the researchers to develop (1) profiles of the general types of appropriations made by groups as well as which members made and controlled them, and (2) maps of appropriation phases" (p. 133). This was important because it allowed the researchers to apply these to a sample of 18 groups in answering the two research questions: "What effects does restrictiveness in GDSS design . . . have on structuration processes?" and "What is the relationship between appropriations of the GDSS and group outcomes, controlling for restrictiveness?" They concluded that restrictiveness reduced the amount of structuring behavior devoted to controlling the system itself and increased the amount of behavior devoted to working with system products. In addition, groups that engaged in faithful appropriations (i.e., ones that either had no ironic bids or that rejected ironic bids) had greater change in consensus than those that did not.

Poole and DeSanctis's work is the most comprehensive and richest description of structurational processes yet offered and is an important contribution not only to the small group literature, but also to the study of new communication technologies (see Poole & DeSanctis, 1990). Perhaps the most significant aspect of this research is that it presents a reasonably thorough explanation of the process by which agents make structuring moves to appropriate structures and thereby produce and reproduce them in group contexts (Poole et al., 1996, p. 125). However, later in this chapter I will argue that Poole and DeSanctis's theory must be informed by a more complete conceptualization of the individual agent, an area in which cognitive theory can be informative.

RECONSIDERING CURRENT APPROACHES
TO STRUCTURATION THEORY

As discussed above, structuration theory has become one of the most significant theoretical perspectives in the field of small group communication (Cragan & Wright, 1990); in fact, it could be argued that the efforts of scholars in this area have constituted *the* dominant approach to the study of small group communication in the past 15 years. However, now that the theory has been a part of the small group literature for some time, it is fair to begin to assess how *well* Poole and his colleagues have been able to articulate a systematic structurational perspective on small groups.

Although my focus in this section is upon asking some important questions about current approaches toward this theory, my primary purpose is not to degrade them; rather, it is to identify the hurdles that must and can be overcome by structuration researchers in order to maintain the momentum that they have built up over the past few years. I contend that if these issues are resolved, structuration might become the dominant theoretical perspective not only in the field of small group communication, but also in the wider area of small group theory as a whole. Thus this essay is necessarily incomplete; the next step is to articulate a research program that is designed to clear these hurdles (something I am currently pursuing; see Seyfarth, 1999).

Key Issues for Structuration Theory

In their most recent review of the structuration literature, Poole et al. (1996) posit six key issues that any form of structuration research should address (see Table 9.2). They present these issues in describing what an ideal structuration theory should look like, and they imply that current approaches are theories in progress; although each of the current approaches has attempted to deal with these issues, there is yet to emerge a complete statement that fully resolves all of these issues. Poole et al. note: "These are not a set of stages for research. Working on any single problem can also produce insights for others. . . . Ideally, the finished theory should be seamless—it would incorporate all analyses into a complete whole" (p. 127).

I do not propose to construct such a seamless theory here. However, I do hope to address at least two of the issues that Poole and his colleagues have highlighted: identifying the relevant structures that are used to constitute the system and explaining how systems work. For the sake of the flow of my argument, I deal with these in reverse of the order that Poole et al. list them. These two issues are the ones most in need of being addressed at this point in time and therefore are the most relevant to the advancement of current knowledge of structurational processes; moreover, these are the ones perhaps most currently amenable to improvement.

Identifying the Structures Used to Constitute the System

One of the issues that Poole et al. (1996) believe that good structurational theories must address is the question, What structures are used to constitute the system? They note that such analyses "must identify the array of relevant structures which are used to constitute the system. This may involve identification of both potential and active structures. All such identifications are, of course, reifications

TABLE 9.2
Key Issues for Structuration Theory to Address

1. Structuration theory must develop an analysis of how systems work, which requires identification of causal links that characterize the system's operation and members' interpretive maps.
2. Structuration theory must identify the array of relevant structures that are used to constitute the system.
3. Structuration theory must identify structuring moves or processes by which agents appropriate these structures, producing and reproducing them in activity.
4. Structuration theory must clarify the mediation of one structure by others as well as the contradictions between structures and their role in the structurational process.
5. Structuration theory should shed light on how social institutions are reproduced or shaped by the process in question.
6. Structuration theory should describe how the subjects or actors themselves are produced and reproduced in structuration.

SOURCE: Adapted from Poole et al. (1996, pp. 125-126).

that 'freeze' the modalities of structuration for purposes of analysis" (p. 125). Giddens (1984) speaks of a similar goal for structurational theories; he calls this the search for the "structural principles," which are the principles that organize "societal totalities" (although the same notion might be taken to apply to the context of small groups). He states: "The identification of structural principles, and their conjunctures in intersocietal systems, represents the most comprehensive level of institutional analysis. . . . The study of structural sets . . . involves the isolating of distinct 'clusterings' of transformation/mediation relations implied in the designation of structural principles" (p. 185).

Both Poole et al. and Giddens highlight an important notion: In order to "explain how systems work," it is necessary to identify the most relevant sets of structures (i.e., the structural principles) that are implicated in specific structuration processes. Although Giddens's work in this area has largely remained at a macro level of analysis (e.g., he offers an analysis of the structural sets that underlie capitalistic systems), Poole and his colleagues point out that similar analyses might be performed at the micro level of small group decision making. Although Poole and his colleagues have taken some strong steps toward identifying these structures, there is still additional work in identifying the relevant structures that constitute the "system" of the decision-making small group. That work centers on identifying the structures that Giddens (1984) calls "memory traces."

A review of the approaches that Poole and his colleagues have taken toward a structurational view of small group communication makes clear an implicit assumption in their theoretical framework—something I call the *overt-sequential assumption*. Simply stated, this assumption is that the structures that are implicated *overtly* are the only ones being appropriated at a particular point in time. This assumption might further be seen as grounded in two more basic notions: (a) that only one structure (or, at least, one *source* of structure) is appropriated at a time, and (b) unless a structure is brought into the group discussion, it is *not* being appropriated by the group. On the surface, this would seem to be an intuitively obvious assumption, given that this sequential assumption is a foundation for a great deal of research in communication theory (see Fisher, 1978; Fisher & Hawes, 1971; Hewes, 1979; Poole, Folger, & Hewes, 1987; Street & Cappella, 1985). However, the problem with this assumption is that it forces researchers to overlook the fact that structures exist not only in their use, but also as what Giddens (1984) calls the "memory traces that orient the conduct of knowledgeable human agents" (p. 17).[10]

The Distribution of Valence Model

To some degree, the entire theoretical foundation of the DVM is premised on this assumption, given that Poole et al. (1982) posit that "the factors determining social action exist only in the stream of ongoing interaction. . . . 'external' factors only have bearing on action in so far as they are produced and reproduced by group members using them in interaction. Even seemingly stable factors such as a majority decision scheme of the group's task are mediated by interaction" (p. 3; but see Seibold et al., 1980, for the first articulation of this notion). Poole et al. argue, therefore, that the effects of external factors are *derived from* interaction, which is the opposite of how most models portray communication process—that is, that interaction is guided by external factors.

The source of this argument is Giddens's (1979, 1984) articulation of the concept of "structure," which similarly focuses on how structures exist only in their use. However, the central issue here is that there is more to the definition of structure than Poole and his colleagues have considered in their foundational premise. If one looks closely at how Giddens defines structure, it is clear that the DVM encompasses only part of this definition, because Giddens (1984) posits that "structure exists, as time-space presence, only in its instantiations in such practices *and as memory traces that orient the conduct of knowledgeable human agents*" (p. 17; emphasis added). Although structures may be identified as they are "instantiated" in the flow of human action, they also exist at another level that is not so observable; that is, at the level of the "memory traces" that group members use to orient their conduct.[11]

Adaptive Structuration Theory

Whereas Poole et al. (1982) clearly make the assumption a foundation of their work with the DVM, Poole and DeSanctis (1990, 1992) are a bit less explicit in their construction of AST. However, the assumption is still as prominent in, and perhaps even more significant to, Poole and DeSanctis's overall research program as in the DVM. The reason for this is apparent in the way that Poole and DeSanctis actually describe the structurational process that they identify in their examination of how small groups appropriate group decision support systems.

Remember that Poole and DeSanctis use two coding systems (or "sensitizing categories") to study the process by which small groups appropriate GDSSs: They simultaneously analyze the way the group appropriates the structure (again see Table 9.1) and the source of the structure that is appropriated (see Table 9.3). Therefore, every single communication act is analyzed in two ways: (a) how a structure is appropriated and (b) where it comes from. In this manner, the appropriation of communication technology is clearly studied as a *sequential* process; for example, first a group might initially focus on appropriating the technology (in a certain manner, which is the "how it is appropriated" category), then the GDSS outputs (again, in a certain manner), then back to the technology, then the task outputs, and so on.[12]

At first glance, the example Poole and DeSanctis offer of the coding scheme seems to validate this assumption. When one reads through the sample transcript presented in Table 9.4, it appears that the focus of the group clearly shifts: first, the members focus on the GDSS itself (i.e., advanced information technology system, coded A), then on the outputs of the GDSS (AO), and, finally, again on the GDSS itself (A). However, this sequential analysis misses many of the structures that are "accumulating" in the group structuring process. If one looks more closely at the sequence of statements, one can see that for group members to understand what is going on, they must not only focus on the mechanics of the GDSS, they must also continually maintain an understanding of what is occurring throughout the overall process; that is, they must maintain coherent memory traces (or, in the less clumsy language of cognitive science, a *mental model*) of the previous actions of the group members in order to "co-orient their conduct as knowledgeable human agents." This, too, is a structurational process.

An examination of some of the key sections in Table 9.4 should make this point clear (but for an analysis of a similar type of example, see Giddens, 1984, pp. 330-331). The first four lines refer to the group members' previous decision to weight the criteria they have generated for the task of allocating a $500,000 budget. Although these statements involve using the GDSS (as Poole & DeSanctis, 1992, indicate by assigning them an A code), they make no sense unless group members understand that weighting the criteria is one part of the overall task work (T) that they have to do, and that to weight the criteria, they must use the criteria they have generated previously, which are listed on the screen in front of them (which is a GDSS output, or AO). Likewise, the seventh and eighth codes highlight the fact that the members are viewing the public screen (i.e., AO); however, for these members to interpret this information, they must also bring to bear their conception of how the GDSS itself (A) works (it takes their individual weights and averages them), and they must also know why this weighting process is necessary in light of their larger responsibilities toward the task (T).

Finally, the last statement is a bid to move back to the main agenda that is a part of the GDSS itself; accordingly, Poole and DeSanctis code this as A. However, to

TABLE 9.3
Major Sources of Structure and Examples of Each

Structure Source	Definition	Examples in GDSS Context
AIT (A)	advanced information technology; includes hardware, software, and procedures	keyboard input devices, viewing screens, group note taking, voting modules, decision models
AIT outputs (AO)	data, text, or other results produced by AIT software following input by members	displays of group votes, lists of ideas, opinion graphs, modeling results
Task (T)	task knowledge or rules; includes facts and figures, opinion, folklore, or practice related to the task at hand	a budget task, customary ways of preparing budgets, specific budget data, budgeting goals and deadlines
Task outputs (TO)	the results of operating on task data or procedures; the results of completing all or parts of a task	budget calculations, implications of certain budget figures for other budget categories
Environment (E)	social knowledge or rules of action drawn from the organization or society at large; decision procedure for votes; references to corporate spending and reporting policies	applying a "spread the wealth" principle to budget allocation; applying "majority rule"
Environmental outputs (EO)	results of applying knowledge or rules drawn from the environment	implications of corporate spending policies for the budget process; the results and implications of applying a "majority rule" decision procedure to votes that have been taken

SOURCE: Adapted from DeSanctis and Poole (1994, p. 129).

interpret such a statement, group members must have an understanding of why it is necessary to move back to the agenda (which will refocus them again on their task, T). Additionally, they must have a conception of what the outputs of the GDSS (AO) have told them; in this situation, they "didn't get much of a spread," so it was necessary to go back and reevaluate what they should do next as a group.

Thus, although this "sequential" perspective does broadly capture a single structure that surfaces in the discourse of the individual members, it also misses much of the less overt structuring behavior that is occurring via the mental traces, or schemata, of the actors. It makes it appear that only one structure (or, at least, one *source* of structure) is appropriated at a time, when, in fact, there are multiple structures that operate in any such process. It also makes it appear that unless a structure is brought into the group discussion, it is *not* being appropriated by the group members, when, as the preceding analysis demonstrates, a variety of additional "covert" structures must underlie any such "overt" structuring process.[13]

TABLE 9.4
Sample of AST Codes

Appropriation Code	Group Member	Conversation
A-1b	5	Should we enter weights on these now?
A-1c	1	Yeah,
A-6b	1	let's each do our own weighing
A-1b	All	(typing on keyboards)
A-6h	1	Did we all enter?
A-6g	4	It's entered, yeah.
AO-AO-3a	5	What's "the most important thing," one and three say almost the same thing (referring to outputs on public screen).
AO-1a	1	Well, we didn't get much of a spread.
	5	hmmm
A-1c	1	Ok, let's go back to the main agenda (referring to a GDSS screen).

SOURCE: Poole and DeSanctis (1992, p. 26).

Implications

What the above analysis suggests is that rather than viewing structuration as a necessarily sequential process, we may better characterize it as a process of "model construction"; while on the surface certain structures may seem to take center stage for stretches of time, *below* the surface group members are continually developing a "theoretical understanding" of what is happening in the group (see Holland, Holyoak, Nisbett, & Thagard, 1986). Moreover, they are also continually applying that understanding—as a structure—in order to interpret what is happening in the group and to contribute to the group itself. This is a process of "model construction," because as time passes, group members create a more complex understanding (i.e., mental model) of what has happened and is happening in the group. Figure 9.1 clarifies this logic. In Figure 9.1a, the sequential perspective is displayed as a series of blocks that get placed one after the other;[14] however, in Figure 9.1b the model construction perspective highlights the notion that group members simultaneously implicate a variety of structures in order to generate small group processes. They start out applying more than one structure at t_1 and the number of structures that they apply fluctuates as the constructed model becomes either more or less complex.[15]

Poole and DeSanctis's (1992) notion of the "ironic" use of certain structures provides a final example of this process. They note that the way they identified "ironic appropriation" groups was by focusing on "how the groups dealt with ironic appropriation bids. . . . To determine reactions to ironic appropriations, we consulted the transcripts wherever one occurred and traced out reactions until it was clear whether the group accepted or rejected the appropriation" (p. 38). This process of "accepting" ironic appropriations is exactly the sort of process that is best conceived as a "model construction" process grounded in the mental models that group members use to orient themselves toward the group's work. This process might be spelled out as follows. First, at some point, an individual member makes an ironic move regarding the technology (this would be captured by Poole & DeSanctis's coding system). Next, other group members either immediately accept the move and act on it (also captured by the coding system) or debate the acceptance of the move (also captured by the coding system) and then ultimately accept it.

Once group members have accepted the ironic appropriation and consider it to be the "right" way to use the system, future ironic appropriations of the move become more difficult to identify. The primary reason for this relates to the way that group members use the past to interpret and to act in the present. What this means is that group members remember the way the group used past structures, and those mental models form the frame from which they interpret and construct their actions from that point on. Later in the group process, there will be less and less discussion about the ironic appropriation in the group; as the appropriation becomes a part of the group members' routine, they will often invoke it without any explicit discussion.[16] In other words, as an appropriation becomes "sedimented" into the habits of the group, there are fewer debates about it, because the appropriation simply becomes part of "how the group does things." Moreover, the ironic appropriation also frames the moves that group members *should not* make in the group, as it may seem to the members that the group has "decided upon" certain issues, and there is therefore little reason to bring them up again in the future. In this manner, the ironic appropriation may lead to a result that is similar to the "nondecision-making" identified by Bachrach and Baratz (1962).

Explaining How Systems Work

Poole et al. (1996) also suggest that structuration theory must develop an analysis of how systems work. Such an analysis "defines the general field in which structuration occurs and its 'surface' indicants. It forms a foundation for the analysis of the constitution of the group system. By implication, this requires identification of causal links that characterize the system's operation and members' interpretive maps" (p. 125). Essentially, what Poole and his colleagues highlight here is the relationship between system and structure; to some degree, good structurational theories must characterize this relationship if they are to explain how knowledgeable agents produce and reproduce social systems. However, because structuration is also premised on the notion that agents are not always knowledgeable about the conditions of their own actions, this implies spelling out the relationship between the intentional actions of agents and the *unintentional*

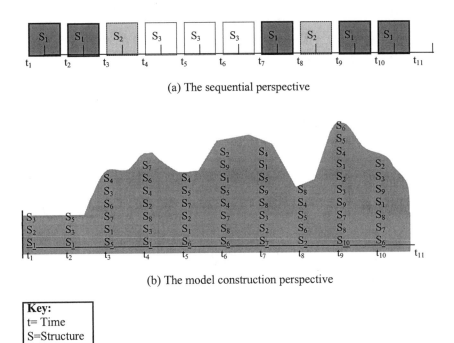

(a) The sequential perspective

(b) The model construction perspective

Key:
t= Time
S=Structure

Figure 9.1. Sequential and Model Construction Perspectives on the Structuration Process

consequences of those actions, both of which result in the pattern of social behavior that characterizes a small group system.

As noted earlier, Poole and his colleagues have had some success in presenting explanations of "how systems work" in terms that have begun to provide answers to some questions that are highly relevant to the field of small group behavior. Although all of the approaches reviewed above share the context of small group decision making as the "general field in which structuration occurs," each approach has a unique explanation of how such a system works as a result of the diversity of issues it addresses. For example, in a nutshell, the multiple-sequence model (Poole, 1983b; Poole & Doelger, 1986) posits that developmental patterns of group development (i.e., the system) are constructed by agents using collective task representations and coherency strategies (i.e., structures), with limits being placed on structuring by key contingency variables. In contrast, the argument-as-structure model (Seibold et al., 1981, 1983) posits that group argumentation processes (i.e., the system) are constructed by agents who use generalized argument strategies (i.e., structures). Despite the differences between these approaches, their common concern is the explanation of how systems work. However, a central issue must be resolved if structurational researchers are to provide a complete explanation of small groups as systems. This issue is bound up in something I call the *group-as-agent* assumption.

Another aspect of Poole and his colleagues' work, citing Warriner's (1956) argument that groups are "real" entities, is the consistent assumption that groups—to some degree—can be considered to be "agents." For example, Poole et al. (1985) observe:

> The subject is not a basic unit of action, but rather a produced and reproduced position in the field of structuration. The importance of the subject is emphasized by our cultural and social suppositions, but neither our culture nor a considered perspective on the nature of action *requires* that individual persons be the only units capable of action. We hold that *groups* can act, can produce and reproduce social structure in the course of acting. (p. 82)

They go on to suggest that one of the consequences of this line of reasoning is that groups may be seen as entities

> where causation and action meet: the "situated group" joins the "situated agent." For instance, just as one's memory may fail, causing one to forget an important point and resulting in loss of credibility at a public hearing, the group may have records (minutes, notes, and research reports) which, if destroyed, impair its ability to act successfully in the future. (p. 83)

Although this group-as-agent assumption underlies all four of the approaches to structuration in a variety of ways, it perhaps comes to greatest prominence in an intuitive reading that is often made of Poole and DeSanctis's (1992) study on the appropriation of GDSS as technological "structure." Poole and DeSanctis indicate that if groups faithfully appropriate the GDSS technology, then this will result in greater consensus change—a measure that many small group researchers see as an indication of higher decision quality. Poole and DeSanctis (1990) see this as initial evidence in support of the "double contingency" proposition in adaptive structuration theory, positing that "*given* GDSS design and other contextual conditions, $n_1 \ldots n_k$, *and* stable group appropriation processes, *then* predicted outcomes of GDSS use will result" (p. 188). Now, if one takes into account Poole et al.'s (1985) previous statements regarding groups as actors, an intuitive reading of Poole and DeSanctis's 1992 study is that their results indicate strong *agency* effects—that is, the way the group (qua agent) appropriates the GDSS technology (i.e., structure) is one of the key moderating variables that affects the outcomes of the group. Thus, in this instance, the group is the primary "agent" being studied.

This is especially interesting in contrast to Poole and Roth's (1989b) study of the MSM, in which they identify what seem to be some limits on the structuring process. In discussing their results, Poole and Roth note that for the global properties of the group decision path, the contingency variables of the MSM seem to control the decision path so tightly that they prevent much active structuring by agents. Specifically, they note that their model's ability to predict global decision paths "suggests determination of decision paths is much stronger and the influence of group action much weaker than proposed by Poole (1985; Poole & Doelger, 1986)" (p. 586). On the other hand, the model was less predictive of the complexity and distribution of the group activities, which they take as evidence that "structuring processes have more scope for play at this level. Overall then, choice of path seems to be strongly constrained, but groups have greater freedom regarding local organization of interaction and content emphases" (p. 586). In other words, although Poole and DeSanctis (1992) seem to have uncovered strong "agency effects," Poole and Roth's research (1989b) seems to demonstrate that there are occasionally limits on group agency—what I call *system* effects, for shorthand purposes.

Although these readings are intriguing—and, as I argue elsewhere, the analogue between groups and agents is useful (Seyfarth, 1999)—a strong argument might be made by other structuration scholars that such intuitive readings simply should not be made. The primary reason is that the group-as-agent assumption that Poole and his colleagues make explicit in their 1985 piece seems to be ultimately inconsistent with the logic of structuration theory. In short, as Giddens might contend, groups must be considered to be systems *composed of* agents, not agents in and of themselves.

Giddens originally formulated structuration theory partly in response to his criticisms of traditional functionalist approaches to social science, which displayed a characteristic tendency to impute teleology to entire social systems, much the way that Poole and his colleagues seem to be doing in their conception of the group as an actor. In his 1979 book, Giddens points out that such tendencies are one of the characteristic weaknesses of functional approaches; moreover, he argues that it is dangerous to impute "purposes, reasons or needs" to social systems, because only *human individuals* can have these. Most strongly, he argues that any theory that imputes such a "teleology" to social systems must be viewed as invalid. He elaborates on this in his later work:

> To say that the existence of social state A needs a social practice B to help it to survive in similarly recognizable form is to pose a question that then has to be answered; it does not itself answer it. The relation between A and B is not analogous to the relation that obtains between wants or needs and intentions in the individual actor. In the individual, wants that are constitutive of the motivational impulses of the actor generate a dynamic relation between motivation and intentionality. This is not the case with social systems, except where actors behave in cognizance of what they take to be social needs. (Giddens, 1984, pp. 12-13)

Later, in a discussion relating to the sociological debate over methodological individualism, he explains this idea further:

> A further question raised by [this debate] is: are collectivities actors? What does it mean to say, for example, "The government decided to pursue public policy X?" Or, "The government acted quickly in the face of the threat of a rebellion"? . . . If collectivities or groups are not agents, why do we sometimes speak as though they were, as in the above examples? We tend to do so when there is a significant degree of reflexive monitoring of the conditions of social reproduction, of the sort associated especially with organizations, although not exclusive to them. . . . It is important to understand that "The government decided . . ." or "The government acted . . ." are shorthand statements because in some situations it may matter a great deal which individuals were the main initiators or executors of whatever decisions were taken (or not taken) and whatever policies followed. (pp. 220-221)

A strong form of this argument is that the group-as-agent assumption simply does not make sense when one considers the overall logic of structuration theory. If one thinks about it, the notion of "group as agent" may present a confounding situation for the theoretician, both figuratively and literally. On one hand, the small group is conceived of as a *system* itself, one that is produced and reproduced by knowledgeable human agents who use structures to produce an observable pattern of activity. On the other hand, the small group is also conceived of as an *agent* itself, one that "can act, can produce and reproduce social structure in the course of acting" (Poole et al., 1985, p. 82). If both of these are true, is there any value in distinguishing agents from systems at all? Might we begin at any level of analysis and identify the properties of agents and the properties of systems identically?[17]

Although this hard-line case against group agency seems to have at least some merit, this is not the position I take in this essay (or in the research that I have conducted that arises from these criticisms; see Seyfarth, 1999). Although it may seem disingenuous to raise this criticism and then partially back away from it, I do so only to point out that there are some important knots to untie in this question of group agency. At the very least, this criticism makes clear that some separation between the conception of agent and system is not only analytically useful but necessary—especially if researchers are to capitalize on the other propositions that are also a part of the logic of the theory (e.g., practical consciousness, the stratification model of the agent, or the unintended consequences of intentional actions).

The reason it is necessary for me to tread lightly as I describe the hard-line version of this case is that, to some degree, it *is* possible to think of some small group situations as approximating this idea of group agency, even though such an idea does violate some of the logic of structuration theory. For example, consider a highly cohesive group of three assembly-line workers performing a simple task in their skill set. It is probably fair to say that such a group approaches something most people would call "intentionality," as the group members share similar representations of the task environment, similar representations of a shared goal state, and even similar representations of the sequence of actions they should perform in order to accomplish the goal state. In this scenario, it is not much of a stretch to think of this group as exhibiting agency.

As such, I do not take the position here that hard-line advocates of structuration theory might, which would seem to preclude any possibility of such a notion as "group agency." However, I do believe that it is important to establish a more interesting position; that is, one that attempts to sort out when groups have properties that are similar to those of agents and when they do not. In other words, assuming that groups may occasionally be thought of as agents, how does such agency relate to Giddens's structurational assumption that systems are produced and reproduced by the structures implicated by *individual* actors? And perhaps more important, is this the same type of agency that may be ascribed to individuals? In summary, the final issue we must dealt with in order to provide a better explanation of "how systems work" is the question of where "system" ends and "agent" begins, and vice versa. Hard-line structuration theorists might posit that "groups are not agents; humans are agents." [18] However, the more subtle questions that need to be answered are, How are groups like agents, and how are they not?[19]

IMPLICATIONS FOR FUTURE RESEARCH

Although I have identified in this essay a number of directions that might be taken in future applications of structuration theory, I want to emphasize strongly that the reason I have presented these criticisms has been to develop those areas, and *not* to criticize for its own sake. In this final section, I briefly outline some of the key ideas that have guided a program of theory construction that is nearing completion. Space limitations prohibit a thorough discussion of this new perspective, thus my comments in this section are intended to be purely illustrative—and in many ways are bound to be a little unfulfilling—because I am unable to deal fully with the intricacies of the approach in this context (for a full explication of these ideas, see Seyfarth, 1999).

For future research to address the issues on which I have focused in this essay—identifying the relevant structures that constitute systems and explaining how systems work—there must be some shifts in the ways structurational processes are studied. These shifts can be summarized as follows: Future researchers must (a) incorporate the study of "mental traces" (i.e., mental models) into current analyses of the structuration process, and thereby provide more concrete analyses of the key structures that are appropriated by agents to constitute social systems; and then (b) build on this individual-level foundation by theorizing about the relationships that may exist among *multiple* cognitive structures. I contend that these relationships—which I call different *patterns of structural appropriation*—are the key to generating *group*-level processes. Moreover, they allow—to some degree—for a conception of *group* agency that is still consistent with Giddens's original theorizing. To explain these goals further, I briefly address each in turn below.

Using Cognitive Concepts in the Analysis of Strategic Conduct

Giddens (1984) posits that although it is important to have a sophisticated analysis of the "effects" of both agents *and* systems to understand structurational processes, it is also occasionally helpful to "bracket" one or the other in order to understand fully how that mechanism contributes to the observable social phenomena that it generates. He further notes that two possible strategies are available to the researcher: institutional analysis, which focuses on the repetitive patterns that characterize system reproduction, or the "analysis of strategic conduct," which focuses on

> modes in which actors draw upon structural properties in the constitution of social relations. . . . [This means] giving primary importance to discursive and practical consciousness, and to strategies of control within defined contextual boundaries. Institutionalized properties of the settings of interaction are assumed methodologically to be "given." We have to take care with this, of course, for to treat structural properties as methodologically "given" is not to hold that they are not produced and reproduced through human agency. (p. 288)

Traditional interpretations of this sort of methodological approach have tended to assume that such analyses are inherently hermeneutic and, as such, require some sort of qualitative approach; in fact, the example that Giddens provides of this type of analysis is Willis's (1977) ethnographic account of "how working-class kids get working-class jobs." However, I maintain that cognitive approaches to social science offer another equally valuable way to accomplish the same objective.

Rather than focusing specifically on how such links should be drawn between cognitive theory and structuration theory, I offer some general comments on how cognitive approaches can meet the goals for current applications of structuration that I have identified above. Generally, cognitive approaches offer highly developed explanations of the individual that are quite compatible with Giddens's conception of the human agent. Moreover, these models tend to be fairly explicit about the ways that individual-level processes serve as mechanisms that generate observable social phenomena. Current cognitive models, which tend to focus on how individuals implicate *mental models* (Holland et al., 1986)—in both a *controlled* and an *automatic* manner (Bargh, 1984)—to interpret their world, as well as to act in it, line up quite clearly with Giddens's (1984) "stratification model of the acting self," which he uses to explain the active agent. These models have the added advantage of years of theoretical and empirical development behind them.

As an illustration of the manner in which this may work, consider how a key axiom of Giddens's description of structures—that is, that they are "both the medium and the outcome of action"—can be applied to mental models, which may also be viewed as both the medium and the outcome of action. Intuitively, mental models may be seen as the *medium* of action, because individuals draw on these models to make decisions about how to act and interpret the actions of others. However, such models may also be seen as the *outcome* of action, because the successful use of a mental model reproduces it as a meaningful basis for future action. Such a notion would be clearly supported by cognitive theorists who believe that memory is much like a "storage bin" (see Wyer & Srull, 1980, 1986). These theorists posit that as one mental model (i.e., structure) is used successfully, it is thrown onto the top of the mental "heap" and is, therefore, more likely to be used again in the future (this effect has been found for frequently used concepts as well as recently used concepts; Fiske & Taylor, 1991, p. 263). In this manner, the reproduction of mental models takes on many of the features of the "priming" process studied by cognitive scientists.

Using Cognitive Concepts to Articulate Patterns of Group Action

Despite the points raised above, it is also important to remember that this analysis by itself illuminates only *one* of the mechanisms that generate small group behavior: the intentional actions of agents. Although one key conclusion should be that this is a necessary component of any complete explanation of a social phenomenon, the analysis cannot end there. Here, I discuss some issues that demonstrate the necessity of situating this cognitive perspective in a larger system of propositions, one that also includes the *unintended consequences* of intentional actions. This is an area in which pure cognitive approaches tend to fall short, and care must be taken to avoid a reductionist move (as McPhee, 1995, has warned; however, for examples of cognitive models that attempt to overcome this potential weakness, see Hutchins, 1990, 1991; Weick & Roberts, 1993).

The essence of the argument is as follows: Once the cognitive representations of each group member are understood—at least on a basic level—the next move is to consider how the cognitive representations of each member relate to the cognitive representations of each of the *other* group members and then how those patterns themselves generate group phenomena. In other words, a fundamental axiom of this perspective is that group behavior is not determined by the structures (i.e., mental models) that a single individual appropriates, nor is it determined by a single set of structures that all group members appropriate; rather, it is determined by the pattern of structures appropriated by each agent in the group. As such, the area of focus for researchers should be the way that each of group member's individual mental model relates to the models of all of the other group members, thereby generating the observable patterns of behavior that we call "group" phenomena.

Although I can only briefly introduce these here, I contend that there are three archetypal patterns that characterize group activity and that suggest a key distinction between when groups may be considered agents and when they may not. The first type of pattern, *quasi-intentionality,* is the one in which a group's activity is most comparable to individual agency. This is a situation in which all members appropriate *similar* structures to generate the observable group activity. In other words, all members share similar mental models and use them in a nearly identical fashion to structure activity. This may be distinguished from the second type of pattern, *mediation,* which is also based on Giddens's theorizing. Mediation is observed in situations in which group members appropriate *different* but *complementary* structures to generate the observable group activity. With this type of pattern, members generate a coherent social order; however, it is not one that any of them fully intend, given that they all use sets of structures that are markedly different from one another. Finally, another alternative is a situation characterized by *contradiction,* in which members appropriate *different* and *noncomplementary* structures to generate the observable group activity. Although this pattern of structural appropriation does not always result in observable social conflict, it does tend to generate a type of outcome that Giddens (1984) has called "perverse consequences."

Drawing Together the Implications

Although the ideas in this section are suggestive, much more space would be necessary for me to develop fully this perspective on structuration theory. The important points to note are that in order to understand small group processes, researchers must (a) expand on their analyses of the mental structures of individual agents and the ways that agents engage in "model construction" as they participate in small group processes and then (b) build on this individual-level foundation by theorizing about the relationships that may exist among *multiple* cognitive structures. The research program I am currently completing is devoted to developing this perspective and then situating the model in order to provide a better explanation of small group communication processes.

SUMMARY

In this chapter, I have provided an extensive review and analysis of current situated approaches to structuration theory and outlined some of the hurdles that these approaches currently face. In the first section I introduced structuration theory and reviewed the four areas of small group communication research on which Poole and his colleagues have focused their efforts. I then introduced the six key issues that Poole et al. (1996) believe good structurational theories must address and used two of those issues to frame an in-depth analysis of Poole and his colleagues' own theorizing. Specifically, this analysis centered upon these two questions: (a) How well do Poole and his colleagues identify the relevant structures that are used to constitute the system? (b) How well do Poole and his colleagues explain how systems work? Finally, I briefly outlined two key implications that these critiques have for future research in this area and commented on how these implications are currently guiding a research program in progress.

To be sure, Poole and his colleagues have come a long way in their work with structuration theory, and small group researchers across the social sciences—not just in the area of small group communication—are in Poole et al.'s debt for bringing this important theoretical framework into the study of small group processes. However, despite the great strides taken in the past 15 years, I have demonstrated in this chapter that there are some important areas that still deserve further theoretical development. Therefore, future work in the areas alluded to in the final section of this essay will be crucial to maintaining the momentum that structurational researchers have established over the past several years. As such, this chapter serves not only as a summary of where we are so far, but as a signpost toward the future.

NOTES

1. I use the terms *situated* and *applied* interchangeably to denote approaches that are not direct extensions of structuration theory itself, but use structuration as a metatheory to inform the work that the researcher takes in a particular context. Because structuration theory is a metatheory, it cannot be "proved" or "falsified" in a traditional sense. However, researchers who incorporate structurational assumptions into their work *can* evaluate the value of these assumptions in situated contexts.

2. Giddens calls this a "double hermeneutic." For a concrete example of the double hermeneutic in action, consider the efforts of small group researchers to determine whether there truly are coherent phases of group decision making. Assuming for a moment that it is possible to identify such phases of decision making, these phases are undoubtedly influenced by group members' mental representations regarding how to engage in decision making, and these "scripts" are undoubtedly influenced by standard patterns for decision making that have been taught for years in small group discussion by social scientists. For an example of a study that struggles with this very dilemma, see Honeycutt and Poole (1994).

3. A brief note is necessary here in regard to Weick's theory of organizing, as it may appear to some readers that Weick's theory already deals with some of the dilemmas introduced in this section. Although Weick's theory of organizing is in many respects similar to structuration theory (due in large part to their both being influenced by Schutz's [1967] phenomenological theory), structuration is a bit more advantageous in its ability to account for change *and* stability. Although Weick (1979) attempts to deal with both, his theory ends up emphasizing change over stability. For example, he states that "the image of organizations that we prefer is one which argues that organizations keep falling apart and that they require chronic rebuilding. Processes continually need to be reaccomplished" (p. 44). This is one of the most valuable insights of Weick's work, but this image must also be balanced by one that accounts for the relative stability in the ways organizations are continually rebuilt. Weick (1990, p. 18) seems to have accepted this point and has drawn some linkages between his approach and structuration theory (e.g., Weick, 1990, 1993), but he has yet to do so comprehensively.

4. Although I focus here on Poole and his colleagues' work on structuration theory in the small group setting, the theory has been applied to a large number of other areas. In fact, Banks and Riley (1993) have described structuration as a possible conceptual center point around which *all* communication research might be based. Additional areas studied using Giddens's framework include organizational climate (Poole, 1994; Poole & McPhee, 1983), organizational culture (Riley, 1983; Seyfarth, 1996), power (Brass & Burkhardt, 1993; Conrad, 1983), group decision making (Banks & Riley, 1993), new communication technologies (Barley, 1986, 1990; Contractor &

Eisenberg, 1990; Contractor, Seibold, & Heller, 1996), communications media and rhetorical theory (Orlikowski & Yates, 1994; Yates & Orlikowski, 1992), contract negotiations (Keough & Lake, 1991), institutional theory and managerial strategic choice (Whittington, 1992), organizational structure (McPhee, 1985; Ranson, Hinings, & Greenwood, 1980), critical organizational theory (Mumby, 1987, 1988), organizational change and innovation (Lewis & Seibold, 1993, 1996; Van de Ven & Poole, 1988, 1995), and symbolic organizational processes (Smith, 1983).

5. Poole also notes that there is another class of structures that are necessary to ensure "coherency" in decision paths. These *coherence moves* create connections between statements and allow the group to make transitions from one step to another. Coherence moves cover a broad range of strategies, including *elementary devices,* which link and separate conversational elements; *alignment moves,* which allay misunderstandings or problems that arise in conversations; and *structuring moves,* which call upon extralinguistic resources (e.g., power, expertise) to remedy certain problems in the flow of the discourse. It is important to acknowledge these strategies as structures that explain how the sequence of phases is managed at the micro level. However, for the sake of simplicity, I only mention these points here and then elaborate on how these structures fit into the program I introduce later in this essay.

6. Although Jarboe's (1988) investigation into the nature of input-process-output explanations may have weakened Hewes's stance a bit, his basic questions in this area remain significant concerns, as Poole et al. (1996) acknowledge.

7. There is a second area in which researchers have recast traditional input variables as interactional, and that is in the study of choice shift (also discussed as polarization, or risky or cautious shift). This approach was laid out in the dissertation work of Meyers, who was a student of Seibold's. Meyers's (1989a, 1989b) research revolves around challenging another noninteractional approach to small group decision making: persuasive arguments theory (see Vinokur & Burnstein, 1974). Generally, her results do demonstrate the value of interactional explanations over the noninteractional PAT explanation; however, her tests do not reveal the precise relationships among the input variables, the interactional variables, and the group outcomes as well as do those of Poole et al. (1982). For an example of a piece that directly links her research program to structuration theory, see Meyers, Seibold, and Brashers (1991); for the most recent statement of Meyers's work relating argument structures to structuration theory, see Meyers and Brashers (1997).

An additional point that should be made here is that many of these same problems are found in other areas of small group communication, the most notable of which is Gouran and Hirokawa's functional approach to small group decision-making effectiveness (see Gouran, Hirokawa, Julian, & Leatham, 1993). Although this work has demonstrated some very general support for the value of communication, the studies have been plagued by inconsistency (see Stohl & Holmes, 1993; for a recent example of such inconsistent results, see Salazar, Hirokawa, Propp, Julian, & Leatham, 1994). For the most cogent summary of this argument against the value of communication as an important variable in understanding group processes, see Hewes's (1986, 1990, 1996) string of arguments.

8. Meyers et al. (1991) have since refined their coding scheme by including a separate category for "agreement." In a manner similar to Canary et al. (1987), Meyers et al. found argument to be characterized predominantly by assertions, elaborations, and agreement statements. For other examples of work in this tradition (but outside of the area of small group communication), see Brossman and Canary (1990) and Canary et al. (1987).

9. Given that this is a review of theoretical perspectives, it may seem odd that I focus so much on this methodological aspect of AST. The reason I need to discuss the coding system in this context is that Poole and DeSanctis do not conceive of this system as purely methodological. Rather than viewing it as an interactional coding scheme, they propose that it should be regarded as a set of "sensitizing categories" in the tradition of Glaser and Strauss (1967). "The primary value of the system is not limited to the identification of specific appropriation moves for quantitative analysis. Just as valuable are identification of key events in the structuring process and support for system-

atic qualitative analysis" (Poole & DeSanctis, 1992, p. 24). Therefore, I find it necessary not only to include this scheme in my review, but to evaluate it, as I do later in the essay.

10. A similar argument with a slightly different rationale has also been made by Hewes and Planalp (1987; Planalp & Hewes, 1982), who claim that such sequential models are "transindividual" approaches to communication science. Although my analysis here is separate from these arguments and based on a different underlying rationale, it is similar in spirit. For a more extensive review of these points, see Seyfarth (1999).

11. It should also be noted that Folger and Poole (1982) have constructed one tool that may be used to deflect some of this criticism in their construct of *representational validity.* This form of validity indicates that the schemes coders use to analyze sequential interaction are in some way parallel to the interpretative schemes group members apply to the actual interaction. Although Poole et al. (1982) establish the representational validity of their coding scheme (and Poole, 1980b, does the same in his work on the MSM), this still makes a dangerous assumption: Because the very notion of representational validity *assumes* intersubjectivity among participants, it does not allow for *any* individual differences in interpretations. In other words, it argues that all cognitive processes are manifest in social processes. Although it is perhaps true that participants are able to think along the same general paths at times, it is doubtful that this characterizes groups at all points in time.

12. This sequential assumption is a foundation for a great deal of research in communication theory, not just AST (see Hewes, 1979; Poole et al., 1987; Street & Cappella, 1985).

13. Two additional sources of evidence for this notion are found in widely divergent literatures. For one, take Bachrach and Baratz's (1962; see also Conrad, 1983) classic example of the professor who plans to make an argument against a long-standing policy at an upcoming faculty meeting but then remains silent during the meeting. Bachrach and Baratz argue that this professor chooses not to act because of his perception of the existing power relationships on the faculty; this illustrates their notion that there are "two faces" of power (a notion with which Giddens, 1984, p. 15, strongly agrees). This also presents an example of a "covert" structuring process; in this case, the structures used in this process (i.e., the perceptions of the existing power relationships) actually lead to what Bachrach and Baratz call *nondecision-making.* A second source of evidence for this process may be found in Aristotle's (1954; see also Cooper, 1989) discussion of the *enthymeme,* which points out that *rhetors* (i.e., arguers) often leave the major premises of their arguments unstated; the reason for this is that audiences are often quite capable of "filling in" major parts of arguments themselves. Moreover, this is actually an effective argumentative strategy, because it is both more efficient and more persuasive than other strategies. Aristotle argues that by filling in the missing parts of an argument, audience members often *persuade themselves.* This process is also an example of a "covert" structuring process, as it focuses on how audience members themselves must supply the "structures" that lead to persuasion.

14. To be accurate, the MSM does not posit that there is only one such string of blocks, but rather at least three strings—what Poole (1983b) calls "activity tracks." Space limitations prevent a full discussion of the subtleties that this possibility raises, but my general argument is that although this is a more complex version of the sequential assumption, it still does not escape the arguments against the sequential assumption generally.

15. Space limitations prohibit my providing a great deal of elaboration upon this model. However, it is important to note at least briefly that a full model would account for (a) the reasons mental models occasionally become less complex, (b) "chunking" processes that may organize the complexity of mental models, and (c) a more focused discussion of *which* mental models, specifically, are being appropriated. For such a discussion, see Seyfarth (1999).

16. Of course, members may also later challenge an ironic appropriation; however, that would thereby remove the group from consideration as an ironic group. For the purpose of this example, I focus on groups that do not revert to faithful appropriations.

17. It is important to emphasize that there is no inherent reason for social scientists to be purists with Giddens (or any other theorist, for that matter) as they translate structuration theory to applied

research. Some slight modifications may, in fact, be necessary to address the concerns of the particular area of application. However, some aspects of the theory are so foundational that altering them would require a researcher (a) to present an extensive rationale that demonstrates some consistency with the original statement of structuration theory or (b) to identify his or her theory as a quasi-structurational explanation.

18. One may make an opposing point to this argument by noting (as many cognitive scientists do; see Minsky, 1985) that humans are *also* systems, in addition to being agents. Although I do not spend time arguing this point extensively, there are some important differences between the types of systems (and "agents"; again see Minsky, 1985) that cognitive scientists study and the types of systems that are characterized in structuration theory. While analogues between the individual cognitive system and social systems may be useful (see Hutchins, 1991; Nelson & Mathews, 1991), they should not be overstated.

19. Interestingly, Contractor and Seibold (1993) make a similar point in their critique of AST, but the implications of their argument are a bit different. Although they agree with the general point that AST must do more to specify the generative mechanisms that produce either faithful or ironic appropriations, their argument is that these generative mechanisms might be uncovered by an increased focus on *unintended* consequences (which might benefit from the study of self-organizing systems). My argument is a bit different from (but not incompatible with) Contractor and Seibold's, in that I contend that Poole and DeSanctis's (1992) approach does not deal with the issues of *intentional* actions as clearly as it might. As I explain later, the important thing is not to determine which is more important—the intended or the unintended—but rather to specify how each type of "social force" acts as a mechanism that generates the observable behavior that characterizes the small group *system*.

REFERENCES

Abric, J. C. (1971). An experimental study of group creativity: Task representation, group structure, and performance. *European Journal of Social Psychology, 1,* 311-326.

Aristotle. (1954). *The rhetoric* (W. R. Roberts, Trans.). New York: Modern Library.

Bachrach, P., & Baratz, M. (1962). Two faces of power. *American Political Science Review, 56,* 947-952.

Bales, R. F., & Strodtbeck, F. L. (1951). Phases in group problem-solving. *Journal of Abnormal and Social Psychology, 46,* 485-495.

Banks, S. P., & Riley, P. (1993). Structuration theory as an ontology for communication research. In S. A. Deetz (Ed.), *Communication yearbook 16* (pp. 167-196). Newbury Park, CA: Sage.

Bargh, J. A. (1984). Automatic and conscious processing of social information. In R. S. Wyer, Jr., & T. K. Srull (Eds.), *Handbook of social cognition: Vol. 1. Basic processes* (pp. 1-43). Hillsdale, NJ: Lawrence Erlbaum.

Barley, S. R. (1986). Technology as an occasion for structuring: Evidence from observations of CT scanners and the social order of radiology departments. *Administrative Science Quarterly, 31,* 78-108.

Barley, S. R. (1990). The alignment of technology and structure through roles and networks. *Administrative Science Quarterly, 35,* 61-103.

Berger, P. L., & Luckmann, T. (1967). *The social construction of reality: A treatise in the sociology of knowledge.* Garden City, NY: Doubleday.

Brass, D. J., & Burkhardt, M. E. (1993). Potential power and power use: An investigation of structure and behavior. *Academy of Management Journal, 36,* 441-470.

Brossman, B. G., & Canary, D. J. (1990). An observational analysis of argument structures: The case of *Nightline. Argumentation, 4,* 199-212.

Budd, R. W. (1977). Perspectives on a discipline: Review and commentary. In B. D. Ruben (Ed.), *Communication yearbook 1* (pp. 29-36). New Brunswick, NJ: Transaction.

Canary, D. J., Brossman, B. G., & Seibold, D. R. (1987). Argument structures in decision-making groups. *Southern Speech Communication Journal, 53,* 18-37.

Canary, D. J., Brossman, B. G., Sillars, A. L., & LoVette, S. (1987). Married couples' argument structures and sequences: A comparison of satisfied and dissatisfied dyads. In J. W. Wenzel (Ed.), *Argument and critical practices: Proceedings of the Fifth SCA/AFA Conference on Argumentation* (pp. 475-484). Annandale, VA: Speech Communication Association.

Canary, D. J., Ratledge, N. T., & Seibold, D. R. (1982, November). *Argument and group decision-making: Development of a coding scheme.* Paper presented at the annual meeting of the Speech Communication Association, Louisville, KY.

Conrad, C. (1983). Organizational power: Faces and symbolic forms. In L. L. Putnam & M. E. Pacanowsky (Eds.), *Communication in organizations: An interpretive approach* (pp. 173-194). Beverly Hills, CA: Sage.

Contractor, N. S., & Eisenberg, E. M. (1990). Communication networks and new media in organizations. In J. Fulk & C. W. Steinfield (Eds.), *Organizations and communication technology* (pp. 143-172). Newbury Park, CA: Sage.

Contractor, N. S., & Seibold, D. R. (1993). Theoretical frameworks for the study of structuring processes in group decision support systems: Adaptive structuration theory and self-organizing systems theory. *Human Communication Research, 19,* 528-563.

Contractor, N. S., Seibold, D. R., & Heller, M. A. (1996). Interactional influence in the structuring of media use in groups: Influence in members' perceptions of group decision support system use. *Human Communication Research, 22,* 451-481.

Cooper, M. (1989). *Analyzing public discourse.* Prospect Heights, IL: Waveland.

Cragan, J. F., & Wright, D. W. (1980). Small group communication research of the 1970's: A synthesis and critique. *Central States Speech Journal, 31,* 197-213.

Cragan, J. F., & Wright, D. W. (1990). Small group communication research of the 1980's: A synthesis and critique. *Central States Speech Journal, 41,* 212-236.

Davis, J. H. (1973). Group decision and social interaction: A theory of social decision schemes. *Psychological Review, 80,* 97-125.

DeSanctis, G., & Poole, M. S. (1994). Capturing the complexity of advanced technology use: The theory of adaptive structuration. *Organization Science, 5,* 121-147.

DiMaggio, P. J., & Powell, W. W. (1991). Introduction. In W. W. Powell & P. J. DiMaggio (Eds.), *The new institutionalism in organizational analysis* (pp. 1-38). Chicago: University of Chicago Press.

Fisher, B. A. (1970). Decision emergence: Phases in group decision-making. *Communication Monographs, 37,* 53-66.

Fisher, B. A. (1978). *Perspectives on human communication.* New York: Macmillan.

Fisher, B. A., & Hawes, L. C. (1971). An interact system model: Generating a grounded theory of small groups. *Quarterly Journal of Speech, 57,* 444-453.

Fiske, S. T., & Taylor, S. E. (1991). *Social cognition* (2nd ed.). New York: McGraw-Hill.

Folger, J. P., & Poole, M. S. (1982). Relational coding schemes: The question of validity. In M. Burgoon (Ed.), *Communication yearbook 5* (pp. 235-247). New Brunswick, NJ: Transaction.

Giddens, A. (1979). *Central problems in social theory.* Berkeley: University of California Press.

Giddens, A. (1984). *The constitution of society: Outline of the theory of structuration.* Cambridge: Polity.

Giddens, A. (1993). *New rules of sociological method* (2nd ed.). Stanford, CA: Stanford University Press.

Glaser, B. G., & Strauss, A. L. (1967). *The discovery of grounded theory: Strategies for qualitative research.* Chicago: Aldine.

Gouran, D. S., Hirokawa, R. Y., Julian, K. M., & Leatham, G. B. (1993). The evolution and current status of the functional perspective on communication in decision-making and problem-solving groups. In S. A. Deetz (Ed.), *Communication yearbook 16* (pp. 573-600). Newbury Park, CA: Sage.

Harré, R., & Madden, H. (1975). *Causal powers.* Totowa, NJ: Rowman & Littlefield.

Hastie, R., & Pennington, N. (1991). Cognitive and social processes in decision-making. In L. B. Resnick, J. M. Levine, & S. D. Teasley (Eds.), *Perspectives on socially shared cognition* (pp. 308-327). Washington, DC: American Psychological Association.

Hewes, D. E. (1979). The sequential analysis of interaction. *Quarterly Journal of Speech, 65,* 56-73.

Hewes, D. E. (1986). The socio-egocentric model of small group communication. In R. Y. Hirokawa & M. S. Poole (Eds.), *Communication and small group decision-making* (pp. 265-289). Beverly Hills, CA: Sage.

Hewes, D. E. (1990, November). *Challenging interaction influence on group decision-making: Extending the socio-egocentric model.* Paper presented at the annual meeting of the Speech Communication Association, Chicago.

Hewes, D. E. (1996). Small group communication may not influence decision-making: An amplification of socio-egocentric theory. In R. Y. Hirokawa & M. S. Poole (Eds.), *Communication and small group decision-making* (2nd ed., pp. 179-212). Thousand Oaks, CA: Sage.

Hewes, D. E., & Planalp, S. (1987). The individual's place in communication science. In C. R. Berger & S. H. Chaffee (Eds.), *Handbook of communication science* (pp. 146-183). Newbury Park, CA: Sage.

Holland, J. H., Holyoak, K. J., Nisbett, R. E., & Thagard, P. R. (1986). *Induction: Processes of inference, learning and discovery.* Cambridge: MIT Press.

Honeycutt, J. M., & Poole, M. S. (1994, November). *Procedural schemata for group decision-making.* Paper presented at the annual meeting of the Speech Communication Association, New Orleans.

Hutchins, E. (1990). The technology of team navigation. In J. Galegher, R. E. Kraut, & C. Egido (Eds.), *Intellectual teamwork: Social and technological foundations of cooperative work* (pp. 191-220). Hillsdale, NJ: Lawrence Erlbaum.

Hutchins, E. (1991). The social organization of distributed cognition. In L. B. Resnick, J. M. Levine, & S. D. Teasley (Eds.), *Perspectives on socially shared cognition* (pp. 283-307). Washington, DC: American Psychological Association.

Jarboe, S. (1988). A comparison of input-output, process-output, and input-process-output models of small group problem-solving effectiveness. *Communication Monographs, 55,* 121-142.

Keough, C., & Lake, R. (1991). Values as structuring properties of contract negotiations. In C. Conrad (Ed.), *The ethical nexus: Values, communication, and ethical decisions* (pp. 171-189). Norwood, NJ: Ablex.

Lewis, L. K., & Seibold, D. R. (1993). Innovation modification during intra-organizational adoption. *Academy of Management Review, 18,* 322-354.

Lewis, L. K., & Seibold, D. R. (1996). Communication during intraorganizational innovation adoption: Predicting users' behavioral coping responses to innovations in organizations. *Communication Monographs, 63,* 131-157.

Locke, E. A., & Latham, G. P. (1990). *A theory of goal setting and task performance.* Englewood Cliffs, NJ: Prentice Hall.

Masuch, M. (1985). Vicious circles in organizations. *Administrative Science Quarterly, 30,* 14-33.

McPhee, R. D. (1985). Formal structure and organizational communication. In P. Tompkins & R. D. McPhee (Eds.), *Organizational communication: Traditional themes and new directions* (pp. 149-178). Beverly Hills, CA: Sage.

McPhee, R. D. (1995). Cognitive perspectives in communication: Interpretive and critical responses. In D. E. Hewes (Ed.), *The cognitive bases of interpersonal communication* (pp. 225-246). Hillsdale, NJ: Lawrence Erlbaum.

McPhee, R. D., & Poole, M. S. (1980, November). *The theory of structuration as a metatheory for communication research.* Paper presented at the annual meeting of the Speech Communication Association, New York.

Meyer, J. W., & Rowan, B. (1977). Institutionalized organizations: Formal structure as myth and ceremony. *American Journal of Sociology, 83,* 340-363.

Meyers, R. A. (1989a). Persuasive arguments theory: A test of assumptions. *Human Communication Research, 15,* 357-381.

Meyers, R. A. (1989b). Testing persuasive argument theory's predictor model: Alternative interactional accounts of group argument and influence. *Communication Monographs, 56,* 112-132.

Meyers, R. A., & Brashers, D. E. (1997, November). *Argument in group decision-making: Explicating a theoretical model and investigating the argument-outcome link.* Paper presented at the annual meeting of the National Communication Association, Chicago.

Meyers, R. A., & Seibold, D. A. (1990). Perspectives on group argument: A critical review of persuasive arguments theory and an alternative structurational formulation. In J. A. Anderson (Ed.), *Communication yearbook 13* (pp. 268-302). Newbury Park, CA: Sage.

Meyers, R. A., Seibold, D. R., & Brashers, D. (1991). Argument in initial group decision-making discussions: Refinement of a coding scheme and a descriptive quantitative analysis. *Western Journal of Speech Communication, 55,* 47-68.

Minsky, M. (1985). *The society of mind.* New York: Simon & Schuster.

Mintzberg, H., Raisinghani, D., & Theoret, A. (1976). The structure of "unstructured" decision processes. *Administrative Science Quarterly, 31,* 246-275.

Mumby, D. K. (1987). The political function of narratives in organizations. *Communication Monographs, 54,* 113-127.

Mumby, D. K. (1988). *Communication and power in organizations: Discourse, ideology and domination.* Norwood, NJ: Ablex.

Nelson, R. E., & Mathews, K. M. (1991). Cause maps and social network analysis in organizational diagnosis. *Journal of Applied Behavioral Science, 27,* 379-397.

Nutt, P. C. (1984). Types of organizational decision processes. *Administrative Science Quarterly, 29,* 414-450.

Orlikowski, W. J., & Yates, J. (1994). Genre repertoire: The structuring of communicative practices in organizations. *Administrative Science Quarterly, 39,* 541-574.

Planalp, S., & Hewes, D. E. (1982). A cognitive approach to communication theory: Cogito ergo dico? In M. Burgoon (Ed.), *Communication yearbook 5* (pp. 49-78). New Brunswick, NJ: Transaction.

Poole, M. S. (1980a, November). *Structuration and the problem of reification.* Paper presented at the annual meeting of the Speech Communication Association, New York.

Poole, M. S. (1980b). *A test of four models of decision development in small groups.* Unpublished doctoral dissertation. University of Wisconsin–Madison.

Poole, M. S. (1981). Decision development in small groups I: A comparison of two models. *Communication Monographs, 48,* 1-24.

Poole, M. S. (1983a). Decision development in small groups II: A study of multiple sequences in group development. *Communication Monographs, 50,* 206-232.

Poole, M. S. (1983b). Decision development in small groups III: A multiple sequence model of group decision-making. *Communication Monographs, 50,* 321-341.

Poole, M. S. (1985). Task and interaction sequences: A theory of coherence in group decision-making interaction. In R. L. Street & J. N. Cappella (Eds.), *Sequence and pattern in communicative behavior* (pp. 206-224). London: Edward Arnold.

Poole, M. S. (1994). The structuring of organizational climates. In L. Thayer & G. Barnett (Eds.), *Organization/communication: Emerging perspectives IV* (pp. 74-113). Norwood, NJ: Ablex.

Poole, M. S., & Baldwin, C. L. (1996). Developmental processes in group decision-making. In R. Y. Hirokawa & M. S. Poole (Eds.), *Communication and group decision-making* (2nd ed., pp. 215-241). Thousand Oaks, CA: Sage.

Poole, M. S., & DeSanctis, G. (1990). Understanding the use of group decision support systems: The theory of adaptive structuration. In J. Fulk & C. W. Steinfield (Eds.), *Organizations and communication technology* (pp. 173-193). Newbury Park, CA: Sage.

Poole, M. S., & DeSanctis, G. (1992). Microlevel structuration in computer supported group decision making. *Human Communication Research, 19*, 5-49.

Poole, M. S., & Doelger, J. A. (1986). Developmental processes in group decision-making. In R. Y. Hirokawa & M. S. Poole (Eds.), *Communication and group decision-making* (pp. 35-62). Beverly Hills, CA: Sage.

Poole, M. S., Folger, J. P., & Hewes, D. E. (1987). Analyzing interpersonal interaction. In M. E. Roloff & G. R. Miller (Eds.), *Interpersonal processes* (pp. 220-256). Newbury Park, CA: Sage.

Poole, M. S., & Holmes, M. E. (1995). Decision development in computer-assisted group decision-making. *Human Communication Research, 22*, 90-127.

Poole, M. S., & McPhee, R. D. (1983). A structurational analysis of organizational climate. In L. L. Putnam & M. E. Pacanowsky (Eds.), *Communication in organizations: An interpretive approach* (pp. 195-219). Beverly Hills, CA: Sage.

Poole, M. S., McPhee, R. D., & Seibold, D. R. (1982). A comparison of normative and interactional explanations of group decision-making: Social decision schemes versus valence distributions. *Communication Monographs, 49*, 1-19.

Poole, M. S., & Roth, J. (1989a). Decision development in small groups IV: A typology of decision paths. *Human Communication Research, 15*, 323-356.

Poole, M. S., & Roth, J. (1989b). Decision development in small groups V: Test of a contingency model. *Human Communication Research, 15*, 549-589.

Poole, M. S., Seibold, D. R., & McPhee, R. D. (1985). Group decision-making as a structurational process. *Quarterly Journal of Speech, 71*, 74-102.

Poole, M. S., Seibold, D. R., & McPhee, R. D. (1986). A structurational approach to theory building in group decision-making research. In R. Y. Hirokawa & M. S. Poole (Eds.), *Communication and group decision-making* (pp. 237-264). Beverly Hills, CA: Sage.

Poole, M. S., Seibold, D. R., & McPhee, R. D. (1996). The structuration of group decisions. In R. Y. Hirokawa & M. S. Poole (Eds.), *Communication and group decision-making* (2nd ed., pp. 114-146). Thousand Oaks, CA: Sage.

Ranson, S., Hinings, B., & Greenwood, R. (1980). The structuring of organizational structures. *Administrative Science Quarterly, 25*, 1-17.

Ratledge, N. T. (1986). *Theoretical and methodological integrity of a structurational scheme for coding arguments in decision-making groups*. Unpublished doctoral dissertation, University of Southern California.

Riley, P. (1983). A structurationist account of political culture. *Administrative Science Quarterly, 28*, 414-437.

Salazar, A. J., Hirokawa, R. Y., Propp, K. M., Julian, K. M., & Leatham, G. B. (1994). In search of true causes: Examination of the effect of group potential and group interaction on decision performance. *Human Communication Research, 20*, 529-559.

Schutz, A. (1967). *The phenomenology of the social world*. Evanston, IL: Northwestern University Press.

Seibold, D. R., Canary, D. J., & Ratledge, N. T. (1983, November). *Argument and group decision-making: Interim report on a structurational research program*. Paper presented at the annual meeting of the Speech Communication Association, Washington, DC.

Seibold, D. R., McPhee, R. D., Poole, M. S., Tanita, N. E., & Canary, D. J. (1981). Argument, group influence, and decision outcomes. In G. Ziegelmueller & J. Rhodes (Eds.), *Dimensions in argument: Proceedings of the Second Summer Conference on Argumentation*. Annandale, VA: Speech Communication Association.

Seibold, D. R., & Meyers, R. A. (1986). Communication and influence in group decision-making. In R. Y. Hirokawa & M. S. Poole (Eds.), *Communication and group decision-making* (pp. 133-155). Beverly Hills, CA: Sage.

Seibold, D. R., Poole, M. S., & McPhee, R. D. (1980, April). *New directions in small group research*. Paper presented at the annual meeting of the Central States Communication Association, Chicago.

Seyfarth, B. (1996). *A structurational account of organizational culture: A description of the model and an exploratory test involving mission statements.* Unpublished master's thesis, University of Minnesota, Minneapolis.

Seyfarth, B. (1999). *Are reasons structures? A cognitive-structurational approach toward explaining small group processes.* Unpublished doctoral dissertation, University of Minnesota, Minneapolis.

Smith, C. W. (1983). A case study of structuration: The pure-bred beef business. *Journal for the Theory of Social Behavior, 13,* 3-18.

Stohl, C., & Holmes, M. E. (1993). A functional perspective for bona fide groups. In S. A. Deetz (Ed.), *Communication yearbook 16* (pp. 601-614). Newbury Park, CA: Sage.

Street, R. L., Jr., & Cappella, J. N. (Eds.). (1985). *Sequence and pattern in communicative behaviour.* London: Edward Arnold.

Van de Ven, A. H., & Poole, M. S. (1988). Paradoxical requirements for a theory of organizational change. In R. E. Quinn & K. S. Cameron (Eds.), *Paradox and transformation: Toward a theory of change in organization and management* (pp. 19-80). Cambridge, MA: Ballinger.

Van de Ven, A. H., & Poole, M. S. (1995). Explaining development and change in organizations. *Academy of Management Review, 20,* 510-540.

Vinokur, A., & Burnstein E. (1974). Effects of partially shared persuasive arguments on group-induced shifts: A group problem-solving approach. *Journal of Personality and Social Psychology, 29,* 305-315.

Warriner, C. H. (1956). Groups are real: A reaffirmation. *American Sociological Review, 21,* 549-554.

Weick, K. E. (1979). *The social psychology of organizing* (2nd ed.). New York: Random House.

Weick, K. E. (1990). Technology as equivoque: Sensemaking in new technologies. In P. S. Goodman, L. S. Sproull, & Associates, *Technology and organizations* (pp. 1-44). San Francisco: Jossey-Bass.

Weick, K. E. (1993). Sensemaking in organizations: Small structures with large consequences. In J. K. Murningham (Ed.), *Social psychology in organizations: Advances in theory and research* (pp. 10-37). Englewood Cliffs, NJ: Prentice Hall.

Weick, K. E., & Roberts, K. H. (1993). Collective mind in organizations: Heedful interrelating on flight decks. *Administrative Science Quarterly, 38,* 357-381.

Whittington, R. (1992). Putting Giddens into action: Social systems and managerial agency. *Journal of Management Studies, 29,* 693-712.

Willis, P. E. (1977). *Learning to labour: How working-class kids get working-class jobs.* Farnborough, England: Saxon House.

Wyer, R. S., & Srull, T. K. (1980). The processing of social stimulus information: A conceptual integration. In R. Hastie, T. M. Ostrum, E. B. Ebbeson, R. S. Wyer, D. Hamilton, & D. E. Carlson (Eds.), *Person memory: The cognitive basis of social perception* (pp. 227-300). Hillsdale, NJ: Lawrence Erlbaum.

Wyer, R. S., & Srull, T. K. (1986). Human cognition in its social context. *Psychological Review, 93,* 322-339.

Yates, J., & Orlikowski, W. J. (1992). Genres of organizational communication: A structurational approach to studying communication media. *Academy of Management Review, 17,* 299-326.

CHAPTER CONTENTS

10 U.S. Public Relations History: Knowledge and Limitations

KAREN S. MILLER
University of Georgia

This analysis of the literature on public relations history indicates that the field has been dominated by a business history approach. Most scholars have studied public relations in its corporate context, and most have utilized business history's dominant paradigm, which calls for a general theory of PR history based on the review of a large number of case histories. But the business history frame is both flawed and inadequate for a complete understanding of public relations history. Political and social histories show that public relations was emerging and apparently would have emerged even if big business had not. In reality, these histories are intertwined. No single strand of PR history can be understood except in relation to the others, and none should be given a privileged position in public relations historiography.

PUBLIC relations is an interdisciplinary field with ties to business, political science, psychology, and media studies, among other areas. The study of the history of public relations could, then, be explored from any number of angles—cultural, intellectual, social, or political history, to name a few. However, most of the best research on public relations has adopted the business history frame, focusing on corporate PR to the detriment of other areas of practice, and business history's dominant paradigm has restricted understanding of corporate public relations. These choices have seriously undermined current understanding of public relations history.

I begin this chapter by describing the dominant business history paradigm and its relationship to public relations historiography. I then examine criticisms of the dominant paradigm and demonstrate how these criticisms suggest different ways to analyze corporate public relations. Finally, I outline some alternative

---

Correspondence: Karen S. Miller, Henry W. Grady College of Journalism and Mass Communication, University of Georgia, Athens, GA 30602-3018; e-mail KarenM@arches.uga.edu

Communication Yearbook 23, pp. 381-420

approaches to public relations history, discuss public relations as political and social history, and conclude with an agenda for further research.

BUSINESS HISTORY AND PUBLIC
RELATIONS HISTORIOGRAPHY

The study of business history has been dominated by a paradigm based on the work of Alfred D. Chandler, Jr., who revolutionized the field with his books *The Visible Hand* (1977) and *Scale and Scope* (1990). Before these books were published, business historians typically wrote biographies and case histories of individual firms; occasionally they examined trade associations or conducted general studies on topics such as labor relations (Hidy, 1970). But, as McCraw (1988) notes, Chandler "insisted on asking a very different set of questions, and in so doing he transformed the nature of the field" (p. 10).

The thesis of *The Visible Hand* may not seem so revolutionary. Chandler argued that the modern business enterprise took the place of market mechanisms in coordinating the activities of the economy and allocating its resources. Technological innovations in communication (the telegraph) and transportation (the railroad), Chandler asserted, enabled innovation in production and distribution, which led to increased volume of output and greater numbers of transactions, which in turn required greater efficiency for high-volume production and distribution. Organizations were therefore subdivided into operating units, with several units integrated into a single enterprise under a managerial hierarchy. Managers monitored and coordinated the production and distribution flow more efficiently than the market could, at least in those industries where administrative coordination permitted greater productivity, lower costs, and higher profit. Large enterprises altered the basic structures of the sectors of the economy that they dominated as well as the economy as a whole. In short, Chandler concluded, the visible hand of management replaced the invisible hand of the market on the supply side of the economic equation.

What was revolutionary about this book was its approach. Chandler organized and synthesized the histories of an enormous number of individual firms in order to generalize business history, essentially developing a model that explained the rise of big business. As McCraw (1988) says, Chandler described the forest by examining all the trees, moving "toward a historical theory of big business, a working model of its evolution" (p. 1). Other scholars had previously developed synthesized histories of business. Most notable of these is Galambos (1970), whose "organizational synthesis" of American business history suggested that "some of the most . . . important changes which have taken place in modern America have centered about a shift from small-scale, informal, locally or regionally oriented groups to large-scale, national, formal organizations" (p. 280). But Chandler went farther, developing a model to explain changes in industry and creating a powerful new paradigm that others have used to structure their own research (Lamoreaux, 1991).

Chandler and Corporate Public Relations Histories

Chandler's approach to business history has also affected many public relations histories. Of the significant scholarly works, most authors who have chosen the business history frame have looked at public relations through a Chandlerian lens, tending to generalize and to consider public relations almost exclusively in the context of big business. The following paragraphs examine how four leading public relations historians—N. S. B. Gras, Alan Raucher, Richard Tedlow, and Stuart Ewen—have explained the rise and growth of the field based on the business history frame. All place the advent of public relations in the broader context of the rise of big business.

Writing decades before Chandler published *The Visible Hand,* Gras (1945) began the effort to generalize the history of PR. Although he did not create a theory of PR, he did develop a chronological model that describes the development of public relations history in terms of changes in the role of business in society. From the 12th to the 18th centuries, Gras argues, "the chief public relations of business . . . was dependence on the public for a recognition of its ways and means of operation" (p. 108). The second period, the 18th and 19th centuries, was characterized by a belief that the public should keep its hands off business so that businesses could freely compete. Business asked for little more than police protection. From 1901 to 1945, Gras asserts, beliefs about the relationship between business and government shifted again, with business leaders developing a new policy of pleasing yet fooling the public and moving toward a policy of informing the public. Gras documents the growth of public relations counseling and internal corporate PR departments, which he sees as the culmination of the changing relationship between business and the public.

In *Public Relations and Business, 1990-1929,* Raucher (1968) also attempted to develop a generalized history of corporate PR. Basing his discussion heavily on the ideas and activities of the "father of public relations," Ivy Lee, Raucher concludes that corporate public relations was initiated primarily as a political device, especially for the railroads. Companies hired publicity men who claimed to be completely aboveboard in their operations; this was intended to demonstrate that business cared what the public thought. Raucher discredits the idea of public relations as a "two-way street" of communication between management and the people, as practitioners since Ivy Lee's time have claimed, because practitioners did not utilize reliable methods of registering public opinion. They said, for example, that they could interpret the true sentiments of workers better than could the unions. Rather than a two-way street, corporate public relations was simply a business strategy rooted in industry's effort to cope with the size and social complexity of bigness and the new methods of communication. Growth and complexity "certainly created the need for new policies, but alone they did not determine which kinds of policies would be adopted." The "vocation specializing in public relations grew out of the need for communicating through the mass media" (Raucher, 1968, p. 150). PR is thus located firmly within the rise of business bigness.

Tedlow's (1979) *Keeping the Corporate Image* is based explicitly on Chandler's attempt to show how modern business enterprises adapted to bigness. Moving on a case-by-case basis through some of the major events in public relations history, Tedlow first disproves the popular thesis that PR emerged in response to muckraking (see, e.g., Ross, 1959, discussed below). Business had been attacked before the Progressive Era began, PR continued after muckraking ended, and nonbusiness organizations, including churches and universities, experimented with press bureaus at the turn of the century even though they were not necessarily the subjects of muckraking. Tedlow therefore attributes the timing of the rise of corporate PR to other changes taking place at the same time as muckraking. His basic argument is that "business bigness, a search for order within corporations themselves encouraging an impersonal approach to management and at the same time suggesting the organization of the publicity which great corporations naturally attracted, high literacy rates, nationally available periodicals, and vigorous reform politicians all played a part" in the rise of corporate public relations (p. 18). Like Raucher (1968), Tedlow (1979) argues that mass communication was an important part of the development of public relations, but he puts additional emphasis on American faith in public opinion. Politicians and business leaders, he says, "never doubted that the locus of power lay with public opinion. What is more, they accepted this situation as right and proper" (p. xvi). If the public turned against business, its leaders had to set them right. PR was only one of the efforts made in response to rationalize bigness—Taylorism, welfare capitalism, and advertising were others. Again, like Raucher (1968), Tedlow places PR within the larger context of the growth of big business and the opposition it faced from government, public, and labor.

Tedlow's (1979) book serves as a model of the ways the Chandlerian approach can inform the study of public relations history, because it draws general conclusions about the history of public relations based on selected cases. First, Tedlow explains when and why corporations started to use public relations techniques, arguing that PR was a managerial strategy that began in the 1880s with the rise of large corporations, especially railroads and utilities. Second, the book sheds light on the policies and practices of individual people and businesses, such as Theodore Vail and Arthur Page at AT&T, without reducing their stories to "great man" studies. Additionally, Tedlow's use of the business history frame allows for examination of what business leaders generally thought about certain issues, as in the discussion of the ways PR techniques were used to defeat the major strikes that followed World War I. Finally, Tedlow assesses the effects of particular campaigns, such as the 1930s free enterprise campaign of the National Association of Manufacturers, which he concludes may have changed some minds, but "its extremism provided a convenient foil against which defenders of the New Deal could crystallize sentiment" (p. 69). All of these issues are important and worthy of study by PR historians, making it clear that the Chandlerian approach has much to offer public relations historians.

Ewen (1997) shows the extent to which the business history frame has dominated PR historiography. His book *PR! A Social History of Spin* is primarily a history of the ideas that have shaped public relations. Ewen explores the changing meanings of *public, public opinion,* and *persuasion* and the ways these meanings have been applied to visual and verbal propaganda. But, perhaps because of the dominance of the business history frame in PR historiography, the scope of Ewen's book is very narrowly defined. Ewen describes four basic eras in 20th-century public relations, beginning with the Progressive Era. By 1914, Ewen asserts, the public, meaning middle-class Americans, had been convinced by muckraking journalism that private enterprise should be responsive to public concerns, but they also feared revolt from below. This tension shaped the thinking of the first generation of public relations men, such as Ivy Lee, who dispensed facts and created a demeanor of openness to counterbalance traditional corporate secrecy. The second era is marked by the post-World War I trend toward social psychology and the belief that public opinion could be managed with appeals directed at emotions. "Old distinctions between the *public* and the *crowd* were giving way," Ewen writes, "to ideas of an all-inclusive mass audience, driven, for the most part, by its sentiments" (p. 143). Reason employed by experts, such as Edward Bernays, could save society from its unreasonable nature. These insights, newspaper chain ownership, commercial radio, and new public opinion measurement techniques combined to cause a dramatic spread in organized propaganda after World War I. "In the simultaneous unfolding of a national media system and of a modern machinery for measuring public opinion," Ewen argues, "a social infrastructure" for the "two-way street" model of public relations was being built (p. 186).

The Great Depression changed views of big business, and, Ewen (1997) reasons, public relations had to respond. President Roosevelt's fireside chats, for instance, reflected a change in PR thinking in their repudiation of disdain for the public, given Roosevelt's clear intention to educate and reason with listeners. New Deal photography likewise changed visual communication, as pictures told stories about real conditions instead of being "color-coded daydreams of advertising" (p. 276). Big business found itself fighting labor, the consumer movement, and government intervention, and it responded with campaigns that linked business to the public interest, typified by the one sponsored by the National Association of Manufacturers. World War II forged a reconciliation between the Roosevelt administration and big business, and manufacturers' reputations improved. But business leaders still made widespread plans for after the war; even during the war, PR advertising highlighted corporate war participation and included exuberant visions of postwar America. Welfare capitalism would replace the welfare state. This fourth period of public relations history marked a return to the idea of a public driven by its emotions. Ewen points to Earl Newsom's work for Standard Oil of New Jersey as an example, indicating that, "to be effective, information must be calculated to stir an audience, to provoke an enduring psychological bond between

the *public* and the *corporate*" (p. 380). This renewed belief in psychological methods of persuasion was influenced in part by the introduction of television—highly
centralized in production and overwhelmingly privatized in reception—projecting
an image to a public that never assembled.

Although Ewen (1997) expands upon the business history frame by putting public relations in the context of the larger society rather than describing it as only a
business strategy, almost all of his examples of PR practice relate to corporations.
He discusses, for instance, Ivy Lee's work for the Rockefellers, AT&T, Bernays's
Light's Golden Jubilee, Byoir's campaign to stop antichain legislation for A&P
grocery stores, and the free enterprise campaigns of the National Association of
Manufacturers. Even the examples of political PR—the Roosevelt administration
and Whitaker and Baxter's American Medical Association campaign in particular—are presented as part of the relationship between political and economic
forces. Ewen addresses public relations largely in its corporate context.

All of the authors discussed above have made significant contributions to our
understanding of the history of corporate public relations, but their attempts to
generalize that history have been premature. Scholars agree that one of Chandler's
strengths is his copious reading of the histories of business enterprises, which he
synthesized into a model that attempts to explain why big business is the way it is.
Chandler drew upon almost innumerable life stories and monographs on individual businesses, whereas the public relations literature is extremely limited and
therefore inadequate for generalization. Tedlow (1979) does not explain, for
example, why he examines Ivy Lee's contributions to PR, but not Hamilton
Wright's or Pendleton Dudley's. Raucher (1968) selects such corporations as
AT&T for study but ignores a multitude of others, and Ewen (1997) characterizes
the post-World War II period as a return to a view of the public as irrational without
examining the approaches of some of the period's leading practitioners—
Benjamin Sonnenberg and T. J. Ross, to name two. It is difficult to argue that these
authors have chosen the most important people or cases for examination when so
little of the history has been documented.

Building a Foundation:
Biography and Autobiography

There are, of course, some sources for historians to build upon. First, a few
book-length autobiographies have been published by public relations luminaries.
These life stories describe the philosophies and strategies of some leading American practitioners, although they are sometimes self-serving or promotional in
nature. McCann (1976) recounts his career in the publicity and advertising department of United Fruit, a career that led him to conclude that "public relations was
helping to screw up the world" (p. 152). Although United Fruit conducted some
activities that McCann believed were useful, such as establishing a sports foundation that brought famous coaches and athletes to Latin America, for the most part
his experience was negative. By contrast, Sattler (1993) reviews his long associa-

tion with Earl Newsom and the Ford automobile account with much more pride. PR staff should have access to management, in Sattler's opinion, but PR's function cannot be primarily one of counseling if it is to contribute to a company's overall success. Harlow (1980) places public relations in the context of his own career, which began in 1912, viewing its history as a steady rise to professional status; in a follow-up article, Harlow (1981) suggests that PR began because an "aid or substitute for loss of the owner-employee intimacy once enjoyed by small concerns had to be devised" (p. 34). Macnamara (1993) and Rogers (1980) regale readers with tales of Hollywood press agentry, such as the lies Rogers told to get starlet Rita Hayworth on the cover of *Look* magazine. He suggests it was his job to try to influence the public on behalf of his clients, but his publicity tactics either garnered media coverage or they did not, and he provides little explanation of how or why the coverage in turn influenced the public. Wood also emphasizes the tactics he used in his long career working with such clients as NBC, Woolworth, and Kodak (see Wood & Gunther, 1988).

Of particular importance is the autobiography of John W. Hill (1963), founder of Hill and Knowlton, which was for decades the largest agency in the world. Like Tedlow (1979), Hill argues that public relations is rooted in "the basic fact that public opinion, confused, obscure, and unpredictable as it may often seem, is the ultimate ruling force in the free world" (p. 2). He describes his early career as a journalist covering business in Cleveland, Ohio, where he learned that both journalists and corporations needed assistance to get information about industry to the public. He opened a corporate publicity office in 1927 and took on Don Knowlton as a partner in 1933. Eventually Hill opened a separate agency, Hill and Knowlton of New York, which obtained some of the largest accounts in the world, including the steel, tobacco, and aviation industry trade associations. Hill describes the strategies and tactics behind the programs his agency planned for several of its largest accounts, but given that the book was written primarily to promote H&K to potential clients, he sometimes glosses over problems and controversies the agency faced. Still, the book provides an unparalleled inside look at a major PR agency.

The most influential autobiographies are those of pioneer Edward L. Bernays (1965, 1971). Bernays began his career as a publicist for theater, music, and ballet, and then became a government propagandist during World War I. In 1919 he formed an independent consulting agency, where he and his wife, Doris Fleischman, created some of the most famous PR campaigns in American history. During the 1920s they promoted soap carving to sell Ivory for Procter & Gamble, popularized gelatin as a dessert and hair nets as sanitary necessities for restaurant employees, and organized Light's Golden Jubilee to honor Thomas Edison while enhancing the image of General Electric and Westinghouse. The most famous PR counsel and certainly the best self-promoter, Bernays (1971) argues that public relations "helps validate an underlying principle of our society—competition in the market place of ideas and things" and makes "it possible for minority ideas to be more readily accepted by the majority" (p. 297). Bernays's autobiographical works revealed to many for the first time the tricks of the trade, and because of the author's prominence and longevity (he lived to be 103), they have had considerable influence on PR historiography: Bernays is never ignored in PR histories. Ewen (1997), for example, bases much of his book on Bernays's career and writings, even though Bernays was not a typical practitioner. Many of his PR brethren scorned him, and he did not join the Public Relations Society of America until 1971.

Published and unpublished biographies also describe important careers, but they too are limited in number. Ivy Lee, considered the "father of public relations," has been most closely examined. Hiebert (1966) provides an excessively admiring biography of Lee, arguing that he "believed implicitly in the power of public opinion and sought to serve the people, whom he considered the kings of democracy" (p. xi). Hainsworth (1987) reviews Lee's relationship with I. G. Farben, the German dye trust, prior to World War II, and states that Lee's advice to his clients, "including the Germans, was to tell the truth" (p. 41). Ballinger (1994) found that Lee was able to influence press coverage of the Ludlow massacre on behalf of his client, the Rockefeller family, but that Upton Sinclair did the same on behalf of the workers and those who died in battle against the armed guards hired by Lee's client.

Recent biographies of women in public relations agencies demonstrate that studying more individuals can illuminate different aspects of public relations history as a whole. Henry (1997, 1998) shows that Bernays did not work alone in developing his philosophy and strategies. Doris Fleischman was an integral part of the counseling firm Bernays founded, and she possessed abilities that made her more effective for some parts of the job than even her highly celebrated husband. For instance, when the NAACP retained the Bernays agency to promote its 1920 annual convention, the first to be held in the South, Fleischman went to Atlanta to work with newspaper editors and the governor because "she knew how to avoid antagonizing people" (Henry, 1997, p. 53). Fleischman also developed a newsletter that the agency used to attract new clients and to promote the field of public relations generally. Despite such contributions, she has not been given attention or credit in general histories of public relations.

Biographies of two Hill and Knowlton executives also provide perspectives that are different from those found in previous research on public relations history. It has been shown that Jane Stewart, one of the agency's first female executives during the 1960s, approached her job differently than many men because she was female (Miller, 1997). For example, she developed a collaborative management style that united people and focused them on shared goals, and she recognized the importance and value of women in the opinion-formation process, making them a formal part of public relations research. Smith's (1997) biography of one of Stewart's colleagues, Mary L. T. Brown, shows both how women were targeted by public relations campaigns and how PR women were hired to target female audiences. Brown, who became Hill and Knowlton's director of women's activities in 1960, produced special campaigns for the agency's industrial clients by focusing on women as consumers. For example, for the American Iron and Steel Institute,

Brown promoted steel doors as safety measures for women, sending news releases on pink paper to newspaper and magazine editors who came to know her by name.

Feminist research on women in public relations, then, offers evidence that not enough histories of individuals have been written to allow for generalization about this field. Women, at least the three women mentioned above, did not have the same philosophy or managerial style as their male colleagues, nor did they necessarily use the same strategies and tactics. Fleischman and Stewart are both remembered for their cooperative styles; Stewart and Brown both thought of women as audience more than did male practitioners, at least so far as can be determined from the current literature. Not all PR practitioners have been alike, and closer examination of a larger number of practitioners will undoubtedly allow us to refine our understanding of corporate public relations.

Institutional History

Institutional histories of public relations are also lacking. Golden (1968) presents brief historical examinations of several corporate PR departments, including General Motors, Standard Oil of New Jersey, and Du Pont, but focuses most closely on contemporary descriptions of the departments. Jarvik (1992) provides an analysis of Mobil Oil's sponsorship during the 1970s of the PBS television program *Masterpiece Theatre*; he argues that Mobil's sponsorship of the show was fundamentally a political strategy: "Mobil's crusade promoted big business, a hands-off Government energy policy, and made it seem that Mobil was the underdog, all in the name of high culture" (p. 271).

Ross (1959) and Cutlip (1994) both review the histories of numerous agencies and make the point that the public is largely unaware of the behind-the-scenes machinations of PR practitioners. Ross (1959) writes that surges of social reform were led by opponents of big business and that PR was business's answer to detractors. The attitude behind William Vanderbilt's famous "public be damned" remark was no longer possible, according to Ross, after Ida Tarbell, Lincoln Steffens, Upton Sinclair, and others turned their energies to exposing the problems of American business. "What PR is trying to sell, in an ultimate sense, are the merits of a particular corporation and the merits of the capitalist system," Ross writes (p. 26), arguing that PR does serve useful functions. PR agents urge reticent clients to talk, coach them to put their best foot forward, and occasionally change corporate policy to reflect public desires. A strength of Ross's book, which was written for a popular audience, is that unlike most PR histories, it continues beyond World War II; thus Ross devotes several chapters to agencies that have been ignored by other historians, including Ben Sonnenberg, Earl Newsom, and Ruder and Finn. (Ross also includes one chapter on nonprofit PR, discussed below.)

Cutlip (1994) provides the most comprehensive history of American public relations agencies to date. He does not attempt to develop a theory to explain the rise and growth of public relations; instead, his primary contribution is that he retrieves the previously forgotten stories of numerous public relations pioneers.

He begins, for instance, by describing the first known agency, the Publicity Bureau, which opened in Boston in mid-1900, and the first Washington agencies, Smith & Walmer and Thomas R. Shipp, all of which predate the firm founded by the "father of public relations," Ivy Lee. Although he spends considerable time on the best-known practitioners—Lee, Bernays, Hill, Byoir, and Newsom—Cutlip also includes chapters on Hamilton Wright, apparently the first American practitioner to run an international agency; John Price Jones, a pioneer in fund-raising; Steve Hannagan, one of the best publicists of his time, as evidenced by the popularity of the Indianapolis 500 automobile race, Miami Beach, and the ski resort at Sun Valley; and Harry Bruno, who was associated with the fledgling aviation industry. While arguing that "it is a basic democratic right that every idea, individual, and institution shall have a full and fair hearing in the public forum" (p. xii), Cutlip also suggests that practitioners wield an unseen power that has a profound impact on the business, political, social, and cultural life of the United States.

One author has examined the historical role of public relations in a trade association. Pratt (1983) includes public relations as one of the three most important functions of the American Petroleum Institute from its inception in 1919. The API created a formal public relations division as early as 1924. By collecting and disseminating statistics about the industry, the API established itself with government officials, allowing industry representatives to lobby effectively because of their direct access to federal policy makers.

Summary: Corporate Public Relations Historiography

Biographies and institutional histories are important because they document the strategies and tactics employed by leading practitioners, provide opportunities for assessment of the effectiveness of PR activities, and highlight the primary legal and ethical issues practitioners have faced. The literature on corporate public relations thus suggests several important themes. The first of these is freedom of speech and the right of practitioners to disseminate their employers' views in the marketplace of ideas. A second theme has been effectiveness, but no consensus has been reached on this issue. The relationship of public relations to the rise of big business has been another important topic, as has the perceived importance of public opinion in society.

Too much remains unknown, however, about individuals, agencies, and corporations. For example, little is known about minority PR practitioners such as African Americans Ofield Dukes, who promoted everything from Motown singers to Lever Brothers, and D. Parke Gibson, who owned an advertising/public relations firm in New York City during the 1960s. Little is known of the histories of agencies founded outside New York, even ones that became large and influential, such as Carlton Ketchum's agency, which opened in Pittsburgh in 1919. Post-World War II agencies such as Selvage & Lee and Burson-Marsteller have also not been the subjects of published research.

Corporate PR departments have been ignored even more than agencies. Of the thousands of potential subjects, scholars have usually selected only three businesses for close examination: the railroads during the 19th century, the Rockefeller-owned Colorado Fuel and Iron at the time it retained Ivy Lee, and AT&T. Westinghouse, which apparently had the first corporate PR department, has not been examined in terms of its public relations function. The dozens of large companies in varied industries that opened internal PR departments after World War II—Ford, Allis-Chalmers, the Pennsylvania Railroad, Gulf Oil, Chrysler, and Northwestern Mutual Life—have not been studied.

In sum, the dominant paradigm in business history suggests that historians should gather as many data as possible on individuals and organizations, then develop generalized histories that explain the subject as a whole. In public relations historiography, general histories based on a limited number of cases, autobiographies, biographies, and institutional histories have identified basic themes and documented important careers and significant events. But much work remains. A definitive history of corporate public relations cannot be written without studies of more people, more agencies, and more companies.

CRITICISMS OF CHANDLER AND THEIR RELEVANCE TO PR HISTORIOGRAPHY

The tendency to generalize in PR historiography is troubling not only because of insufficient evidence, but because of criticism leveled at Chandler's work, criticism that should be considered by public relations scholars as well. Although many issues have been raised regarding Chandler's model, three are especially relevant to public relations history: power as a managerial motive, the relationship of business to the political state, and entrepreneurship. These issues and their significance to PR historiography are examined in this section.

Power as a Managerial Motive

First, Du Boff and Herman (1980) question Chandler's assertion that the incentive for growth was efficiency rather than the drive for power, noting, "In the framework employed by Chandler, power seems to be an incidental consequence of the growth of large firms: it is thrust upon managers by technological advance, widening markets, and the drive for efficiency" (p. 92). U.S. Steel, which cornered 60% of the steel market when it was created, is one example in which power, specifically market control, was clearly a factor in managerial decision making.

Power is relevant to public relations historiography in that the motives for introducing the public relations function into a corporation are just as important as the outcomes. Although companies and practitioners often describe the motive for PR as putting forth industry's voice in the marketplace of ideas, the real motive may be market *control* of ideas, particularly relating to labor. Fones-Wolf (1994) reviews post-World War II business campaigns that aimed to sell free enterprise to the American people. Industry leaders feared their workers' loyalty to unions and to government intervention in business, she argues, leading them to seek victories over organized labor at the bargaining table, in Congress, and, perhaps most important, in workers' opinions. They sought to educate Americans about the benefits of the free enterprise system through an aggressive public relations campaign that targeted everyone from union members to schoolchildren. "The labor movement could never match the resources available to the leaders of American business," Fones-Wolf concludes. "As a result, the political and cultural landscape of the postwar era was increasingly dominated by the images and ideas produced by a mobilized business leadership" (p. 287).

Research on the creation of corporate culture also shows ways that companies attempted to control or at least influence the way people thought about business. Marchand's (1991) analysis of the General Motors "family" campaign of the 1920s, in which advocacy advertisements used the metaphors of family, community, neighborhood, and ministry to promote what was essentially a giant holding company, indicates that the primary target and biggest beneficiaries of the campaign were dealers and managers of the various divisions, rather than the general public. A review of General Electric's campaigns during the 1920s likewise shows that public relations activities were essentially attempts to create a corporate culture (Marchand, 1989).

Nye (1985) has examined the idea of corporate culture by analyzing photographs to uncover the ideologies presented by General Electric to various audiences. For example, to engineers GE presented itself as science. The *General Electric Review,* which went to engineering students, technicians, and officials who would buy GE products, included close-up, uncluttered photos of machines and only rarely included people. By contrast, to workers, GE was corporation as community, with photos in *Works News* (for line employees) that emphasized team ideals: formal group pictures, corporation-sponsored sports teams, and the like. Although there was no single coherent ideology, Nye argues, the photographs were taken and utilized for specific audiences, thus revealing what the corporation wanted certain people to think.

In my own examination of national and local public relations campaigns conducted by the American Iron and Steel Institute and the United Steelworkers of America during the 1946 steel strike, I found a slightly different picture (Miller, 1995). Although both management and labor tried to saturate the marketplace of ideas with their own views about the strike at the national level, local newspapers in one strike town presented both sides and advocated a peaceful settlement to the negotiations rather than arguing the merits of either side's case. In other words, the public relations campaigns had little impact on the resolution of the strike and certainly did not harm labor's position. Although power may be management's motive for introducing public relations activities, it is not at all clear that business control of the marketplace of ideas is necessarily the result. Still, motivation and the desire for control appear to be fruitful areas of research for historians of corporate public relations.

Ideology and the Relationship of Business to the Political State

Du Boff and Herman (1980) also criticize Chandler for downplaying the role of the political state in the growth of big business. Numerous historians have demonstrated the importance of the state and federal governments in the development of U.S. big business. For example, Dunlavy (1991) found that about 40% of all railroad capital in the 1830s came from the states, and a leading business history textbook documents the extent to which government regulations shaped the growth of railroads (Blackford & Kerr, 1990). Such evidence indicates that political economic issues cannot be ignored in generalized histories.

This criticism of Chandler is relevant for several reasons. Dunlavy's (1991) comparative approach would be equally useful for public relations scholars. Studies of countries with different government and media systems would shed light on the rise, growth, and philosophy of public relations in the United States. Culbertson's (1996) analysis of research on public relations in other countries suggests that "a nation's political system and culture shape its practice of public relations" (p. 6); presumably, the same has been true historically.

Second, the emphasis on political economy is important because corporate public relations has always been related to the political economy. In fact, two public relations historians—Carey (1997) and Olasky (1987)—locate public relations in the sphere of political action, although from different perspectives. Olasky (1987) asserts that "for over a century, many major corporate public relations leaders have worked diligently to kill free enterprise by promoting government-big business collaboration" (p. 2). He argues that PR practitioners supported the regulation of big business in order to eliminate competition and to ensure their own profits. He then recounts many of the same episodes from public relations history as Gras (1945), Raucher (1968), Tedlow (1979), and Ewen (1997), including those concerning the railroads, Ivy Lee, the Depression, and Bernays's career, reinterpreting them with a libertarian bent.

Carey (1997) also suggests that corporate PR is primarily a political measure, but in his view, it has been used to inhibit true democracy by restricting public discussion about business. U.S. corporate propaganda emerged because of the two opposing forces of increased popular franchise and the union movement, and the growth of corporate power, which clashed to create a climate in which business leaders perceived a need to protect corporate power against democracy. They developed internal and external programs that identified free enterprise with cherished values and government and unions with tyranny and oppression. By taking corporate power out of the sphere of public discussion, Carey argues, propaganda has closed minds and society. Both Olasky (1987) and Carey (1997) reject a progressive interpretation that views public relations as becoming more ethical or corporations as increasingly motivated by the public interest, and both do so because of PR's role in the political economy.

Two articles on military public relations also indicate the importance of political-economic considerations in public relations historiography. Thelander's (1966) analysis of the U.S. Navy's campaign for naval and industrial preparedness before World War I shows that Navy Secretary Josephus Daniels used the Naval Consulting Board, an advisory group chaired by Thomas Edison and consisting of several leading businessmen, to conduct a publicity campaign to gain public support for a bigger, better-equipped navy. Miller (1996) documents the U.S. Air Force's cooperation with the aircraft manufacturers' "Air Power Is Peace Power" campaign after World War II, arguing that air advocates fashioned a climate of opinion that favored air power and helped to establish a policy of peacetime armament. These articles suggest that greater attention is needed to the role of public relations in the development of the military-industrial complex specifically, an area that has gone virtually uninvestigated, in addition to the political economy in general.

Another stream of business history research also touches on the government-business relationship, focusing on ideology. In *Scale and Scope,* Chandler (1990) argues that the characteristics of certain industries, particularly capital-intensity and ability to take advantage of economies of scale, meant that those industries were destined to become monopolies or oligopolies. Scranton explicitly challenges this point in *Proprietary Capitalism* (1983), a study of the Philadelphia textile manufacturers during the 19th century. Scranton not only argues that alternative forms were possible, he shows that they existed. The textile manufacturers of Philadelphia "had erected a manufacturing system that stood as a fully realized alternative to the corporate industrial model" (p. 3). These businesses remained family or partnership owned, in contrast to the more famous corporations in Lowell, Massachusetts. The oligopolies Chandler describes were not inevitable— nor, Scranton argues, did they necessarily represent the best competitive route for business firms to take.

The existence of alternative forms to big business is important to public relations historiography for two reasons. First, scholars should consider alternatives to public relations rather than assume that it had to emerge exactly as it did. Tedlow (1979) and Raucher (1968) briefly mention several alternatives to public relations available to corporate managers: Communication accountability could be placed in the hands of lawyers or advertising agencies; corporate leaders could speak directly to the public themselves; they could manipulate advertising contracts to sway editorial opinion; they might provide information to sympathetic third parties, such as legislators, so that those parties could serve as conduits to the press and public. Instead, corporate leaders chose to institutionalize public relations by hiring managers and creating departments in charge of releasing information and, sometimes, seeking input from publics. Raucher (1990) also notes that the PR agency was not a preordained form. In addition to establishing independent consultancies, PR pioneers found work by expanding the services of existing advertising agencies to include PR and creating public relations departments within corporations and other institutions. Problematizing public relations—that is, starting with the assumption that it need not have emerged the way it did—makes explicit the thinking of its originators. Historians could study public relations agencies that failed to determine what makes agencies appealing or unappealing to clients.

Second, because alternative forms of business did exist, some scholars argue that the missing link in Chandler's model is ideology. Like Scranton, Sklar (1988) rejects Chandler's economic determinism, asserting that big business was not the natural outcome of some suprahuman law of economics; instead, it was constructed. Several preconditions helped to guarantee the relative peacefulness of the transformation. These included the expanding market and nationalist sentiment after the Spanish-American War, a president who favored corporate capitalism, the disenfranchisement of black Americans, the weakening of trade unionism (especially following the Homestead and Pullman strikes during the early 1890s), and the fact that no politically effective segment of the population saw itself as threatened by the new system. Lawyers, intellectuals, journalists, educators, members of the clergy, engineers, politicians, and so on all supported corporate capitalism, especially "corporate liberalism," which Sklar defines as a mutual adaptation of corporate capitalism and American liberal tradition that resulted in neither totalistic statism nor a corporate state, but administered markets and a regulatory government.

This interest in corporate liberalism is reflected in research that examines the role of PR in government-industry accommodation. Galambos (1975) reviewed trade journal coverage of big business and found that public acceptance of the corporate state was nearly complete by 1940. Considering the devastation of the Great Depression, attacks against big business were feeble in comparison to earlier periods. The image of business was thus directly related to its public acceptance, and the public relations role of creating corporate cultures is doubly important.

Although Chandler neglects the role of ideology, most PR historians have not made the same mistake. In addition to discussions of the political role of corporate public relations by Raucher (1968), Olasky (1987), Tedlow (1979), and Carey (1997), one history explicitly addresses the ideological role of PR. Galambos and Pratt (1988) consider the rise of public relations as a part of the gradual process of government-business accommodation. In the 19th century, they argue, both business and politics were local, grassroots affairs, with entrepreneurs enjoying a measure of political authority and respect in their cities or towns. Big business never enjoyed that public goodwill at the local level, but a new political system emerged along with the new economy. Individual influence and a local power base became less important than effective state and national lobbying, making both effective legal representation and media campaigns necessary to build public understanding and confidence. Business in 1900 was not equipped to carry out these activities, but public relations and public affairs soon became permanent staff functions in the large combines. "Public relations grew directly out of the perception on the part of managers, especially corporate officers, that liberal or progressive political campaigns were generating an intensely negative concept of business and threatening to create an ever more restrictive political economy" (p. 96). Thus PR departments labored hard to alter negative images of the corporation, gave input on corporate decisions, and reported on public perceptions and how the business might avoid antagonizing publics. By the 1920s, Galambos and Pratt argue, the "two-way street" of information between the public and the business firm was in place, with the public relations department serving as the conduit, and business was more in touch with its social environment than it had been since the rise of business bigness. The corporate commonwealth is the uniquely American relationship between business and government, whereby corporations remain privatized yet are regulated in the public interest.

Scholarship on institutional advertising also shows the role of public relations in government-business accommodation. The case of AT&T is instructive. Its ads at the turn of the century "combined a subdued element of advocacy with such other purposes as employee instruction, morale building, and the enhancement of corporate prestige" (Marchand, 1987, p. 130). An ongoing motif of these ads was the identification of the company with democracy, both democracy of service to all and democracy of ownership by many shareholders, all the while promoting the virtues of private monopoly in the hopes of avoiding government imposition of utility status on the telephone company. Griffith (1983) analyzes the Advertising Council's campaigns to "sell America to Americans" after World War II, showing that the council's political philosophy reflected an emerging corporatist ideology, opposing New Deal policies that threatened private enterprise, yet viewing the state as a powerful instrument for sustaining economic growth. "Mistrustful of the untutored responses of ordinary citizens, the Council feared that Americans did not truly understand the economic system," and that they could be misled by propaganda, Griffith notes (p. 395). The Advertising Council and many individual companies thus began to promote the American way of life (and business).

This research suggests that the role of public relations in creating an ideology and a political climate that supports big business is another fruitful area for research. Several important campaigns have been examined, but additional information can only enhance our understanding of PR, business, and society.

A Bigger Picture:
The Entrepreneurial Paradigm

In addition to these specific criticisms of Chandler's model, historian Harold Livesay (1989) has raised a larger question. Perhaps more important than any particular flaw in the model is what Chandler omits: small businesses and entrepreneurs. Small business did not die with the rise of big business, but it has taken a decidedly secondary position in the business history literature in the Chandler era. Livesay has led the charge, arguing that the entrepreneurial paradigm should not be abandoned. "The study of large-scale organizations," he asserts, "leaves too many recent phenomena unexplained and inexplicable" (p. 2). Chandler cannot account for the role of individuals, although Livesay argues that "given the right manager, any form of organization can work or be reorganized until it does work, whereas the wrong people can cripple the most vigorous firm despite the presence of a structure thought to be self-correcting" (p. 3). Furthermore, small business is a source for future large businesses, and together small businesses have had a dynamic impact on the economy.

The entrepreneurial paradigm has much to offer public relations historiography. Sullivan's (1968) unpublished master's thesis is illuminating. Sullivan traces the development of the public relations function at Parker Pen, a manufacturing company in Janesville, Wisconsin. Formed in 1891, the firm was a partnership that began growing to a substantial size during World War I and had its first million-dollar sales year in 1918. Parker's top management remained "primarily a family affair," "paternalistic," with a distinctive character and "way of doing things" (pp. 42, 45). Sullivan asserts that this character was an important part of the public relations programs and policies the firm developed over the years. The public relations function, like the top management, tended to stay under the control of only a few individuals. Eventually, PR became part of the policy-making process, although perhaps only in small ways. In 1947, for instance, the company made all of its financial information public for the first time.

What does this study of a medium-sized firm tell us about the history of PR that other studies have ignored or failed to uncover? It reveals how one company's management looked at public relations: with reluctance. Not until 1946 did Parker Pen introduce a PR person or consider public relations part of the overall approach to doing business. Sullivan's study also documents some specific campaigns undertaken by the company to promote products, a function often overlooked in favor of the political aspects of PR, which figured as the main activities during the early years of the department. It shows how an individual, PR director Alan Center, could affect the course of a company. It shows that public relations was not the two-way street that its practitioners often claimed, because Parker Pen's PR department made no attempts to ascertain public needs or desires, only to send information out from the firm. More such studies would make invaluable contributions to our knowledge about public relations generally.

Summary: Public Relations History and Criticisms of Chandler

The above discussion of criticisms of the dominant business history paradigm points out many flaws in public relations historiography. Not one published book has examined the history of a corporate PR department or trade association over time. No monograph has traced the development of a single counseling agency's philosophy or strategies and tactics. Small agencies, agencies that failed, PR departments in small or medium-sized firms, and virtually all organizations outside New York City have been ignored. No one has examined organizations that have tried approaches other than PR. The deficiencies in the literature are such that Pearson (1990), in a review of approaches taken by four PR historians, can conclude only that "for the left, public relations is seen as serving the private interests of individuals, from the right public relations is seen as threatening these interests" (p. 37).

ALTERNATIVE APPROACHES:
POLITICAL HISTORY

Livesay's (1989) criticism of business history's dominant paradigm can be expanded and applied to public relations historiography. The biggest problem with the current public relations literature is not so much that it is flawed; rather, the problem is simply that too much has been left out as a result of researchers' adhering so closely and so frequently to the business history frame. Public relations could be viewed from many other perspectives, and a slowly emerging literature has begun to present a very different picture, one that looks at public relations as more than just corporate. In this section I consider PR as political history and describe how research in this area has been delegitimated by the extensive use of the business history frame.

Election Campaigns

Public relations in the political sphere can include several different kinds of work, including political campaigning, publicizing the actions of elected and appointed officials, lobbying, fund-raising, and seeking support for government policy. Public relations historiography provides only a sketchy picture of these processes, and no author has definitively explained the rise and growth of political PR. The most common approach, however, has been to criticize the role of public relations in the democratic process, generally because PR is said to subvert the marketplace of ideas. As Cutlip (1976) notes, public relations practitioners "have come to constitute an influential and integral component of the nation's public information system—the system upon which our citizens must depend to make their political judgments and their daily decisions" (p. 7). There is at least one history relating to congressional public relations. Richard Nixon's first press secretary, William Arnold (1975), relates funny or interesting stories, such as the time he was left behind on an airplane trip because the plane was too heavy and Nixon's staff chose to take along the mimeograph machine rather than the press secretary. But this is quite unusual. Only two areas of political PR have been explored to any degree in the literature: election campaigns and public information campaigns conducted by the federal government.

Only two authors have considered the role of formal public relations in political campaigning, and both are critical of the function. Kelley (1956), however, does see PR as an improvement over bossism. By turning to propaganda, he argues, political parties moved campaigning into the hands of specialists who guide the actions of politicians toward the people and vice versa. He notes, "The problem now becomes one of finding what it means for our system of government to have a political discussion increasingly monopolized by members of a restricted skill group" (p. 38). He believes that just as big advertising expenditures can be used to keep competitors from entering the field, public relations activities can drown out ideas.

Bloom (1973) traces changes in campaigns, starting with Samuel Adams, and the increasing importance of public relations in policy making, beginning with President Eisenhower. He argues that public relations is only one part of the campaign process, but that with the increasing importance of television and of "image," it is becoming a more dominant part. PR is not, he notes, a part of classical democratic theory, which posits the press as an intelligence service for the people. But the complexity of both government and society means that reporters can no longer keep up, and they must depend on public relations practitioners to help them. Written in the aftermath of Watergate, Bloom's unhappy conclusion is that "public opinion is not really a weapon that the people can confidently hold in reserve as part of their revolutionary arsenal. Instead, it has become a factor subject to professional management" (p. 248).

Because of the importance of elections to a democratic society, it is almost shocking how little is known about the historical role of formal PR in political campaigns. For example, Democrats started the first permanent publicity bureau in 1929, and the first political PR agency was Whitaker and Baxter, formed in California in 1933, but no major historical study has been published about either one. Kelley (1956) does review several of Whitaker and Baxter's campaigns, especially one against "socialized medicine" for the American Medical Association, but not such significant contributions as the agency's campaign during Richard Nixon's first run for office. Charles Michelson's (1944) autobiography provides some insights regarding the Democratic National Committee's public relations tactics during the 1930s and 1940s, indicating that the publicity director "was not of the policy-making group" during that time (p. xvi), but no other author has investigated party public relations policies. The first U.S. representative to hire a press secretary, Frank O'Hair of Illinois, did so in 1912; the first senator to do so, Hiram Johnson of California, waited until 1918. These press secretaries might have had impacts on the election process, but they have not been studied. The passage of the 17th Amendment, which was ratified in 1913 and established direct election of senators, might also have had an impact on the adoption of formal public relations in election campaigns, but that relationship is likewise yet to be examined. The emphasis on the business history frame in public relations historiography has apparently discouraged scholars from studying other areas that are just as important, if not more so, to understand.

Information Campaigns

Information campaigns conducted by U.S. presidents and other officials have fortunately not been so neglected. Two areas of research, presidents and the press and executive branch PR, including war propaganda, have been most popular. Below, I review the literature on federally sponsored campaigns to influence public opinion, noting that research on this topic has been particularly preoccupied with determining the effectiveness of such campaigns.

There has been to date but one general history of political PR, written by a British historian. Pimlott (1951) explains several reasons for the growth of government PR, including increasing bigness of government and of the population, decreasing acceptance of alternatives to open communication (such as bribery of members of Congress), and changes in the media industry as a whole. He asserts that although executive branch agencies were forbidden in 1913 from employing publicity agents except with congressional consent, the federal government has justified the use of PR in two ways: one reportorial, suggesting that a democratic government must report to its citizens, and the other administrative, suggesting that measures will not succeed without public support and understanding. He concludes that the professionalization of government information specialists should help to protect citizens. Although now almost five decades old, Pimlott's book provides a good starting point for research on formal public relations in politics.

Although several of the colonies used public relations techniques to promote settlement (Cutlip, 1995), most histories place the beginning of government public relations with propaganda during the American Revolution. Davidson (1941) and Berger (1976), for example, review government-sponsored initiatives ranging from pamphlets and broadsides to John Adams's letters to the editor and army rumor-mongering. "As propagandists, the Americans demonstrated great ability," Berger writes, but the new country's leaders "never lost sight of the fact that words were no substitute for 'an arm of flesh' " (p. 199). Propaganda, then, was only one part of the war effort, and not the most important part. Miller (1936), however, suggests that propaganda was effective because British officials were alarmed by the successes of American propaganda, believing that Sam Adams had turned citizens in New York and Philadelphia into fire-eating patriots. In short, even the genesis of American government propaganda is not fully understood. This is symptomatic of the state of the literature on political public relations.

Presidential Press Relations

Chandler's influence on corporate public relations historiography is most evident when that literature is compared to the state of the literature on presidential press relations. There exist dozens of autobiographies and biographies of political public relations practitioners, especially White House press secretaries, yet there has been very little generalization. By reading these life stories—which are nearly nonexistent in the corporate PR literature—scholars can see the gradual institutionalization of presidential media relations.

Press Relations from the 19th Century to the Progressive Era

Several authors have traced the history of president-press relations, beginning as early as the first president, George Washington (Pollard, 1947), and Amos Kendall, who joined Andrew Jackson's "Kitchen Cabinet" in 1829 (Endres, 1976). Kendall's duties included writing speeches, performing straw polling, serving as an advance man, and building a favorable image of the president. Cutlip (1994) contrasts the press relations of Abraham Lincoln and Jefferson Davis during the

Civil War, showing that Lincoln was much more adept at dealing with the press and public. Davis, he writes, had a tendency to keep secrets, which brought criticism from Confederate newspapers. Davis did hire James Spence, a British propagandist, to recruit support in England. Tebbel and Watts (1985) discuss George F. Parker, who worked for Grover Cleveland as what was essentially a press secretary, although he lacked an official title. Parker later became Ivy Lee's first partner when the two formed an agency, Parker and Lee, in 1905.

Hilderbrand (1981) indicates that the McKinley administration's efforts "marked the beginning of self-conscious presidential management of public attitudes in foreign affairs" (p. 4). Prior to the 1890s, presidents recognized the value of publicity, but they used it only rarely, in part because they needed public support for foreign policy so sporadically. However, the executive became an increasingly dominant force in leading public opinion, and presidents employed increasingly sophisticated techniques for directing public views of foreign affairs. Hilderbrand suggests four reasons for these changes: improvements in technology of the mass media; the development of the business of public relations; Progressive ideology, which emphasized the power of the people; and the rapid expansion of the U.S. role in world affairs. McKinley laid the foundation for changes in executive management of public opinion on foreign policy through such activities as appointing a secretary to the president, John Addison Porter, who held nightly press briefings and whose assistant, George B. Cortelyou, drew up numerous press handouts. McKinley also opened a room inside the White House to reporters, drawing them away from the North Portico, where they had traditionally waited to interview the president's visitors.

Such activities quickly became institutionalized, Juergens (1981) has shown, during the Progressive Era. The starting point for most histories of presidential opinion management is Theodore Roosevelt (Cornwell, 1965; Juergens, 1981; Pollard, 1947; Smith, 1990). Juergens's (1981) examination of the administrations of Theodore Roosevelt, William Howard Taft, and Woodrow Wilson indicates that as power flowed to the executive branch with increased regulatory power and an increased role for the United States in foreign affairs, both the modern presidency and the "watchdog" Washington press corps came of age. Ponder (1994) goes even farther, asserting that presidential publicity—"the ability of the chief executive to appeal to the citizenry through the developing media of mass communications" (p. 257)—was central to the transformation of presidential power. Presidents and reporters were thrown into a relationship of mutual need and mutual antagonism, Juergens (1981) argues, that continues today. The liaison between these antagonists became the press secretary—in Wilson's case, Joseph Tumulty (Bloomfield, 1965), often considered the first modern press secretary.

Press Relations Since World War I

Following the institutionalization of presidential press relations during the Progressive Era, the literature tends to fall into three general categories: examinations of the relationships between individual presidents and the press, biographies and autobiographies of press secretaries, and the development and institutionalization of the techniques of opinion management. These areas are discussed in turn below.

Press relations of individual presidents. Many authors have examined relationships between particular presidents and the press. Pollard (1947, 1964) provides a chapter-by-chapter synopsis of each president's relationship with the press, from Washington to Johnson. He presents information on such topics as the president's attitudes toward a free press, use of a press secretary, and format and style of meetings with reporters. Cornwell (1966) likewise examines how each president from Theodore Roosevelt to Truman attempted to lead public opinion, discussing, for example, whether or not they employed speechwriters and how adept they were at using the mass media.

Based on the work of Pollard (1947, 1964), Cornwell (1966), and many others, it is clear that the story of presidential press relations after World War I is one of expansion. Like the Wilson administration, Herbert Hoover advanced the degree and sophistication of governmental public relations. Hoover's humanitarian campaign to help feed the needy on behalf of the Food Administration during World War I catapulted him to public prominence (Ponder 1995), but Liebovich (1994) notes that President Hoover's approach to the press was uneven. Hoover saw the press as a tool, but he could not understand why reporters disliked being treated as such; and although he had strong links to certain influential magazine and newspaper editors, he had a roller-coaster relationship with the White House press corps, depending on how compliant reporters were with his wishes.

Theodore Roosevelt may have originated many White House public relations techniques, but it was his cousin Franklin who perfected them. As Ewen (1997) points out, FDR's administration used many forms of verbal and visual communication to keep the public informed about government measures to combat the Great Depression. Winfield (1990) shows the development of FDR's media skills and explains in detail how Roosevelt and his press secretary, Steve Early, controlled press conferences, making sure that reporters always got a story—but only the story they wanted to tell. FDR, like his cousin, is credited with many innovations in press relations, particularly regarding his use of radio, photojournalism, and newsreels. Recognizing that although he could control the press conference, he could not control the press, he turned to these alternative forms of communication to reach the public (Schoenherr, 1976).

Williams (1984) and Liebovich (1989) disagree to a certain extent about the effectiveness of Truman's relationship with the press. Williams calls Truman the "newspaperman's president," whereas Liebovich asserts that Truman lacked the diplomatic skills and patience to work well with the White House reporters. Virtually everyone agrees that the sometimes testy Truman suffered in comparison to his predecessor, Franklin Roosevelt, whose charisma made him a media natural.

The major public relations innovation during the Eisenhower and Kennedy administrations involved the increasing use of television. Allen (1993) points out that, although Kennedy is remembered as the television president, Eisenhower was actually the first to make extensive use of TV, experimenting with televised fireside chats, news conferences, and cabinet meetings and hiring a television consultant. Ike also allowed his press secretary, James Hagerty, to contribute to policy making. Kennedy's best-remembered innovation was to allow the live television broadcast of news conferences, but Pollard (1964) notes that Kennedy also enjoyed unusual intimacy with certain correspondents, inviting them to swim in the White House pool with him, or dining in their homes. The president was often criticized, however, for his administration's efforts to "manage" the news.

President Lyndon Johnson, like Truman, languished in comparison to his charismatic, fallen predecessor. Cornwell (1966) explains that Johnson tried to rely on small group meetings with reporters, something he was accustomed to because of his years in the Senate, rather than the colorful spectacle of the Kennedy-type press conference. He also began using planned and impromptu television announcements and had television facilities installed in the White House for such events.

Maltese (1992) shows that the ever-expanding White House public relations apparatus changed significantly in 1969, when President Richard M. Nixon created the White House Office of Communication. This office functioned in addition to the White House Press Office, and its four staff members, directed by Herbert Klien, coordinated the flow of information from the entire executive branch. Nixon used the office as a political tool to influence, not just inform, the public. Not surprisingly, when the administration's lies to public, Congress, and the media were exposed during the Watergate scandal, the entire White House public relations operation was discredited.

The Nixon experience did not slow the growth of White House PR, although Nixon's successors had to live down the precedent he had set. Rozell (1989, 1992) has investigated the relationships between Ford and Carter and the press by examining newspaper coverage and interviewing reporters and White House staff members. In his study of Carter, he analyzes changing eras in presidential press coverage and concludes that one of the biggest problems President Carter faced was simply timing, with a traumatized press being determined not to be manipulated by a president following Watergate.

The above-mentioned examinations of the media relations of individual presidents show that there has been considerable interest in the White House as a source and as a manager of news. Presidential opinion management techniques have been studied extensively; there is also a sizable literature on White House press secretaries.

White House press secretaries. The history of the White House press secretary is the single best-documented aspect of political public relations, but even in this area the research is flawed. Biographies and autobiographies of the press secretaries abound, but a major problem with the autobiographies in particular is that the press secretary authors have very often used their pens to promote their presidents or to continue their debates with the press. The ever-loyal Joseph Tumulty (1925) painted Woodrow Wilson as a heroic martyr to the cause of world peace, even though Wilson and his wife had all but broken with the press secretary by the time Wilson died (Blum, 1951; Smith, 1964). In his *With Kennedy* (1966), Pierre Salinger did much the same thing, with only occasional references to the actual work of the press office, such as preparing Kennedy for press conferences or planting questions with reporters by telling them they would get an interesting answer if they asked about a specific issue. Salinger's (1995) later book provides a little more detail, showing that he had a very basic approach to public relations, simply trying to "create a climate in which it was as easy as possible for the reporters to cover our campaign" (pp. 75-76). Jerald terHorst (1974) does not discuss himself or the press office until the epilogue of his book about Gerald Ford. Ron Nessen (1978) and Jody Powell (1984), secretaries for Ford and Carter, respectively, both wrote books that include diatribes against journalists they disliked.

Another problem with biographies and autobiographies is that they often focus more on the exciting events that press secretaries have witnessed or people they have met than on the day-to-day operations of the White House press office. Jim Brady's biographer describes his recovery from gunshot wounds suffered during an attempt on President Reagan's life; very little of the book discusses Brady's strategies or policies as press secretary (Dickenson, 1987). Larry Speakes (1988), who took Brady's place after the shooting, focuses in his book somewhat more on press operations, but he usually concentrates on how the press office handled specific events, such as the Reykjavik summit with the Soviet Union. Speakes also analyzes the pros and cons of his own performance, explaining that he had to fight Nancy Reagan's desire to hide the president's cancer from the public, and evaluates certain reporters. Speakes's successor, Marlin Fitzwater (1995), likewise includes in his book "insider information" on summits between Reagan and Gorbachev, the U.S. invasion of Panama, and events during the Bush administration.

The most analytic press secretary autobiography, Jody Powell's (1984), suggests that the relationship between the press and the president is seriously flawed. Powell, who was Jimmy Carter's press secretary, somewhat bitterly argues that the press fails to provide the president with an adequate channel of communication while failing to provide the nation with the information the people need for self-government. Both the White House and the press are flawed, he says, because both adhere to artificially imposed deadlines, base their stories on inadequate information, make decisions based on what the other is doing, become overly defensive, and fail to punish mistakes or incompetence from within.

Although there are abundant studies of the modern president's influence on public opinion, these very often ignore the role of the public relations staff or press secretary in shaping executive policy. Studies of the Cuban missile crisis, for instance, attend to neither Pierre Salinger's counsel to President John F. Kennedy nor his contributions to influencing press coverage when the country was on the brink of nuclear disaster (Salinger, 1966, 1995). In their study of the Kennedy administration, Kern, Levering, and Levering (1983) examine three sets of factors that influenced Kennedy's relationship to the press. In the category of "internal conditions," they include such elements as "the quality of presidential activity directed toward the press; his overall press strategy; his news conferences, special messages, backgrounders, and leaks," but not the public relations expertise of his press secretary and staff (p. 11). Small (1988) similarly asserts that in both the Johnson and Nixon presidencies, "no systematic attempt was made to coordinate the flow of public opinion, nor were any specific aides responsible for its monitoring" regarding the Vietnam War and foreign policy (p. 14).

Even when they do include a president's press advisers in their analyses, scholars fail to place the role of the press secretary in the context of public relations historiography generally. Anderson (1968) examines the careers of important presidential advisers, including several press secretaries, but considers only what each contributed to his president's administration. Eisenhower's press secretary, James G. Hagerty, was included so often in high-level discussions that he became part of the decision-making process (Tebbel & Watts, 1985), but his career has not been analyzed in terms of his impact on public relations practice. (Hagerty did leave behind a diary; see Hagerty, 1983.) Williams (1984) and Liebovich (1989) both analyze Harry Truman's press relations, but not in terms of how his press advisers contributed to the development of public relations or even whether they typified public relations after World War II. In his unpublished dissertation on Franklin Roosevelt's press secretary, Steven T. Early, Schoenherr (1976) describes Early's daily routine and shows that his philosophy of public relations was that "he was as much the representative of the press in the White House as he was a representative of the administration to the press" (p. 46). Schoenherr concludes that because Early accepted the right of the press to criticize the president, he never became an intimate adviser to FDR. This is an idea that deserves further analysis, but because Schoenherr focuses on the individual rather than the vocation, it is an idea that goes unexplored.

Techniques of presidential press relations. Another group of authors who have written on political public relations history focus on the development and institutionalization of specific presidential PR tactics over time, but they never compare the use of these tactics to other areas of public relations practice. Smith (1990), for example, traces the development of the presidential press conference, discussing the format of the questions (written versus spoken), the ground rules (whether or not direct quotation was allowed, for instance), where the conferences were held, and which reporters attended. Similar analyses of presidential press relations have included discussion of techniques such as leaks, trial balloons, photo opportunities, and radio addresses. Cornwell (1965) analyzes each president's attempts to lead public opinion, from Theodore Roosevelt to Truman, noting which ones had press secretaries and how adept they were at working with reporters. Spragens (1979) evaluates the television-age presidents and their press secretaries. Pollard (1947, 1964) provides a progressive history in which presidents move from reliance on unsophisticated partisan newspapers for publicity to the ultimate form—the live, televised press conference. Unfortunately, none of these authors provides any context based on how these or similar tactics were used in corporate or nonprofit public relations during the same periods.

In fact, political PR is virtually always treated in isolation from other areas of public relations history. One example will suffice. Spragens (1980) interviewed former White House staff members and reporters to learn about tactics, such as the use of briefing books, as well as philosophies of public relations. He discusses a conflict of opinion about the role of the press secretary as policy adviser or as technician. For Spragens, Jerald terHorst, who resigned because he disagreed with Ford's decision to pardon Richard Nixon, represents a policy adviser; his successor, Ron Nessen, took the role of technician, believing it was his job to serve as the president's spokesperson regardless of the decisions the president might make. This reflects a long-standing debate among public relations counselors about client choice (Should practitioners represent only those clients with whom they agree, or do all clients deserve representation?), but neither corporate nor political PR historians have drawn from each other to analyze this debate.

Executive Branch Public Relations

As with presidential press relations, several authors pinpoint the Progressive and World War I eras as key periods for the development of executive branch public relations. Ponder (1994) argues that the World War I Committee on Public Information (CPI) was only the continuation of a trend toward centralization of executive branch news: "As early as 1889, Jeremiah Rusk, the first Secretary of Agriculture, found that newspaper editors were willing to print departmental reports as news if they were written in a summary form and sent to editors on a timely basis" (p. 259). By the time Wilson took office in 1913, many federal agencies had their own press bureaus; the first was the U.S. Forest Service, headed by Gifford Pinchot, in 1905 (Ponder, 1990). Several members of Wilson's cabinet hired their own publicists or met with reporters independently, leaving Wilson frustrated by leaks and unhappy with press coverage. Ponder reports that Wilson considered forming a federal news agency as early as 1913.

The Committee on Public Information

The Committee on Public Information, the federal government's propaganda arm during World War I, is the government PR agency that has been studied most extensively in terms of its contribution to the development of public relations. Most of the biographies of Bernays include analysis of his years in the CPI, most histories of World War I at least mention the committee, and the general histories of corporate public relations lavish great amounts of attention on this first large-scale effort at federal propaganda. Drawing upon and espousing Progressive ideals, the CPI under former muckraking journalist George Creel used nearly every form of mass and interpersonal communication—posters, pamphlets, radio and films, press releases, school materials, speeches, and more—to rally Americans and allies and to neutralize the enemy (Creel, 1947; Vaughn, 1980). Hilderbrand (1981) suggests that the CPI was in some ways a temporary aberration, but it was also the "era's highest expression of executive desire for control and centralization of information" (p. 164).

Most people believed that the Creel committee had been extraordinarily effective, and many historians agree. George Creel (1920) himself was so sure of the CPI's success that he subtitled his memoir *The First Telling of the Amazing Story of the Committee on Public Information That Carried the Gospel of Americanism to Every Corner of the Globe*. Mock and Larson (1939) argue that the CPI uttered the "words that won the war." "Through every known channel of communication the Committee carried straight to the people its message of Wilson's idealism, a war to end war, and America to the rescue of civilization," they conclude (p. 5). Vaughn (1980) asserts that the CPI "succeeded all too well," because it "organized patriotic enthusiasm where it existed and created it where it did not" (p. 4). Raucher (1968), although arguing that the war was not a watershed moment in public relations history, points out that "what is most noteworthy about the work of the Creel Committee was the scope of its operations" (p. 72), with a single clipping bureau amassing 15,000 newspaper stories in a span of 18 months.

The Office of War Information

The World War II Office of War Information (OWI) has been given some attention, but the definitive history of that office has yet to be written. Bishop and Mackay (1971) provide a summary of OWI activities and a history of the formation of the agency, which was composed of three prewar agencies. One of these was the National Emergency Council (NEC), created by Franklin Roosevelt in 1933, a little-remembered but important government agency that helped the administration gather information and feedback from the public. The NEC, Bishop (1966) recounts, made regular informal surveys on as many as 50 different topics, produced special reports as needed, and maintained a clipping service, all to keep the administration informed about public opinion on issues and events. Roosevelt called the NEC "my legs and ears and eyes" (quoted in Bishop, 1966, p. 16). This is a rare example of two-way communication in political public relations history.

Winkler (1978) argues that the excesses and the apparent success of the CPI's propaganda left Americans with a bitter taste in their mouths, and this led the Roosevelt administration to take a more restrained approach. Under the direction of respected radio commentator Elmer Davis, the OWI "was to provide truthful information to the American public and meanwhile to develop campaigns—like those on behalf of bond-buying or salvage—to secure certain actions by that public" (p. 35). Even efforts in Europe, such as radio propaganda, were news based rather than emotional. But other scholarship on the OWI shows the efforts were far-reaching and not simply factual. Honey (1984) demonstrates that magazine editors used government-suggested story lines and themes in fiction about women war workers, both to recruit women and to create a more supportive environment for them. Koppes and Black (1990) confirm that the OWI was more than just factual with their examination of government influence over Hollywood films that were designed to end isolationism and instruct Americans on which side to take.

Many authors have documented American propaganda efforts overseas during World War II and during the Cold War that followed. For example, Laurie (1996) reviews propaganda campaigns aimed at Nazi Germany, showing that OWI campaigns were infused with liberal, New Deal ideologies despite their espoused goal of nonpartisanship. Shulman (1990) and Green (1988) analyze the Voice of America and the U.S. Information Agency, respectively, to show how Americans attempted to influence foreign audiences. Such analyses are very often concerned with the effectiveness of American propaganda in the Cold War against communism.

Summary: Political Public Relations

At this point, scholars have assembled bits and pieces that explain small parts of the history of government PR, but there is no comprehensive history and, as is the case with corporate PR, many of the individual parts have yet to be explained. For example, Ritchie (1991) provides one of the best discussions available of the origins of public relations in Congress in a few pages in his analysis of the Washington press corps. Why did the government form the CPI during World War I but not create such a committee during the Spanish-American War, not so many years before? Why did government agencies continue to hire public relations specialists even after Congress had prohibited them from doing so—and why did Congress feel compelled to ban the practice? The literature thus far suggests that the Progressive Era was key not only to corporate PR but to political public relations. Hilderbrand (1981) makes a strong case that the Progressives realized the usefulness of opinion management, but not the possibility of its application to goals they did not share, at least in the case of foreign policy. Kelley (1956) argues, "This has been the chief motive back of the vast expansion of public relations programs by businesses, industries, and interest groups: to control government policy by standardizing and enforcing public opinion" (p. 218). All of these ideas must be carefully investigated if we are to understand the historical effects of public relations on society.

Moreover, there is no theory to explain the rise and growth of political public relations as a specialized function, the reasons for the technician and policy adviser roles and why each one is adopted, or the relationship between the growth of political PR and the growth of corporate and other areas of public relations practice. A fairly sizable literature on White House public relations, including biographies, autobiographies, and general histories on presidential-press relations, is available to scholars. Compared with corporate public relations, there is much more research for scholars to draw upon in developing a generalized history of executive branch public relations—yet no such generalized history has been written. In short, Chandlerization has not yet taken place, and Chandler's influence on corporate PR historiography is made doubly clear. His model of generalization has not been adopted in other areas of public relations historiography.

This emerging literature on political public relations indicates that understanding the rise of public relations as solely (or even mostly) due to the rise of big business is insufficient. Despite the fact that historians of corporate public relations have recognized as much and have included discussions of the Creel committee and other noncorporate aspects in their discussions of the rise and growth of PR, the widespread adoption of the business history frame has in essence delegitimated research on other forms of PR activity (although this was by no means the intention of historians, who have a rightful interest in public relations in its business context). The business frame defines corporate as the norm, and public relations activity that took place before the rise of corporate PR—which includes a great deal of the history of political public relations—is therefore defined as an "antecedent" rather than "real" public relations. Raucher (1968) separates the vocation of public relations from the business policy of public relations, arguing that the vocation was new in name and specialization, but many of the functions it would eventually carry out were old. Public relations did not spring up full-blown in corporations. It had been developing for many years, but the business history frame has encouraged scholars to consider PR only after 1900 and only as a full-time vocation.

ALTERNATIVE APPROACHES:
SOCIAL HISTORY

If, as political PR historiography suggests, other approaches are both useful and necessary, then the redefinition of PR beyond the business history frame could begin with analyses of areas that are usually considered "antecedents." These commonly include press agentry, advertising, reform movements, civic voluntarism, fund-raising, and showmanship, in addition to political campaigning and war propaganda. Such PR activities often include public relations at the grass roots, conducted by the people rather than at the people. In this section, therefore, I examine research on the antecedents of public relations and on PR for nonprofit organizations, and I arrive at conclusions about public relations that are very different from those the corporate literature suggests.

The "Antecedents" of Public Relations

Circus promotion historiography shows how one antecedent has been ignored as part of the development of modern public relations. Publicity genius Phineas T. Barnum is the best known of these promoters. Wallace (1959) suggests that Barnum had an "instinctive understanding of what startled, amazed, astonished, titillated, thrilled" the public, and Saxon (1989) similarly attributes Barnum's success to "his almost intuitive knowledge of human nature . . . ; to his willingness to risk all that he had . . . ; and to his then skillfully exploiting public opinion through the press so as to build interest in his acquisitions to a perfect furor" (p. 74). Harris (1973) finds a greater level of sophistication in Barnum's appeals to the public. Barnum capitalized on the Jacksonian challenge to notions of social order, which placed authority in the hands of the "common man," to glorify doubt and celebrate individual judgment, and asked audiences to judge for themselves the authenticity of the Fiji mermaid or the aesthetic quality of Jenny Lind's voice. All of these authors agree that Barnum was a publicity genius and describe his use of techniques that are still current, but none places him in the context of the rise of public relations.

A notable exception to the tendency among historians to allow the business history frame to dominate has been the research of the "father of public relations education," Scott M. Cutlip. His *Public Relations History* (1995) traces the antecedents of modern public relations, again starting long before corporations institutionalized public relations as a function of business. Based primarily on secondary sources, the book serves essentially as reinterpretation of American history with a view toward understanding the people and events that contributed to the development of the field. In addition to circus promotion, war propaganda, and political campaigning, Cutlip includes a wide range of publicity and press agentry activities, including those not sponsored by government or industry. Many campaigns, such as Clara Barton's tireless efforts on behalf of the American Red Cross, were conducted by nonprofit organizations.

Olasky (1985) also considers grassroots public relations in his examination of General Lafayette's visit to the United States in 1824-1825. "Each community invited Lafayette on its own and made preparations to receive him properly as he passed by on the grand tour," Olasky writes (p. 4). The citizens of Murfreesborough, North Carolina, formed three committees, one to invite Lafayette to the city, a second to arrange his reception and housing, and the third to choose a speaker to welcome him. Olasky's point is that citizens working as community boosters utilized many of the strategies and tactics later adopted by corporate practitioners, albeit for different reasons.

McBride's (1989, 1993) dissertation and book on the work of 19th-century women reformers redefine PR by demonstrating that decades before corporations institutionalized public relations, Wisconsin women used nearly every modern technique of public relations in reform campaigns for the abolition of slavery, temperance, and woman suffrage. McBride (1989) argues that these public opinion campaigns contributed to "the rise and growth of mass communication in general and, specifically, to the modern profession of public relations which arose only after 1920" (pp. 391-392). McBride (1989) criticizes the current literature on PR history because it focuses on what is predominant today—an emphasis on PR's corporate and political origins—when in fact the social reform origins of public relations run much deeper (McBride, 1993).

McBride's work on Wisconsin women is complemented by recent unpublished research on women's reform movements. Byerly (1993) shows that suffragists had a coherent strategy for shaping public opinion about women and women's rights, and they orchestrated a carefully planned campaign of interpersonal and mediated communication to reach their goal. Farmer (1997) notes that the suffragists "skillfully employed such public relations tactics as media relations, publicity, public education, propaganda, literature, public speeches and conventions, and political lobbying" (p. iii). Their tactics were ahead of their time. For example, to reach the ethnic communities in New York, "the suffragists held block parties with street dancing for each foreign group, which included native costumes, music, and suffrage speeches in the native tongue" (Farmer, 1997, p. 54). Such sophisticated targeting of audiences was not typical until years later in corporate public relations. Garner (1995) shows that beginning in 1912, Margaret Sanger used many techniques to promote birth control, including grassroots lobbying, long before many corporations or industries institutionalized them.

One of the most important examples of reform movement public relations is described by Hon (1997), who analyzes the PR elements of the civil rights movement by focusing on the Southern Christian Leadership Conference (SCLC), headed by Martin Luther King, Jr. Although the movement clearly did not utilize formal public relations, such as retaining external counsel, Hon identifies many public relations elements in the campaign, including alliance building, political advocacy, consumer boycotts, and grassroots communication. The SCLC conducted citizenship and political education campaigns designed to recruit volunteers, increase voter registration, and train citizens in nonviolent methods to resolve social problems. "Largely through its effective communication strategies and programs," Hon concludes, "the SCLC eradicated state-supported segregation and disenfranchisement of African Americans, both predominant obstacles to advancement" (p. 201).

Civil rights PR is a dramatic example of the democratic possibilities of public relations from the bottom up, but another social history indicates that some of the same tactics used by the civil rights movement had previously been used to subjugate black citizens. Shotwell's (1974, cited in Cutlip, 1994) unpublished master's thesis on the Southern Publicity Association, an Atlanta agency headed by Elizabeth Tyler and Edward Young Clarke, shows that the agency was largely responsible for the revitalization of the Ku Klux Klan during the 1920s. The firm's previous work for nonprofits, notably the Red Cross, the Salvation Army, and the YMCA, prepared it to recruit volunteers and raise funds, lessons it then applied to the nearly moribund Klan beginning in 1920. Within 3 months after the Klan's Imperial Wizard retained Tyler and Clarke, 48,000 new members had joined. The publicists coached the Klan's leader on public speaking, gave tours of the organizations, and worked with the news media to secure press coverage. They recognized, Shotwell explains, the suspicions and frustrations of white Protestant Americans and articulated them, in effect mobilizing public dissatisfaction.

PR for Nonprofits

Cutlip's (1990) book on fund-raising, first published in 1965, documents the origins of fund-raising for nonprofit organizations beginning with Harvard College in the 17th century and including large-scale philanthropic efforts of such "robber barons" as Andrew Carnegie and John D. Rockefeller. Like corporate and political PR historians, Cutlip asserts that World War I was "the catalyst that set off the nation's first great explosion of public giving" (p. 529).

Two of the institutional histories that focus mostly on corporate PR also contain information on nonprofit public relations. Ross (1959) includes a chapter titled "The Nonprofit Field" that briefly describes the PR activities of such groups as the Methodist Church, the American Cancer Society, and the Congress of Industrial Organizations. Cutlip (1994) discusses nonprofit and political campaigns conducted by several different agencies. For example, he describes the Birthday Balls organized by Carl Byoir and Associates, which were held on Franklin Roosevelt's birthday to raise money for polio research during the Depression. Such inclusion is not typical, however; public relations for nonprofit organizations is perhaps the single most neglected area in PR historiography.

An article on church public relations indicates that research on nonprofit PR can be informative. Ferré (1993) shows that public relations grew increasingly popular for churches at the same time it was being institutionalized in big business. Decreasing attendance and the demise of the Protestant press at the beginning of the 20th century led some religious leaders to experiment with publicity techniques, "creating a corps of amateur and professional publicists," acceding "to the rising authority of urban newspapers and business practices" (p. 515). Some ministers prepared sermons with an eye toward the headlines. Others wrote slogans or held competitions, such as father-son look-alike contests. There was enough demand for church PR that in 1913 Ivy Lee's partner, George F. Parker, left their firm to become a publicist for the Episcopal Church.

Another area of research on nonprofit organizations concerns higher education. After the Civil War, Bonfiglio (1990) argues, greater competition for enrollment and the rise of the mass media led to a need for college recruitment as well as a need for larger universities. Much as a hierarchy grew in big business, university administrations began to expand. Unlike the corporate model, however, universities did not rely on outside counsel but turned quickly to "in-house" public relations departments. The first of these, the University of Michigan's publicity office, opened in 1897. By 1937 there were 205 such offices in American higher education. One example, the University of Wisconsin's press bureau, is described briefly by Bronstein and Vaughn (1998). In 1909, Wisconsin's publicity director, Willard Bleyer, launched a weekly press bulletin that brought stories about the school to newspapers nationwide. Bleyer's work dovetailed with the Wisconsin Idea, a partnership between the university and the state aimed at improving living conditions for all citizens, and Progressive ideals that had also fueled government and corporate public relations. Bonfiglio (1990) notes another difference from the corporate model, however, in that universities did not band together to promote themselves until 1981, when the Council for the Advancement and Support of Education instituted a campaign to promote higher education as a whole.

Summary: Public Relations as Social History

The social histories reviewed above, which have often examined public relations from below, strongly contradict the findings of corporate PR historiography. Public relations was used not to suppress workers or subvert democratic processes but by ordinary and sometimes oppressed citizens to inform and persuade. Olasky (1985) notes that "the decentralist and vountaristic emphases of early 19th century public relations have clearly been superseded in this century by paid, concentrated labors" (p. 10), but these antecedents deserve greater attention.

Together, the analyses of public relations as social history suggest the same thing as political histories: that the rise and growth of PR cannot be attributed solely to the rise of big business. The emphasis on the corporate frame has detracted from our understanding by infusing PR historiography with a decidedly institutional bias. But social histories have shown that individuals and public organizations such as reform groups, whether or not their aims were socially beneficial, were as important as corporations in the development of PR techniques and in the development of public relations as an occupation. As Byerly (1993) asserts, "Before the profession of public relations, there was the practice" (p. 16). To understand that practice and the profession that followed, historians must "examine much earlier periods" and "look for a more inclusive cast of PR actors" (p. 16), and thus adopt a broader definition of what constitutes the field.

In sum, public relations is not simply an occupation of paid counselors. Redefining PR so that it includes the philosophies, strategies, and tactics employed by individuals and communities, nonprofit and social organizations, and political advocates and institutions provides a broader base for understanding how and why people choose to utilize and institutionalize formal public relations practices in all kinds of organizations, including corporations. Byerly (1993) suggests that such a redefinition will democratize the way scholars study and conduct research on public relations. With so much of public relations historiography focusing on corporate PR, teaching materials such as textbooks also very often reflect a corporate or institutional bias. In reality, public relations history cannot be understood until all of its elements have been examined individually and then generalized in a Chandlerian model that blends many histories and not just business histories.

CONCLUSION: AN AGENDA FOR FURTHER RESEARCH

In this chapter, I have shown that the dominant paradigm in business history research, a Chandlerian model in which a general theory about the rise of big business is developed based on many individual case studies, has had a significant impact on the historiography of public relations. Although it has flaws, and despite the fact that it has been applied without prerequisite scholarship, the Chandlerian lens has shed light on many important aspects of public relations history. Important themes identified in this chapter include the role of public relations in the marketplace of ideas, the historical effectiveness of PR, PR's relationship to the rise of big business, and the perceived importance of public opinion. But I have also shown here that the business history frame is simply too limiting for public relations. Because of the reliance on the corporate frame, most general histories of PR concentrate almost exclusively on its business aspects, neglecting other potentially profitable areas of inquiry, such as political, social, intellectual, and cultural histories.

This review has also shown that, although severely limited in quantity, research that has utilized other historical lenses has proven insightful. It is clear that public relations activities began long before they were institutionalized by corporate entities; it is clear that the Progressive Era was a watershed moment for public relations in every area of society; and it is clear that many different groups and individuals have used and been affected by the use of public relations strategies and tactics. Several scholars have made pleas for a more inclusive history of public relations (Byerly, 1993; Creedon, 1989; Garner, 1995), calling particularly for greater attention to women's history and social reform movements. But even that is not enough. Political and social histories show that public relations was emerging and apparently would have emerged even if big business had not. And the corporate histories have relied on evidence from political and nonprofit PR (e.g., Raucher, 1968, on John Price Jones's fund-raising activities; Tedlow, 1979, on the CPI) to explain how the field advanced. In reality these histories are intertwined, an idea best represented by the career of the PR pioneer George F. Parker, who worked for a president, a corporate counseling firm, and a church, all before World War I. No single strand of PR history can be understood except in relationship to the others, and none should be given a more privileged position in public relations historiography.

Throughout this chapter I have advanced the elements of a research agenda for public relations history. Put together, the new agenda would include many elements. Scholars must examine not only the many big-city counseling firms and corporations, but civic, voluntary, and religious groups; labor unions, consumer groups, and trade associations; women's and minority groups; small businesses, nonprofit organizations, and political groups; and agencies outside of New York. An analysis of public relations as a whole during the Progressive Era would seem to be particularly important, given that scholars in so many areas have indicated the significance of that period. Research on individuals and on practitioners' groups should also be continued. For instance, a group called the Wise Men formed in 1938 in New York City and included such luminaries as Tommy Ross, Claude Robinson, Pendleton Dudley, Paul Garrett of General Motors, and Carlisle MacDonald of U.S. Steel, but it has not been studied. Comparative studies are also relevant. Because of the importance of the Progressive Era and World War I to

American public relations, a comparison between the Creel committee and Britain's Wellington House (Kunczik, 1997), for example, would be productive. The adoption of American public relations practices around the world is another important topic. Intellectual histories, such as an exploration of the meaning of *publicity* to Progressives, would further explain the ideas that have contributed to the development of PR, and cultural histories could illuminate the ways in which public relations has influenced society as a whole. Continued research on the political and social roots of public relations is also imperative. Until such wide-ranging studies are completed, scholars will not and cannot fully understand the history of public relations.

REFERENCES

Allen, C. (1993). *Eisenhower and the mass media: Peace, prosperity, and prime-time TV.* Chapel Hill: University of North Carolina Press.

Anderson, P. (1968). *The presidents' men.* Garden City, NY: Doubleday.

Arnold, W. A. (1975). *Back when it all began: The early Nixon years.* New York: Vantage.

Ballinger, J. R. (1994, August). *The muckraker and the PR man: Upton Sinclair, Ivy Lee and press coverage of the Ludlow massacre.* Paper presented at the annual meeting of the Association for Education in Journalism and Mass Communication, Atlanta, GA.

Berger, C. (1976). *Broadsides and bayonets: The propaganda war of the American revolution* (Rev. ed.). San Rafael, CA: Presidio.

Bernays, E. L. (1965). *Biography of an idea: Memoirs of public relations counsel Edward L. Bernays.* New York: Simon & Schuster.

Bernays, E. L. (1971). Emergence of the public relations counsel: Principles and recollections. *Business History Review, 45,* 296-316.

Bishop, R. L. (1966, July). How the New Deal kept abreast of public opinion. *Public Relations Journal, 22,* 16-18.

Bishop, R. L., & Mackay, L. S. (1971, May). Mysterious silence, lyrical scream: Government information in World War II. *Journalism Monographs, 19.*

Blackford, M. G., & Kerr, K. A. (1990). *Business enterprise in American history* (2nd ed.). Boston: Houghton Mifflin.

Bloom, M. H. (1973). *Public relations and presidential campaigns: A crisis in democracy.* New York: Thomas Y. Crowell.

Bloomfield, D. M. (1965). Joe Tumulty and the press. *Journalism Quarterly, 42,* 413-421.

Blum, J. M. (1951). *Joe Tumulty and the Wilson era.* Boston: Houghton Mifflin.

Bonfiglio, R. A. (1990). *The history of public relations in American higher education in the twentieth century: From self-interest to national interest.* Unpublished doctoral dissertation, Columbia University.

Bronstein, C., & Vaughn, S. (1998, June). Willard Bleyer and the relevance of journalism education. *Journalism and Mass Communication Monographs, 166.*

Byerly, C. M. (1993, August). *Toward a comprehensive history of public relations.* Paper presented at the annual meeting of the Association for Education in Journalism and Mass Communication, Kansas City, MO.

Carey, A. (1997). *Taking the risk out of democracy: Corporate propaganda versus freedom and liberty.* Urbana: University of Illinois Press.

Chandler, A. D., Jr. (1977). *The visible hand: The managerial revolution in American business.* Cambridge, MA: Belknap.

Chandler, A. D., Jr. (1990). *Scale and scope: The dynamics of industrial capitalism.* Cambridge, MA: Belknap.

Cornwell, E. E., Jr. (1965). *Presidential leadership of public opinion.* Bloomington: Indiana University Press.

Cornwell, E. E., Jr. (1966). The Johnson press relations style. *Journalism Quarterly, 43,* 3-9.

Creedon, P. J. (1989, Autumn). Public relations history misses "her story." *Journalism Educator, 44,* 26-30.

Creel, G. (1920). *How we advertised America: The first telling of the amazing story of the Committee on Public Information that carried the gospel of Americanism to every corner of the globe.* New York: Harper & Brothers.

Creel, G. (1947). *Rebel at large: Recollections of fifty crowded years.* New York: G. P. Putnam's Sons.

Culbertson, H. M. (1996). Introduction. In H. M. Culbertson & N. Chin (Eds.), *International public relations: A comparative analysis* (pp. 1-13). Mahwah, NJ: Lawrence Erlbaum.

Cutlip, S. M. (1976). Public relations in government. *Public Relations Review, Summer,* 5-28.

Cutlip, S. M. (1990). *Fundraising in the United States: Its role in America's philanthropy.* New Brunswick, NJ: Transaction.

Cutlip, S. M. (1994). *The unseen power: Public relations, a history.* Hillsdale, NJ: Lawrence Erlbaum.

Cutlip, S. M. (1995). *Public relations history: From the 17th to the 20th century.* Mahwah, NJ: Lawrence Erlbaum.

Davidson, P. (1941). *Propaganda and the American revolution, 1763-1783.* Chapel Hill: University of North Carolina Press.

Dickenson, M. (1987). *Thumbs up: The life and courageous comeback of White House press secretary Jim Brady.* New York: William Morrow.

Du Boff, R. B., & Herman, E. S. (1980). Alfred Chandler's new business history: A review. *Politics and Society, 10,* 87-110.

Dunlavy, C. A. (1991, Spring). Mirror images: Political structure and early railroad policy in the United States and Prussia. *Studies in American Political Development, 5,* 1-35.

Endres, F. F. (1976). Public relations in the Jackson White House. *Public Relations Review, Fall,* 5-12.

Ewen, S. (1997). *PR! A social history of spin.* New York: Basic Books.

Farmer, S. L. (1997). *Communicating justice: The National American Woman Suffrage Association's use of public relations to win the right to vote.* Unpublished master's thesis, University of North Carolina, Chapel Hill.

Ferré, J. P. (1993). Protestant press relations in the United States, 1900-1930. *Church History, 62,* 514-527.

Fitzwater, M. (1995). *Call the briefing!* New York: Times Books.

Fones-Wolf, E. A. (1994). *Selling free enterprise: The business assault on labor and liberalism, 1945-1960.* Urbana: University of Illinois Press.

Galambos, L. (1970). The emerging organizational synthesis in modern American history. *Business History Review, 44,* 279-290.

Galambos, L. (1975). *The public image of big business in America, 1880-1940: A quantitative study in social change.* Baltimore: Johns Hopkins University Press.

Galambos, L., & Pratt, J. (1988). *The rise of the corporate commonwealth: U.S. businesses and public policy in the twentieth century.* New York: Basic Books.

Garner, R. B. (1995, March). *The case for a more inclusive history of public relations.* Paper presented at the Southeast Colloquium of the Association for Education in Journalism and Mass Communication, Gainesville, FL.

Golden, L. L. L. (1968). *Only by public consent: American corporations search for favorable opinion.* New York: Basic Books.

Gras, N. S. B. (1945, October). Shifts in public relations. *Bulletin of the Business Historical Society, 19,* 97-148.

Green, F. (1988). *American propaganda abroad: From Benjamin Franklin to Ronald Reagan.* New York: Hippocrene.

Griffith, R. (1983). The selling of America: The Advertising Council and American politics, 1942-1960. *Business History Review, 57,* 388-412.

Hagerty, J. C. (1983). *The diary of James C. Hagerty: Eisenhower in mid-course, 1954-1955* (R. H. Ferrell, Ed.). Bloomington: Indiana University Press.

Hainsworth, B. E. (1987). Retrospective: Ivy Lee and the German dye trust. *Public Relations Review, 13*(1), 35-44.

Harlow, R. (1980). A timeline of public relations development. *Public Relations Review, 6*(3), 3-13.

Harlow, R. (1981). A public relations historian recalls the first days. *Public Relations Review, 7*(2), 33-42.

Harris, N. (1973). *Humbug: The art of P. T. Barnum.* Boston: Little, Brown.

Henry, S. (1997). Anonymous in her own name: Public relations pioneer Doris E. Fleischman. *Journalism History, 23*(2), 51-62.

Henry, S. (1998). Dissonant notes of a retiring feminist: Doris E. Fleischman's later years. *Journal of Public Relations Research, 10,* 1-33.

Hidy, R. W. (1970). Business history: Present status and future needs. *Business History Review, 44,* 483-497.

Hiebert, R. E. (1966). *Courtier to the crowd: The story of Ivy Lee and the development of public relations.* Ames: Iowa State University Press.

Hilderbrand, R. C. (1981). *Power and the people: Executive management of public opinion in foreign affairs, 1897-1921.* Chapel Hill: University of North Carolina Press.

Hill, J. W. (1963). *The making of a public relations man.* New York: David McKay.

Hon, L. C. (1997). "To redeem the soul of America": Public relations and the civil rights movement. *Journal of Public Relations Research, 9,* 163-212.

Honey, M. (1984). *Creating Rosie the Riveter: Class, gender, and propaganda during World War II.* Amherst: University of Massachusetts Press.

Jarvik, L. (1992). PBS and the politics of quality: Mobil Oil's "Masterpiece Theater." *Historical Journal of Film, Radio and Television, 12,* 253-274.

Juergens, G. (1981). *News from the White House: The presidential-press relationship in the Progressive Era.* Chicago: University of Chicago Press.

Kelley, S., Jr. (1956). *Professional public relations and political power.* Baltimore: Johns Hopkins University Press.

Kern, M., Levering, P. W., & Levering, R. B. (1983). *The Kennedy crises: The press, the presidency, and foreign policy.* Chapel Hill: University of North Carolina Press.

Koppes, C. R., & Black, G. D. (1990). *Hollywood goes to war: How politics, profits and propaganda shaped World War II movies.* Berkeley: University of California Press.

Kunczik, M. (1997). *Images of nations and international public relations.* Mahwah, NJ: Lawrence Erlbaum.

Lamoreaux, N. R. (1991). Chandler's own economies of scale and scope. *Reviews in American History, 19,* 391-395.

Laurie, C. D. (1996). *The propaganda warriors: America's crusade against Nazi Germany.* Lawrence: University Press of Kansas.

Liebovich, L. W. (1989). Failed White House press relations in the early months of the Truman administration. *Presidential Studies Quarterly, 18,* 583-591.

Liebovich, L. W. (1994). *Bylines in despair: Herbert Hoover, the Great Depression, and the U.S. news media.* Westport, CT: Praeger.

Livesay, H. C. (1989). Entrepreneurial dominance in businesses large and small, past and present. *Business History Review, 63,* 1-21.

Macnamara, P. (1993). *Those were the days, my friend: My life in Hollywood with David O. Selznick and others.* Metuchen, NJ: Scarecrow.

Maltese, J. A. (1992). *Spin control: The White House Office of Communications and the management of presidential news.* Chapel Hill: University of North Carolina Press.

Marchand, R. (1987). The fitful career of advocacy advertising: Political protection, client cultivation, and corporate morale. *California Management Review, 29,* 128-156.

Marchand, R. (1989). The inward thrust of institutional advertising: General Electric and General Motors in the 1920s. *Business and Economic History, 18,* 188-196.

Marchand, R. (1991). The corporation nobody knew: Bruce Barton, Alfred Sloan, and the founding of the General Motors "family." *Business History Review, 65,* 825-875.

McBride, G. G. (1989). *No "season of silence": Uses of "public relations" in nineteenth-century and early twentieth-century reform movements in Wisconsin.* Unpublished doctoral dissertation, University of Wisconsin–Madison.

McBride, G. G. (1993). *On Wisconsin women.* Madison: University of Wisconsin Press.

McCann, T. P. (1976). *An American company: The tragedy of United Fruit* (H. Scammel, Ed.). New York: Crown.

McCraw, T. K. (1988). Introduction. In T. K. McCraw (Ed.), *The essential Alfred Chandler: Essays toward a historical theory of big business* (pp. 1-21). Boston: Harvard Business School Press.

Michelson, C. (1944). *The ghost talks.* New York: G. P. Putnam's Sons.

Miller, J. C. (1936). *Sam Adams, pioneer in propaganda.* Boston: Little, Brown.

Miller, K. (1996). "Air power is peace power": The aircraft industry's campaign for public and political support, 1943-1949. *Business History Review, 70,* 297-327.

Miller, K. S. (1995). National and local public relations campaigns during the 1946 steel strike. *Public Relations Review, 21,* 305-323.

Miller, K. S. (1997). Woman, man, lady, horse: Jane Stewart, public relations executive. *Public Relations Review, 23,* 249-269.

Mock, J. R., & Larson, C. (1939). *Words that won the war: The story of the Committee on Public Information, 1917-1919.* Princeton, NJ: Princeton University Press.

Nessen, R. (1978). *It sure looks different from the inside.* Chicago: Playboy.

Nye, D. E. (1985). *Image worlds: Corporate identities at General Electric, 1890-1930.* Cambridge: MIT Press.

Olasky, M. N. (1985). A reappraisal of 19th-century public relations. *Public Relations Review, 11*(1), 3-12.

Olasky, M. N. (1987). *Corporate public relations: A new historical perspective.* Hillsdale, NJ: Lawrence Erlbaum.

Pearson, R. (1990). Perspectives on public relations history. *Public Relations Review, 16*(3), 27-38.

Pimlott, J. A. R. (1951). *Public relations and American democracy.* Princeton, NJ: Princeton University Press.

Pollard, J. E. (1947). *The presidents and the press.* New York: Macmillan.

Pollard, J. E. (1964). *The presidents and the press: Truman to Johnson.* Washington, DC: Public Affairs.

Ponder, S. (1990). Progressive drive to shape public opinion, 1898-1913. *Public Relations Review, 16*(3), 94-104.

Ponder, S. (1994). Presidential publicity and executive power: Woodrow Wilson and the centralizing of governmental information. *American Journalism, 11,* 257-269.

Ponder, S. (1995). Popular propaganda: The Food Administration in World War I. *Journalism and Mass Communication Quarterly, 72,* 539-550.

Powell, J. (1984). *The other side of the story.* New York: William Morrow.

Pratt, J. A. (1983). Creating coordination in the modern petroleum industry: The American Petroleum Institute and the emergence of secondary organizations in oil. *Research in Economic History, 8,* 179-215.

Raucher, A. R. (1968). *Public relations and business, 1900-1929.* Baltimore: Johns Hopkins University Press.

Raucher, A. R. (1990). Public relations in business: A business of public relations. *Public Relations Review, 16*(3), 19-26.

Ritchie, D. A. (1991). *Press gallery.* Cambridge: Harvard University Press.

Rogers, H. C. (1980). *Walking the tightrope: The private confessions of a public relations man.* New York: William Morrow.

Ross, I. (1959). *The image merchants: The fabulous world of public relations.* Garden City, NY: Doubleday.

Rozell, M. J. (1989). *The press and the Carter presidency.* Boulder, CO: Westview.

Rozell, M. J. (1992). *The press and the Ford presidency.* Ann Arbor: University of Michigan Press.

Salinger, P. (1966). *With Kennedy.* Garden City, NY: Doubleday.

Salinger, P. (1995). *PS: A memoir.* New York: St. Martin's.

Sattler, J. E. (1993). *Fifty years ahead of the news: A lifetime of practical public relations.* Kalamazoo, MI: Sattler International.

Saxon, A. H. (1989). *P. T. Barnum: The legend and the man.* New York: Columbia University Press.

Schoenherr, S. E. (1976). *Selling the New Deal: Stephen T. Early's role as press secretary to Franklin D. Roosevelt.* Unpublished doctoral dissertation, University of Delaware.

Scranton, P. (1983). *Proprietary capitalism: The textile manufacture at Philadelphia, 1800-1885.* New York: Cambridge University Press.

Shotwell, J. M. (1974). *Crystallizing public hatred: Ku Klux Klan public relations in the early 1920s.* Unpublished master's thesis, University of Wisconsin.

Shulman, H. C. (1990). *The voice of America.* Madison: University of Wisconsin Press.

Sklar, M. J. (1988). *The corporate reconstruction of American capitalism, 1890-1916: The market, the law, and politics.* New York: Cambridge University Press.

Small, M. (1988). *Johnson, Nixon, and the doves.* New Brunswick, NJ: Rutgers University Press.

Smith, C. (1990). *Presidential press conferences.* New York: Praeger.

Smith, G. (1964). *When the cheering stopped: The last years of Woodrow Wilson.* New York: William Morrow.

Smith, P. C. (1997). *Breaking new ground in public relations: A biography of Mary L. T. Brown.* Unpublished master's thesis, University of Georgia.

Speakes, L. (1988). *Speaking out: The Reagan presidency from inside the White House.* New York: Charles Scribner's Sons.

Spragens, W. C. (1979). *The presidency and the mass media in the age of television.* Washington, DC: University Press of America.

Spragens, W. C. (1980). *From spokesman to press secretary: White House media operations.* Washington, DC: University Press of America.

Sullivan, R. A. (1968). *Evolution of a corporate public relations function.* Unpublished master's thesis, University of Wisconsin.

Tebbel, J., & Watts, S. M. (1985). *The press and the presidency: From George Washington to Ronald Reagan.* New York: Oxford University Press.

Tedlow, R. S. (1979). *Keeping the corporate image: Public relations and business, 1900-1950.* Greenwich, CT: JAI.

terHorst, J. F. (1974). *Gerald Ford and the future of the presidency.* New York: Third Press.

Thelander, T. A. (1966). Josephus Daniels and the publicity campaign for naval and industrial preparedness before World War I. *North Carolina Historical Review, 43,* 316-332.

Tumulty, J. P. (1925). *Woodrow Wilson as I know him.* Garden City, NY: Garden City.

Vaughn, S. (1980). *Holding fast the inner lines: Democracy, nationalism and the Committee on Public Information.* Chapel Hill: University of North Carolina Press.

Wallace, I. (1959). *The fabulous showman: The life and time of P. T. Barnum.* New York: Alfred A. Knopf.

Williams, H. L. (1984). *The newspaperman's president: Harry S Truman.* Chicago: Nelson-Hall.

Winfield, B. H. (1990). *FDR and the news media.* Urbana: University of Illinois Press.

Winkler, A. M. (1978). *The politics of propaganda: The Office of War Information, 1942-1945.* New Haven, CT: Yale University Press.

Wood, R. J., & Gunther, M. (1988). *Confessions of a PR man.* New York: New American Library.

AUTHOR INDEX

SUBJECT INDEX

Adaptive structuration theory:
- analysis of, 359-362
- principles of, 352-354

Adolescents:
- compliance resistance strategies used by, 134
- dieting in
  - age of onset, 276
  - growth and developmental effects, 276
  - parental influences, 276-277
  - peer pressures, 276-278, 297-298
  - reasons for, 276
  - social conformity and, 277
  - *See also* Eating disorders; Thinness
- music for altering mood of, 111-112
- rebelliousness of, 111-112

Advertising:
- body image effects, 293-294
- guilt-based persuasion for, 31, 80-85
- in weight-loss industry
  - gender-based differences, 275
  - regulatory agencies, 274

Alienation, shame and, 21

Anger:
- conflict management using, 258
- guilt arousal and, 91-92
- maintenance of, for hedonistic purposes
  - avoidance of diversionary stimulation, 109
  - description of, 107-108
- shame and, 12, 19-20

Anorexia nervosa. *See* Eating disorder(s)

Anticipated guilt, 18, 88-92

Anticipated regret, 88-89

Appraisal, of emotions:
- in children, 26
- guilt, 7-8
- individual differences in style of, 8
- shame, 7-8

Argumentation, effect on small group decision-making processes:
- cognitive rules, 352
- distribution of valence model and, 350-351
- persuasive arguments theory and, 352
- structuration theory application to, 350-352

theoretical rationales, 351

Attribution theory:
- of compliance resistance with request interactions, 131-132, 154-155
- of sexual harassment, 183, 185

Avoiding style, of conflict management, 236-237, 241-242, 248, 257

Behavior. *See* Anger; Nonverbal behavior; Verbal behavior

Blaming, shame and, 12

Body image:
- definition of, 272
- disturbances in, 272, 294
- mass media messages regarding
  - description of, 271
  - female attractiveness standards, 288-289, 293-296
  - idealized characterizations, 288-290, 292
  - television advertising and programming, 293-294
- social comparison theory and, 289-290
- *See also* Dieting; Eating disorders; Thinness

Bulimia nervosa. *See* Eating disorder(s)

Business history approach, to public relations:
- alternative forms, 394-395
- Chandler's participation, 382-383
- criticisms of, 391-397
- entrepreneurial paradigm limitations of, 396-397
- origins of, 382-383
- political state involvement, 393-396
- power as managerial force, 391-392
- principles of, 382
- public relations history and, 383-386

Children:
- dieting in
  - age of onset, 276
  - growth and developmental effects, 276
  - parental influences, 276-277
  - peer pressures, 276-278, 297-298

ABOUT THE EDITOR

MICHAEL E. ROLOFF (Ph.D., Michigan State University, 1975) is Professor of Communication Studies at Northwestern University. His research interests include interpersonal influence, conflict management, bargaining and negotiation, and social exchange within intimate relationships. He has published in *Communication Monographs, Communication Research, Human Communication Research, Journal of Language and Social Psychology,* and *Personal Relationships.* He is currently coeditor of *Communication Research.*

ABOUT THE CONTRIBUTORS

A. DAWN ADKINS (M.A., University of Montana, 1997) is a doctoral student in the Department of Speech Communication at Texas A&M University. Her teaching and research interests include health communication, interpersonal communication, intimate relationships and sexual health.

RONALD BISHOP (Ph.D., Temple University, 1996) is Assistant Professor of Communication at Drexel University in Philadelphia. His research interests include the impact of the mass media on body image, sourcing practices in journalism, and the relationship between public relations and journalism. The *Journal of Communication Inquiry* recently published his paper on boundary work done by journalists in their coverage of Princess Diana's death, and the *Journal of Popular Culture* will soon publish his narrative analysis on television collectibles programs. In 1997, his chapter on cable television was included in *Mass Media and Society,* a textbook edited by Alan Wells and Ernest Hakanen.

DANIEL J. CANARY (Ph.D., University of Southern California, 1983) is Professor, Hugh Downs School of Human Communication, Arizona State University. He has also taught at Pennsylvania State University, Ohio University, and California State University, Fullerton. His research interests focus on couples' maintenance behavior, conflict management, and gender differences in close relationships. He serves as the Associate Editor of Communication for the *Journal of Social and Personal Relationships* and is a member of the editorial boards of several communication journals.

SUSAN HAFEN (Ph.D., University of Ohio) is Assistant Professor in the Department of Communication & Journalism at the University of Wisconsin-Eau Claire. Her teaching and research interests include organizational communication (especially organizational gossip), cultural diversity, and environmental communication (particularly animal-human relationships). Her research slants toward feminist, critical, and postmodern perspectives.

DANETTE E. IFERT (Ph.D., Northwestern University, 1994) is Assistant Professor in the Department of Communication at West Virginia Wesleyan College. Her primary research interest focuses on interpersonal influence, particularly the role that obstacles and refusals of requests play in the development of request interactions. Her other research interests include the role of peer influences in classroom communication and taboo topics in romantic relationships. Her work has appeared in *Communication Research, Personal Relationships, Communication Quarterly,* and the *Journal of Language and Social Psychology.*

LAURA L. JANSMA (Ph.D., University of California, Santa Barbara, 1997) is an Instructor at the University of California, Santa Barbara, and an organizational consultant; gender and communication define both roles. Her research on the effects of pornography on men's attitudes and behaviors toward women has appeared in *Communication Monographs*. Her sexual harassment research focuses on bases for and assessment of mitigation strategies.

MIN-SUN KIM (Ph.D., Michigan State University, 1992) is Associate Professor in the Department of Speech at the University of Hawaii at Manoa. Her research interests focus on the role of cognition in conversational styles among people of different cultural orientations. She has applied her models (based on conversational constraints) in the areas of requesting, re-requesting, conflict, and styles. Her publications have appeared in several journals, including *Human Communication Research, Communication Monographs, Communication Research, Communication Quarterly, Journal of Communication, International Journal of Intercultural Relations, Howard Journal of Communication, Research on Language and Social Interaction, Journal of Asian Pacific Communication,* and *Folia Linguistica,* as well as in *International and Intercultural Communication Annual.* Her most recent research, concerning self-construals and re-requesting styles, just appeared in *Communication Monographs.* She is currently investigating individuals' predispositions toward verbal communication in different cultures, and she is working on a book about non-Western perspectives on interpersonal communication.

TRUMAN LEUNG (M.A., University of Hawaii at Manoa, 1997) is the Coordinator of the University of Hawaii Community Colleges International Affairs Outreach Program of the Pacific and Asian Affairs Council. He has taught at the Beijing University of Aeronautics, China, as well as served as an Instructor at Kapiolani Community College. His research interests include cross-cultural conflict management styles, specifically focusing on Chinese-U.S. communication.

KAREN S. MILLER (Ph.D., University of Wisconsin–Madison, 1993) is Assistant Professor in the Henry W. Grady College of Journalism and Mass Communication at the University of Georgia. She won the Nafziger-White Dissertation Prize from the Association for Education in Journalism and Mass Communication in 1995 for her research on Hill and Knowlton of New York. A revised version of her dissertation has been published under the title *The Voice of Business.* She has also published articles on public relations and media history in *Business History Review, Public Relations Review, American Journalism,* and the *Journal of Public Relations Research.*

DANIEL J. O'KEEFE (Ph.D., University of Illinois, Urbana-Champaign) is Associate Professor in the Department of Speech Communication at the University of

Illinois, Urbana-Champaign. His research concerns persuasion and argument. His work has appeared in *Human Communication Research, Communication Monographs, Argumentation and Advocacy,* and other journals, as well as the *Communication Yearbook,* and he has received the Golden Anniversary Award and the Charles Woolbert Award from the National Communication Association. He is the author of *Persuasion: Theory and Research* (1990).

SALLY PLANALP (Ph.D., University of Wisconsin–Madison, 1983) is Professor in the Department of Communication Studies at the University of Montana in Missoula and Adjunct Professor of Management Communication at the University of Waikato, Hamilton, New Zealand. Her teaching and research interests include interpersonal communication, close relationships, and communication and emotion. Her recent work has appeared in *Cognition and Emotion, Journal of Social and Personal Relationships,* and *Communication Theory,* as well as the *Handbook of Communication and Emotion.* She is also the author of a book titled *Communicating Emotion: Social, Moral and Cultural Processes* (1999).

BRYAN SEYFARTH (Ph.D., University of Minnesota at Minneapolis-St. Paul, 1999) is a Consultant for Cogos Consulting, Inc., a knowledge management consulting firm based in Cambridge, Massachusetts. At Cogos, he is a codesigner of Andromeda2000©, an advanced groupware system that allows distributed work groups to coordinate their work and to communicate more effectively. As a graduate student, he focused his research efforts on the theory of structuration, with an emphasis on understanding the ways organizational members use communication to create and re-create a variety of work processes. Although his research interests have become more technical in nature, they still revolve around the ways small groups and organizations can use communication technologies to transform their work processes.

ELAINE D. ZELLEY (M.A., Pennsylvania State University, 1998) is currently a doctoral student in speech communication at Pennsylvania State University. Her research interests include relational maintenance behaviors, supportive interaction, and the role of interpersonal communication in the manifestation of and recovery from disordered eating.

DOLF ZILLMANN (Ph.D., University of Pennsylvania, 1969) is Professor of Communication and Senior Associate Dean for Graduate Studies and Research at the University of Alabama. His research has addressed the choices and effects of media content generally. He has explored the news function, educational television, and media entertainment at large. His entertainment research spans the psychology of comedy, suspenseful and violent drama, horror, tragedy, erotica, sports, and music. Independent of media choices and effects, his research has focused on emotional behavior, especially on the agonistic emotions of fear and anger and their relation to sexuality. Among his recent publications are *Connections Between Sexuality and Aggression* (1998), "The Psychology of the Appeal of Portrayals of Violence" (in *Why We Watch,* 1998), "Anger" (in the *Encyclopedia of Mental Health,* 1998), "Musical Taste in Adolescence" (in *The Social Psychology of Music,* 1997), and "The Psychology of Suspense in Dramatic Exposition" (in *Suspense,* 1996).